KATHARINE HEPBURN

By the same author

Polanski: A Biography
Orson Welles: A Biography
If This Was Happiness: A Biography of Rita Hayworth
Bette Davis: A Biography

KATHARINE HEPBURN

BARBARA LEAMING

WEIDENFELD AND NICOLSON LONDON

First published in Great Britain in 1995 by
Weidenfeld and Nicolson

The Orion Publishing Group
Orion House, 5 Upper St Martin's Lane, London WC2H 9EA

Second Impression March 1995

ISBN 0 297 81319 6

A catalogue record for this book is available from the British Library

Filmset by Selwood Systems, Midsomer Norton
Printed in Great Britain by Butler & Tanner Ltd, Frome and London

CONTENTS

ILLUSTRATIONS

Between pp. 118–119

Fenwick, Kate's childhood home by the sea in Connecticut (AP/Wide World Photos)

Katharine Houghton Hepburn, Kate's mother (Connecticut Images)

Dr. Thomas Norval Hepburn, Kate's father (Alfred Webster Collection)

Mrs. Hepburn in 1911 with her three oldest children, Tommy, Kathy (Kate), and baby Dick (Connecticut Images)

Tommy and Kathy (Alfred Webster Collection)

Mary "Aunty" Towle and Kathy at Fenwick (Connecticut Images)

A family portrait taken shortly before Tom committed suicide in 1921 (Alfred Webster Collection)

Kate in the male role of Oliver in *The Truth About Blayds* at Bryn Mawr College in 1927 (Springer/Bettmann Film Archive)

Kate as Pandora at Bryn Mawr's 1928 May Day celebration (Alfred Webster Collection)

Kate as Antiope in *The Warrior's Husband* on Broadway in 1932 (The Bettmann Archive)

The aspiring actress (Alfred Webster Collection)

Kate and John Barrymore in *A Bill of Divorcement*, her first film (Alfred Webster Collection)

Kate in *Christopher Strong* (both Connecticut Images)

Kate as Jo in *Little Women* (Connecticut Images)

Kate and George Cukor on the set of *Little Women* (UPI/Bettmann)

Margaret Sanger and Mrs. Hepburn at the 1934 birth control hearings in Washington, D.C. (UPI/Bettmann)

Mrs. Hepburn delivers a speech at Carnegie Hall in 1935 (AP/Wide World Photos)

Kate on the set of *Alice Adams* with director George Stevens (UPI/Bettmann)

Kate as Mary of Scotland (Alfred Webster Collection)

Kate and John Ford on the set of *Mary of Scotland* in 1936 (Alfred Webster Collection)

John Ford on his yacht, the *Araner* (AP/Wide World Photos)

John Ford (AP/Wide World Photos)

John Ford and his wife, Mary (AP/Wide World Photos)

John Ford with his daughter, Barbara (AP/Wide World Photos)

Kate and Dennis Hoey in the 1937 Theater Guild production of *Jane Eyre* (UPI/Bettmann)

Howard Hughes (UPI/Bettmann)

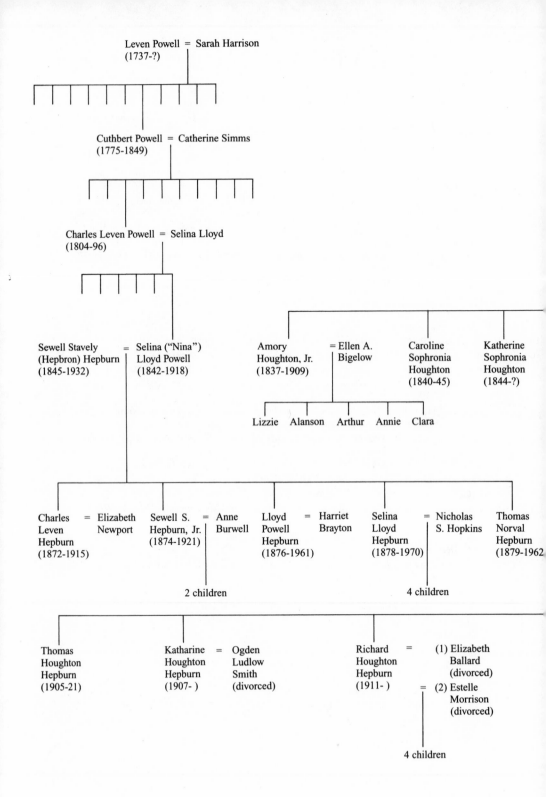

KATHARINE HEPBURN
forebears and family

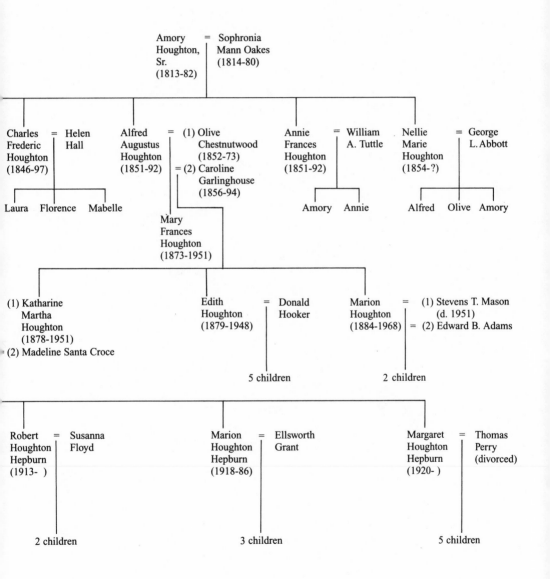

Amory Houghton, Sr. (1813-82) = Sophronia Mann Oakes (1814-80)

Charles Frederic Houghton (1846-97) = Helen Hall

Alfred Augustus Houghton (1851-92) = (1) Olive Chestnutwood (1852-73) = (2) Caroline Garlinghouse (1856-94)

Annie Frances Houghton (1851-92) = William A. Tuttle

Nellie Marie Houghton (1854-?) = George L. Abbott

Laura   Florence   Mabelle

Amory   Annie

Alfred   Olive   Amory

Mary Frances Houghton (1873-1951)

(1) Katharine Martha Houghton (1878-1951) = (2) Madeline Santa Croce

Edith Houghton (1879-1948) = Donald Hooker

Marion Houghton (1884-1968) = (1) Stevens T. Mason (d. 1951) = (2) Edward B. Adams

5 children

2 children

Robert Houghton Hepburn (1913-) = Susanna Floyd

Marion Houghton Hepburn (1918-86) = Ellsworth Grant

Margaret Houghton Hepburn (1920-) = Thomas Perry (divorced)

2 children

3 children

5 children

PROLOGUE

A little over fifty years ago, the superintendent of Prospect Lawn Cemetery in the village of Hamburg, New York, looked up in astonishment as the door to his office flew open and Katharine Hepburn swept in. He stared at the familiar freckles and fine bones, the fox-colored hair and piercing blue eyes. The movie star's sudden arrival was so baffling and unexpected he hardly knew what to say.

She did not introduce herself. If he doubted for a moment that this really was Katharine Hepburn, he could doubt no more when he heard her distinctive nasal voice ask him to help locate the grave of Alfred and Caroline Houghton. Her manner was intent, direct, no-nonsense; she did not explain why she wanted to see the grave.

The superintendent, who also ran a small monument business, checked the records. He found a card recording Carrie Houghton's purchase of a burial plot on November 1, 1892. Then he led Hepburn across the road to section A, lot #12, in the old graveyard. He left her there to study the dates carved on the small, upright double marker of her maternal grandparents.

In 1993 when I visited Katharine Hepburn in her Manhattan townhouse for the first time, she was still trying to find out about Fred and Carrie. Without inquiring how I knew, she asked probing questions about what I had been able to learn.

There is a strong sense in Kate's family that their story begins with the mysterious events surrounding Fred Houghton's violent death in 1892, and Carrie's death eighteen months after that.

"Did you find out yet? Do you know why Fred Houghton

1

killed himself?" Kate's younger brother Bob, then eighty, asked several times with unmistakable urgency as I was researching this book. In a family fraught with secrets, Bob was sixty before he learned that their grandfather had taken his own life.

For Kate, who discovered their older brother Tom hanging by the neck in a New York attic in 1921, the past seems to hold a special lure and danger. Certainly she does not talk freely or openly about the past, not even, it seems, with her family. When I interviewed Bob and Kate, each was eager to know what the other had said about certain highly charged subjects.

Bob told me that some topics, particularly the story of Fred and Carrie Houghton, were simply never discussed in the household. Young Tom's name was rarely mentioned after he died. One reason the past continues to exert such a powerful hold over all the Hepburns is that they know so little about it.

As I probed Katharine Hepburn's life for this biography, as I read her private correspondence and the letters of those who knew and loved her, I have come to understand how much her own story is part of a larger family saga. She responded to the suicides in her family by turning herself into a relentless life-force. In relationships with dark, self-destructive men like Spencer Tracy, John Ford, and the poet H. Phelps Putnam, she attempted to answer questions she had been forbidden to ask about her brother Tom or the others.

That is the story I have tried to tell. It is a story of the power of the past, and one woman's struggle to come to terms with and triumph over it.

Although I interviewed Katharine Hepburn and many others for this book, I saw early on that I was going to have to piece the narrative together for myself. No one has ever known the whole story until now.

My research began on a hot afternoon in a dusty, airless storeroom in Buffalo, New York, about ten miles north of the cemetery where Fred and Carrie Houghton are buried. As I opened the first of two large brown boxes marked "CARRIE G. HOUGHTON," an avalanche of brittle, yellowed letters, papers, and documents poured out. Reading them allowed me to enter a vanished world.

PART ONE

Go into thy closet and when thou hast shut the door, pray to thy Father which is in secret and thy Father which is in secret will reward thee openly.

MATTHEW 6:6

ONE

On a sunny Friday afternoon, October 28, 1892, forty-one-year-old Fred Houghton and his younger sister Nellie Abbott left a massive stone house on Pine Street in Corning, New York, to ride in her carriage.

For two months, Fred had been desperately ill, paralyzed with the worst of the depressions that had plagued him all his life. His always fragile hold on himself had shattered completely as he sank into a mist of impenetrable despair. Finally, two weeks previously, their oldest brother, Amory Houghton, Jr., had traveled four hours to rural West Hamburg, outside Buffalo, New York, to bring him to Corning to recover.

Fred, who had spent nearly a lifetime struggling to escape his brother's shadow, seemed somehow to have expected Amory to come. Large and corpulent, with fragrant, well-trimmed whiskers, Amory, head of the Corning Glass Works, was the richest and most powerful Houghton; another brother, Charlie, worked for him there. Without protest, Fred packed his bag and followed Amory out of the farmhouse overlooking Lake Erie, where Fred lived with his second wife, Carrie, and their three daughters.

Two weeks in Amory's thickly curtained guest room with a constant stream of Houghton relatives coming and going seemed only to plunge Fred into a deeper crisis. He lay in the enormous canopied bed for days at a time. On all sides, Ellen Houghton's cut-glass collection, hundreds of precious bowls, goblets, and decanters, sparkled with dizzying white light and prismatic color.

Of the seven Houghton siblings—three brothers and four

sisters—Fred and Nellie had always been closest. Amory, fourteen years older than Fred, seemed like another generation. As children, Fred and Nellie had been inseparable. Yet in the days since Amory had brought him here, Nellie had not been able to persuade Fred to accompany her on a carriage ride to the suspension bridge. She whined, pleaded and cajoled; but nothing would change his mind. Fred's resistance would have troubled her deeply for it had never been that way between them before.

That Friday, when Fred unexpectedly sent word to his sister to come for him after the midday meal, she must have thought that this was the sign of improvement the Houghtons had been waiting for, the turning point in Fred's terrible bout of depression.

Somewhere in the black coat he wore against the west wind that swept across Corning that day, Fred concealed a revolver. He had brought it with him from West Hamburg. For two weeks the gun had lain hidden in the guest room.

The fashionable streets where Amory and the other Houghtons lived occupied a hill above the glass works. As Nellie's horse trotted down to the Chemung River, Fred would have seen the factory's eight chimneys, each more than one hundred feet high, spewing clouds of black smoke across the landscape. He would have seen the great pile of sand at the mouth of the sand shed, and Amory's workmen, their faces swathed in dark masks, shoveling the fine white powder into wheelbarrows on their way to the mixing room. Small boys known as runners appeared at regular intervals with tin lunch pails overflowing with beer.

Seated beside his sister, Fred must have felt the revolver pressing against him. Nellie had always been sensitive to his every mood and whim. Perhaps he thought she would guess his plan. Perhaps he was counting on her to stop him in time.

At four o'clock, Nellie's carriage headed back uphill. They paused at the corner of Third Street, and Fred climbed down. Nellie watched him for a moment as he slowly walked up the stone path to Amory's house. She turned her horse around and proceeded to Second Street, then one block over to Cedar, where she lived with her husband George Abbott, a business associate of Amory's.

When Fred did not appear at supper, Amory assumed he had agreed to dine with the Abbotts. Several hours later, when there was still no sign of him, Amory grew worried. In recent days he had observed his brother's desperation at close range. He trudged around the corner, hoping he would find Fred lingering at Nellie's.

Late into the night, search parties combed the woods and quarries around Corning.

Nellie Abbott, tortured with guilt, remembered that she had never actually seen Fred go into the house. It was the last image she had of him: slowly approaching, never quite reaching, the front door. She had merely assumed that she had brought him home safely. Amory guessed that Fred had waited for Nellie to lose sight of him before he turned and vanished into the gathering darkness.

No one ever knew precisely what path Fred took that night. The noisy streets near the glass works were crowded with men and boys milling among the saloons that catered to factory workers. Others, laughing and drinking from flasks, were on their way to the cockfights in a shack on the bank of the Monkey Run.

It must have been raining when Fred reached Walker's Lumber Yard at the foot of Cedar Street, almost at the riverbank. Whether he had headed there deliberately or whether he had been wandering in wild confusion and despair, the quiet and solitude suited his purpose.

At 6:30 on Saturday morning the rain had begun to taper off when two railroadmen, Ira Miller and J. H. McCarthy, were moving a boxcar down the Fall Brook railroad switch which cut through the lumber yard. They saw Fred Houghton's body stretched across the track. His light brown hair was matted with blood from the gaping wound in his forehead. He seemed to have been lying in the rain for hours, the gun still tightly clutched in his right hand.

That morning when the police reported Fred's suicide to the Houghtons, Nellie Abbott seemed to take it hardest. Why hadn't she saved him? Why hadn't she known? And even if she had failed to suspect what he was about to do, was there anything she might have said or done that afternoon which could have changed his mind?

Nellie's many questions would never be answered. Fred's body had been discovered at the foot of Cedar, the street where the Abbotts lived. Had Amory been wrong about Fred's plan to trick her? Had Fred turned around at Amory's door only to follow her home?

Was there something more Fred wanted to say to her? But why had he failed to come in? When he reached her house, why had he kept on walking?

And if indeed Fred had planned to kill himself all along, why had he chosen to involve his sister? This perhaps was the most frightening and unsettling question. Surely Fred could have slipped out of Amory's house on his own; there was no need to make Nellie his unwitting accomplice. He of all people knew how sensitive she was and how much she loved him. He would have known the years of unanswered questions and regret to which he was condemning her.

Could his cruelty to her have been intentional? Or by that time, was he just too far gone to care?

While it is impossible to know precisely why Fred Houghton killed himself, family letters, including Fred's correspondence with his first wife, Ollie Chestnutwood, offer significant clues.

Born on March 5, 1851, Alfred Augustus Houghton spent a troubled childhood in Cambridge, Massachusetts, and Brooklyn, New York. Fred was nothing like his tough, aggressive, beefy older brothers. Amory, Jr. and Charlie seemed to have inherited their father's ferocious drive, energy, and ambition. Fred, moody and lethargic, could hardly rouse himself from bed some mornings. Known as the "artistic" Houghton, he read books, studied philosophy, and played Schubert and Chopin on the violin. He dreaded following his brothers into the glass manufacturing business.

Amory, Jr., in his late twenties, was already their father's partner at the Brooklyn Flint Glass Company when Fred was still a schoolboy. Fred measured everything he did in terms of Amory's achievements, and felt inadequate in comparison. Shrewd and undeniably brilliant as a businessman, Amory was famous for his lacerating tongue. He took pleasure not just in winning, but in mocking and humiliating his adversaries, including business associates and family members who opposed him. Even Charlie, so much more resilient than Fred, could hardly bear to work with Amory and briefly left the firm in 1866, when he was twenty.

Two years later, Fred was next in line to work at the family's new factory in Corning when his father intervened. Amory, Sr. was a rich man now, but he had started poor as a carpenter's apprentice. Dressed in rags, with dirt on his face and under his fingernails, he had often watched the rich boys at Harvard and dreamed of what it would be like to have their advantages. Now, to show how far the Houghtons had come, he announced plans to send his eighteen-year-old youngest son to Harvard.

When Fred Houghton entered the freshman class in the fall of 1869, for the first time he perceived himself as having an identity and purpose in his large family. He was to have something that even his brother Amory, superior in all things, lacked; neither Amory nor Charlie had gone to college. By now, Charlie had been sucked back into Amory, Jr.'s orbit and was unhappily working in Corning. Fred rejoiced that Harvard had saved him from Charlie's miserable fate. Although his father and brothers planned for Fred to enter the firm after graduation, he secretly dreamed of a career as a scholar or a diplomat.

That spring, as Fred completed his first year at Harvard, his father's business failed. The new factory in Corning proved too expensive to operate. In September 1870, a court placed the Corning Flint Glass Works in receivership. Nathan Cushing, a Boston businessman, swooped in to buy the bankrupt factory.

Amory Houghton, Sr. was ruined. Fred's return to Harvard in the fall was out of the question.

The family pinned its hopes on Amory, Jr. when Nathan Cushing, the new owner, appointed him manager. Amory, at thirty-four, recognized the opportunity of a lifetime. He blamed his father's failure on waste and vowed personally to oversee every penny the newly reorganized company spent. Not a single particle of white sand would escape his meticulous attention, if that was what it took to make the business profitable.

Within months it became evident that Amory's frugality and precise management were going to work. By 1872 Nathan Cushing agreed to allow Amory to return the factory to family hands by purchasing it on credit. As always, Fred was astonished by his brother's confident mastery of the situation. He cheered along with the other Houghtons when Amory single-handedly retrieved their father's business. But by then, Fred was convinced that his own life had been ruined.

After withdrawing from Harvard, Fred worked briefly for Amory in Corning. Amory demanded that his brother arrive at the factory punctually at 8 a.m. to set an example to the workers. Fred's habitual lateness caused Amory to set another sort of example; he was fired.

In the months that followed, Fred worked with scant enthusiasm to become a lawyer. He studied law books and court papers in a Brooklyn law office, but the dreams he had once nurtured at Harvard, the newfound identity and sense of purpose, had vanished. Fred was back where he started, living under his brother's shadow, which suddenly seemed more gigantic, oppressive, and inescapable than ever.

In 1872, the year Amory rescued the factory, Fred married nineteen-year-old Olive Chestnutwood. Levi Chestnutwood's five daughters had been friends of the Houghton girls in Brooklyn. The brash and cantankerous Kate Houghton, Fred's oldest sister, was the intimate of Frankie Chestnutwood (whom she always addressed as "Frank"). Nellie, the youngest Houghton, considered frail, kind-hearted Ollie her best friend.

Marriage does not seem to have assuaged Fred's torments. The first Mrs. Houghton catalogued her husband's peculiar obsessions and nighttime terrors: Upon retiring he would search their bedroom for intruders, in the closets, behind the curtains, and under the bed. Even in his own house on Adams Street in Brooklyn, he would rise repeatedly throughout the night to check the latch on the bedroom door. The bride euphemistically referred to Fred's anxiety attacks as his tendency to "feel sick in the night," and plied him with brandy to relieve the pain.

When Ollie was eight months pregnant in 1873, she dreamed that she was safe in bed with Fred's arm wrapped tightly around her. "When I got awake and found you were really not there, I could hardly believe it, you do not know how disappointed I was," she wrote from her father's house in Buffalo.

Fred was back in Brooklyn; on account of Ollie's poor health, he had brought her to Buffalo to give birth to "little Houghton" with her mother, Mary, and sister Frankie nearby. Frankie feared that the bout of ague, the cold, hot, and sweating fits Ollie suffered during the first year of marriage, had left her too weak and thin to sustain the pregnancy; and apparently there was much truth to it. But in Ollie's letters to Fred, the "little wife" seemed more concerned with her husband's delicate health and spirits. "Dear Fred, How I would love to see you this morning, it seems too bad that little H. should have separated us for so long a time," she wrote. "If you will only keep well, it won't be so very long until we are together again."

Their daughter, Mary Frances Houghton, was born on August 25, 1873. Three months later, on November 19, Ollie died in her father's house. She had never become well enough to go home. At twenty-two, Fred Houghton was a widower with a baby daughter he could hardly find the strength or the sanity to care for. Alternating between feelings of guilt, rage, and despair, he wondered how he would go on himself.

Not long after Ollie's funeral, Fred closed the house in Brooklyn and moved in with the Chestnutwoods. In the beginning, he saw this as a temporary arrangement until he got his bearings.

Fred remained with Ollie's family for three years. During that time, Frankie's husband, John Linen, completely and unexpectedly turned Fred's life around.

Although everyone spoke of the house on East Eagle Street where they all lived as Levi Chestnutwood's property, John Linen had been discreetly paying the bills since his father-in-law had failed in business. When it seemed that old Mr. and Mrs. Chestnutwood might lose their home, John Linen asked permission to move in. Linen, president of the large and successful Buffalo Scale Company, obviously did not need to live under another man's roof; but the generous rent he and Frankie paid allowed Levi Chestnutwood to keep his property without the loss of face involved in accepting a handout.

John Linen exercised similar tact in his assistance to Fred Houghton. He hired him to work with Levi Chestnutwood in the management of Buffalo Scale. Recognizing that Fred was tortured with self-doubt, Linen skillfully nurtured his confidence. No man had ever taken an interest in Fred before, certainly not his brothers, and his career flourished under Linen's patient guidance. When Fred married Caroline Garlinghouse in 1876, when he started a new family, when he rose through the ranks to become vice-president of Buffalo Scale, it seemed to him that he owed it all to John Linen, without whom he still probably would have been nothing.

To most eyes Fred Houghton was a success: a prominent businessman, a loving husband and father, the owner of a seven-acre gentleman's farm outside Buffalo. To his neighbors in West Hamburg, he was one of a small group of wealthy Buffalonians who acquired houses there in the 1880s when the railroad service improved. Fred and Carrie Houghton, their three daughters and several servants, became familiar figures in the rustic lakefront community.

Harry the coachman took Mr. Houghton to the Athol Springs train station every morning and picked him up at night; once or twice a week, Harry drove Mrs. Houghton to Hamburg village to place orders at the grocer and butcher. The family swam in Lake Erie, rode horses on the beach, and tramped through the fields to pick wild strawberries. The girls had their own pony cart and two of the first bicycles at the lake.

Nellie Abbott, who spent summers at Cloverbank, near Fred and Carrie's farm, had never seen her brother so active or in better spirits. But in private, with only his wife and daughters to see, "recurrent, chronic depression" continued to torment Fred. In 1877, the year after Fred remarried, John Linen had fallen gravely ill. Linen, who was only forty at the time, recovered; yet Fred seemed never to get over his own unutterable terror at the prospect of losing him.

Fifteen years later, this terror returned in force as John Linen lay dying at his home on Niagara Street in Buffalo. It was autumn 1892; with his wife, Frankie, and son, Georgie, at his bedside, he lingered in excruciating pain until January 10, 1893. Meanwhile, responsibility for the day-to-day functioning of Buffalo Scale fell on vice-president Fred Houghton, who quickly crumbled under the pressure.

Now that John Linen needed him, Fred was helpless, unable to think or act effectively. It was a nightmare. Convinced of his own worthlessness, Fred terrified his wife and daughters with talk of killing himself. At any other time in their marriage, Carrie would have turned to John Linen; but that October, there was really only Amory Houghton, Jr. to ask for help.

Kathy was Fred and Carrie's oldest daughter. On Sunday mornings after breakfast, the child would disappear upstairs to her bedroom overlooking Lake Erie. Walking softly on the fragrant grass matting that covered the creaky floors of the farmhouse, she slipped into her closet to pray in secret.

The deaths of several of Kathy's young first cousins haunted her. In 1888, her father's brother Charlie Houghton and his sister Annie Tuttle had both lost children; and Kathy had asked permission to go to the Episcopal church with her half-sister, Mary Frances.

Ollie's daughter lived in Buffalo, where she was being raised by her grandmother and aunt. Theirs was the only home Mary Houghton had ever known. When Fred remarried, he left Mary with Frankie Linen, whose own daughter (also named Mary Frances) had died in infancy. In the Chestnutwood household, Mary Houghton, pale and severe, was openly regarded as having replaced Frankie's dead child. Because of this, and because Mary's mother had died shortly after Mary was born, Kathy, like the other children, associated Mary with the mystery of death.

Kathy, whose father often privately spoke of death as something he longed for, made the ten-mile train trip to Buffalo every

Sunday with her governess to pray with Mary and old Mrs. Chestnutwood. On Easter Sunday 1889, Fred and Carrie left the children with the governess while they went horseback riding. Eleven-year-old Kathy secretly took her younger sisters, Edith and Marion, into Buffalo alone to attend church. It must have seemed to Kathy that her father's adamant rejection of God made her own prayers and those of her sisters all the more necessary.

Despite Kathy's fervent churchgoing, the threat of death crept closer to home. Nellie Abbott was Kathy's favorite Houghton relative, in part because Fred always seemed happiest in her company. When six-month-old Amory Abbott died suddenly in 1890, Kathy was terrified she had done something wrong. Hadn't she faithfully prayed with Mary that the dying would stop?

Kathy seized on a line in her Bible: "Go into thy closet and when thou hast shut the door, pray to thy Father which is in secret and thy Father which is in secret will reward thee openly." She stopped going to church. Perhaps God wanted her to express her devotion in a less showy manner. Perhaps if she prayed in secret with only God to see and hear, her prayers would be answered and her father would stop wanting to die.

Not long after the death of Nellie Abbott's baby, all the Houghtons came to West Hamburg. Amory Houghton, Jr., staying at Fred's, was given Kathy's room while she doubled up with Edith.

It was Sunday morning. Everyone, Fred and Carrie, Edith and Marion, Uncle Amory and the others, had gone out, probably to visit the Abbotts at Cloverbank. Kathy, left alone in the house, ran up to her own room. Hardly had she gone into the closet, dropped to her knees, and begun to pray, when she heard slow, heavy, awkward footsteps on the grass matting.

Uncle Amory, who suffered from gout, walked with difficulty. The bedroom door creaked open and the wheezing fat man dragged himself to the iron bed. Cringing among the dresses in her dark closet, Kathy heard her uncle's enormous laced boots, first one then the other, drop to the floor.

For as long as Uncle Amory remained there resting his swollen feet, Kathy struggled to keep silent. Every time the bed squeaked, she felt certain Amory had heard something and was on his way to find her. The child promised herself that if he opened the closet door, nothing would make her tell what she was doing there or for whom she had been praying.

Fred Houghton's body was loaded onto the Lackawanna Express in Corning on the afternoon of Saturday, October 29, 1892. Fletcher and Cook's undertaking rooms, where the police had deposited him that morning, provided a temporary coffin. An undertaker from the firm of Brady and Drullard waited at Buffalo, where Fred was to be cremated according to specifications in his will, made seven years previously.

All day Sunday, the Houghtons and their many friends and business associates arrived at the Iroquois Hotel in Buffalo. Only nine months before this, Amory, Charlie, Nellie, and the others had gathered here for the funeral of their sister Annie Tuttle, who had died in childbirth. But Fred's death aroused very different thoughts and emotions in the family, for unlike poor Annie he had chosen to die. He had chosen, whether consciously or not it hardly mattered, to subject the Houghtons to the stigma of suicide.

Although it was then common practice (and still is) to avoid scandal and disgrace by falsely attributing certain suicides to natural or accidental causes, there would have been no possibility of doing that with Fred, who was found with a bloody wound in his forehead and a gun still clutched in his right hand. Amory Houghton, Jr., aware that these and other grim details would be copiously described in newspapers in Corning, Elmira, Buffalo and other upstate New York cities and towns, moved quickly to dispel the rumors of inherited insanity that swarmed like locusts around families in which suicide occurred.

In nineteenth-century America, suicide was widely believed to be a form of madness that ran in families. In even the most prominent family, a single suicide might be a sign that the stock was deteriorating, and the harbinger of suicides in generations to come. Amory's confident assertion to the press that simple "overwork" had

driven Fred to commit suicide may have successfully controlled
newspaper coverage in upstate New York; but it was unlikely to
ease his family's painful anxieties about what Fred had done and
what it meant for themselves and those they loved.

At the time, no one could have pondered these questions more
fully or with greater urgency than Fred's widow. The Houghtons
of Corning had each other to cling to if that was what they cared to
do. But Carrie Houghton, at thirty-six, was alone and isolated, with
three young daughters to consider, when Amory's telegram
announcing her husband's suicide arrived in West Hamburg.

Carrie, small and outspoken, with unruly nut-brown hair and
enormous dark eyes, had been married to Fred since she was nineteen and he was twenty-five. Although she considered herself an
intelligent, even a superior woman, Carrie had always depended on
Fred to make the family's major decisions, particularly where the
outside world was concerned.

Her first independent decision, to send Fred to Corning two
weeks before, had been a disastrous mistake. She must have realized
that when the telegram arrived. She had entrusted her husband to
the one man whose power and influence he dreaded; and in doing
so she had confirmed Fred's worst nightmares about what was to
become of him without John Linen's protection.

All at once, more decisions faced her. Whatever guilt Carrie
may have felt would have to be put aside. She had to act quickly
before Amory arrived and took over as everyone in the family
(including Fred) would have expected him to do.

Amory had already sent precise instructions for where and
how to bury Fred. He had checked; there was a space beside Ollie
in the Chestnutwood plot at Forest Lawn Cemetery in Buffalo.
Amory knew Carrie's age and (although he had yet to read the will)
had a fair idea of Fred's assets. Property would have to be sold, of
course, and the proceeds invested. The strictest economies must
be instituted. But Amory would take care of all that later. In the
meantime, he calculated that under the circumstances, the young
widow would almost certainly need, perhaps even want, to remarry.
Better to bury Fred with his first wife, which had the advantage of

costing the estate nothing. The space at Forest Lawn was theirs for the asking.

Carrie found all this unacceptable. To her, Fred's suicide was an ugly statement on their sixteen-year marriage. Everything they had built, everything Carrie believed was meaningful and important, Fred had publicly called into question with a single gunshot.

Carrie harbored no bad feelings about Fred's first wife. Ollie's family, especially John and Frankie Linen, had always been exceedingly kind to the second Mrs. Houghton and her daughters. Still, she could not bring herself to bury Fred with Ollie. To do that must have seemed like an admission of something Carrie didn't feel: that her own life with Fred, the children they had created, the values they had shared, the music they had made together, had been worthless.

As late as Sunday, Amory and the other Houghtons expected Fred to be buried in Forest Lawn. That afternoon Carrie drove by carriage to another cemetery, Prospect Lawn, about three-quarters of a mile from the center of Hamburg, in Water Valley. She paid fifty dollars for a double grave for her husband and herself.

On Monday morning a cold rain pounded Buffalo as Amory Houghton, Jr., stooped beneath an immense black umbrella, led the mourners to the 8:15 local train to Athol Springs in Hamburg. At the lakeshore station, a grim row of carriages from Brady and Drullard waited in the fog to carry the visitors along rutted, rain-slicked dirt roads. The stout, red-faced, bearded brothers, Amory and Charlie, and their plump wives, Ellen and Helen, shared a carriage whose great wooden wheels slashed deeply into the mud.

When the mourners reached Prospect Lawn, the widow had another surprise in store for them.

Amory and Charlie, raised as Congregationalists, had been affiliated with the Episcopal Church for many years; both served as vestrymen at Christ Church of Corning. Fred, under the influence of the popular orator Robert G. Ingersoll, had become a freethinker, a scoffer, and an atheist. The families of atheists often gave them religious burials in the hope that God might accept their poor, wretched souls after all. This is what Amory assumed would be done with Fred; but Carrie had other ideas.

There was no minister to say a prayer for Fred Houghton's soul when his wife and daughters placed his ashes in the earth. Fred, having deemed his life a shambles and a failure, had chosen to die (as Ingersoll would have said) without taking gods, heavens, or hells into account. Amory's objections notwithstanding, Carrie wanted at least to give Fred the dignity of burying him in accordance with his beliefs.

After the funeral, the family sat down to lunch at Fred and Carrie's farm. It had started to rain again. The sound of water drumming on the roof could be heard throughout the house, which was crammed with old books, drawings and penny prints, and shabby, comfortable, mismatched furniture. Persian and Smyrna rugs were scattered everywhere on the grass matting.

Toward evening, Amory entered Fred's study to sit at the pine desk and examine his brother's financial records.

It was all much as Amory had expected. The estate was pathetically small. There was some minimal life insurance, but that would take many months to collect. There was the seven-acre farm, but Fred had mortgaged it heavily. There were more than one hundred shares of capital stock in Buffalo Scale Company, valued at perhaps $100 a share; but the imminent death of the firm's president and the suicide of its vice-president made this a poor time to sell.

Carrie brought out her husband's will. Everything, whatever that might mean, was left to her, much as Amory would have anticipated. What Amory had failed to anticipate, and what shocked him greatly (although he must have struggled to conceal his shock from Carrie), was Fred's having appointed her, not Amory, executor. Fred advised but did not require Carrie to ask for Amory's advice on financial matters. It was unthinkable, an insult and an outrage. Fred, as if to make his intentions toward Amory even clearer, gave John Linen the right to buy the Buffalo Scale stock from Carrie at any price Linen deemed fair. In this matter Amory's advice, were Carrie to ask for it, would not be a factor.

As Amory studied the will, Carrie must have known how angry it would make him. She would already have suspected the precarious financial circumstances in which Fred had left her, and how desperately she needed Amory's help and counsel to bail her out. Yet when Amory, obviously expecting her to ask for advice, looked up from the two-page will, Carrie was pointedly silent.

T W O

On Saturday morning, November 5, exactly one week after Fred's suicide was discovered, Roland Crangle, a young process-server from the Erie County Surrogate's Court, climbed the steps up to the front porch of the Houghton farmhouse in West Hamburg and knocked on the door.

When Kathy answered, Crangle must have guessed that the slender, graceful child with fine light chestnut hair and green eyes was the fourteen-year-old. He unfolded one of three sheets of heavy creamy-white paper. He read off her full name, Katharine Martha Houghton, and handed her an impressive-looking document with a gold seal in the lower left-hand corner. Then he called out two other names: Edith Houghton and Marion Houghton. As Kathy's sisters, aged twelve and nine respectively, peered out from behind her, Crangle served them with summonses to appear on November 17 at a court hearing to ratify their father's will.

At a glance, Kathy and Edith, the two oldest, hardly looked or acted like sisters. One was soft and feminine, the other scrawny, angular, and boyish.

Kathy was a clothes-horse. With her mother's encouragement she sketched her own costumes for the seamstress to sew. She collected rich, colorful fabrics—velvet, silk, taffeta, and dimity. She had a flair for dramatic excess. Her dresses had more lace, braid, ribbons, and bows than anyone else's; her skirts were always a foot or two fuller and her waists a fraction of an inch tighter. She wore

20

her hair pulled back loosely with a bright silk ribbon to show off her blazing eyes and long, elegant neck.

Edith was a tomboy. A fringe of dark sandy bangs covered her forehead. Her thick wild hair flew in every direction. Edith lacked the patience to be measured for new clothes, so her gingham dresses were often comically short or tight. She always seemed to have a rip in her elbow from climbing trees or falling down in a race with the local farm boys. She would have preferred to wear a boy's shirt and trousers but her mother wouldn't hear of it.

Kathy and Edith adored each other. Almost certainly, their father's troubles had made them closer than they might otherwise have been. They pulled together to shield Marion, whom they regarded as the baby. The older girls had developed well-defined roles for coping with the hurt, fear, and confusion Fred's violent mood swings provoked. Early on, Kathy taught herself to rein in her anxieties in front of others and forced herself to appear to respond calmly, but Edith was by temperament unable to keep her feelings in check. Kathy's reassuring equanimity kept the sisters going. Edith's agitated outbursts gave voice to the turbulent emotions they all felt.

The girls trusted their mother to rescue Fred from his fits of despondency and immobility. Eventually, he probably would have come out of his dark moods without Carrie's efforts; but repeated successes made her appear almost omnipotent to the girls.

Ollie Chestnutwood had naively done what she could to soothe her husband with brandy and baby-talk. She did not live long enough to develop other, possibly more effective means of bringing Fred out of his pain. Carrie, in the early years of marriage, experienced similar bewilderment. Gradually she taught herself to be vigilant for the first signs that Fred was about to slide into torpor and despair. She learned that it was her duty to leap in and save her husband from the black depths into which he threatened to drag them all.

Carrie transformed herself into a determined advocate of life. When Fred wanted to withdraw, she forced him into the open air.

When he crawled into bed, she roused him for a brisk walk in the woods or a horseback ride on the beach. When the blood drained from his face, she gave him the latest, most controversial book to force him to stop thinking about himself. When his eyes flashed with terror, she dragged him into the living room and pressed a violin into his hands; then she began to play the piano. Fred joined in and soon the exquisite sounds of Schubert and Chopin would fill the house and pour out over the lake.

The children's world crumbled when Fred killed himself in 1892. They had often heard their father talk of death. They were intimate with his pain and knew that sometimes he experienced an overpowering disgust with life. But somehow Carrie had always been able to save Fred from himself; and when she did not, suddenly everything her daughters knew to be true was open to question.

Sometime between Crangle's arrival to summon them to court and the hearing on November 17, Amory Houghton, Jr. returned to West Hamburg. Down to the penny, he laid out for Carrie what she had, what she owed, and what was owed to her. It was a grim picture.

He explained the mortgage. He explained the inadvisability of selling Fred's stock. He pointed out that Buffalo Scale owed Fred a little over $4000. Her husband's life insurance, when and if she finally collected it, would amount to $3000. Out of that, funeral expenses must be paid, as well as legal fees connected with the administration of the estate. Three physicians and a nurse who had treated Fred during his final siege had submitted claims. Carrie's debts came to $1000, which left her—an uneducated, unskilled widow—with about $6000 to live on for the rest of her life. Should Carrie's daughters fail to marry, perhaps they would have to live on it too.

He waited. When Carrie still did not ask for his help and advice (as Fred's will suggested she should), Amory wished her well and returned to Corning.

The hearing at Erie County Surrogate's Court was to have been routine. Relatively little was at stake. Kathy, Edith, and Marion, who accompanied Carrie to the hearing, were not about to contest

Fred's decision to leave everything to their mother. Still, they were minors, so the surrogate, Jacob Stern, had appointed Buffalo attorney Charles Bullymore temporary guardian to represent the interests of Fred Houghton's daughters. Carrie, of course, remained the permanent guardian of her girls.

Amory Houghton, Jr. came from Corning to observe the proceedings. Young Georgie Linen, John's son, attested that the signature on the document was indeed Fred's. William Tuttle, the widower of Fred's sister Annie, swore that he had witnessed the signing in 1885. Roland Crangle rose in court to certify that he had personally handed summonses to three of Fred Houghton's daughters in West Hamburg and a fourth in Buffalo.

Crangle's humdrum testimony threw everything into chaos. Suddenly, Jacob Stern had a great many questions. Fred's will made no mention of these living arrangements. Why were Fred's daughters living apart? Wasn't Carrie Houghton Mary's mother? If not, what was Mary's legal status? Was there no one to represent poor Mary's interest in the estate? How could Bullymore represent Carrie's daughters as well as Mary when their interests were so obviously at odds? When Fred Houghton wrote his will, had he made no special provision for his eldest daughter?

Until this moment, no one seemed to have given more than a glance to the drab, thin, painfully shy nineteen-year-old who had left her prayer vigil at John Linen's deathbed to attend the hearing with Georgie and their grandmother, Mary Chestnutwood. Suddenly, Mary Houghton was the center of all discussion, probably to her great embarrassment.

Technically, Mary had no permanent guardian. With Fred's death she became an orphan. At the time Fred wrote his will, Levi Chestnutwood was already gone. Perhaps Fred had expected that John Linen would assume guardianship, although Linen's relationship with Mary had never been formalized and Fred knew it. As far as the court was concerned, John Linen's imminent death left Mary in a treacherous legal limbo.

Carrie and her daughters listened as the arguments about Mary shot back and forth. To the girls, already frightened by Fred's suicide, the debate about their half-sister (who Mary Houghton was and where and to whom she belonged) must have been deeply unsettling. The court clerk hastily scratched out Mary's name from page after page of legal documents where she had been listed with Carrie's daughters. Although Mary had lived with the Linens all her life, the surrogate, in light of John Linen's health, appointed William Tuttle Mary's permanent guardian.

Mary's plight triggered powerful emotions of anger and indignation in Carrie. Fred had done nothing to provide for his eldest daughter. He had not even mentioned her in his will. He had left her penniless and wholly dependent on the kindness and charity of others. Weeks after Mary's status was finally settled and the surrogate admitted Fred's will for probate, Carrie could not stop thinking about Ollie's daughter.

Mary Houghton served as a grim warning of what could happen someday to Carrie's daughters if she did not act to protect them now. Ollie Chestnutwood Houghton, in the months before she died, had allowed herself to dream that Fred was her protector, his arm wrapped tightly around her in the night. Carrie, realizing finally that she and her daughters did not have that luxury, sent word to Amory Houghton, Jr. to ask for help.

It was winter. Snow and ice blanketed the dirt roads, making them impassable to anything but a horse-drawn sleigh. There was little traffic; many of the lake houses stood empty. Small boys from Hamburg village grabbed onto the backs of sleighs headed out to the lakeshore to deliver groceries or the rare visitor.

In December, Carrie struck a bargain with Amory.

She and he were in the master bedroom of the farmhouse going through Fred's old clothes together. Amory was convinced that there was much treasure to salvage from Fred's cupboard. There was no question that any of the coats or trousers they examined would actually fit Amory, but he was interested in the material, which could be cut up and reused. Amory, who had once fired Fred for habitual lateness, was also keenly interested in Fred's gold pocket watch. He offered Carrie $300 for the lot.

When she accepted, no cash changed hands. Amory added the

sum to the other monies Carrie had already asked him to invest. In large part, this consisted of the more than $10,000 Amory advanced Carrie and the girls against the future sale of Fred's stock. When the $3000 life insurance was paid in March, this too Carrie promised to send him.

Carrie gave Amory control over her finances. She agreed to live on the small sums he doled out from her income. She agreed to make a full and detailed accounting of even her most trivial monthly expenditures, to conceal nothing, and to allow Amory to demand changes when he felt that she or the girls were being wasteful. And she reiterated that she wanted her brother-in-law to take charge of her life; he had not forced his help or advice on her, he had not even suggested any of this until she asked him to step in.

If Carrie mentioned it at all, she certainly did not emphasize what she hoped to do with the money his investments earned. Knowing Amory's violent opposition to women's education, she would have said little or nothing about her plans to send Kathy, Edith, and Marion to college.

Carrie, to guarantee her daughters' independence, had agreed to give up her own.

In all the years Carrie had lived at the lake, winter had always been a bleak, harsh, desolate time, and the winter of 1892–3 seemed the worst by far. Like most of the businessmen who used their lakefront farms as vacation homes, Nellie Abbott, her son Ted (named after Fred), and daughter Ollie (after Ollie Chestnutwood) had returned to town. With the exception of Carrie's friend Sarah Deane in Buffalo, there was no one but Amory to confer with that winter as he shuttled regularly between Corning and West Hamburg to discuss financial arrangements and urge her to sell the farm.

Carrie, awake at night beneath a pile of blankets, listened to the flapping arms of a windmill in the distance. Life with Fred had taught her that introspection was dangerous; to allow oneself to think too much was to stray perilously close to the edge.

Naturally, Fred's suicide would have posed a great many painful, difficult, perhaps unanswerable questions for Carrie and the children. Why had he done it? Why hadn't he left a note? Did his act of self-destruction mean he hadn't loved them?

Carrie, for better or worse, chose finally to leave all such questions unasked and unexplored.

Following the disgrace of his brother's suicide, Amory would not have been surprised (and might even have been somewhat relieved) to see Carrie take up "the shawl and the sofa," as neurotic female invalidism was sometimes described; but Carrie, with three young children to care for and no one she trusted to take her place, was determined to avoid that fate at any cost.

The brutal fact of Fred's suicide could hardly be concealed from the girls; Edith especially would have read the detailed accounts in the Buffalo newspapers. Still, in the interest of protecting her daughters from the nightmare thoughts that presumably had done Fred in, Carrie discouraged the girls from talking about the suicide, asking questions, or even thinking about it. Carrie enforced the rule of silence even when she and the children were alone together; when Carrie was absent, Kathy kept Edith and Marion in line. Their father was dead and that was that.

Carrie's insistence that they keep the suicide a family secret had the unintended effect of making it seem shameful to the children. The suicide in their past became a hidden source of guilt, fear, and perplexity that was all the more threatening and powerful for remaining off-limits.

Kathy had a cozy room upstairs at the lake house that she called her study. The three sisters had their own bedrooms, but Kathy was allotted a separate space for painting and drawing. She took art lessons with a private instructor and dreamed she would become a great artist some day. The study, with its low, sloping ceiling, was not much larger than a broom closet. There was a tiny stone fireplace with a soft white fur rug in front. Fred had carved a mantelpiece from a rough old barn beam so that Kathy could display her plaster casts of children, saints, and animals. From floor to ceiling she covered nearly every inch of wall space with overlapping engravings and illustrations from old books. Her favorite image showed the artist Rosa Bonheur's donkey looking over a fence.

Several times a week Kathy invited Edith and Marion to her retreat. She coaxed her sisters to pose naked on the fluffy white rug near the fire, while she drew countless studies in her sketchbook. Edith was always long, slim, and bony; when she tilted her head forward, her sharp spine poked out beneath the skin. Marion, soft and round, had not yet shed her baby fat.

These sessions were among the rituals that helped the girls survive the long, lonely winter after their father died. Another was afternoon tea, which Carrie served in gold and white porcelain cups and saucers at an immense round wooden table draped with a starched white cloth.

Before Fred died, Carrie and Sarah Deane had frequented the lectures on women's rights at the Women's Union Coterie in Buffalo. Carrie, sipping mint tea beside the fire in her living room, led the children in discussions based on all she and Sarah had heard. As far as Carrie was concerned, no topic was too controversial or advanced for the girls. She encouraged her daughters to discuss almost anything except the one subject that undoubtedly troubled them most.

Determined to put the past behind them once and for all, that spring Carrie decided to sell the farm and move to cheap rented quarters in Buffalo, near Sarah Deane and her husband, Elisha. The lake house was full of painful memories and (with its mortgage and staff of servants) far too expensive to maintain. On May 2, 1893, Carrie signed the property over to her brother-in-law. Amory invested an additional $11,000 on Carrie's behalf, nearly doubling her principal.

The widow spent the next three weeks selling off much of the best furniture and other possessions she and Fred had taken sixteen years to accumulate. The horses went first, then the carriage, then little Marion's cart and pony. Carrie allowed the girls to decide what few things each would take to their new life in Buffalo. They spent their last night at the lake in September.

When the children opened the front door of the rented row house on Hodge Avenue that fall, the aroma of grass matting filled their nostrils. Carrie had stripped the mats from the floors in West Hamburg. The tattered Persian and Smyrna rugs, which she hadn't had the heart to sell, brightened the dingy rooms. Carrie had set up the tea table where her daughters would see it right away, and laid it out with silver and china and a cut-glass tea caddy. Her piano was here, and two of Fred's violins.

The girls were not supposed to talk or think about their father, but his presence loomed everywhere. The shelves groaned with hundreds of his books. There was the chess table where Edith had played with Fred when he was in high spirits, and the willow rocking chair where the sisters had watched him sit for hours staring into the flames.

In the rabbit warren upstairs, Carrie had done her best to reproduce the children's bedrooms at the lake. When Kathy warily peeked in at her new room, she discovered her favorite lace and cotton curtains. Three plaster casts from Kathy's study (one of Saint George, the others of children) and the engraving of Rosa Bonheur's donkey decorated the oak night table beside her bed. There was space for little else.

A great deal was missing, of course, but Carrie encouraged her daughters to view their losses positively. The sale of household possessions had provided an additional $4000 for Amory to invest.

Carrie's obsession with preparing the girls for college helped sustain her through some very difficult times. While at first her plans were vague, she seemed to relish the irony of using Amory's business acumen to help create precisely the kind of independent woman he despised. In November, a more specific image of that new woman began to take shape in Carrie's mind when she read newspaper accounts of M. Carey Thomas's election to the presidency of Bryn Mawr College in Pennsylvania.

The life of the brilliant, rebellious, iconoclastic thirty-six-year-old daughter of wealthy Baltimore Quakers was already the stuff of legend. From childhood, M. Carey Thomas (the M. was for Martha, which she rejected in favor of the androgynous Carey) knew she was destined for better things than wifehood and motherhood. She vowed that she would never allow herself to be financially or emotionally dependent on any man, her physician father included. She aimed to have a career as a doctor, geologist, naturalist, or scholar. Warned that girls were by nature less intelligent because their brains were smaller and lighter, Thomas declared: "By the time I die my brain shall weigh as much as any man's if study and learning can make it so." She signed her diary "Jo March" in identification with the tomboy heroine of Louisa May Alcott's *Little Women*.

She completed undergraduate studies at Cornell University in two years, then applied to be the first woman graduate student at Johns Hopkins University. There, Thomas was forbidden to attend classics seminars with men because a woman's presence might diminish concentration. One professor, however, is said to have invited her to attend his Greek seminar if only she would agree to sit concealed behind a large wooden screen.

Carey Thomas rejected "the crumbs," as she scolded the Hopkins administration before decamping for Europe to receive her doctorate *summa cum laude* in German philology at the University of Zürich. It was, she wrote home to her mother, "the highest possible degree—a degree which no woman has ever taken in Philol. before and which is hardly ever given."

In 1884, Thomas, aged twenty-seven, applied for the presidency of the new Bryn Mawr College for women, where her father James Carey Thomas was a trustee. With typical aplomb, she guaranteed that she "could make the college more of a success than anyone else." Instead, the board of trustees appointed her dean of the faculty, professor of literature, and assistant to Bryn Mawr's first president, James E. Rhoads. Carey Thomas held these posts for nine years. During that time she established the "Bryn Mawr standard" and radically altered the very nature of women's education in America.

Many nineteenth-century educators believed that the purpose of a woman's education was to make her pleasing to her husband and a softening influence at home, especially with her young sons. To paraphrase Rousseau, women were educated (if they were educated at all) to counsel, console, and care for their men, and to make life sweet and agreeable.

At Bryn Mawr, Carey Thomas instituted rigorous entrance requirements including preparatory work in Latin and Greek. She designed the nation's toughest entrance exams with an eye toward the notoriously difficult Harvard exams. She limited the faculty to holders of doctorates and founded distinguished graduate programs and fellowships modeled on Johns Hopkins and the German university system. She promised women the finest university education available to anyone, male or female, in the United States.

Mrs. Houghton's plans crystallized as she read about Carey Thomas's appointment to the Bryn Mawr presidency upon Dr. Rhoads's retirement. Certainly, Thomas's passion for creating self-reliant women would have exerted a powerful attraction. As Carrie told her daughters, she had desperately wanted to go to college when she was young; but her father had disapproved. The tale of how the headstrong Quaker overcame extraordinary obstacles to obtain her degrees had an exhilarating effect on Carrie Houghton; like a great many American women that November, she identified with Thomas's struggles and found vicarious comfort in her triumph.

It has been said that the obstacles facing any young woman who applied to Bryn Mawr made the prospect of acceptance seem like nothing less than "entrance into paradise." That winter, one year after Carrie buried her husband, she discovered a sharp new focus for her energies. She dedicated herself to preparing her daughters to meet the Bryn Mawr standard.

At the lake, private tutors had given the girls only a smattering of Latin, German, French and other academic subjects. Eager to compensate for the deficiencies that would almost certainly keep them out of Bryn Mawr, Carrie consulted anyone in Buffalo who might help. At the Buffalo Library early that winter, she approached Ellen M. Chandler, assistant to the superintendent, J. N. Larned. Miss Chandler quizzed Kathy and Edith about their training and background, then urged Mrs. Houghton to subscribe at once to Mr. Larned's work-in-progress, *History for Ready Reference and Topical Reading*. The first two volumes were available at five dollars each.

In Carrie's reduced circumstances, ten dollars was a considerable sum; and it was scarcely the sort of expense of which
Amory (who demanded to know where every penny went) would
approve. Nonetheless, Carrie paid out of her monthly pittance and
signed a contract for the complete set. Kathy and Edith could begin
studies in history, politics, and economics immediately.

By the time of Kathy's sixteenth birthday on February 2, 1894,
Carrie had learned about Miss Baldwin's School for girls in Bryn
Mawr, Pennsylvania. Florence Baldwin, the daughter of a Con-
gregationalist preacher, had founded the school in 1888 to train
students to pass the Bryn Mawr entrance exams. It was James
Rhoads, the president of Bryn Mawr, who had suggested the idea
for a preparatory school to Miss Baldwin, a fellow parishioner at
Bryn Mawr Presbyterian Church. Tall and imperious, with dark
eyes, a beak nose, and upswept hair tightly wound into a bun on top
of her head, Florence Baldwin hinted at her own standards when
she told the faculty: "We shall probably have some girls each year
who do not belong here, but we shall not have the same girls two
years!" Of her first five graduates, four passed the Bryn Mawr
entrance exams. Miss Baldwin's School was all Carrie Houghton
might have hoped for; sending Kathy, Edith, and Marion there
would nearly guarantee acceptance to Bryn Mawr.

But after the trauma Carrie and the children had just been
through, they did not want to live apart. In the aftermath of Fred's
suicide (which they continued to avoid as a topic of conversation),
mother and daughters found the idea of separation far too painful.

Finally, Carrie and the girls agreed they might move to
Pennsylvania together. In early spring, Carrie would take Kathy to
meet Miss Baldwin and have a look at Bryn Mawr. If they liked
what they saw, Carrie proposed to rent a small house there for
September. That way the girls would not have to board; they could
go on living with their mother when they began school in the fall.

On May 13, 1894, Carrie Houghton would be thirty-eight.
Shortly before her birthday, she and Kathy entered the dark gray
stone archway to Carey Thomas's Bryn Mawr.

The Pembroke Arch is still there today, but the privileged,

highly charged, hermetically sealed world Mrs. Houghton and her daughter discovered when they stepped through it has mostly vanished. It was a world of theater, ritual, and masquerade that symbolically set off the scholar from other young women.

Bryn Mawr girls wore full academic dress: handsome gowns of fine black serge or nun's veiling and close-fitting black caps with a square flat top and a tassel. The costume was modeled on the Oxford scholar's gown that Alys Pearsall Smith, Carey Thomas's cousin, had brought from England in 1885. Small distinctions were crucial. Undergraduates wore their sleeves to the wrist; the sleeves of graduate students fell dramatically to the foot of the gown.

To be at Bryn Mawr in its "golden age" was to be assured that there was no activity more important or of greater consequence to society than one's academic work. The college provided every possible luxury and amenity; nothing of the mundane world and its time-consuming petty demands must impede or distract the passionate young scholar. Thomas, with her disdain for traditional domestic roles, strictly ruled out all housework and other "feminine nonsense." Maids scrubbed the girls' spacious private rooms, laundresses washed their clothes, and waitresses served trays of milk and sugar-flecked biscuits in the student parlor every morning promptly at eleven. Professors who intended to be absent from class were required to notify Thomas's office, so that the president's assistant could send respectful notes of explanation to the girls, whose precious time must not be wasted. Even the most eminent international scholars, scientists, authors, and experts whom Thomas had personally recruited to teach at Bryn Mawr were not exempt.

All this had nothing to do with the pampering many wealthy girls received from indulgent fathers and husbands, who put women on a pedestal only to render them incapable of independence. In an era when women were commonly regarded as scarcely able to think or act for themselves, Carey Thomas demanded that Bryn Mawr students be treated with dignity and respect; everything must be done to nurture feelings of confidence and self-worth.

In an America whose Constitution did not yet give women the vote, Bryn Mawr girls ruled themselves through the nation's first student self-government. Students made their own rules of conduct and set their own punishments; and by and large the president hesitated to interfere even when she believed them mistaken.

"You can do it!" was Carey Thomas's revolutionary message to Kathy Houghton and the other young women who passed through Pembroke Arch for the first time. Thomas did not guarantee to make every girl a "professional scholar" in four years, only to give her the power and capacity for independence that came with "mental discipline and the intelligent comprehension of things."

Enthralled by the supportive community of women she and Kathy had discovered at Bryn Mawr, Mrs. Houghton asked Florence Baldwin to reserve three places for her daughters, promising to send the $75 fee as soon as she found a house for the fall and returned to Buffalo.

Suddenly, for a very short time that spring, everything seemed possible. Carrie had finally discovered a way to guarantee her daughters' future. Amory, as expected, opposed the move; but aside from making a good deal of noise, there was little he could do to stop them. Though Amory controlled Carrie's finances, she remained free to spend her pittance as she wished. According to her calculations, everything about their new life in Bryn Mawr was safely within her means. The modest house she and Kathy had chosen cost no more than the one she was already renting. At Baldwin the tuition for day students was less than what she would have had to pay tutors in Buffalo.

Carrie set the date of the move for late August. That way she would have the girls settled into their new home before the fall term began. She sub-leased the house in Buffalo to W.G. Rappleye, director of the University Preparatory School, promising that the house would be empty by September. The children excitedly announced the impending move to Sarah Deane, Ellen Chandler, and almost anyone else who would listen.

Afterward, Carrie could not remember exactly when the sharp pain in her abdomen started; but sometime in early summer, as she and the children prepared to leave Buffalo, she became aware that something was very wrong.

The pain became increasingly severe. She lost considerable weight. Perhaps at first Carrie told herself that she was exhausted from all she had been through lately; and there may have been some truth to it. But then she started to spit up blood. When she finally decided to see Dr. Charles Stockton, he suspected advanced cancer of the stomach, and urged her to go to New York City immediately for exploratory surgery.

Everything was happening much too quickly. Carrie, more than ever, must have realized how entirely alone she was. She hadn't made a will. There was no family member she trusted to raise her children should anything happen to her.

In June, a surgeon in New York City told her that she had "inoperable" stomach cancer.

As her condition deteriorated steadily throughout July, Carrie struggled to maintain focus. Before the illness, she had very nearly had her daughters on the path to Bryn Mawr. Every element was in place. But now, only weeks later, there was no telling what would happen to Kathy, Edith, and Marion after their mother was gone.

Carrie realized that even if she devised a plan, she could not depend on her relatives to honor her wishes. Amory Houghton, Jr. certainly would never agree to give the girls a university education; but probably neither would her brother, Frederick Garlinghouse, or her cousin, Mack Smith. The notion of an educated, independent woman was antithetical to everything these men believed in. Carrie, much as she longed for her daughters to have a home, could scarcely bear to think of them under the same roof with Amory, Frederick, or Mack.

By the end of July, Carrie had a plan that must have shocked a good many people when they learned about it. She decided that her daughters must not live permanently with any of their relatives. Instead, she wanted the children to live together in Bryn Mawr exactly as they had planned before Carrie became sick. She tentatively secured the services of a housekeeper, Mrs. Prince, to care for the girls while they attended Baldwin as day students. Carrie hoped to get the girls to Bryn Mawr before Amory, Frederick, or Mack could stop them. Once they were safely there, Florence

Baldwin (of whom it was said that "her word was better than a man's bond") could be trusted to take care of the rest.

Carrie wanted Kathy, Edith, and Marion to remain together as a family; at this point the sisters had only each other to depend on. Carrie's written instructions make clear that she wanted to spare her daughters having to spend school vacations with relatives, as boarding students might be compelled to do. She did not want the girls suddenly to find themselves, like Mary Houghton, poor relations dependent on the kindness and charity of others.

Nonetheless, when Carrie became too weak to care for the girls, she reluctantly sent eleven-year-old Marion to spend the rest of the summer with Mack Smith and his wife Nettie in Canandaigua, New York. She planned for Marion to rejoin Kathy and Edith in Bryn Mawr in September.

In the second week in August, Carrie, in the final stages of illness, arranged to enter Hornell Sanitarium in Hornellsville, New York. She sent Kathy and Edith to stay with Nellie Abbott in Corning, a few miles away.

On August 13, removal men arrived at Hodge Avenue to crate up the family's belongings. Carrie ordered everything placed in storage until the house in Bryn Mawr was ready. The movers agreed to come back next week for Carrie's wooden bed and hair mattress, dressing table, heavy sash curtains, and a few other pieces of furniture in her room.

On August 15, Carrie, confined to bed, wrote her last will and testament in indelible ink, in the presence of her lawyer Henry Lyon and her friend Sarah Deane. She left her estate to "my three children, Katharine, Edith, and Marion, share and share alike." She expressed her wish "that the arrangements I have made for the education of my children at Bryn Mawr shall be carried out." She gave details of the house she had rented for them there and of the housekeeper she had hired, but left final approval on these and other decisions to Kathy. Carrie's failure to appoint Amory Houghton, Jr. or any other guardian was a significant gesture, especially in light of the trouble that had ensued when Mary Houghton was discovered to have no legal guardian.

Necessarily, the financial arrangements were another matter. Carrie had faith in Kathy's ability to carry out her wishes for the girls' education and living arrangements, but what would a sixteen-year-old know of money and investments? Carrie had to depend on Amory to continue to use his acumen on the girls' behalf.

That Carrie agonized over whether to appoint Amory executor is suggested by her decision to make Frederick Garlinghouse and Mack Smith his co-executors. From experience, Carrie had to have known how angry this would make Amory; but she evidently could not bring herself to give him total financial control over her girls. She must have hoped that her brother and cousin, whatever their limitations, would at least provide a counterbalance.

While Carrie left all major financial decisions to the executors, she asked that her money "be kept in good interest-bearing securities." She asked the executors to pay as much as possible of the girls' expenses at Bryn Mawr out of the interest from her estate, and to divide what was left equally among her daughters when the youngest, Marion, turned twenty-one. Finally, the mother directed Amory, Frederick, and Mack to pay her girls "a monthly allowance of five dollars for their personal wants and amusement."

Two days later, Carrie left the house on Hodge Avenue for the last time. She was assisted by Miss Richardson, a nurse from Buffalo General Hospital. A hired carriage took them to the train station for the trip to Hornellsville.

On Friday afternoon, August 17, 1894, a phaeton from Page House Livery waited in the heat for the Buffalo express. Newspapers in rural western New York were calling the summer of '94 the most arid in twenty years. In Hornellsville, where it hadn't rained for weeks, the Canacadea Creek was nearly bone dry. The railroad station was surrounded by miles of parched, brown fields and hills.

The phaeton driver knew it would be easy to pick out his passenger when the express pulled in. Most of the patients at Hornell Sanitarium came there to die. Carrie Houghton, a small, skeletal figure wrapped in a heavy wool shawl, may yet have retained some hope as Miss Richardson helped her down. The sanitarium advertised a special "system for removing and curing cancerous tumors" whose results were said to be "most remarkable and unprecedented" even with patients other physicians had declared incurable.

The phaeton rolled through a wooded ten-acre private park to Hornell Sanitarium, a five-story brick building that overlooked the valley. Carrie, undoubtedly exhausted after the trip, would have to be assisted up a flight of broad wooden steps to the front entrance. Probably she met her new doctor, Clarence L. Starr, before being escorted to her apartment in a separate wing with other cancer patients.

New patients at Hornell were often kept awake by the loud, continuous hum of a massive rotary fan outside the building. The fan, attached to a mile of pipe, pumped fresh air medicated with balsam, creosote, or carbolic acid into flues in the brick partition walls.

Carrie had a great deal to think about in the night. A formidable task faced her next week when Kathy was set to visit for three days. The children had not yet seen her will and Carrie had no way of knowing whether they ever would. It is a measure of how little Carrie trusted her executors that she felt compelled to explain the details to her oldest daughter. She had to be certain that Kathy knew and understood her wishes.

Carrie had to find the words to explain the responsibility she was leaving Kathy and to give the child some idea of what faced her should the executors oppose Carrie's plans. The mother would have known how frightened and confused the girls must be only a year and a half after their father's suicide. Carrie had been their anchor through all the changes and dislocations. What must they be going through in anticipation of losing her?

On Monday, August 20, the phaeton took Kathy up Bald Hill. The following day, Carrie left her bed for the last time to walk with her daughter in the tree-shaded grounds. At the risk of wounding Edith, who remained in Corning, she had asked to see Kathy alone. Carrie knew her girls. Edith, exceptionally intelligent and articulate, was also fractious and excitable. Her strong opinions and intense enthusiasms could get the better of her. Bursting with life, fourteen-year-old Edith had difficulty focusing on one thing at a time.

Carrie's message to Kathy was to allow nothing to distract the girls from the goal their mother had set. No matter what the executors might do or say, it was up to her to keep the sisters together and get them to Bryn Mawr. Kathy, who returned to Corning the next day, remembered her mother's words as "a divine command."

Frederick Garlinghouse arrived from Pittsburgh the following week. Carrie asked him to walk down to the Hornellsville business district to purchase indelible ink, pens, and paper. She wanted to write letters to her daughters. On Thursday morning, at Carrie's request, Frederick sent a telegram to Mack Smith in Canandaigua, asking him to bring Marion. Kathy and Edith were summoned from Corning.

On Saturday, more than 8000 people attended the bicycle races at the farmers' club fair in Hornellsville. It was the day Kathy, Edith, and Marion came to say goodbye. They were with their mother when she died at Hornell Sanitarium on Sunday, September 2.

Frederick stayed in Hornellsville to wind up his sister's affairs. Mack and Nettie Smith took the girls to Buffalo in anticipation of the funeral on Tuesday.

The girls wanted to be alone with their sorrow—but where? Although they thought of Buffalo as home, the house on Hodge Avenue was no longer theirs. Edith and Marion looked to Kathy to decide what to do next. She decided they would stay with Mary Houghton, who still lived with Frankie Linen and Mary Chestnutwood on Niagara Street, until it was time to leave for Bryn Mawr. Before the train reached Buffalo, the sisters had agreed. It probably never occurred to Kathy that Mack Smith would object.

At the station, when Kathy told Mack her plans, he flatly declined to allow Marion to accompany her sisters. Kathy and Edith were free to go to Mary Houghton, but Marion must stay with the Smiths at the Iroquois Hotel. Mack Smith may have sincerely believed that Marion was too young and upset to be sent off with her sisters; but Kathy saw this as the first of the battles Carrie had asked her to fight to keep the girls together. It must have been hard for Kathy to understand when Mack ended the discussion by simply taking Marion with him. Kathy and Edith headed for Niagara Street in defeat.

Frankie Linen and Mrs. Chestnutwood took the girls in. Tormented with guilt that she had betrayed her mother's wishes by allowing Marion to go off with the Smiths, Kathy vowed to retrieve the child on Tuesday after the funeral. By that time, Mack Smith would be headed back to Canandaigua. Kathy planned to take her sisters to Bryn Mawr within days.

Carrie's body, which Frederick had ordered wrapped in a hammock, arrived on the Buffalo express Monday night. Amory shipped a casket and black robe from Corning. To give the undertaker time to prepare the body, Carrie's funeral was scheduled for 1:30 on Tuesday afternoon at the home of Sarah and Elisha Deane.

On Tuesday morning, Carrie's executors met at the Iroquois Hotel to examine the will and decide how to proceed. As Carrie had predicted, Amory found much of the document unacceptable. What Carrie could not have anticipated was how quickly her brother-in-law assessed the dynamics in the room and seized control.

Frederick Garlinghouse, a consulting and contracting engineer who specialized in bridges, steel buildings, roof trusses, and girders, seemed mainly concerned about the time and money he had lost in Hornellsville. He made clear that the major business of Carrie's estate must be settled by September 6, when he would be returning to Pittsburgh. As his sister lay dying, Frederick had noted the 55 cents she had asked him to spend for indelible ink, pens, and paper, the 25 cents it had cost to telegraph Mack Smith, and the $1.05 to call Kathy and Edith in Corning. Evidently the sisters had been out when Uncle Frederick telephoned to summon them to Hornellsville, requiring him to call three times at 35 cents a call.

It was not difficult to see what Carrie's brother was about. To give him something to ponder, Amory declared that Frederick couldn't have a penny until he submitted a properly itemized bill.

Mack Smith, by contrast, was eager to be actively engaged in every aspect of Carrie's estate. He seemed to bask in the colossal presence of Amory Houghton, Jr., with whom he sought every opportunity for involvement. He was desperate to be thought of as the millionaire's partner, confidant, and friend.

Mack was also keen for the money he could earn were Kathy, Edith, and Marion to board permanently in Canandaigua. He strongly agreed with Amory that Bryn Mawr was out of the question; Frederick didn't care.

In time to leave for Carrie's funeral, the executors voted to disregard her instructions. They agreed to send the girls to Canandaigua. Mack Smith would be paid to provide room and board, and handle the estate's day-to-day paperwork. Amory, freed from having to take his nieces to Corning (which he probably would have done rather than allow them to go to Bryn Mawr), would invest their money and approve all expenses. The girls' applications to Baldwin and the rented house in Bryn Mawr would have to be cancelled immediately.

Kathy and Edith knew nothing of this when they arrived at Sarah Deane's with Mary Houghton and Frankie Linen. Kathy had waited all morning to see Marion. But when Mack Smith arrived, he or Nettie kept a proprietary arm around Marion throughout the funeral service. Fifty camp chairs had been set up in Elisha Deane's living room; Kathy and Edith weren't even seated next to their sister. Marion, anxious for affection, clung to her cousins. Later that day, after Carrie was buried beside Fred in Prospect Lawn Cemetery in Hamburg, Marion returned to the Iroquois Hotel with the Smiths.

Kathy still had not been told the executors' plans when Amory and the others met with Carrie's lawyer Henry Lyon at his office on Wednesday morning. Lyon had helped Carrie draw up her will and witnessed her signature three weeks before. Still, he acquiesced when Amory instructed him to list the girls' permanent address on court documents as c/o Mack Smith, Canandaigua, New York.

Amory argued that Carrie had been too sick to think clearly when she wrote her will; obviously the girls would be better off living with relatives than in rented quarters with only a hired woman to care for them. Amory would not have mentioned that the relatives expected to be paid.

By afternoon, a process-server arrived at Frankie Linen's house to notify Kathy and Edith that Mr. Lyon had submitted their mother's will to the surrogate, Jacob Stern. Hardly had the girls read the document when Amory Houghton, Jr., Mack Smith, and Frederick Garlinghouse paid a surprise visit. Uncle Frederick was due to return to Pittsburgh the next day, so the executors were anxious to settle matters quickly.

Amory was shocked and annoyed by the resistance he met when he told Kathy and Edith they were to go to Canandaigua with the Smiths. In case Amory thought she was unfamiliar with the will, Kathy cited the provisions her mother had described, especially the house in Bryn Mawr. She also mentioned her promise to Carrie to keep the girls together. At that point, Amory would have guessed that he already held the winning card. Mack Smith had Marion. She had spent much of the summer with the Smiths and had formed a noticeable attachment. Amory declared that there was little he could do should Kathy and Edith run off; but twelve-year-old Marion must go to Canandaigua. He left it at that.

When Amory signaled Mr. Smith and Mr. Garlinghouse (as he always called them) that it was time to leave, Kathy had not yet made up her mind. Her mother had been buried just the day before, and already the child was being required to make a momentous decision.

She agonized for days. Unlike Edith, who would eagerly have gone to war with Amory, Kathy recognized the need for a strategic retreat. Her mother had been right: Kathy possessed the ability to focus and do whatever was required to reach a goal. In this case, it appears to have taken Kathy several days to remember that her aim was not a rented house in Bryn Mawr. Nor was it a year at Miss Baldwin's. Her mother had intended the house and the preparatory school as means to an end. Carrie had asked her to keep the sisters together and get them to Bryn Mawr—the college. Whatever Kathy decided, she must have that goal constantly in sight.

Kathy's tactical skills came from watching her mother, who had negotiated a strategic retreat of her own after Fred's death. Whatever Amory said or did to provoke her, Carrie resisted the personal struggle that had consumed her husband. Carrie had never allowed herself to hate Amory. She realized that going head-to-head when she was powerless to budge him could only divert her from the real goal.

Sometime in the week between September 5 and September 13, Kathy, still staying at Frankie Linen's, sent word to Amory that she and Edith would go to Canandaigua on one condition. Making a demand was an important gesture; if Amory accepted or even entertained it, that meant the sixteen-year-old had engaged her uncle and forced him to negotiate.

Amory can only have laughed when he received Kathy's demand to take the Bryn Mawr entrance exams, scheduled to begin on September 24. Kathy could not possibly pass. He knew that Carrie had planned to send her to Miss Baldwin's for the 1894–5 school year to prepare her for a first attempt in June 1895; and he knew that even then further work at Baldwin was likely to be needed. It was inevitable that Kathy would return from the week-long exams in humiliation and defeat. Strange to say, Kathy must have known that too. Guilty about having agreed to go to Canandaigua, she probably wanted to show that she was not reneging on her promise to Carrie. Her insistence that she take the exams proved that Bryn Mawr remained her goal; she and her sisters would just have to get there some other way.

To pay for Kathy's ill-fated trip to Bryn Mawr, Amory made a great display of deducting $200 from her mother's estate. If Kathy insisted on squandering her paltry inheritance, so be it.

At 2:30 p.m. on Monday, September 24, Kathy failed the two-and-a-half-hour exam in plane geometry. At 9 a.m. on Tuesday, she failed the three-hour test in algebra. On Wednesday morning at 9, she failed Latin grammar and composition; and that afternoon at 2, she failed physical geography. On Thursday morning between 9 and 10:30, she failed the exam in Virgil, which required applicants to "translate simple passages at sight." Girls usually took the Bryn Mawr entrance exams in two parts; had Kathy passed at least some subjects, she would have been invited back for tests in French, German, English, and modern history.

Amory was waiting for Kathy when she returned to Frankie

Linen's in anticipation of leaving immediately to join her sisters in Canandaigua. After her experience, Amory would have been the last person she expected or wanted to see.

Even with a child as his adversary, it was the sort of painful moment Amory relished. He announced that while Kathy had been wasting time and money in Bryn Mawr, he had been right here on Niagara Street negotiating the sale of Fred's Buffalo Scale stock to Georgie Linen. Amory might have sold Fred's 108 shares to Georgie at any time; he chose Friday, September 28, the day Kathy was due back from Bryn Mawr.

THREE

When Kathy was a little girl she would watch her mother at the dressing table, where Carrie kept two heavy cut-glass perfume bottles. The intricately faceted bottles with flat bases, long slender necks, and pointed stoppers had been a wedding present from Fred.

Carrie would pin up her hair. Then she would dab the etched tip of the stopper behind each ear. Kathy, mesmerized by the glittering facets, sometimes reached out to touch them. Carrie always caught the child's hand, explaining that the perfume bottles, with their six- or seven-inch necks, were very delicate; if Kathy wasn't careful, they would break.

As far back as the sisters could remember, the bottles had stood on Carrie's dressing table at the lake; later they had been among the personal treasures Carrie had brought to Hodge Avenue. Now they were in storage, along with nearly everything else Carrie owned at the time she died.

The week Kathy took the Bryn Mawr exams, Mack Smith had conducted a "private sale" of a small number of Carrie's household items, including her wooden bed (to Sarah Deane) and Kathy and Edith's iron beds. Marion's extreme upset led Nettie Smith to allow the twelve-year-old to keep her brass bed. Shortly after Kathy arrived from Buffalo, Mack announced that he and A. H., Jr. (as he always referred to Amory) had arranged to ship the remainder of their mother's possessions to Canandaigua. When the crates arrived, under no circumstances were the sisters to touch anything before they had asked permission of Mack or Nettie.

Amory had instructed Mack that Carrie's daughters must buy whatever they wished to keep. Until Mack had estimated the value of each item, Kathy, Edith, and Marion would be permitted to borrow a few things; but Mack warned that he or Nettie must fill out receipts. If an item was not returned later, Amory expected the sister who signed the receipt to pay for it.

All this must have seemed very abstract to the children. They must have wondered why they were being required to buy things they already considered theirs. And they can hardly have comprehended that for the next nine years, until Marion turned twenty-one, Amory would obsessively track every penny the girls spent. In the end, he and the other executors would deduct each sister's monthly allowance and all expenses from her portion of Carrie's estate.

Above all, Amory expected his nieces to be "businesslike." Every time they bought a piece of candy or the funny paper, they were to submit a signed receipt to Mack Smith. He recorded the item and sum in his ledger and submitted the receipt, no matter how trivial, for Amory's approval. Amory replied in a spidery hand on ruled paper trimmed to the exact size of his message. That the head of "the largest glass factory in the world" took the time to quibble over hundreds of receipts for items as insignificant as a button or a spool of thread and sums as small as a penny suggests the extent of Amory's preoccupation; he even annotated the girls' weekly laundry bills.

Mack apparently derived immense pleasure from lecturing the children on the accounting procedures he called "the Canandaigua plan." The sisters must sign here, Mack and Amory must sign there; and finally, nothing was valid if Mack failed to pound the receipt with his rubber stamp:

MACK S. SMITH, EXECUTOR, ETC.

ESTATE OF CAROLINE G. HOUGHTON, DECEASED

In addition to the weekly five dollars room and board Mack and Nettie billed each girl, there were numerous other charges. They even had to pay extra for bath water.

The imminent arrival of Carrie's possessions promised to bring Mack important new responsibilities. Amory assigned him to make a complete descriptive inventory: from Carrie's piano down to the last silver-plated nut-pick and bon-bon spoon. He was also to assess damage: a broken pitcher, a cracked mirror, a cut-glass basket with a chipped handle.

For days Kathy could think only of her mother's perfume bottles. She wrote to ask Mary Houghton to rescue the delicate bottles from Balk and Steuart before the crates were shipped to Canandaigua. Kathy was sure the long slender necks would break in transit.

When Mary applied at the warehouse, Mr. Balk informed her that she needed Mack Smith's permission to remove anything. After considerable back-and-forth, Mack reluctantly agreed. Mary took Carrie Houghton's scent bottles to Niagara Street; and at length, Kathy went to Buffalo and lovingly transported them by hand to Canandaigua.

After the trip, Kathy plunged into round-the-clock work with a private tutor. She paid Mr. E. H. Eaton with her own money, charged against Carrie's estate. On the basis of a suggested reading list from Bryn Mawr, Kathy estimated it would take her two years to prepare.

At Kathy's insistence, Edith and Marion were enrolled as day students in the college preparatory program at Miss Caroline Comstock's Granger Place School "for the thorough education of young ladies." Edith, who had borrowed her father's violin from the crates, began private lessons with Mr. Victor Bentley.

As quickly as possible after dinner with the Smiths, the sisters would retreat to Kathy's room where the glittering perfume bottles were set out on a table. For at least an hour, they read aloud to each other from their father's books. Kathy and Edith always began with a book they hoped would be "improving" to Marion and ended with something they considered entertaining (usually the English ballads and love songs their parents had favored). As intellectuals and free thinkers who valued art, music, and literature, Fred and Carrie had always looked down on the provincial cousins in Canandaigua.

Living with the Smiths, Kathy and Edith struggled to remain a unit apart and keep their identity as Fred and Carrie's children. Kathy, echoing her father, derided Mack and Nettie as "conventional."

Marion, traumatized after the loss of Fred and Carrie, continued to be drawn to the Smiths. She loved her sisters, but she longed to have parents again; Mack and Nettie, whatever their shortcomings, fitted the bill. Because Kathy and Edith were older, they had had more opportunity to develop a sense of themselves based on Fred and Carrie's values. Marion, by contrast, was extremely malleable. Kathy and Edith feared that she could easily turn into a "Smith" as Mary Houghton had long ago become a "Linen." They did what they could to keep the child from forgetting whose daughters they were.

There were frequent bittersweet reminders. On January 31, the sisters were spending the holiday with Mary in Buffalo when Ellen M. Chandler, assistant to the superintendent of the public library, appeared. When Miss Chandler heard that the Houghton girls were in Buffalo, she rushed to Niagara Street to present them with the latest installment of J. N. Larned's *History for Ready Reference and Topical Reading*: the subscription their mother had taken out when they first set their sights on Bryn Mawr.

By the time the girls returned to Canandaigua, Kathy had dramatically revised her plans.

After three months with the Smiths, it must have been the vision of Mary Houghton at home with her aunt and grandmother that made Kathy abandon the idea of staying with Mack and Nettie for two years. In 1892, the sight of Mary at Surrogate's Court had galvanized Carrie to make her daughters independent. Now, Carrie's girls were orphans like their half-sister; but Mary at least had a loving home with people who treated her as a daughter. Frankie Linen's house was another world from Canandaigua, where the Smiths regarded Kathy, Edith, and Marion as paying lodgers.

Kathy traveled to Corning to appeal to Amory. She wanted to take the Bryn Mawr exams in late May; and if she did well, she wanted him to permit Edith and Marion to transfer to Miss Baldwin's.

This time, there was no explosion from Amory; he listened indulgently as the child spoke her mind. He appeared to approve, even to encourage, Kathy's feelings of superiority to the Smiths; yes, she was right to feel closer to her Houghton uncle, and to believe that she could turn to him for sympathy and support—Fred's daughter deserved the very best the rich and powerful family had to offer. But didn't she realize that college was strictly for "dull, middle-class" girls? Amory told Kathy that no girl who was "really correct" would want to go.

He echoed the opinion of most wealthy Americans at the time; the old money of New York, Boston, and Philadelphia, and the new rich who aped them, tended to educate their daughters with tutors and in finishing schools. Well into the 1890s, a majority of female collegians were middle-class "calico" girls, who sought the financial independence and stability of a teaching career. According to popular wisdom, the calico girl's search for marketable skills and knowledge left her with little time or inclination to cultivate the social graces that distinguished the wealthy "velvet" girl. The female collegian was said to be "indifferently dressed," to lack "small talk and spontaneity," and to have "bad manners, when not utterly mannerless." Higher education was thought to make women rude, aggressive, and masculine.

Amory Houghton, Sr., like other members of the new rich, had sent his son Fred to Harvard as a sign of the family's rising fortunes; Amory, Jr. did the same with his oldest son. Alanson Houghton, Kathy's first cousin, had graduated from Harvard in 1886, and did graduate work in political economy at the universities of Gottingen, Berlin, and Paris.

A son at Harvard added immeasurably to a family's prestige, but the daughter who sought higher education could be a source of embarrassment, especially to the new rich, who were sensitive to any inference that their daughters needed to earn a living. Carey Thomas recalled that when she had pursued graduate studies in Europe, certain members of her family perceived it to be as much of a scandal as if she had eloped with the coachman.

Uncle Amory, whose sister Annie had married and had her

first child at fifteen, warned that if Kathy went to Bryn Mawr she would never marry. He reflected a belief common in nineteenth-century America; prominent physicians argued that the stresses of a college education left women unsuitable for marriage and child-bearing. Too much study and the poor health it entailed killed a woman's sexual desire and made her undesirable to men. In a popular caricature, the college girl was a bloodless, sexless monster. Cramming for exams made her features sallow and her eyes pearly white. She was prone to anemia, neurasthenia, degeneration of the sex organs, uterine disease, and madness.

Dr. Edward Clarke, professor at the Harvard School of Medicine, claimed that female collegians who worked too hard diverted blood from the ovaries to the brain, damaging their capacity to have healthy children. Another prominent physician, Silas Weir Mitchell, declared that the strain of intellectual exertion caused many college women to break down, leading inevitably to a life of "the shawl and the sofa." When Dr. Mitchell dined with Carey Thomas in 1888, he warned that "no woman could study and be well." Mitchell conceded that for all her academic degrees and honors Carey Thomas looked healthy enough, but assured her that she had "some secret disease that must show itself sooner or later."

In all apparent sincerity, Amory insisted that he was only trying to protect his niece when he urged her to give up the idea of Bryn Mawr. He proposed instead to send her to a French finishing school in New York City, where the feminine accomplishments (embroidery, drawing, singing, and playing the harpsichord) were taught. That would be more appropriate for a Houghton.

With the clear eye he used in business, Amory had assessed his opponent. He would have known Kathy's reputation as a clothes-horse. He would have guessed that she was not a natural bookworm like Edith. (Kathy's work with Mr. Eaton was an uphill struggle, but Edith's days of study at the Granger Place School were pure joy.) He would have calculated that the French finishing school and all the fun and luxury it implied had to be more appealing than Bryn Mawr.

It was—as Kathy probably would have been the first to admit; but a sense of duty to Carrie kept her from giving in.

Kathy and Edith decided that the only chance of getting Amory to capitulate was to make the Smiths want them to leave. This would be a formidable task, as Mack and Nettie were clearly delighted to have the extra income the girls provided; and Mack would scarcely want to give up the chance for almost daily correspondence with his hero. In desperation the sisters devoted an hour each night to pounding the floor of Kathy's room, directly above the living room where Mack spent evenings on his inventory of Carrie's possessions. When Mack or Nettie ran upstairs, the children insisted nothing was wrong. All this had an unintended result. Instead of throwing the girls out, Mack relished yet another opportunity to confer with Corning.

Amory, exasperated, promised to put an end to the nonsense. He notified the girls that he was taking them to court to have himself appointed guardian; that way, they would have to do as he commanded and settle down at the Smiths.

From Mary Houghton, Kathy learned that a seventeen-year-old had the right to approve anyone the court might name; the younger sisters, fifteen and twelve, would have to accept their uncle. Kathy quietly found a lawyer who agreed to replace Amory as her guardian.

The court date arrived and the sisters stood before the judge. Naturally, Amory assumed he would be appointed to supervise all three girls, until Kathy produced the attorney's letter and explained to the judge why she did not want her uncle. When it became evident that a stranger would be named to look after Kathy, Amory withdrew his petition.

It seemed a great victory. If Kathy did well in the entrance exams, Amory would permit Edith and Marion to begin at Miss Baldwin's in the fall. He even volunteered to escort Kathy to Bryn Mawr at the end of May and stay with her until she completed the week of tests. Eager for her powerful uncle's affection and approbation, Kathy misinterpreted the offer as a first sign of support. To celebrate, she took Edith and Marion to the most fashionable milliner in Buffalo to buy felt sailor hats for a triumphant return to Canandaigua.

In the last weeks of May, Kathy logged nearly one hundred hours with her tutor. Mack and Nettie used every opportunity to remind her that she was ill-prepared and would almost certainly fail.

Shortly before Kathy was due to leave, she discovered that Amory had invited Mack and Nettie's daughter to come along to Philadelphia. The exams began on Friday, May 31. On Thursday afternoon, when they checked into a hotel, Amory put the two girls in one room. Kathy, who had planned to study all evening and retire early, struggled to conceal her agitation. She did not want to offend her uncle, who had taken a rare week off just to be with her.

All smiles and joviality, he seemed to do everything to make her visit pleasant and comfortable. Amory had never shown such kindness before. To Kathy's amazement, he insisted on taking the girls to the theater and a late supper. He kept them out until long past midnight. Even when Kathy guessed what Amory was up to, she fought back her suspicions. It was hard to accept that Amory wanted to exhaust her for the exam tomorrow, or that he had deliberately placed her in a room with another girl to make study or rest impossible. In her loneliness, Kathy needed to believe that Amory had actually begun to care for her.

By Friday, however, there could be no mistaking what her uncle and cousin were trying to do. Day after day they insisted on accompanying Kathy to Bryn Mawr and hovered like vultures while she took exams in plane geometry, algebra, Latin composition, Latin prose authors, Virgil, modern history, and German grammar and translation. Whenever Kathy looked up or took a break, their presence made her feel defensive; she knew they were waiting for her to fail.

But Kathy did not fail. While her scores were poor in some areas, this time she performed well enough overall to be invited back. In late September she faced exams in English grammar and punctuation, English composition, French grammar and translation, and physical geography. Even if Kathy were admitted for the fall, she would have to retake any tests she had failed.

Because of the inferior quality of women's preparatory education, it was common for Bryn Mawr applicants to fail parts of the matriculation exam. Girls who failed as many as four out of the fifteen subjects required for entrance might be admitted on the condition that they pass the tests before the beginning of their sophomore year.

After the German exam on June 4, when Kathy returned to Canandaigua she discovered a thick package waiting. With Carrie's plans finally about to come to fruition, the mother's last gift to her daughters, the final installment of J. N. Larned's *History for Ready Reference and Topical Reading*, could hardly have arrived at a better time.

In the fall, Edith and Marion were to board with Florence Baldwin. If Kathy did well in September, she would enter Bryn Mawr as a freshman; otherwise she would join her sisters.

On June 19, when the spring term at Granger Place ended, the girls traveled to Buffalo to visit their half-sister Mary Houghton, intending to spend several days at Niagara Street. No sooner had Kathy arrived, however, than a sudden impulse overcame her. She left Edith and Marion with Mary and returned to the train station to buy a ticket to Hamburg. She had not been there since Carrie's funeral.

Perhaps because Carrie discouraged the girls from talking or thinking about the past, the lake house where they grew up would always retain an exceptionally powerful hold on their imaginations. Now that Kathy had kept her promise to her mother, it must have seemed fitting to go back.

At 6 p.m., after spending some time outside her father's house, Kathy appeared suddenly at Cloverbank, where Nellie Abbott was in residence for the summer with her children and a maid, Mary Higgins, who recorded in her diary the family's pleasure and excitement at Kathy's unexpected arrival. Kathy would always remember Aunt Nell as the one Houghton who treated her with dignity. Nellie's love for Fred made her regard his children with a warmth and tenderness they discovered nowhere else. Nellie of all people knew what Amory must be putting them through. Still, she was powerless to protect her husband from Amory's mockery at work, so what could she possibly do for the girls?

For years to come, Fred's suicide and the shame it had caused the Houghtons would remain the subtext of Kathy's difficult encounters with Amory; but with Aunt Nell, the many painful questions the suicide provoked made for a powerful and lasting bond of affection and understanding. The woman who never forgave herself for having failed to avert her brother's death had much in common with the child whose prayers for her father had gone unanswered.

"The Houghton children," as Florence Baldwin described them, arrived in time for Kathy to begin three days of exams on September 23. Temporarily she boarded with Edith and Marion, hesitating to reserve a room at the college in case she was denied admission at the last minute. Girls frequently traveled across the continent for the fall exams only to be sent home in disgrace.

Shortly after Kathy completed the final session, physical geography, on September 25, she learned that Bryn Mawr had admitted her with the maximum number of conditions. Had she failed one more test, she would have been rejected. Set to begin a full load of courses a week later, on October 1, 1895, Kathy had one year to retake the four tests she had failed.

In many ways it was the least of the pressures Kathy faced as she prepared to move to a shared suite in the gray stone Pembroke West dormitory at the south end of the campus. After many months of fighting to get to college, suddenly Kathy was uneasy about living apart from her sisters. She was uneasy about whether she ought to have insisted that Marion come with them to Bryn Mawr, when the child had obviously been content with the Smiths. She was uneasy about entering a classroom after years of private study; and she was uneasy about her readiness for what Carey Thomas called "true collegiate courses," when almost all of her recent work had taken the form of desperate cramming with Mr. Eaton.

Admission to Bryn Mawr was an immense personal triumph, of course; but the turbulent three years since Fred's suicide had left her ragged at the edges. For a full year after Carrie died, Kathy had been on a perpetual war footing as she prepared for the entrance exams and struggled with her uncle and cousins. She was scarcely in a state of mind to begin immediately on an academic program that would have posed formidable difficulties to almost any freshman: courses in Latin prose composition, Horace, Livy, English literature, rhetoric and essay writing, and French literature.

More daunting, however, would have been the prospect of living and working closely with strangers. Only naturally, the other Bryn Mawr girls would want to know who Kathy was, where she lived, and who her parents were. Until this, most people she encountered, whether in Hamburg, Buffalo, or Canandaigua, would have heard about Fred Houghton and known to avoid the subject. Not so the Bryn Mawr students and faculty, from whom Kathy would have somehow to keep her father's suicide a secret.

The nineteenth-century myths surrounding suicides had terrifying implications for their children, who were believed to carry the seeds of madness. According to one authority, Dr. Forbes Winslow, the madness might erupt at any time, often dooming the child to repeat a parent's act of self-destruction. At a less serious level, the taint might manifest itself in sudden outbursts of violence or other antisocial behavior. In such cases, the full-fledged "disposition to suicide" was thought likely to recur in subsequent generations. The belief that the grandchild of a suicide might kill himself (perhaps without suspecting the "hereditary predisposition") irreparably damaged the marriage prospects of any young man or woman with a known history of suicide in the family.

Fred and Carrie had been passionate devotees of Robert G. Ingersoll. In contrast to the prevalent "medical" view of suicide, the controversial freethinker argued that self-destruction was often a rational, "perfectly justifiable" act; where there was no hope, said Ingersoll, the failure to commit suicide "would be a mistake, sometimes almost a crime." It is impossible to know whether Fred Houghton clung to this doctrine in the last hours of life. But for

Fred's children, there could be little comfort in anything their father might have believed.

In 1895, many Bryn Mawr parents would have shuddered at the prospect of allowing their daughters to enter into close daily contact with the child of a suicide. Carey Thomas herself placed considerable emphasis on students' family backgrounds and the mental characteristics girls inherited from their parents; in the case of one student who went "quite mad" on campus, the president made no bones about suspecting that the poor child had inherited insanity from her father.

That first semester at Bryn Mawr, Kathy attempted to bury the past by reinventing herself as Kate Houghton, niece of the prominent businessman Amory Houghton, Jr. of Corning, New York.

Kate simultaneously concealed and called attention to herself with flamboyantly stylish clothes of her own design made at Mrs. Alanson Houghton's dressmaker in Elmira. Her stiff, wide, floor-length skirts were stuffed with horsehair up to the knees to make them stand out as though made of fluted metal. The seamstress had sewn a protective mohair braid underneath at the bottom; still, Kate held up the long, heavy back breadths when she walked with a calculated swish of white lace pleated ruffles. Each gargantuan leg-o'-mutton sleeve, also lined with horsehair, was nearly the size of her entire torso. She wore an immense black velvet bow at the back of her head above a pompadour, and boasted a tight-laced fifteen-inch waist.

Eager to be thought glamorous and a fashion-plate, Kate apparently had no idea that many Bryn Mawr girls would regard her as merely frivolous. On October 1, the day classes began, Carey Thomas met with the Student Self-Government Association to lament the large number of students who violated "propriety" by wearing gym suits to lectures. Rules notwithstanding, at Bryn Mawr the fashion trend was toward freer, looser, and shorter; Kate, so proud of her wasp waist, rustling street-sweeper skirts, and layers of white lace undergarments, instantly set herself apart.

Tense and afraid to talk to anyone, she was politely condescending to any girl who insisted on addressing her. In the evening, as often as possible she avoided the noisy, crowded, huge vaulted dining hall above the carriage entrance that connected Pembroke East and West, and slipped off campus to take meals in Edith's tiny room at Miss Baldwin's.

By the last week of October, crates filled with the objects Kate had purchased from her mother's estate arrived from Canandaigua. In the private bedroom of the suite she shared with a "sophisticated" junior from New York City, she carefully unpacked the long-necked perfume bottles, gold-and-white porcelain teacups and saucers, and a small cracked mirror with a painted wood frame. Much of the cutglass she had asked Mack to send had shattered in transit. The scent bottles, a vase, a decanter, an ice-cream dish, the tea caddy, and other pieces survived—enough to give Kate the aura of a Corning Glass heiress.

There were four of Carrie's moth-eaten Persian and Smyrna rugs, her pine writing desk and tea table, and the down quilt and heavy sash curtains from her bedroom. There was the dark wood grandfather clock from the front hallway at the lake, and a small yellow clock from Fred's desk.

Edith and Marion, who had received similar deliveries across the street, appeared at Pembroke West to make their selections from the boxes of Fred's books and the twenty-one remaining prints and drawings; the sisters divided everything "share and share alike." About one picture, however, there could be no question to whom it must belong: Kate wistfully regarded the engraving of Rosa Bonheur's donkey as all that remained of her childhood ambitions.

She set it aside until after she had walked Edith and Marion home. When she returned, without a word to her roommate she excitedly put the picture on the mantelpiece in the shared study. How Kate decorated her bedroom was for her alone to decide. The study was another matter; visitors would judge both girls by the objects displayed there.

Kate's roommate cast a chilly glance at the donkey and pronounced it "absurd for a college room." At an institution obsessed with critical values and the capacity to discriminate good art from bad, a sepia photograph of an acknowledged masterpiece or a cast of a famous sculpture would have been a more acceptable choice.

Constantly on the defensive after many months of struggle with Amory, Kate wildly overreacted and refused to remove the print. The engraving was the first authentic fragment of the past that Kate had permitted herself to expose at school. When her roommate criticized it, she seemed somehow to question Kate's entire background: not just the happy memories associated with the image, but also perhaps the family secret Kate was so anxious to conceal. The incident seemed to confirm all her worst fears of personal rejection; it was as though Kate had placed the picture in the shared room in order to test her roommate's response.

To avoid further humiliation, Kate adopted a pose of considerable arrogance and superciliousness. To prevent other girls from rejecting her, she rejected them first. She was aloof and unreachable. She would rather have died than allow anyone to see how lonely she was. She masked her insecurity with disdain.

Terrified that she would fail at college, Kate appeared to do everything to sabotage her grades. After many months of fighting to be admitted to Bryn Mawr, suddenly she seemed determined to get herself kicked out. She committed the "expelling offense" of smoking when she joined several girls who tested a tobacco pipe in the nearby Harrington family cemetery. She cut classes and refused to study. She affected the pose of a happy-go-lucky, spoiled rich girl who had better things to do. She declared schoolwork a nuisance and insisted she was more interested in "living." Skittish and highly-strung, she often sought release by sneaking out of the locked dormitory at night to go horseback riding with Edith.

On the rare occasions when Kate appeared in Latin Prose Composition, the professor, Gonzalez Lodge, complained that she was a "drag" on the other girls. Known for his warm, sympathetic, personal interest in all students, Lodge quickly sensed that something was wrong. He alone at this point seems to have noted the disparity between Kate's "extreme," attention-seeking costumes and her rigidly guarded personal reserve—but quite what to make of it the professor had no idea.

Kate might not have lasted out the year had she failed to make a first close friend at school: Mary Towle of Wakefield, Massachusetts, who lived in a single room down the hall. Awkwardly large and fat, with an enormous nose, tiny shoulders, broad hips, and a "great big seat," Mary reminded people of a sea lion. A devotee of horoscopes and ouija boards, she broke the ice by making Kate guffaw with laughter at predictions delivered in a solemn, clear, cultivated voice.

The sea lion and the fashion-plate made a curious pair on campus. The clumsy, near-sighted, comical Mary always leaned slightly forward as she walked; Kate, slender and graceful, held her head so high it seemed to be attached to an invisible balloon. Unlike Kate, who strained to conceal her thoughts and feelings, Mary was forever throwing up her hands, shrieking with horror, and making disgusted faces; friends described her as an emotional whirligig.

Mary Towle became Kate's best friend, sidekick, foil, and protector. She fussed and fretted over her, and called her "darling." Mary was Kate's one-woman claque. Kate's roommate was only too happy to change places with Mary; unlike her, Mary admired and approved of everything Kate did.

From the moment Mary moved in, their study echoed with the laughter of girls having tea and cake or making melted cheese sandwiches over the gas jet. This was all Kate's doing; thrilled by the affection and affirmation Mary provided, Kate plunged into Bryn Mawr social life with the ferocity of a child who has been starved of fun with other young people. Suddenly, she was working as hard to make and keep friends as she initially had to avoid them. She attracted visitors by always keeping a plentiful stock of food in her room.

Most girls' families regularly sent packages of goodies from home. While Mary Towle and her other new friends were busy studying, Kate slipped into the village to buy the sweets she implied were shipped from Corning. To the consternation of Mack Smith, who continued to oversee the sisters' finances and report regularly to Amory, Kate ran up huge bills at local food shops. Pretending to be rich and loved was a costly proposition. By January, Kate negotiated an increase in her monthly allowance from $5 to $30—but even that scarcely covered expenses.

Kate took pride in the number of milk-white calling cards she received inviting her to other girls' rooms. In the dormitories, entertaining was an elaborate ritual that began with the calling card slipped under one's door at night: "Could you please call on me in my rooms for coffee?" "Could you come for tea this afternoon?" "May I invite you for dinner?" The girl's name was engraved in black; in the upper left-hand corner, she wrote in ink the day and hours she planned to be "at home." Wary of being left out, Kate accepted every invitation.

The Student Self-Government Association set daily "quiet hours" when girls were presumed to study or attend classes; entertaining was strictly forbidden. Kate and a few others regularly violated quiet hours, especially the prohibition on gatherings after 10 p.m. during the week. The oil lamp often blazed in Kate's study long past midnight as she held court with friends.

She imitated her father's tendency to sleep late. With a persistence that had to be deliberate, Kate slept through Carey Thomas's immensely popular speeches at morning chapel.

On the eve of exams, when Kate gleefully disclosed a shocking lack of preparation, Mary Towle and her friend Bertha Rembaugh stayed up all night to force Kate to cram. Kate regarded the last-minute attempt to avert failure as a "most amusing situation." She seemed to enjoy skirting the edge and provoking poor Mary to fits of panic. It was a cry for attention, a way of expressing her own worst fear: that she shared her father's capacity for self-destruction.

Kate escaped Carey Thomas's attention until rumors of late-night horseback riding with Edith reached the president. Probably anticipating yet another engraved invitation, Kate opened a small square cream-colored envelope to discover a summons to the Deanery. Kate vowed to Mary that if Thomas scolded her, she would continue to ride at the risk of expulsion.

"Miss Houghton, I understand that you ride horseback at night," Thomas began in a melodious voice. Her heavy eyelids half-closed over blazing eyes. She said that riding at night must be great fun. She failed to see why a competent rider like Kate shouldn't be allowed to go out when she pleased. Still: "It would be a great personal favor to me if you would stop it. I am trying to build up the college and there is a great deal of prejudice against women going to college. The people in the neighborhood are shocked when girls ride horseback at night."

And that was it. No blistering tirade. No reprimand. No threats. No angry insistence that Kate abide by the rules or else.

One of Thomas's trademarks was the respect she accorded students. She treated girls as rational human beings capable of making up their own minds; she did not dictate, she reasoned. She listened to what they had to say and took them seriously. Instead of humiliating Kate as Amory no doubt would have done, Thomas calmly explained why she hoped Kate would comply. Then she let her decide.

Thomas used this strategy whenever student actions blighted "the good name of the college." Because a great many people violently opposed the very idea of an educated woman, nothing must be done to jeopardize the school's image. Thomas encouraged the girls to think of Bryn Mawr as an experiment that had to work.

Those people who wanted the experiment to fail were constantly scrutinizing Bryn Mawr students for evidence of the deleterious influence of higher education. When twenty girls swam naked in the college pool; when they went out bicycling or walking in short skirts on Sunday morning; when they paraded up and down Montgomery Avenue wearing basketball costumes and no hats on Sunday afternoon; and even when they painted a black moustache on a terra cotta statue of Hermes that the president's friend, Mary Garrett, had donated to the college, Thomas usually (sometimes grudgingly) agreed there was "really no harm" in what they had done. Still, their actions had been "spoken of" outside Bryn Mawr; and "for the good of the college" the president hoped they would stop.

In compliance with Carey Thomas's request Kate stopped riding at night, but (to judge by the extensive charges she ran up with Florence Baldwin) she continued regularly to disappear from the dormitory to dine in seclusion with Edith. Despite Mary Towle,

Bertha Rembaugh, and the other friends Kate had made at Bryn Mawr, her strongest bond was still with her sister.

Though Kate often spoke to Mary and the other girls of "my family in Corning," she really had nowhere to go during Easter recess. Pretending that she was on her way to her uncle's, she packed her bags and left Pembroke West only to sneak across the street to stay with Edith.

In Edith's cozy room at Baldwin, decorated with Fred's bookcases, willow rocker, and chess table, they planned for the time when Edith would finally share Kate's rooms at Bryn Mawr. (Mary Towle intended to room with her younger sister, Sarah, also an incoming freshman.) Edith was to take the Bryn Mawr entrance exam the following May.

Kate, Edith, and Marion spent Christmas 1896 in Corning, where they found Nellie Abbott in a fit of agitation. Aunt Nell was convinced that something was very wrong with her fifty-year-old brother, Charlie Houghton, but no one in the family would listen. Mary Higgins noted Mrs. Abbott's frustration when no one else seemed to observe what she had perceived all too clearly.

Amory laughed at his sister when she tried to warn him about Charlie's fragile mental state. In recent months Charlie had sunk into a deep depression, possibly triggered by ill health and a bout of typhoid fever. Amory, anxious to avoid the specter of inherited insanity, denied anything was wrong.

As vice-president of Corning Glass, Charlie was far too important to the family business for Amory to permit damaging rumors to take hold. Charlie's gregarious personality was useful in sales and marketing; his famous charm and cordiality made him the perfect front man. He was exceedingly popular with the factory workers and their families, whom he made a point of knowing by name. In the business community, the Houghton brothers were widely regarded as complementing each other brilliantly. People tended to fear Amory but liked and trusted Charlie.

Although Charlie loathed travel, Amory shrewdly kept him

out on the road much of the year. Amory pressured his brother to subordinate his life to business duties: Charlie obediently spent so much time traveling that he had had to postpone marriage to his childhood sweetheart, Helen Hall, until he was thirty-two.

Charlie always followed Amory's orders, but in time his unconscious appears to have rebelled. It can hardly have been accidental that Charlie developed a series of compulsions that made travel impossibly difficult. He acquired an obsessive fear of riding in a horse-drawn carriage and of traveling on or near a large body of water. Wary of poison, Charlie dreaded dining cars, preferring the safety of his own large hamper of food. Terrified to travel alone, he was known to plead for a colleague to accompany him to California.

Charlie's phobias were reminiscent of the obsessions that had tormented Fred, but Amory led the family in dismissing them as Charlie's "peculiarities." Charlie, apparently to avoid giving discomfort to others, continued his duties despite the pain. By contrast with their nakedly sensitive younger brother, Charlie tended to mask his panic behind a display of ebullience. In recent years, however, two events had affected him greatly. In 1888 Charlie's seven-year-old daughter Florence had died, and four years later Fred took his own life.

After the suicide, Charlie was a changed man. Amory had successfully managed the upstate New York press coverage, but Charlie knew only too well that Fred had hardly been driven to kill himself by "overwork." Charlie comprehended as perhaps no one else could the younger brother's desperate fear of returning to Amory's domination. He became morbidly preoccupied with Fred's death and what it might mean for him.

Charlie's condition was appallingly obvious at Amory's 1896 holiday gathering. Throughout the fall Nellie had been unable to lure Charlie to Cedar Street for dinner although he lived only a block away. Christmas at Amory's, however, was a command performance.

Fred's daughters were well acquainted with the signs of severe depression. It must have been terrifying for them to see their father's brother like this, especially in the house where Fred had spent his last days.

Charlie had replaced Fred as Amory's whipping boy. Tongue-lashing his despondent brother, Amory seemed to declare that it was business as usual as he held court in the billiard room. He denied the terror lurking in the room that history was about to repeat itself. He challenged fears that the Houghtons could be doomed to self-destruction. He insisted (to himself as much as others) that Fred's suicide had been a one-time aberration, a sign merely of unforgivable weakness and not a taint of blood.

In the weeks after Kate and her sisters returned to Bryn Mawr, Charlie's mental deterioration continued. But to everyone's amazement, he appeared suddenly much improved as he prepared to go to the office on Monday, March 29, 1897. Accompanied by his daughter Mabelle, he strolled downhill to the factory. His amicability seemed to have returned as he warmly greeted friends and acquaintances along the way, often stopping to shake hands and chat.

Mabelle walked with her father to the factory gate but turned to go shopping before she actually saw him step inside. Later an employee would faintly recall seeing Charlie pass the office about 10 or 11 a.m.

When Charlie failed to appear at his desk by noon, the staff assumed he had gone out of town on business. Only after he missed dinner that evening did Amory's two sons initiate a "quiet" all-night search. Until they knew Charlie's fate, they wanted to keep their father and especially their aunt Nellie from hearing about the disappearance. With a sense of inevitability, the search party combed the woods and quarries around Corning and the river flats where Fred's body had been found.

At 5 a.m., two searchers entered the sand shed at Corning Glass. Charlie Houghton's corpse lay beside a mountain of white sand. He had fired two bullets into his temple. At 7 a.m., a boy delivered Arthur Houghton's message to the Abbott house: "Dear Aunt Nellie, Uncle Charles is dead. He shot himself in the sand shed, last night, in the factory." Amory's sons ordered the body promptly removed to Fletcher and Cook's undertaking rooms before the factory workers arrived for the day. The bloody wound in Charlie's temple and the revolver at his side made an autopsy unnecessary.

In every detail Charlie's death mimicked Fred's. Like Fred, he had pretended to get better. He had gone out with someone he loved dearly, almost certainly planning to kill himself afterward. He had appeared to go inside only to slip off unseen.

That morning, no sooner had Amory learned of his brother's death than he went to the local press to insist that ill health had caused Charlie's mind to become "temporarily unbalanced." But this time, even Amory was powerless to prevent the *Crockery and Glass Journal* from pointing out that Fred Houghton had "committed suicide in 1892 in much the same way." The deaths of prominent brothers offered a mesmerizing spectacle. That the family was rich and powerful made the case even more irresistible. Inevitably the question arose, Who among them would be next?

In private, the Houghtons blamed a strain of madness in the Oakeses, the family of Amory, Sr.'s wife, Sophronia.

Kate and her sisters remained in Bryn Mawr. Accounts of Charlie's death in the *New York Times* and other papers also mentioned their father's suicide, and Kate, who had often emphasized her identity as a Corning Houghton, was frantic that her classmates and their families who read the news items about Charlie might make the connection with her.

During Easter recess, April 14–22, Kate stayed on alone at Pembroke West. Edith spent the holiday in seclusion at Miss Baldwin's, studying for the entrance exam in late May.

Before this, Kate had seemed almost ready to settle down and apply herself at Bryn Mawr. Surrounded by loyal friends, she appeared calmer and less tightly coiled. Their steady support was finally about to pay off when the blow of Charlie's suicide undid everything. Any young person whose father and uncle had committed suicide was bound to be anxious about her own fate; worse, the Houghton sisters had no adult with whom to discuss the terrifying questions Charlie's death provoked.

That Easter, Kate wrestled with her demons alone.

Nellie Abbott, mindful of what the girls were going through, invited them to Cloverbank for the summer. Charlie's suicide had revived and intensified Nellie's feelings of powerlessness in the family: Why, she kept asking, had Amory refused to listen to her? Fred's daughters provided the best tonic for Nellie's spirits.

"Lots of confusion as usual," Mary Higgins noted fondly in her diary, the day nineteen-year-old Kate and seventeen-year-old Edith arrived. (Marion, fourteen, would stay nearby with a friend.) Nellie wanted to give the girls at least the semblance of home. She assuaged her own pain by trying to make them feel calm and secure. Kate especially was grateful for the simple pleasures of driving to Hamburg village in the Abbotts' new phaeton; taking Ted and Ollie for a swim in Lake Erie; picking wild strawberries; or just sitting on the porch for long talks with Aunt Nell. It meant the world that Kate was free to ride her horse on the beach at night. Nellie even encouraged her habit of sleeping late, whatever inconvenience that might entail.

Nellie took in another young person that summer. As a favor to the devoted Mary Higgins, Nellie allowed the maid's seventeen-year-old sister, Margaret, to come in July. The Higgins girls, daughters of an impoverished stonecutter who eventually found work at Corning Glass, had grown up near the railroad track where Fred shot himself. Mary and another sister, Anna, had saved their earnings as domestics to give Margaret a better life at a private boarding school, Claverack College and Hudson River Institute. It was a strange moment for the observant, exceptionally intelligent and ambitious girl to enter the Abbott household, when the Houghtons were still privately reeling from Charlie's suicide. Even before Margaret Higgins met Kate and Edith, she almost certainly knew more about the secretive sisters than most people outside the family did.

Whatever good Aunt Nell's pampering had accomplished was swiftly undone when Kate and Edith accompanied her to Buffalo to meet Amory's train on July 27. After a short stay at Cloverbank, Amory planned to take his sister and nieces on a boat trip up the St. Lawrence River to Quebec. Understandably, he had been profoundly unsettled by his brother's death. Based on the circumstances of the suicide, especially Charlie's decision to shoot himself at the factory, a good many people in Corning interpreted the act as a final defiant gesture against Amory.

Amory dealt with pain by lashing out at others; scarcely had he arrived at Cloverbank when he designated a new scapegoat. For Kate the four-week boat trip was a nightmare. Amory used almost any pretext to disparage her. His voice quivering with anger, he repeatedly compared her to her weak, pathetic father.

Kate had stuffed her trunk with her best clothes but lost the key. In front of Edith, Aunt Nell, and others, Amory lambasted her carelessness and stupidity. Although Kate found the key soon afterward, Amory's tirade had flustered her to the point where she quickly lost it again.

Amory reserved the worst abuse for Kate's tendency to sleep late. The man who had once fired his own brother for being late flew into a red-faced rage when Kate regularly arrived for breakfast a few minutes after everyone else had begun. Every time he produced his pocket watch to see exactly how late she was, Kate felt a pang of horror; it was Fred's gold watch, which Amory had bought from Carrie in 1892 after his death.

F O U R

That fall of 1897, the music of Schubert and Chopin poured out the windows of rooms 33–35 at Pembroke West. Edith played Fred's violin and Kate accompanied her on Carrie's piano. At Kate's request, Mack and Nettie Smith had shipped the piano from Canandaigua on October 18 along with a barrel of their mother's crockery.

Kate was in her junior year when Edith entered Bryn Mawr as a freshman. Everyone seemed fascinated by the gaunt, angular, long-limbed Edith. Some girls said she looked and acted more like Kate's brother than a sister. There was something wild and defiant about her. In tattered, loose-fitting shirts and trousers, Edith always seemed deliberately disheveled. Nobody knew whether she dressed as a boy for comfort, theatrical effect or a little of both. She knew how to keep people guessing.

Her reputation as an actress in male roles preceded her, Edith having famously appeared as a handsome soldier in Miss Baldwin's production of *The Heart of the Princess Asra*. Her manner on stage was said to be "graceful and gentlemanly."

Edith could run the fifteen-yard dash in two seconds. She could throw a basketball $76\frac{1}{2}$ feet. She was a basketball hero, a champion gymnast, a crack chess player and team leader, and unquestionably one of the sharpest minds in her class. She seemed "never to feel fatigue or discouragement." Other freshmen erupted in loud, boisterous cheers when she entered the dining hall.

Edith was a mass of contradictions: ugly and beautiful, truant and studious, angry and sweet, aggressive and painfully vulnerable.

A first-rate science student, she defied rules by wearing her basketball costume, a short black velvet skirt and loose white cotton blouse with sleeves rolled up above the elbows, to work in the lab at Dalton Hall. Her boundless enthusiasm, expressed in sharp, impatient motions, resulted in stacks of itemized bills for broken lab equipment, shattered beakers, funnels, flasks, test tubes, and other damage. She exuded an air of roughness that classmates found simultaneously appealing and frightening. She was impulsive and quick to take offense. She was known to grow rowdy on the basketball court or at the chess club, and flew into a spluttering rage when things didn't go her way.

Only with Kate did Edith seem never to lose her temper. While the sisters did not always agree, Edith deferred to Kate in all things. The younger sister recognized that she might never have reached Bryn Mawr without Kate's ferocious persistence.

The three-room, first-floor corner suite in Pembroke West was their first real home since Carrie's death, and they were unabashed in their delight simply at living together again. Sharing a sense of high drama, they enjoyed cultivating their mystique. Although 33–35 constantly overflowed with friends and admirers, the sisters made it obvious that there was no one on earth they would rather talk to or be with than each other.

Edith was by no means an anomaly at Bryn Mawr, where girls often dressed and acted as boys on stage and off. At Vassar, masculine costumes stopped at the waistline; in campus productions Vassar girls wore men's vests and coats, but "legitimate trousers" were strictly forbidden, requiring students to make do with divided skirts. Smith had similar regulations. At Bryn Mawr, by contrast, girls freely wore "the masculine dress complete" on stage and continued to pose as men at the all-girl dances or "masquerade balls" that followed. (Men were kept out of Bryn Mawr dances until 1929.) It was usually the older girls, imbued with the glamour of superior power, who wore male attire and invited younger students to dances.

Before they set foot outside the privileged space of the stage performance or the all-girl dance, however, they were expected to change back into floor-length skirts, or to be certain that the masculine costume was "entirely covered," lest outsiders see or (worse!) photograph them in trousers. Carey Thomas grew agitated when girls so much as "crossed the campus in men's dress" or appeared "in the main halls where there was any possibility of being seen through the windows." Rumors of girls who masqueraded as boys in the college dining halls or even at private parties in student rooms drove the president to distraction.

It was not that Thomas disapproved of acting or dressing as a boy. Probably better than most, the woman who had signed her childhood journal "Jo March" could sympathize with the impulse. Still, Thomas feared that pictures of Bryn Mawr students in men's dress would seem to substantiate the claim that college made girls monstrous by perverting their sexual identities.

The forbidden images might also call attention to a deeply suppressed aspect of life at Bryn Mawr and other women's colleges. It found expression in rough, aggressive, disorderly play on the basketball court. It erupted in personal fouls, savage quarrels, and bloody physical injuries. It was suggested in the volcanic passions of student "smashes" when girls pursued, courted, and fell deliriously in love with one another. There were sparks of it in the class cheers, singing, jostling, and rowdiness that broke out in the dining and residence halls, causing the president to plead repeatedly for order. The legendary "ceremony and graciousness" of Bryn Mawr concealed a bubbling undercurrent of violence and aggression that constantly threatened to burst forth into public view.

Part of this was simply the sudden, intoxicating jolt of finding oneself in a private, all-female world that vigorously encouraged intellectual and professional ambitions; for the young woman who had been sheltered, patronized, and tautly restrained all her life, this newfound dignity and intellectual scope could be a heady experience that pleasantly burned the throat, blurred the vision, and made one a bit unsteady on one's feet. Gloriously drunk on the milk of paradise, girls roughhoused like excited children who can barely measure the consequences of their own growing strength.

Yet the liberation Bryn Mawr offered was incomplete. Eager to free the mind, Carey Thomas stopped short of relaxing the tightly drawn corset string and the ladylike decorum it symbolized. Girls allowed, even prodded, to think for themselves for the first time soon longed to unbutton their wasp waists, kick off shoes with toothpick toes, and elude the chaperones Carey Thomas insisted accompany them to the theater and opera in Philadelphia.

On Lantern Night, when sophomores passed the light of knowledge to freshmen who wore caps and gowns for the first time, many students had their first heart-pounding glimpse of the secret life of Bryn Mawr. The initiation ceremony for Edith's freshman class took place on Tuesday, November 2, 1897. By 9 p.m., Carey Thomas, her companion Mamie Gwinn, and their guests had gathered on a rooftop to observe the spectacle. Black-gowned sophomores, clutching lanterns of filigreed tin lined with red isinglass, emerged from the dark grotto of Pembroke Arch singing the Greek hymn "Pallas Athene, Thea." In front of Denbigh Hall, each sophomore presented a lantern to a younger student. The freshmen replied with their class hymn, "Sofias"; they marched through the college halls with lanterns swinging. This was the part of Lantern Night outsiders were permitted to see. What followed was another matter; but by then the president's party would have dispersed.

Sophomores burst into freshmen rooms to seize caps and gowns. The purpose was to humiliate younger girls by forcing them to appear before Carey Thomas at Wednesday morning chapel without proper academic attire. For 364 days a year, girls might wait for formal engraved invitations before calling on others, but on Lantern Night they threw off their masks of ladylike courtesy and reticence and broke in any way they could. They destroyed doors and ransacked rooms. They left freshmen quarters in a shambles.

The marauders went to bed at 3:30 but were too keyed up to sleep. Within the hour they were dancing across the campus, shouting for friends to join them. At daybreak, they triumphantly hung three black gowns in a gnarled tree near the athletic field, and wrestled with freshmen who tried to retrieve the gowns. Finally, the sophomores broke into Pembroke West, locking a terrified student named Patty Williams in her bedroom. Realizing that Patty's cap and gown were locked in with her, one girl crawled out on the ledge and smashed the bedroom window with her fist. She was about to plunge through the jagged glass when her classmates pulled her back.

The ritualized violence of Lantern Night gave vent to unruly impulses that Carey Thomas hoped to keep in check through the rest of the year; it attempted to unleash the energy of those impulses while containing and neutralizing their threat to the social order. To whatever extent Thomas dissembled with college trustees and the occasional enraged parent who complained about outbursts such as Lantern Night 1897, the president knew and accepted that Bryn Mawr girls inevitably often played the same games of power and aggression as men. Thomas preferred to keep all that secret, however, "for the good of the college."

Bryn Mawr girls were expected to keep a good many secrets from the outside world, but no secret was more strictly guarded than that of Carey Thomas's tempestuous private life. Thomas openly shared the Deanery with the ethereal, languid Mamie Gwinn, who had lived and traveled with her in Europe. They did not think of themselves as lesbians, but their relationship included physical as well as emotional intimacy. Unspoken, however, was that Miss Gwinn, a professor of English, had embarked on a love affair with Alfred Hodder, a married faculty member notorious for liaisons with students.

"This roused Carey to fury," recalled Bertrand Russell, the husband of Thomas's cousin Alys and a houseguest at the Deanery, "and every night, as we were going to bed, we used to hear her angry voice scolding Miss Gwinn in the next room for hours together."

Carey Thomas's intimacies with another woman, Mary Garrett, heiress to the Baltimore and Ohio Railroad fortune, further complicated matters. Hardly would Miss Gwinn leave every two weeks to visit her family when Miss Garrett would arrive from Baltimore. She always left, Russell noted, "at the exact moment of Miss Gwinn's return." This state of affairs persisted until 1904, when Mamie Gwinn finally eloped with her male lover and Mary Garrett took up permanent residence at the Deanery.

Only naturally perhaps, Carey Thomas felt a deep and abiding sympathy for a tomboy like Edith Houghton. Still, the brazen, unbridled Edith, standing with feet apart and hands stuffed in pockets, posed a considerable risk to the college. She was full of mischief. She attracted too much attention. She thumbed her nose at campus codes of secrecy and discretion. Her behavior was often— as Carey Thomas liked to say—"unwise."

Several quite innocent escapades during Edith's freshman year caused Thomas to characterize her as "very high-spirited and very thoughtless." One February night after Pembroke's doors were locked, Edith and a friend, disguised as working men, slipped off campus for a moonlight walk in the woods. A neighbor's complaint led to Edith's first reprimand from the Student Self-Government Association. She received another black mark for allowing herself to be photographed in "men's costume" outside Pembroke West on a Sunday morning "in full view of the people going to church."

On March 12, 1898, "Mr. and Miss Houghton," as Edith and Kate were billed, appeared together in the Bryn Mawr production of Goldsmith's *She Stoops to Conquer*. The performance took place in the brick gymnasium where Carey Thomas watched intently from a first-row seat with the pale Miss Gwinn beside her. Afterward, Edith cockily posed for photographs as Young Marlow outside Pembroke West. Later that night, she hosted a candlelit supper in 33–35 for a group of girls all wearing men's coats and trousers.

Edith's activities, much "spoken of" in the days that followed, resulted in a final stern warning from the Self-Government Committee. Carey Thomas noted that Edith's next offense, whatever it might be, would be "dealt with very severely."

Things started to come crashing down around the sisters. The college had put a stop to their musical evenings after a series of anonymous complaints and Kate, under duress, sadly shipped her mother's piano back to Canandaigua. Then suddenly, she was besieged by creditors. As if by cabal, nearly every shopkeeper in town demanded to be paid that spring. What with all the lavish entertaining she and Edith had done, Kate's food expenses had escalated dramatically. With her cultivated air of superiority and self-assurance, Kate had had little trouble persuading local tradesmen to open accounts without Amory's approval. No one seemed to doubt she was a blithe and extravagant heiress who needed only to ask "my uncle" for the money.

Finally, Eddie Burns at the livery stable begged Kate to settle a $75 bill. Burns, who had always shown exceptional kindness to the sisters, explained the personal circumstances that caused him to need cash immediately.

That night, girls jammed into 33–35 to attend a bizarre public auction. On a cash-only basis with no returns permitted, Kate and Edith sold off the dregs of their mother's estate. Kate, preening in the study, was auctioneer. Edith instructed customers to shout bids from the hallway; no one was to come within ten feet of the items on sale.

Again and again, Kate whipped up the girls to increase their bids. When she gingerly showed off sparkling pieces of fine cut-glass, she concealed that she and Edith had just glued them back together. When she displayed her famous dress collection, she hid rips, stains, moth holes, and patches. Edith swiftly collected the cash, nudging girls out the door before their purchases turned to dust.

On Friday, November 4, 1898, Carey Thomas, on a business trip to New York City with Mary Garrett, wrote to Amory Houghton, Jr. about Edith: "Dear Sir: I very much regret to inform you that we have been compelled to suspend your niece, Miss Houghton, for a period of thirty days, beginning at noon, Monday, November 7th. During this time she will not be permitted to attend lectures or to appear on the college grounds; and under the rules of the college governing undergraduate students, she will not be permitted to reside in Bryn Mawr or in Philadelphia unless she is able to live with members of her immediate family. Unless these conditions be observed she will be liable to suspension for the entire year. Your niece brought upon herself last year a reprimand and was then informed that any further offense would be severely dealt with. She has recently been concerned in a peculiarly outrageous case of hazing."

Although Carey Thomas did not provide details of the case to Amory, the facts were well known at Bryn Mawr. On Lantern Night 1898, Edith and four other sophomores had taken the violence to a level beyond anything the college had previously experienced.

After the ceremony, Edith and her friends had entered one of the locked residence halls with a set of stolen keys. They roused two freshmen from bed and blindfolded them. The younger girls, half-naked and wrapped in blankets, were forced out of the building. Edith's group led them off campus through the woods to the old cemetery where girls often went to smoke, securely tied the freshmen to a tree, tore off their blindfolds and blankets, and left them there alone all night. Wild with excitement, they danced back to Bryn Mawr to boast of what they had done.

The next day, a notice from Evelyn Walker, President of the Student Self-Government, was delivered to 33–35 Pembroke West, summoning Edith to defend herself before her peers. Although the younger girls were physically unscathed after the ordeal, they remained frightened, disoriented, and very upset.

To Edith's amazement, there was considerable outrage on campus about quite how far she and the others had gone. There was outrage about the peril to which the victims had been exposed; and outrage about potential damage to Bryn Mawr's reputation. "Parents will not trust their daughters to us if there is even danger of their being subjected to such risks," declared one furious college trustee. Edith, standing before the student board on November 3, made a great show of failing to see what all the fuss was about. Since hazing had never occurred "in this form" before at Bryn Mawr, how were the sophomores supposed to know it was objectionable? They had merely regarded it as "a piece of fun." With a wink to the others, Edith insisted she would never have tied up the girls and left them out all night if she "had realized that it was against the rule of the Self-Government."

Edith had tangled with Evelyn Walker and the other board members before. The board agreed that as a result of past infractions, Edith, the ringleader, was "in a very different position from the other students" involved in the hazing. The Student Self-Government issued severe reprimands to the others. Edith alone was barred from campus for thirty days.

Edith bristled at criticism of any kind. She seemed thunderstruck that the board had treated the matter so seriously. She insisted her punishment was a major injustice and threatened to quit school if they went through with it. Evelyn Walker, pointedly ignoring her, communicated the decision to Carey Thomas before the president left for New York.

It was Carey Thomas's duty to notify Edith and her Uncle Amory, but she did not relish the prospect. Although Thomas shuddered to think of the "disastrous consequences" that might have attended the hazing, privately she admitted to Mary Garrett that in past years she had indeed always "smiled on" the practice. And it seemed such a shame to sabotage a first-rate student by barring her from classes; yet that was the penalty the Student Self-Government had devised and Thomas was required to enforce it. There was considerable feeling among Edith's admiring professors that suspension was too harsh a punishment, and Carey Thomas was inclined to agree. Still, the president adamantly opposed undercutting the authority of the Student Self-Government no matter how wrong-headed or misguided their decisions. Women, Thomas believed, must learn to exercise political power by governing themselves; and to do that they must be allowed to make mistakes. There was no other way.

The president knew next to nothing about Amory Houghton, Jr. or his relationship with the sisters when she contacted him in Corning. As far as Thomas was concerned, it was up to the uncle whether Edith should be sent home or to some other location. Calculating that her letter would reach him on Saturday, Carey Thomas anticipated the uncle's reply some time before Edith's Monday noon deadline.

On Friday afternoon, Edith went into seclusion with Kate to await word from the president. Frantically she paced back and forth, waving her long skinny arms and decrying her unjust fate. Her speech was continuous, loud, high-pitched, and often irrational. She could not seem to sleep or rest. Edith knew she was to go home on

Monday—but where exactly was home? Other than Bryn Mawr, she had no home. The suspension brutally highlighted her status as an orphan with no place to go. She lived with Kate in 33–35. To be driven from their nest was unthinkable.

In private, Edith's bravado shaded into terror. Where would she go? There was always Aunt Nell in Corning, but that would put her within Amory's reach: the last thing Edith wanted under the circumstances.

On Saturday morning, a packet of three letters arrived from New York: "Dear Miss Houghton: It is a great grief to me to send you the enclosed formal notice and I am exceedingly sorry business detains me in New York, so that I am compelled to send it to you instead of seeing you in person. . . . I am writing by this mail to your uncle Mr. Houghton and I enclose a copy of my letter to him as I think you may wish to see it."

Amory's name plunged Edith into a new crisis. Almost certainly he had received Carey Thomas's letter by now and Edith would hear from him directly. Waiting for the inevitable explosion from Corning added an unbearable new pressure. With mounting stridency, Edith continued to insist that she had done nothing wrong; but the general uproar against her gave the sisters cause to wonder.

To the Bryn Mawr community, the hazing episode represented student violence and aggression taken too far. Edith and the others had stepped over the line; and students and faculty grappled with the undeniable fact that women were capable of such impulses. To many on campus, the hazing seemed like an eruption of madness, all the more disturbing because of the credence it appeared to give to popular medical theories that the exertions of a college education could drive women insane.

To Kate and Edith, however, the episode was terrifying for reasons they dared not discuss with anyone. Not even the benevolent Carey Thomas could have comprehended quite what they were going through in private. As any child whose father and uncle had committed suicide might have done, the sisters feared a connection between the "outburst" and their family history. Had a taint of blood driven Edith to go further with the violence of Lantern Night than any girl before her?

The sisters had seen mature men, Fred and Charlie, react to overwhelming pressure by taking their own lives. Watching Edith in the throes of a desperate crisis, Kate grew frantic over what she might do next.

Each passing hour that weekend brought fresh torture as the Monday deadline approached and still there was no word from Amory. The sisters dreaded hearing from him, yet his silence seemed ominous.

Kate had never revealed their personal circumstances to any other student. She had told no one of their family history or of their troubled relations with Amory. Close friends like Mary Towle and Bertha Rembaugh had suspected that Kate's family life was hardly as she painted it. Nonetheless, she preferred to conceal her pain behind a façade of blithe spirits and extravagant spending (lately often with money borrowed from Mary Towle).

Now, however, the crisis with Edith was too much to bear entirely on her own. As always, Kate felt responsible for her impulsive sister; she needed to protect her, but how? Edith's mental state seemed dangerously fragile as she veered between fits of anger and despondency.

It is a measure of Kate's desperation that she confided at least some of her fears to Edith's friend and mentor, Mary Helen Ritchie. Kate disclosed almost everything—except the family history of suicide; about that she still could not bring herself to speak.

A notorious figure at Bryn Mawr, Mary Helen Ritchie, twenty-five, was a graduate fellow in Latin, working on a thesis entitled "A Study of Conditional and Temporal Clauses in Pliny the Younger." Like Edith, she preferred men's coats and trousers and played male roles in school theatricals. She was a champion athlete and served as umpire at Bryn Mawr basketball games. Carey Thomas, a staunch admirer, noted that Miss Ritchie "was afraid of nothing, her plumed feather was always erect and waving in the wind." Detractors called her haughty manner "affected" and whispered that she regularly invited undergraduates to smoke cigarettes in her flat in the Low

Buildings. People said she was not a "good specimen" of a college woman.

On the night of Sunday, November 6, when Carey Thomas returned to the Deanery, Mary Helen Ritchie was waiting. The president hurriedly put on cap and gown to talk to her.

Thomas had fully anticipated that the hazing incident would have serious repercussions in the week to come. From New York she had sent details to various trustees and knew they were not about to take the episode lightly. "We know it will obtain publicity," one trustee was already grimly warning. Thomas hoped to minimize that publicity and play down the inevitable campus controversy over Edith's punishment. With all this swirling in her mind, the last thing the president expected was complications with Edith herself.

Mary Helen Ritchie told Thomas that in recent years the sisters had been "brought up without father or mother," and that for all of Kate's boastful talk of her rich uncle in Corning, the girls really lived "about with relatives." Banished from Bryn Mawr, Edith was desperately ashamed to admit that she had "nowhere to go." For the first time, Thomas learned that the girls' uncle was "exceedingly severe" and that Kate feared the psychological effect of his wrath on her sister.

Next, Mary Helen Ritchie ushered Kate into the Deanery. The girl Carey Thomas saw now was not the flighty, frivolous creature known for cutting classes and constant entertaining. She was not the thoughtless, arrogant beauty whom the president had chastised for late-night horseback riding. She was brave, strong, serious, and responsible. She was passionately concerned for her sister's well-being. She was articulate and persuasive about why Edith's was no ordinary case. The transformation was amazing.

In the light of what Mary Helen Ritchie and Kate told her about Amory, Thomas agreed to find someplace other than Corning for Edith to wait out the thirty days. The terms of the suspension prohibited Edith from remaining in the immediate area of the college, but Kate's anxieties convinced the president to waive that rule.

Thomas proposed to send Edith to Miss Mary Stevens, who

rented out rooms in nearby Germantown. By Monday morning, Stevens had agreed to take Edith strictly as an experiment; noting that her house was characterized by quiet monotony, she wondered whether a girl of Edith's nervous temperament would fit in.

All that was missing was some word from Amory. When there was no letter from him in the morning mail, Thomas reluctantly extended the deadline. Amory's letter, dated May 7, was delivered to the Deanery on Tuesday morning. Thomas read it with shock and disgust; to Mary Garrett she described the letter as savage. Far from being upset about Edith's suspension, Amory criticized the mildness of her punishment. He angrily declared that his niece ought to be shot—a very strange remark from a man whose brothers had died of self-inflicted gunshot wounds. His choice of words suggests that like Kate, Amory immediately associated Edith's outburst with the family history of suicide.

Edith was not wanted in Corning. Amory wrote that he had instructed her to consult with Thomas about the thirty days in question.

Thomas sent a note to Pembroke West, advising Edith to visit Germantown that same afternoon. To assuage Miss Stevens's fears, Thomas advised Edith to arrive without luggage, so that the two could have a pleasant talk first. But Edith was already gone when the president's message arrived. Amory's vitriolic letter had sent his niece flying directly to Germantown.

Miss Stevens took one look at the shivering, overwrought child and announced that there was no room for her. Edith obviously was much too upset to be sent away immediately, however. Inside with Miss Stevens, she made a show of declaring that she would probably go home in two weeks anyway. She proudly insisted that before the hazing, she had not meant to stay another year in college.

Then suddenly Edith's façade dissolved and the pain started to pour out. She had to talk to someone. Miss Stevens, warning Edith not to run away from criticism, urged her to prove herself worthy of Thomas's trust and confidence.

Edith hesitated to return to Bryn Mawr, where a second deadline had passed; but there was nowhere else for her to go. Thomas conferred with Mary Helen Ritchie throughout the day. By 7 p.m. they had agreed: Edith would be entrusted to Mrs. Hanna Chalfant, proprietor of Upland, a small, secluded country inn in Chester County, about thirty miles from Philadelphia. Mrs. Chalfant, who often gave shelter to Bryn Mawr girls in trouble, agreed to allow Kate and Marion to spend four days with their sister at Thanksgiving.

Still, Kate was wildly uneasy about sending Edith off for the month alone. She dreaded making a mistake as her mother had once done with Fred. She had to be sure that Edith would be all right. Thomas, sensing that the sisters needed to spend one more night together, rented a room for them in the nearby home of Rose Herman, a former student. Early the next morning, Edith left for Upland.

At the outset of her final exams, January 30–February 7, 1899, Kate blacked out and struck her head in Mary Helen Ritchie's smoke-filled flat in the Low Buildings. The president's sister, Helen Thomas, a reader in the English department, was one of a group of women who witnessed Kate's fall. Dr. Walter Christie was summoned; he declared that the blow to Kate's head was likely to have a temporary effect on her mind.

The incident seemed to realize Kate's worst fears about herself. Like other members of her family, she had snapped. Something terrifying and irrational had suddenly erupted in her. Now it was no longer a possibility; it had happened and others had seen it.

As the fall semester drew to a close, it had become increasingly evident to Mary Helen Ritchie and others that the hazing and its calamitous aftermath had taken an immense personal toll on Kate. She had studied even less and cut classes more than usual. Due to graduate in June with a dual major in history and political science, she had been unable to muster the usual spurt of delirious energy to cram for exams; she seemed tense, raw, exhausted, and dangerously highly-strung.

During Edith's month at Upland it had been Kate who faced the other students and took the heat for her sister. She publicly insisted that she did not take the hazing very seriously even as she agonized about its implications for Edith and herself.

Somehow Kate had survived a much-dreaded German oral on January 7. Unable to focus in anticipation of her final exams, however, she pretended not to care if she failed to graduate with her class. Gonzalez Lodge, professor of Latin and secretary of the faculty, reported to Carey Thomas that by then Kate had put herself "under a cloud" with many of her classmates. Now that they were seniors, some of the same girls who had once been amused and delighted by the spectacle of Kate's last-minute cramming sessions expressed bitter resentment at her flippancy, which appeared to insult all that Bryn Mawr offered women.

Edith, by contrast, had swiftly put the hazing behind her. Immediately she returned she plunged into feverish study. Not only did she catch up with the other sophomores, she soared beyond them. A month in the country with Mrs. Chalfant appeared to have had a wonderful clarifying effect; suddenly Edith knew exactly what she was doing at Bryn Mawr and what she wanted. She had taken Mary Stevens's advice to heart: She would do everything possible to prove herself worthy of Carey Thomas's interest.

Forswearing her loss of control on Lantern Night, Edith went to great lengths to demonstrate prodigious self-discipline. She excelled at every subject. She appeared in every production. She spoke at every gathering. She participated in every sport. By an act of will, the pariah transformed herself into the college's undisputed star.

Kate, in the days following her collapse, failed ten out of fifteen hours of exams, seriously jeopardizing her graduation. Though the doctor recommended that she be permitted to make up exams in the spring, Carey Thomas feared that to allow one student to retake exams would only encourage others to seek the same privilege. Kate would receive no decision until the faculty discussed the case in May. If they decided against her, she would have to return to Bryn Mawr for an additional semester.

That spring, anyone crossing the campus who happened to glance at Pembroke West would have seen a curious sight. The lower parts of the windows of 33–35 were pasted over with heavy paper. No one could see in or out. Kate had covered the glass to force herself to concentrate on an exhausting program of round-the-clock study. Idly gazing out at girls in billowing white skirts and straw hats on their way to the village offered too much temptation.

Dr. Christie's explanation that a blow to the head had caused her failure allowed Kate temporarily to suppress fears about what had really happened to her mind; she seemed anxious to prove that she was back in control. She crammed with Mary Towle and Edith. She hired tutors, Mlle. de Bouneville and Miss Chamberlain. She demonstrated the same furious determination to get out of Bryn Mawr as she once had to get in.

After Kate passed her orals, Carey Thomas continued to hesitate to allow her to make up the failed exams. Thomas changed her mind only when a group of seniors—the same girls who had complained about Kate—testified that "a great change had come over the feeling of the senior class about her." Suddenly, Gonzalez Lodge reported, "everyone in the class would be glad for her to get her degree." With the overwhelming support of her classmates, Kate retook and passed the tests. Final exams, May 24–June 6, were now the sole remaining obstacle to graduation.

Meanwhile Edith, starring in a campus production of *The Amazons*, the latest of many theatrical successes, had begun to give serious thought to a career as an actress. Regular forays into Philadelphia to see Richard Mansfield, Eleanora Duse, John Drew, Julia Marlow, Ellen Terry, Ethel Barrymore, Henry Irving, and the other celebrated actors who appeared there suggested tantalizing possibilities; she talked of joining a theatrical company to tour the world.

Carey Thomas had very different ideas for her. The president made no bones about wanting Edith to become a doctor, as Thomas herself had once hoped to do. Thomas belonged to the Women's Fund Committee known as "the Ladies" that had guaranteed $500,000 (much of it provided by Mary Garrett) to open the Johns Hopkins Medical School in Baltimore, Maryland, in 1893 on the condition that women be admitted "on the same terms as men." She urged Edith, a chemistry and mathematics major, to set her sights on Hopkins.

In the spring of her sophomore year, Edith announced plans to accelerate work at Bryn Mawr and enter medical school early. Attendance at the Harvard Annex (Radcliffe) that summer and an increased course load in the 1899–1900 academic year would enable her to graduate in three years instead of four—the sort of extreme gesture that greatly appealed to the actress in Edith.

Only a few months after Amory declared that his niece ought to be shot, he wrote a worried letter about her to Carey Thomas. Almost certainly he was thinking about his brothers when he speculated about the effects too much pressure might have on Edith. Amory said nothing about Edith's family history, however; had he done so, Carey Thomas, a believer in the heredity of mental weakness, would have been unlikely to reply, as she did on May 26, that she approved of Edith's plan to finish a year ahead of her class.

In the midst of all this back and forth over Edith, Kate plunged into final exams. She was exhausted from the many weeks of cramming. She was keyed up with a desperate need to prove that her blackout and the failure that followed had been an aberration. She was anxious about Edith having to cope with next year's pressures alone; and about herself, suddenly facing life beyond Bryn Mawr without her sister (and without Mary Towle, who was staying on for a graduate degree).

She successfully completed tests in German literature, German reading, and French literature; then precisely as she had done five months before, she blacked out in the exam room.

Kate awakened in a bed at Bryn Mawr Hospital. She insisted that she felt all right but doctors forbade her to return for exams in Faust, German composition, and German idealism. Within days, Carey Thomas sent word of a faculty ruling that Kate's remaining exams were to be postponed until fall. It was almost with a sigh of relief that Kate declared her intention to stay at Bryn Mawr with Edith for an additional year. She would take an M.A. and graduate side by side with her sister in the class of 1900.

———————

It was the fashion among college seniors that year to describe themselves as "the last class of the century."

At Bryn Mawr, two events in the 1899–1900 academic year suggested that a watershed had been reached in women's higher education. The first, in November, was the public unveiling of John Singer Sargent's austere portrait of the Bryn Mawr president. Seated in an ornately carved armchair, the heavy-lidded Thomas struck a reserved and distant pose. Viewed from below, she appeared monumental, a colossus, her flowing jet-black academic gown dominating the pictorial composition.

Before its unveiling, the portrait was locked in a room at the Deanery where Thomas could see it from the bay window of her bedroom. "It really looks alive," she assured Mary Garrett. "Mamie and I pay it frequent visits." Her preoccupation was not wholly egotistical. To be painted by Sargent in those robes guaranteed that Bryn Mawr's president and all she stood for had entered history. The portrait was a monument to "the cause" of all educated, independent, self-reliant women. It confirmed the extent to which Thomas herself had come to symbolize the conviction that women are "competent to follow and succeed in the highest pursuits of men."

The first annual May Day celebration on May 1, 1900, aimed to communicate that conviction to the wealthy and prominent Philadelphians whose support Carey Thomas had long been eager to attract. Five tall maypoles, decorated with flowers, ribbons, and streamers, rose on the campus lawn and one hundred red, gold, blue, and white embroidered silk banners rippled from windows in Denbigh and Pembroke East and West. The colorful festival of Elizabethan masques, music, and dances brought some 3000 guests to the campus—"among them the most important people socially in Philadelphia," the president crowed in a letter to the trustees.

Hoping to dispel the myth of the female collegian as an invalid or an androgynous freak, Evangeline Walker Andrews, a Bryn Mawr graduate and faculty wife, had designed the pageant to give visitors "their first idea of the gaiety and energy and health of normal college women." Heralded by a blast of twelve trumpets, Kate Houghton, Mary Helen Ritchie, and Mary Towle marched in the procession of Elizabethan revelers—milkmaids, shepherdesses, clowns, mummers, chimneysweeps, rustics, jesters, maypole dancers and flower girls—that preceded the arrival of the Lord and Lady of the May.

Edith Houghton, a rawboned, hollow-cheeked Robin Hood, emerged from the cavern of Pembroke Arch on a white horse. She was accompanied by Maid Marian and a band of Robin's men. To assuage the perpetual fears about girls being seen in men's dress, Edith wore several very short skirts that passed for a tunic over leather leggings. She intended the performance to be her last. On May Day, she renounced acting in favor of a career in medicine, Hopkins having accepted her for the fall.

It was now six years since the death of Carrie Houghton, for whom Bryn Mawr had represented all she hoped her daughters might achieve. Kate and Edith, about to graduate, had fulfilled their mother's dream.

Bryn Mawr women learned to be aggressive, ambitious, and powerful. They learned that they were rational human beings in charge of their own destinies. They learned to stop obeying unquestioningly and to think and speak for themselves. They tasted the manna of political power, and the scope they exercised in student self-government probably posed a far greater threat to the status quo than anything they studied in chemistry or Latin. But when they finally left the rarefied, privileged, nestlike existence Carey Thomas had created for them at Bryn Mawr, how would they function? What would the man's world beyond Pembroke Arch make of an Edith Houghton?

And what of Kate Houghton? In the end, Kate had thrived on the support and esteem of Bryn Mawr's community of women. She had seen what it is to be treated with dignity and respect. She had enjoyed the company of people who did not disparage and humiliate her. What would become of Kate when she returned, as seemed almost inevitable, to her "family in Corning"?

She did not return.

Throughout their lives, Kate would often be overcome by the need to "talk about things" with Edith as she could talk to no one else. As Kate later described it to Edith, suddenly she would feel "crazy to see" her. That spring, in consultation with Edith, Kate decided to try for medical school. Hopkins's principal attraction to both sisters appears to have been the sense in which it formed a continuum with Bryn Mawr.

There were at most seventy-five places in each Hopkins class and several hundred applicants for each one. The Ladies had insisted on exceptionally rigorous entrance criteria; poorly prepared women would only disgrace the committee and make it difficult for other women to be admitted. Lacking the science background—the "preliminary medical course"—that the Ladies required in addition to French and German, Kate had devoted the 1899–1900 academic year at Bryn Mawr to chemistry and physics.

When Edith moved to Baltimore in the fall, Kate would accompany Mary Towle to Cambridge, Massachusetts, where Mary was to begin a Ph.D. in English at Radcliffe. Kate applied to do additional work there in chemistry and mathematics, specifying that she did not plan to pursue a Radcliffe degree. Marion Houghton was still not ready to take the Bryn Mawr entrance exam, so Carey Thomas arranged for her to go to Baltimore with Edith for two years of additional preparation at the Arundell School.

Kate hoped to be ready to apply to Hopkins for the fall of 1901.

F I V E

---

dith Houghton, like other first-year Hopkins medical students, spent much of her time in one of several small dissecting rooms. On each of three zinc-covered tables lay a draped cadaver. The heavy air reeked of chemicals and mummified flesh.

Students, in teams of five or six, unwrapped only the area of the body to be cut apart and examined. Out of deference to the women among them, there was no gratuitous stripping or exposing. Usually they began with the arm, carefully noting muscles, nerves, and blood vessels. They ended, several months later, with the neck and head.

The students sometimes fainted. In Edith's class one young man passed out during a dissection. His head fell on the shoulder of the woman beside him. She deposited him in a heap on the floor, then resumed the dissection exactly where he left off—all without seeming to miss a beat.

Edith and the other women knew the almost impossibly fine line they were expected to walk. They must show themselves ready to leap in and do everything a man could. They must not appear squeamish. At a time when some girls' schools still pasted heavy paper over textbook pictures of the human body, women medical students must demonstrate that anatomy would not unnerve them. On the other hand, they must avoid seeming too eager. Decorum must be observed if the charge was to be even partly contradicted that no decent, respectable woman could listen to the detailed discussion of medical topics in the presence of men. How, it was asked, could her male classmates continue to respect her?

As late as 1900, when twelve women graduated in a class of forty-three, the belief persisted that some Hopkins women had gone into medicine to pursue "abnormal sex interests." The female student who showed too much coolness of mind when she examined men laid herself open to charges of sexual perversion. At the Johns Hopkins Hospital that year, Dorothy Reed, an intern who had been a leading light of the class of 1900, was flatly told that only the "desire to satisfy sexual curiosity" would lead her or any woman to ask to work in a male ward.

It was common knowledge that the Hopkins trustees had never really wanted to admit women; only the desperate need for cash to open the long-planned medical school before the faculty they had hired found work elsewhere compelled the trustees reluctantly to accept Mary Garrett's money—and her inflexible terms. There was considerable resentment among both students and faculty that women had been allowed to buy their way into Hopkins, and one professional journal publicly lambasted the school for "selling its privileges."

Dorothy Reed noted that some women at Hopkins grew "embittered and supersensitive from association with the men of their classes who made them feel they were not wanted." Male students harassed "hen medics" with cruel practical jokes and smutty "biological" humor; and the faculty members were often just as bad. One lecturer, in an attempt to fluster and embarrass the women in his audience, devoted nearly an hour to comparing the cavernous tissues of the nasal passages to the corpus spongiosa of the penis.

"From the start he dragged in the dirtiest stories I ever heard, read, or imagined, and when he couldn't say it in English he quoted Latin from sources not usually open to the public," Reed recalled. "Nearly fifty years have passed since this night, but much he said is branded in my mind and still comes up like a decomposing body from the bottom of a pool that is disturbed."

Many women students reacted to such incidents by cultivating a thick hide. Reed claimed to have developed an independence and arrogance at Hopkins that were foreign to her original nature. The only way to survive medical school, it seemed, was to ask no favors as a woman and try not to look for discrimination and insults everywhere.

Any woman who expressed ambivalence about her medical studies was a topic of immense concern to Mary Garrett and the other Ladies. Were she to fail or drop out permanently, not only would she squander an invaluable opportunity for herself, she would cast doubt on all other women who wanted to come to Hopkins. Edith, along with other female students, was often summoned to Mary Garrett's mansion on Monument Street, where a footman stood behind each guest throughout dinner. From first to last, conversation focused on the progress and prospects of women at Hopkins. During Edith's first term, no student can have been more feverishly discussed or agonized about than Gertrude Stein, then in her fourth year.

Stein's last two years at Hopkins were fraught with difficulty, the result of deep ambivalence about her medical career. She was already pursuing her studies in "a half-hearted way" when intense jealousy over her lover May Bookstaver's ongoing relationship with another woman made it impossible for her to work at all. It seemed all too likely to the Ladies that Stein would complete four years of medical school without earning her degree: a blow to the cause of women at Hopkins.

With all eyes on Gertrude Stein, no one seemed to notice that Edith Houghton was experiencing a similar attack of uncertainty.

A backstage encounter with the actor Richard Mansfield had revived the theatrical ambitions Edith had abandoned under pressure from Carey Thomas. Mansfield, who portrayed Beau Brummell, Cyrano de Bergerac, and Richard III to great acclaim, invited Edith to join his company. He arranged for her to go to Paris in May to study acting. By October 1901, she would be ready to make her debut in Booth Tarkington's *Beaucaire*, the light comedy Mansfield was preparing to open at the new Garrick Theater in Philadelphia. At Christmas, Edith told Kate of her decision to abandon Hopkins.

As it happened, Edith lasted only a few restless months in Paris, where she lived in the Latin Quarter with a family named Le Frappe and studied acting with a colleague of Mansfield's. She returned to Baltimore in the fall and resumed medical work with a vengeance. Edith told her friend Florence Sabin (an intern whom Mary Garrett had asked to look after the younger women at Hopkins) that she had finally realized a stage career was not for her.

It was then quite common for women to drift in and out of the medical school, taking more than the customary four years to finish. Edith's brief absence had a more lasting impact on her sister. Kate abruptly dropped the idea of medical school: What was the point of applying to Hopkins if Edith wasn't going to be there? She withdrew from premedical studies at Radcliffe on December 30, 1900.

By this point Kate was receiving a monthly stipend from her mother's estate; instead of submitting her bills to Mack Smith, she was expected to pay for everything herself out of the $91.66 Amory sent like clockwork. Suddenly, Kate found herself regularly getting through that amount long before the month was up. She traveled, she stayed at hotels, she bought expensive clothing for herself and gifts for friends. Her allowance was scarcely sufficient. When Kate asked Amory for more, he deducted the amount from future payments, so that she was almost always short of cash.

In October, Kate decided to tour the museums and art galleries of Europe with Mary Towle, who had left Radcliffe after a year of course work. Kate had only enough money (most of it borrowed from Mary Towle) for the cheapest passage. She wrote to Corning for an advance of three more payments, but this time Amory balked. In the light of past advances, he refused to send a penny until December 13. Amory was tired of Kate's living beyond her means. Besides, he objected to the idea of two young unmarried women traveling abroad without a chaperone.

Kate went anyway. She arrived in Paris with a scant ten dollars and the address of the family with whom Edith had stayed. She persuaded the Le Frappes to allow her and Mary Towle to board on credit. In December, the friends settled their bill and left for several months in the south of France and Italy.

If Kate seemed anxious to prolong her travels in Europe,

perhaps it was because the mask of the tourist allowed her to conceal—from herself as much as anyone else—that she had no home and no prospects. Although she gave her address as "Corning, New York," she must have sensed the pathetic existence that awaited her there now that she had abandoned any idea of a career.

Mary Houghton, Kate's half-sister in Buffalo, lingered as a symbol of what happened to unmarried women without money, career, or a home of their own, who accepted the permanent hospitality of older relatives. Her grandmother, Mrs. Chestnutwood, had died in 1899; but Frankie Linen lived for another twenty years and Mary Houghton was expected to care for her until the end. She served as Frankie's devoted companion in the home of Georgie Linen, who was married and had his own family. The "family claim" ruled out any other life for a woman like Mary Houghton; and so it probably would for Kate should she succumb to temptation and take up residence with Aunt Nell.

Instead, upon her return to the United States that fall, Kate discovered another of the roles available to a young woman in impecunious circumstances. An invitation to Chicago to stay with her school friend Ethel Hooper was followed by another to spend several weeks with Mary Towle's family in Wakefield, Massachusetts; and before Kate knew it, she was drifting from one extended visit to another.

In an era of big houses, cheap servants, and arduous travel, wealthy families invited guests to house parties that often lasted weeks at a time. As every hostess knew, the well-mixed gathering must have its share of unattached women and men. Attractive single women served as bait for the unmarried men; there must be just enough pretty girls on the guest list to keep the males interested and amused. Usually a young woman in Kate's position was also expected to divert and entertain the hostess's husband and his married friends; but she must not go so far as to antagonize the wives.

Kate walked a perilously thin line. She must be flirtatious without seeming fast. She must keep the married men interested without tarnishing her reputation. Above all, whatever Kate did, she must not arouse the jealousy of the hostess or of other married women. If that happened, she would not be invited back and word would quickly spread for other hostesses to beware.

The "visiting girl" depended on an almost uninterrupted series of invitations; she could ill afford to incur the displeasure of even a single hostess. She must do everything to make herself a desirable guest. She must dress beautifully, she must always seem pleasant and in a good mood, she must be clever, witty, and charming without appearing learned or immodest. She must work hard at seeming always to have fun. She must never moan or complain; she must keep her troubles to herself. No one wanted to hear about Kate's money worries or her frantic need to keep her calendar filled—that was her problem.

With no home of her own, Kate had to have someplace to go every day of the year. She had to make herself constantly available without seeming over-eager. When there was a gap between house parties, she had to be certain that she had money enough to stay at the Cotocheset, an inn in Wianno, Massachusetts, on Cape Cod.

Although Kate pretended to live in Corning, she obviously could not repay hostesses by inviting them to her family home. (Only Mary Towle seems to have accompanied Kate to Amory's.) This probably accounts for Kate's strong sense of earning her keep by accommodating her hostesses' special needs. Their demands could be crassly insulting. One woman offered Kate an expensive Grueby vase if she would agree, in effect, to seduce her husband. Kate had been invited to spend a week at the young couple's home outside Boston. The woman explained that it was her husband's custom to go off on hunting trips with a dissolute friend who drank too much; she wanted Kate to use her charms to stop him.

That the hostess offered to pay for her services suggested the appalling position in which Kate had placed herself. For all of Kate's pretenses, her desperate lack of money was only too evident. It was an ugly, unpleasant episode all around. The cucumber-green vase proved an immense temptation and at length Kate did everything in her power to earn it. The husband remained at home; and within days, apparently thinking his wife oblivious, he was writing love sonnets to Kate. Penniless, unattached, and unprotected, she was fair game.

Wherever a visiting girl went, she was on perpetual display. Everyone knew and accepted that such women were usually in search of a rich husband. Their only capital was physical allure and perhaps a talent to amuse. Their shelf-life was limited; novelty was all. They must snare a man before hostesses and guests wearied of them and the invitations stopped.

Kate turned twenty-five on February 2, 1903. On the house-party circuit, twenty-five was relatively old for an unmarried woman in her circumstances. She had other drawbacks. There was a distinct edge to her personality. She was neither docile nor obedient. She was over-educated—at least by most men's standards.

The passivity of her situation horrified her. Sensitive to the demeaning experience of being endlessly looked over, judged, and compared as if she were a piece of merchandise, Kate finally insisted that it would be far more dignified actively to go after the man she wanted. She knew only that she hadn't seen him yet and that she would not accept a man who was "at all second-rate." More than anything, Kate wanted to fall "violently in love."

Many years later, Kate would tell her children that she had fallen in love with Tom Hepburn's arms, and Tom recalled his passion for Kate's broad shoulders.

It was typical of their marriage that when Kate and Tom talked about each other it was often in strongly physical terms. They were never reticent about the powerful sexual attraction that formed the basis of their relationship. When Kate reminisced about their first meeting, she depicted herself as the aggressor. After many months on passive display in the sexual marketplace of the house parties, Kate had finally spotted the man she wanted. She knew nothing about him, only what she could see; yet she recalled telling herself, "That's going to be my husband."

He had thick, dark, mahogany-red hair and finely chiseled features. He was 5 feet 11 inches and about 175 pounds. He had powerful shoulders and rock-hard muscles developed playing fullback on his college football team, as it was then done, without helmets, shoulder guards, or thigh pads. He moved with an acrobat's speed and agility and seemed to enjoy being watched and admired. His brilliant blue eyes darted constantly between what he was doing and his audience of the moment. He loved the rumor that nurses at Hopkins Hospital spied on him from the windows whenever he passed on the street. He seemed well aware that Kate, like most women, found him devastatingly attractive.

Everyone always said that Tom had the most perfect hands they had ever seen, smooth and white with long, elegantly tapered fingers. They were the picture of a surgeon's hands.

Tom worked his way through medical school teaching tumbling and gymnastics. He was fencing with his classmate Edith Houghton in her flat on North Wolfe Street near the hospital when Kate first saw him. He wore a form-fitting, high-necked white padded jacket and white trousers.

"The most beautiful creature!" Kate whispered to her sister when the fencers took a break.

To Kate's astonishment, Edith did not seem to share her enthusiasm. Unlike most women, Edith failed to defer to Tom. She did not treat him as God's gift to the universe. She thought him arrogant, vain, self-dramatizing, and even a little foolish. She maintained a lightly mocking attitude that appeared to irritate and fluster him. Still, the alphabet ruled and Hepburn, Houghton, and another second-year medical student, Donald Hooker, sat together in a good many classes and became friends.

When Kate expressed too much interest in her sister's fencing partner, Edith pointed out that the twenty-three-year-old Thomas Norval Hepburn was hardly a catch. He was a poor Southern farm boy. As far as Edith could tell, Tom and his older brothers, Charles, Sewell, and Lloyd, seemed to have spent their childhood doing somersaults from the family hayloft. Their father, the Reverend Sewell Stavely Hepburn ("Brother Hep"), was a traveling Episcopal minister in far-flung, impoverished country parishes in Maryland

and Virginia. Edith warned Kate not to risk her future with the likes of Tom.

"Never mind my future!" Kate replied. "My present is all that matters. I'd marry him even if I knew it meant I'd die in a year and go to hell!"

It was the last day of Kate's visit to Baltimore. Between invitations, she was headed to Bryn Mawr in the morning to see Marion, then in her freshman year; as a Bryn Mawr graduate, Kate would be able to stay in one of the college residence halls until her next house party. To Edith's chagrin, that night she had to attend a medical society meeting. She asked what Kate would like to do while she was out. Kate said pointedly that she wanted "the young man with the red hair" to keep her company. Would her sister arrange it?

In Tom's experience, no proper Southern girl would have been so bold as to summon him like that, hours after they first met. The evening was tense, awkward, highly charged. Edith's furry lap dog sat between them on the couch the entire time.

Kate had felt sexual attraction like this before but tended to reject potential suitors for fear of the sort of children they would produce. Rather than admit what was really on her mind, Kate would pick out some physical imperfection that disqualified a young man as the prospective parent of her child. In fact, she was actively searching for a man whose strong and healthy bloodline would overpower a possible genetic weakness in her own background.

Tom always talked openly, even boastfully, of the Powell bloodline, his "inheritance" as he called it. Edith depicted Tom as something of a hayseed, but he emphasized the lost romantic grandeur of his "family forebears." He constantly pointed out that Nina Hepburn, his mother, came from one of Virginia's most distinguished families. The Powells—he would say—were "F.F.V.," a first family of Virginia.

Tom, his brothers, and a sister, Selina, may have grown up dirt poor, but their aristocratic mother had enjoyed an idyllic girlhood at Llangollen, the family estate near Upperville, in Loudoun County. Tom knew by heart the litany of his maternal ancestors: Nina's great-grandfather, Leven Powell, was a founder of the Minute Men and a colonel in the Revolutionary War. He served with his friend and commander George Washington at Valley Forge, and was a delegate to the Virginia convention which ratified the Federal Constitution. A Federalist, he was elected to the Sixth Congress in 1799. Nina's grandfather, Leven's son Cuthbert, served as mayor of Alexandria, Virginia. After making his fortune as a ship-owner and merchant, he built Llangollen, a brick mansion with four large white columns. A Whig, Cuthbert Powell was elected to the Twenty-Seventh Congress in 1841.

Nina's father, Charles Leven Powell, had the reputation of a family failure. After graduating from Yale in 1823, the gentle, scholarly, "ineffectual" Charles was repeatedly frustrated in his attempts to establish a law career. Unable to support his wife, two sons, and three daughters on his earnings as a lawyer, Charles finally returned to Yale for an M.A. in 1860. He and his wife, Selina Lloyd Powell, opened a girls' boarding school in Winchester, Virginia. Mrs. Powell's childhood friend Mary Custis was now the wife of Robert E. Lee, and the Confederate general's daughters became the school's most illustrious pupils.

Nina was nineteen when the war began, precipitating the Powell family's downfall. Her father's school, in the middle of the war zone, had to be shut down; Nina's two brothers, Lloyd and Charlie, were slaughtered in the first and second battles of Manassas; and Llangollen and the family fortune were lost.

From the time when Tom was a little boy, Nina's stories had always made the Civil War loom large in his imagination; as children, he and his brothers would play with abandoned military equipment in the old battlefields where the Confederacy had lost the war.

Like Kate and Edith, Tom was haunted by the image of a lost Eden—but with a difference. At this point, he used every opportunity to talk about his family tragedy and the vanished glory of Llangollen. Kate, by contrast, regarded the tragedy in her past as a source of shame; the Houghton family history of suicide must be kept secret at any price, especially now that she was actively seeking a mate.

Tom Hepburn accompanied Kate to the station in the morning and helped her onto the train. She traveled to Philadelphia in a romantic haze. At Bryn Mawr, Marion was incredulous when Kate insisted that she had just spent an evening with the man she was going to marry.

There was a note from him the next morning. Kate made a display of being shocked and disillusioned when Tom, who held a master's degree from Randolph-Macon College in Ashland, Virginia, wrote "warf" for "wharf." Kate taunted him by sending a dictionary with the suggestion that he learn to spell. It was typical of Tom's unshakable self-confidence—Edith would have called it arrogance—that he replied with a declaration that history's great men had never been able to spell. He warned Kate to abandon all hope that he would ever learn.

In the months that followed, Kate single-mindedly pursued Tom Hepburn. Determined, she said, not to let him get away, she stayed frequently at Edith's tiny flat. The more time Kate spent with Tom, the more she liked him. And it appeared that Tom felt the same way about Kate except for one thing: He never touched her. He kept his distance. They never even kissed.

Accustomed to men's unwanted advances as Kate was, she did not know what to make of Tom. She lamented to Edith that he was "more a sitter than a suitor." His reserve seemed so uncharacteristic. If Tom Hepburn was anything, he certainly was not shy.

The relationship progressed to the point where Edith arranged a dinner party for the couple with Don Hooker and a few of the other second-year students. Kate and Tom, walking in the woods that afternoon, became so absorbed in each other that they forgot Edith's plans. They dined at a country inn, talked for hours, and returned to Edith's apartment quite late. Kate lingered at the entrance to the building before heading upstairs to the inevitable explosion. Years later, she could still vividly remember hoping that Tom would kiss her good-night, and her perplexity and disappointment when he did not.

There was a simple explanation, although Kate would have no inkling of it until after they were married. In sexual matters, Tom had been determined "to learn from the mistakes" of his older brothers.

Years later Tom Hepburn would tell his son that while Virginia tradition forbade gentlemen "to sexually violate the daughters of your family's friends," it was considered acceptable for white men to have intercourse—and illegitimate children—with black women. According to local custom, the women were supposed to be "delighted to have sex with the young masters of the house because they would like to have children that were nearer white than black." In this manner, Charlie Hepburn and Lloyd Hepburn contracted gonorrhea and Sewell Hepburn contracted syphilis.

Tom, in childhood, had always refused to take orders from the older boys; whenever Charlie, Sewell, or Lloyd tried to force him to do something, little Tom would break away, shouting, "You ain't the boss of me!"

In later life, his brothers' experiences with venereal disease led Tom to decide that although his sexual appetites were every bit as strong as theirs, he would not—as he said—let sex "boss" him. Tom's ego was much too large to allow anyone or anything to dictate his actions; and he fought his own desires as vigorously as he fought other people.

Displays of self-control were a Powell tradition: Cuthbert Powell was legendary for claiming to derive satisfaction from drastically minimizing his own personal desires. And when Nina's brother Charlie Powell broke a sacred promise to his mother not to chew tobacco, she famously declared: "Charlie, this life wouldn't be a warfare, if there were nothing to war against!" Tom Hepburn, determined to master his own will, planned to resist sex before marriage. He insisted the pleasure would be the greater for having been deferred.

Kate obviously presented an immense challenge. Although Tom had had many girlfriends in Virginia, none had pursued him quite like this. Kate, in an unabashed effort to become part of Tom's life, signed on to teach at Baltimore's Calvert School in the 1903–4 school year.

When Kate proposed that they spend time alone together that summer, Tom assumed the young lady was inviting him to Corning. But that wasn't what Kate had in mind at all. At this stage she probably did not want Tom to see the fluster and forgetfulness to which Amory was capable of reducing her. She told Tom that her family would expect the young couple to go out a good deal, scarcely allowing them any time to themselves.

Tom took the cue to invite Kate to Waverley, a waterfront mansion in Gloucester County, Virginia, the home of his older sister Selina and her husband, Nicholas Snowden Hopkins. Tom assured Kate that the Hopkinses would be only too eager to cooperate with their desire for uninterrupted privacy.

When Amory heard about Kate's plans, he fired off a furious letter, forbidding her to go. The trip, he said, could only end in humiliation. Kate replied firmly that she was over twenty-one and would go where she pleased when she pleased. She insisted she knew what she was doing.

Prior to the trip, Tom warned Kate that Southerners were naturally suspicious of outsiders. They knew and resented the opinion Yankees had of their customs. At Randolph-Macon, Tom and the other football players had enjoyed shocking and appalling Yankee visitors: As a boy, Tom had learned the bizarre trick of pretending to hang himself by the neck, skillfully positioning his muscles so as to allow him to breathe. The Randolph-Macon football team used Tom's technique to stage mock hangings of blacks as a nasty prank on visiting teams from the North.

Nobody played tricks on Kate during the two weeks she and Tom visited Waverley, but the locals did view her with considerable suspicion and alarm.

The Colonial-style brick house built by Captain Phillip Tabb after the War of 1812 had a marble porch and steps and a broad hall with a curved staircase. Situated in a grove of elm trees, Waverley overlooked North River, a tidal estuary that connected with Mobjack Bay. Weatherworn tombstones, etched with the skull and crossbones, suggested that Waverley had risen on the site of an earlier house. Kate slept alone in one of the huge upstairs bedrooms. Enormous wooden folding screens were set up for privacy. A maid served her breakfast in bed.

Tom's sister and brother-in-law, as promised, kept their distance. They left the young couple to spend days alone on a sailboat. Kate seemed to relish the idea that a number of Tom's old girlfriends, shocked by the Yankee girl's willingness to travel with a man to whom she was not even engaged, might be watching intently with spyglasses from the shore.

At Waverley, Tom's attentions persuaded Kate that he had indeed finally fallen in love. By the end of the holiday, she was certain they had settled things between them. They took a paddle-wheeler to Old Point Comfort, where Kate happily bought a boat ticket to Boston. Tom accompanied her as far as Newport News, a three-hour trip. But when he talked about the next seven years, Kate noted that her name never once came up. She had no place in Tom's plans. She had misunderstood. Tom had not fallen in love after all. Whatever Kate had assumed, he obviously had no intention of marrying. She struggled to conceal the crashing disappointment.

Tom got off at Newport News, leaving Kate to sink into her steamer chair—as she recalled—in a sort of coma. Dazed, she scarcely moved for the rest of the trip, endlessly turning over in her thoughts how she could have been so mistaken about his feelings. She told herself that Tom was not a serious suitor after all.

To cover the hurt and humiliation, Kate headed for the Cotocheset on Cape Cod, where she threw herself into a round of activity with various young men. She played golf, she sailed, she went to parties and dances. By her own account, she "jollied up" nearly every man she met, in a conscious effort to restore her confidence. She needed the reassurance that men found her attractive. And she wrote long letters to Tom Hepburn detailing her escapades.

That fall Kate arrived in Baltimore with significant ammunition. She had had a marriage proposal. Billy Buckminster, a regular on the house-party circuit, offered stability, security, and a home of her own. Kate did not say yes or no; and she strategically withheld the news from Tom until the right moment.

Edith had moved to larger quarters at the Saint Paul residence in Baltimore, which Kate shared, and Tom visited almost daily. The housekeeper predicted that before long Mr. Hepburn would hang his hat there; but still Tom did not propose.

More and more he seemed to talk and think only of work. As third-year students, Tom, Edith, and their friend Don Hooker put on the white duck laboratory coats of the "embryo physician." The year was devoted to practical work in the dispensary clinics at Hopkins Hospital, where they wrote up patients' histories, did physicals and blood and urine analysis, and heard themselves called Doctor for the first time.

It has been said of Hopkins's eminent and flamboyant senior faculty of the period—Drs. William Osler, William Halsted, Howard A. Kelly, and William Welch—that "they comprised the most extraordinary group the world of medicine ever saw or probably ever will see." Bertram Bernheim, Tom Hepburn's classmate, dubbed them the "doctor-actors."

Osler enjoyed performing autopsies dressed in a silk hat, gray cutaway coat, striped trousers, and spats. With a flourish he would push up his sleeves to point out a heart or kidney lesion, "the blood dripping from his slender taper fingers to the tray below." For flair and showmanship Osler was rivaled by Howard A. Kelly, professor of gynecology and obstetrics, whose lectures were said to be "more enchanting and spectacular than a variety show." Kelly, a connoisseur of the poisonous serpents of North America, would often show off his vast collection. Now and then a deadly rattlesnake bit his finger, but the doctor-actor always made a display of waving away students who rushed to help. Kelly, sucking the wound, would resume his lecture at the usual rapid clip without disclosing that an assistant had carefully milked the snake's venom in advance.

William Halsted, surgeon-in-chief at Hopkins Hospital, where he developed the Halsted mastectomy, struck a very different note. He was silent, distant, and melancholic. Women especially thought him intimidating and even a bit sadistic. Dorothy Reed, for one, complained that he "frightened the students to death and made them feel like fools." Other students, more sympathetic, detected the flicker of tragedy in Halsted's eyes. There was a story behind his aloofness and apparent lack of warmth or emotion: In Halsted's pre-Hopkins bachelor days in New York City, his brilliant career had nearly been destroyed when cocaine addiction landed him in a private mental hospital. After that, Halsted abandoned the *bon vivant*'s life for a mode of existence characterized by forbearance and self-denial. To acolytes like Tom Hepburn, it was hardly that Halsted could not express his feelings, it was that he dared not.

Tom Hepburn's preoccupation with his brothers' downfall made him particularly susceptible to Halsted. Tom, always striving to master his own will, found comfort and inspiration in Halsted's victorious struggle against his personal demons. Like other students who joined the unofficial Halsted school, Tom began assiduously to ape the master. He emulated Halsted's perfectionism and mania for control in the operating room, as well as his Brahmin reserve in most personal and professional relations. Before long, Tom came to be known as Halsted's "special student." When professor and protégé passed on the street, they bowed silently in acknowledgment. Soon there was talk that Halsted had nominated young Hepburn for a fellowship to study surgery with Professor Czherney in Heidelberg, Germany, in the summer of 1904.

The possibility that Tom might go abroad without her threw Kate into a panic. They were riding a horse-drawn carriage around the park when she told him of her decision to accept Billy Buckminster's proposal. Tom grew indignant.

"The best thing about our relationship," she went on, indicating Tom and herself, "is that whenever one of us marries it will not hurt that relationship at all."

"I don't know how you can say that," Tom snapped. "If I don't marry you, I shall never marry anyone."

"May I take this as a proposal?" Kate asked.

He answered that he had been proposing "for the past six months" and assumed Kate had understood. When she said she had been waiting for him to "put it in so many words," Tom laughingly accused Kate of being too literal.

Soon afterward, they told Edith and Don Hooker that they

were engaged to be married that spring. In Tom's circumstances, it was a risky business: At Hopkins, medical students were not supposed to have spouses and most of the country's best hospitals ruled out married interns. Almost anywhere Kate and Tom went, they would have to conceal their status.

They probably would have been unable to marry just then had Kate not come into her legacy: Marion, a Bryn Mawr sophomore, had turned twenty-one on November 22, 1903. Kate knew that throughout the fall, Amory, Mack Smith, and Frederick Garlinghouse had been working madly to finalize the business of the estate. But she can hardly have expected that very much money was left. When Amory had sold Fred Houghton's West Hamburg farm, Carrie's net worth had come to $58,289.52. It was not an enormous sum considering that the girls would have to live on it for nine years and more; but at least Kate's constant pounding had forced the executors to realize Carrie's last wish that her daughters attend Bryn Mawr. Carrie had also asked Amory to invest some of her funds on the girls' behalf; and although Kate may not have realized it yet, through his shrewd and meticulous management the estate had grown to $88,000.

The executors met at the Buffalo Court House on December 1, 1903. Mack Smith arrived with a tally of every penny the girls had spent. Frederick Garlinghouse was anxious to sign the papers and go home, but Amory insisted on one last opportunity to confirm that everything was in order.

The fat man disappeared behind a mountain of bills, receipts, and correspondence. By this time, the inflamed joints in his feet caused ceaseless agony; no doctor in Corning dared call the condition "gout," however, for fear of implying that Mr. Houghton, a devout teetotaler, had a secret fondness for the bottle. Amory called out to Mack Smith to help pull off his boots, so he could put his throbbing feet up on a chair, as was his custom. Amory's lips moved silently as he reviewed the ledger. It was all there in maddening detail. Mack seemed not to have missed even an ounce of bath water. When every last penny was accounted for, the sisters were left with $57,440.47. Of that, Kate received $18,216.60, Edith $19,562.30, and Marion

$19,661.57. For Kate and Tom, the sum would be just "enough to get started on."

Not surprisingly, Amory was deeply suspicious when Kate announced her engagement shortly thereafter. It must have seemed that Tom Hepburn was merely after the money, which Kate had left with Amory for safekeeping. A visit to Corning was promptly arranged.

When the train approached Elmira, Kate was plunged into a fit of agitation. Fearful she was leading Tom to slaughter, Kate implored him to take a drink to steady his nerves, but Tom refused. The disagreement occasioned their first big argument. Tom insisted he was not about to meet the Houghtons with liquor on his breath. He believed alcohol would "obstruct self-control"; and Tom, true to form, would have none of that. As a boy, Tom had once become drunk on hard cider at a party; unable to control the wagon on his way home, he vowed never to touch a drop of alcohol again.

In Corning, they headed directly for Pine Street, where, much as Kate had anticipated, the Houghtons and their circle had collected in the billiard room. Everyone seemed to want a look at Kate's fiancé.

Amory sat in a corner. His foot, swathed in white bandages, rested on a stool. His face was twisted with pain. His jowls shook like jelly when he spoke.

"Look at my foot," Amory barked at Tom, "and tell me what you think is the matter with it."

All eyes were on Tom as he undid Amory's surgical dressing and studied the foot.

"I think, sir, that you have the gout," he said without blinking an eye.

Silence.

"I knew that I had," Amory exclaimed, "but no one dared tell me!"

Everything was fine after that. Tom seemed to have passed a test. Had the uncle smelled weakness, he probably would have eaten Tom alive as he had liked to do with Fred and Charlie Houghton; but Tom had been forthright and Amory respected him for it. At

Amory's invitation, in the morning Tom accompanied him to Corning Glass. Amory had never shown such warmth to Kate, who was disconcerted by their instant rapport.

When Amory raised the subject of his niece, Tom, admitting that he had no money, emphasized his education and above all his "inheritance" as a descendant of the Powells of Virginia. He spoke of the two U.S. congressmen. He spoke of the connections with George Washington and Robert E. Lee. He spoke of Llangollen. That night, when Kate's uncle and fiancé returned from their day together, Amory informed her that she was one "very lucky" young woman. Tom Hepburn, Amory declared, was "a diamond in the rough."

Amory waited until Kate returned to Baltimore before he poured out his wrath on her. On February 1, 1904, Kate asked Amory for $1000 from her account; she intended to repay Mary Towle the balance of a debt run up during the past seven years. The request provoked a vicious letter from Corning.

"My opinion of you is the same as it has always been—that you are an extravagant, deceitful, dishonest, worthless person," Amory wrote on February 4, two days after Kate's twenty-sixth birthday. "You have squandered thousands of dollars and left your honest debts unpaid. But I do not think you are capable of comprehending the mistakes that you have made. Now that you are paying up Mary Towle, how would it do to pay the various other accounts that you owe? When you see Tom, please tell him that I do not think he could do worse."

So there it was. Hardly had Amory met Tom Hepburn when he made an ally of him—against her.

Amory saved the worst for last. He wrote in a postscript: "When you were a little girl and went into Buffalo and got trusted for some dry goods which you were not allowed to keep (they were returned) your father remarked 'Kathy is a feather head.' It is true. Kathy is a feather head; always has been, and doubtless always will be."

This was Amory at his most heartless. He calculated the one point that would cut the deepest. How could Kate challenge Amory's recollection? It was a cruel claim to make to a daughter who would always wonder why her father had killed himself. Amory seemed to imply that Kate was among the causes of her father's misery, and that someday Tom might stop loving her too.

Under Halsted's influence, Tom had become absorbed by the "mechanics" of surgery. Halsted encouraged students to view surgery as a series of problems: Would constricting metal bands placed around the great blood vessels relieve swelling? Was silk thread effective for joining the lips of a wound? What was the best way to suture the ends of a divided loop of the small intestine? This emphasis on technique fit Halsted's carefully cultivated air of personal and professional reserve.

Edith, in contrast, was passionately interested in people. She thrived on contact with patients. She immersed herself in their stories and private dramas. She befriended the sick, visited homes, assisted families, and attended funerals. Her experiences in the dispensary clinics provided a set of preoccupations that stayed with her all her life. In later years, she would trace the beginnings of her personal and political awakening to an encounter with a farmer named Jacob Abners in March 1904.

Edith was on her way out to lunch when she noticed a large, awkward, and powerful man, aged about forty, in the dispensary waiting room. He clutched his five-day-old son with enormous, knotted hands. The infant was crying. By turns Abners rocked him back and forth on the hard bench and paced to and fro in the corridor. He held him over his shoulder. He hummed a broken tune, but nothing would stop the baby's screams.

Father and child were still there when Edith returned just before 2 p.m. Abners struggled to give the baby a bottle. The baby, stubbornly refusing, continued to shriek. Edith approached to ask whether a nurse was needed. As Abners turned to reply, the bottle flew from his hand and shattered on the floor.

"Ain't this dispensary ever goin' to open?" he asked impatiently.

"Yes, presently," said Edith. "What have you come in for?"

"The little un's eyes," he said.

He turned the child to her. Edith noted the inflamed, swollen eyes; pus had nearly glued them shut. As a third-year medical student, she knew that almost certainly the condition was "directly traceable to venereal infection"—and incurable. But for the moment, she could barely admit it to herself, let alone tell the father.

"Your first child?" she asked.

"Yes, and ain't he a dandy? If it weren't for these eyes, he'd be a beauty—was, when he was first born, only a little too red. Pretty, know your Pop?"

Edith watched him tickle the baby's chin. The baby tried to rub his eyes but Abners stopped him.

"Look out you don't carry it over to your own eyes," Edith said firmly.

"I wish it was my eyes 'stead of his," said Abners, who had started to cry himself.

Edith took the man's history. He had been married for a year. His wife, aged twenty-two, was also very ill, but Abners ascribed her fever to anxiety over the baby.

Finally, the supervising physician returned from lunch and Edith asked him to examine the tiny patient. In the consulting room, the doctor took one look at the child's eyes and snapped at Abners, "When did you last have gonorrhea?"

Abners seemed not to know what he meant.

"Oh, you know, the clap, tripper," said the doctor, annoyed.

"Why, now, I almost disremember," said Abners, apparently sincere. "I was somewheres about twenty-nine or thirty or so. I've always lived a decent life, except that one time I went up to market with one of the men, and it was then I got caught. I learned my lesson but I got over it all right, though. Haven't noticed it for years. It's a long time I've thought of it even."

"Well, that's where the baby got these eyes from," the doctor said coldly.

"Good God!" said Abners. "Do you mean I done that without even knowing, and then this had to be?" Abners, wild with anger, grabbed the physician's arm. "Say man, what are you doctors for, anyhow, letting people do such things? It's your fault, not mine, that he's blinded. I didn't never mean any ill."

The doctor scribbled a prescription. Abners crushed it in his palm.

"A curse on you and all your kind," said Abners. "May the curse you've let fall on me come back on your own head."

"I don't see where it's my fault, my man," said the doctor.

"You should have told us. You were the only ones as know'd. Suppose there was a rotten bridge on the road, and the commissioners was the only ones that know'd it would give way and they didn't tell no one and didn't mark it, and suppose someone drove over it and got killed or maimed. Who'd you blame, the man that fell in or the road commissioner? Well, it's the same with the health commissioners. They know the holes and we don't; and I say they ain't earning their pay."

The doctor indicated he was ready for the next patient. Edith, filled with compassion for the farmer, knew it was her cue to lead him back to the waiting room. She pointed out the desk where he could get the prescription filled, and was about to return to the consulting room when Abners caught her hand.

"You've a good heart," he told Edith. "You'll tell 'em, won't you? And in time, too?"

Years later, Edith still vividly recalled returning the man's grip as she nodded silently. Although she may not yet have realized it, she had committed herself to expose the "tragedy of venereal disease" in an era when 60 percent of young unmarried American men were said to have gonorrhea and 10 to 15 percent to have syphilis. No adequate cure existed.

Women's statistics were especially disturbing. Gynecologists estimated that "fully 75 percent of the major operations performed upon the generative organs of married women were occasioned by gonorrhea, contracted from their husbands." A man's contacts with prostitutes also affected children as yet unborn. In Edith's words: "Eyes that are blind from birth, tongues that cannot speak, and ears that cannot hear, these are the heritages of incontinence." Like Jacob

Abners, many American men, thinking themselves cured of venereal disease when symptoms disappeared, fathered children with physical and mental defects. Some never forgave themselves when they realized what they had done.

Given the fear of an inherited taint in Edith's family background, it is not surprising that she was deeply affected by the cases of Jacob Abners's son and other innocent children. And given Edith's experience of Carrie Houghton's powerlessness, it is easy to understand why the fate of young Mrs. Abners had the galvanizing effect it did.

Within days of Abners's visit, Edith received "a somewhat crumpled and streaky-looking envelope, addressed in a labored hand." The envelope was from Abners. When Edith opened it, she discovered his wife's obituary.

Edith, weighing the impact on wives and children, came to view venereal disease and prostitution as "women's issues." Inevitably, perhaps, she was drawn to Howard A. Kelly's gynecological clinic, where a great many women like Mrs. Abners were to be found. She grew enraged over the conspiracy of silence that surrounded the transmission of venereal disease from husband to wife. Even if a wife were dying of venereal infection, she must never be told the cause; and afterward, her death must be cloaked in mystery. Doctors even had a euphemism to cover the often fatal appearance of gonorrhea in young brides; grotesquely, they called it "honeymoon appendicitis."

Part of this was medical etiquette—physicians were not supposed to disclose a husband's secret. But doctors were also motivated by concern for the women. It could be perilous for a married woman to know she had venereal disease. In a case that sent shock waves through the clinic, a Baltimore man divorced his wife on the grounds that her infection proved she had committed adultery—this in spite of the fact that, as everyone knew, it had been he who had infected her.

Edith's indignation crystallized around the case of Mrs. Hutchins. The beautiful dark-haired nineteen-year-old, married for only seven months, had unknowingly contracted gonorrhea from her lawyer husband. When she was carried into the hospital the doctors on duty were surprised she wasn't already dead. Without explaining the procedure or its consequences, they performed a hysterectomy. Edith observed the operation, keenly resentful that the poor woman had no idea why she was ill or what the outcome of the surgery must be.

In the days that followed, Mrs. Hutchins lay in great pain. She begged for a soporific, but it was forbidden. Edith, unable to put Mrs. Hutchins out of her thoughts, visited regularly.

The husband, whose photograph was prominently displayed on the night table, kept the room filled with fragrant hyacinths. When Edith met Mr. Hutchins, she thought him charming and cultured—and quite sincerely concerned for his wife. Yet, knowing that he had secretly caused the woman's misery, Edith pitied and loathed him all at once.

Eventually, Mrs. Hutchins's pain appeared to subside. Edith found her resting comfortably.

"You're getting better, Mrs. Hutchins," Edith said quietly. "Soon you'll be able to go out on the bridge."

"Yes, I am better. I feel as if I had been down into the pit. The agony—the agony you will never know."

Mrs. Hutchins closed her eyes and Edith could see she was crying.

"Tell me, Doctor," Mrs. Hutchins said softly, "tell me, shall I be able to have children?"

The last thing on earth Edith wanted was to answer that question. "You must take good care of yourself, Mrs. Hutchins, and rest and not worry," she said, disgusted with her own evasion. She avoided the patient's enormous brown eyes. "You mustn't let any trouble prey on your mind, it will not be good for you."

Mrs. Hutchins's chin trembled, but she did not pursue the topic. Thereafter, Edith took a nurse whenever she visited Mrs. Hutchins. She limited conversation to trivial subjects, but the question lingered as a painful subtext.

Finally, the patient was to go home. Edith was off-duty when the supervising physician informed Mrs. Hutchins that she would never have children. She showed no emotion until after he left. Then, dissolving in tears, she sank her teeth into her wrist and hand. A frantic nurse summoned Edith, who threw on her white laboratory coat and rushed to the hospital.

"He told me, he told me this afternoon," Mrs. Hutchins wept uncontrollably. "Oh, Doctor, I can never have any children!" Again she chewed at her wrist.

"Now, now, Mrs. Hutchins," said Edith, "it isn't as bad as all that. Lots of people haven't any children. You are young, you have your husband."

"That's the worst of it, that's the worst of it. He will divorce me now that I am childless. He's longed for them so. The first boy was to be called by his name. He's thirty-six and he settled down just to have children. He wants someone to carry on the name. He doesn't love me for my own sake. It's all on account of the children. Oh, my God, what shall I do?"

Edith fought the impulse to tell Mrs. Hutchins the nature of her infection—and where she had contracted it.

"I'll talk to your husband," said Edith. "He will see things in the right light."

"No, no, he won't. It's no use. I know him. He will look upon me as the barren fig-tree in the Bible and he'll think I ought to be chopped down and thrown into the fire. Oh, why did it have to happen anyway, why did it have to happen?"

At length, Mr. Hutchins did divorce his wife. The case and others like it haunted Edith. "The woman was so sinned against," she recalled, "and yet the burden of disappointment was in such large measure hers alone to bear."

Ignorance about venereal disease was so deeply ingrained that even medical students patronized prostitutes. In search of cheap lodgings, the young men would unknowingly rent rooms in buildings used for prostitution. Many had their sexual initiation on their first night in Baltimore when prostitutes appeared at the door to solicit them. "Infection naturally followed in a certain proportion of the cases," Edith wrote, "and vacancies in the class occurred, which were listed in the record under curiously deceptive headings." That year, one medical student with gonorrhea secretly married without telling his bride.

Edith confronted her classmates about their involvement with prostitutes. She visited brothels, houses of assignation, and road-houses. She searched out women known to have transmitted venereal disease and begged them to come to Howard Kelly's clinic. She consulted doctors and law enforcement officials. In one case, she tracked down a prostitute's mother.

Kelly himself was an advocate of social purity and a relentless vice crusader. Although Edith did not share Kelly's religious convictions, she admired his forthright approach: Kelly stormed Baltimore's brothels to implore prostitutes to change their way of life. With funds from his lucrative private gynecology practice, he even offered to subsidize some of the women until they found other employment.

Influenced by his sister Dora (Mrs. Lawrence) Lewis, Kelly believed that giving women the vote would do much to combat social problems like prostitution and venereal disease when legislators were forced to deal with issues that most profoundly affected women.

Don Hooker, who sat between Tom Hepburn and Edith Houghton in many classes, was another Kelly acolyte. Like Edith, he was—she wrote—"vitally interested" in the impact of the "social evil," as prostitution was known. He too had resolved to study the problem after graduation in hopes of checking the spread of venereal disease. Edith called their shared preoccupation "a fortunate circumstance." Among their classmates it was no secret that Don Hooker had arrived at Hopkins with a strong prejudice against female medics, but his working relationship with Edith appeared to change him.

Though rich, Don Hooker did not cut a dashing figure like his friend Tom Hepburn. No one rushed to the window when he passed on the street. He was a bluff, easy-going, affectionate man, who would reach out spontaneously to people with his large, steady, comforting hands. Where Edith was all excitement, enthusiasm, and frantic nervous energy, he radiated calmness and equanimity.

Don assumed the role of Edith's "stabilizing factor." They conducted marathon conversations about what she described as "the dawn of a new day in the relation between the sexes."

They agreed that every intelligent man and woman must give considerable thought to the "discreet and careful choice of a co-parent." They agreed that marriage should never be based merely on sexual attraction. They agreed that "genuine friendship and congenial tastes are at the basis of all happy human relationships" and that "marriages between men and women students at professional schools are conspicuously happy marriages." In their view, happy was the couple who shared values and interests and worked for a common cause.

S I X

N ina Hepburn was a plump little white teapot of a lady. She would drawl miserably: "I am poverty stricken because the South lost the war, and the Yankees took my 2000-acre plantation, and I have no money, and I'm married to a minister, and I have five children."

Nina believed she had married considerably beneath her station. She had a fiery temper and no sense of humor. She suffered bouts of depression. With Charles, Sewell, Lloyd, Selina, and Tom, she had been a harsh taskmaster and a merciless disciplinarian. According to Nina's grandson, "when she felt that her disciplinary rules were being infringed, she would not infrequently overreact with sudden scoldings and punishments."

Nina's second eldest, Sewell, once ran away from home to escape her wrath. Brother Hep, who fetched him back, implored Nina to leave the poor, frightened boy alone. In later years, family members would say that Nina had driven her older sons "too hard," causing them to become self-conscious and overwrought. But to Nina's way of thinking, she was simply trying to enforce a standard of conduct in line with Powell tradition.

Charles Leven Powell's sons had not died in defense of slavery; Charles, for his part, owned no slaves. Nina never tired of reminding her children that their uncles Lloyd and Charlie had fallen defending their native state from outsiders; the family called it "our sacred cause." Nina talked of Yankee pillage and butchery. She talked of the hangings of Southern boys in Winchester and of splendid mansions burned to the ground.

When, after the Civil War, General Sherman spoke of "the deep and bitter enmity of the women of the South," he might have been talking about Nina Hepburn: "No one who sees them and hears them but must feel the intensity of their hate." Quivering with rage, Nina would vow that her own sons and daughter were going to "put this family back on the map!" Whenever she was agitated, a telltale bead of perspiration formed in the tiny scar that cut through the center of her forehead.

Tom's wedding to Kate Houghton on June 6, 1904, was precisely such an occasion. Kate's actions that day seemed to confirm all of Nina's most rabid nightmares about Yankee depravity. Brother Hep presided over the strange ceremony in Baltimore. The contingent from New York included Amory Houghton, Jr., Nellie Abbott, and Mary Houghton. Mary Towle, Edith, and Marion, in long white summer dresses, were bridesmaids.

Heads turned in shock and bewilderment as Amory limped down the aisle with his niece. Kate, in a jet black hat and veil and long black dress, looked as if she were at a funeral instead of a wedding. And that, apparently, was her point: The bride wore black to signify the death of the old Kate and the birth of the new. Nina Hepburn returned to Virginia, convinced her baby had married a Yankee madwoman.

After the ceremony, Tom and Katharine Houghton Hepburn, as she would be called, disappeared to Upland in Chester County, Pennsylvania. The bride had asked to spend her wedding night at the country inn to which Carey Thomas had banished Edith after the hazing incident; according to Kate, this private association imbued Upland with an aura of "romantic glamour." Although Tom had borrowed a friend's car to begin a driving trip the next morning, the couple did not stir for ten days.

Tom, having finished his third-year examinations, was due to begin Professor Czherney's surgical fellowship in Germany. An old friend who owned a cattle steamer gave young Hepburn and his bride free passage to Europe.

On their first night at sea, Tom and Kate were sitting out under the stars. She decided that the moment had come to confide her

secrets; now that she was married, she finally had someone besides
Edith with whom to share the burden of her past. Carrie Houghton
had taught her daughters never to speak about the most painful
things, but Kate desperately wanted to try. As soon as she summoned
the courage to begin, however, Tom cut her off.

She tried again, and again he stopped her.

"Aren't you interested in my innermost thoughts?" Kate
snapped.

"Not if those are your innermost thoughts," Tom replied.

His blunt refusal was so unexpected—and humiliating—that
Kate could barely admit to herself quite what had just happened.
Instead, she focused on his necktie and how she had always loathed
it.

Years later Kate could still recall gazing out at the waves as a
powerful feeling of depression swept over her. If she and Tom could
not be emotionally close, if they could not be totally frank with one
another, what was the point of having married? She turned to Tom
and launched into a diatribe against marriage.

Kate felt trapped, panicky, convinced they had made a big
mistake. By the time they returned to the cabin several hours later,
she was certain her marriage was doomed.

"Why did you wear that tie?" she barked as if that were really
the reason she was so upset. Without a word, Tom removed the tie
and tossed it out the porthole.

That night, as Kate would tell the story, Tom showed her how
"wonderful" marriage could be; his attentions seemed to make up
for the brutal emotional rejection on deck. It appears to have been
Kate's first inkling that if the marriage was to work, she would have
to accept the powerful physical connection Tom offered in place of
the frankness and emotional intimacy she craved.

The struggle to set the marriage's ground rules continued as
they visited England, France, Switzerland, and Italy before Tom
reported to Heidelberg. Kate announced that for all his knowledge
of medicine, Tom was woefully ignorant of art history. She dragged
him to museums and galleries, and he dutifully listened to her
lectures on painting and sculpture.

Kate bristled at her husband's attempts to assert control. Tom was often dictatorial and seemed to expect her to obey orders; at times he even sought to discipline her. She found herself wondering what she was doing traveling about Europe with a stranger.

The situation came to a head late one night in Paris, in a tiny Latin Quarter hotel near St. Etienne du Mont. Their room, illuminated by a kerosene lamp, overlooked a garden. For hours, Kate and Tom had been playing chess by the window. They had purchased a small leather set in London and played frequently on boats and trains. Kate almost always lost. This time, however, she refused to go to bed until she was victorious.

"That's enough, let's go to bed," Tom announced suddenly. Ignoring Kate's protests, he rose, blew out the light, and retired. Nothing she said seemed to reach him.

Kate, defiant, lingered in the moonlight. Why, she asked herself, was she allowing this stranger to discipline her when even Amory had never managed to break her spirit? Kate decided to light the lamp in contempt. The matches were nowhere to be found and she realized he must have hidden them.

Tom lay in bed as Kate disappeared into the corridor. Moments later, she returned with a flaming sheet of paper. As she rushed toward the lamp, she saw that in her absence Tom had removed the glass chimney. If he assumed that would keep her from lighting the lamp, he was dead wrong. At once sickening kerosene fumes swirled through the little room.

"If you leave that light going, it will explode," Tom warned from bed.

"Yes, I know it," Kate taunted him, refusing to extinguish the flame.

The risk greatly excited them both; they were dancing at the edge of the precipice, each waiting for the other to pull back first. Finally, it was Kate who flinched. Overwhelmed by fumes, she reluctantly put out the light.

Kate threw on a dressing-gown and fled. On her way out, she told Tom she was going to stay with a girl she knew upstairs. But she did not. She sat outside the door and waited for Tom.

After a while, she returned and perched dejectedly by the window. She studied the trees as they shimmered in the moonlight. She was terrified by how close she had come to allowing the kerosene lamp to explode.

On one level, Kate longed just to crawl into bed beside Tom and forget the dispute. But if she did that, would he expect her always to capitulate? Then she wondered: Was Tom so cold and indifferent that he had actually been able to fall asleep? Or was he only pretending? She came to a decision. If Tom was indeed asleep, she would consider the marriage finished. She could not live with a man who cared for her so little. If Tom was awake, she would patch things up with him.

"If you will give me the matches and the chimney, I will come to bed," she said, testing him.

Without a word, Tom sat up and showed her where he had hidden them.

On the subject of marriage, Brother Hep (who had an auto-biographical gem for every occasion) liked to tell the following story: After the Civil War, Sewell Hepbron, as he was then called, enrolled at the Virginia Theological Seminary in Alexandria. He was twenty-one years old and the son of a blacksmith of Scottish descent. Sewell didn't have a penny to his name, but he was stage-star handsome, lean and sinewy, with wavy red hair, brilliant blue eyes, and high cheekbones. He worked up a sweat chopping his own firewood and slept on a cornshock mattress in a tiny rented bedchamber. He believed in the literal truth of the Bible and despised most religious pomp and ritual.

One day Sewell returned to St. George's Hall at the seminary (a former hospital for Union soldiers) with the news that he had chosen a bride. Nina Powell was a teacher at her sister Rebecca's Arlington Institute for young ladies in Alexandria. Sewell con-tentedly described her as a good, strong, solid specimen. She was two and a half years his senior and seemed well cut out for the harsh existence of a minister's wife in the war-scorched rural South.

Fenwick, Kate's childhood home by the sea in Connecticut. This house was destroyed in the hurricane of 1938.

Katharine Houghton Hepburn, Kate's mother, was a leader of the women's suffrage movement in the United States.

Dr. Thomas Norval Hepburn, Kate's father.

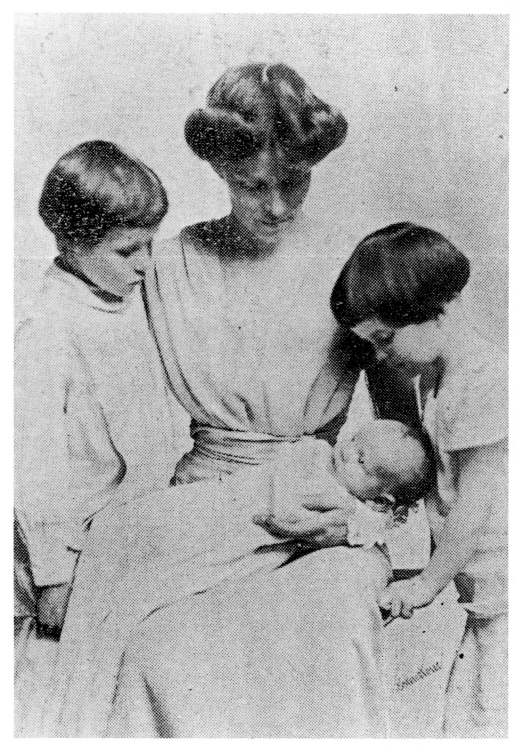

Mrs. Hepburn in 1911 with her three oldest children, Tommy, Kathy (Kate), and baby Dick.

Tommy and Kathy.

Mary "Aunty" Towle and Kathy at Fenwick. Kathy cut her hair like a boy and borrowed her brother's clothes.

A family portrait taken shortly before Tom committed suicide in 1921. The children are (l. to r.) Kate, Marion, Bob, Tom, and Dick. Mrs.Hepburn holds baby Peg.

Kate (2nd from r.) appears in
the male role of Oliver in
The Truth About Blayds at
Bryn Mawr College in 1927.

Kate as Pandora at
Bryn Mawr's 1928
May Day celebration.

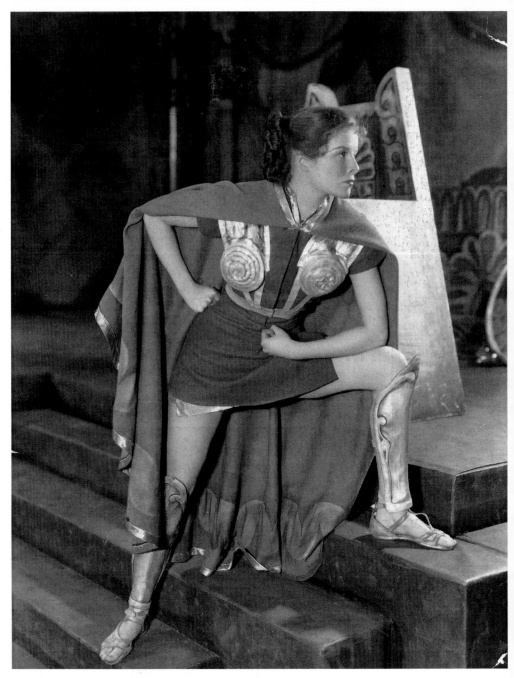

Kate as Antilope in *The Warrior's Husband* on Broadway in 1932.

The aspiring actress.

Kate and John Barrymore in
A *Bill of Divorcement*, her first film.

Kate in *Christopher Strong*.

Kate as Jo in *Little Women*.

Kate and director George Cukor on the set of *Little Women*.

Margaret Sanger and Mrs Hepburn
at the 1934 birth control hearings
in Washington,D.C.

Mrs.Hepburn delivers a speech at
Carnegie Hall in 1935.

Kate on the set of *Alice Adams* with director George Stevens (in dark glasses).

Kate as Mary of Scotland.

Kate and director John Ford on the set of *Mary of Scotland* in 1936.

John Ford on his yacht, the *Araner*.

John Ford.

John Ford and his wife,
Mary, play cards at home
on Odin Street.

John Ford with his beloved
daughter, Barbara. A model
of the *Araner* is in the
background.

Kate as Jane Eyre and
Dennis Hoey as Mr.Rochester
in the 1937 Theater Guild
production of *Jane Eyre*.

Howard Hughes.

Sewell's classmates stopped him there, pointing out that he talked about Miss Powell as though she were a horse. How did he feel about the girl? Did he love her? Was he at all romantically inclined? When he spoke of his future wife, why did he have to be so dry and practical?

Sewell replied that the level-headedness needed to buy a horse was even more critical to the prudent selection of a woman. He could always sell off a bad horse later, but once he picked a wife he'd have to keep her no matter what. A man had better choose with care.

Brother Hep had another favorite marriage story: During her engagement, Nina, in a letter to her mother, made the mistake of referring to Sewell by his first name. Mrs. Charles Leven Powell was quick to correct her: To speak so familiarly was an intolerable sign of disrespect, especially as Nina's fiancé was soon to be a minister of the Gospel. The great-granddaughter of Lieutenant-Colonel Leven Powell must not show such poor manners. Nina, her mother counseled, must always speak of and address her fiancé as "Mr. Hepbron."

Some thirty-three years later, when Tom Hepburn and his bride visited Ashland, Virginia, immediately after their honeymoon, someone—Tom most likely—would have had to tell the story to Kate to explain why Nina always solemnly addressed her husband as "Reverend Hepburn." (Sewell had changed the family name from "Hepbron" to "Hepburn" in 1881 to conform with what he believed to be the original Scottish spelling.) Even in bed, Nina Hepburn reportedly never called her husband by his first name.

Kate had anticipated the visit to Ashland with considerable trepidation. Brother Hep, with his bushy eyebrows, shaggy moustache, and stiff white clerical collar, cut a formidable figure. He suffered from intermittent tics of the head and hands, which he banished with a shot of whiskey. The pulpit was his stage; in church, an air of high drama made him seem distant and intimidating. At home, however, he would throw his wiry arms around visitors, squeeze hard, and plant a firm kiss on the cheek. He greeted his sons in the same manner, and his warmth and folksy effusiveness instantly put Kate at ease.

Kate quickly came to love him. She loved the well-worn stories of his traveling rural ministry in Maryland and Virginia, and Reverend Hepburn loved having a fresh and receptive audience to tell them to. He talked of riding horseback on rutted dirt roads encrusted with sand and red-clay mud; he talked of tending the sick, the lonely, and the dying, and of assisting at operations, births, and amputations; he talked of performing an appendectomy with only a bottle of whiskey to kill the patient's pain; and he talked of his custom of retreating to the church antechamber after the Sunday sermon to yank out parishioners' rotten teeth with a pair of dental forceps.

It must have been hard for Kate to understand why Tom seemed not to appreciate his father. Tom bitterly resented the financial hardship and deprivation to which Sewell had subjected Nina. In Hanover County, Virginia, where the Reverend Hepburn's territory covered some four hundred square miles, he was loved and revered as the so-called "Bishop of Hanover," yet he earned barely enough to support a wife and five children. He claimed to have traveled a distance several times the earth's circumference, but his income never exceeded $600 a year.

Nina supplemented her husband's pitiful salary by the sale of eggs, butter, and poultry. She practiced every economy and forswore every personal pleasure. She made, cleaned, and mended all of her family's clothes. For want of schools in the rural South, she educated the children herself.

Tom was Mrs. Hepburn's favorite and he idolized her. He spoke in glowing terms of the spartan "discipline" that had allowed Nina to run her household and prepare her children for the future. He said she had always been forced to work "too hard" and had tragically "wasted" her prodigious energies and talents. Blaming his father for Nina's threadbare existence, Tom vowed to earn a solid living and give his own wife every opportunity for fulfillment.

Kate and Tom returned to Baltimore in the fall of 1904 to begin his final year at Hopkins. Like other married students, he practiced discretion. His marriage was an open secret among classmates, but he did his best not to flaunt it before the college authorities.

The talk at Hopkins that year focused on Edith, and her relationship with Don Hooker. Florence Sabin, now an associate in the anatomy department and Edith's closest friend and confidante, reported frequently to Mary Garrett and the other Ladies. In their view, the appalling precedent was Gertrude Stein, who had left after her fourth year without a degree. But there was a crucial difference: Edith had impressed the Women's Committee with her "high standing in the medical courses." She promised to be a first-rate doctor and a credit to their efforts to advance women's opportunities in medicine.

Hopkins men were often heard to grumble about the "economic waste" of accepting women when so many of them married and "did not go into practice or scientific work." So the Ladies reacted with shock and dismay when Edith Houghton and Don Hooker announced their engagement. Edith (according to her friend Elizabeth Daly) had missed a good deal of work that fall due to illness. She withdrew from medical school with only one semester to go.

Had she gone mad? Had she lost all sense of purpose and direction? Even an intimate like Florence Sabin thought Edith's decision out of character.

But Edith had her reasons. Don had been chosen to study venereal disease with the distinguished genito-urinary specialists Alfred Blaschko and Max Marcuse in Germany. If she remained at Hopkins to make up course work, Don would have to go to Berlin alone—and Edith could not bear to miss out on the experience. Florence Sabin failed to comprehend that by this point, the social and ethical preoccupations Edith shared with Don were far more important to her than becoming a doctor. Edith was in love, and for better or worse, she poured her passion into their life's work together. She and Don were married in Baltimore on June 14, 1905.

As Halsted's protégé, Tom Hepburn was in the running for some of the best internships in the country that spring. He had the opportunity to stay in Baltimore; but that meant having to contend with Edith. She and Don were due to return in a year, Don having been offered a teaching post at Hopkins. Tom hoped to remove Kate from her sister's orbit; and although he and Don remained good friends, Tom always quietly resented Hooker's inherited wealth and Yale education. Living in the same city would highlight Tom's status as the poor brother-in-law.

Also, by this point Tom was eager to escape the South and "begin again." Known in the family as "a great competitor" and a man who "did not like to lose," Tom associated the South with defeat and ruin. Now that he had his medical degree, he voiced disdain for all "sentimentality about the pre-war days of the Old South."

"What is past is past," he would say.

There were excellent offers from New York City, but Tom refused to live in the shadow of his brothers who were already established there. Charlie worked as a lawyer in Manhattan, Lloyd as an insurance broker. (Sewell was a physician in Annapolis, Maryland.)

Tom accepted a considerably less prestigious offer from Hartford, Connecticut. He had heard about Hartford Hospital from his classmate Arthur Davis, who had already signed on there. In 1905, there were only two operating tables and the practice of surgery consisted mainly of "fracture work, laceration repairs, and drainage of abscesses." Dr. Thomas Norval Hepburn would be a very big fish in a small pond.

Hartford, unlike New York, seemed "a wonderful place to raise a large family." Kate was four months pregnant when she and Tom left Baltimore that June; but she did not pretend to share her husband's enthusiasm about the move. Hartford was a far cry from Baltimore, where Kate had a great many friends and social acquaintances in the exceptionally large community of women college graduates who lived there. Baltimore had the reputation of a haven for educated women, who thrived on its network of women's clubs, cultural events, and discussion groups. As far as Kate could see, there would be nothing like that in Hartford. With the exception of Arthur Davis, she knew no one there.

Worse, an intern's schedule guaranteed that Tom would have little time for her. That was why interns weren't supposed to have wives, let alone pregnant wives. And that was why interns were required to live in special quarters. If Tom's supervisors discovered that he wasn't really sleeping at the hospital, he could lose everything he had worked for.

Kate and Tom knew they were skating on thin ice when they rented quarters at 29 South Hudson Street, across from the physicians' entrance to Hartford Hospital. The risk made the hideous, red two-family house all the more appealing. They thrilled to the idea of violating staff rules virtually under the noses of Tom's supervisors. The address was a statement: At the age of twenty-five, Tom Hepburn was still crying, "You ain't the boss of me!"

According to Kate, she and Tom knew better than to ask permission to live together. A house officer, as interns were known, was on twenty-four-hour call. Tom had to be able to reach the wards as quickly as if he were at the dormitory.

Once installed, Kate unrolled her mother's Persian and Smyrna rugs. She put up her heavy sash curtains and set up her tea table with faded gold and white china. On the dresser, she placed an old wooden box with three small drawers, and on top of that Carrie's cut-glass perfume bottles. Framed photographs of Fred and Carrie hung on the bedroom wall, but Kate never talked about her parents.

The expectant mother spent most of her time alone. With Edith out of the country, she had no one with whom to share the anxieties their family history provoked. There was reason for optimism, however. Unlike Fred and Charlie Houghton, Tom Hepburn, with his Powell "inheritance," was notably strong and vigorous; and it was widely believed that the potent influence of one "nervously superior" parent could "breed out" certain nervous disorders from the stock.

On November 8, 1905, Katharine Houghton Hepburn, aged twenty-seven, gave birth at home. Mary Towle and Marion Houghton (now a Bryn Mawr senior) both thought that the healthy baby boy with soft, curly blond hair resembled his mother. Brother Hep christened him Thomas Houghton Hepburn. Kate and Tom called him Tommy, and named Mary Towle his godmother.

There were great expectations all around. For Nina Hepburn and her son Tom, the newborn seemed destined to recapture the Powell glory. Of Charles Leven Powell's five children, only Nina had had children of her own. She had always been exceptionally demanding of her first son, and she encouraged Tom to do the same with his. In Nina's view, no matter how large the family, the oldest child set the standard. In the beginning, it was agreed that Tommy would go to Yale like his great-grandfather; he would attend the Johns Hopkins Medical School like his father; he would be handsome, athletic, and fearless.

Tom's schedule left little time for the baby. Indeed, the birth had to be kept secret at the hospital, where Dr. Hepburn spent most of his waking hours. With her husband on call seven days a week, Kate had only little Tommy for company; he was her main source of happiness and fulfillment. For nearly two years, Tommy saw his father relatively little. With no other child to divide his mother's attentions, mother and son formed an exceptionally close bond.

Tom was usually just across the street, but Kate could never visit him. Hoping to catch an occasional glimpse of him in the hospital window, she was left to imagine his life there.

He talked about the wards, long, dark, hall-like rooms with many beds on either side. He talked about the patients, poor people who could not afford their own doctor at a private facility like Prospect Hospital, where most significant surgery was performed. Conditions were primitive. Although a bacteriologist had been on the staff since 1896, many crusty older physicians remained skeptical that bacteria caused infection. They made a point of rejecting sterile instruments and antiseptic technique. Before entering the operating room, they changed into old shirts and trousers to prevent their good clothes from being splattered with blood. They performed surgery "with their bare hands, with no washing." Patients often went home sicker than when they arrived.

Tom reported his horror of opening abdominal cavities, fearful that patients would contract an infection and die. Still, he managed to hone his skills as a surgeon; he did not want to be a general practitioner, he did not want to treat pneumonia or the common cold. Tom asked to exchange his rotations in medicine for surgery, arguing that the more he operated, the better. He craved experience at every type of surgery. He insisted that specialization limited a man's horizons. Part of this, admittedly, was economic: He didn't want "to lose all those stomachs and thyroids and gall bladders to somebody else." But it was also Tom's nature to balk at restraint: He needed "the freedom to go from a gall bladder to a prostate to a kidney."

Dr. Hepburn viewed each operation as an "athletic stunt," requiring "every last ounce of energy." Waiting to rush into the operating room reminded him of his days as a fullback on the Randolph-Macon football team. The doctor-actors of the Johns Hopkins Medical School had strongly influenced Tom, and his panache soon became legendary; at Hartford Hospital, it was said that Dr. Hepburn handled surgery as a "dramatic performance."

Tom's first year as a house officer was abruptly cut short when he contracted typhoid. The infection could prove fatal; the death rate then was about 300 per 100,000. Tom suffered fever and exhaustion. He lost considerable weight.

When Kate fell ill and was unable to care for Tom or the baby, the Reverend Hepburn brought them to Shepherd's Delight, his 260-acre farm in Kent County, Maryland. His brother, Thomas Hepbron, for whom Tom had been named, had died of typhoid fever in 1854 at the age of twenty-one; and Brother Hep was not about to take any chances with his son and grandson. That summer, he and Nina lovingly nursed Tom and Kate back to health.

The seventeenth-century white farmhouse had been in the family since 1832 when Brother Hep's uncle, Colonel Tom Hepbron, and his illegitimate daughter, "Cousin Mary," moved in. Brother Hep had inherited Shepherd's Delight upon Cousin Mary's death in 1897. When Kate felt better, she and Nina walked in the boxwood garden on the south side. Tom mended split-rail snake fences and built a log cabin at the edge of an orchard.

Charlie Hepburn visited from New York with his wife, Elizabeth Newport, a Powell cousin, to see Kate's baby. Charlie knew what it was to be a first son; he knew the special demands and expectations. Nina had always required him to serve as a model of conduct, a teacher and protector. She liked to tell the story of Charlie's victorious twenty-round fistfight with a hooligan who made the mistake of picking on young Sewell. Even as an adult, Charlie Hepburn was said to carry the burden of "an over-developed sense of duty and responsibility."

For Kate, the summer provided a respite from Tom's work; after months of loneliness, she loved having him around. Mary Towle came to Shepherd's Delight to take care of the baby, freeing Kate to spend even more time with her husband.

Kate had not been pampered and fussed over like this since she and Edith had stayed with Nellie Abbott after Charlie Houghton's suicide. She and Tom moved into the log cabin as soon as he completed it. In August, they conceived their second child there.

As with Kate's first pregnancy, the timing was deliberate. Tom took immense pride in his ability to determine exactly when they had children. It was part of his preoccupation with self-control and not letting sex "boss" him. He let it be known that he and Kate were "very fertile," so they could have children "any time" they wanted.

Tom, perhaps in part because of long-standing ambivalence about his father, rejected religion. He called Christianity "bunk." Recalling the countless times in boyhood when he heard the Reverend Hepburn preach, Tom insisted to Kate, "I never believed a word he said!" According to Tom, people who believed in the reality of God were "either lower-class or uneducated." Still, he and Kate attended services at St. Luke's Church in Church Hill, Maryland, about fifteen miles from Shepherd's Delight.

One Sunday, Kate cringed with embarrassment and indignation as the Reverend Hepburn delivered a sermon on the "Giant Selfishness." Kate was sure his words were directed at them and that everyone in the church knew it. How could she have been so foolish as to believe that the Hepburns had enjoyed coddling her all summer? Just when Kate's defenses were down, the Reverend Hepburn had humiliated her in public—or so Kate thought.

She angrily confronted him afterward. "Why did you talk to

us from the pulpit instead of telling us how you really felt?"

"If the coat fits, put it on," Brother Hep laughed. His walrus moustache shook with merriment. "I wasn't thinking of you at all. I wrote that sermon twenty years ago with a very selfish woman in the church in mind. After the service she came up to me and said, 'I think that sermon was very fine and will do Mrs. Brown a lot of good.' It never occurred to her that it was aimed at her until I told her so."

The incident highlighted Kate's abiding feelings of guilt and of being unloved. For all of the kindness the Hepburns had shown her, Kate still seemed to feel completely secure only with her sisters.

Edith, bursting with stories, plans, and excitement, returned from Germany in time for Don to assume his post in the Hopkins physiology department. As always, she never stopped talking or moving. She wore dark, severely tailored, hip-length jackets with long matching skirts. She brushed her hair away from her face and knotted it on top in a Psyche knot.

Edith had spent the year doing case work with the street-walkers of Berlin. She raged against government legalization and regulation of prostitution; she argued that licensing would do nothing to stop the spread of venereal disease and would merely create a class of officially degraded women. She had had violent disagreements with her husband's supervisor. Dr. Blaschko insisted that prostitution was a necessary evil as "male continence was unthinkable." Edith, an abolitionist, demanded that the law make prostitution a "copartnership offense" with grave consequences for men who buy sex.

"A term in the penitentiary would convince the average man that intercourse with prostitutes was not worth his while," she declared.

Scarcely had she and Don arrived back in Baltimore when they founded the Guild of St. George, a facility for unwed mothers and their children. The sexual double standard encouraged men to have intercourse with a variety of partners before (and during) marriage. But a woman known to have had pre- or extramarital sex was "ruined"—particularly if there were illegitimate children. No "respectable" house in Baltimore would rent rooms to unwed mothers. In Edith's view, many of these outcasts, deprived of the possibility of marriage or the means of earning a living, were driven into prostitution. She vowed to give them a "new lease on life."

Back in Hartford, Kate awaited her second baby. While Tommy resembled Kate, she wanted a child who looked like her husband. On May 12, 1907, she gave birth at home. The nurse showed her a girl with blue eyes.

Kate said, "Hold her up to the window so I can see."

Sunlight poured over the child's hair.

"Yes," Kate said contentedly, "it's red."

Tom Hepburn dubbed her Redtop. Brother Hep christened her Katharine Houghton Hepburn. But from the first, everyone called her Kathy.

Kathy's birth provoked a crisis. Once again, after everybody made a fuss over the baby, they all left and Kate was alone. Tom returned to the hospital. Brother Hep went back to Shepherd's Delight. Edith resumed work at the Guild of St. George. A nurse, a maid, and a cook left Kate with little responsibility. She was idle, bored, restless. For nearly fifteen years, she had been hurtling toward one goal or another. Now she was there—or so she was supposed to think.

Kate had discovered personal happiness with her husband. She had a family. She had financial security. But somehow her days lacked meaning. She wanted direction and purpose. Was this all Bryn Mawr had prepared her for?

Mary Towle, adrift since leaving the Radcliffe doctoral program, announced plans to follow Bertha Rembaugh to law school. Tom, excitedly preparing to enter private practice, seemed about to begin life. Kate wondered whether she had anything left to do—except turn thirty in February. Her discontent crystallized one morning when she took the children out for a stroll. She wheeled the newborn in a pram. Little Tommy, not quite two, toddled at his mother's side.

"Now I have done this," Kate thought, "and now what? Am I just going to continue to the end of my life? It will take many, many years for these children to grow up, and is my life only to take care of them?"

A letter from Baltimore was waiting at home. Edith's timing could not have been more perfect. She wrote with passion about a lecture on venereal disease that she and Don had heard at the Maryland State Medical Society.

Dr. Prince A. Morrow, unlike most American physicians, went well beyond public health and disease control to raise ethical issues in human sexuality. He argued that men should be held to the same standard of sexual conduct as women. It was a message Edith had been waiting to hear. Edith and Don joined Morrow's Society for Sanitary and Moral Prophylaxis to help humanity emerge from what she was soon calling "the dark ages of sex." Don chaired a committee to undertake a statistical study of the prevalence of syphilis and gonorrhea in Baltimore.

At any other time, Kate might have read the letter and forgotten it. Edith always seemed to be on one soapbox or another. This time, however, Edith's fury was contagious. It spoke directly to Kate's craving for a purpose that transcended her duties as wife and parent.

Kate knew better than to announce to Tom that she wanted to join Edith's vice crusade. She told her son years afterward: "The way to handle Dad if you wanted him to accept an idea was to present it to him. Then two or three weeks later he'd come back with it and say, 'You know, I thought such-and-such.' He wouldn't acknowledge the fact that you had given him the idea. But he had the idea, which is what you were trying to accomplish anyhow."

When Tom came home, Kate showed him a pamphlet Edith had sent. She asked if he knew anything about venereal disease.

Soon afterward, Tom recounted an experience in the gynecological ward at Hartford Hospital. A young bride, dying of gonorrheal peritonitis, had been infected on her honeymoon. When Dr. Hepburn made inquiries, he discovered that the bridegroom's friends had taken him to a brothel several days before the wedding "to get a little practice."

Rather than talk about his brothers, Charlie, Sewell, and Lloyd, it was typical of Tom to discuss a case of venereal infection that meant nothing to him personally. Still, he had broached the subject; and Kate reacted as if she were hearing about it for the first time. With a fervor that must have surprised her husband, she pledged to educate herself on this aspect of his work. As if at Tom's instigation, Kate joined Prince Morrow's society. She read every piece of literature. She memorized statistics and corresponded with Edith.

Tom's two years as a house officer were nearly finished. He rented space for a private office at 42 High Street. Although he would be affiliated with Hartford Hospital, he no longer had to live there—or pretend to. The Hepburns could move to a larger, nicer house.

Tom found a gabled Victorian Gothic cottage at 133 Hawthorn Street in the Nook Farm district. It was set in a bumpy woodland near a winding, dark brown, malodorous stream called the Hog or Meandering Swine. The house was red brick with black trim, and it had shutters and fireplaces. There were cherry, hemlock, pine, and pink and white hawthorn trees. There was the ruin of a clay tennis court, once the site of outdoor dancing parties. A thrush sang in the woods and quail whistled in the ravine. After a heavy rain, great numbers of toads hopped about on the gravel walks.

The writer Charles Dudley Warner and his wife Susan had occupied the house in the nineteenth century; his little book *My Summer in a Garden* was based on their life there. Warner's friend and neighbor Mark Twain had been a frequent visitor. Harriet Beecher Stowe had lived nearby. The community was bursting with exotic gardens and architectural follies. Residents had carved a labyrinth of secret footpaths and byways in order to visit each other without being seen on the street.

When Tom showed the Warner house to Kate, she described it as a "fairy palace." She ran her fingers across the words cut in stone over the fireplace: "Listen To The Song of Life." She rushed into the Stowe conservatory at the south end of the living room. The glass wall was encrusted with vines. Sunlight cast intricate leafy shadows over the bare floor.

Kate excitedly opened the straw basket she had brought. She removed a tattered white cloth and spread it out. She arranged frayed linen napkins and tarnished silver-plated teaspoons. She unpacked her mother's old china pot and placed it in a pool of light. Kate and Tom, celebrating Carrie's tea ritual on the garden-room floor, initiated the cottage as their own.

For Tom, the historic house in one of Hartford's best neighborhoods signified status and position. (Notoriously antiquated heating and plumbing had made it affordable.) It was a proper residence for an up-and-coming doctor and his family. This was how a descendant of the Powells of Virginia ought to live—at least for now.

Kate cared little for status or position. Music had been played here and books and ideas had been discussed. 133 Hawthorn Street reminded her of her cozy, secure, much-loved childhood home.

Nook Farm prided itself on hospitality. Within days of Kate and Tom moving in, a parade of neighbors arrived to invite them to dinners and dancing parties. Their first engagement was a large dinner at the home of Mr. and Mrs. Richard M. Bissell. The president of the Hartford Fire Insurance Company occupied the old Mark Twain house, a turreted black-and-vermilion brick Victorian edifice, said to have been modeled on a Mississippi riverboat.

Kate sat quietly throughout the meal in the cavernous dark oak dining room, which sparkled with silver wall ornaments from Tiffany's. After dinner, Tom remained with the men for brandy and cigars. It was an important evening for a young doctor eager to make contacts. Kate accompanied the women to the parlor.

Later, she contended that it had all been quite innocent. She insisted that she had not planned to shock Mrs. Bissell and the others. She sincerely believed that her new neighbors would want to join Edith's crusade to help mankind emerge from "the dark ages of sex."

Kate, a woman possessed, lectured on the ravages of venereal disease. All her reading and thinking came pouring out: Syphilis.

Gonorrhea. Prostitution. Lesions. Chancres. Defective children. Oblivious to the tense silence in the parlor, she unburdened herself of nightmare images she had been storing up for months. Kate and Tom went home that night with no idea of the scandal she had created.

For some time afterward, it seemed to Kate that there was no woman in Hartford to share her newfound sense of purpose. None of Kate's neighbors wanted to discuss, let alone act on the issues that preoccupied her. By contrast, her sister had quickly discovered a network of activists in Baltimore.

Edith had concluded that until American women had the vote, government would do little to combat the "social evil" and the degradation of all women it symbolized. As the sex that gave birth and nurtured children, women were thought to possess a greater capacity for caring and moral concern; reformers theorized that womanly virtues expressed at the polls would do much to improve the quality and moral tone of American life.

Edith joined the suffragists who gathered at the home of Elizabeth King Ellicott. Carey Thomas's cousin and childhood friend had been one of the Ladies responsible for opening Hopkins Medical School to women, and she went on to organize the Equal Suffrage League of Baltimore. Edith's friend Florence Sabin served as treasurer. Carey Thomas and Mary Garrett were honorary vice-presidents. Howard A. Kelly led the Men's League. Edith's position, as chairman of the Lecture Committee, put her in touch with leading figures in the international women's movement.

Mrs. Emmeline Pankhurst, founder of the Women's Social and Political Union in England, soon ranked among Edith's idols. A grandmotherly figure in a high boned collar with a lace ruffle, Mrs. Pankhurst, widow of a Manchester barrister, was the unlikely ideologue of militant tactics. In 1905, her daughter, Christabel, and another woman, Annie Kenney, had heckled Sir Edward Grey at Free Trade Hall in Manchester. "Answer the question!" they cried repeatedly. "What will the Liberal Party do about votes for women?" Pandemonium erupted as the women were dragged from their places and hurled out the door. When Pankhurst and Kenney tried to address a crowd of jeering bystanders, police manhandled and arrested the suffragists. The immense publicity that followed convinced Mrs. Pankhurst that provoking government violence against women could be a powerful political weapon.

In years to come, Emmeline Pankhurst was to have a tremendous impact on the fight for the enfranchisement of American women. But when Kate Hepburn, at Edith's urging, attended her first public appearance in Hartford, there were more than 1400 empty seats. Still, some 200 women had come to Parsons' Theater. "If this movement means anything to you," exhorted Mrs. Pankhurst, "if the result would be worth anything, then you ought to be willing to do something for it, to make it a part of your lives." After many months of reading and thinking in isolation, Kate was thrilled to discover a community of women with concerns and goals similar to her own.

Kate met her first comrade. In the weeks that followed she and Emily Pierson, a teacher in Bristol, Connecticut, were inseparable. Through the Hepburns' cook, Ida, they arranged to practice public speaking before a local church group. Kate lectured on "Woman Suffrage and the Home." Emily, considerably more at ease addressing an audience, discussed "Working Women and the Vote."

Soon afterward, a Nook Farm neighbor visited Kate to warn: "My dear, you must not take up this cause. Everyone in town who is anyone is against it. You will be socially ostracized. People have been very nice to you. They have called on you and asked you to dinner and dances, but if you take up this cause no one will have anything to do with you." The woman, whom Kate had met at Mrs. Bissell's, took this opportunity to enlighten her on the shock and disgust her comments on prostitution and venereal disease had generated.

Kate agonized about all the neighbor had said and implied. The prospect of being shunned did not seem to matter as much as the damage to her husband's career. Tom's practice had been slow in getting started. The general practitioners who had traditionally performed surgery in Hartford hesitated to refer patients to Dr. Hepburn. A specialty in surgery was a new thing; and in the beginning, older physicians preferred not to lose patients to the young upstart.

When Tom came in that night, Kate told him about their neighbor's visit. "Do you think it will hurt in your work if I take up this cause?" she asked.

"Of course, it will," Tom replied, "but do it anyway." As always, the thing Tom hated most was any attempt to "boss" him, to dictate what he should think or do. The neighbor could hardly have calculated a more effective means to influence him to support Kate's work. "If you don't stand for the things you believe in, life is no good," Tom continued. "If I can't succeed anyway, then let me fail."

Tom and Kate were not talking about exactly the same thing, however. He backed her, but only up to a point. For all of Tom's lip-service to progressive ideas, he retained an old-fashioned view of the roles of husband and wife. He never stopped thinking of himself as the one who worked; he never stopped thinking of Kate's work as part-time volunteerism. Her involvement in the women's suffrage movement must not interfere with her duties at home. When Tom returned from work, he expected to find Kate "behind the tea set." If she was a few minutes late, he could be every bit as upset and judgmental as Amory had been when Kate arrived late for breakfast.

When Kate and Emily committed themselves to women's suffrage, the movement was in a phase activists called "the doldrums." Suffragists were then concentrating on winning the vote state by state, rather than through an amendment to the federal Constitution that would enfranchise women in all states. No new states had been won since Utah and Idaho had granted women the vote in 1896. (Women had voted in Wyoming since 1869, and in Colorado since 1893.) In Connecticut, the women's movement was nearly extinct. Isabella Beecher Hooker had founded the Connecticut Woman Suffrage Association in 1869; but since her death in 1905 no vibrant young leadership had emerged.

Kate, Emily, and their friends Josephine Day Bennett and Annie Porritt formed the tiny Hartford Political Equality League. Subsidized by Emily, who had money of her own, they presented speakers at Unity Hall and ran advertisements in local newspapers.

Soon, the Connecticut Woman Suffrage Association invited younger women working independently in Hartford and Greenwich to join forces. Kate, elected vice-president on October 22, 1909, plotted with the Greenwich activists to wrest control of the moribund organization.

On the night of November 5, Kate received word that Amory Houghton, Jr. had died in Corning, at the age of seventy-two. His wish to die "in the harness" as head of Corning Glass had been granted. The Reverend W. C. Roberts eulogized: "A masterful mind; a sympathetic spirit; a charitable disposition; all blended to a well-balanced character given to the work of Christ Church in unstinted measure. As to his benefactions and wise counsels, the half has not been told."

Kate refused to attend her uncle's funeral. Amory had destroyed his brothers. He had thwarted and humiliated Kate, and made her feel foolish and incompetent. For all she had accomplished in getting through Bryn Mawr and starting a family of her own, she still half-believed much of what Amory had said about her. With his unerring instinct for weakness and insecurity, he had always known precisely what would hurt most.

Long after Kate appeared to have beaten Amory, he was still capable of goring her with invective. Amory was dead, but his words remained: "Kathy is a feather head; always has been, and doubtless always will be." Kate, beginning a decade of struggle for women's rights, was determined to prove him wrong.

S E V E N

From the time little Kathy took her first halting steps, Tommy Hepburn knew he was responsible for her. Beneath a mass of tousled blond curls, his eyes radiated the seriousness and intensity with which he regarded his obligations as big brother.

In those days, Mrs. Hepburn dressed the children in fashionable Russian outfits of skirted blouses with standing round neckbands and side-buttons, and tiny matching bloomers. Wherever Kathy went, Tommy was there, protectively holding her tiny hand. With its deep ravine and clumps of trees and tree stumps, the bumpy lawn at Hawthorn Street was a minefield for small children, and Kate expected Tommy to see that nothing happened to his sister. Tommy idolized his mother and was eager to please.

Nina Hepburn had taught her daughter-in-law to hold the oldest child accountable for those younger. That was how Nina had handled her own large family. When one of the smaller children misbehaved or had an accident, Nina automatically blamed Charlie or Sewell. She punished the older boys even if they were in no way involved. She hardly cared why something went wrong—only that Charlie or Sewell had failed to prevent it. Nina punished without warning or explanation. She broke a child's will, forcing him to submit unquestioningly to his parents' superiority.

Kate, in consultation with Edith, rejected Nina Hepburn's emphasis on severe punishment and blind obedience. The sisters concurred that the first five years of childhood "are of determining importance in the development of the individual."

Edith, who gave birth to a son, Donald, in September 1908, believed that "the evil effects of corporal punishment are so profound and so intimately connected with perversions and fixations of various kinds that it is not too much to recommend its complete abrogation in behalf of gentler methods of discipline."

Rather than dictate arbitrarily, Kate preferred to reason with her children. Like Carey Thomas, she made a point of explaining why she wanted something done: Tommy must look out for his sister and refrain from teasing her because as the older child he knew better. Kate insisted on always treating the children with dignity. She vowed to bring them up to use their own judgment.

"Parents aren't always right," she liked to admit. In this, Kate consciously drew on her memories of Amory Houghton, Jr. and Mack Smith, who had fought relentlessly to impose their will on her.

The Smiths had assumed that like all children, the Houghton sisters were invariably up to no good. Mack and Nettie "had no idea how to handle children," Kate declared, "and did nothing but inflame the child's sense of itself." From their poor example, Kate learned to "handle children to make them think, and enhance their self-respect and joy of living." That, Kate and Edith agreed, was how Carrie Houghton had raised them.

Kate remembered the Easter when their parents went off on a riding trip and without a word to the staff, eleven-year-old Kate had secretly taken Edith and Marion to church in Buffalo. The governess, trembling with anger, had punished them harshly. But when their parents came back, Carrie did not seem angry. She listened with interest and appreciation as the girls recounted their adventures in Buffalo. Only then did Carrie patiently explain that frightening the servants had been "unkind." Instead of punishing the children, Carrie helped them to understand why their actions had been wrong.

Now that Kate was a mother, she encouraged Tommy and Kathy to have their say on all subjects. Like Aunt Nell, she developed a knack for making children think that what they were saying was the most interesting thing in the world. When she put Tommy and Kathy to bed at night, she let them babble on endlessly about whatever was on their minds. Kathy, she discovered, had a "red-headed temper" like Dr. Hepburn's; Tommy was sensitive and easily wounded like his mother.

An English nurse, Lizzie Byles, minded the children all day while Kate was immersed in suffrage work. But bedtime was Mrs. Hepburn's private time with them. She closeted herself with Tommy and Kathy for as long as they seemed to need. Dr. Hepburn was forbidden to enter the room. Kate believed that children would naturally form the habit of retiring early if she made the experience pleasant enough. If she simply ordered them upstairs or tried to bribe them, they were all too likely to resist.

She sat on the edge of the children's beds. She talked and sang. She fussed over them and read fairy tales and Bible stories. Kate and the children thrived on their nightly bedtime ritual; the familiar, comforting scent of her "4711" eau de cologne lingered long after she turned out the lamp and went downstairs.

Dr. Hepburn claimed teatime as his special time with the children. Even if he had to be brusque with patients, he made a point of getting home every afternoon by five. In good weather, tea was served alfresco, with gnarled tree stumps for tables and chairs. The children adored their father. Dr. Hepburn, redolent of pipe tobacco, roughhoused with them; he taught them the acrobatic stunts Charlie and Sewell had taught him.

He swept Kathy off the ground to stand on his powerful shoulders. He flipped Tommy upside down and held his ankles while the boy stood on his head. Later, he encouraged them both to walk on their palms and do flying somersaults off his shoulders.

Dr. Hepburn might be sipping tea and chatting with Mrs. Hepburn when suddenly he would order Tommy to show how fast he could run. The family reacted to Dr. Hepburn's voice as if it were "the thunderous truth of God from on high." Tommy, anxious to please, would break into a sprint. But when he glanced back from the other side of the lawn, there was no look or word of praise from his father. It was Dr. Hepburn's custom to tell the children when they did poorly, but never when they excelled. "I expect you to do well," is all he would say, "that's the norm." Dr. Hepburn could be critical to the point of cruelty, but by all accounts "he never gave a compliment."

Kate privately reassured the children that their father loved them but "just plain couldn't express that kind of thing." She attempted to compensate by bubbling with enthusiasm over the children's accomplishments and gently consoling them when they failed.

Still, poor little Tommy constantly pushed himself harder in the hope that Dr. Hepburn would finally be satisfied. He struggled to run faster and graduate to more challenging gymnastic feats. The child longed for his father's approbation. Dr. Hepburn appears not to have realized that his failure to praise made the boy fear he had disappointed him.

Dr. Hepburn also pushed Kathy—quite literally, when he placed the terrified three-year-old on her first bicycle and sent her flying down a steep hill in Keney Park. But Kathy was a girl; and for all of Dr. Hepburn's ostensible support of women's rights, he expected his son to carry the family banner. Tom believed it imposs-ible for a woman to manage a career and a family, and he made no bones about expecting Kathy to marry one day; so the pressure remained squarely on Tommy.

Tommy was four when he developed nervous twitches in the face, diagnosed as chorea or St. Vitus's dance. Dr. Hepburn would have recognized the symptoms from his studies with William Osler at Johns Hopkins. An authority on the disorder, Osler had inves-tigated some 410 cases at the Philadelphia Infirmary for Nervous Diseases. He noted that in children the "irregular, involuntary con-traction" of the muscles was frequently triggered by "worry and stress." Children like Tommy Hepburn were understandably fright-ened when they could not control their own movements. Frequently, parents first realized that something was wrong when the child inexplicably overturned a glass or upset a plate at the dinner table. The most extreme symptoms, such as rapid winking of the eyes and contortions of the nose and upper lip, tended to coincide with self-consciousness about being observed or judged.

"Parents should be told to scan gently the faults and way-wardness of choreic children," Osler declared. Although physicians frequently prescribed mild physical exercise, Osler warned that competition "should be emphatically forbidden."

Such advice was lost on Dr. Hepburn. The father refused to accept his son's inability to control the tics, which he referred to as Tommy's "habits." Since boyhood, Dr. Hepburn had struggled to conquer his own will, and he expected his son to do the same. His demands placed further pressure on Tommy, who fought desperately to master his facial expressions.

Osler reassured parents that "recovery is the rule." Almost always the tics disappeared as mysteriously as they emerged. Still, so long as Tommy continued to twitch, his condition publicly reflected on Dr. Hepburn—or so the father seemed to believe. Dr. Hepburn could hardly overlook a possible connection between his son's chorea and the Reverend Hepburn's tics of the head and hands.

William Osler, noting that it was common for choreic children to experience night terrors, emotional outbursts, and acute melancholia, alluded darkly to "families with pronounced neurotic taint." Kate seemed to have successfully buried the past when she married Tom and gave birth to a healthy son and daughter; but Tommy's condition revived painful questions of family fate as she watched her son show signs of the melancholia that had afflicted her father.

In 1910, certain streets in Hartford were off-limits to a woman like Mrs. Hepburn. A physician's wife was not supposed to know about the eleven houses of prostitution, several within walking distance of the police station. Most men would have been well aware of them, and the police kept up-to-date records.

The municipal government practiced an unofficial policy of toleration, which sent out the message that Hartford's approximately 200 prostitutes were a necessary evil. Now and then, the illegal houses were raided and fines collected; but invariably, they quickly reopened.

At Hartford's "best high-priced house," noted for "scrupulously clean" bed linen, a prostitute reportedly accommodated twenty-five men in a night. Patrons of the "cheaper houses" were accustomed to beds or heavy tables "with no linen on them, just a piece of dark, dirty oilcloth." Cubicles were separated by a plywood partition that rarely reached the ceiling, or a filthy curtain hung on an iron pole. The prostitute, often seventeen or under, charged 50 cents. Half went to the girl, half to the house. Beyond that, the proprietor collected the first seven dollars she made each week, to cover board and medical expenses.

At Hartford Hospital that year, at least 287 patients entered with diseases directly traceable to venereal infection. Many were women unknowingly infected by their husbands. In Connecticut, most cases went unreported. According to Tom Hepburn's mentor at Hartford Hospital, Oliver C. Smith, few of the state's twenty hospitals willingly received or treated venereal disease patients. That children were often born blind or deaf as a result of a father's infection was well known in the medical profession; yet with few exceptions, prostitution and venereal disease remained "forbidden topics for discussion or action."

On May 13, 1910, Kate and Tom Hepburn were among approximately 100 prominent Connecticut physicians, lawyers, and professors to gather at the Hunt Memorial Building in Hartford to found "an organized movement against the moral and physical diseases having their origin in illicit sexual relationship." Tom Hepburn was appointed secretary and member of the executive committee of the Connecticut Society of Social Hygiene. Kate Hepburn was named to the publications committee, responsible for preparing and approving "sex literature," mainly pamphlets on prostitution. Tom agreed to represent Connecticut at the founding of the American Federation for Sex Hygiene (later the American Social Hygiene Association) in St. Louis, Missouri, on June 6, 1910. Elected to the national executive board, he collaborated with Prince Morrow and Harvard president emeritus Charles Eliot on a governing constitution and by-laws.

The Hepburns made an exceedingly effective and charismatic

team. People sympathetic to their views were enthralled by the couple's passion and forthrightness. There was a palpable electricity between them, intellectual and physical. In a crowded room, they appeared instinctively to think and act as one.

Young and attractive, the Hepburns epitomized the pleasures of a strong monogamous bond. Many of their social purity fore-runners had expressed acute discomfort with human sexuality not strictly in the service of procreation; by contrast, "Kit" and "Hep"— as they called each other—were astonishingly open about their sexual happiness. They almost purred with contentment. Their delight in each other bordered on exhibitionism. Their example proclaimed that if only all married couples discovered such bliss, the bawdy houses and disreputable districts would hold little appeal.

At home, the Hepburns made a point—some thought a display—of talking openly in front of the children about their work. No aspect of prostitution or venereal disease was taboo. No detail was too graphic or frightening. Mrs. Hepburn read and annotated pamphlets with titles like "House of Bondage" and "Panders and their White Slaves."

The Hepburns cultivated an air of consummate frankness; they obviously enjoyed shocking and disconcerting people with plain talk about sex. Much remained pointedly unspoken, however. Certain subjects, off-limits, were never broached. Dr. Hepburn never talked about the gonorrhea that afflicted two of his brothers or the syphilis of a third. The openness was in fact a façade; it concealed a singular lack of emotional candor. Tom had set the rules during their honey-moon when he stopped Kate from attempting to share the painful burden of her family history.

The social hygiene agenda as it evolved in the early 1910s allowed both the Hepburns to think and talk obliquely about emotionally charged personal issues without seeming to refer to themselves. Although social hygiene emphasized problems of "present health," the movement intersected with eugenics (the science of improving the human race by the careful choice of parents) in a preoccupation with "faulty" or "nervously defective" inherit-ance. The Hepburns subtly expanded their ken to include inherited taints and defects not caused by venereal disease. Dr. Hepburn, acting on behalf of the Hartford society, arranged for Edith Douglas, an investigator from the Eugenics Records Office of Cold Spring Harbor, Long Island, New York, to spend a year in Connecticut, documenting the "family histories of defective children." The purpose was to establish the hereditary, rather than environmental, basis for insane, criminal, and other antisocial behavior.

The proceedings of the Connecticut Society of Social Hygiene—prepared and distributed by Dr. Hepburn—are peppered with eugenic slogans like "the improvement of the race" and "the protection of our race stock against hereditary deterioration." There was much talk of the "inherited tendency" to crime and insanity, and vociferous interest in a mandatory "operation for the prevention of procreation" in cases where genealogical study discovered an irreversible family fate. The eugenics and social hygiene movements combined to argue that there were those in society who ought to be discouraged, even prevented, from multiplying. On the other hand, Americans of "better"—usually Yankee—stock were urged to avoid "race suicide" by having large families. Theodore Roosevelt was speaking to widespread fears about non-Anglo-Saxon immigrants and their potential impact on the fabric of society when he asked American families to produce a minimum of six children.

There was considerable irony in Dr. and Mrs. Hepburn's preoccupation with eugenics. Like other prominent figures in the social hygiene movement, they advertised themselves as people of superior stock; yet Dr. and—especially—Mrs. Hepburn were troubled by unanswered questions about their own family histories. At the moment, their concerns focused on Tommy. Eugenicists argued that St. Vitus's dance tended to appear "in the offspring of nervous parents." From the eugenic standpoint, a child's tics were "evidence of heredity that is nervously weak and constitutionally inferior."

In October 1911, the talk at the Connecticut Woman Suffrage Association convention in Bridgeport centered on Kate Hepburn. Not all of that talk was positive. There was a buzz of voices in the auditorium when, every three hours, Kate disappeared from the stage, giving over the podium to Grace Seton.

The year before, Kate's group had staged a coup at the annual convention. Kate, vowing to "jump in and stir things up at once," seized the presidency. Emily Pierson became state organizer. Annie Porritt, Grace Seton, Valeria Parker, and Caroline Ruutz-Rees joined the board. Kate outlined an ambitious strategy to pressure the state legislature to vote on suffrage for the first time.

Two months after she assumed the presidency, Kate became pregnant. She concealed the fact from her supporters, many of whom would have been furious; the women had every reason to expect her to hold the post at least until the state legislature voted. As it was, a newborn baby would force her to step down after only a year. Dr. Hepburn never doubted that a baby ruled out any position so demanding as the CWSA presidency; and at this point, Kate would have been inclined to agree.

The curious part was that, as she later confided to Grace Seton, the pregnancy had been no accident. Kate implored her friend not to tell the others that even as she was being installed as president, she had been planning to have a baby as soon as possible. Plagued by self-doubt, and eager to preclude the possibility of failure and humiliation, Kate told herself that she wanted to keep the presidency for one year only. It was a gesture of self-protection. That way, she was responsible for her own fate; her decision not to seek re-election made it impossible for others to vote her out.

When she could no longer conceal her pregnancy, Kate certainly did not reveal that it had been deliberate. Much as she had feared, there was dismay among the younger suffragists that she planned to drop out so early in the game. Strange to say, Kate shared their dismay. She had had a change of heart; several months into the presidency, she realized how much she enjoyed the work. She loved pressuring legislators and helping to set up local suffrage groups. And best of all, she discovered that she was terrific in the job. She excelled at running a large organization.

Her self-doubt, the legacy of many years of listening to Amory, was unfounded. The more time she spent in the job, the more she saw that Amory had been wrong about her. She was no "feather head," incapable of effective action. By then, however, Kate, well into her pregnancy, had no choice but to step down. The prospect was devastating.

Richard Houghton Hepburn, born at home on September 8, accompanied his mother to the CWSA convention the following month. Although a nanny came along to help, Kate could not see how she was going to conduct the meeting and care for a screaming baby. In Bridgeport, however, she discovered that there had been nothing to fear. Little Dick was exceptionally quiet and tranquil. While mother attended to convention business, baby lay peacefully in an open desk drawer backstage. When it was time to nurse him, Kate turned over the podium to Grace Seton.

The experience came as a revelation to Kate, who suddenly realized that even with a baby she could have retained the CWSA presidency. It was a very poignant moment. To her dismay, she saw that there was no need to abandon a job she had come to love. But it was too late. The agenda called for her to turn over the presidency to Maud Hincks of Bridgeport. Worse, Kate had alienated a good many supporters; the women, angered by her decision to step down, had come to doubt her seriousness. Unless Kate did something to prove herself, they were unlikely to follow her lead again. She left the meeting heartbroken yet determined to win back their trust.

Kathy, aged four, began kindergarten at the West Middle Public School that fall. Tommy was in the first grade. In the aftermath of the convention, Kate, accompanied by the baby, addressed suffrage groups throughout Connecticut. But that was no substitute for the exhilaration she had known as president.

Kate recaptured some of that intensity of feeling when she and Jo Bennett risked life and limb in the fight to put Hartford's vice lords out of business.

When Mayor Edward Smith shut down eleven houses of prostitution as an experiment, a *Hartford Times* editorial and other prominent voices called for some houses to be reopened under a policy of segregation. Prostitution was not going to disappear, they argued, so at least limit it to one part of town. Kate, outraged, swept into action. Echoing Edith's argument that legalized prostitution created a class of officially degraded women and thereby degraded all women, Kate mobilized opposition in the suffrage and social hygiene movements. The vice campaign was her crash course in political pressure tactics.

She organized rallies and gave speeches and interviews. She harangued legislators. She demanded that the mayor appoint a vice commission to recommend a policy for the city. She targeted major vice lords by name.

Kate was tangling with some very dangerous characters. For many months, the Hepburns were subjected to anonymous threatening letters and telephone calls. Every time the phone rang, Kate was reminded of the peril to which she had subjected herself and her children.

Jo's husband, M. Toscan Bennett, an attorney appointed to the new vice commission, kept Dr. and Mrs. Hepburn apprised of the investigation into Hartford's web of commercialized vice. The Bennetts, who lived nearby on Park Terrace, were the Hepburns' best friends and frequent visitors to the cottage. Large and fat, the garrulous Toscan Bennett favored heavy wool suits with big, rough leather buttons which fascinated the Hepburn children. His behavior with Mrs. Bennett was another source of fascination. He treated her like one of the boys. Suddenly in mid-sentence, he might turn to his wife and call, "Oh, Jo, by the way, will you change the tire on the car?" Mrs. Bennett, in her long skirt, would dash out to fix the flat, allowing her husband to return to his conversation.

The vice commission recommended that the brothels be closed permanently, and that the city move to shut down restaurants, saloons, and other fronts where prostitution was known to occur. To Kate's indignation, the city seemed inclined to bury the report. She provoked further threats on her family by publicly speculating about connections between commercialized vice and politics.

When the city printed only 500 copies of the report, she persuaded the CWSA to reprint it for sale at their storefront in the Hartford shopping district. From Mrs. Pankhurst, Kate had learned the strategy of provoking the authorities to act against suffragists;

by her own account, she hoped that the municipal government would try to stop them from selling the report.

When the city council voted to postpone a resolution endorsing the commission's recommendations, Kate placed a large poster in the window: "Mothers Of Hartford—Do You Know How The Following Members Of The Hartford City Council Who Claim To Represent You Voted In Regard To The Suppression Of Commercialized Vice In Your City?" Reasoning that the politicians' wives and daughters were likely to pass the window display, Kate laughed that perhaps they would put "a little domestic pressure" on the men to alter their views.

The vice campaign, and the tremendous publicity it generated, established Kate as a suffrage leader. It was her baptism as an activist. It gave her an identity in the national women's movement; from then on, she was the woman who had stood up to the vice lords in Connecticut. Although she did not manage to abolish prostitution in Hartford, she had demonstrated her courage and effectiveness. The eleven houses were permanently closed; a vice commission had been appointed, and its report widely distributed; most important, people throughout the state were becoming increasingly aware of what Kate liked to call "the woman's point of view."

In 1912, the Hepburns and the Hookers spent their first summer together in a sprawling three-story shingled cottage at Fenwick, overlooking Long Island Sound. The twenty-four-year-old house perched precariously on a sandbar. Howling winds shook the screens and rattled the porches on the lower floors. Waves pelted the stony beach and wooden bulkhead. Rain drummed on the roof and leaked through the windows. On foggy nights, bells and horns thundered from the Lynde Point and Saybrook Breakwater lighthouses. One occupant compared the cottage to a "sailing ship" or a "castle perilous on the ocean."

Even in tranquil weather the cottage was exceedingly noisy. Everybody could always hear everybody else in the house. Doors slammed and feet pattered on the ceiling. There were voices and laughter and snippets of conversation. Music mingled with the clatter of plates. Children called and rushed up and down creaky stairs. After lunch, while Mrs. Hepburn took a nap on the second-floor porch, Kathy, Tommy and their friends would play on four swings on the lower porch. They screamed and threw pillows and took turns trying to kick the ceiling.

Adults slept on the second floor, children in the attic. There was no electricity, only smoky kerosene lamps; no indoor plumbing, only porcelain chamberpots and an outhouse. Sometimes birds began to sing in the middle of the night. Lying in bed, one heard the din of crickets and cicadas, and a windmill spinning in the distance.

Eighteen years after Carrie Houghton had abandoned West Hamburg to take her daughters to Buffalo, Kate and Edith rediscovered the atmosphere of their father's house on Lake Erie. Their response to Fenwick was deep and emotional. Once again the sisters were together in a large, comfortable vacation cottage with shimmering pale blue water in front and tangled green and yellow fields behind.

That summer, Tommy, six, and Kathy, five, had their first pungent taste of living at close quarters with their tempestuous, passionate, idealistic, argumentative, tomboyish, flamboyant aunt Edith; many decades afterward, Kathy would remember the experience as a kind of "paradise."

Dr. Hepburn, wary of Edith's sharp tongue and unruly influence, had long been determined to keep the sisters apart; but his $2000 yearly salary did not allow him to buy the cottage on his own, so he invited Dr. Hooker to share the purchase price and expenses. Tom sweetened the deal by volunteering to convert the unfinished third floor into children's rooms. In the beginning there were five children in the house, Edith having given birth to Russell Houghton Hooker, known as Houghty, on October 10, 1911.

Edith cut a controversial figure in the insular, ultra-conservative summer colony of Hartford insurance executives, where most wives and daughters were "antis," violently opposed to women's suffrage. They regarded her as a dangerous firebrand out to destroy the American home. If possible, by this time Edith was more outspoken and confrontational than ever. Now head of the newly formed Just Government League and editor of the *Maryland Suffrage News*, she had spent the past few years making a name for herself in Maryland with street-corner speeches, delivered from her husband's open car.

"I see you are all men here!" she would cry, standing on the seat. "What man has failed to accomplish, woman, the mother, may yet win!"

Angry faces and wagging tongues appeared in the windows of surrounding buildings.

"Please let us vote as soon as possible," she kept on. "We intend to talk until the day of doom!"

Edith welcomed, even relished, derision and abuse, and patiently answered the most insulting questions.

"What would you do with the baby while you went to vote?" someone yelled.

"Well," said Edith so all could hear, "we have to leave the baby every day while we attend market. Sometimes the baby is asleep or we leave her with kind neighbors. If we can leave her every day in the year to attend to the buying of home necessities, we can leave her one day in the year to vote."

A little boy challenged Edith to explain why women always chase kids who play ball on the street. The crowd seconded the question with rowdy applause and hoots of approval.

"That may be true," said Edith, bravely struggling to drown out the hecklers, "but they are only sorry that the boys don't have regular ballfields, which they would have if women could vote."

At Fenwick, Edith burst into the living room at the same high pitch of excitement that galvanized her street-corner speeches. She threw her nervous hands about and wore holes in the rugs with her frantic pacing. She had strong opinions on everything. Unlike Kate, who preferred quietly and subtly to manipulate her husband (in ways that the children probably did not yet understand), Edith thrived on eyeball-to-eyeball confrontation—particularly with Dr. Hepburn, whose views on child-rearing and discipline she abhorred.

"I am so straightforward and abrupt a creature," Edith would say, "that you never need fear that I have any cards except those that are laid flat on the table." She even chastised her beloved sister for smoking cigarettes: "Tobacco smoking by women is proof of their subjugation to men!"

Edith loved to occupy center-stage. She mesmerized the children with accounts of her adventures. At Bryn Mawr, Edith had broken athletic records and dressed as a boy. She had been to medical school and worked side by side with Dr. Hooker and Dr. Hepburn; she had traveled to Paris to study acting. That summer, she was planning her debut as a figure of national prominence in the suffrage movement; Dora Lewis, Howard A. Kelly's sister, had arranged for Edith to address the National American Woman Suffrage Association on the "social evil" at the annual convention in Philadelphia in November.

In the meantime, she spurred little Kathy and the other children to put on the first plays at Fenwick. The living room, dining room, and porch opened onto one another, permitting the kind of large audience Edith preferred. To Kathy—the only girl in the house—Edith was a vivid and glamorous role-model. Edith taught the child to dream of becoming a physician, an actress, whatever Kathy wanted to be.

The Valley Railroad that crossed South Cove to the Fenwick peninsula brought other extraordinary women to Kathy's "extended family." Edith's great friend Florence Sabin came from Baltimore, where she had attracted international renown for her work on the lymphatic system. An unmarried "career woman" who had dedicated her life to medical research, Dr. Sabin was "Aunt Florence" to Edith's children; she regarded the Hooker family circle as her second home.

Mary Towle enjoyed a similar relationship with Tommy and Kathy, whom she loved and indulged as if they were her own. "Aunty" had recently been admitted to the bar in New York City; she lived in Greenwich Village and practiced law with Bertha Rembaugh. Dressed in a tent-like black bathing costume that extended to her thick white calves, Aunty presented a comical picture as she crawled on hands and knees over the wooden bulkhead; she never swam, preferring to sit absolutely motionless in the water.

The Hepburns subjected Aunty to a great deal of affectionate teasing. Dr. Hepburn (who dreaded her visits) would comment sarcastically on the prodigious quantities of flounder, fluke, shad, eel, and bluefish she liked to devour. Aunty, in turn, coughed, sighed, groaned, made nauseated faces, and threatened to leave whenever Dr. Hepburn's "sex" talk (deliberately?) offended her delicate Victorian sensibilities. Squeamish to the point of hysteria, Mary Towle was an anomaly in a household where the adults prided themselves on being hard to shock.

Mrs. Hepburn, by her own account, was not invited to visit the neighbors—with the notable exception of Jo Bennett's mother, Katharine Beach Day, an ardent suffragist. Jo's late father, George H. Day, vice-president of the Pope Manufacturing Company in Hartford, an early automobile maker, had purchased a summer cottage in 1888; and it was through the Bennetts that Kate and Edith had discovered Fenwick. Kate worried that the summer colony would punish the Hepburn and Hooker children for their parents' controversial views. Ostracized by the neighbors, she hoped to spare Tommy and Kathy the hurt she was experiencing.

She stocked the ice chest with ginger ale and root beer and invited the neighborhood children to come in any time they liked. She encouraged them to play loud games in the "secret passages" Dr. Hepburn had constructed in the attic. On rainy afternoons, when other people were far from keen to have fifteen or twenty children noisily charging up and down stairs, Mrs. Hepburn instructed Tommy and Kathy to invite all their friends. She noted that as a result, her children "didn't feel unpopular but felt very superior."

Mrs. Hepburn became pregnant again in July, and decided to be absolutely open and honest with Tommy and Kathy about how the pregnancy had happened.

"No child unless he is a moron can be expected not to be interested in how he was born," she declared. Mrs. Hepburn wanted Tommy and Kathy to "feel that their parents can be relied on to tell them the truth . . . and can be trusted as a source of information." In her view, the youngsters must not grow up regarding their parents as "close-mouthed strangers." She feared that if parents failed to explain where babies come from, the children would only get "distorted information" somewhere else.

She took Kathy aside. Calmly and thoroughly she gave a short, well-rehearsed speech on reproduction. She made a point of describing Dr. Hepburn's role as well as her own. Then she waited for Kathy's response.

"Then I can have a baby without getting married," Kathy exclaimed suddenly. "That's what I shall do. I don't want any man bossing my children."

E I G H T

On March 3, 1913, Edith led a contingent of Maryland women preparing to march among the 5000 suffragists who had converged on Washington, D.C. Edith had designed a special parade unit costumed as Amazons. Brandishing immense silver shields, Edith's "women warriors" planned to ride up Pennsylvania Avenue in horse-drawn chariots.

As women from many states waited for the procession to start, there was a general sense that something terrible was about to happen. More than half a million men, many already drunk, clogged Pennsylvania Avenue. One marcher later recalled her alarm "that the noise from the avenue was deafening—and not cheering." Even before the procession began, there was chaos among the women who could hardly find space to assemble. And there was little hope of marching through the solid mass of bodies that confronted them; rowdies had cut the restraining ropes that were to have separated suffragists from the crowd.

Inez Milholland, in a white Cossack suit and sky blue cape, appeared on a white horse to lead the parade. "There was no division between the parade and the crowd," recalled one marcher, "and the crowd was a seething mob of men who surged around the struggling marchers, shouting obscenities. There were few police in sight, and those who were in sight were making no effort to control the crowd."

"I'd like to meet you after dark!" men howled at the suffragists. "You ought to get yourself a man! You can get what you want without that!" Boys climbed onto the floats, taunting the women with lewd remarks. One drunk grabbed the foot of a terrified little girl, refusing to let go. Another man was nearly crushed beneath the wheels of a float. Instead of protecting the women, police laughed and shouted insults of their own. "If my wife were where you are, I'd break her head!" jeered one officer. Tears streaming down their cheeks, the suffragists took more than an hour to march the first ten blocks. Some older women, shaken and exhausted, were compelled to withdraw, but most pressed on. There were 175 requests for ambulances.

Yet Edith and others in the inner circle around Alice Paul, the organizer, considered that the parade had gone as planned—even better. Not by accident had Edith designed a contingent of "women warriors"; the costumes suggested the new direction the "Alice Paul militants" believed the women's movement must take.

Alice Paul, a disciple of Mrs. Pankhurst, was a four-year veteran of the rough-and-tumble British suffrage movement. Jailed for activities with the militant Women's Social and Political Union, she went on a hunger strike. Prison authorities pried open her delicate jaws with a steel implement and forcibly fed her with a dirty india-rubber tube inserted through the mouth into the stomach. Repeated on numerous occasions, the ordeal, known as "hospital treatment," had permanently damaged her ability to digest food. Paul, small, pale, and sickly, appeared an unlikely harbinger of a "new race of women" whose "ideal is strength." Speaking sometimes barely above a whisper, Paul declared that the time had come to stop begging and to seize women's rights. In emulation of the British militants, she argued that suffragists must give up attempting to reason with the oppressor; women must force the government to enfranchise them.

Paul's message spoke powerfully to many American suffragists, especially younger women like Edith who were impatient with NAWSA's pace. Between 1910 and 1912, Washington, California, Oregon, Arizona, and Kansas had given women the vote. The addition of five states was cause for rejoicing in NAWSA, committed as it was to winning suffrage state by state. But Alice Paul sneered at the time it would take to enfranchise all American women that way. She wanted to revive interest in the Susan B. Anthony women's suffrage amendment to the federal Constitution, introduced in 1878: "The right of citizens of the United States to vote shall not be denied or abridged by the United States or by any state on account of sex." Passage of the amendment would give women the vote in all states in one fell swoop.

It had been twenty-five years since the U.S. Senate voted against women's suffrage. Suffragists had long ago made state work their priority, and though NAWSA maintained a Congressional Committee in Washington, D.C., it was a hollow affair. In 1912, its chairman Elizabeth Kent received a pittance of $10 to conduct federal work. Alice Paul, promising to do her own fundraising, wrested control of the Committee from Kent, giving herself and her associate Lucy Burns a base of operations in Washington.

In the manner of Mrs. Pankhurst, Paul wasted no time in planning a bold gesture to advertise her arrival: a women's parade on the eve of the presidential inauguration of Woodrow Wilson in March 1913. Aware of the many reporters and photographers who would be in town for the inauguration, Paul envisaged pictures of Washington's first women's suffrage procession in newspapers around the world.

"What politicians had not been able to get through their minds we would give them through their eyes—often a powerful substitute," recalled one follower. Paul appointed Hazel Mackaye, a pageant designer, to choreograph the procession. Echoing Mrs. Pankhurst's Manichean concept of a struggle between feminine good and masculine evil, Paul ordered Mackaye to create a pageant whose beauty of form, shape, and color provided a powerful visual image of womanly peace and order versus male violence and chaos.

Paul anticipated that violence might actually be part of the spectacle. Like Mrs. Pankhurst, she was not averse to attracting attention and sympathy by provoking action against suffragists. On the day of the demonstration, Paul exulted that the police had—in suffragist Doris Stevens's words—unintentionally "played into the hands of the women." Photographs of men attacking suffragists showed the lengths to which men were willing to go to prevent "women warriors" from seizing their rights.

On the afternoon of March 3, Woodrow Wilson was astonished to discover no cheering crowds at Union Station when he arrived for his inauguration; they were watching the suffrage parade instead. For Wilson, it was a first inkling of what was to be a major source of tension in his presidency: the persistent demands of Alice Paul and her disciples.

At Fenwick, Edith arrived all afire. As always, she was intent on sharing her enthusiasms with her sister. Kate, in the final month of a fourth pregnancy, had been unable to accompany Edith to Washington. Giving a speech while pregnant was one thing; marching with thousands of women in a hostile and dangerous environment was another. She gave birth to her third son, Robert Houghton Hepburn, at home in Nook Farm on April 4, 1913. Edith was soon writing to Alice Paul, imploring her to take a week's vacation with the Hepburns and the Hookers. Edith longed for Kate to meet and become involved with her.

But Paul declined to leave Washington. Mrs. Hooker had failed to understand that she devoted all her time to suffrage. She never took a vacation. She forswore anything so frivolous as pleasure and diversion until women had the vote. Paul had scant patience with women who cited the pressure of husbands and children; in her view, the suffragist was permitted only one commitment.

Personal experience with Amory made Kate and Edith particularly receptive to the militant agenda. They had seen male power at its cruelest and most naked. They had survived an ugly and primitive struggle with their uncle. Amory rarely sugar-coated his actions. He did not flinch from declaring, as he had to Carey Thomas, that his niece ought to be shot. Alice Paul's message that men were capable of great violence to protect their power and authority came as no surprise to the sisters.

With the arrival of Alice Paul, the action in the women's movement shifted from the states to Washington, D.C. That created a problem for Kate, who, much as she sympathized with Paul's tactics, could hardly leave a demanding husband to spend time in Washington. Edith, who lived nearby in Baltimore, could easily slip into town for a few hours as often as she liked. Kate, far away in Connecticut, did not have that luxury.

Edith, reeling with excitement about the Washington procession, seemed to think or speak of little else. She held forth with colorful details; she displayed her own pen-and-ink drawings of women warriors brandishing shields and riding in chariots; she rhapsodized about how women voters with their "motherly" instinct for nurturing and good were about to change the world.

Her exhilaration was contagious. Six-year-old Kathy, under the spell of her aunt and mother, was soon trumpeting a cause of her own. George C. Ingham and his son Frank operated a fish-house on the stony beach several hundred yards east of the Hepburn–Hooker property. Tall, erect, rawboned men in leather hipboots, they claimed ancient rights to maintain a shed on the beach and a network of stakes and nets in the water.

Kathy Hepburn became a frequent visitor to the fish-house. The Inghams taught her to handle a small boat in rough waters. They cooked shad Indian-style on a long plank before an open flame. They showed her how to fillet a flounder. They told marvelous stories about Fenwick history and taught the child to love the sea and the open horizon.

That summer, the Fenwick Association of wealthy cottage owners declared that the Inghams were operating a fish-house illegally. Eager to banish all commercial enterprises from the summer colony, the governor of the Borough of Fenwick ordered the fish-house to be destroyed. Kathy Hepburn went wild. Emulating her mother and aunt, the child frantically rushed about winning support for the fishermen. The Inghams must seek an injunction! They must sue for damages! Kathy, irate at the injustice of it all, appealed to Dr. Hepburn to supply the name of a good lawyer.

She ran along the waterfront, where shrieking gulls swooped in to pick off schools of tinker mackerel. The slippery grey and black stones beneath her feet were tufted with eel grass. The tiny, freckle-faced child with a Dutch bob and sunburnt nose raced toward the vast white Saybrook Breakwater lighthouse.

"I'm going to change the world!" Kathy shouted. "I'm going to change the world!"

Kate would remember these years as the best of her life. On October 22, 1913, she retrieved the presidency of the Connecticut Woman Suffrage Association. Hartford's Unity Hall was decorated with the purple, white, and green suffrage colors. On stage, while she waited for Maud Hincks to present her with Isabella Beecher Hooker's gavel, Kate could see the ten enormous silk banners, each representing a state where women already voted, that hung from the balcony. She was determined that Connecticut would soon be among them.

Earlier that year, the Connecticut legislature had voted on suffrage for the first time. The women lost badly, but Kate considered it a triumph that the men had finally considered the amendment. There would be another vote in 1915. That gave her two years to attract legislative support.

At thirty-five, Kate Hepburn was very different from the woman who had become president in 1910. This time, she was committed to remain until state suffragists won the vote; and she was convinced, as she had not been first time out, that she was the right person to lead them.

Kate exuded vitality and a passion for life. Strikingly beautiful with large, intense green eyes and lofty, arched brows, she dressed to show off the tiny waist she retained even after four babies. Rejecting the dark, severely tailored suits Edith preferred, Kate wore light-colored dresses with tightly sashed waists; a favorite was pale lavender linen with a matching broad-brimmed hat. When collarless dresses became the fashion, Kate continued to wear tight, stiff, high necks to flatter the graceful sweep of her neck and shoulders. She believed that when speaking to men, it was in her interest to appear "feminine" and non-threatening.

Suddenly everything seemed to have come together for her.

Fenwick summers had brought Edith back into Kate's daily life; the Hepburns and the Hookers had reached a plateau of friendship and intellectual harmony. At Nook Farm, Jo and Toscan Bennett and their children, two girls and a boy, had built a house next door to the Hepburns. Kate, living in a house she loved, was surrounded by an extended family who shared her political beliefs and goals. They all lived with the accent of history, confident of the weight and rightness of their actions.

No sooner had Kate taken over as CWSA president, however, than her determination and leadership were tested. Several board members opposed her involvement in Mrs. Pankhurst's American tour to explain the British suffragists' shift to a "new and stronger policy of aggression." In the past, although British suffragists had smashed windows and perpetrated other acts of "symbolic militancy," women had largely been the victims of violence. Now, Mrs. Pankhurst was leading her followers in a campaign of "guerrilla warfare" against the government. Women burned country homes and theaters, blew up empty railroad carriages, and cut telephone and telegraph wires. They used acid to destroy golf courses frequented by prominent Liberal politicians; they burned "votes for women" into the turf.

When the French liner carrying Mrs. Pankhurst docked in New York City that October, immigration officers escorted her to Ellis Island, as it was feared that she had come to urge suffragists to imitate British violence. Kate encouraged Connecticut women to barrage President Wilson with telegrams, urging him to admit Pankhurst. After two and a half days, when the president let her in, not everyone was happy. "She's classed with dynamiters, arsonists, seditionists, silly fulminators, nihilistic flourishers and mannish Amazons," one police official told reporters.

It was hardly an image with which most Connecticut suffragists cared to be identified, and CWSA board members demanded that Kate dissociate herself from Mrs. Pankhurst's appearance in Hartford on November 13. Kate notified the board that she would indeed be involved with the Pankhurst visit. To pull back, she argued, would demonstrate "the most ignominious disloyalty." Kate arranged the lecture independently; CWSA sponsorship was not implied. In Hartford, Mrs. Pankhurst was the Hepburns' houseguest.

By and large, Kate emerged victorious from the showdown. Mrs. Pankhurst spoke to a standing room only audience at Parsons' Theater. Still, the episode suggested the tensions that Kate would have to contend with as CWSA president. To lead effectively, she would have to walk a tightrope between her own strong attraction to the Paul militants and the more cautious approach her constituency favored.

Kate, whose involvement with Pankhurst brought her national attention, was invited to address the forty-fifth annual NAWSA convention in Washington, D.C., taking place from November 29 to December 5, 1913. As Edith had discovered the year before, a slot on the program was a first step to becoming a national leader. Kate, scheduled to appear on the final night, was to speak on the vice campaign in Hartford. By the time she delivered her address, however, all hell had broken loose.

Alice Paul had addressed the convention on the efforts of the Congressional Committee—and to a lesser extent, her Congressional Union, founded that spring to raise money for the federal campaign. Paul's remarks opened a floodgate of resentment against her. Much of that resentment focused on her Pankhurstian insistence on holding the party in power responsible: In the event that the Democratic majority in Congress should fail to pass the Anthony amendment, Paul wanted suffragists to work against all Democrats, friend and foe alike. Many women thought it "bad politics" to punish legislators who had supported their cause.

NAWSA, repudiating Paul's involvement with the British militants, dismissed her as chairman of the Congressional Committee. She refused to remain on the committee under new leadership. The fate of the Congressional Union, however, was entirely in her hands. Paul could disband it; she could attempt to affiliate with NAWSA; or she could proceed independently, forming a rival suffrage organization with distinct aims and tactics.

Edith Hooker argued for the latter. She urged Paul to establish the CU as a separate entity with its own constitution. Paul wasted no time appointing Edith to the CU executive board.

In the light of Kate's status as Connecticut's "unquestioned leader," Paul hoped that she too could be persuaded to join. But that, Edith feared, might not be so easy. While there was no question of Kate's strong sympathy with Paul, the combined pressures of Dr. Hepburn and the largely moderate CWSA membership blocked her involvement with the militants. Still, Kate did attend two days of small private sessions at Edith's home in Baltimore, in anticipation of a mass meeting in Washington, D.C. on Sunday, January 11, to discuss the CU's future.

For suffragists who had often observed Edith in public, the dynamics of her relationship with Kate were a marvel and a mystery. To Edith, Kate would always be the shrewd older sister capable of miracles. The pain and secrets they had shared as children intensified their palpable joy in each other's presence now.

Edith, usually forthright and abrupt to the point of high-handedness, actually seemed to defer to Kate, who argued against a democratic constitution and the "red tape" that would involve. Kate believed in the dictatorship of a radical elite. Mrs. Pankhurst's society in England prided itself on operating without the trappings of a constitution, she declared, so why shouldn't Alice Paul's? Kate's speech electrified the group.

Still, she resisted both Edith's and Alice Paul's efforts to persuade her to join the board or even just to remain for the Sunday afternoon open meeting, where all the big decisions would be made. She had strong opinions and much to contribute. She obviously longed to see how things turned out. Yet like Cinderella frantic to get back before midnight, Kate hurried home after the Saturday session.

From her office on Pratt Street Kate oversaw sixty-one local suffrage organizations and 18,000 CWSA members. She answered hundreds of letters and queries, approved press releases, coordinated statewide lectures, meetings, and rallies, and met with legislators and other

Connecticut officials. Much in demand as a speaker, Mrs. Hepburn traveled constantly—always careful, however, to allow time to get home before Dr. Hepburn.

For all of Tom Hepburn's vigorous, apparently sincere public support of his wife's work, at 5 p.m. he expected to find her "behind the tea set," preferably looking as though she had spent the afternoon at home doing nothing more strenuous than reading. Although he knew perfectly well that Kate worked all day, he liked to maintain the illusion that she was the lady of leisure Nina Hepburn could never be. Kate's frantic pace notwithstanding, Dr. Hepburn wanted her to make it all seem effortless.

She accommodated her husband by carefully calculating train schedules. When she had a speaking engagement in some distant corner of Connecticut, she left early in the morning. Kate delivered her address at lunch and returned to Hartford on the next train. The need "to get right back" was a motif of her arrangements. When that seemed impossible, Jo Bennett's mother, Mrs. Day, often proved a godsend, lending Kate her car and driver, Crocker. Kate needed only to rush in the door moments before Tom's arrival; Fanny Ciarrier, the live-in factotum, blind in one eye, took care of everything else.

At home, Kate changed into beaded tunic dresses with high-waisted dark tops and narrow silky skirts. The Hepburns welcomed a steady stream of houseguests—suffrage and social hygiene campaigners passing through Hartford—and gave constant dinner parties. Mrs. Pankhurst made a particular impression on little Kathy; far from being frightened, the child experienced a curious surge of excitement on hearing details of the force-feedings in England.

Mrs. Hepburn's balancing act worked—but only because, by and large, she was there when Dr. Hepburn wanted her. So long as she was working in Connecticut or New York City, Mrs. Hepburn, with a little ingenuity, could satisfy her husband's demands. Washington, however, was simply too far from Hartford.

That was why Kate had so abruptly left Baltimore on the eve of the CU meeting in Washington, which she had obviously wanted to attend; and why in the months that followed, she worked tirelessly to mediate between NAWSA and the militants. Although her natural sympathies were with Alice Paul, working in Washington on a daily basis was out of the question. At a distance, Kate could never wield the power and influence she did in Connecticut, where she believed herself achingly close to persuading legislators to allow a suffrage referendum.

Mrs. Hepburn's efforts to make peace between NAWSA and the CU reflected a desire to avoid having to choose between them; she wanted to give up neither the personal satisfaction of daily work in Connecticut nor the exhilaration of commitment to the militants. Kate worked behind the scenes to persuade NAWSA to accept the CU as an auxiliary member. Alice Paul, for her part, had little hope of being accepted back in the fold; nor did she much care. Paul's sole concern was to prevent the National from withdrawing from her big event on May 2 in support of the Anthony amendment.

This year, instead of confining the pageantry to Washington, Alice Paul coordinated simultaneous demonstrations in every state. Mrs. Hepburn organized the first suffrage parade in Hartford. Jo Bennett carried the CWSA flag. Dr. Hepburn and Toscan Bennett marched with suffrage husbands. Fanny Ciarrier led a contingent of waitresses; nanny Estelle Rivoire was head marshall of nursemaids. Little Kathy Hepburn, costumed as a puritan in a white linen bonnet and white apron tied around the waist, waved a "votes for women" banner in the children's procession. The parade culminated at Park Casino where Connecticut suffragists, like others across America, passed a resolution calling for immediate action on the federal amendment.

On May 9, delegates from every congressional district in the country converged on Washington. Mrs. Hepburn and Mrs. Hooker were on the bill to address a mass rally at the Belasco Theater. Afterward, white-clad suffragists, bearing armloads of purple, white, and yellow flowers, marched up Pennsylvania Avenue to the Capitol to present the resolutions as proof of "overwhelming public opinion in favor of real democracy."

Although NAWSA reluctantly participated in the parades, it was common knowledge that the moderates had decided to cast out

Alice Paul. When the decision was announced, Connecticut had to choose sides. In Maryland, Edith instantly broke with NAWSA. Kate, powerfully drawn to the militants, was desperate to do the same thing, yet knew she must not. That would mean giving up the efficacy she enjoyed in Connecticut.

She could no longer keep a foot in both camps. When Alice Paul invited the CWSA president to join the CU board, Kate's constituency would not hear of it. Although Kate, Jo Bennett, Emily Pierson, Annie Porritt, and a few others greatly admired Paul, most members were moderates. Connecticut suffragists, having chosen to stay in the National, did not want a president with divided loyalties. If Kate wanted to lead in Connecticut, she had no choice but to turn down Alice Paul's offer.

The sight terrified people. On the front lawn at Hawthorn Street, Dr. Hepburn had rigged up a mechanical contrivance. First Tommy, then Kathy would climb a sixty-foot swinging ladder affixed to the sturdy branch of an elm tree. There the child grabbed onto a trapeze attached to a pulley on a long rope. Dr. Hepburn had stretched the rope between the tree branch and the rear boundary of the heavily wooded property. The course slid steadily downward. The child, sitting or hanging by the knees, flew past the gabled roof at breakneck speed, traversing the rear lawn before hitting the ground with a thump.

Dr. Hepburn drilled Tommy and Kathy to be fearless. He took them on rounds at Hartford Hospital. In the operating room, they stood on a table to see over his shoulders. He wanted his children to be "matter-of-fact about seeing things."

"Didn't bother me at all," Kathy insisted afterward.

At home, a neighbor called to alert Mrs. Hepburn that Kathy had climbed to the top of a hemlock tree, the better to survey distant woods and meadows. "Yes, I know," said Mrs. Hepburn resignedly. "Don't scare her. She doesn't know that it's dangerous."

With their mother committed full-time to the CWSA, Dr. Hepburn became the dominant presence in the children's lives; and the older children often supplied the attention and worshipful companionship a man of his ego required.

Dr. Hepburn bought a sneakbox, Butterfly class, for eight-year-old Tommy to take part in the sailing races in South Cove at Fenwick. Fourteen feet long, the boat had a sprit sail and no jib. It was shaped like a watermelon seed. Sneakboxes overturned easily; and the eleven boys who raced under the direction of yachtsman Marcus Potter needed to be quite deft to keep from plunging comically into the water.

The races were no laughing matter to Dr. Hepburn, however. He had an insatiable appetite for victory. Acutely sensitive about having less money than his neighbors, Dr. Hepburn was often heard to remark that unlike Toscan Bennett and Don Hooker, he had to earn every penny. Each time Tommy raced, he was carrying the Hepburn banner. The family honor was at stake—much as it had been in Charlie Hepburn's famous twenty-round fistfight.

Like his uncles Charlie and Sewell, Tommy drove himself relentlessly to live up to a demanding parent's expectations. The symptoms of St. Vitus's dance had largely subsided by the time Tommy had entered the West Middle School, but he remained highly-strung and extremely sensitive. Even so, Dr. Hepburn ignored Osler's dictum that "the competition for prizes should be emphatically forbidden." He fueled the child with an all-consuming need to win.

Dr. Hepburn constructed a springboard and tower for diving contests. He put gym mats in the attic, so the children could compete on rainy days. Tommy, lean and agile, acquired the reputation of being one of Fenwick's best competitive athletes. He won so often that officials decided to limit the blue ribbons one boy could earn.

He ran track. He swam. He wrestled. He played tennis and golf. On the lawn of the neighboring Morgan Brainard cottage, he was a vigorous participant in games of capture the flag, prisoners base, and kick the can.

His sister learned to be equally competitive. The pressure was principally on Tommy, but Kathy did her best to keep up. A fierce red terrier of a child, Kathy was almost always at his side. She, too, ran, swam, wrestled, and played tennis and golf—all to earn the praise Dr. Hepburn appeared incapable of offering.

Sent out as little gladiators to vanquish the other kids, Tommy and Kathy were enacting a drama that was not really theirs and can scarcely have concerned them. It was Dr. Hepburn's drama, and his mother's. The competition always came down to one thing: Dr. Hepburn's fight to retrieve his rightful place in the world.

His sons seem to have grown up regarding him as a harsh, omnipotent figure, who mercilessly drove them; but Kathy, from the first, appears to have sensed something of the pain and vulnerability behind her father's bluster. Probably this was because as a girl, she was not subjected to the same degree of pressure. Kathy struggled constantly to win, less to prove her worth to Dr. Hepburn (as Tommy did) than to gratify and comfort him.

This competitive spirit, deeply ingrained, soon appeared to drive Kathy even when Dr. Hepburn wasn't around. Whatever the activity, she insisted on doing it better than anyone. Some of the children described her as a "show-off." One little girl spoke of hating her "passionately." Another, Lil Smart, who sat behind her at school, dunked Kathy's hair in the inkwell in exasperation.

Assigned to distribute gas-filled purple, white, and green "votes for women" balloons at a country fair, Kathy propelled herself to give out the most. She forced balloons on people as though her life depended on it. When an adult declined and kept walking, she darted about his legs. "Votes for women," the urchin cried in a raucous, faintly menacing voice. With outstretched arm, she persisted in offering the balloon on a six-foot string. "Here take it," she pressed. "Votes for women."

In March 1915, Mrs. Hepburn led hundreds of women who took possession of the state Capitol to harangue legislators; only seventy-one had voted for the amendment two years before. Led by little Kathy Hepburn, flower girls rushed about with baskets of purple, white, and green bouquets, which they pressed on legislators. Mrs. Hepburn, Emily Pierson, Annie Porritt, and Jo Bennett called the roll of a contingent of working women: a hat trimmer, a stenographer, a teacher, a furrier, a clock factory worker, a telephone operator, and others; each rose to say, "I favor the bill and am a believer in suffrage."

For all that, on April 6, 1915, the amendment was defeated by 124 votes to 106. In the noisy gallery of the House of Representatives, Mrs. Hepburn, with Tommy and Kathy at her side, rejoiced at the closeness of the vote. "It is a wonderful advance on the vote of two years ago," she insisted to reporters. "It marks the growing strength of the suffrage movement, and it is a certain indication of success when next the House of Representatives of this state has an opportunity to vote on a woman suffrage measure."

N I N E

On Tuesday and Thursday afternoons, Dr. Hepburn took a train to New York City to meet with Dr. Edward Keyes at Bellevue Hospital at the foot of East 26th Street. Keyes taught the Hartford physician to use a cystoscope, a thin, cylindrical instrument for examining the inside of the bladder. After years of competition with general practitioners who insisted on doing all their own surgery, Tom hoped that knowledge of the cystoscope and urethral catheters would improve his income.

In 1913, Don Hooker, aware of Tom's financial woes, had offered to boost his yearly earnings of approximately $2000 to $10,000, by inviting him to lead the American Social Hygiene Association, formed when the American Federation for Sex Hygiene and the American Vigilance Association merged. That way the two couples, the Hepburns and the Hookers, would be able to spend most of their time together in political and social endeavor without Tom's being distracted by the need to earn a living. It is not too much to suppose that Edith, eager for her sister's companionship, had a hand in the offer.

Proposed with sincere good intentions, the plan was unlikely to appeal to Dr. Hepburn. Tempting as the money may have been, Tom had no desire to abandon the drama of surgery for what he perceived as humdrum administrative work. Nor did he wish to be beholden to anyone, Edith's husband least of all.

In Hartford, Dr. Hepburn borrowed money for cystoscopic equipment; and soon colleagues were referring all their urological cases to him. Aside from the boost to his income, urology appealed to Dr. Hepburn because—he made clear—there were as yet "no authorities" in the field. He thrived on the "excitement of exploration and of trying something new."

In New York, Tom would visit his brother Charlie, who lived not far from Bellevue at 144 East 22nd Street. That spring of 1915, Charlie was in the throes of what family members described as a "nervous breakdown." Employees at the apartment house would say that Mr. Hepburn had appeared "despondent" for months.

To most observers, Charlie Hepburn had no good reason to seem so hopeless and dejected. His haunted state of mind was a mystery. Always the handsomest of Nina Hepburn's boys, at forty-two he retained the apple-red cheeks and delicate Cupid's-bow lips that had made him irresistible in youth. Charlie was a successful attorney, by all accounts "well known in his profession." His personal finances were sound. For twenty-four years, he had been married to Elizabeth Newport, a poet and novelist. To all outward appearances, their inability to have children was the only cause for sadness.

Still, Charlie's depression deepened. At his law firm, Roberts and Hepburn, he was increasingly unable to function. On the afternoon of Thursday, April 15, Julian G. Roberts sent him home with the suggestion that he take a long rest. Charlie, accustomed to driving himself well beyond the brink, promised he would be back the next day.

Throughout the night, Elizabeth could hear Charlie wildly pacing the floor in the next room. The lack of sleep notwithstanding, he seemed somehow considerably improved in the morning—or so Elizabeth insisted afterward.

Just before 8:30 a.m., Charlie put on his hat and coat. He pulled a glove onto one hand and was about to put on the other when he disappeared into the living room, which looked out on the steeple and pale green crucifix of Gustavus Adolphus Lutheran Church.

Elizabeth thought nothing of it. She went to the kitchen to talk to the maid for a few seconds before returning to the bedroom to finish dressing, it having been agreed that she would drop her husband downtown at the office. Moments later in the kitchen, the maid heard the screech of police whistles from the street. When she dashed to the living room to see, she found the window wide open.

Four flights below, Charlie was impaled on the iron picket fence at the entrance to the superintendent's basement office. Unconscious, he hung face-down from a six-foot spike; a sharp metal curlicue cut through his right leg below the knee. His hands touched the sidewalk, a glove still clutched in one palm.

Joseph Boggs, the superintendent, had heard something crash against the fence and rushed upstairs. Patrolman Fackman of the East 22nd Street precinct, who had witnessed the plunge, was already there. The two men slowly lifted Charlie Hepburn off the stake. His hat fell off as they struggled to free him. His scalp was covered with blood.

By this time, Charlie's wife had joined the maid at the front window.

Boggs and Fackman carried Charlie, his leg bleeding profusely, two steps up to a small vestibule. While they waited for an ambulance from Bellevue Hospital, the policeman improvised a tourniquet. Elizabeth identified her unconscious husband, then reportedly became hysterical, refusing to say why he might have tried to commit suicide. She told police only that he had been despondent.

At Bellevue, doctors listed his condition as serious. Although he never regained consciousness, police charged Charles Leven Hepburn with "attempted suicide." He died at 4:55 p.m. Dr. Edgar T. Ray, who prepared the death certificate, tactfully gave the cause of death as shock and internal injuries due to a fall.

Charlie's law partner, anxious to avoid the stigma of suicide, did his best to portray the leap as an accident. "Mr. Hepburn did not commit suicide in my opinion," Julian G. Roberts insisted to the press, and Elizabeth agreed. Although no one had been in the room with him at the time, they speculated that he might have become dizzy. Employees at the apartment house, however, spoke openly of Charlie's months of despondency; and even Mrs. Hepburn had initially confirmed this to the police.

"ATT'Y HEPBURN DIES AFTER SUICIDE LEAP", the page one headline of the *New York American* declared. "LAWYER LEAPS FOUR STORIES.

Charles L. Hepburn Hurls Himself from Window at Home",
announced the *New York Evening Journal.*

Charlie's nervous breakdown had been no secret in the family.
Still, the Hepburns clung to the somewhat comforting theory of
accidental death, difficult as that theory may have been to substantiate. It was hard to conceive quite how a strapping, athletic
man, dressed in business clothes and about to leave for work, would
have suddenly pitched out of a small window without having
intended to do so. Elizabeth must have known this on some level;
she declined to accompany her husband's ashes to Shepherd's Delight
for the funeral. That task fell to Lloyd, the least driven of the
Hepburn boys.

Cloaking the death in silence and denial, the family ruled out
suicide. Among themselves, they would speak of Charlie's death as
"an accident resulting from a nervous breakdown." This delicate
phrasing, which cushioned the Hepburns from the stigma of suicide,
reflected the belief that Nina had driven Charlie too hard.

The circumstances of Charlie's death were a bitter blow to his
mother. Relentlessly, often cruelly, as Nina may have pushed her
boys—especially the two oldest—she sincerely believed she had been
pursuing a noble cause. Nina's father had been weak and ineffectual;
her brothers were killed in battle; her husband never earned enough
to support her and the children. She had always borne down on her
sons to "put this family back on the map!"—and the Hepburns,
while recognizing her role in Charlie's tragedy, seemed not to blame
her.

Sewell Hepburn, now the oldest, was notably absent from the
funeral. He had always been closest to Charlie, whom he idolized.
Of the three remaining brothers, Sewell took the suicide hardest. In
boyhood, when Sewell ran away to escape Nina's strong hand, it
had been to join his older brother at the Episcopal High School in
Alexandria, Virginia. And when a bully tormented Sewell at school,
it had been Charlie who, famously, had fought twenty rounds to
defend him. Led by Nina, the family mythologized that fight as a
confrontation between good and evil—and good had triumphed.

Charlie's decision to kill himself left Sewell without a protector.

Sewell would never fully recover from the shock of losing him.

Tom Hepburn also missed the funeral.

In Hartford, Kate had been in high spirits after the vote in the Connecticut legislature when the news from Bellevue Hospital brought her up short. That very day, she had been writing to thank people for participating in the 1915 campaign and to urge them to keep going for two years more.

Having long ago put the suicides of father and uncle behind her, Kate was confronted with the eruption of suicide in Tom's supposedly robust family. No less than in 1892, when Fred Houghton killed himself, there continued to be wide popular and medical belief in the hereditary character of suicide. In a household where matters of heredity and eugenics were often discussed, Charlie's suicide presented an especially chilling prospect.

Kate entered into an unspoken pact with Tom not to allude to the circumstances of his brother's death. Charlie Hepburn was gone and that was that; they simply did not mention it. "What is past is past," they agreed.

That would not quite do to answer a child's inevitable questions, however. Uncles Charlie and Sewell were familiar figures to Tom's children; every summer all the Hepburns gathered at Shepherd's Delight, where Nina and her imperious older sister, Aunt Bec, held court. Dr. and Mrs. Hepburn always made an issue of being candid and open with the children; their mysterious silence about Uncle Charlie succeeded only in calling attention to, and raising questions about, his death. Eager not to be thought a "close-mouthed stranger," Mrs. Hepburn had been quick to tell Tommy and Kathy how a little brother had been born; but she pointedly refused to tell how or why Charlie died. Tommy, in particular, would have been curious about his fate. Kate's having emulated Nina's policy of holding the oldest child responsible taught Tommy to identify with his uncle; Charlie and Tommy shared pressures the others escaped.

At Fenwick that summer, dismal weather kept cottage owners indoors more than usual. The tense aftermath of Charlie's suicide was the worst time for Dr. Hepburn to find himself at close quarters with his irrepressible sister-in-law. Alone or with the other Hepburns, Tom and Kate may have been able to maintain their silence on the subject of Charlie, but that would hardly be possible with Edith. The years of Edenic happiness at Fenwick ended when Edith openly challenged the iron hand that Dr. Hepburn, like Nina Hepburn before him, used to discipline the children.

The Hepburns and the Hookers had always had strong philosophical differences about child discipline. Edith believed in "total freedom of choice and action" for children. Dr. Hepburn required obedience. Edith, quoting Charlotte Perkins Gilman, mockingly defined obedience as "the subordination of the intellect and the abrogation of the will." Surely, Edith argued, parents ought to have better goals.

Dr. Hepburn had the reputation of a "spanking dad." At the dinner table, when a child talked out of turn, Dr. Hepburn would slap the child across the face.

Edith demanded that he stop. She protested vehemently against all forms of corporal punishment, and worried about the long-term repercussions of parental brutality. She took Charlie's suicide as a warning; if Kate and Tom were willing to ignore it, Edith was not. From their own medical studies with William Osler, Dr. and Mrs. Hooker knew the disastrous effects heavy demands and fierce punishment could have on a choreic child.

Edith's protests made Dr. Hepburn dig in his heels; he did not like to be told what to do, certainly not with his own children, and certainly not by Edith. That he was deeply torn, however, is suggested by the confession, many years later, that he never liked to hit the children; doing so, he told his son Bob, always made him feel as if he had "lost control." And control—of himself and his household—was the thing that mattered to him most.

Dr. Hepburn enlisted Kathy to help embarrass Edith. The Hepburns and the Hookers were sitting in the dining room at Fenwick when Kathy, on cue, knocked over a glass of milk. Whether Dr. Hepburn consciously chose one of the characteristic involuntary movements by which parents often first recognize St. Vitus's dance in children is impossible to say. More likely, the overturned glass was an unconscious expression of why the subject of discipline was so highly charged for him. On some level, perhaps, he knew it was a mistake to drive his son so, yet something in his character made it impossible for him to stop.

He dragged Kathy upstairs; and soon Edith and the others heard a particularly fierce beating. Edith, furious, was indignantly preparing to leave Fenwick when Dr. Hepburn and Kathy reappeared. Dr. Hepburn permitted Edith to berate him for a while before disclosing that it had all been a joke. Father and daughter grinned wickedly. The terrible pounding Edith heard had been a tennis racket whacking a pillow, and Kathy's shrieks of agony had all been faked.

Edith was not amused; but she agreed to stay. She believed that a child who takes pleasure in "cruel jokes" on others has herself often been the victim of a parent's "harsh treatment."

Obedient at home, Kathy became quite the scrapper outside. When children taunted her about the Hepburns' politics, she put up her fists. She cultivated a violent tone of voice. When she opened her mouth, her snarling manner seemed to say, "What the hell are you gonna do about this?" She exulted in her ability to intimidate.

That summer, Kathy cropped her "red red" hair half an inch from her scalp to prevent boys from yanking a fistful. She wore Tommy's old white shirts and knee-length white linen trousers and called herself "Jimmy" like his best friend, Jimmy Soby. Fanny boasted that Kathy and Tommy "beat up on those kids that plagued them. Kathy beat up on the biggest bully of the lot—beat up on him plenty."

The hellion was still wearing her brother's raggedy clothes when she returned to West Middle School in the fall. The teacher, "old lady Seymour," stalked up to the child's desk.

"Katharine!" she cried. "In my class little boys wear pants and black stockings and little girls come in pretty dresses. As I know you live nearby, you go home and put on a pretty dress and come back to class."

Mrs. Hepburn was at CWSA headquarters when Kathy turned

up at Hawthorn Street; but Fanny quickly provided a dress and Kathy was soon back in class.

The next day, however, all heads turned when Kathy Hepburn reappeared in Tommy's clothes. She strode to her seat as if nothing were wrong.

"Katharine!" boomed Mrs. Seymour, hovering again.

The teacher repeated yesterday's speech and Kathy repeated her disappearing act. But when she returned, she was still in Tommy's shirt and trousers. Mrs. Hepburn swept in behind her.

"Mrs. Seymour, you don't tell my daughter how to dress," she said for the entire class to hear. "That is my concern, not yours."

In this period, Kathy regularly accompanied her mother to the Saturday meetings of Heterodoxy in Greenwich Village, a radical discussion group attended by "the most unruly and individualistic females you ever fell among." According to one member, Elizabeth Gurly Flynn, Heterodoxy afforded "a glimpse of the women of the future, big-spirited, intellectually alert, devoid of the old 'femininity.'"

Nina Wilcox Putnam, a dress-reformer in a Botticellian tunic, looked on in astonishment as little Kathy Hepburn, "natural as a young savage," ran about screaming and snatching sweets from the women's plates.

"I want her to express her true self, fully!" Mrs. Hepburn explained. "We never suppress her."

It would soon be ten years since Katharine Houghton Hepburn, about to turn thirty, had experienced the crisis of meaning that propelled her into suffrage work. Twice the Connecticut legislature had defeated the amendment. A third vote loomed in April 1917. Kate had devoted her thirties to rushing toward this last hurdle, which only naturally took on immense personal significance. At the beginning of the year, she met with CWSA headquarters secretary Catherine Flanagan and executive board members including the original team of Emily Pierson, Jo Bennett, and Annie Porritt to map out the final three months of the state campaign.

On January 2, 1917, eight days before the militants planned to begin the drastic, unprecedented, and enormously controversial measure of picketing the White House, Mrs. Hepburn was struggling to persuade Connecticut state legislators that all suffragists were not Amazons and wild women. She wanted to show the men that CWSA leaders were, in her words, "women of their own kind with whom they could be at ease."

Publicly, Mrs. Hepburn continued to agree with moderates that "even a rock eventually gives way under the constant dripping of water." NAWSA insisted that gentle persuasion, not force, would finally win the vote. To resort to force of any kind (including political pressure) would "debase" the movement, causing the reasonable, peace-loving sex to imitate male aggression and violence. The point, NAWSA argued, was to raise male-dominated society to the moral level of women, not bring women down to the level of men.

Privately, however, Mrs. Hepburn longed to stand with Edith and the other militants, who served notice that they would not abandon the silent vigil outside the White House until women had the vote. Edith, wearing an ankle-length black coat and a Merry Widow hat trimmed with willow plumes, joined Maryland women lined up along Pennsylvania Avenue between the east and west iron gates. They carried signs like "Mr. President, What Will You Do For Woman Suffrage?" and "How Long Must Women Wait For Liberty?" In the first weeks, whenever the dark-blue presidential limousine passed the Silent Sentinels (as the pickets were called) Wilson, pretending to be in sympathy with the women, stiffly raised his hat and flashed clenched teeth. He left it to Representative Emerson of Ohio to demand that Alice Paul call off the pickets as "an insult to the president."

There were bitter laments in moderate suffrage circles. In peacetime, the CU's confrontational tactics would be bad enough; but with the coming of war, picketing the White House seemed unpatriotic and potentially destructive to the cause of women's rights.

Alice Paul replied that American suffragists had faced a similar dilemma at the outset of the Civil War. The earliest suffragists had also been staunch abolitionists. In response to Republican assurances that women would be granted the vote at the end of the war, they abandoned the suffrage campaign for war work. But the assurances were hollow. When black men were enfranchised after the war, women continued to beg for their rights. Paul and her re-christened National Women's Party had no intention of allowing American women to be deceived again.

On April 6, the United States declared war on Germany. From then on, the Silent Sentinels, poised at the White House gates, were widely reviled as "pro-German traitors" and "scum of the earth." Rumors flew that the NWP pickets were financed by the Germans. NAWSA ideologue Anna Howard Shaw, pleading with Alice Paul to call off the pickets, argued that no matter what their frustration suffragists must observe the "proprieties."

On April 23, Edith Hooker led forty Maryland women through the White House west gate to urge President Wilson to regard suffrage as a war measure. How could Wilson justify fighting for democracy abroad, Edith asked, when American women were denied the privileges of democracy at home?

Her friend Dora Lewis posed a similar question when she and Lucy Burns displayed a banner intended to embarrass Wilson before the representatives of Alexander Kerensky's new provisional government in Russia. The czar had abdicated in February, and already Russian women had the vote. "President Wilson and Envoy Root are deceiving Russia," the banner proclaimed. "They say 'We are a democracy. Help us to win the war so that democracies may survive.' We women of America tell you that America is not a democracy. Twenty million women are denied the right to vote. President Wilson is the chief opponent of their national enfranchisement." As soon as the Russians entered the White House, a mob of government clerks in straw hats and white suits attacked grandmother Dora Lewis and Lucy Burns. Shouting epithets at the women, who struggled to hold their ground and stare straight ahead, the men ripped the banner from its supports and tore it to ribbons.

At Fenwick, the Hepburn–Hooker cottage rocked with news of the escalating violence against suffragists. Repeatedly, Edith rushed to Washington for emergency NWP board meetings. On her return, her voice would sweep through the cottage like a strong blast of wind.

Edith described crowds of boys, government clerks, and sailors who pummeled women, knocking them to the ground, twisting arms, and seizing banners. She described the ultimatum by Major Raymond Pullman, Chief of Police, that in view of the war police would hereafter arrest the pickets; and Alice Paul's reply, "We think it is our duty to go out." She described the shrieks of the mob, "Traitor!" and "Take it to Berlin!" And she described the imprisonment of Dora Lewis and others who, for the first time in the suffrage struggle, acted with the knowledge that they faced arrest. Thus began the "real militancy," declared Alice Paul, who was herself dragged the width of the White House sidewalk when a sailor tore off her tricolor sash as a souvenir.

Kathy, brought up to be fearless, thrilled to the news from Washington. Flying through the air hanging by her knees, and doing half-gainers and one-and-a-halfs off the diving board at Fenwick pier, had taught her to crave the danger and intensity she discovered in Edith's reports from the front.

Subjected to physical brutality, many suffragists shared Mrs. Hooker's elation in having shattered the smug mask of chivalry and gentility, the "proprieties" that concealed insidious psychological violence against women. The violence was finally out in the open, and many suffragists felt the better for it; this was how the men of America and their government responded when women peacefully demanded their rights.

The decision Mrs. Hepburn dreaded was fast approaching. Time and again she had resisted joining the militants. Although she had often found herself saying one thing and believing another, the CWSA presidency allowed her to balance suffrage work with a demanding husband's inflexible requirements. But in April, when the Connecticut legislature rejected women's suffrage yet again, Kate took this third defeat very hard. Having devoted ten critical years of her life to a losing strategy, she quietly declared herself "disgusted" with state work.

On the morning of Saturday, August 18, the telephone rang at Fenwick. Edith picked up to hear Connecticut NWP president Lillian Ascough report that Catherine Flanagan, on vacation from CWSA headquarters, had been brutalized and arrested with other Silent Sentinels. Flanagan was sentenced to thirty days in the government workhouse. Already, Connecticut moderates had denounced her.

Throughout the morning and afternoon, Kate conferred with Jo Bennett. Cheered on by Edith and Kathy, Mrs. Hepburn and Mrs. Bennett decided to resign as CWSA officers—but not before they had used their titles to lend weight to statements of support for Flanagan.

Dr. Hepburn was expected that evening. By and large, he slept at Fenwick only one night a week. Since the war began, his office had overflowed with patients of doctors called to military service. Exempted on account of family responsibilities, he suddenly had as many operations on his calendar as he could possibly handle. All day in the operating room, he would rush back and forth between tables 1 and 2. For years Tom had been desperate to earn money like this, and he was determined to seize the opportunity. He longed to be the successful Hartford surgeon who played bridge and discussed the stock market with other prosperous men at the University Club. More than ever, he wanted a wife "behind the tea set" when he came home—and all that that implied. He envisaged a life more settled, comfortable, and conservative.

Before Tom arrived, Kate and Jo made statements to the Hartford papers. Identifying themselves as CWSA president and treasurer respectively, they signed pro-Flanagan letters to be published in *The Suffragist*, the militant organ. "I admire Miss Flanagan very much for being willing to go to jail for her convictions," Kate wrote. Having said that, there was no turning back. Even if she changed her mind about resigning, Kate could scarcely continue as CWSA leader when the parent organization, NAWSA, adamantly opposed picketing.

Dora Lewis immediately nominated Mrs. Hepburn to the NWP board. Kate replied on September 26. After years of resisting what she really wanted to do, she excitedly agreed to serve as soon as the CWSA replaced her. At the time, Mrs. Hepburn did not know that she had become pregnant in August, probably on the night Dr. Hepburn discovered that she had joined the militants.

The fighting began in November, and there was much to fight about. But instead of having it out over the simmering, largely unspoken tensions in the household, Dr. and Mrs. Hepburn angrily debated the Bolshevik Revolution. Kate hurled a steaming coffee pot at her husband. The battles were so furious that friends worried divorce might be imminent.

Mrs. Hepburn declared herself a supporter of Lenin's proletarian dictatorship. Bitterly recalling Amory's harsh treatment of his employees, she hailed the revolution of workers and peasants and welcomed the leadership of a radical elite. Dr. Hepburn replied that the unquestioned rule of a single vanguard party went against every principle his "family forebears" in Virginia had fought and died for. At the very moment Dr. Hepburn began to earn a substantial income, his wife called for the downfall of capitalism. And just when Tom started to listen to the financial talk at the University Club with an eye to making some shrewd investments of his own, Kate advocated the abolition of the stock market.

The arguments coincided with Dr. Hepburn's insistence that they move two blocks away to 352 Laurel Street. For seven years, the Hepburns had rented the Hawthorn Street cottage month by month. Kate knew that the Arrow Electric Company next door planned to expand their factory, and in 1917 the sword of Damocles dropped. Tom received notice that Arrow Electric intended to demolish the Warner cottage and build on the site.

Heartbroken, Kate resigned herself to the move. It was a bad moment to lose a much-loved home, just when she was abandoning that other defining aspect of her life, the CWSA presidency. The nondescript Laurel Street property made the impending move all the worse. Even Dr. Hepburn admitted that the new house lacked charm.

Tom, having signed a two-year lease, was in the midst of painting and improvements that included the installation of a gymnasium for the children, when "133" received a reprieve. It would not be torn down after all. Mrs. Hepburn called her husband with the news; but he did not share her exultation. As though Kate were an imbecile with no concept of money, Tom explained that he had poured a good deal of cash into Laurel Street. Abandoning the investment was out of the question.

Kate dutifully packed their things and moved. About politics and world affairs she argued fiercely and refused to back down; about household and family, she deferred to her husband. It was only a short stroll to "133," but for a year Mrs. Hepburn refused to walk or drive past. After that, when she wandered there for the first time and saw the old cottage, she burst into tears.

Dr. and Mrs. Hepburn had been happy and harmonious in Hawthorn Street, but the move to Laurel Street marked a turning point. From then on, Dr. Hepburn was constantly heard to say that Mrs. Hepburn thought money grew on trees. Patronizing and supercilious, he inculcated the children with the idea that their mother was a spendthrift, whose privileged background as a Corning Houghton and Bryn Mawr bookworm had never required her to learn the value of money. Echoing Amory's charge that she was a "feather head," Dr. Hepburn portrayed their mother as frivolous and impractical, a spoiled rich girl, while he, the poor Southern farm boy, was a realist, who had to earn every penny the hard way.

Mrs. Hepburn never challenged any of this. She did not disclose that it was Amory's and Mack's nickel-and-diming that had taught her to scorn money and accounting for how she spent it; she never explained that far from having been bookish and intellectual at Bryn Mawr, she had been so troubled that she barely graduated. To reveal any of those things, Mrs. Hepburn would have had to tell the children something of her past; and that she was unwilling, perhaps unable, to do. Mrs. Hepburn was a stranger in her own household, cut off and alone in the presence of those she loved most.

That fall of 1917, Kate wanted to stand vigil with the Silent Sentinels, but her pregnancy made it impossible to risk mob violence and arrest. Almost certainly, Dr. Hepburn had intended to keep her off the picket line that way. By the time Mrs. Hepburn officially joined the NWP board, Alice Paul was in prison, fighting attempts to commit her to St. Elizabeth's mental asylum as suffering a "mania of persecution."

Just how far some powerful American men—including, apparently, the Wilson administration—were willing to go became clear on November 15; nothing in the mob and police violence thus far had quite prepared suffragists for this. The women called it the Night of Terror. Under orders from W. H. Whittaker, super-intendent of the Occoquan Workhouse, as many as forty guards with clubs went on a rampage, brutalizing thirty-three jailed suffragists. They beat Lucy Burns, chained her hands to the cell bars above her head, and left her there for the night. They hurled Dora Lewis into a dark cell, smashed her head against an iron bed, and knocked her out cold. Her cellmate Alice Cosu, who believed Mrs. Lewis to be dead, suffered a heart attack. According to affidavits, other women were grabbed, dragged, beaten, choked, slammed, pinched, twisted, and kicked.

After many months of Wilson's paternalistic, two-faced treat-ment—assuring suffragists that he supported them even as he stead-fastly declined to further their cause—it came as no surprise when the president feigned ignorance of the brutalities at Occoquan. Smooth and civilized as always, Wilson left the dirty work—degrad-ing and intimidating the women in hopes of scaring them off—to the cruder figure of Whittaker. The hooligans who brutalized suffragists on the Night of Terror expressed a president's, perhaps a nation's, pent-up rage.

More surprising to militants was NAWSA's refusal to condemn the escalation of violence against women. The moderates went so far as to question whether the violence had actually occurred.

In December, little Kathy Hepburn stood at her mother's side on stage at the Belasco Theater in Washington, D.C., to honor eighty-one suffragists who had served jail terms, including veterans of the Night of Terror. Kathy watched excitedly as Mrs. Hepburn decorated each white-clad "prisoner of freedom" with a silver pin in the form of miniature jail bars with the words "Votes for Women". The child was furious when Mrs. Hepburn—four months pregnant—failed to receive a pin of her own.

War fever prevented most Americans from viewing the women as heroines. In the eyes of many, the militants seemed only to confirm their disloyalty when they provoked the government. At best, suffragists were said selfishly and unthinkingly to endanger the lives of American soldiers; at worst, they were rumored to be German-financed. The Bolshevik Revolution further aroused public hysteria about traitors and spies. Suddenly, Americans sniffed pro-Germans and Reds everywhere.

Mrs. Hepburn's association with the NWP made her a contemptible figure in many quarters of Hartford. At night, rocks crashed through the windows on Laurel Street. Other children menaced, taunted, harassed, and pummeled the young Hepburns. Bob Hepburn, small for his age, depended on his brother Dick to rush in and save him. Tommy, drilled to take responsibility, kept a keen eye on them all. Kathy, for her part, declared that if people were hostile, it must be because the Hepburns were "superior" to everyone else.

A month before Kate was due to give birth, Nina Hepburn died in Maryland on March 15, 1918. She was seventy-five. Her miserable, angry, unfulfilled life had taken a turn for the worse after the death in 1915 of her oldest son. Charlie Hepburn's suicide had triggered the physical and psychological decline that led to Nina's demise.

Nina Hepburn cast a shadow over the birth of Tom and Kate's fifth child on April 24. When Dr. T. Weston Chester delivered Marion Houghton Hepburn at home on Laurel Street, Dr. Hepburn gasped in astonishment. Pointing to a tiny scar on the baby's forehead, he insisted it was identical to his mother's. There was even the bubble of perspiration that appeared when Nina was most unhappy. Mrs. Hepburn declared that if you believed in reincarnation, you would be sure that Nina's soul had come back to earth. Dr. Chester, flustered, mistakenly recorded the sex as male on the birth certificate.

Kathy Hepburn created a commotion at school the next day

when she boasted to her classmates that she had watched her mother give birth. Scandalized parents endlessly repeated Kathy's story until it snowballed into a rumor—used to discredit Mrs. Hepburn politically—that the eccentric Hepburns had "forced" their children to watch the birth of new members of the family.

T E N

Years of striving to please his father had taught young Tom Hepburn—as he was called now—to press harder than most boys. At the Kingswood School, housed in the old Mark Twain house recently vacated by the Bissells, Tom excelled at football, baseball, basketball, and track.

The Kingswood School football field, at the bottom of a hill to the west of the main building, was only 90 yards long, but that did not faze the black-gowned English headmaster. Rats the size of groundhogs scampered along the edge of the Meandering Swine on the south end of the football field. Foul odors from the soupy brown stream wafted over the boys as they played. Once a boy dove into the filth and swam across to retrieve a football; he compared the experience to a volcanic mud bath.

When it rained and the playing field was too wet for practice, Tom Hepburn and his teammates ran the length of Woodland Street. Something always compelled the Hepburn boy to outdistance his friends. It was as if he heard his father thundering at him to run faster and faster—although of course Dr. Hepburn was nowhere in sight.

Kingswood's top athlete, James Thrall Soby, known as Jimmy, was Tom Hepburn's best friend. Jimmy's father, Charlie Soby, a cigar manufacturer, had made a fortune as principal investor in the coin mechanism used for pay telephones. Like Tom, Jimmy was sensitive, highly-strung, and given to brooding and nightmares. In both boys, a veneer of good looks and physical prowess concealed an inner core of sadness and desperation. Jimmy admitted that he hated being banged around on the football field, yet he drove himself to the point of damaging the nerves in his head.

Jimmy had experienced his first nervous collapse at the age of seven, when the headmistress of Miss Wheeler's School taunted him and called him a spastic. Dr. William Porter of the Hartford Retreat, a private mental institution, advised Jimmy's parents to remove the overwrought child from the school. Jimmy received private tutoring until he entered Kingswood in 1916. Dr. Porter treated him again when at length Jimmy suffered a second collapse, characterized by uncontrollable trembling and clouded vision.

At Kingswood, Tom Hepburn and Jimmy Soby enjoyed the reputation of daredevils; they were each other's best audience. Tom would walk the narrow wood beam that stretched like a tightrope across the top of Mark Twain's old coach-house. Riding a horse named Easter Belle, Jimmy would swoop down to earth to catch a white handkerchief with his teeth. Anxiety about being watched, however, could make Jimmy awkward and clumsy—sometimes dangerously so. When he fell wildly in love with Kathy Hepburn's friend Gertrude "Timmy" Robinson, Jimmy caught her attention by shouting "Hooray for Yale!" as he ran across her family's Forest Street porch. He hoped to dazzle her; instead the star athlete tripped over his own feet, tumbled down the porch steps, and broke his arm in three places.

Boys never made fools of themselves over Kathy Hepburn, not at that time anyway. Then in her first year at the Oxford School in Hartford, Kathy was skinny, angular, and painfully self-conscious about her freckles. She had let her hair grow to shoulder-length and parted it on the left. In a household where both parents frequently walked about naked, Kathy could see that she was not developing anything like her mother's feminine roundness; only the example of "stringbean" Aunt Edith provided any comfort. When Tom escorted twelve-year-old Kathy to her first dance, she struggled to make herself inconspicuous. "Who's that goofy-looking girl standing against the wall?" she heard a boy exclaim seconds before Tom knocked him to the floor.

Kathy was more in her element accompanying Mrs. Hepburn

to New York City to help out with "Aunt" Bertha Rembaugh's 1919 campaign to be elected Justice of the Municipal Court. Aunty Towle's law partner was the first woman to run for the post since New York state had granted women the vote. Slender and energetic, with golden brown skin and strong, dark, capable hands, Bertha Rembaugh reminded some people of a tanned, crinkly-eyed old sailor. Master of her own thirty-one-foot sloop, she would disappear to sea for weeks at a time. In addition to a heavy litigation schedule, she was a regular at Night Court, where she volunteered to defend prostitutes; she was one of the first New York lawyers of reputation to go near such cases. In 1918, Rembaugh astonished her friends and colleagues when she became a single mother, adopting a baby daughter.

Running as a Republican in the heavily Democratic first district, Bertha Rembaugh had scant chance of winning. She anticipated little fanfare; but her candidacy fired the imagination of a good many women, who, like Mrs. Hepburn, flocked to Greenwich Village to work on her behalf.

Suffragists were in the final throes of the struggle to push through the federal amendment. Before long, they hoped, women would be running for political office throughout the United States. The first breakthrough had come on January 10, 1918, when the House of Representatives passed the amendment by 274 votes to 136. But it would be eighteen months before the Senate said yes; and another fourteen months after that before the thirty-six required states ratified the amendment. Meanwhile, militants found new ways to express frustration over the delay.

Bells rang, flames leapt, and the smell of smoke drifted ominously across the White House lawn as women built "watchfires of freedom" in a bronze cauldron filled with firewood. Germany signed an armistice agreement on November 11, 1918. Wilson's struggle to carve his place in history as champion of world peace suggested new ways to embarrass him. Disgusted with the president's empty promises, the women burned his "useless, impotent words" on freedom and democracy. The spectacle on the pavement in front of the White House provoked many arrests. Sentenced to five days in prison, Jo Bennett went on a hunger strike.

In Hartford, Mrs. Hepburn answered angry protests against the escalating militance. "You have become used to looking upon women as naturally servile and second-rate," she harangued a crowd. "You are willing to have them beg politely for their freedom but not demand it. Well, there are some women in this country who are neither servile nor second-rate and who have the spirit to protest and will continue to protest against the present position of American women until it is changed. They are among the most worthwhile women in this country, the kind you men really like in spite of all your old-fashioned notions."

When Congress finally passed the Nineteenth Amendment on June 4, 1919, Mrs. Hepburn had a personal stake in making certain that Connecticut was one of the thirty-six states necessary for ratification. But when Governor Marcus Holcomb refused to hold a special session of the state legislature, which had adjourned until spring 1921, Kate sadly advised Alice Paul to avoid wasting time and money in Connecticut.

Kate was pregnant through much of the ratification process, having conceived her sixth child at Fenwick in August 1919. As the number of states to ratify approached the magic number, Dr. Hepburn keenly anticipated that she would soon withdraw from public life. The war had enabled him to build a lucrative practice; afterward, the return of a good many doctors permitted reduced hours in the operating room and a more civilized work schedule. Best of all, from Tom's point of view, the arrival of Dr. Bernard "Red" Spillane in 1919 allowed him to refer all syphilis and gonorrhea patients to the new physician, freeing him to focus on surgery.

Dr. and Mrs. Hepburn had been fighting about politics since 1917; by this time, the fights had become an established feature of life in the Hepburn household. Dr. Hepburn's disagreement with his wife's Marxist sympathies was very fierce and very serious. Still, as so often with the Hepburns, there was a distinct element of exhibitionism in their debates. To those who knew the couple best it was obvious that they loved to perform—for friends, for the children, and often just for themselves. Dr. and Mrs. Hepburn had clearly come to thrive on all the fighting. The arguments were stimulating, physically and emotionally, to both of them. Instead of diminishing on account of the discord, their physical passion for each other remained exceptionally strong. Dr. Hepburn, in particular, seemed to relish Mrs. Hepburn's ability to fight back.

Kate, having long been deeply hurt by her sense that Amory never liked her, would always be powerfully drawn to her husband's Amory-like bullishness and strength. No matter how bitterly they argued, he made her feel safe and protected as her weak father had failed to do. And she knew he adored her. In the end, she always deferred to him.

Mrs. Hepburn gave birth to Margaret Houghton Hepburn at home on Laurel Street on May 17, 1920. From the first, everyone called the newborn "Peg." To Kathy, at thirteen, little Marion and Peg sometimes seemed more like her own children than her sisters.

That summer of 1920, there were fourteen young cousins in residence at Fenwick. Edith had five children; in addition to the boys, she had had twins, Edith, Jr. and Elizabeth, in 1916, and a third daughter, Beatrice, in 1918. Kate and Edith's younger sister Marion, who was married to attorney Stevens T. Mason, brought her three children, two girls and a boy, from Detroit.

In later years, Mrs. Hepburn insisted on recalling the summer as extraordinarily peaceful, despite the large number of children in the house. She attributed the astonishing absence of quarrels to her policy of holding the oldest responsible. Kathy remembered that summer less fondly; in contrast to her mother, she felt beleaguered by the interminable noise and chaos and desperately longed for quiet and privacy.

Shortly after the thirty-sixth state, Tennessee, approved the Nineteenth Amendment and the ratification was certified on August 26, 1920, prominent Connecticut Democrats approached Mrs. Hepburn at Fenwick. They asked her to run for the United States Senate. A huge honor, the invitation testified to Kate's reputation as a political leader.

Ironically, some of the most militant suffragists reacted to victory with panic, depression, and despair. The violent struggle had made them feel intensely alive; danger made their hearts pound with excitement. Some women dreaded sinking back into a stultifying life of comfort and propriety, where they might never experience such sensations again.

For Kate and Edith, women's suffrage had always been a means, never an end in itself. From the outset, the sisters had been principally interested in social reform. Edith, for her part, spoke of enfranchisement as merely a "first step toward progress." After the Nineteenth Amendment became law, she announced plans to return to her original concerns: "The enfranchisement of women has released the power essential to a successful, constructive campaign against sexual promiscuity and its attendant infections." That summer, Edith began work on a book to show American women how to use their newly won political power to achieve reform.

Kate hoped for the chance to do exactly that in the U.S. Senate. She had given her husband the six children he wanted: the minimum Theodore Roosevelt recommended if America was to avoid "race suicide." At 42, she was unlikely to have another baby. Perhaps now, Dr. Hepburn, so much happier and more successful in his own work, would make some accommodation to Kate's career. But when she called with the news, he snapped sarcastically, "Well fine, Kit, when do we get our divorce?"

His reply closed the subject.

Young Tom Hepburn's marked nervousness in the spring of 1921 led Dr. and Mrs. Hepburn to attempt to "divert" him with a five-day trip to New York City in the company of Kathy and his godmother, Mary Towle. Two days after Easter, Aunty went with Tom and Kathy on the train to New York; she promised to send them back on Sunday, April 3.

Photographs of Tom in this period show a broad-shouldered, strikingly handsome and robust fifteen-year-old on the brink of intense young manhood. He seems to have inherited Mrs. Hepburn's generous mouth and nose and Dr. Hepburn's long, tapered fingers.

In a last family portrait, the towering oldest son, wearing a somber suit and tie, rests a large hand gently but protectively on Dick's shoulder. Seated in the lower left-hand corner, Kathy, at thirteen, seems to have outgrown her "Jimmy" phase. The urchin with a giant chip on her shoulder and a furious glint in her eye had metamorphosed into a graceful, astonishingly demure young lady in a diaphanous full-skirted white party dress.

Suddenly, when the Nineteenth Amendment became law, Mrs. Hepburn was no longer a pariah in Hartford and even something of a heroine. Rocks ceased to crash through the windows at night, bullies stopped picking on the children, and Kathy shook off the burden of having constantly to defend with her fists the family honor. There was another decisive change in Kathy's life: No longer the only girl in the family, she had two small sisters to look out for. The experience mellowed and matured her by bringing out the nurturing instincts she possessed in abundance.

Still, Tom assumed responsibility for his sister at the outset of their Greenwich Village holiday. That was the way the family had always done things. In New York, he purchased and took charge of two parlor car tickets for the return trip. Then they headed downtown to Aunty's old-fashioned little red brick house at 26 Charlton Street. The children knew the house well, having stayed there on numerous occasions with their mother.

Tom carried his suitcase up three flights to an attic storeroom stuffed with spare furniture, crates, and boxes. Beneath a sloping roof and exposed wooden beams, a freshly made cot filled a tiny alcove. An extra metal bedspring lay nearby.

Kathy slept in a cozy downstairs room on the same floor with Aunty, who was pleased to note that both young people, accustomed to a houseful of noisy children and babies, seemed delighted to have some privacy. Tom, enthusiastic about everything, told Aunty that the trip was the happiest experience of his life. Indeed, until Friday night all appeared to go wonderfully.

In two months, Mary Towle was to begin work for United States Attorney Col. William Hayward, wartime commander of the famous Black Tigers regiment. As Assistant U.S. Attorney for the

Southern District of New York, she would be the first woman to hold the post in a federal judicial district east of the Mississippi. Mindful of the example she would set, Aunty planned to pour all of her energy into the job; but she had plenty of time now to show her "niece" and "nephew" the sights. Others anxious to entertain Tom and Kathy included Charlie Hepburn's widow, Aunt Betty Newport; and Uncle Lloyd Hepburn, who promised to take them to the tower of the Woolworth Building on Saturday.

On Friday evening, Tom seemed to be in exceedingly high spirits when Aunty took the young people uptown for the 8:30 screening of a new Fox film based on Mark Twain's *A Connecticut Yankee in King Arthur's Court*. In the dark of the movie theater, however, Tom's mood shifted violently when the image of a hanging flashed onto the screen. Billed as a comedy, the silent film plunged the boy into a fit of agitation. Deeply shaken for the rest of the evening, Tom confided to Kathy that the hanging scene had given him "the horrors"—she alone would understand.

The year before, Kathy and Dr. Hepburn had discovered Tom hanging by the neck from a noose at home on Laurel Street. The boy insisted he was only trying the mock-hanging stunt Dr. Hepburn had often described from his own youth. Any parent would likely be appalled by the sight of a child playing with nooses—especially a troubled child of Tom's "nervous temperament" (Dr. Hepburn's words). In a family with a history of three suicides, the incident should have set off clanging alarm bells.

But the Hepburns—candid about sex and all things controversial—tended resolutely to avoid speaking of their most troubling thoughts and emotions; and it was certainly no different now. Eager to accept Tom's explanation, Dr. Hepburn instructed the boy not to try the stunt again. With that, the subject was closed; and father and son apparently said no more about it.

Between the time Tom, Kathy, and Aunty left the cinema and Saturday morning when Lloyd Hepburn was set to pick up his niece and nephew, Tom struggled to regain his composure.

Uncle Lloyd, the easy-going, light-hearted, ebullient brother—

so different from Charlie and Sewell—failed to recognize that anything might be wrong with the boy. After a day of sightseeing, he
returned Tom and Kathy to Aunty's. The dutiful older brother
marched upstairs to pack for the two of them in anticipation of the
evening's festivities, particularly concerned that everything be ready
to go first thing in the morning.

On Saturday night, he played his banjo and sang with Aunty
and Kathy in the living room. To Aunty's relief, "the horrors" of
the previous night appeared to have evaporated and Tom seemed
sincerely happy and expansive.

"You're my girl, aren't you?" he assured Kathy. "You're my
favorite girl in the whole world."

They all went to their rooms at ten o'clock.

Sometime after Tom shut the garret door, he removed his
trousers, carefully laid them out and put a suitcase on top, so they
would be neatly pressed in the morning. No one heard a sound from
the attic all night.

The next morning, Kathy enjoyed a leisurely breakfast with
Aunty. In deference to Mrs. Hepburn's rule of no set hour for the
children's breakfast, Aunty hesitated to rouse Tom. Finally, at nine,
she sent Kathy to see what was keeping him. Kathy dashed up three
flights and knocked on the attic door.

"Sleepyhead," she called in mock disapproval. Last night, Tom
had been so insistent they leave on time.

When Tom failed to respond, Kathy tried the doorknob, but
the garret was locked. Alarmed, she forced the door and went in.

She brushed against something, turned, and screamed. Tom
was hanging by the neck from a rafter. His knees were bent, his feet
touched the floor. His skin was a bluish-purple color.

Evidently, sometime during the night, he had ripped up a
bedsheet and braided the strips of cloth to improvise a rope. He tied
one end to the large metal bedspring lying on the floor. Then he
fashioned a noose, tossed the rope over a rafter, and fitted the noose
to his neck. He climbed up on a packing case and jumped. But the
rope was too long; Tom's feet hit ground and he found himself
standing again.

To judge by what he did next, he must have wanted to die very much.

Bending his knees and pitching his weight forward, Tom applied all his strength and will to pull at the metal bedspring and tighten the noose. He died of slow strangulation. Since his feet always touched the floor, there was nothing to prevent him stopping at almost any time—except the determination to destroy himself.

Alerted by Kathy's scream, Aunty raced up three flights. Hysterical, she sent Kathy to fetch Bertha Rembaugh two houses away—Aunt Bertha would know what to do. She told Mary Towle to notify the police.

When Patrolmen Peter O'Rourke and John Taylor arrived, they placed an emergency call to St. Vincent's Hospital. Shortly thereafter, Dr. Condy determined that Tom had been dead for three to five hours. That meant he had probably killed himself sometime between 4 and 6 a.m. Tom's body was removed to the morgue, where Dr. Gonzalez, the assistant medical examiner, registered the cause of death as "asphyxia by hanging (suicide)."

Meanwhile, the police asked Mary Towle some preliminary questions; when she said Tom had spent Saturday with Lloyd Hepburn, they summoned the uncle from West 184th Street.

One more telephone call remained to be made.

In Hartford, Bob Hepburn and his mother were lingering over breakfast when the telephone on the dining-room table rang. It was the day before Bob's eighth birthday.

Throughout his childhood, the telephone seemed to ring constantly; the small, freckle-faced boy with bright green eyes and a short Buster Brown haircut loved to watch his mother persuade callers to make a speech, appeal yet again to a hostile legislator, or perform some other dread task. Mrs. Hepburn called this being a good "manager." No matter how serious the crisis, in the child's adoring eyes she always appeared unruffled. Bob's mother never seemed to mind how much noise he or the other children made; but he knew that when she talked on the telephone, it was time to be quiet until she finished. This time, however, she said nothing.

She listened for a second or two. Then without a word, she

slumped face down like a rag doll onto the dining-room table. Still and silent, Kate lay there as if the life had been pounded out of her.

Eventually, she sat up and seemed herself again; but in that moment, the child had glimpsed something so terrible the image would haunt him for the rest of his years.

Dr. and Mrs. Hepburn, accompanied by Jo Bennett, were to arrive in New York on Sunday afternoon. Until then, the police extensively interviewed Kathy, Mary Towle, Bertha Rembaugh and Lloyd Hepburn.

No one doubted that Tom Hepburn had taken his own life. To those who had glimpsed the death scene, the only possible question was, why? Tom's death had been neither fast nor easy. What would make him want to destroy himself so badly? Had there been any warning signs? Could anything have been done to save him?

Kathy, it seemed, knew the most. She was closest to Tom, the one family member in whom he was known to confide. Before the Hepburns arrived, Kathy told the police everything she could remember about the events leading up to the discovery of the body. Still reeling from the shock, she detailed Tom's Friday night experience of "the horrors" and the "struggle" to recover afterward.

Mary Towle and Bertha Rembaugh provided information about Tom's history of nervous problems. They described the St. Vitus's dance that had afflicted him in childhood, and the recent bout of nervousness from which the trip had been intended to divert him.

Lloyd Hepburn struck a different note. Although he certainly didn't mention it now, in 1915 his brother had jumped out a window and impaled himself on the iron picket fence of an apartment house only a short walk away. At the time, the family had rejected the obvious conclusion that Charlie had taken his own life, and now again Lloyd instinctively recoiled from the taint of suicide. Lest his younger brother be blamed or stigmatized on account of the boy's actions, Lloyd's comments to police emphasized that Dr. and Mrs. Hepburn were "model parents."

Finally the Hepburns arrived. As they entered Mary Towle's

house, Dr. Hepburn waved away a crowd of newspaper reporters. Jo Bennett helped support the pale, grimly silent figure of Mrs. Hepburn.

Hardly were the Hepburns inside the door when, like many parents whose children have taken their own lives, Dr. Hepburn staunchly denied that Tom could have committed suicide. It was the first time that anyone had questioned the assumption that Tom had killed himself. Tom's body having been removed to the morgue, the death scene was merely an idea to Dr. Hepburn, not something he had actually witnessed. According to police statements, the father insisted that an intruder must have strangled his son and that the hanging was merely someone's clumsy attempt to cover up murder. Police checked out Dr. Hepburn's suspicions but found no evidence of an intruder.

Flailing for control—a position Dr. Hepburn did not like to find himself in—he demanded to inspect the attic. Perhaps some clue remained to give them all a better understanding of what had happened.

On the top floor, Dr. Hepburn studied the parlor car tickets his son had purchased for the return trip. He studied the trousers which still lay beneath the suitcase Tom had carefully rested on them the night before. And he studied the cot: There were no signs of turbulence, of twisting or turning. He claimed to have found traces of the exact spot on the sheet where the boy had lain undisturbed through the night.

When he came back downstairs, Dr. Hepburn reluctantly admitted to police that, yes, Tom probably had taken his own life. But he emphasized that only a "sudden, irresistible impulse," a "temporary mental aberration," could have driven the normal, happy, athletic, successful Tom to kill himself.

This stress on suddenness—as if Tom's death were a tragedy no one could have anticipated—was the father's attempt to let himself off the hook. Mindful of family whisperings that Nina Hepburn had driven Charlie to his death, and of Edith's tirades against his own harshness as a parent, Dr. Hepburn did his best to sever Tom's final act from the life that had preceded it.

"My son was normal in mind and body and the taking of his own life can be accounted for only from a medical point, that he was suddenly afflicted with adolescent insanity," Dr. Hepburn told newspaper reporters gathered outside the little red brick house. "He was an athlete, bronzed with health and exercise." According to Dr. Hepburn, young Tom had expressed the wish to "enter Yale University, to study surgery, and as he said 'follow in father's footsteps.'" Pressed on the medical examiner's statement that Tom had been a victim of St. Vitus's dance and "nervous all his life," Dr. Hepburn pointed out that the nervous twitchings associated with chorea had long been a thing of the past. He insisted the boy was "without a care in the world."

"God knows why he did it," said the father. "God alone knows why."

When Dr. Gonzalez filed his report, the Medical Examiner's Office released Tom's body to an undertaker for shipment to the New York–New Jersey Crematorium across the Hudson River. Dr. and Mrs. Hepburn, Kathy, and Jo Bennett accompanied the body on the ferry. They traveled in tense silence. Dr. Hepburn had long ago forbidden his bride to share her "innermost thoughts." Mrs. Hepburn suffered alone. Forgoing their usual physical intimacy, husband and wife stood pointedly apart from one another. Dr. Hepburn disliked tears and all other "manifestations of weakness."

Kathy had never seen her mother cry before. The child stood with Dr. Hepburn on the bow. About twenty feet away, Jo Bennett did what she could to comfort Mrs. Hepburn. But even with her closest friend, Mrs. Hepburn could not bring herself to say a word about Tom's death.

At the crematorium, Dr. Hepburn arranged to pick up Tom's ashes in Springfield, Massachusetts, for burial at the end of the week. He called his father at Shepherd's Delight and his brother Sewell in Annapolis before they read about Tom's suicide in the papers. The Reverend Hepburn, whose faith had been tested by Charlie's unnatural death, took the news very hard. Offering to preside over the burial, he said he would leave Maryland on Wednesday.

Dr. Hepburn returned to Hartford. Mrs. Hepburn and Kathy

remained in New York. Edith, who was scheduled to go to the White House on Wednesday along with other NWP leaders to confer with President Warren Harding about the suffragists' new goals, rushed to her sister's side as soon as she heard the news.

In New York, the Monday morning newspapers informed their readers that young Tom Hepburn's mother had been a leader of the Alice Paul militant suffragists. Her companion, Mrs. Bennett, had run for the U.S. Senate in 1920 on the Farmer-Labor ticket, which advocated the socialization of U.S. railroads and utilities. In a burst of utopian enthusiasm, Toscan Bennett, a founder of the radical National Labor Party, had recently announced plans to move his family to a "little soviet" in Katonah, New York, the Brookwood Labor College for the education of workers—and this, too, found its way into accounts of Tom's death.

In Hartford, however, young Tom was identified principally in terms of his father. "DR. HEPBURN'S SON, 15, HANGS HIMSELF WHILE VISITING IN NEW YORK" blasted the front-page headline of the *Hartford Courant* when Dr. Hepburn returned to Laurel Street.

Tom's suicide was the fourth such death in the family— although at this point only Dr. and Mrs. Hepburn and the Hookers may have known it. In the eugenic vocabulary of which Drs. Hepburn and Hooker were so fond, an individual with suicides on both sides of the family might be "doomed by heredity." Unwilling to be "bossed" by anyone or anything—certainly not by the past— Dr. Hepburn railed against the possibility that he had lost his son to a family fate beyond his own mastery.

Perhaps more than any parent who denies the fact of a child's suicide, Dr. Hepburn, obsessed with an ideal of control, needed to discover some other explanation. He found it as early as Monday when Kathy called from New York.

Mrs. Hepburn, a broken woman, remained taciturn and remote. She was in no mental condition to discuss with Kathy the meaning of what the child had seen. When Kathy called her father, by her own account she did not doubt that her brother had committed suicide; how could she, having observed the evidence of Tom's fierce struggle to destroy himself? Rather, she wanted to talk about the hanging episode the year before. Tom's death might have led anyone to review the earlier incident, especially his insistence that he was merely practicing a stunt. Kathy needed to talk out her feelings with her father.

But Dr. Hepburn's need was the greater. By the time the conversation ended, instead of concluding that the earlier hanging might well have been an aborted suicide attempt, Dr. Hepburn was insisting that Tom had died during a botched effort to try the old "hanging stunt." From then on, he would declare that a "mistake in judgment" had caused Tom's death. He wasted no time in releasing a detailed statement to the press, in which he adamantly denied that Tom had committed suicide.

"I am convinced that I have done the boy an injustice," he wrote. "In the first place, his whole life and temperament does not coincide with the suicide theory. While subject as a small boy to a few facial habits, he had outgrown them and was in the best mental condition that I have ever seen him. That he had no intention of taking his own life is borne out by the fact that he had purchased tickets and parlor car seats for his return to Hartford with his sister. He had fixed his trousers under a suitcase so that they might be freshly pressed for the journey. The bed showed that he had slept without restlessness, for it was only depressed in the spot where he lay. He left no note or sign of mental distress. To theorize that a normal healthy boy committed suicide after a good night's sleep is unbelievable.

"I am now convinced that the boy was the victim of an accident as the result of a foolish stunt. I had entirely forgotten that he considered himself an expert in hanging by the neck in such a way as to look as if he were dying, to the entertainment of his brothers and sisters. He used to fix a bow-knot in the rope and untie it in time to prevent being choked. I warned him about a year ago of the danger of this stunt, but had not thought of it since that time.

"Friday night he saw a moving picture in which I am told there is the picture of a hanging. That must have recalled his old stunt, and when he awoke the next morning he decided to rehearse it for a performance when he got home. He could find only a strip of cotton cloth to use, and the material was such that his bow knot did not slip as he expected. And so the poor boy was strangled to death as the result of a boyish idea.

"The accident theory would explain all the findings. Tom's sister called me up today to recall to my mind his hanging stunt of a year ago, and volunteered the same explanation at which I had arrived. In view of the fact that I have given the world my opinion that the boy committed suicide, and have thereby cast a blot upon his memory, I feel anxious to repair this damage in so far as I am able."

Dr. Hepburn's statement contained a jarring contradiction. One moment he referred to Tom's stunt as though it were something the boy often did for the entertainment of the other children, and the next he spoke about a seemingly isolated incident of the previous year which he claimed to have forgotten until Kathy reminded him of it. The discrepancy betrays Dr. Hepburn's terrible struggle to deny the obvious reality of his son's suicide.

Dr. Hepburn's account was at odds with the evidence of everything Kathy had just seen with her own eyes; no wonder she didn't believe it. It required that no further mention be made of her brother's experience of "the horrors" at the movie theater; indeed, Tom's acute agitation over the last few months would undermine Dr. Hepburn's point that the happy, carefree boy had merely been engaging in a bit of fun. And it required Kathy to suppress her memory of the death scene. The picture her father painted left out key specifics— the bent knees, the feet touching the floor. Far from swift and unanticipated, Tom's death had been agonizingly slow and deliberate. His only "mistake in judgment" had been to fashion a rope too long, so that he had to pitch his weight forward to tug at the metal bedspring and tighten the noose. According to police, the boy had done "hard work to die."

While the train tickets, the trousers neatly pressed beneath the suitcase, and the undisturbed bed did indeed suggest an intention to go home that morning, Dr. Hepburn omitted an essential detail: Tom had ripped up a bedsheet and painstakingly braided the strips of cloth to improvise a rope. Anyone acquainted with the kind, meticulous, responsible boy knew that under normal circumstances he would never have deliberately destroyed his hostess's property.

At a moment when Kathy needed to try to come to terms with the terrifying image of her brother's self-destruction and the painful questions it raised, other pressures worked on the traumatized thirteen-year-old to revise that image, to blur and erase details that contradicted Dr. Hepburn. Eventually, by her own account she was no longer certain of exactly what she had seen or experienced. Her memories took on a nightmarish cast. One story in particular, shot through with feelings of helplessness and anxiety, sounds unmistakably like the dream it probably was. In contrast to Kathy's own initial testimony, in this later version Mary Towle did not rush upstairs when Kathy screamed upon opening the attic door. Instead, hoping to protect the highly-strung, emotional Aunty, Kathy dashed across the street to a house with a doctor's sign.

A woman opened the door a crack. Kathy never saw her fully.

"My brother's dead," Kathy called.

At first the woman said nothing, then: "What?"

"My brother—he's dead."

"Then the doctor can't help him, can he?"

"No."

The woman slammed the door, leaving the frantic child to conclude that, yes, it was "too late for the doctor to help."

Like the girl in the dream, Kathy herself finally accepted that forcing the doctor—Dr. Hepburn, that is—to confront the actual death scene would do nothing to bring Tom back to life. Helpless to save her brother, she could still perhaps protect her father. Displaced in the dream, the desire to protect Aunty probably expressed Kathy's wish to shield Dr. Hepburn from the pain and guilt associated with his son's suicide. If the dream eventually came to seem like truth, that may have been because it so perfectly articulated the child's motive for remaining silent.

Although Kathy may have seemed the weaker partner in their new relationship, the decision to protect her father attested to prodigious inner strength. Sensing Dr. Hepburn's desperate need to deny the truth, Kathy sacrificed whatever chance to heal she might have had. Their pact of silence, and the terrible burden of suppressing her most troubling memories and emotions, left Kathy with questions that would drive her for the rest of her life.

Dr. Hepburn must have sensed that Kathy knew a truth he could not bear to live with; he was careful never to discuss Tom's death with her again. He did discuss it with his son Bob in later years but probably only because with Bob—who had been too young to understand fully at the time—he felt relatively free to tell the story according to his own specifications.

After Dr. Hepburn released his statement to the press on Monday afternoon, he called the Reverend Hepburn and his brothers Lloyd and Sewell to explain that Tom's death had not been a suicide after all. Dr. Hepburn's protestations of remorse for having "cast a blot" on Tom's memory were probably a way of transferring guilt from things too painful to deal with directly: Had Edith been correct that he pushed his son too hard? Worse, had he ignored the boy's cry for help the year before?

By the time Mrs. Hepburn and Kathy returned to Hartford, history had been revised, the stigma of suicide lifted. On Tuesday morning, April 5, the text of Dr. Hepburn's statement appeared in the *New York Times* under the headline "SAYS SON'S HANGING WAS BOYISH 'STUNT'".

In Annapolis, Dr. Sewell Hepburn was in emotional turmoil.

Ill and depressed in the years since Charlie's suicide, Sewell had stopped working for a time. He had been a frequent visitor to Hartford, where he received treatment from his brother Tom for the long-term effects of syphilis. At Dr. Tom Hepburn's urging, Sewell had recently resumed his own active medical practice.

First Charlie, now young Tom had succumbed to what was beginning to seem like a family fate. Both were oldest sons with all the expectations and responsibility that entailed; both had finally cracked under the pressure. In 1915, the Hepburns had refused to accept that Charlie had taken his own life; and now again, young Tom's death was being written off as an accident. About nine o'clock on Tuesday night, Sewell told his wife, Annie, that he had to go out for an hour or so to make house calls. Their seventeen-year-old daughter Eleanor was away at St. Hilda's Hall in Charlestown, West Virginia. Shortly after her husband left, Annie went upstairs and fell asleep waiting for him.

Some time late that night, Sewell closed himself in the garage of his home at 54 State Circle. He sat in the driver's seat of his car with the motor running. When Annie found him there in the early morning hours, he was dead.

At Shepherd's Delight the next morning, the Reverend Hepburn was about to leave for Hartford when he received word of his son's "sudden death." Every detail pointed to the conclusion that Sewell had taken his own life, yet he was reported to have suffered a fatal heart attack while "doing some work on the car" in the middle of the night. Dr. J. O. Purvis, a close family friend, did his best to dispel the specter of suicide with the explanation that syphilis had weakened the blood vessel walls, resulting in "acute dilation" of the heart. There was no autopsy.

Hands shaking, the Reverend Hepburn hitched his mare Mayfly to the buggy. He left for Annapolis to bury Sewell at Cedar Bluff Cemetery on Friday. Lloyd Hepburn promised to meet him there. The trip to Connecticut to bury young Tom was postponed until the following week.

Meanwhile, Bob Hepburn accompanied his father to the crematorium in Springfield, Massachusetts. When the question of an urn arose, Dr. Hepburn barked that he didn't believe in "any fancy thing to control the ashes." They drove home with Tom's remains in a candy box.

Several days later, at Cedar Hill Cemetery in Hartford, the Reverend Hepburn said a short prayer over the grave where Dr. and Mrs. Hepburn and the children buried the ashes. The parents avoided mentioning Tom after that.

"What is past is past."

PART TWO

I have taken up the heat of life from her.

H. Phelps Putnam

E L E V E N

I t seemed to young Bob Hepburn that his sister had never acted that way before. Suddenly that spring, Kathy, now fourteen, went to bed early each night and rose at 5:30 a.m. before anyone else in the Laurel Street house was up. Careful not to wake the others, she slipped downstairs and ate breakfast alone. Whenever Bob got out of bed, he knew he would find Kathy bent over her desk, "furiously attacking her studies" with a "great seriousness" and "tremendous drive" she had never before shown for schoolwork.

Kathy was so immersed in her books she seemed oblivious to the little boy watching her with such perplexity; or was she only pretending? Her blue eyes remained downcast, riveted to the page.

Bob brooded endlessly about what he later described as Kathy's "sea change" after Tom died. The close contact with death had transformed her. Kathy had always been very talkative with her brothers and sisters; now suddenly she was silent, moody, and withdrawn. She avoided situations like the breakfast table where she would have to speak; schoolbooks allowed her to escape her brothers' painful questions.

Bob wondered about the relationship Kathy had tacitly entered into with Dr. and Mrs. Hepburn. Whatever had happened in New York had created a mysterious bond that seemed to exclude the other children; Kathy and her parents shared a secret the others were not privy to. Seemingly keen to distance herself, Kathy referred to her brothers, as well as the baby sisters, as "my kids." She called her father and mother "my friends."

The Hepburns had produced their family in carefully spaced pairs: Tom and Kathy, Dick and Bob, Marion and Peg. In Tom's absence, the dynamics shifted drastically as Kathy formed a new grouping with Dr. and Mrs. Hepburn; they talked quietly and spent time together in ways that forever set them apart from the rest of the household. They did not, however, talk about young Tom.

When the family returned from burying the ashes, Dr. Hepburn insisted that life go on as if nothing had changed. Mrs. Hepburn could not bring herself to utter Tom's name; when she absolutely had to refer to him, she would speak cryptically of her child who had "left home" or "gone away." With friends like Jo Bennett, Mrs. Hepburn tensed up visibly at any mention of Tom or the circumstances of his death; and people quickly learned to avoid the subject.

"Don't regret your daily chores," Mrs. Hepburn would tell the children. "They are what keep you from going insane."

Dr. Hepburn, for his part, lost himself in work, zealously courting affiliations at Bristol, New Britain, Rockville, and other Connecticut hospitals. Eager to deny what the suicides of two brothers and a son seemed to say about his Powell "inheritance," he dreamed of building a grand new house in Connecticut that would finally "put this family back on the map!"

In the weeks that followed Tom's death, Kathy bravely returned to the Oxford School to finish the ninth grade; but the questions and curiosity of her classmates proved unbearable, and for all her frantic studying she could not seem to keep up with the work.

It was not that anyone doubted Dr. Hepburn's "accident" theory; on the contrary, throughout Hartford there was palpable relief at the father's having dispelled the specter of suicide. Young people terrified by the thought that Tom's death could possibly have been intentional, and parents fearful that their own children might do something similar, were eager to accept that a "mistake in judgment" had caused the boy to die. Kathy, who knew differently, could hardly describe the scene in the attic to anyone; she could not talk about what had really happened for fear of hurting her father.

Such reticence was foreign to her. At a moment when Kathy

most needed their friendship, her pact of silence cut her off from the other girls. Brought up to be forthright and always to speak her mind, now she had no choice but to isolate herself emotionally. Jo Bennett thought that Kathy "got the brunt" of Tom's death.

The child's mind played tricks on her. As if to eliminate the wrenching thought that something might have been done to save Tom before he took his own life, she eventually forgot that an entire day had separated his Friday night experience of "the horrors" and her discovery of the body Sunday morning. Her unspoken doubts and fears seemed to focus on one question: She wondered whether Tom had really said, "You're my girl, aren't you? You're my favorite girl in the whole world" before going upstairs to die, or whether she had only imagined that he had. After what Tom had done, it was important for her to know that he had loved her and had not meant to hurt her.

Never one to mince words, Edith knew that Tom had taken his own life; but she did not share Kathy's willingness to protect Dr. Hepburn. At this point, among people close to the Hepburns, Edith alone knew that Tom was the fourth suicide, Sewell the fifth; she pulled back in horror as though to protect her own family from contagion. After nine summers with the Hepburns at Fenwick, Edith refused to return. She and Dr. Hooker built their own cottage, Little Island Camp, in Greenville, Maine. At a moment when, more than ever, Mrs. Hepburn needed the emotional comfort only Edith could provide, her departure would have been devastating; it was a blistering indictment against Dr. Hepburn for having ignored her warnings.

Many years before this, the deaths of Fred and Charlie Houghton had forged a powerful bond between the sisters; Tom's suicide exploded that bond forever. Edith, the one person Mrs. Hepburn had always been able to talk to in complete frankness and sympathy, abruptly flew out of her life. Now, in effect, Mrs. Hepburn lost a sister as well as a son; they would see each other again certainly, but the old intimacy was gone.

To make matters worse, that May when Edith completed the manuscript for *The Laws of Sex*, she included a diatribe against parents whose harshness causes children to suffer "world-weariness, sometimes culminating in suicide." Although Edith did not name names, her brother-in-law would know precisely who she had in mind. In a passage that would raise eyebrows when the book was published later that year, Edith speculated that some adolescent suicides can be traced to an adult's stern warnings that masturbation leads to "St. Vitus's dance or a characteristic facial expression."

After years of locking horns with Edith, Dr. Hepburn seemed relieved to be rid of her. He bought out Dr. Hooker's interest in Fenwick, which had been vastly improved in recent years with the installation of electricity and plumbing. The Hepburns told friends that Don Hooker's long-standing love of the Maine woods and mountains had caused him to decide to spend summers there. But the explanation must have rung false to anyone who knew the sisters. That Edith would so frivolously abandon Kate, particularly at a time like this, was unimaginable.

"I was really lonesome," said Mrs. Hepburn of that first summer at Fenwick without Tom or Edith. "I pictured the people in the other homes in a warm happy atmosphere. The wind howled and the waves dashed on the shore, and there I was alone." In a noisy house where everyone could always hear everyone else, Mrs. Hepburn felt the absences all the more deeply. Two months after her son's death, the isolation was so excruciating that she feared she was losing her mind.

Dr. Hepburn was in Hartford throughout the week; Mrs. Day, Jo's mother, had left Fenwick in 1917; and Jo had gone off to live at the Brookwood Labor College in Katonah, New York, with her husband and their two daughters. Eager to fill the empty places at her large table with anyone who might agree to come, Mrs. Hepburn astonished her neighbors with a barrage of invitations to bridge luncheons. It had long been the custom among many conservative Fenwick residents to look the other way when the radical Mrs. Hepburn and Mrs. Hooker, arm in arm, passed on the stony beach. But now, the neighbors came anyway; and when they did not return her invitations, she invited them again and again until they did.

By her own account, she simply could not bear to be alone with her thoughts. In the many unavoidable hours of solitude, she would comb over the summer of 1920, struggling to reassure herself that her child-rearing methods had worked and that young Tom, looking out for the smaller children, had maintained perfect harmony. The sight of a child lighting a smoky kerosene lamp convinced her that the whole house might suddenly go up in flame. She ordered heavy ropes installed in every room on the third floor, so that the children could jump out the windows and let themselves down to safety.

In an attempt to exhaust herself physically, Mrs. Hepburn took up fancy diving. On one occasion, eschewing the long black stockings that were *de rigueur* for the bathing costume of any proper lady, she strode bare-legged to the Fenwick pier diving board. Just when she had started to gain social acceptance in the community, her natural rebelliousness jeopardized everything. By the time she realized that she was creating a scandal among the neighbors, it seemed too late to turn back.

Pretending not to notice, she gave her customary diving exhibition, including the back jack-knife and Flying Dutchman, then strode back to the cottage as if nothing were wrong. It is a measure of how much Mrs. Hepburn's life had changed, however, that she dared not appear without the long black stockings again.

Kathy, too, struggled to exhaust herself physically; but unlike her mother, she seemed to crave solitude. The gaunt, nervous, unreachable, suspicious girl forced most people to keep their distance.

At the shore, Kathy continued her habit of rising before anyone else. But here, it was impossible to conceal the sounds of rapid footsteps on creaking floorboards. When she threw open the front door, the cries of fishhawks and gulls flew in with a gust of sea breeze. To Bob, it seemed that the same "tremendous drive" that had compelled Kathy to study so furiously in the weeks after Tom's death infused just about everything she did that summer.

Daily she propelled herself through the Fenwick golf course, whose fourth hole ran by the tiny bell tower of St. Mary's-by-the-Sea, where Kathy had begun to attend Sunday services, often with Aunty Towle. She played golf with lightning speed like her father, who regularly joined her on weekends. "Hep races along as though he were trying to catch a train," Mrs. Hepburn would say, smiling at the sight of father and daughter, in matching jodhpurs, swinging golf clubs in the distance. "Kathy behaves the same way."

Watching his sister, Bob sensed that somehow she was trying to become Tom.

Eventually, there was talk that Kathy planned to be a doctor as Tom would have been had he lived. Lest there remain any doubt about her intentions, Kathy abandoned her May 12 birthdate, appropriating Tom's birthday for her own; and her parents cooperated with the practice. Many decades later, people would still believe, and biographers record, that she was born on November 8.

In the aftermath of Tom's death, Kathy became Dr. Hepburn's clear favorite, leaving Mrs. Hepburn to compensate their sons by showering them with affection. Because Dr. Hepburn would never judge a girl as harshly as he did the boys, it was easier for him to accept Kathy as Tom's replacement. However much they tried, Dick and Bob simply could not measure up to the idealized "perfect son" Tom became in their father's memory.

"Tom was the best of the children," Dr. Hepburn once remarked to Bob, although he had certainly never praised the boy when he was alive.

As Kathy fought to make herself a champion athlete, she usurped Dick's position as oldest "son". The sensitive, handsome nine-year-old would often have occasion to wonder why his father seemed so much closer to Kathy and always took her side; and she would wonder whether she had ruined Dick's life.

As the summer drew to a close, Kathy recoiled at the prospect of facing her classmates' questions again, so Dr. Hepburn agreed to allow her to withdraw from the Oxford School; she would be tutored privately as Mrs. Hepburn had been when she was Kathy's age. It seems a curious decision, especially when one considers that Dr. Hepburn continued to insist that Tom's death had been an accident; if he really believed that, why should he have encouraged his daughter to isolate herself from girls she had known all her life? Ostensibly, the reason was that her best friends were both going off to boarding school in Simsbury, Connecticut, and Kathy didn't want to be at

Oxford without them. Also, freed from a rigid schedule of classes, Kathy would have time to take daily lessons with the golf pro at the Hartford Golf Club on Asylum Avenue.

As always, however, much went pointedly unspoken in the Hepburn household, and although father and daughter avoided discussing it, there could be no disregarding the "sea change" that even her eight-year-old brother had noticed; far from having improved during the summer, Kathy seemed only to have withdrawn more deeply into herself.

Suddenly, as if something had clicked in Mrs. Hepburn's memory, she announced that Kathy must prepare for the Bryn Mawr entrance exams.

When Dick and Bob returned to school in September, their sister remained at home. For the next three years, in Hartford, in a neighborhood where she knew almost everyone, Kathy lived a strange, lonely existence, cut off from almost all young people outside the family.

Although Kathy wasn't old enough to get a driver's license, her mother allowed her to take the car, an old Reo, during the day. The precedent was Mrs. Day's having permitted Jo to drive from the age of eleven. When Kathy was finished with her daily tutoring sessions and golf lessons, she frequently spent hours alone in a local movie theater, paying for tickets with money earned raking leaves, shoveling snow, and mowing lawns.

Instead of friends her own age, there was only her mother's garrulous Irish seamstress, Mary Ryan, to talk to; companionless, Kathy waited impatiently all week for her Thursday visits. On other days, when Dick and Bob finally came home, Kathy entertained them with a miniature theater she had constructed in a wooden box. Narrating the stories and fairy tales she had begun to invent while her brothers were at school, Kathy fit cardboard actors and bits of delicately painted scenery into grooves cut in the tiny green stage.

Evidently, the silence and denial that shrouded Tom's suicide did not eliminate the agonizing fears and doubts associated with it. Time and solitude could not make the haunting images go away. Prohibited from dealing directly with the enigmatic, nightmarish scene she had discovered when she broke into Mary Towle's attic, Kathy developed an obsession with forbidden doors.

In early spring, sometime around the anniversary of Tom's suicide, she began to break into summer cottages at Fenwick before they had been opened for the season. She forced doors, windows, and skylights. Far from being acts of gratuitous mischief, the break-ins allowed Kathy to replay terrifying feelings she was not supposed to think, let alone talk, about.

Theft was never the aim. Like many people who have suffered a traumatic experience, Kathy was drawn to repeat a version of that experience in an attempt to master it. At Fenwick, she sought only to explore the dark, silent premises of someone else's house, then depart without consequence. Each break-in gave the child an opportunity to repeat the terrible moment in New York when she forced the attic door and entered; this time, however, everything was going to be all right.

Her accomplice in all this was the spunky Ali Barbour, on Easter vacation from boarding school. Physically fearless, Kathy probably would never have dared to become a housebreaker without Ali, daughter of one of Hartford's wealthiest families, to cheer her on. Kathy entered however she could, then let Ali in, often by the front door. On one occasion, she came close to death when she plunged through a skylight and landed in the third-floor corridor, narrowly missing a straight drop between circling banisters to the marble ground floor.

In addition to their exploits as housebreakers, Kathy and Ali were part of a girl gang known as the Mystic Pigs; they attracted considerable notoriety at Fenwick when, Edith-style, they tied up a younger girl with ropes, abandoning her in a deserted shack.

With Ali, her protector, present at the shore, Kathy began to experience some relief from the isolation that characterized her life in Hartford during the school year. They revived Edith's tradition of staging theatrical productions at Fenwick. When it was announced at St. Mary's-by-the-Sea, where Ali's father played the organ, that a Navajo Indian reservation in New Mexico needed $75 for a Victrola, the girls mounted a show to raise the money. Dick

Hepburn wrote a scenario based on *Beauty and the Beast*. Mrs. Hepburn brought a trunk of old costumes that had been stored away in Hartford after Edith's departure. Ali's mother volunteered her cottage porch for a stage; the audience could sit on the lawn. Tickets sold for a dollar, prompting one parent to withdraw his daughter from the company when Ali, starring as Beauty, refused to lower the price. Kathy, in the role of the Beast, wore a grey flannel bag over her head, red glass eyes, long floppy grey ass-ears, and white cardboard tusks.

For nearly two years after young Tom's suicide, Mrs. Hepburn had withdrawn from public life. While Mrs. Hooker went on to fight alongside Alice Paul for an Equal Rights Amendment to the constitution, an emotionally shattered Mrs. Hepburn occupied a good deal of her time playing bridge with the sort of women she had previously scorned. In a sense, she had never completely come alive again after collapsing on the dining-room table the day Kathy discovered Tom's body in Mary Towle's attic.

Finally, in January 1923, Jo Bennett and Katharine Beach Day, hoping to draw Mrs. Hepburn back into the fray, persuaded her to dine with them and Margaret Sanger, the leader of a movement to legalize birth control and make it available to all women. Mrs. Sanger had come to Hartford to launch a battle in the legislature to change a Connecticut law, the most restrictive in the nation, which made it illegal to prescribe or use any form of birth control. Mrs. Bennett and Mrs. Day were convinced that Mrs. Hepburn's skills and experience in state politics would prove invaluable; besides, it would do her a world of good to become politically involved again.

As far as anyone knew, Mrs. Hepburn's prior acquaintance with Mrs. Sanger had been limited to a support dinner at the Brevoort Hotel in Greenwich Village in 1916 on the eve of Mrs. Sanger's trial for transmitting "indecent" literature through the U.S. mails. Mrs. Hepburn had attended the event as the guest of Mrs. Day, an early and consistent financial backer of Margaret Sanger. At the time, no one had guessed that Mrs. Hepburn and Mrs. Sanger were not strangers, having met in Nellie Abbott's cottage at Cloverbank in 1897, the summer after Charlie Houghton committed suicide.

Margaret's older sister was Mary Higgins, Nellie Abbott's maid. That summer, Kate and Edith and several friends had been listening to a singer, Miss Milligan, in the Abbott living room, when young Margaret, refusing to remain in the servants' quarters, boldly joined the other young people. Having grown up poor in Corning where the Houghton name was all, Margaret made a point of positioning herself with Kate and Edith. Mary Higgins recorded the occasion in her diary.

A quarter of a century later, Margaret Sanger was a figure of international renown, a celebrated author, speaker, and ideologue, who hobnobbed with leading writers, artists, and intellectuals. But her sister still worked as Nellie Abbott's maid at Cloverbank; and Margaret avidly corresponded with her, keeping up on Houghton family gossip. More than most people could have possibly understood, for all of Margaret's sophistication it still meant the world to her to sit on the sofa with Amory Houghton, Jr.'s niece, whom she regarded as a kind of royalty.

Mrs. Hepburn, for her part, seems to have been considerably less sure of how she felt about encountering this figure from her past. Margaret Sanger had intimate knowledge of a part of her life which she had worked very hard to bury. The maid's sister knew the history of suicide in Mrs. Hepburn's family. She alone among the women in Mrs. Hepburn's circle was capable of making the dreaded connection between that history and the circumstances of Tom's death; she alone held the threat of exposure.

Yet it was Margaret Sanger who finally drew Mrs. Hepburn out of her self-exile from political activism. Making an alliance with Mrs. Sanger, the person she would have seemed most likely to avoid, was a very strange gesture for a woman as secretive as Mrs. Hepburn. Nonetheless, for the first time since 1921, she agreed to commit herself to a cause in which she believed passionately. She would work on Mrs. Sanger's behalf, petitioning the state legislature much as she had done during the fight for the vote.

Later, she would permit birth control publicity, with a strong eugenic slant, to advertise the Hepburns as a model family. For Mrs. Hepburn, there appears to have been an element of denial in all of this: If Margaret Sanger, the one outsider who knew the story of her family background, accepted that she and Dr. Hepburn were the sort of superior people who should breed, perhaps it was really true; perhaps young Tom had not taken his own life as her father and uncle had unquestionably done.

Despite Mrs. Hepburn's startling new involvement with Margaret Sanger, she still shrank from discussing her background with her own children even when it might have relieved some of the terrible pressures on them after Tom's death.

As the time approached for Kathy to follow Mrs. Hepburn's footsteps to Bryn Mawr, the precedent of her brilliant mother seemed utterly overwhelming; how could she ever live up to it? Kathy had no inkling of the academic difficulties Mrs. Hepburn had experienced, or the grave personal problems that had nearly prevented her from earning a degree. It might have helped her to know something about that history, but unreservedly as Mrs. Hepburn loved her children she simply could not bring herself to talk about the past. The day Mrs. Hepburn was to take her daughter to see Bryn Mawr (as Carrie Houghton had escorted her in 1894), Kathy was so nervous that she had a serious automobile accident in the morning. The front of the old Reo was destroyed when she collided with another car and knocked over a police telephone on Asylum Avenue.

Kathy took the Bryn Mawr entrance exam in two parts, and for all her anxiety she did considerably better than her mother had. In June 1924, three years after Tom's death, Kathy was admitted with "no conditions", one of thirteen daughters of Bryn Mawr alumnae in her class. She asked to live in the gray stone Pembroke West dormitory, where her mother and Edith had once held court.

Mindful that campus life might prove something of a shock after three years in isolation, Dr. and Mrs. Hepburn encouraged Kathy to take the most expensive private suite. As a further safeguard, Mrs. Hepburn had persuaded Ali Barbour to apply, although Ali had no interest in college and dropped out after a year; she and Kathy were among six Connecticut girls accepted.

That June, Mrs. Hepburn returned to Bryn Mawr for the twenty-fifth reunion of the class of 1899. It was a time for taking stock, for assessing what she and her classmates had accomplished in a quarter of a century. Once before she had arrived with a terrible secret, and it was no different this time. Then she had one suicide to conceal; now there were five, including that of her own son. Somehow, Mrs. Hepburn needed to face the other women in her class before she sent her daughter to Bryn Mawr.

When the alumnae procession emerged from the dark cavern of Pembroke Arch, Katharine Houghton Hepburn startled onlookers with her costume of tight black satin breeches and short matching jacket. Aware that many in her daughter's generation believed the suffrage struggle had been a waste of time when it was personal and sexual freedom, not the vote, that women needed, Mrs. Hepburn wore a self-mocking banner across her chest: "OATS FOR WOMEN." And when she participated in the class debate over the battle for enfranchisement, she insisted on taking the position: "The Nineteenth Amendment is a failure." Mrs. Hepburn argued the point with such fervor and conviction that one might almost have wondered whether she really meant it.

T W E L V E

I n the early years of this century, shortly after Kate and Edith Houghton left Bryn Mawr, Carey Thomas poured much of her passion and energy into the construction of the turreted Jacobean library and monastic cloister, where she planned to be buried in a tomb modeled on that of Bishop Fernandez de Madrigal at the Cathedral of Avila.

She raised money. She met with architects. She quarreled with trustees. She pored over drawings and sepia photographs of the world's great cloisters. She traveled to Europe with a flexible steel tape measure to take measurements in the Wadham College dining hall at Oxford, the Doge's Palace in Venice, the Germanische Museum in Nuremberg, and other dramatic settings. She ordered copies of gargoyles, bronze tablets, fountainheads—anything that might prove useful when construction began on the building intended to communicate her idea of Bryn Mawr to future generations.

In 1906, black-robed students and faculty first walked up the broad teakwood stairway to the cavernous reading room, with its vaulted roof, rows of tall desks, and massive windows decorated with tracery. The quiet, stately arched cloister at the Library's center embodied Carey Thomas's vision of a sheltered, hermetically sealed existence far from the doings of "horrid" men. In the courtyard arcade, a fountain spouted a single clear jet of water symbolizing the purity and tranquility that, in Thomas's view, were among the pleasures of a woman scholar's life.

On May Day 1924, two years after she retired as president at the age of sixty-five, Carey Thomas, on her way to see a student performance in the cloister, was denied admission to the Library. A freshman, failing to recognize her, refused to let her in without a ticket. This awkward moment encapsulated the enormous changes that had taken place at Bryn Mawr since the end of the war.

Carey Thomas continued to occupy the Deanery after she stepped down, but the "quiet lady in black" no longer set the college standard; in a decade when most well-to-do American families expected to send their daughters to college, Miss Thomas, and the ideals and aspirations she stood for, seemed like relics of a vanished world. The woman scholar's sheltered life, cut off from intimacy with men during college and after, held little appeal to many post-war college women mesmerized by flappers and the Jazz Age.

"I think a woman gets more happiness out of being gay, light-hearted, unconventional mistress of her own fate, than out of a career that calls for hard work, intellectual pessimism, and loneliness," said Zelda Fitzgerald in 1924. "I don't want my daughter to be a genius, I want her to be a flapper, because flappers are brave and gay and beautiful." Far from the shining examples they once had seemed, scholars like Carey Thomas, and professionals like Mary Towle and Florence Sabin, were mocked as "dried-up old maids" or "female celibates, women too refined to have a husband."

At Bryn Mawr, the 1925 appointment of Helen Taft Manning as dean of the college appeared to signal a shift in values. The daughter of former U.S. President William Howard Taft, and an attractive woman with two children and a handsome, successful husband, Professor Frederick Johnson Manning of Swarthmore, Dean Manning offered proof that the new woman could "have it all"—both marriage and a demanding career. Lest she seem to side with the widespread backlash among young people against politics and social responsibility, Helen Taft Manning told Bryn Mawr girls that she found post-war youth "disappointing." She noted with dismay that instead of taking an interest in progressive issues as their mothers' generation had, young women of the 1920s seemed interested mainly in having fun, meeting men, and cultivating experience for its own sake.

"There are too many 'drink-deepers' among us," Dean Manning warned, "and they are taken too seriously."

The single clear jet of water still spouted from the cloister fountain when seventeen-year-old Kate Hepburn (as Kathy would call herself from now on) arrived at Bryn Mawr on Monday, September 29, 1924; but the secluded, self-enclosed existence it symbolized was in the process of disappearing. Almost every month, it seemed, the old rules and traditions were eroded a little further.

Student costume was the most visible change from Mrs. Hepburn's and Mrs. Hooker's day. On campus, girls no longer wore the traditional black cap and gown that had once set the scholar apart from other young women. Students came to class in skirts and sweaters, often with dirty tennis shoes and heavy woolen socks. Meanwhile, the *College News* fed fantasies with illustrated advertisements for flapper outfits on sale in local stores for one's off-campus sprees.

After several decades of women's struggle, post-war college women preferred causes like smoking and the right to seek pleasure off-campus. Mrs. Hooker had insisted that "tobacco smoking by women is proof of their subjugation to men"; but to Kate's generation, a cigarette signified the personal liberation associated with sexual awakening. When President Marion Edwards Park, an 1898 Bryn Mawr graduate, acquiesced by allowing girls to smoke in the dormitory reception rooms known as "showcases," the students hailed it as "a very liberal move." Other voices in the surrounding community, indeed throughout the nation, criticized Carey Thomas's successor for having sanctioned what she had failed to suppress.

President Park did not, however, acquiesce to demands that men be permitted to attend Bryn Mawr dances. When Ali Barbour dragged Kate Hepburn to the welcoming Freshman Dance at 8 p.m. on Saturday, October 4 in the college gymnasium, their only potential partners were other girls.

Fearful that girls would sneak into the village to meet men, Marion Edwards Park strictly required students to sign out whenever they left the campus in the evening, giving the name of their hostess and the precise time they expected to return before closing hours. Girls were forbidden to own an automobile lest they use it as a "mobile room" for encounters with the opposite sex.

For all that, according to Kate's classmate Alice Palache, from the first there were quite a few "fast girls" in their class, identifiable by a penchant for cigarettes and lipstick; they regularly met men in Philadelphia. Back on campus, over midnight cups of muggle—a sickeningly sweet concoction of cocoa and condensed milk heated on a gas jet—fast girls regaled classmates with stories of having "gone the limit," as sexual intercourse was called.

That November of Kate's freshman year, there was much fanfare when Margaret Sanger appeared at Taylor Hall, under the auspices of the Liberal Club. To members of Mrs. Hepburn's and Mrs. Hooker's generation, Margaret Sanger brought the message that birth control would benefit society by lowering the population of the defective, the feeble-minded, and the unfit, allowing America to produce a "race of thoroughbreds." To post-war college women, however, Mrs. Sanger stood for quite a different idea: that marriage must be something more than an institution for procreation. Sexual pleasure was every woman's right. "She must not seek to crush down the passion which wells up from her deepest nature. On the contrary: she should and must abandon herself to it utterly," Mrs. Sanger wrote in her book *Happiness in Marriage* (1926).

During one of Kate's many visits to Baltimore during her Bryn Mawr years, Mrs. Hooker brought her to a meeting of NWP activists, where the conversation turned to the upcoming generation.

"Now what is it that college girls want most?" Edith asked her niece, expecting Kate to list the social reforms superior young women were especially keen to accomplish.

"They want to fall in love and get married!" Kate gleefully blurted out.

Mrs. Hooker and her colleagues were appalled; but Kate spoke for many in her generation who were eager to discover, in Margaret Sanger's words, "that joyful ecstasy which is the legitimate fruit of marriage."

Already, Ali Barbour, Kate's best friend, had met the man she wanted to marry. During freshman year, she took up with Moreau D. Brown, a Yale man from Philadelphia, who planned on a banking career at Brown Brothers, the family firm; and soon, Ali was one of the girls who regularly left campus on weekends to spend time with their beaux. Never really having wanted to go to Bryn Mawr in the first place, Ali rhapsodized about leaving school at the end of spring semester to become engaged.

That year, unlike the exuberant Ali Barbour, Kate seemed to shrink from all that life had to offer. As much as possible, she hid in her two-room first-floor suite. Avoiding contact with other girls, she went to bed very early and rose at 4 a.m. to use the bathroom before anyone else was up. She took cold showers, in keeping with Dr. Hepburn's theory that an icy plunge bath would drive negative thoughts from the mind.

A calamitous visit to the dining hall above the carriage entrance that separated Pembroke East and West convinced her not to return. Dressed in a French blue skirt with buttons down the front and a matching Icelandic knit sweater, Kate, feeling rather like a wet mouse, hesitantly entered the large, noisy dining hall. She knew no one there. Ali Barbour lived with two friends, Alita Davis and Mary "Megs" Merrill, in Merion Hall, another dormitory. Eager to escape notice, Kate had begun to make her way across the room when the distinct, confident, ironic voice of a New York sophisticate rose above the din as though to recite the opening line of a play.

"Self-conscious beauty!"

Nervousness always made Kate's skin blotch beneath her freckles. Although she dared not look in the other girl's direction, there could be no doubt precisely who was meant. Kate bravely went through the motions of eating her dinner—but after that she took her meals alone.

Ali would appear at Number 3 Pembroke West with extra food saved from visits to the dining hall with Alita and Megs. Kate hoarded whatever scraps Ali brought. Breakfast was usually fruit and cereal, eaten alone in her suite. Most other times, Kate used her $75 monthly allowance to dine off-campus.

Some nights, Kate was so lonely that she escaped to Merion to sleep on Ali's floor. Yet she craved obscurity; she went to great lengths to remain invisible.

Kate loved athletics but dared not try out for anything. Although she did swim on the team during freshman year to fulfill an academic requirement, otherwise she pretended to be inept. Much as she longed to join girls like the dynamic Alice Palache, who excelled at tennis, field hockey, track, basketball, and other sports, Kate just shrugged her shoulders and insisted that she was awful.

She was a puzzle to the few students who did notice her. For all the time Kate spent in her rooms, she barely studied. There was little to distract her, yet she could not seem to concentrate. She appeared serious and intelligent, but anything beyond rote memorization was obviously beyond her capacities.

As in her mother's day, maids still scrubbed the girls' rooms, made their beds, and attended to other "feminine nonsense," so that students might devote their time to study. Academic standards remained high—ironically, higher perhaps than in earlier decades, when women's preparatory education was not all it should have been. In 1924, Marion Edwards Park rejoiced at America's new attitude to women's education when she pointed out that for the first time in Bryn Mawr history, every girl in Kate's class had entered without any conditions. "The college has never admitted a class with so fair a start, with so little impedimenta."

Once admitted, however, most girls found course work extremely demanding. While the rare student like the athletic Alice Palache, the daughter of a Harvard mineralogy professor, seemed effortlessly to shine in every subject, with plenty of time left over for extracurricular activities, most girls who wanted to do well needed to devote five weeknights and usually one whole day on the weekend to study.

It was no longer possible, as in Mrs. Hepburn's era, barely to squeak through one's courses without being detected. Had Mrs. Hepburn attended Bryn Mawr somewhat later, she would have run into the merit law, instituted in 1907, which demanded that students do superior work in at least sixty of the 120 required hours. No student who failed to achieve a grade of merit or better in half of her courses was permitted to graduate; and more often than not, the dean weeded out deficient girls long before that. The moment of truth came at the end of junior year; any student who had not achieved the necessary merit grades was forced to withdraw. Until then, mediocre—that is, merely passing—work might cause a girl to be asked, but not yet required, to leave. In any event, from freshman year on, the girl who fell below the 50 percent merit standard was forbidden to participate in student productions and other extracurricular activities that might take time from her studies.

By the spring semester of 1925, the merit law had caught young Kate Hepburn in its net. A poor showing in her first exams ruled out participation in the Freshman Show that February—although it was unlikely she would have tried out anyway.

As freshman year drew to a close, Kate was tortured by a sense of having disappointed her father, who did little to discourage the notion. Kate's inability to master a basic chemistry course, coupled with poor grades overall, made it painfully obvious that she was not going to become a doctor as young Tom ("the best of the children") would have been had he lived. Thwarted in her struggle to become Tom, or at least to take his place in the family, suddenly Kate's whole existence was being called into question. "Thank God, I hope I'll die," Kate told herself when she suffered an appendix attack at the outset of sophomore year; it was an alarming sentiment in a girl whose brother had committed suicide less than five years before.

That Dr. Hepburn insisted, against tremendous opposition at the hospital, that he alone must perform his daughter's appendectomy suggests how fearful he was of losing her. It was unheard of for a doctor to operate on a close family member, but having lost one child already, he could not bring himself to entrust Kate to anyone else.

Since Tom's death, Dr. and Mrs. Hepburn had kept a keen eye on their daughter. They seemed sensitive to the pattern of suicide on both sides of the family: the suicides had occurred in pairs, at five- or six-year intervals. There remained a tacit understanding in the household that Dr. and Mrs. Hepburn's relationship with "Kath"—as the parents called her—was different from that with the other children. Bob sensed it; and Dick was often heard to grumble about his big sister's special treatment. Even when Dr. and Mrs. Hepburn had to pay for damages after a Fenwick neighbor accused Kate of housebreaking, they hesitated to punish her; nor was there a harsh word when she wrecked the car.

Due to the appendectomy, Kate started sophomore year ten days late. As if in a nightmare, she could not seem to focus or keep up with other students. Under excruciating pressure to do better, Kate helplessly watched her grades plummet. Ali Barbour, Alita Davis, and Megs Merrill had all dropped out after freshman year, leaving Kate forlorn and more alienated than ever. From first to last, the year was an unmitigated disaster.

Tempers flared on Laurel Street when, following Kate's last exam on May 29, Helen Taft Manning advised (but did not yet require) Kate to withdraw from Bryn Mawr. Dr. Hepburn lashed back with a sarcastic letter. He pointed out that if he had a patient in the hospital and didn't know what was wrong, he wouldn't just send him home, as the dean proposed to do with Kate. Never a man who liked to be bossed, Dr. Hepburn angrily refused to permit his daughter to leave until she was required to at the end of junior year.

As he had done with Tom, he pushed Kate very hard. He insisted that anything begun must be finished no matter what. Ignoring the precedent of a son and two brothers who had cracked under pressure, he expected Kate to return to Bryn Mawr in the fall.

She did not want to return. Instead, she shocked her father with a sudden announcement: She planned to drop out of Bryn Mawr to become an actress.

It does not seem such a strange goal when one considers that Kate came from a family in which both parents considered themselves to be performers. Dr. Hepburn saw himself in the tradition of the doctor-actors at the Johns Hopkins Medical School. He spoke of the operating room as a stage, where he enacted the life-and-death drama of surgery. Mrs. Hepburn, for her part, was proud of her reputation as one of the suffrage movement's best public speakers. Like her husband, she loved to put on a show. Since her childhood

Kate had often watched, and thrilled to the excitement in the room, when her flamboyant parents performed.

Kate herself had experienced the thrill of performing when, in the years before Tom's death, Edith had led the children in putting on plays at Fenwick, and afterward when the tradition was revived without Edith. Like Dr. Hepburn, Edith had once been a Hopkins doctor-actor; like Mrs. Hepburn, she was one of the most effective suffrage speakers. But Edith was something more: For a brief time, on deciding that medicine was not for her, Edith had pursued a stage career under the tutelage of Richard Mansfield. At Fenwick, Edith had often enthralled Kate and the other children with tales of her theatrical studies in Paris. Now that Kate's plans to enter medicine had come to nothing, a stage career seemed a viable alternative.

But Dr. Hepburn would not hear of it. To have a daughter of his on the stage, with all the publicity that would entail, was unthinkable. The association with Edith made the whole idea especially distasteful.

On some level, Dr. Hepburn, who had recently shown himself to be deeply concerned about his daughter's state of mind, must have known that he was taking a terrible chance when he sent Kate back for junior year. She had been miserable at Bryn Mawr; there was every reason to believe she would fail.

Kate did not fail. She did not crack under pressure as men in the family had done. The year before, she had drifted perilously close to the edge of the slope; she had felt the attraction of darkness; now she embraced life.

In the 1926–7 academic year, anyone who climbed the teakwood stairway to the reading room of the M. Carey Thomas Library was likely to see an unprecedented sight. At one of 134 tall desks, the dark, boyish, curly-haired Alice Palache, famous for gliding through the most difficult courses with minimal effort, pored over stacks of books with her new best friend, Kate Hepburn. Palache— as she was always known—was to Kate what Mary Towle had been to Kate's mother: the one who helped her back into the world after a period of loneliness and isolation.

They made a strange twosome. Kate was pretty; Palache, plain.

Kate was a loner; Palache, gregarious and popular. Kate participated in nothing; Palache led several campus clubs and teams, and was active in others. Kate was timid; Palache, cocksure and "intellectually snobbish." Kate was among the worst students in the junior class; Palache, among the best. Sometimes, seated beside Palache in the immense, silent reading room, Kate, struggling to concentrate, imagined she could hear the cogs in her friend's brain "going round and round."

Palache, for her part, diagnosed Kate's problem as never having learned to study properly. Kate was "plenty smart," Palache insisted; but she made the mistake of trying to get through a subject like philosophy by mechanically memorizing "reams and reams and reams" of material, when reflection and rigorous analysis were required. The art history–French major spent so much time helping Kate study that Kate would always say Bryn Mawr ought to award Palache two diplomas.

Buoyed by Palache's friendship, Kate was determined to earn enough merit grades to stay. She spent whole days in the library. Once she remained all night. After two years of self-imposed solitude, she was ready to emerge from her shell and participate in campus life; but first she had to earn the privilege.

When the first light of dawn poured through the window tracery, Kate finally left her desk. She did not, however, return to Pembroke. A groined-vault passageway led to the monastic cloister, where Kate threw off all her clothes and bathed in Miss Thomas's fountain.

Dr. Hepburn loved to show off his perfect, smooth, pointed fingers. Mrs. Hepburn would get out the family's well-worn copy of *Cheiro's Book of Palmistry*, which explained that tapered fingers signified an artistic personality. But the feature he always seemed proudest of was his stiff, straight thumb. When young Bob tested his own thumb, it bent right back—but not Dr. Hepburn's. No matter how hard anyone tried to push back that thumb, it remained rigid. According to Cheiro, this characteristic signified a strong will.

By 1927, Dr. Hepburn had realized his dream of building a large, impressive brick house to rival Cuthbert Powell's Llangollen. In old Virginia—he would say—"the people who were anything" all had big houses like the one that rose now at 201 Bloomfield Avenue in West Hartford, opposite the Hartford Golf Club. Having practiced medicine in Hartford for twenty years and brought his yearly salary to approximately $45,000, Dr. Hepburn wanted a home that would properly convey his position in the community.

His need intensified when his fellow doctors at Hartford Hospital failed to elect him chief of surgery. As Dr. Hepburn strode into the staff meeting where the top position was to be filled, he simply assumed that as senior surgeon he was entitled to lead. His colleagues thought otherwise; they chose H. Gildersleeve Jarvis, a physician with less seniority perhaps but a more palatable personality.

While the family always wistfully spoke of the Nook Farm cottage as Mrs. Hepburn's house, Bloomfield Avenue was strictly the doctor's. To build it, he sold the stocks he had begun to purchase during World War I, which, in the economic boom ten years later, were worth several times their original value. He also took out a $10,000 bank loan. At Bloomfield Avenue, Dr. Hepburn became much less concerned with his "family forebears"; from then on, it was understood in the household that "things didn't begin with them, they began with him."

Not long after the Hepburns moved in, Kate invited Alice Palache for the weekend to play tennis. The grand establishment was unlike anything the college professor's daughter was used to; everything was almost "too big." Palache soon discovered that in this bustling, talkative, volcanic family, where giant egos were perpetually colliding, the hub of activity was neither the living room nor the kitchen.

A curved staircase led to a spacious upstairs hallway. A guest room was on the right; down a long corridor were the children's rooms and a master suite. Finally, in the corner, overlooking a beech tree, was the warm, sunny, comfortable room, adjoining the master bedroom, that all acknowledged as the symbolic center of the house.

The dressing room was Dr. Hepburn's lair, and there the family tended to congregate. He had installed cork flooring so that his feet would not freeze when, as was his custom, he emerged from the bathtub to greet visitors. He liked to debate current events while soaking in the tub or shaving at the basin, where he might catch a rear view of himself in the mirror on the opposite wall. The only concession to privacy was the separate closet that held the toilet. A small cupboard contained his two suits and two pairs of shoes.

It bothered Dr. Hepburn not at all that Kate's guest was a twenty-year-old woman who had never seen her own father undressed. Palache was scarcely accustomed to carrying on a conversation about "transcendent problems of the world" with a naked man in his late forties. To Kate, his nakedness obviously was routine; Palache, however straitlaced she considered herself, had little choice but to get used to it. In the dressing-room, the girls would sit on a pillow-strewn, upholstered sofa with short Queen Anne legs. Dr. Hepburn, striding back and forth with nothing on, argued fiercely with Palache, whose political views always seemed to arouse his ire.

When Mrs. Hepburn entered the dressing room, husband and wife would hug and kiss a good deal, which shocked Palache almost as much as the casual nudity. "I find him beautiful," Mrs. Hepburn, approaching fifty, would say without blushing. She boasted that unlike many men his age, the doctor had "no seat." Yet in moments of exasperation, she was known to call her husband an "old blowhard" and to define the male—with obvious reference to Dr. Hepburn—as a creature who "butts and struts and makes a noise."

Palache felt as if she had landed on another planet. Her own family, so much more inhibited and constrained, certainly never discussed topics like prostitution, venereal disease, and birth control. Professor Charles Palache, an Episcopalian, had always forbidden his tomboy daughter to play with friends on Sunday. Dr. Hepburn, thumbing his nose at churchgoers, led the family on nature walks in the hills. Spotting a group of birch trees, he would send the children scrambling to see who could climb up and bend one over first.

Initially, Dr. Hepburn mistook Palache, with her big nose and thick dark eyebrows, for a "Mary Towle" whom he could tease and bully with sex talk and nudity. Soon he had to admit that he had misjudged her. Instead of running out screaming with horror as Aunty tended to do, Palache stood firm and fought back. He admired her spark. The sturdy, competitive young woman was quite capable of out-arguing him; and the more they disagreed, the fonder of her he seemed to grow. Dr. Hepburn made it clear that he trusted her "to be with Kate"—and by all accounts, Palache did not take that trust lightly.

With Palache's help, by the spring of 1927 Kate had earned enough merit grades to be eligible to appear in a school show. She was cast in the male role of Oliver in A. A. Milne's *The Truth About Blayds*. Following a two-night run on campus in April, the production would travel to the Colony Club in New York for a performance to benefit the New York Alumnae Regional Scholarship. The Varsity Players hired a professional drama coach, Mr. Walter Greenough, to direct.

Already notorious on campus as the girl who had gone naked in the cloister fountain, Kate, determined to look like a boy, used fingernail scissors to cut off her hair. Palache declared Kate's haircut "the most godawful-looking thing you've ever seen in your life."

"As the young Oliver, Katherine [sic] Hepburn was a trifle amateurish, a bit too conscious that she was on the stage, but she made an engaging boy, roguish and merry," proclaimed the *College News* on April 20, 1927. To celebrate her first review, Kate and Palache, disguised as men in blazers and white trousers, spent the evening in Philadelphia. Spotted hailing a cab, they returned to Bryn Mawr to find themselves summoned before the student self-government. The high esteem in which Palache was held ensured that they received only a severe reprimand, accompanied by a warning not to violate campus rules again.

"Why don't we go abroad this summer?" Kate asked Palache soon afterward. Although Palache served as her protector, Kate was usually the instigator of their adventures.

"Yes, well why not!" replied Palache, who had toured Europe with her mother in 1921. "I have some money."

"I haven't got any money," said Kate. "I haven't got any money at all."

"I've got $500 in my savings bank."

"I've got some antique furniture, my mother's," said Kate. "Maybe she'd let me sell it."

At the end of the term, Kate went home first. Several days later, Palache, en route to Connecticut with her suitcases, had no idea whether Kate had permission, let alone the cash, to sail to Europe. Professor Palache, eager for his daughter to learn self-reliance, had said only, "It's your own money. I guess you can do with it what you please."

As the train pulled into Hartford, Palache saw her friend dancing along the old-fashioned wooden platform. Kate, full of glee, waved a piece of paper. It was a $500 check from Dr. Hepburn.

"I'm not going to go to any of your silly old cathedrals or any of your art stuff because I'm not interested," Kate warned before they purchased tickets to Plymouth, England.

"All right, fine with me," Palache agreed.

"No," Kate went on. "We won't do that. We're just going to see England, Wales, and Scotland."

Round trip in student-third class cost $210, about the same as steerage. Professor Palache warned each girl to keep $100 as a reserve, which left $190 for hotels, food, and all other expenses. In London, Palache was about to pay $75 for a secondhand car, a little Morris Cowley, when Kate suddenly put on a big act for the owner.

"Mr. Seymour, is this car safe?" she inquired with great dubiousness.

Palache watched in wonder as Kate, wisps of hair flying about her face, delivered a long, impassioned speech, like something out of a stage play, about the dangers two girls faced in the countryside and all the horrible things that might happen should the car break down. Undone by the performance, Mr. Seymour offered to buy back the car for $75 if Kate returned it in the same condition; perhaps that would prove his confidence in the vehicle.

The next morning, the girls rolled the top down and threw their incongruously expensive luggage on the back seat. Kate, wearing a floppy straw hat to keep her nose from turning red, insisted on taking the wheel. A speedy driver, Kate shot into the right-hand side of the road. She had gone no more than half a block when she screeched to a halt, face to face with another car; it was a very close call.

"You drive!" Kate snapped as she leapt out to exchange places with Palache.

That was the last time Kate drove during the trip. She also refused to carry her own money. On the rare occasions when Kate went off on her own (as when she arranged a rendezvous with a young man she had met on the boat), Palache gave her only enough cash to get where she was going and back again.

The girls laughed and sang as they drove, Kate holding onto her straw hat, which constantly threatened to blow away.

"What's that over there?" said Kate, pointing across the fields.

"That's Salisbury Cathedral," said Palache, who had been dying for her to ask. "You won't be interested."

"Well, now. Wait a minute," said Kate.

"It's just one of those old musty things you don't want to see."

"I think we'd better go and look at it," Kate declared, changing her mind in a flash. From then on, much as her father would have done, Kate acted as if visiting all the cathedrals they could find had been her idea in the first place.

Some nights they slept in pubs, where Palache had to ram a chair under the doorknob to prevent drunken men from bursting in. Other nights they slept twisted up in the car, which was much too small for comfort. Kate composed a poem cataloguing the various dreadful penny toilets they encountered along the way.

Vowing to spend no more than five dollars a day, they existed on tomato sandwiches, sliced and buttered with a large carving knife. Kate's sole indulgence was chocolate, Palache's cigarettes.

As they worked their way north, they dreamt of watching the sunrise at Loch Katrine. After many hours of driving, they stopped at a farm on the road to the lake.

"What do girls like you want hay for?" the farmer inquired.

Kate and Palache explained that they planned to spend the night on the lakeshore.

"Aren't you afraid of gypsies?" laughed the farmer.

"Gypsies! What gypsies?" Kate blustered. "No, we wouldn't be afraid of gypsies!"

The farmer, greatly amused, helped them fill the back of the car.

It was quite late by the time the girls found a secluded spot, just above the lake, to camp out. They stretched out in the hay with the carving knife between them. Exhausted, they quickly fell asleep.

Kate awakened several hours later. A dense fog had rolled over the lake that would prevent them from watching the sunrise. Suddenly, at the water's edge, Kate saw the red tip of a burning cigarette.

Heart pounding, she grabbed the knife and rushed down to discover . . . Palache.

"My dear Miss Hepburn," wrote Marion Edwards Park on October 20, 1927. "In view of your failure to keep the regulation which forbids a student to smoke in her college room, the Bryn Mawr Association of Self-Government has asked me to notify you of your suspension from the college halls and from all college exercises from Sunday October 23rd at noon to the evening of Friday October 28th. Your absences from classes during the week will be regarded by the college as though they were unexcused cuts . . . I am sending a copy of this letter to your father in order that he may understand your return home at this time."

President Park did not go into details, but the facts of the case were well known on campus. When the semester began on October 5, Kate Hepburn, recently returned from Europe, had remained in Hartford to attend Ali Barbour's wedding to Moreau D. Brown, missing the first week of classes. Not long after she arrived at Bryn Mawr, the student self-government received an anonymous report about smoking in her new tower room at Pembroke East. As president of the undergraduate association in charge of this year's May

Day celebration, Palache had become quite close to Marion Edwards Park; she defended Kate against the students who demanded her expulsion, and eventually the five-day suspension was agreed to.

Even that milder punishment suggests the strong emotions the topic of smoking generated among students. By this time, President Park had emerged as a heroine for having taken the lead among women's college presidents by permitting smoking in restricted areas. Student leaders, grateful to Park for her "willingness to bear the criticism of the country in taking what was considered by many a radical stand," insisted on strict enforcement of the new smoking rules—thus the uproar over Kate's seemingly minor infraction.

Thirty-two years before this, Edith had been terrified at the prospect of Amory Houghton, Jr.'s receiving a similar letter from Carey Thomas; but Kate knew her father much too well to suffer any trepidation. On October 22, Dr. Hepburn replied with a long letter, full of bluster, in his daughter's defense. Kate departed insisting she was happy for the opportunity "to play golf all day long" in West Hartford.

For all the solemn voices that were heard against her, the incident made Kate Hepburn a school star. Her exploits snowballed into legend—or "campus dirt," depending on whom one talked to. Classmates described her as "full of high jinks." Splashing naked in the cloister fountain; dressing as a boy; and now, smoking scented cigarettes in her tower room, she seemed to enact the Twenties motto, "Out with inhibitions!"

Kate made real other girls' fantasies of doing things strictly because they were fun. She was self-dramatizing and brave. It was as if one of the heedless, hedonistic flappers pictured in *College News* advertisements had magically sprung to life—but with a new twist: This gallant good-time girl, her blazing red hair dragged back into a charwoman's bun, wore baggy, unflattering cast-off clothes rumored to be held together with safety pins. Her nose shone as though polished, but she appeared not to care.

And it didn't matter: "Katherine [sic] Hepburn . . . was so extraordinarily lovely to look at that it was difficult to form any judgment on her acting," declared one bedazzled student reviewer when Kate appeared in G. Martinez Sierra's convent drama, *The Cradle Song*, in December. After that, young girls at the nearby Shipley School, who happened to see the production, declared themselves "in awe" of her. Suddenly, people on and off campus were talking about Kate Hepburn.

All long limbs and frantic energy, Kate was notorious for shinning up and down drainpipes and vines after dormitory closing hours. Palache, who lived in Merion, slipped out by fire escape. With two other close friends, Elizabeth Rhett and Adele Merrill, they would sit on a nearby hill to watch the moon, or "joyride" in the new two-toned yellow and black Chrysler which Liz illegally kept garaged in the village. Palache named the group the Three Musketeers and D'Artagnan.

When asparagus was in season, the foursome, who considered themselves "very exclusive," dined regularly on asparagus and Hollandaise sauce, which seemed all the more delicious because the King Of Prussia Inn was inexplicably off-limits to Bryn Mawr girls. Back on campus, Kate and Palache, rocking with laughter, would take turns jumping to catch the bottom rung of the Merion fire-escape ladder and pull it down to the ground.

Long past midnight, over cups of muggle in Palache's room they would listen to other girls' descriptions of having "gone the limit." Palache tended to dismiss the stories as mere boasting and exaggeration, although she quietly admitted to being envious if any of it were true. Never having had a date, Palache liked to say that a woman should always keep a man around as a "doormat."

And what did Kate think?

"Take 'em or leave 'em alone!" was Kate's credo as far as men were concerned. For the moment, other matters preoccupied her.

"What are you going to be?" Kate asked Yale art student Robert McKnight when they met at a dance in New Haven.

"I'm going to be the greatest sculptor in the world," said McKnight. "What about you?"

"I'm going to be the greatest actress in the world."

She appeared to believe it. Based on *Cradle Song*, and almost certainly with a good word thrown in by Palache, Kate had been cast as Pandora, the lead role in John Lyly's sixteenth-century comedy *The Woman in the Moon*, which would be performed in the cloister on May Day.

It is difficult to exaggerate the excitement on campus in anticipation of the week of May 4, 1928, when visitors from across the nation, family, friends, alumnae, and other interested parties, would pour into Bryn Mawr, filling every conceivable boarding house and hotel room. At Palache's urgent request, Dean Manning asked professors to lighten the workload as Bryn Mawr's seventh quadrennial Elizabethan festival, billed as the "greatest" May Day ever, approached.

All year long, girls had practiced tumbling, singing, and Morris-dancing—the latter performed with a set of brass bells worn on each leg. They practiced the lute, the pipe and tabor, and the viol. They rehearsed plays and conducted a raucous Miss America-style beauty pageant for Maid Marian, Queen of the May. Contestants marched two by two through the gymnasium as classmates shouted comments on their appearance and "how well they would look on a horse." The pageant ended with all thirty-four "prospective queens" being asked to join hands "like a Greek frieze" and skip merrily out of the room. Kate, nominated to appear in the beauty pageant, promptly withdrew.

Wintry cold lasted well into the spring that year. When Kate wasn't rehearsing *The Woman in the Moon*, she spent a good deal of time with two wealthy young men in their late twenties, Ludlow Ogden Smith and John G. Clarke, Jr., who shared a primitive, whitewashed cottage, set in a meadow, about forty minutes outside Bryn Mawr.

Jack Clarke's family, listed in the Philadelphia Social Register, owned Robindale, a gloomy, three-story Victorian house adjoining the Bryn Mawr campus at Yarrow Street and Morris Avenue. Jack, a tall, brash, good-looking war veteran, and his sisters, Louise and Agnes, were said to have vowed never to marry or have children of their own, their mother having been committed to an insane asylum. Clarke's father, who had built Robindale in 1896 when Kate's mother was at Bryn Mawr, tended to look the other way when, at all hours, students sneaked into an old tool shed on his property to smoke; and it was there that young Jack and his best friend Luddy first ran into Kate and her friends.

Tall and broad-shouldered, with rosy cheeks and thinning black hair doused in tonic and brushed straight back, Luddy, at twenty-eight, seemed incredibly mature and sophisticated to Kate. He came from a socially prominent Philadelphia family; the Smiths owned Sherraden, a rambling house on the Main Line at Strafford, but had lived in town since shortly after the death of Luddy's older brother Lewis, a lieutenant in the U.S. Navy, in 1919.

Luddy, too, had served in the war; he remained in France afterward to study at the University of Grenoble. He spoke several languages and talked knowledgeably about art, classical music, and photography, which was his passion. Friends described him as sensitive, gentle, and always a bit sad. But Luddy could also be silly. He made the girls laugh with a trick he had of touching the tip of his nose with his tongue.

When the girls visited the suave older men at their country retreat, Luddy, as was his custom, coaxed the visitors to disrobe. Palache was indignant, but Kate, for whom nudity was no big deal, astonished their host by blithely posing naked on the living-room sofa.

Her attitude toward sex set her apart from girls who thought the Twenties generation had invented female passion. Where many of her contemporaries perceived themselves to be in rebellion against their suffragist mothers' Victorian sensibilities, Kate came from a household where sex was treated matter-of-factly and a beautiful body was nothing to be ashamed of.

She threw back her neck, shook out her red mane, and grinned at the shy photographer.

The name H. Phelps Putnam has been forgotten for more than half a century, but in the late twenties and early thirties he was worshiped as one of America's finest young poets. When he published his first volume, *Trinc*, in 1927, at the age of thirty-three, Edmund Wilson hailed it as "one of the best books of English poetry of the time." Others heard, in his poems of sex, "strong drink," and the pleasures of male friendship, a powerful, authentic new voice of the post-war generation. His name was uttered in the same breath as those of Ernest Hemingway, F. Scott Fitzgerald, and Edna St. Vincent Millay.

Since his Yale days, Putnam, dark and handsome, with a hoarse, harsh New England voice, had been legendary for his romantic exploits. Like e. e. cummings, he was said to be "fatally irresistible to women." Malcolm Cowley described him as Byronic. Edmund Wilson, who envied Putnam's success with women as much as he admired his verse, called him "the woman's ideal poet: attractive and unreliable."

"I am a hobo with a low repute," Putnam, drunk as a fiddler, would introduce himself to girls at Greenwich Village parties. He wore a broad-brimmed black slouch hat, which, in the words of one observer, gave him the air of a Yale man "disguised as a decadent artist of the 1890s." Famed for his seductive conversation, he invited women to travel with him "down the outrageous highway of delight." He called liquor "the dew miraculous," the gin flask in his coat pocket "bottled fire."

Putnam's friends marveled at the "large portions of time and emotion" he devoted to the many women in his life. Putnam, for his part, never really tried to hide what he called "the Bad Boy side of my character." At times he rather flaunted it. "Though I have never picked pockets, I have stolen money," he liked to say. "Though I have never been kept by a whore, my way has been paid now and then by nice though frail ladies."

During Putnam's forays to New York, his wife Ruth waited in their modest, cat-filled, top-floor apartment at his parents' house in Jamaica Plain, a Boston suburb. He always returned. "Kind girl, I am a weary child," he addressed her in "Song to Ruth," one of several poems in *Trinc* in which the wife appears.

"Why do we marry, people like us?" he once asked a fellow poet. "It's damned silly for us. Being married makes it harder for us . . . just plain goddamn harder. Ask me about it—I know."

On Saturday nights, the devoted Mrs. Putnam would serve a superb dinner to a group of Yale graduates who gathered to hear her husband recite work-in-progress from the notebooks he carried with him everywhere. The coterie, whose voices and personalities Putnam wove into his poems, included the young writers F. O. Matthiessen, Charles Walker, Russell Davenport, and Professor Frederick Johnson Manning, husband of the dean of Bryn Mawr.

Close friends knew that Putnam was often in pain from "asthmatic, strangling breath" and a host of other ailments, real and imagined. Grotesque fantasies of hanging, nooses, and strangulation figured prominently in his poetry, notebooks, and correspondence. He pictured himself suddenly transformed from "a man to a strangling beast, choking for life." He wrote of the daily struggle, increasingly difficult, "to make a half dead corpse into a man," and his longing for a "soul-mate" to help ease the pain. In the final poem in *Trinc*, a "troubled girl" stands beneath a noose and cries, "Come, lift me up, I too will hang, I shall be sisterly."

He avowed that if he drank too much, it was only because alcohol liberated him from "the thick noise of disease" to provide "static clarity."

The critical success of *Trinc* brought excruciating new pressures. Now, it seemed, everyone expected Phelps Putnam to fulfill the promise he had shown in that first volume—and to do it quickly. In March 1928, Edmund Wilson sent a copy of *Trinc* to F. Scott Fitzgerald, with an eye to persuading Fitzgerald's and Hemingway's publisher, Charles Scribner's Sons, to do Putnam's next book. Repeatedly Wilson urged Putnam to waste no time planting himself at the top of the profession.

All this had the effect of blocking Putnam. Success had its drawbacks; suddenly, magazines were clamoring for new work, and he complained bitterly, to Edmund Wilson and others, of the difficulty of writing with a time limit.

"I have such noble thoughts once in a while," Putnam groaned. "It would be nice if I could write about them."

By the end of April, the pressure to produce had made Putnam physically ill. In a broil with his emotions, he fled Jamaica Plain. On

May 2, 1928, Putnam wrote to the poet Stephen Vincent Benet to report that he had moved in temporarily with Fred and Helen Manning on Roberts Road in Bryn Mawr to try to recover his soul. In a moment of intense personal crisis, it was only natural for Putnam to turn to the man he called "bleak friend, my rare unswerving company."

Since college days, when they had regularly talked through the night about "sex, philosophy, God and man," Phelps Putnam and Fred Manning had been the closest of companions; and they remained so, although the womanizing, hard-drinking, bohemian poet was precisely one of those "drink-deepers" about whom Helen Taft Manning had so vociferously warned Bryn Mawr girls. Dean Manning encouraged the men to do their carousing as far away as possible from Bryn Mawr, where Putnam's sister, Frances, was currently a senior.

Whatever Putnam may have expected, there was little peace at Bryn Mawr that week as the college geared up for Friday and Saturday's May Day revels. The town was packed. The looming presence of alumnae made it impossible for Fred Manning to share the usual bottle, so Putnam drank alone.

When the poet, clutching his notebook, stumbled out for a walk, he was lost in a dizzying throng, which seemed to grow larger and louder by the hour as visitors poured in from across the country. Beautiful young women, costumed as jesters in cap and bells, ribbons, and gewgaws, paid no attention to him as they rushed past on their way to rehearsals.

"It had never been so lovely for May Day," President Marion Edwards Park later recalled. "The cold had held back so many of the blossoms that suddenly everything burst out, whether it was time or not, in the luxurious warmth."

Phelps Putnam accompanied Fred and Helen Manning down the passageway to the cloister, where Elizabethan music mingled with the splashing of the fountain. A large crowd waited for the first act of Lyly's *The Woman in the Moon*. Dr. and Mrs. Thomas N. Hepburn were there, as were Ludlow Ogden Smith and John S. Clarke, Jr., the men responsible for those nude photographs, which had been much talked about by the Bryn Mawr girls when Kate brought blowups back to the campus.

As Pandora, Kate wore a loose-fitting, long white Grecian gown that exposed arms slightly fleshy from a few too many midnight cups of muggle. Her hair floated freely in the breeze and her scratchy voice reminded Putnam of a sandstorm. He arranged to have "the child" invited to lunch at Dean Manning's.

In the weeks that followed, Kate, infatuated with Phelps Putnam, would often climb out her window for a late night stroll— alone. Palache did not accompany her on these walks, nor did Kate go to her friend's room afterward to hear girls boast about having "gone the limit." Putnam, back with his wife in Jamaica Plain, had sent Kate a copy of *Trinc*, on whose title page was the black-and-white image of a serpent curled around a vine. Still in the throes of writer's block, "Phelpie" wanted Kate to join him in New York, where he hoped to work on a new volume of poems.

T H I R T E E N

"Well, that's done!" Dr. Hepburn was heard to exclaim from his red plush seat at Goodheart Hall when Kate received her diploma, with a major in history and philosophy, on the morning of Thursday, June 7, 1928.

Professor and Mrs. Charles Palache also were there, having missed May Day on account of its being too expensive to make two trips from Cambridge. Professor Palache was exceedingly proud of his daughter for having lined up a job as research trainee in the Boston investment firm of Scudder, Stevens and Clark. The soaring stock market made 1928 an especially exciting time to begin. One of three college women hired, Palache would earn $18.75 a week and live at home.

Kate waited for the long drive home to Connecticut to announce her plans.

"I have a job, Dad. I'm an actress."

Silence.

Although she probably did not tell her parents every detail, this is how it happened: After Kate appeared as Pandora, Jack Clarke had given her a letter of introduction to the producer Edwin Knopf, who had a stock company in Baltimore. On the weekend of May 12, Kate's twenty-first birthday, she and Liz Rhett drove down to Maryland; they stayed at Edith's house, called Upland after the country inn to which she had been banished after the hazing incident. Kate's connection with the flamboyant Mrs. Hooker, who was much admired in Baltimore social and political circles, cannot have hurt when she applied to the local stock company. Knopf told Kate to get back to him when she finished college.

After her last exam on June 2, Bob McKnight, the Yale art student, drove Kate to Baltimore, where Knopf hired her as one of four ladies-in-waiting in *The Czarina*, starring Mary Boland. Rehearsals were to begin on Monday, June 11, four days after graduation.

Father and daughter fought loudly and bitterly all the way to West Hartford. He accused her of being a show-off and an exhibitionist. He derided her vanity. He deplored the publicity a stage career would bring to the entire family. He outlined "the sordid ways of theatrical folk" and called acting nothing but "a shortcut to a life of prostitution." Wifehood and motherhood were the goals Kate should be aiming for! Career and marriage were incompatible, Dr. Hepburn reminded her, and women who attempted both ended up "floundering failures." This last point was no doubt his way of cutting off Mrs. Hepburn, who had immediately expressed support for Kate's plan.

The fireworks continued at home. Little Marion and the others, listening to their father shout, decided that Kate must have inherited her dramatic ability from him. Dr. Hepburn forbade Kate to go to Baltimore. If she insisted on taking such a foolish step, he would cut off her allowance. He failed to see why he should have to invest in something he disapproved of.

Kate said she didn't blame him and would ask for nothing. Whether or not the family supported her, she planned to leave on Sunday. She would be in Baltimore a week, perhaps two, then go on to New York. It was her life, Kate declared, and she had a right to live it exactly as she pleased!

Yell as he might, there came a point in family squabbles when Dr. Hepburn, sensing he had lost control, abruptly lowered his voice and indignantly demanded that others do the same. Nothing whatsoever had been resolved when father and daughter swept out of the house to play golf at the Hartford Golf Club across the street.

Soon after she left for Baltimore, however, Dr. Hepburn sent ten dollars to the Bryn Mawr Club, where she had taken a room. It wasn't

Kate's allowance, he insisted to Mrs. Hepburn, just his bridge winnings, "ill-gotten gains" he might as well pass on to their daughter.

"Let's have dinner," Kate called to her fellow lady-in-waiting Marie Simpson after the first rehearsal, at which Kate had distinguished herself by sitting cross-legged on the floor instead of accepting a chair like everybody else.

"I don't have any money," said Marie, a petite, fine-boned redhead.

"That's nothing!" Kate assured her. "I have ten dollars. A man gave it to me."

Over dinner—which cost 50 cents for each girl—Kate regaled Marie with stories of her friend Palache and their adventures in Europe together. Instead of revealing that she was staying at the Bryn Mawr Club, Kate declared that she was being put up in a fraternity house.

In Baltimore, Kate wore baggy trousers, dirty tennis shoes, and a man's faded green sweater. Wisps of red hair curled out from under a battered felt hat. A straw basket with a strap around it appeared to contain all her possessions.

Experienced company members took Kate under their wing. Mary Boland showed her how to circle her eyes with makeup and urged her to abandon her "golf course stride." Actor Kenneth MacKenna encouraged her to speak slower and avoid getting so worked up that her voice cracked, as it tended to do when she appeared in minuscule roles in *The Czarina* and a second Boland vehicle, *The Torch-Bearers*. When her two-week engagement was over, MacKenna sent Kate to New York with a letter of introduction ("Stands awfully and never sits in a chair if there's an inch of floor available") to Frances Robinson-Duff, a voice and drama coach.

Kate ran up three flights of stairs when the servant at the East 62nd Street townhouse forbade her to use the hand-pulley elevator. She dashed into the studio unannounced, to find a corpulent woman in her fifties waiting on a gilt and velvet throne beside a music stand cluttered with Delsarte charts. Walking in the rain from Aunt Betty Hepburn's apartment had left her soaking wet. Water dripped from Kate's tousled hair and down her nose.

"I want to be an actress," Kate said. "I want to learn every-thing."

To Phelps Putnam, New York in the summer was always a kind of hell. The fetid air of the city made it hard to breathe. Wandering the hot streets, he studied women with "quivering breasts" and flesh "sculptured by their plastered clothes"; he imagined office girls oblivious to work, "conscious of underclothes against their nerves."

At night he made the rounds of speakeasies, of which he favored Tony Soma's smoky, airless basement on West 49th Street, where he traded witticisms at Robert Benchley's table and guzzled whiskey from heavy white coffee cups. Afterward, in bed with a woman, Putnam, aware of each breath, dreaded the moment when his "soul-mate" might see him change into "a shrivelled, wheezing aged man with centuries of death piled high on his chest."

It was July 1928. He woke up in the sun-flooded riverfront tenement apartment he had borrowed from Russell Davenport, who was off working on *Through Traffic*, a first novel. Half-asleep, Putnam looked through an open door and saw Kate, who had just stepped out of the tub; she stood naked before a mirror.

As Kate did up her hair, she sang: "Well, the lady done wrong, / Yes, the lady done wrong— / Well, she sold her reputation / For the sake of a song."

As late as July 12, Putnam, still in Massachusetts with Ruth and the cats, had written to F. O. Matthiessen that he planned to accompany Fred Manning to Canada, but Kate's presence in New York changed all that. He headed for Davenport's empty apartment at the foot of East 54th Street, and Kate arrived from Aunt Betty Hepburn's with her straw basket.

At night Kate lay in Putnam's arms in a dark room filled with the passing shadows of riverboats. He marveled at "the candor of her lust." He held her naked body, "white and exquisite," and com-pared it to a dagger, "unsheathed and glimmering in my hands."

Kate did everything in her power to seduce him. Dr. Hepburn, who observed Kate's strong physical attraction to Putnam when she

Kate on the set of *Bringing Up Baby*.

Howard Hawks, Cary Grant, and Kate on the set of *Bringing Up Baby*.

Kate plays tennis in 1940.

Dick Hepburn, Kate's brother.

James Stewart, Kate, and George Cukor on the set of *The Philadelphia Story*.

Kate and Cary Grant in *The Philadelphia Story*.

Kate in *The Philadelphia Story*.

Spencer Tracy, George Stevens, and Kate on the set of *Woman of the Year.*

Kate and Spencer Tracy in *Woman of the Year,* their first film together.

Spencer Tracy and his son Johnny at the Riviera Polo Field.

Spencer, Louise, and Johnny Tracy at a polo match in 1939.

Spencer Tracy, Kate, and George Cukor on the set of *Keeper of the Flame*.

Tracy and Hepburn in *The Sea of Grass*.

Kate and Constance Collier in *Stage Door*. Collier later became Kate's acting coach as she prepared to appear in Shakespeare.

Kate and William Prince in *As You Like It* on Broadway in 1950.

John Huston and Kate during the filming of *The African Queen*.

Kate and Humphrey Bogart in *The African Queen*.

Tracy and Hepburn in *Pat and Mike*.

Spencer Tracy returns from Europe in 1951 after Kate left for Africa.

John Ford during the filming of *The Last Hurrah*. Kate had persuaded him to work with Tracy again for the first time in twenty-eight years.

Robert Helpmann and Kate in George Bernard Shaw's *The Millionairess* in London in 1952.

Kate in her dressing room during a rehearsal for *The Millionairess*.

On the set of Eugene O'Neill's
Long Day's Journey Into Night.

Kate in *Long Day's Journey Into Night*. In the background are Dean
Stockwell, Ralph Richardson, and Jason Robards.

In 1963, Tracy hides from photographers as he is wheeled into the emergency entrance of St.Vincent's Hospital in Los Angeles. Kate had summoned an ambulance when he collapsed at the beach.

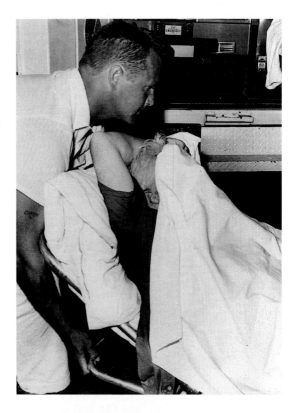

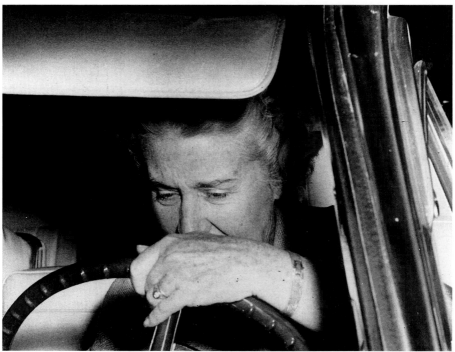

Louise Tracy leaves the hospital late that night.

Kate and Spencer on the set of *Guess Who's Coming to Dinner,* his final film.

Spencer Tracy a few weeks before his death in 1967.

Kate and Peter O'Toole in *The Lion in Winter,* her first film after Tracy's death.

Kate in the film version of Euripides's *The Trojan Women.*

Kate accepts an award from Planned Parenthood for her work and her mother's in support of women's rights.

brought the poet to Fenwick one weekend, compared his daughter to "a young bull about to charge." Yet something kept Putnam from consummating the relationship. He kissed and caressed her but did not have sexual intercourse with Kate.

He observed and listened. He relished what he called Kate's "tricks," as when she improvised that little song to catch his attention. He delighted in her "chattering" and eyes "turned carelessly" to his. He appreciated when her head "drooped" with love and enjoyed it when her anger, mob-like, "swept into murderous action." While she studied voice with Frances Robinson-Duff on East 62nd Street, Putnam thought and wrote about Kate—endlessly. "I do not know how I should speak of her," he wrote—yet the words poured out as they had not in a very long time. It seemed that Kate's energy and nervous intensity had blasted away his writer's block.

When he escorted her to Tony's, she didn't walk so much as burst into his world. Wide-eyed, she blazed through the crowd like a hurricane. Instead of wearing rouge and lipstick, she appeared to have scrubbed her freckled face with alcohol until it gleamed. Instead of jewelry, she sported safety pins where buttons happened to be missing. Her pathetic little cap had a rather prominent hole in it.

Seated at the table where Benchley regularly held court with Dorothy Parker, Kate kept getting up to go to the bathroom. With an irritating nasal twang, she explained that, following Dr. Hepburn's advice, she drank prodigious quantities of water every day. Her jaw dropped when Benchley invited the group, ladies included, for a nightcap at Polly Adler's brothel, where he kept a black kimono.

Kate admitted to feeling like a "country bumpkin" among Phelpie's witty, sophisticated friends, but they quickly recognized "a certain style of her own, a presence, a manner that defies description." She was at once audacious and shy; discourteous and kind; awkward and graceful; masculine and feminine. People called Kate an "original," a "personage"—"like no one else one knows."

Twenties New York thrived on such unlikely discoveries. Intellectuals like Edmund Wilson prided themselves on spotting new vitality in the oddest corners, where stodgier minds would never deign to probe. Anything startling, fresh, new, fast, and angular intrigued them. In nightclubs, circuses, vaudeville houses, dives, and movie theaters, they valued "high-pressure performers" whose quality of "demoniac possession" irritated, jarred, jolted, and disturbed. They prized the "machine-like energy" of Eddie Cantor and the "whining and nasal voice" of the Follies dancer Miss Ada Mae. They cheered silk-hatted vaudeville clown Herbert Williams, whose plaintive cry, "This is very embarrassing for me!", possessed the "quality of a bad dream—or of a French Dadaist drama." They savored nightclub hostess Texas Guinin, whose brassy greeting, "Hello, sucker!", seemed more honest, forthright, and engaging than much of what passed for contemporary highbrow culture.

There were "two Americas," the novelist John Dos Passos insisted. One was staid, bourgeois, and constipated; the other rebellious, sexual, and creative. Knowing the "right places" in a city like New York meant the ability to find one's way into the raucous America of light and energy hidden on certain backstreets within the torpid, repressive wasteland of post-war politics and culture.

From this perspective, guzzling rotgut whiskey from thick white coffee cups seemed like a blazing act of protest against the triumph of puritanism and stultification that Prohibition symbolized. Two months after she graduated from Bryn Mawr, Kate was dazzled that Phelpie knew his way about smoky places like Tony's, where glimmers and intimations of that "other" America might be found. It probably never occurred to her that she was about to be the floor show.

Putnam soon realized that he had the beginnings of a major new poem. Long before this, he had been known as a lyric poet who freely wove into his work the personalities and voices of friends and lovers. Some players, like Ruth Putnam, Fred Manning, Russell Davenport, and Charles Walker, appeared by name; but even when the poet failed to identify characters, they were instantly recognizable to his circle. The knowledge that friendships and love affairs provided material for Putnam's poetry invested those relationships with a peculiar intensity and self-consciousness, as though every word and gesture were being recorded for posterity.

The poem about Kate, more ambitious than anything he had

written before, was suffused with images of warmth, light, and energy. Putnam would call it "The Daughters of the Sun," a reference to the morning sunlight in the apartment that became a symbol of the poet's renewal. Only once did the "strangulated necks" of his earlier work appear, and that was when the speaker, "delirious" with light and love, revisited the "strangling friends" he had "left among the damned."

For Kate, such images were highly charged; how could they be otherwise? The poet who had once written "Come, lift me up, I too will hang, I shall be sisterly" led Kate into shadowed psychological terrain off-limits since her brother's death. Like Tom, Putnam envisaged himself hanging by the neck; but this time, it was in her power to save him.

The relationship remained unconsummated. He called Kate "my nourishment, my sister and my child" and hesitated to make love to her. At the time, Putnam suggested that despite Kate's eagerness, he had left her "unbroken" because his own passion was "too ecstatic to endure." Years later, he would blame the visit to Fenwick, when Dr. Hepburn threatened to shoot Putnam if he allowed Kate to seduce him.

And then, there was Edmund Wilson, who, when he learned that Putnam was finally at work on a major new poem, laughingly warned him to beware of the erotic entanglements that had sapped his energies in the past. Putnam had already suffered one nervous breakdown. Wilson predicted that if he wasn't careful now, the sky might suddenly fall on his head.

Putnam, clutching his notebooks, fled to Nova Scotia to work in "catastropheless beatitude." Of Kate, whom he abandoned in New York, he wrote: "I have taken up the heat of life from her."

In the days when F. Scott Fitzgerald lived in Great Neck on the North Shore of Long Island, he discovered the blue lawns and yellow cocktail music that provided the atmosphere for *The Great Gatsby*. The thick, intense heat, undisturbed by the soft Manhasset Bay breeze, caused Zelda Fitzgerald to laugh that perhaps she was already experiencing the afterlife.

In the summer of 1928, the Fitzgeralds were long gone, but the glittering Gold Coast world of Jay Gatsby remained. At the height of the great bull market of the Twenties, paper fortunes were made overnight, and the tipsy merrymaking showed no sign of petering out. Ring Lardner, weary of Great Neck's "social sewer," had finally decamped to East Hampton; but the porch where he and his young friend Scott Fitzgerald had sat and sipped whiskey or Canadian ale still looked out on the "almost continuous house-party" next door at the rented home of newspaper editor Herbert Bayard Swope and his wife, Maggie.

Guests and gatecrashers, writers, artists, actors, producers, gangsters, politicians, and millionaires still roared up the circular gravel drive of the big white house on East Shore Road that Mrs. Swope called her own "seething bordello of interesting people." The actress Ruth Gordon noted that among "the steady pour-through" of weekend guests one was sure to find "everybody anybody wanted to meet." Regulars like Harpo Marx and the theater critic Alexander Woollcott played croquet, chased through the bushes on treasure hunts, and feasted on steak and champagne in the middle of the night.

The large number of stage personalities in Great Neck, most of whom flitted through the Swopes' parties, caused Zelda Fitzgerald to compare the place to "Times Square during the theater hour." At the Great Neck Theater, plays headed for Broadway previewed before a discerning audience of show people and opinion-makers.

On a sweltering Saturday evening in August after Phelps Putnam had abandoned her, Kate arrived in Great Neck, where the Edwin Knopf company was to put on one performance only of *The Big Pond*, co-written by George Middleton. The playwright's wife, the suffragist Fola La Follette, was an old crony of Mrs. Hepburn's and Mrs. Hooker's; and Middleton himself was a great admirer of Edith's. Initially hired as an understudy, Kate had been catapulted into a major role when Knopf fired his leading lady days before the opening in Great Neck. With a nod from Middleton, Kate was assigned to play Barbara, an innocent American in love with a dashing Frenchman portrayed by Kenneth MacKenna. The comedy was to open at the Bijou Theater on Broadway later in the month.

As soon as she arrived in Great Neck, instead of going directly to the theater, Kate took a walk in the pine woods. Desperately nervous, she needed to spend some time alone before making her entrance. Perhaps only Palache knew about the "theatrical intestines" that caused her to go to pieces "within herself" in anticipation of facing an opening-night audience. When she found a clearing, she had a quiet supper consisting of a box of blackberries and a bottle of milk. Struggling to calm herself, she filled her lungs with soft, salty air from Long Island Sound.

The stage manager was in a dither when Kate strolled into the theater about ten minutes past eight. Moments before she was to go on, the lace panties she wore beneath a dress from Bergdorf Goodman began to tickle. Grumbling that she had never worn lace underclothes before, she suddenly stripped off the panties, tossed them to a shocked stagehand, and swept on stage with a blast of personality. Palache always said Kate knew how to work herself up.

Some in the audience probably recognized Kate from her nights at Tony's with Phelps Putnam. People roared approval when she did her first turn, mimicking Kenneth MacKenna's French accent. The thunderous applause seemed to lift Kate up and out of the play. Her confidence soared. She flew about the stage with unrestrained excitement and talked so quickly that she was impossible to understand.

There were two ways of looking at the calamitous performance. Knopf and his backer Lee Shubert cringed with embarrassment when Kate's voice rose nearly to a falsetto. Instead of acting, Kate was "acting up."

What appalled Knopf and Shubert thrilled and delighted audience members like Arthur Hopkins. Hepburn was bad, Hepburn was inept, Hepburn was often incomprehensible—but she possessed the heat of life. And to a certain Twenties cast of mind, that was all that really mattered. Short, fat, and Buddha-like, Hopkins returned to his gray clapboard home in Great Neck confident that he had spotted a diamond in the dross. Soon afterward, when he heard that the fools had fired her, Hopkins, one of Broadway's most respected producers, summoned Kate to his office above the second balcony at the Plymouth Theater.

Hopkins had made a discovery like this the year before. In 1927, a skinny, androgynous New York society girl with close-cropped taffy-colored hair, a crooked smile, and an emphatic arm-swinging stride had won instant stardom in a small role in Philip Barry's silken comedy *Paris Bound*. Hope Williams was instantly dubbed "the Park Avenue swagger girl."

Eager to repeat the magic with Kate, Hopkins offered her a small role as a student in *These Days*. Katharine Clugston's new play depicted life at a smart finishing school, where the tormented headmistress, Miss Van Allstyne, drills her pupils with lessons about "the nastiness of sex." Set to preview in New Haven and Hartford, *These Days* would open at the Cort Theater on Broadway in November. Kate, evicted from the East 54th Street tenement when Russell Davenport returned, moved to the Park Avenue apartment of her Bryn Mawr classmate Megs Merrill, who was married to Armitage Watkins, an investment banker. They were away for the summer, so Kate mostly had the place to herself.

With Phelps Putnam temporarily out of the picture, Kate took up again with Ludlow Ogden Smith and Jack Clarke. They regularly squired her about Manhattan, where they had rented apartments in Murray Hill. Luddy, especially, was eager to dance attendance. Living on Park Avenue and keeping company with the wealthy Philadelphians, Kate, with her prominent cheekbones, aristocratic head, and dangling arms, gave people the impression that she was an insouciant society girl in the manner of Hope Williams.

When Luddy drove Kate to the shore in August, the Hepburns were caught up in the small-boat racing fever that swept the colony. The races in which Tommy Hepburn had once carried the family banner had been discontinued during and after the war. In the winter of 1927–8, however, Fenwick residents formed a committee to revive sneakboat racing, and a fleet of fifteen "pumpkin seeds" was constituted. Dr. Hepburn, to whom winning was everything, plunged into the competition with great urgency. Passing over Dick, Dr. Hepburn designated Bob skipper of the Hepburn boat, number 14. Holding the sheet and tiller, Bob repeatedly led the family to victory as Tommy had done.

Dick, for his part, played the role of family mischief-maker. In West Hartford, Marion and Peg took to locking themselves in the bathroom to escape his pranks, after Dick put Peg on an ice cake one winter and sent her flying down the Meandering Swine. On another occasion, Dick produced Tommy's sneakbox, which had long been in storage at Fenwick. "Just get in the boat and sail, it's the best way to learn!" Dick beckoned his younger sisters. The girls, who were hardly old enough to have known Tommy, could not resist climbing into his boat. Just then, a powerful southwest wind hit the sail, and the sneakbox swept into Long Island Sound.

The fourteen-foot boat required considerable experience to keep upright. Dick watched from the east end of Fenwick pier as Marion struggled with the sheet and tiller. Having lost control, she and Peg were about to crash into the lighthouse breakwater when Bob and his friends, running along the stony beach, plunged into the water to save them.

On Luddy's first night at Fenwick, the Hepburns had all gone to bed and Luddy was about to retire when he heard rushing footsteps on creaking floorboards. He opened his door to discover the children, pretending to be ghosts, running every which way in the dark. Unable to see clearly, he followed the laughter downstairs to the shadowy main hall. Suddenly, he heard the voice of God thunder from the staircase.

Dick, seizing the moment, threw on the lights, and Luddy looked straight up at Dr. Hepburn, naked but for a skimpy old shirt that left his private parts exposed.

Thus, Dick and the others welcomed Kate's beau into the family.

Phelps Putnam, back from Nova Scotia, attended his sister's

wedding on September 8 in Massachusetts. When he turned up in New York soon afterward, he clutched a draft of "The Daughters of the Sun."

Edmund Wilson was about to leave for a rented beach house in Santa Barbara, California, to revise his novel *I Thought of Daisy*. Intending to dine with Putnam, he arrived at the poet's borrowed apartment. As Putnam put on a fresh shirt, Wilson stared in shock at his bare back. A girl—Putnam left it to his friends to guess who—had ripped and bloodied the flesh with her fingernails. It seemed to Wilson that Putnam displayed his wounds with "conscious pride." He laughingly warned Putnam to beware lest thwarted passion drive the child to tear him "in small pieces."

Wilson wept when he heard Putnam read his long poem about the girl with the "fox-colored hair" and the poet's resolve to seek "the energy of solitude." F. O. Matthiessen called the passages about Kate "the high point" of Putnam's eloquence. Wilson proposed that when Putnam finished fiddling with words and phrases, he would provide an "impassioned" introduction to Maxwell Perkins, chief editor at Scribner's.

While Kate rehearsed her modest role in *These Days* under Arthur Hopkins's direction at the Plymouth Theater, Putnam's recitations were making her something of a legend about Manhattan, it being no secret in certain circles that she was the girl of whom Putnam wrote:

> I do not dare to lie, once having heard
> The daughter of the Sun at morning sing—
> She bathed and with long lifted arms
> Bound up her smoldering hair again, and sang,
> Leaving this sluggard lover in her bed.
> And I was filled with light to such excess
> That I became delirious.

The descriptions Phelpie had scribbled in notebooks, the affectionate details he had related to friends, all somehow found their oblique way into "The Daughters of the Sun."

Kate's "sluggard lover" came back into her life with all the ambiguity that had clouded their relationship during the summer. The man whom Archibald MacLeish once called "Hamlet" still could not seem to make up his mind about her. Putnam had done perhaps his best writing in praise of Kate, yet work remained his true passion. The poem made clear that Putnam was powerfully drawn to her, yet he persisted in leaving Kate "unbroken." Still they spent a good deal of time together; and at one point, Kate had her first taste of being expected to keep a low profile while Mrs. Putnam visited New York to attend the wedding of one of their friends.

Phelpie did not seem to know what he wanted. In November, he impulsively followed Kate to New Haven, where she was to appear in the first tryout of *These Days*. Six months had passed since Putnam, hoping to recover his soul, had first set eyes on her at Bryn Mawr. Since that time, he had produced "The Daughters of the Sun"; and Kate, without experience or training to speak of, was about to open on Broadway. He checked into the Taft Hotel, vowing to bring her there after the performance to celebrate.

Too nervous to wait in his room until it was time to meet Kate for an early dinner, he spent hours wandering about New Haven. When he turned up at F. O. Matthiessen's, the Yale professor was out; but Mrs. Matthiessen permitted Phelpie to guzzle as much of her husband's good whiskey as he pleased. By the time he was ready to see Kate, Hamlet had begun to waver. He left Matthiessen a strange note to say that depending on what happened with Kate, he might be back for a nightcap. In either event, he begged Matthiessen not to mention the visit to Ruth Putnam.

Luddy, for his part, had waited patiently in the wings through-out the fall. With Phelps Putnam back, Luddy was relegated to a secondary role. He continued regularly to drive up to Connecticut with Kate, who appeared to enjoy bossing him about. It seemed to Bob Hepburn that Luddy, so sweet, sensitive, and eager to please, was no match for his strong-willed sister, whom the family recognized as a "natural boss" like Dr. Hepburn.

Bob was not alone in the belief that Luddy "needed protection." Mrs. Hepburn worried that Kate, indeed the entire family, would "run roughshod" over the poor, besotted fellow. Just from the way

Luddy watched Kate, one could tell that she "astounded" him. He used every opportunity to kiss and hug her; and it was obvious that she was physically attracted to him as well.

Luddy's feelings for Kate were strong, clear, and direct; yet Phelps Putnam, "born to dark hysteria," remained the more fascinating figure. At times, Kate seemed ready to give up everything to nurse and nurture the poet if only he would make his move.

"Do not dream too long, do not wait—" Putnam wrote; yet that is exactly what he did on opening night in New Haven. When the "sluggard lover" crawled back to Manhattan the next morning without having taken Kate to bed, Luddy seized the initiative.

Where Putnam had been ambivalent, Luddy was persistent, attentive, and unrelenting. He actively wooed Kate. Jack Clarke and his sisters were away from the Murray Hill apartment they shared when Luddy brought Kate there and asked her to go the limit. After months of waiting for Phelpie, Kate saw no reason to refuse.

Phelps Putnam withdrew from Kate's life, vowing to devote himself to his art. On the basis of his poem about her, critics were predicting that he had it in him to become a sort of American Chaucer or Rabelais. Putnam, for his part, indicated that he thought of himself and of the poetry he planned to write more in terms of Dante. For years Edmund Wilson and other admirers waited for him to produce his next great work, but it never happened. "The Daughters of the Sun" had been the pinnacle of his career. Putnam wrote almost nothing of note after that. He died twenty years later, frustrated and largely forgotten.

In June 1928, Philip Barry, in residence at his Villa Lorenzo in Cannes, France, wrote to Stephen Vincent Benet that he was completing a new comedy of manners for Arthur Hopkins about people who are too rich and have forgotten how to have fun.

Barry wrote *Holiday* with Hope Williams, "the Park Avenue swagger girl," in mind. She would play Linda Seton, the single ray of light and life in a family devoted to the worship of money and determined to snuff out Linda's originality and individuality. "She's developed the queerest—I don't know—attitude toward life," Julia Seton, Linda's stylish sister, says of her. "I can't make her out. She doesn't think as we do at all, any more."

Linda balks at her financier father's snobbery and insularity. She decries the family's "general atmosphere of plenty with the top riveted down on the cornucopia." She longs to escape the social conformity and superficial values that have stifled her sister and brother. "Do you know any living people?" Linda asks a visitor to the Seton mansion. "That's a cry from the heart." Linda senses that there are "damn few" such people, and hopes she might be one of them. She is—although beside Julia, the "boyish" Linda "seems a trifle gauche, and almost plain." Yet that is precisely the quality her creator prizes in her. She alone in the Seton family appears capable of thinking and acting for herself. She needs only the spur of a kindred spirit to find the courage to break loose.

That was exactly what had happened when Philip Barry and Arthur Hopkins prodded Hope Williams to shock her aristocratic family by going on the Broadway stage.

The actress Lynn Fontanne, appalled by Hope's swaggering walk, sent her to school to change it. After a first lesson, which consisted of walking naked with mirrors on all sides, Williams refused to return; and it was a good thing she did, as her "unladylike" flat-footed stride was the first thing audiences loved about her when she made her professional debut in *Paris Bound*. All Williams had to do was lope across the stage for theatergoers to erupt in appreciative laughter and applause.

The first tryout of *Holiday*, starring Hope Williams, was scheduled for November 18, 1928 at the Shubert Theater in New Haven, with the Broadway opening on the 26th. *These Days*, Arthur Hopkins's other production, opened in New York on November 12 and closed the same week, massacred by the critics, though Lawrence Langner of the Theater Guild later recalled that Kate Hepburn had "flashed like a comet" in her small role. The morning after *These Days* folded, Hopkins sent Kate back to New Haven to understudy for Hope Williams in the role of Linda Seton.

Kate's reputation preceded her. Donald Ogden Stewart, an

actor in the company, had been at Phillips Exeter Academy with Phelps Putnam; he was one of Phelpie's Yale roommates and closest friends. Philip Barry had known both Putnam and Stewart at Yale.

As a writer preoccupied with those moments when life breezes into the room in the form of a quirky character "like no one else one knows," Barry studied Kate intently through round, steel-rimmed glasses. Watching rehearsals from the stalls, Kate threw both legs over the seat in front of her. Childlike, she licked intently at an ice-cream cone.

She was staring at Hope Williams, slim, immaculate, and imperturbable. In the past few months, Kate had often been mistaken for a New York society girl; but Williams, with her upturned nose and cap of hair parted on the side, was the real thing. The high-flown manner of the finishing school came naturally to her. Williams spoke with astonishing brusqueness yet appeared to underplay every line. Noël Coward once described her speech as possessing "a kind of beguiling tonelessness." Even the wittiest remarks she delivered deadpan.

It was all very bewildering and intimidating to Kate, who was unable to crack the code of word and gesture in which Williams seemed to communicate with her co-stars Babs White and Beatrice Stewart. The trio, who had been at finishing school together, agreed that Kate was too "fresh and perky" for her own good; she would never get to play Linda Seton if they could help it.

When *Holiday* opened to glowing reviews, Kate regularly arrived at Broadway's Plymouth Theater an hour before anyone else. While another understudy watched from the auditorium, Kate, on the darkened stage, recited passages from Shakespeare.

"How are you feeling tonight?" Kate would ask whenever Hope Williams, in a Venetian red silk robe, peered out of her dressing-room door. Kate's eagerness strengthened the resolve of Hope and her friends to keep her from going on. On one occasion Beatrice Stewart and her husband Donald propelled Hope Williams, miserable with flu, onto the stage, so Kate wouldn't have her chance.

Again, Luddy seized the opportunity. Now that they had gone the limit, he pressed Kate to marry him at a moment when nothing would have given her greater pleasure than to walk out of the play.

Kate shocked Arthur Hopkins with the sudden announcement that she was giving up her theatrical career to marry Ludlow Ogden Smith, who planned to buy a grand house for her on the Philadelphia Main Line as soon as they returned from their honeymoon in Bermuda. To get Kate to marry him, Luddy had even agreed to change his name when she balked at the prospect of being known as "Mrs. Smith." Declaring that a man beginning a new life ought to have a new name to go with it, he rechristened himself "Ogden Ludlow," although Kate and the rest of the Hepburns continued to call him Luddy or Lud. Luddy's decision to drop the name "Smith" broke his mother Gertrude's heart. Kate's grandfather, whose wife had always respectfully addressed him as "Reverend Hepburn" even when they were in bed together, found the young man's willingness to change his name hard to understand.

In West Hartford to officiate at the ceremony on December 12, Reverend Sewell Stavely Hepburn, now eighty-three, reminded Luddy—as he had all prospective bridegrooms in the course of nearly sixty years of ministerial work—that the level-headedness needed to buy a horse was even more critical to the prudent selection of a woman. Kate, whose mother had worn black to her own wedding ceremony, wore a crushed white velvet dress with gold embroidery around the neck and down the front.

Luddy could not keep his hands off Kate. Now that they were married, he was even more physically demonstrative than in the past. He kissed and hugged his bride. He wrapped his arm around her broad, bladelike shoulders. He made her feel comforted and safe. Unlike Kate's father, who was forever carping and criticizing, Luddy had only words of praise. There was nothing Kate could say or do that would change his mind about her.

Kate was free of shyness or reticence with her husband. Warm, emotional, and affectionate, she did not feel guilty about enjoying herself sexually—why should she? She had grown up with parents who were unabashed in their displays of physical affection. Again and again throughout her childhood, Kate had heard Dr. and Mrs. Hepburn and Dr. and Mrs. Hooker speak of "the complete satisfaction of sexual desire" and "the mutual enjoyment of passion" as essential elements in any successful marriage.

"The mate is not really a mate at all in the deepest sense if he or she fails to comprehend the natural yearning for physical union," Edith wrote. "The emotion of love is embodied in physical passion and love itself is repudiated when it is denied full expression."

The uninhibited atmosphere in Dr. Hepburn's dressing room, which had initially shocked Alice Palache, thrilled and delighted Luddy whenever he and Kate spent time with her family. He treasured the warmth and excitement he perceived in the Hepburn household, which contrasted markedly with the coldness and formality of his own parents. The Hepburns were consummate performers who thrived on an audience; and Luddy loved nothing better than to watch the sparks fly when they debated world events.

Kate's mother tended to quiz her guests on their political opinions and to ignore them afterward if she did not like what she heard. Visitors who said the wrong thing rarely had the chance to talk politics with her again. Only with Luddy, who had voted for Herbert Hoover, did she make a concerted effort. The family knew that she must be very fond of the young man when she quoted Karl Marx to him at every opportunity. If she had disapproved of him, she would never have tried to show him the light.

When Kate and Luddy returned from their honeymoon in Bermuda, they toured stone farmhouses with post-and-rail fences set in the rural fantasy of the Philadelphia Main Line. Suddenly, Kate was stricken. "What am I doing?" she asked herself. "I couldn't live here!"

The house-hunt was abruptly canceled, and Kate told Luddy that she needed to return to New York at once. Instead of offering a protest, Luddy cheerfully agreed to follow; whatever Kate wanted was all right with him. She went directly to Arthur Hopkins's office above the second balcony at the Plymouth Theater to ask for her job back.

"Yes, of course," said Hopkins. "I expected you."

Kate was clearly of two minds about Luddy's readiness to give in. On the one hand, her upbringing had trained her to be egotistical and self-centered. Strong-willed like her father, she expected to get her way and gloated when Luddy instantly changed his plans to suit her. Like her aunt Edith, Kate had found a "saintly" husband who would happily back her in everything. But Kate's situation was more complicated than Edith's. Conflicting impulses fueled her. Perhaps only her family could see that even as Kate gleefully bossed Luddy around, there was a part of her that longed for him to react "strongly," as Dr. Hepburn would have done.

Luddy's charming ability to laugh at his own sometimes comical devotion made it difficult ever to be cross with him; in this, too, Luddy differed from her father, who always took himself very seriously indeed. Even Dr. Hepburn, who might have been expected to give his son-in-law a hard time, appreciated that Luddy so clearly shared the family's concern for Kate's well-being. Still, he left no doubt that he would have handled things very differently when Kate called off the house-hunt and demanded to return to New York.

By any standard, the newlyweds led an unusual life in New York, where Kate had gone back to work as Hope Williams's understudy. At the end of the day, hardly would Luddy return from his job at an insurance brokerage house when Kate would sweep out of their East 39th Street brownstone apartment. She jogged crosstown to the Plymouth Theater, where Arthur Hopkins expected her to sit through every performance lest Hope Williams suddenly fall ill. Hopkins, apparently, was oblivious to the cabal against Kate among the show's Social Register contingent; winter melted into spring and Kate never had a chance to go on.

In his wife's absence, Luddy, an aficionado of toy trains, tinkered with an elaborate miniature railroad he spent many years constructing. The music of Debussy, Stravinsky, Wagner, and the other composers in Luddy's vast record collection blasted on the Victrola. The landlord, an Englishman, sent meals up by dumbwaiter.

Many of Kate's colleagues in the theater never even knew she was married.

It was being said in New York that Hope Williams, in the role of Linda Seton, had created "a type new to the stage." Night after night, the Plymouth was filled with young women "making up their minds to be like her this winter," as the *New York Times* reported. Ironically, although Philip Barry had intended to pillory the very rich for their antagonism to originality and individuality, *Holiday*'s principal effect was to promote that year's "debutante look." Androgyny was in the air. Hope Williams's fame soared with the stock market. The Park Avenue swagger girl tapped into the popular imagination at the bullish close of a decade which had often seen fit to idolize the American rich.

Every night on Broadway, Hope Williams, in the role of Linda Seton, railed against lives "devoted to piling up money." But that was exactly what many Americans dreamed of doing at a moment when great fortunes seemed achingly within reach. Americans in record numbers were pouring their life savings into stocks and securities. Margin trading and artificially low interest rates encouraged people to put down a mere 10 or 20 percent and borrow the rest from the broker.

That spring of 1929, Dr. Hepburn operated on Samuel G. Dunham, president of the Hartford Electric Light Company. The wealthy patient spent several difficult months in the hospital. In August, when he was finally ready to go home, he told Dr. Hepburn to charge whatever he thought fair.

"You've been here a long time," replied Dr. Hepburn, thinking it over. "You're a very well-to-do person. I think it should cost about ten thousand dollars."

"That's all right," said Dunham.

Ten thousand dollars was precisely the sum Dr. Hepburn had borrowed to build his house after he sold off all his stocks. He wasted no time in changing into street clothes to dash over to Hartford National Bank.

"I want to pay off my loan," he told Bob Newell, a bank officer.

"Tom, don't do that," Newell urged. "We can invest this money and you can double it in no time!"

Almost any financial counselor would have given Dr. Hepburn the same advice. Investors large and small were quickly making great sums of money—on paper. In a time of low interest rates, people were not eager to reduce debt; on the contrary, they kept borrowing more to invest.

Not one to be swayed, Dr. Hepburn insisted on paying off the loan although friends and associates thought him a fool. Two months later, paper fortunes worth about thirty billion dollars disappeared in the stock market crash. For years afterward, in the dressing room at Bloomfield Avenue, Dr. Hepburn never tired of reminding Palache and other visitors that he had gotten out of the market and paid off his loan just in time.

Still, the Hepburns did not escape the sting of the Great Depression. Medical bills were among the first that people stopped paying. In one year, Dr. Hepburn's earnings plummeted from $45,000 to $10,000.

After years of listening to Dr. Hepburn deride their mother as a spendthrift, the children were confronted with the unprecedented sight of Mrs. Hepburn cheerfully darning their socks. Yet household chores were the last thing on her mind. In November 1929, Mrs. Hepburn became legislative chairman of Margaret Sanger's National Committee on Federal Legislation for Birth Control. She was an obvious choice to spearhead the drive to change federal laws which classed contraception with obscenity and abortion. As Lucy Burns had said years before, outside of Alice Paul the two women in America who had the best grasp of the federal legislative process were Mrs. Hooker and Mrs. Hepburn.

Since 1923, Mrs. Hepburn had proved a tireless worker in the struggle to persuade Connecticut legislators to change the state law banning the prescription or use of birth control. Much as she had once done on behalf of women's suffrage, every two years she mounted a campaign to push through a birth control bill in Hartford. Her efforts came to a climax at the 1929 session, where, testifying with an official of the American Eugenics Society, Mrs. Hepburn delivered a controversial speech arguing that unfit parents who have children "are common criminals and ought to be in jail." Her provocative remarks seemed to court danger in a town where a great many people were aware of what had happened to her son. At times,

Mrs. Hepburn appears to have kept up the fight to legalize birth control at great psychological cost.

She had been very hesitant about agreeing to work with Margaret Sanger in Washington. Besides Dr. Hepburn's standard objection to his wife spending time away from Connecticut, there was Mrs. Hepburn's own deep ambivalence about Mrs. Sanger. Their relations veered wildly between a degree of intimacy unusual for Mrs. Hepburn and moments of icy distance in which she suddenly sought to draw back; there was almost nothing between the extremes.

It cannot have been easy to face the prospect of working more closely than ever with a woman who reminded her of a past she preferred to forget. Worse, the national publicity the chairmanship would entail threatened Mrs. Hepburn and her family with the exposure of painful and damaging secrets. In the end, she accepted Mrs. Sanger's invitation, but with noticeable reluctance.

The tycoon J. Horace Harding, delegate-at-large to the 1928 Republican national convention that nominated Herbert Hoover for president, did not live to see the Great Crash the following year. Harding, a banker, chairman of the board of the American Express Company, and director of many major corporations, contracted a cold on New Year's Day 1929. Three days later, surrounded by a vast art collection that included paintings by Goya and El Greco, Harding died of "influenza complicated by blood poisoning." He left a stone mansion on Fifth Avenue in New York; a country home, Thornton, at Rumson, New Jersey; and an estate worth many millions of dollars. His debutante daughter Laura, traveling in Europe at the time, was rumored to have inherited seven million dollars as her share alone.

When Laura, a pert brunette with hazel eyes and a golden complexion, returned from Paris, she studied acting with Frances Robinson-Duff. Like Hope Williams, Laura was a graduate of Miss Porter's finishing school and had appeared in society amateur theatricals. Dreaming of a stage career, she worked in summer stock at the Berkshire Playhouse in Stockbridge, Massachusetts; and in

October 1929, she appeared at Chicago's Princess Theater in *Thunder in the Air*. Laura had the small role of a parlormaid until word got out that the seven-million-dollar-girl was in the cast. Upset by the nationwide publicity, she fled the show.

That spring of 1930, Laura was planning to return to the Berkshire Playhouse when Frances Robinson-Duff asked her to talk to Kate Hepburn.

Kate's career had yet to take off. After attending performances of *Holiday* for six months without once going on stage herself, she went to France with Luddy. When she returned, Kate finally had the opportunity to play Linda Seton for one night at the Riviera Theater on Upper Broadway, where the company was preparing for their tour.

It was an unsettling experience. Struggling to imitate Hope Williams, Kate was conscious of getting no response to lines that usually elicited peals of laughter. She wore Hope Williams's costume, which did not quite fit, as Kate was several inches taller.

Soon afterward, Kate landed a part in *Death Takes a Holiday*, but was fired in Philadelphia during previews. And she was dismissed from the Theater Guild production of Turgenev's *A Month in the Country* after the leading lady Alla Nazimova complained to the casting director, Cheryl Crawford: "I don't want that girl in the company. She's never on time for rehearsals. Her excuses are that she's been fencing or taking lessons or playing tennis. Fire her."

It was then that Frances Robinson-Duff put Kate together with Laura Harding. Robinson-Duff hoped she might decide to spend the summer honing her skills at the Berkshire Playhouse, where Alexander Kirkland and Cowles Strickland were preparing productions of *The Admirable Crichton* and *The Romantic Young Lady*.

Kate lasted only two weeks at Stockbridge before walking out in a huff when she was not cast in leading roles. She spent the rest of the summer at Fenwick with Luddy. But those two weeks, during which she roomed with the American Express heiress in a one-bathroom theatrical boarding house run by a decorous English minister and his alcoholic Southern wife, had a lasting impact on Kate.

Poised and sophisticated like a character in a Philip Barry play,

Laura Harding would initiate Kate into the customs and status symbols of the very rich. She would help crack the code that had bewildered Kate when she watched Hope Williams and her friends in the cast of *Holiday*. For many months, raggedy Kate had pressed her nose against a cold window to peek inside; Laura was her ticket to that glittering private party.

Kate was brash, spontaneous, and unconventional. Laura, sleek and impeccably tailored, always knew the thing to do; she knew what good taste was all about. Where Kate's "impossible" gravelly voice cracked and squeaked with unrestrained excitement, Laura spoke in low, carefully modulated tones.

Laura made no bones about disapproving of what she called her friend's bohemian ways. She could smooth Kate's rough edges and eliminate her gaucheries; she could put a little Park Avenue in the girl. Yet those were precisely the qualities that endeared Kate to people like Philip Barry, who, in the meantime, had quietly begun to outline a new heroine "made of platinum wire and sand" based on Hepburn. Daisy Sage, "slim, lithe, a stripling, but with dignity beyond her years and a rare grace to accompany it," differed from Barry heroines like Linda Seton in her lack of a moneyed background. In *The Animal Kingdom*, Daisy sets off sparks when she collides with the deadening social conformity of the status-seekers who surround her.

That season, while Kate appeared in Benn W. Levy's "rose-colored comedy" *Art and Mrs. Bottle* at Maxine Elliott's Theater in New York, she had no idea that Philip Barry was in Bermuda, writing *The Animal Kingdom* for her. Several months later, Kate was rehearsing in summer stock at the Ivoryton Playhouse near Fenwick when the producer Gilbert Miller called to offer her the role of Daisy.

As Kate read the script about a sensitive man torn between his wife and his mistress, it was not difficult to recognize herself in Daisy. And in the lover's insistence to his mistress that theirs is a spiritual relationship between friends, it was not hard to hear echoes of Phelps Putnam.

Clearly, Philip Barry had observed Kate far more intently than she had ever imagined. Like Phelpie, he had "taken up the heat of life from her"; but the playwright at least intended to return the favor by allowing Kate to play Daisy opposite Leslie Howard when *The Animal Kingdom* opened at the Broadhurst Theater in January. Daisy Sage, like Linda Seton in *Holiday*, was the sort of role designed to make a girl a star.

Gilbert Miller, from the first, strongly opposed hiring Hepburn. In the past theatrical season, he had produced Barry's new play *Tomorrow and Tomorrow*, in which the relatively inexperienced Zita Johann had given him a good deal of trouble. The producer did not wish to encounter similar problems with Kate. No matter that Philip Barry had modeled Daisy Sage on her; Kate's credits hardly seemed to qualify her for the part.

Still, Barry prevailed; and Kate went into rehearsal that November 1931 only to be fired five days later after Leslie Howard repeatedly complained that he could not work with "that beanpole." At home with Luddy, Kate bitterly blamed her faux pas of having appeared at the first rehearsal in high heels that made her tower over Leslie Howard. But when she called Philip Barry, the playwright, roused from his bath, offered a very different explanation: "Well, to be brutally frank, you weren't very good."

Phelps Putnam had relished those moments when Kate's anger "like a sudden mob swept into murderous action"; Philip Barry, in a more prosaic vein, compared her fury to a "fishwife's tirade."

"You can't let them do this to me! You've always said I was ideal for this role. I am! I'm it! They're ruining your play! They're gypping me! I won't stand for it!"

Barry shouted in reply: "They're right about you! Nobody with your vicious disposition could possibly play light comedy! You're totally unsuited to the part! I'm glad they threw you out!"

Hope Williams, who had signed a five-picture contract with RKO, could hardly have anticipated that Kate would lose her role in *The Animal Kingdom*. Some months before, she had gasped at the news that Philip Barry had written a marvelous new play for her former understudy. Williams languished in Hollywood without any of the promised film projects materializing; word of Kate's sudden ascendancy came as a bitter blow. Before she went to RKO, Williams had signed with Arthur Hopkins to return to Broadway in the spring of 1932 as the Amazon warrior Antiope in Julian Thompson's comedy *The Warrior's Husband*. Disappointment in Hollywood, coupled with the news about Kate, caused Williams to change her mind. With Hepburn set to become the new Barry girl on Broadway, Hope Williams preferred to launch herself in a serious stage role. Hopkins dropped their commitment to the Thompson play, replacing it with Gretchen Damrosch's *The Passing Present*.

Unable to get Hope Williams for *The Warrior's Husband,* producer Harry Moses decided to offer the role to her *Holiday* understudy.

That March of 1932, you could buy Phelps Putnam's second volume of verse, whose centerpiece was the long poem about Kate, at almost any good bookstore in Manhattan; recently published by Scribner's, *The Four Seasons* already had many fervent admirers, including T. S. Eliot. Or you could stop at the Broadhurst Theater to see the successful production of *The Animal Kingdom* with its finely etched portrait of Daisy Sage, where Frances Fuller played the role Philip Barry had written for Kate. But to see the thing itself, you went to the Morosco Theater.

Every night, for nearly two hours prior to curtain time, Kate, in a greenish-blue bathing suit, bronzed her lean arms, legs, and face with a large jar of greasepaint. She curled her hair Amazon-style over her forehead and at the nape of her neck, nearly always singeing herself in the process. Whenever a maid tried to help, Kate waved her away, insisting she didn't like to be "fussed over." She then donned a brief chainmail tunic and silver leather shin guards. She arranged her hair to curl out from beneath a tall silver helmet.

About ten minutes after the curtain rose, she flung a stag over her shoulder and, bare-legged, hurtled down a long, steep, narrow stairway amid swirling lights at the rear of the stage. She threw the carcass at the foot of the Amazon queen and—very gallant— dropped to one knee.

"Get me a bowl of water, will you?" Kate roared to one of the queen's attendants. "I'm in a terrific sweat!"

Theatergoers went wild.

F O U R T E E N

As the Super Chief screeched to a halt in the Pasadena railroad station on July 4, 1932, Kate smelled orange blossoms and squirmed with pain from the three flecks of steel rail stuck in her bloodshot left eye.

Laura Harding's dogs, a Scottie named Jamie and a Shelbourne terrier called Twig, yapped madly at the parade of Louis Vuitton luggage being wheeled out of Kate and Laura's private drawing room. With the full blessing of Luddy, who could not leave New York because of work, Laura served as Kate's companion as she traveled west to appear in her first film. It had been agreed that they would return to New York in a month or so, as soon as Kate fulfilled the terms of a one-picture deal. As always, Luddy had been delighted to see her so happy and excited.

Despite the scorching heat, Kate wore a Quaker gray-blue silk cutaway coat with padded shoulders over a ruffled turtleneck and long flared skirt. She wore dark blue gloves and a blue straw pancake hat. The New York designer Elizabeth Hawes, self-styled "Panther Woman of the Needle Trades," dressed women to look like "she-wolves"; but the Hollywood agent Myron Selznick, who had never seen his new client before, thought Kate looked like nothing so much as a cadaver.

Holding Laura's arm and squinting in the sunlight, Kate stepped down from the train. Each time she blinked, she felt a stab of pain.

"We got $1500 for that?" Myron Selznick said to his partner Leland Hayward with a laugh, referring to the weekly salary they

269

had negotiated with Myron's brother David Selznick for Hepburn to appear in George Cukor's *A Bill of Divorcement* at RKO.

The buzz about Kate's performance in *The Warrior's Husband* had led to two screen tests. John Ford shot the first test when Fox expressed interest in doing a film version of the play. Shortly thereafter, George Cukor ordered a test of his own, shot by an RKO scout in New York. Watching Kate play a scene from *Holiday*, David Selznick reacted to the test with the violent antipathy that would characterize his personal feelings about her even after she had become a star. He found Kate Hepburn sexually repellent.

Cukor, for his part, had no love for the mannered style of acting Kate affected. He was about to dismiss her as a mere curiosity when something she did on screen suddenly jolted him to attention. It was a simple gesture: lowering a glass to the floor with her back to the camera. Yet the moment moved him deeply.

The crest of emotion did not carry over into their meeting on July 4 as Leland Hayward and Myron Selznick rushed Kate, pancake hat slightly askew, straight from the train station into Cukor's tiny ground floor office at RKO. She had no opportunity to work herself up.

"Mr. Cukor!" she broadcasted through the nose. "I have something in my eye! Do you know a doctor?"

The short, plump director, in a short-sleeved white shirt that showed his hairy arms, studied Kate through wire-framed glasses with thick lenses. What he saw dismayed him.

"I want you to see the sketches," Cukor said. "What do you think of those?"

"Well!" said Kate, with scarcely a glance at the costume designs. "I really don't think that a well-bred English girl would wear anything like that."

Laura Harding tittered in the background.

Kate continued: "I should think she would be wearing . . . do you know Chanel?" Kate pointed to Laura's suit. "Miss Harding has a Chanel."

"What do you think of what you have on?" Cukor snapped.

"I think it's very smart," said Kate, astonished he would ask.

"Well, I think it stinks!" said Cukor. "Now, we can proceed from there."

Cukor possessed a lethal combination of insecurity and arrogance. Eager to be thought of as a man of breeding and social position, he reacted violently to Kate's put-down. Yet it was precisely the put-down that instantly attracted him to Kate and Laura; the women, with their air of "slumming it in Hollywood," seemed to represent a world of East Coast old money from which Cukor, ugly, Jewish and homosexual, felt hopelessly excluded.

To Cukor's surprise, Hepburn responded to his chiding by just letting it roll off her "knife"—as the director described it, echoing Phelps Putnam's image of Kate as a "dagger": shiny, metallic, and blade-thin. Only much later did Kate admit that, accustomed to being slapped across the face by Dr. Hepburn, she was not about to be thrown when Cukor barked at her.

Cukor instructed her to remove her hat. Wearing her hair skimmed back off her face made Kate appear gaunt and skeletal. Her long, fine hair was tightly rolled back in a knot and lanced with protruding hairpins. On close inspection, the hair itself seemed dull and brittle. Cukor ordered it cut to chin length and brushed out to fall in a natural wave. Daily egg shampoos were prescribed to restore the luster. Wearing her hair shorter and fuller around the face would soften Kate's features and call attention to her eyes.

After a private physician finally removed the steel particles from her left eye, Kate returned to the studio in a chauffeur-driven Hispano-Suiza with a flying silver stork on the hood. The battle-chariot of a car, rented by Laura, gave rise to a rumor, soon picked up in the press, that Kate was "heiress to untold millions."

Laura had once fled a show in Chicago when word got out that she was an heiress from New York, yet that was exactly the impression Kate hoped to create about herself. The masquerade would never have worked in Manhattan or on Long Island, but when Kate appeared in Hollywood with Laura Harding at her side, it was hard for people like George Cukor to tell the difference between them. Kate had studied Laura as though she were a part in a play.

As Kate stepped before the movie cameras for the first time on July 9, 1932 on Stage 5 at RKO studios, several factors were working in her favor.

Without a word to Kate, her aunt Edith, who had once had acting aspirations of her own, asked a favor of her old friend Florence Sabin, now an eminent research scientist at the Rockefeller Institute in New York. Long before she entered the Hopkins medical school, Dr. Sabin had worked as governess to Ned Sheldon, a prominent playwright as well as friend and mentor to John Barrymore. When Mrs. Hooker learned that her niece would be playing John Barrymore's daughter in *A Bill of Divorcement*, she arranged for Ned Sheldon quietly to ask the fifty-year-old actor to look out for Kate.

Barrymore, often contemptuous of film work, pleasantly surprised everyone in the first scene he shot with Kate that Saturday morning. At first, he merely walked through the take, which required him to enter his living room, wearing a shabby hat and raincoat, after an absence of many years in a mental institution. As Barrymore fiddles with some pipes on the mantelpiece, Kate, the daughter he has never met, watches without his being aware of her presence.

When the camera stopped, Barrymore, perhaps remembering his promise, shot a guilty look at Kate. He walked over and took her chin in his hands.

"I'd like to do it again," Barrymore called softly, and Cukor was only too happy to oblige. Kate watched with amazement as Barrymore, with new focus, performed the second take in a manner vastly superior to the first.

From that point on, Barrymore seemed to do everything he could to help Kate. There were no hard feelings when she rebuffed the obligatory pass. Barrymore winked at Cukor when Kate did well and pushed her in front of the camera when her innocence of film technique was all too evident.

"Be yourself, draw on your emotions," Cukor urged whenever Kate reverted to her high-flown Philip Barry acting style. It was sound advice—although Cukor can scarcely have suspected the extent to which Kate's own background would fuel her portrait of Sydney Fairfield.

In the course of the film, Sydney learns about the taint of blood that has plunged her father and aunt into madness and might someday affect her own children. A girl who had once sacrificed her own emotional needs to protect a tormented father—and who knew the terror of suicidal instability in her own family—could well understand Sydney Fairfield's pivotal decision: she resolves to stand with her father against the world although that means renouncing a normal life with the young man she had hoped to marry.

Cukor found Kate wonderfully photogenic; from the first she appeared at ease in front of the camera. He marveled at the way her skin seemed to attract light. Yet when David Selznick studied the first footage he continued to be put off by Hepburn's appearance, which one studio bigwig described as "a cross between a horse and a monkey." Selznick's distaste put immense pressure on Cukor, who was responsible for her presence at RKO. *A Bill of Divorcement* was one of Selznick's pet projects; Hepburn's failure with audiences, which Selznick seemed to think inevitable, would be on Cukor's head.

On August 2, Laura Harding, paid $10 for her services, was one of ten young women employed as extras in a party scene. Kate, wearing an organza dress with sleeves cut like angel's wings, descended a staircase and waltzed off with her beau, played by David Manners. Laura, pausing at the foot of the staircase, rested her hand on the newel post. As Laura's young man approached, the ball-shaped top of the newel post came loose in her palm. Flustered, she handed the ball to him; the actor screamed; and Cukor, stamping with rage, dashed over and hit Laura for ruining the shot. The incident, one day before principal photography finished, suggested the tension on the set, where Selznick's dismay with Hepburn and dire predictions for the film were no secret.

As Kate did some retakes before leaving California, RKO seemed most unlikely to pick up her option. Early previews, especially the August 30 screening for the trade papers, changed everything. David Selznick, seated in a darkened theater, heard the audience stir with excitement when Hepburn performed so simple an act as stretching out in front of the fireplace. As Cukor had been when he watched her lower a glass to the floor in her screen test, people were inexplicably very moved.

Although Selznick continued to find Kate personally repellent, the businessman in him could hardly deny the accolades with which the trade press garlanded his new discovery: "*A Bill of Divorcement* is an event, a milestone in motion picture history," proclaimed the *Hollywood Reporter* on August 31. "After last night, there is a new star on the cinema horizon, and her name is Katharine Hepburn. The dynamic way in which this newcomer swept the audience off its feet at the preview is only a forerunner of the way she will capture followers by the millions, all over the country, unless all signs fail. Not many times in the history of celluloid entertainment has there been such a first performance as Miss Hepburn gives."

The *Hollywood Herald* compared Kate to Duse, Katharine Cornell, Greta Garbo, and Lynn Fontanne: "She has a rugged sincerity that is momentarily masculine in its graceful strength, yet in the passing of a few tiny celluloid frames she becomes as soft, as sympathetic, as appealing as a lovely woman can be. She is so real, so genuine—well, darn it all what's her next picture? We want a front seat!"

Before Kate left, she signed a new contract with David Selznick, who was suddenly very eager to pick up the option on her future services before a rival studio snatched her. Kate recognized that if she was going to work steadily in Hollywood, she and her husband were going to have to come to some agreement about their life together. For the moment, however, she and Luddy were determined to put off all serious discussion until they had returned from a celebratory holiday in Europe. There would be plenty of time to make important decisions about their future living arrangements when they got back.

Things did not work out quite as the couple had planned. Their vacation was abruptly cut short when RKO ordered Kate, then in Europe, to report to work immediately to begin her next picture, *Three Came Unarmed*.

Kate and Luddy sailed for New York early; she went directly to Los Angeles, and he returned to his job at an insurance brokerage house in Manhattan. Once again, Laura Harding, who had plenty of free time and no need to earn a living of her own, served as Kate's traveling companion. Kate and Luddy's serious talk about their living arrangements was put off for another few weeks until she came home after completing *Three Came Unarmed*.

But when Kate appeared at the studio, it quickly became apparent that the film was not ready to begin shooting. There were several postponements, and finally *Three Came Unarmed* was dropped from her schedule altogether. By that time it was December, and the separation from Luddy had dragged on much longer than either one of them had anticipated. Their reunion—and big talk—would have to wait until after she had completed *Christopher Strong*, the new film to which Selznick had assigned her. Luddy might have come out to California during Christmas week, but Kate expected to be very busy with work then; she would have little time for him.

Leland Hayward liked to boast about the many famous women to whom he had made love. He referred to them as the girls on his scalp bracelet. Even Greta Garbo had apparently been unable to resist the rangy young man with "pleading" china-blue eyes and close-cropped hair said to be the texture of duck's down.

Hayward wore beautifully tailored dark flannel suits, pink shirts with diamond cufflinks, and the finest linen boxer shorts ordered from London. He owned more than three hundred pairs of tiny shoes and a vast collection of handkerchiefs. He never traveled between coasts with fewer than thirty shirts. He doused himself with bay rum and maintained a bronze tan with an array of sun lamps around his twenty-two-foot office desk, once a refectory table in an Italian monastery.

He spent much of a typical business day stretched out on his office sofa in check-stockinged feet. With three telephones propped on his flat chest, Leland conducted several calls at a time. To spare his delicate nerves, the phones in his office never buzzed; instead, a soft magenta light announced incoming calls.

Thirty years old, unmuscular and unathletic, he prided himself on taking no regular exercise other than nightly lovemaking. It was said in Hollywood that a big part of Leland Hayward's business success was due to the fact that he didn't look or act like an agent— and that the wives of the moguls never stopped talking about him.

Hayward had shown little interest in Kate when she first arrived. Back then, Hepburn's scalp didn't seem worth having. His New York office had agreed to represent her only when RKO asked them to inquire about the young star of *The Warrior's Husband*. By the time Kate returned from her vacation in Europe with Luddy four months later, Leland's attitude had changed entirely. The phenomenal success of *A Bill of Divorcement* made him decide to turn on some of his famous charm.

It was very much in Leland's favor that Laura remembered him from New York, where his father lived in a stone mansion on Fifth Avenue not far from the Harding residence. Before flunking out of Princeton, "adorable" Leland had been head of the stag line at the coming-out parties Laura had attended in Manhattan. Laura, who made a great point of looking down her nose at most people in filmland, instantly warmed to Leland as one of her own kind.

Although Kate had never met Leland before coming to Hollywood, he was familiar to her as well. His father, Colonel William Hayward, had been Aunty Towle's boss in the U.S. Attorney's office in New York, so the name Hayward had often been mentioned in the Hepburn household.

That December, Kate began work on *Christopher Strong* for Dorothy Arzner, one of the few women directors in Hollywood in the period. Leland soon became a fixture at Quinta Nirvana, the Spanish ranch house she rented with Laura in Coldwater Canyon. In the beginning, the trio enjoyed wonderful gossip-filled dinners. They came to view themselves as lonely New Yorkers who had drifted far from home and were superior to their new surroundings. Hayward, a compulsive talker, dazzled Kate with his intimate knowledge of all the players in Hollywood. In attitude and manner, he reminded her of the writers and artists she had met with Phelps Putnam.

Before long, he was regularly spending the night in Kate's bedroom, although he continued to maintain quarters at the Beverly Hills Hotel. At Quinta Nirvana, closets and drawers suddenly overflowed with great quantities of Leland's elegant clothes—a new experience for Kate, who was accustomed to Dr. Hepburn's two suits and two pairs of shoes. Luddy, a typical wealthy Philadelphian, tended to keep coats and trousers until they wore out.

At dinnertime, Leland would have a drink while Kate and Laura ate their meal. As Kate prepared to go to bed early, Leland left for a night on the town. In restaurants and nightclubs, he made contacts and gathered the information essential to his business. Kate, still very much a married woman, always insisted that she would not have wanted to join him on his rounds; but the fact remained that Leland himself had a wife in New York.

Leland was now in his second marriage to the former Lola Gibbs. He had been so obsessed with Lola that he was rumored to have attempted suicide after she divorced him in 1922. They married again eight years later.

It simply would not do for Kate and Leland to be seen about town together, so they conducted their relationship in secret with Laura as a beard. When Leland crawled home at midnight, he knew that Kate would be waiting for him in bed. His mind spinning with the many details he had heard that evening, Leland usually needed to unwind. Rambling on, he shared all the gossip with Kate.

At this point, both partners found the relationship exceedingly comfortable and convenient; beyond sex, there were few demands and no long-term expectations. They were both busy people who poured their time and energy into work.

Totally dedicated to whatever project she happened to be working on, Kate developed the capacity to turn off everything else. According to Palache, this single-mindedness eliminated the need to make decisions. Once Kate committed herself to something, it was to the exclusion of everything—and everyone—else.

In a period when Kate would make five films in a little over a year, she often arrived at the studio as early as 6 a.m. for her daily egg shampoo and did not leave until 6:30 p.m. She worked six days a week. Sundays—Kate's day off—were taken up by tennis and golf; Leland, who hated sports, never joined her.

Laura's high public profile in Kate's life, coupled with the absence of any visible man, gave rise to a rumor that the women enjoyed a sexual relationship. There was no truth to it. That Hepburn shared a bed with Leland Hayward virtually every night he was in town remained largely unknown.

Luddy as yet had no idea that he was being cuckolded. As far as he was concerned, Kate's prolonged presence in Los Angeles was an accident of circumstance. He had every expectation that she would soon return to their apartment in Murray Hill, where they could both calmly plan for the future. If a film career was what Kate wanted, that was what Luddy thought she should have; his work, of course, was secondary. He seemed not to care about newspaper reports that quoted Kate as denying that she was married. His faith in her was absolute.

By this time, Luddy had established himself as very much a member of the Hepburn family; even in Kate's absence, he spent most weekends with her parents in Connecticut. He was especially kind to Kate's sisters, showering them with gifts and taking them on excursions to New York. He and Jack Clarke built a new log cabin with a fireplace and chimney for the girls. Marion, an unhappy child prone to black moods, grew particularly close to Luddy.

Dr. Hepburn came to depend on his son-in-law's mechanical skills—never a Hepburn speciality—to repair Fenwick's notorious plumbing and electricity. When the radio broke, everyone simply waited for Luddy to fix it. At the dinner table, where each family member was expected to perform his or her turn, Luddy's meandering stories were greeted with affectionate cries that he should get to the point.

With Luddy this close to the Hepburns, how could anything go wrong between him and Kate?

That January of 1933, Kate was plunged into a deep personal crisis while filming *Christopher Strong*. Zoë Akins's screenplay portrayed a flamboyant Amelia Earhart-like aviator who begins a sexual relationship with a married man. For the first time on screen, Kate, wearing jodhpurs and leather helmet in the character of Lady Cynthia Darrington, could project the "rugged feminism" that would be an important part of the Hepburn image.

In a sense, Kate was playing precisely the sort of free-spirited woman her mother and aunt had worked to make possible. *Christopher Strong* explored the choices an independent woman must make between love and career. In her depiction of the plight of an unmarried woman who becomes pregnant, Kate was suddenly capable of communicating with an audience larger and more diverse than any Mrs. Hepburn or Mrs. Hooker might ever have dreamed of reaching.

Kate's crisis erupted prior to shooting the sequence where Lady Cynthia, in desperation over the unplanned pregnancy, takes her own life by removing her oxygen mask at an altitude of thirty thousand feet. By no means a quick death, this method of suicide called for the actress to seem to fight the natural impulse to return the mask to her face. Dorothy Arzner saw the moment as a dramatic act of will on Lady Cynthia's part. Unaware of the grotesque echoes of young Tom Hepburn's suicide, Arzner could hardly understand the inner turmoil that led Kate to be absent for two days, January 26 and 27, causing the entire production to be shut down, or repeatedly to leave the set early when she returned.

Kate finished *Christopher Strong* on February 3, and headed for New York soon afterward. In Los Angeles, Kate's single-mindedness had permitted her to concentrate on work—and the undemanding affair with Leland. Going home meant facing her husband; it would no longer be possible to put Luddy out of her thoughts.

Luddy had once seemed worldly and glamorous; he had been there for Kate when she needed to feel loved and protected. Beside a slick character like Leland Hayward, however, the devoted husband lost his luster. After a little over four years of marriage, Kate had outgrown Luddy, and now she faced the difficult task of letting him down gently.

From the beginning, Kate had always believed that she could

tell Luddy anything and that he would not think less of her for it. So she told him the truth: She had slept with another man. When she returned to Los Angeles, she planned to continue sleeping with him. She did not want to hurt Luddy, but there it was.

Kate may have seen her marriage as finished, but her husband didn't view it that way at all: All right, another man had made love to her and no doubt would make love to her again. But it was only an affair. It wouldn't last. Kate didn't know her own mind. Luddy was confident that she would eventually return to him. He loved her too much to let Leland Hayward or any other man come between them. In Luddy's hands, passivity became a powerful weapon.

He wanted to photograph her. At a moment when she was trying to push him away psychologically, he used a camera to get close to her. Kate went on automatic pilot, flirting with the lens while Luddy took pictures much as he had done when they first knew each other.

When they drove up to Connecticut, Kate confessed everything to her mother. Mrs. Hepburn responded with frustrating silence.

As she would have done with any of the children, Mrs. Hepburn did her best to seem aloof, encouraging Kate to make up her own mind about what to do—and whether it was right. At such times, Aunty Towle would scream that Mrs. Hepburn simply had to speak her mind. The mother always resisted. Yet somehow her children knew exactly what she thought. Mrs. Hepburn communicated her feelings silently, in small but unmistakable ways.

There could be no mistaking Mrs. Hepburn's—indeed the entire family's—fondness for Luddy. More than ever now, Mrs. Hepburn made a point of showing him every kindness. She and Luddy were constantly disappearing for long talks together. Although Mrs. Hepburn refused to take sides, she made her position abundantly clear: She was not going to let Kate's affair with Leland Hayward affect Luddy's position in the family.

Mrs. Hepburn had been Kate's staunch supporter when Dr. Hepburn tried to block her stage career. She wanted all three of her daughters to do something more with their lives than Dr. Hepburn had in mind for them. She did not, however, approve of the decidedly commercial turn Kate's career had taken; she would have preferred to see her daughter in something by Shakespeare or Shaw. So long as Kate was not appearing in classic roles, Mrs. Hepburn had a good deal of trouble taking her acting as seriously as Kate would have liked.

And Mrs. Hepburn could not abide Kate's "New York society girl" persona and the values that went with it. As early as 1931, Mrs. Hepburn, eager to counter Laura Harding's influence, had gone so far as to arrange for the more down-to-earth Alice Palache to come to New York to work for Margaret Sanger.

When Kate returned from Hollywood in 1933, Palache, like Luddy and Aunty, was a regular member of the Hepburn family circle. At the dinner table, Mrs. Hepburn made a point of showing great interest in Palache's activities. By contrast, Kate's film career seemed only to bore her. After a lifetime of encouraging Kate to babble on about anything and everything, Mrs. Hepburn, a skilled listener, did not bother to conceal her lack of concern with the comings and goings of Hollywood.

Palache, however, was deeply interested in Kate's affair with a married man—and Kate soon found out why. The previous August, Palache, who had yet to "go the limit," had begun her first serious relationship. Not long afterward, Russell Jones, an advertising account executive, confessed that he had a wife and children in suburban Ardsley. Insisting that his wife was an invalid with whom he no longer had a real marriage, he explained that he had no intention of leaving her until the children were grown up. "We'll do what we can," Palache had replied, seeming to accept his terms.

Kate had settled nothing in her own life when she returned to Los Angeles to begin work on *Morning Glory*, to be directed by Lowell Sherman. Luddy, who insisted on seeing her off that April of 1933, vowed to wait for her no matter what.

At Quinta Nirvana, Kate fell back into her nocturnal relationship with Leland Hayward. Although she was sleeping with her agent, she refused to follow his professional advice: Hayward had urged her to turn down the script by Zoë Akins about a self-centered, stage-struck young actress modeled on Tallulah Bankhead.

Sherman, John Barrymore's brother-in-law, held one week of rehearsals before launching into a frantic shooting schedule that had principal photography completed in nineteen days. Paid $2500 a week—$1000 more than for her first two pictures, and a very substantial salary for a relative newcomer—Kate turned in her most accomplished performance to date as Eva Lovelace, a starving actress who calls attention to herself at a New York party by reciting two scenes from Shakespeare. Hired to understudy for the tempestuous star of a new Broadway show, Eva gets her big break when the leading lady storms out on opening night.

After the intense Sydney Fairfield in *A Bill of Divorcement* and the stark, strident Lady Cynthia in *Christopher Strong*, Hepburn impressed critics with the unexpected "gentleness" of her Eva Lovelace. "At the moment," the *New York Herald Tribune* declared, "Miss Katharine Hepburn is the cinema's wonder girl."

Success did not make Kate blasé—far from it. To those who worked closely with her now, it was evident that she thought herself very lucky to be acting. For all the superb reviews, she saw each new film role as a great opportunity. On a film set, her excitement was contagious. George Cukor, who shared Kate's childlike delight in being allowed to make movies, called her "a force of nature." She wanted—no, expected—everyone around her to share her passion. Kate could hardly abide people who failed to find the work as "thrilling" as she did.

And she needed to be admired. She thrived on enthusiasm and praise. Worship made her blossom. Directors who told Kate she was wonderful found that she did everything possible to live up to what they thought of her. She was quite capable of accepting criticism, but lack of interest, a hint that someone might find her boring, could cause her to wither. George Cukor saw it happen when he directed her as the tomboy Jo March in *Little Women* that summer of 1933.

Every time Kate went before the camera, she sensed someone watching her with disgust. When she looked up and searched the set, she saw the granite-jawed woman hired to tutor the child actress Jean Parker, looking as though she found Kate boring and silly. Her presence had a paralyzing effect on Kate, who could hardly play in front of her.

Finally, when Cukor thought he knew what was wrong, he approached Kate.

"Have you noticed that schoolteacher?" he asked. "What is the matter with her?"

"It's agonizing," Kate confirmed.

"She has been absolutely destroying me because I wonder what she is thinking," said Cukor.

The director saw Kate laugh to herself.

"I'm going to fire her," he went on. "I've never fired anybody but I'm going to fire her."

"Fire her, you're right!" Kate grinned, won over by Cukor's acute sensitivity to her needs.

But when he hesitated, Kate took matters into her own hands.

"I'll fix it!" she declared. With Cukor rooting from the sidelines, Kate marched up to the teacher.

"Do you enjoy this work?"

"What work?" the woman snapped.

"Seeing the scenes and everything."

"No, I don't like working in a studio."

"Why don't you depart?"

Indignant, the teacher walked out and never returned.

Director and actress were not always so in tune. On one occasion, the explosive Cukor slapped Kate hard across the face when she flubbed a shot.

"You amateur!" he yelled.

"Well, that's your opinion," Hepburn shot back for all to hear. She made a point of holding her chin very high.

On another occasion, Kate defended cast members against one of Cukor's tirades: "Just because you don't know what you're doing, don't take it out on us!" she cried.

The remark hit Cukor where it hurt. An expert director of actors, Cukor was notoriously weak on matters of script, camerawork, and editing. He lacked the ability, characteristic of the best directors, to substitute an image for a line of dialogue. Instead of paring down his scripts, he tended to bloat them with additional speech.

For all the sparring, however, Kate and her director recognized each other as kindred spirits who took ravenous pleasure in every aspect of their work. Cukor, who collected eccentric, exciting, theatrical women as friends, soon added Hepburn to his list. There developed a kind of instant intimacy between them. Kate regularly swam nude in his pool, and he confided his perpetual torments about his weight and physical unattractiveness. She began to attend Cukor's Sunday lunches, where she played the innocent little girl with *grandes dames* like Zoë Akins, Ethel Barrymore, Fanny Brice, Ina Claire, and Tallulah Bankhead.

"Of all the dreary, opinionated college girls I ever hoped to meet!" Bankhead exclaimed to Cukor after her first encounter with Kate, insisting that Kate reminded her of nothing so much as "a New England spinster."

And Kate complained: "I must say your friend Miss Bankhead uses all sorts of words. I don't think it's very amusing."

Before Tallulah left for New York, Cukor arranged to show her a rough cut of Kate's work-in-progress. After the screening, she rushed to the set of *Little Women*. Tears pouring down her cheeks, and clutching three wet handkerchiefs, Bankhead fell on her knees before Kate.

"Tallulah!" Cukor turned a cool eye on her. "You're weeping for your lost innocence."

Bankhead provided the first hint that *Little Women* would be Kate's biggest box-office hit to date. The RKO executives and salesmen who fretted about the commercial prospects of a costume drama never counted on Kate's strategy: She played Jo March as a vital, high-strung, modern young woman expressly based on her aunt Edith Hooker.

When Kate finished *Little Women* on August 28, 1933, she had a commitment to do one more picture at RKO, playing an Ozark mountain girl in director John Cromwell's *Spitfire*. After that, she planned to return to the Broadway stage in Jed Harris's production of *The Lake*. Meanwhile, she headed east to see her family and rent a townhouse to replace the nest she shared with Luddy in Murray Hill.

The move would mark a symbolic break with the past. Although Luddy had every intention of moving with her, at least a house with several bedrooms would give Kate some breathing space; perhaps she could see things more clearly there and begin to figure out quite what to do about the husband who would not leave.

House-hunting together, Kate and Luddy settled on a modest brownstone at 244 East 49th Street, between Second and Third Avenues, in Turtle Bay Gardens. To enter, you descended several steps below street level to a small narrow hallway. There was a tiny kitchen to the left and a dining room that gave out onto communal gardens at the back. A steep flight of stairs led to a living room above with two fireplaces. The formal part faced north, overlooking the noisy midtown street. Behind, a sitting room with enormous windows looked out over the gardens. The sun-flooded windows and high ceilings made the sitting room seem much larger than it really was. A staircase in front led to two floors of bedrooms.

Rented for $100 a month, the house was to be strictly a temporary measure until Kate had her life in order.

F I F T E E N

A ctors called Jed Harris "the Vampire". Noël Coward compared him to "that strangely ruthless insect, the praying mantis." Laurence Olivier recalled "the most hurtful, arrogant, venomous little fiend that anyone could meet, let alone be asked to work with." The legendary producer had staged plays including *Broadway, Coquette, The Royal Family, The Front Page*, and *Serena Blandish*. His picture, hands stuffed in trouser pockets, had appeared on the cover of *Time*.

Famous for his "satanic" powers of seduction, Harris, in the words of Ben Hecht, possessed "a Dracula-like hunger for the blood of his victims." He was fueled by a perverse need to put actresses on a pedestal, then tear them down with ridicule and abuse.

Why, then, did people flock to work with him? Arthur Miller put it best: "We tend to obey the crazy."

His clothes were the first thing one noticed: the camel's hair coat with upturned collar flung over his shoulders like a cape, the snap-brim fedora at a rakish angle. Then one saw the dark, gleaming, hypnotic eyes and arched eyebrows, the heavy, jutting lower jaw covered with stubble. Harris, it was said, had the grin of a sorcerer.

Typically he sat with feet up on the desk in his black and gold office at the Empire Theater. Long, thick fingers toyed with a pointed paper knife. In a whispery voice that reminded some women of a snake's hiss, Harris would explain that a "second-rate poetess" had once used the paper cutter to kill herself; "unfortunately," he added, the attempt had been thwarted.

286

When Helen Hayes, who had starred in *Coquette*, heard that Katharine Hepburn was doing *The Lake*, she sent a warning to the young actress: "Don't let Jed direct you. He will destroy your confidence." Worthington Minor, short and plump, was due to direct, while Harris produced. Harris fired Minor after a week, deciding to direct the play himself.

True to form, the thirty-three-year-old Harris mocked, browbeat, and humiliated Kate. Nothing she did was right. During rehearsals before the Washington and Philadelphia tryouts, he repeatedly denounced the artificiality of her performance. He thundered at Kate to stop posing. He castigated her coy sideways glances and girlish cuteness. He ridiculed the way she put a limp hand to her forehead and draped herself over the furniture. He performed a devastating imitation of her daisy-chain enthusiasm.

Crushed and demoralized, Kate could hardly concentrate. How could she work herself up with Harris's judgmental eyes staring at her from the stalls? When Cukor exploded on a film set, Kate always knew that at heart he was very fond of her. Harris's tirades were different. There was never a moment when he seemed to admire anything she did. His approach was all slash and burn.

There was another major pressure on Kate, of which no one but her family was aware. When Luddy, blithe but watchful, met Kate at the train station on November 18, 1933, circumstances had changed drastically since her last trip east.

Leland Hayward had asked Kate to marry him. Eager to move quickly, he planned to divorce Lola and wanted Kate to do the same with Luddy. In California, it had all seemed so easy; but in New York, Kate found herself living again with the poor, sweet, devoted husband whom she did not want to hurt.

Leland commuted regularly between Los Angeles and New York. It took its toll on Kate's nerves to continue to see him while living under the same roof with her husband. Luddy, seemingly unshakable, did not make things easy for her. A messy situation that most men would have found humiliating seemed hardly to embarrass Luddy at all. His presence, both in the townhouse and at Fenwick, gave Hayward the creeps.

Worse, Kate's family was clearly hoping that Luddy would somehow prevail over Leland. Marion, in her diary, repeatedly expressed the fervent wish that "Katy"—as she called her big sister—would not divorce. If *Cheiro's Book of Palmistry* was to be believed, divorce seemed likely: When the fifteen-year-old examined Luddy's hand, she discovered two marriage lines.

The family's opinion was important to Kate in ways outsiders could not begin to comprehend. Despite the brownstone in New York, in Kate's mind her home continued to be with Dr. and Mrs. Hepburn. More than a decade had passed since Tom's suicide, but the bond between Kate and her parents had not weakened. Retreating to West Hartford and Fenwick whenever she could, she thought of herself as never having really left home. For all her success, Kate would always be drawn to the place she called "my father's house."

Although Dr. and Mrs. Hepburn were not usually preoccupied with Kate's career, they seemed very anxious in the weeks before the tryout of *The Lake* at the National Theater in Washington, D.C. As it happened, several strands of their life were to come together that night.

The Bryn Mawr Club of Washington had bought out the entire theater and were selling tickets to benefit mother and daughter's alma mater. Margaret Sanger, aware of the immense audience Mrs. Hepburn's daughter was capable of reaching through motion pictures, wasted no time in attaching herself to the occasion. She implored Dr. and Mrs. Hepburn to stay with her in Washington, and declared herself heartbroken when Mrs. Hepburn announced plans to stay with her sister at Upland. Nonetheless, Mrs. Sanger arranged a buffet luncheon in the Hepburns' honor on the 18th. She reminded Mrs. Hepburn that the Bryn Mawr ladies who had worked on the benefit were all very anxious to meet her.

Dr. Hepburn rarely slept in any bed but his own, so the decision to travel to Washington—and spend the weekend with Edith!—signaled that he too regarded the performance as a very special occasion. On December 18, he planned to visit nearby Alexandria, Virginia, where his great-grandfather Cuthbert Powell had served as mayor in the days before Llangollen and the family fortune were lost; it was Dr. Hepburn's way of announcing that at long last, Nina Hepburn's granddaughter had returned to "put this family back on the map!"

As the time approached for Kate to leave for Washington, she broke down in tears. Jed Harris had driven her to breaking point. At first she seemed inclined to pull out; but the stage manager begged, and she finally consented to go.

At the preview, Kate did little more than walk through the role of newlywed Stella Surrege, who falls in love with her husband shortly after the ceremony only to see him killed in an automobile accident soon afterward. A great many people were rooting for her; but the only eyes she appeared to respond to were those of Jed Harris.

"I can do better than that," Kate insisted to Margaret Sanger, who came backstage after the show.

Kate did not do better. When *The Lake* opened in New York the day after Christmas 1933, the reviews were disastrous.

"Miss Hepburn is not a full-fledged dramatic actress yet," wrote Brooks Atkinson in the *New York Times*. "Her rocket-like success in the talking pictures has set too high the standards by which she has to be judged in the more coherent world of the stage. For the fact seems to be that in the current drama she has a sensitive and remarkably intense personality and an unworldly charm, but she has not yet developed the flexibility of first-rate acting and her voice is a rather strident instrument."

Dorothy Parker, in the *New Yorker*, declared that Hepburn ran the gamut of emotion "from A to B." This review must have seemed especially hurtful to Kate, coming as it did from someone who had sat around the same table with her and Phelps Putnam at Tony Soma's.

By the time Luddy accompanied Kate to West Hartford on the 30th for one night, his days in the townhouse were numbered. Loving Kate as he did, he appeared almost to blame himself for her troubles in *The Lake*; yet he had no intention of leaving until she forced him out.

Kate, due at the theater, left Luddy in Connecticut to celebrate the New Year with her parents. On January 1, he and Marion boarded a train to New York. While they ate dinner on the train, Marion well understood the subtext of Luddy's wistful conversation about people who make the mistake of falling for others. He asked Marion whether she had ever been in love; when she said no, he assured her that was wise. After observing Luddy's pain at close range in New York, Marion promised her diary never to fall for anybody if she could possibly help it; a powerful, one-sided love like Luddy's was just too dangerous. To judge by her diary, she was acutely aware that Kate was giving serious consideration to divorce.

Soon after Marion was sent back to West Hartford, Kate once again tried to distance herself from Luddy—this time somewhat more forcefully than in the past. At this point, Kate was not quite ready to divorce. Nor did she insist that her husband move very far. Instead, Luddy took up residence directly behind Kate on the East 48th Street side of Turtle Bay Gardens.

From his apartment window, Luddy could see into Kate's sitting room and rear bedrooms. Husband and wife remained connected by a communal garden. To visit, Luddy simply walked out his garden door and entered Kate's house through the dining room. That way he could be there whenever she needed him: When the pipes burst or a ceiling crumbled, Luddy was first on the scene.

The Hepburns did not learn about Kate's new living arrangements until late January. At the time Luddy moved out, Mrs. Hepburn was in Washington for the birth control hearings conducted by the U.S. House of Representatives judiciary committee. It was a time of maximum press exposure for Mrs. Hepburn. She appeared in national newspapers, often on the front page, on a daily basis. Reporters and photographers followed her everywhere. At a moment when *Little Women* was shattering box-office records at the world's largest theater, the Music Hall in New York, Kate's stardom created enormous new interest in her mother; suddenly, every time Mrs. Hepburn's name was mentioned in the press, there followed "mother of the actress" or "Katharine Hepburn's mother."

With Amelia Earhart and Charlotte Perkins Gilman, Mrs. Hepburn was a featured speaker at the American Conference on

Birth Control and National Recovery on January 15–17, which Margaret Sanger had organized to kick off that year's campaign. The morning after the final session, Mrs. Sanger and Mrs. Hepburn, arms linked, led a procession of women up Capitol Hill to the first of two hearings on a bill which would permit physicians to distribute birth control information. The large Sanger–Hepburn contingent required the proceedings to be moved to the House caucus room, which quickly filled to capacity. Mrs. Hepburn, her small black hat tilted over one eye, took up the cudgel against the popular radio evangelist Father Charles Coughlin, who predicted that birth control would cause the downfall of American society. "RADIO FATHER VS. MOVIE MA," the newspaper headlines announced.

Privately, Mrs. Hepburn worried about the impact her controversial activities, and the immense publicity they were attracting, would have on Kate, who was under enough pressure of her own already. Mrs. Hepburn discussed some of her fears with Margaret Sanger. Linking Kate to the birth control movement, as her mother's activism inescapably did, could devastate her career. American Catholics were especially fervent in their opposition to birth control; how would the film studios react to the possibility that a large segment of Kate's audience might boycott her pictures?

Worse, Mrs. Hepburn's high profile in the national movement had caused the enemies of birth control, particularly the Catholic press, to place her under a microscope in hopes of discovering anything to discredit her. Aside from being embarrassing to Kate, the history of suicide which contradicted the image of the Hepburns as a model family could have an enormously damaging impact on the birth control movement. Yet for reasons of her own, Margaret Sanger encouraged Mrs. Hepburn to occupy the spotlight instead of working behind the scenes, where the threat of exposure would have been smaller. It was as though Mrs. Hepburn was drawn to, and exhilarated by, the danger, just as she had once been at Bryn Mawr.

Mrs. Hepburn left Washington the day after the hearings. In New York, she collected Kate and Luddy following the Saturday evening performance of *The Lake*. That night, January 20, they arrived in West Hartford, where the family learned that Luddy had moved into a separate apartment. As always, Luddy refused to say a word against Kate; but his pain was evident.

When Kate returned to New York, reporters were waiting. What was her opinion of the birth control hearings? Did she agree with her firebrand mother and Margaret Sanger? Conscious of the uproar her remarks would no doubt create at RKO, Kate announced that she stood with everything her mother had said in Washington. Later, she added: "I detest the newspapers' reference to her as Katharine Hepburn's mother. My mother is important. I am not." She wrote to Margaret Sanger that they must not worry about her for one moment. Kate insisted that Mrs. Hepburn's work was far too urgent to let any potential problems in Hollywood get in the way.

It was a courageous position to take in the midst of her troubles on Broadway. Although Kate had worked hard to improve her performance in the weeks since the calamitous opening, the whole experience had been a major embarrassment. Her sole consolation was that with ticket sales so low, Jed Harris would soon be forced to close down; February 10 was the date talked about.

It never occurred to Kate that Harris would decide to prolong the agony by taking *The Lake* on national tour. The show might be a flop, but a movie star's name on the marquee would guarantee ticket sales.

"My dear, the only interest I have in you is the money I can make out of you," Harris told Kate when she called him at three in the morning to protest.

"How much?" Kate snapped, offering to buy herself out of her contract.

"How much have you got?"

She read off the figure in her Chase National bankbook, $13,675.75. Harris said he would take that and Kate promised to send a check in the morning.

With the nightmare at an end, there remained the Luddy situation to deal with. Leland urged divorce; yet Kate was uncertain whether she could bring herself to do that to Luddy just yet. And did she really want to end one marriage only to plunge quickly into another?

When Kate took Leland to see her family in West Hartford, the visits were awkward and uncomfortable. Prone to severe allergies, he traveled with a pigskin valise full of ointments and medicines. Tramping in the woods with the hardy Hepburns, he broke out in hives. Outwardly polite, Dr. and Mrs. Hepburn dominated the dinner table with political conversation almost certainly calculated to exclude their perfumed visitor, with his fancy suits and diamond cufflinks.

Leland told Kate that he was "crazy about" her mother. Mrs. Hepburn, for her part, was less complimentary. "How can you like him?" she asked Kate. "I don't understand it. His hands are so small."

Bob Hepburn, then a student at Harvard, thought Leland's conversation uninteresting. On several occasions, Bob drove him to Brainard Airport where his plane waited. Each time, Leland would try to discuss Kate with her brother.

"If Kate would only relax!" Leland confided. "She's always so intense." It wasn't hard to see that what Hayward really wanted was, in Bob's words, "a good old-fashioned soft female companion," and that Kate hardly fit the bill.

Still, the lover pressed Kate to end her marriage; and in March she decided to travel to France for four or five weeks. Away from both Luddy and Leland, perhaps she could finally make up her mind. Luddy—ever hopeful that she would come back to him—paid for the trip. As traveling companion Kate enlisted Suzanne Steele, a singer who had given her voice lessons after Brooks Atkinson and others criticized her in *The Lake*.

Preoccupied with her departure on the French liner *Paris* on March 17, Kate seemed almost uninterested in her Academy Award nomination for *Morning Glory*. Her attitude toward awards ceremonies was that she didn't need to attend. When a telegram signed "Katharine Hepburn," thanking the Academy for the nomination, arrived at the awards banquet on March 16, it was widely rumored to have been sent by the RKO studio press department in the east.

On the 17th, all hell broke loose as reporters in New York scrambled to locate Katharine Hepburn, who had been named Best Actress the night before. They found her, with upturned collar and hat pulled over eyes, boarding the *Paris* under an assumed name. Refusing to comment, Kate dashed to her stateroom and slammed the door.

"Can't you see I'm incognito?" she shouted through the keyhole.

"Aw, let us take another picture," cried one photographer. "We got one anyway."

"I'll bet it's lousy!" said Kate.

Before heading to the Riviera, where she planned to do some serious thinking, Kate stopped in Paris to visit Mrs. Hepburn's old friend Jo Bennett. Jo, divorced from Toscan Bennett, had lived on and off in France for a decade. In the beginning, she had been the lover of Harold Stearns, a dissipated writer on whom Ernest Hemingway based the character Harvey Stone in *The Sun Also Rises*. She moved in the Hemingway circle and had been close to the novelist's wife Hadley. Now Jo was contentedly married to the expatriate painter Ricard Brooks.

Kate's brief visit with this old friend from Nook Farm days had a wonderful clarifying effect. Her mind made up about what she must do, Kate sailed home after only four days in France. As it happened, her shipmate was Jo's friend Ernest Hemingway, who helped her face the clicking cameras and reporters' questions when they docked in New York on April 3.

"I was homesick," she explained her sudden return.

"For what?" called reporters.

"I'm sure I don't know."

She did know. The next day, Kate went to Connecticut to tell her family that she had decided to divorce Luddy and marry Leland. She rushed back to New York after supper, leaving Marion to lament the news in her diary.

Luddy reacted stoically when Kate told him of her plan to go to Mexico with Laura to seek a quick divorce. Vowing to wait for her no matter what, Luddy agreed not to block the marriage to

Leland, and instructed his attorney to do whatever Kate asked.

When reporters gathered outside the East 49th Street house to inquire about divorce rumors, Kate slipped out the back door. Relishing the game of cat and mouse, she crossed the communal garden and left through Luddy's apartment, to turn up on the other side of town at a bon voyage party for George Cukor and David and Irene Selznick aboard the White Star liner *Majestic*. Selznick, now at MGM, had invited Cukor to visit England with him in preparation for filming *David Copperfield*. At the party, Kate's unmistakable corncrake voice could be heard above the din assuring the Selznicks that she and Leland planned to be married within a month; the newlyweds would join them in Paris soon after that.

Kate and Laura arrived in Mérida, Mexico, on April 22. Registered at the Hotel Itzé under the name Mrs. Ludlow Smith, Kate claimed to be there to visit the Mayan ruins. Eight days later, she appeared at the Second Civil Court, where she testified that Luddy had been summoned to the divorce hearing but declined to appear. Citing "deep disagreements to life" and "incompatibility," she requested an immediate decree. Her attorney produced a signed petition from Luddy, asking the court to forgo a waiting period before remarriage. As soon as the divorce became final on May 30, Kate would be free to marry Leland.

In the aftermath of the proceedings, it came to Dr. Hepburn's attention that over the years Kate had spent some $100,000 of Luddy's money. Calling that "absolutely outrageous," Dr. Hepburn took the money back from his daughter and forced Luddy to accept it. From then on, Dr. Hepburn replaced Leland Hayward as overseer of Kate's finances. According to Alice Palache, who took over the job after Dr. Hepburn's death, he was a very strict manager. He curbed Kate's natural extravagance and generosity. He forced her to save. He doled out nearly every penny she spent.

News that Leland and Lola Hayward had sought a quick divorce of their own in Juarez, Mexico, sparked rumors that a second Hepburn marriage was imminent. For all her public protests about being hounded by the press, Kate privately claimed to enjoy eluding the newsmen. In a characteristic gesture, she gleefully thumbed her nose at reporters who staked out the Turtle Bay townhouse.

Dr. Hepburn did not share Kate's delight. On June 3, 1934, when he opened the front door at Bloomfield Avenue, he saw a photographer taking pictures of the family home. He charged at him, destroyed his camera, and seized several exposed plates.

When the photographer protested, Dr. Hepburn shouted, "You're lucky I didn't kill you!"

From the very first moment Kate had talked of a stage career, Dr. Hepburn had railed against the publicity it would bring. In the days following young Tom's suicide, he had had enough of newsmen swarming about the house. That chapter had been closed; why risk opening it again?

Kate had divorced Luddy; Leland had divorced Lola; and there was nothing to stop them from getting married, as Kate had told her parents she wanted to do.

Yet she resisted; she stalled; she put him off; she made excuses; she kept saying, perhaps next week or next month. The longer Leland allowed Kate to hesitate, the weaker he seemed in her eyes and the less likely she was to marry him.

To Leland's consternation, not even divorce had flushed Luddy from their lives. The camera-wielding ex-husband had been a fixture at Fenwick that summer. Luddy was forever photographing the Hepburns; now and then he even turned his camera on Kate and Leland—much to the annoyance of Leland, who had no idea how to respond to this apparent insanity. When people spotted Luddy bounding along the stony beach with paunch thrust out, they guessed that a marital reconciliation could be imminent, and reports to that effect soon turned up in the press.

Luddy used every opportunity to assure Kate that although he was probably too good for her, he was determined to hold on until she came to her senses. Just because they were divorced, Luddy liked to say, didn't mean they had to be separated. When Kate complained about his embarrassing presence at Fenwick, he insisted that as an ex-husband he had rights! He vowed not to have sex again until the day Kate returned to him.

In August, Kate went back to Hollywood, having signed a new six-picture deal with RKO. Leland had had every expectation of being married to Kate—and rid of both Luddy and Laura—by the time she headed west, but somehow things had not worked out that way. Laura, too, was still very much in the picture.

Kate once told John Ford that in Los Angeles she preferred to live with no one at her back. Quinta Nirvana, her old place in Coldwater Canyon, had been too small for three people, so she rented a much larger house, perched at the top of Angelo Drive in Beverly Hills; at night the city spread out in the distance like many thousands of fireflies. To reach the property, you ascended a long, steep, narrow, treacherous road, with many sharp turns, off Benedict Canyon. If you didn't know the way—and sometimes even if you did—the drive up felt like a roller-coaster seconds before the plunge.

That September, Kate put on gypsy garb to play the role of Lady Babbie in *The Little Minister*, based on a play by J. M. Barrie. Meanwhile, Leland convinced himself that only Laura's continued presence was standing in the way of his happiness. In the past, Laura had served as a beard when Kate and Leland needed to conceal their liaison. But the American Express heiress was no longer of use to Leland. He urged Laura to stop living in Kate's shadow; it was time to get on with her own life.

When they had first arrived in Hollywood, Laura's presence allowed Kate to maintain a certain emotional distance; emulating Laura, Kate affected disdain for the film world. She pretended to regard making movies as a lark. If she failed, that pose would permit her to say it didn't really matter; she had never been serious about becoming a screen actress anyway. Kate's outlook was very different now that she had won an Academy Award for *Morning Glory* and shattered box-office records with *Little Women*. Still, Laura's influence often forced Kate to revert to a defensive attitude that had little to do with how she really felt about working in films.

Like Palache, Laura was a foil who set off Kate's beauty to advantage. There was little chance that Alice Palache or Laura

Harding would ever outshine Kate in a room. Palache and Laura served much the same purpose for Kate as Mary Towle had for her mother and Florence Sabin for Edith.

As had happened with Luddy, Kate had outgrown Laura. Aside from bringing picnic lunches to Kate's film sets and helping George Cukor select art and antiques for his home, there was little for Laura to do in Hollywood; with few exceptions, the people there found her dull and not particularly attractive. Nudged out of Kate's new life, Laura claimed to be eager to get back to people of her own kind; she insisted that a woman of her background would always be out of place in Hollywood. Leland arranged for Laura to work in his New York office.

Sending Laura away was probably the worst mistake he could have made. From the first, she had been Leland's staunch supporter on account of his New York society pedigree. She found him acceptable as well as adorable. At Quinta Nirvana, the three of them had formed a snug, superior little island; and it served the interests of both Leland and Laura for Kate to remain isolated on that island.

That something had changed in Kate's life became evident during the filming of *Break of Hearts*, directed by Philip Moeller. Since *A Bill of Divorcement*, it had been Laura's custom to flit about the film set while her friend worked. Her presence established a wall around Kate. Now the duenna was gone. Instead of conferring with Laura between shots, Kate was most often observed sitting at the feet of her co-star, Charles Boyer. She would rest her head on Boyer's knee and look up adoringly while the Frenchman spoke of his life. Not long after Boyer began work on February 11, 1935, rumors began that Kate and the married actor were having a fling.

On one occasion, Kate and Boyer were kissing in his car parked on the studio lot when she saw a man's face at the passenger-seat window. Long-jawed with a blunt nose and a small, sensitive mouth, the man looked right at her as though Boyer weren't there. He tightened his lips; otherwise, his face was deadpan and unreadable. His expression never changed. She noticed that his shirt and trousers were splattered with mud.

"I'm George Stevens," he said, reminding her of her appointment to meet him, and abruptly disappeared.

RKO production chief Pandro Berman had been pushing Stevens to direct *Alice Adams*, based on the Booth Tarkington novel; but Kate, whose Academy Award gave her a certain clout at the studio, had final approval. Stevens had minimal directing experience; he had spent much of his career as cameraman and gag man on Laurel and Hardy films and other comedy shorts at the Hal Roach Studios. He was now under contract at RKO where he worked for a modest weekly salary. William Wyler—the director Kate wanted—was what Berman called a "big pay man"; special arrangements would have to be made to bring Wyler to RKO.

Berman and Hepburn agreed that *Alice Adams* could be critical to her reputation. *A Bill of Divorcement, Morning Glory*, and *Little Women* had been immensely successful; but the more recent *Spitfire* and *The Little Minister* were artistic and commercial failures. Coupled with the disaster of *The Lake*, they signaled a career in trouble.

Starting with *The Little Minister*, Leland Hayward had renegotiated Kate's price to $50,000 a film, so the studio could ill afford a string of box-office duds. Berman saw that Hepburn wasn't the sort of star who could carry an inferior picture; she had to have precisely the right material to make audiences sympathize with her. In consultation with Kate, the decision was made to put her into a comedy with a modern look. *Alice Adams* was the story of a lonely, small-town girl's struggle to achieve social recognition.

Other than telling Kate how much he admired her, Stevens had little to say at their awkward first meeting in Pandro Berman's office. Twenty minutes before, Stevens, up to his ankles in mud, had been directing pratfalls elsewhere on the lot; he had not even had time to clean up, so hurriedly had he been ordered to summon Kate to Berman's office. Then he had found her in Boyer's car.

Perhaps it was to compensate for her embarrassment, or perhaps—as Berman suspected—it was because she found the ruggedly handsome Stevens so attractive: Whatever the reason, Kate quickly accepted him to direct *Alice Adams*.

Their second meeting caused her to wonder whether she had made a foolish mistake. Sick in bed, Kate was wearing white pajamas and a dressing gown when she greeted Berman and Stevens, who had come to Angelo Drive for a script conference. She and Berman talked on and on about the book, but nothing they said or did would draw Stevens out. He just sat there in exasperating silence. For Kate, who loved to talk, it was like speaking into a void.

About the only thing Stevens said was: "Booth Tarkington's a fine writer. I'm going to do him more harm that he's going to do me." Otherwise, for an hour and a half, he stared at Hepburn.

Stevens was the sort of man—taciturn, maddeningly mysterious—Kate called "a watcher." She failed to suspect that he was merely trying to conceal that he had not yet read the Tarkington novel. Nor did she guess that Stevens's acute perceptions of her personality made that day would find their way into the film.

They were still crisply addressing each other as "Miss Hepburn" and "Mr. Stevens" the day they shot the scene in which, according to the script, Alice returns in humiliation from a party, throws herself on her bed, and bursts into tears.

"Do you mind if I say something about this scene?" the director asked.

"No," said Kate.

"I think it would be a wonderful idea if instead of throwing yourself on the bed, you walk over to the window and just watch the rain. You put your hands up on the window and just look and look, and finally tears begin to run out of your eyes."

Recognizing a solid visual concept, Hepburn decided that perhaps Stevens was not such a dolt as she had thought. Frustrated by his perpetual poker-face, Kate saw the chance to "wow" him with her skills as an emotional actress.

But when Kate approached the window and touched her fingertips to the glass, a chill shot through her. Cold water had leaked in from the other side. The sting blocked her emotions. She knew she would never be able to cry.

"Cut it! Cut it!" Kate yelled, although it was the director's prerogative to say that. "It isn't any good."

"Certainly, we'll do it again," said Stevens, pretending not to notice that she had usurped his authority.

The same thing happened again. And again. And again. Each time, Stevens was sweet and polite to Kate, who felt herself longing for some kind of stronger response. Desperate to work herself up, she decided to provoke Stevens to hit her. That would make the tears flow, she calculated.

"Mr. Stevens!" Kate blasted for all to hear. "I think it's lovely when you have a new idea like this. But it does make it very difficult for me. I've worked on this script for a long time and I've thought of the scene this way. I think it would have been a much better idea if you'd called me last night."

The director's lips tightened and his face went white. Kate imagined that Stevens wanted to punch her in the face. Indeed, furious at being talked to like that, Stevens was considering walking off the picture.

"What would you like to do, Miss Hepburn?" he said in an extremely measured tone. "Would you like me to change the setup?"

The hateful look in his eye jolted Kate, who called, "Roll 'em! Roll 'em fast!"

Stevens gave the go-ahead. This time she performed precisely as he wanted. She no longer felt the cold water; all she could think of was the director's anger.

"That was great, wasn't it?" Kate beamed at him afterward. "Really hit it."

Stevens, guardedly, said it was fine.

To celebrate, director and actress dined at Lucy's restaurant. Stevens confessed that Kate's arrogance had nearly driven him to resign from the picture. She, for her part, liked the idea that the tough guy could be so easily wounded. Just when things were going beautifully, Leland Hayward appeared at the table. Joining them for a few minutes, he boasted about a deal he had just negotiated. Kate and Stevens listened in silence as Hayward recited a litany of numbers.

When the agent left, Stevens looked hard at Kate. He put his arms around her and kissed her on the mouth.

"George," said Kate, thinking it very sweet of him to have done it.

"Money, money, I can't bear that talk," he said.

Kate knew exactly what Stevens meant.

He continued: "It's what we do that's great, isn't it?"

The incident encouraged Kate to look at Leland Hayward—and herself—with new eyes. Suddenly it was possible to see her fiancé for what he was: an agent preoccupied with money and deals. Indeed, Leland's inability to be an artist would cause him great frustration and disappointment throughout his life. As for Kate, she had come to Hollywood pretending to be something she was not. Only now did she begin to discover—and accept—a more authentic identity. George Cukor warmly encouraged the immense pleasure Kate took in her work, but it was George Stevens who first gave her the confidence to take herself seriously as an artist.

Stevens saw beyond Kate's attempts to appear grand and sophisticated; and he put that understanding into *Alice Adams*. The film is so effective at stripping away Alice's pretensions and discovering her true sensitivity and generosity because Stevens recognized a similar duality in Kate. Director and actress talked about it and he allowed her to explore that conflict in her own nature on camera.

George Cukor, watching the rushes with Pandro Berman, recognized that *Alice Adams* just might be Hepburn's best film to date. (At length, it won her a second Academy Award nomination, but not the prize itself.)

Perceiving in her a piquant quality he called "garçonne," Cukor wanted to star Hepburn in a movie based on Compton Mackenzie's novel *The Early Life and Adventures of Sylvia Scarlett*, about a young woman who eludes police by disguising herself as a boy. Berman opposed the idea from the first, but Kate was so eager to do it that she turned down Arthur Hopkins's summons to return to Broadway in Helen Jerome's stage adaptation of *Pride and Prejudice* In view of her luminous performance in *Alice Adams*, Berman reluctantly gave the go-ahead to *Sylvia Scarlett*.

It was a fiasco. Although Cukor described the atmosphere on the set as ecstatic, he later wondered whether he and Kate had been too much in love with the material, unable to see its flaws. Midway through filming, Kate had the sinking feeling that the script made no sense; but she hesitated to share her lack of confidence with Cukor. She had experienced similar anxieties after George Stevens shot the dinner table sequence in *Alice Adams*; at the time, she feared it was, in her words, "as funny as a baby's open grave." The finished product, however, was a gem of comic timing. Perhaps she was equally mistaken about *Sylvia Scarlett*.

She wasn't. Kate attended the preview with the actress Natalie Paley. Cukor sat with the editors. Intended as an uproarious comedy, *Sylvia Scarlett* didn't get a single laugh.

"Kate, what is wrong? They don't laugh!" said Paley.

"Natalie," said Kate, "they don't think it's funny."

By the time the lights came on, much of the theater was empty. In the back row, Pandro Berman and studio head B. B. Kahane were berating Cukor.

In the bathroom, Kate saw a woman, obviously quite ill, sprawled on a sofa.

"What's the matter?" Kate asked impishly. "Did the picture finish you off?"

Afterward, Cukor and Hepburn drove to the production chief's house.

"Pandro, scrap this and we'll do another picture for you for nothing," Kate implored.

"I never want to do a picture with either of you again," Berman said coldly. He didn't mean it, but the words stung nonetheless.

After a day of retakes on November 4, Leland flew Kate to the east coast in his two-seater plane. He was weary of constantly being asked—by reporters as well as friends and associates—when the wedding was to take place. It was all such a blow to his dignity. And he can hardly have failed to sense that Kate's attitude toward him had altered since the day George Stevens kissed her in Lucy's restaurant—although almost certainly Leland did not know about the kiss or what Stevens had said. There was no apparent explanation for Kate's disillusionment with her fiancé, who had once seemed so glamorous and exciting. In New York, Leland's client Edna Ferber had offered to give the couple an engagement party; at least that would allow him to save face.

Leland's anxiety about whether Kate would go through with a public acknowledgment that they planned to marry, coupled with her own upset over *Sylvia Scarlett*, made the flight particularly tense. When they made a forced landing in St. Louis, it did not help that even the airport mechanics kept asking about his relationship with Hepburn. In a fit of temper, he snapped that he was "not a celebrity or a screen star but only her husband." Immediately he took off someone phoned in the remark to the press.

Reporters were waiting in Pittsburgh. Hayward, overwrought, narrowly missed crashing the plane when he landed. Thus far Kate had successfully eluded the newsmen. But the next morning, November 7, they almost caught up with her at Newark airport.

The propellers were still spinning when Kate, in brown trousers and a scarlet sweater, emerged. Spotting several photographers, she ducked under the forward fuselage. The propellers nearly hit her. Unscathed, she sped off in a waiting car. Left to face the press, Hayward insisted that Kate had bet her friend she could avoid all photographers on the trip east—thus her eagerness to escape.

Asked whether he and Kate were secretly married, as Hayward himself had suggested in Pittsburgh, he shot back: "Do I look like a sap?"

Maybe he did. Scheduled to take a lengthy business trip to Europe, Leland was desperate to get a firm commitment from Kate during their stay in the east. That she permitted Edna Ferber to give an engagement party seemed like a step in the right direction. Yet she continued to vacillate about a specific wedding date.

Finally, Leland came up with a plan to win Kate's heart. On New Year's Eve, Edna Ferber and George S. Kaufman hatched the idea for what would become the play *Stage Door*, about life in a theatrical boarding house. They felt certain they could have the drama ready for Broadway in the fall. Ferber, in confidence, told the idea to her agent. Hayward wasted no time in promising the material to Kate, which of course he had no right to do.

Knowing Kate as he did, Hayward had anticipated how much

Stage Door, reminiscent of *Morning Glory*, would appeal to her. Making Kate promise not to tell anyone about the Ferber–Kaufman play, Leland swore it was precisely the stage vehicle she needed to turn her career around after *Sylvia Scarlett*. Kate sensed he was right.

For the moment, with the promise of the part, Leland looked very attractive to Kate again. Newly confident of her affection, he sailed for Europe on January 25, 1936.

"Poor me," Kate sighed to George Cukor in anticipation of returning alone to her hilltop house in Beverly Hills.

On February 25, she was to begin her tenth film at RKO, *Mary of Scotland*, to be directed by John Ford.

S I X T E E N

Many years later, Kate realized that close as she had
been to John Ford and Spencer Tracy, both red-
headed Irishmen, she had never really understood
either one.

Kate was drawn to the identical quality in both men; she called
it an oversensitivity to life. Like her brother Tom, John Ford and
Spencer Tracy were capable of being devastated by the world. This
raw sensitivity to people and emotions was part of what made Ford
and Tracy such powerful artists; it also wreaked havoc with their
lives.

The precise source of their torments remained an enigma to
her. Why were both brilliant, lavishly gifted men driven to desperate
acts of self-flagellation? Why, with so much success and so much to
live for, did Ford and Tracy seem at times to exert all their strength
to destroy themselves? Kate spent much of her adult life privately
struggling to comprehend the demons that drove them.

Several years before Kate knew either man, Ford and Tracy
had met in New York. It was the spring of 1930.

John Ford, then thirty-four, was already one of the most
revered directors in Hollywood, where he had been working in films
since 1914. A tall, pensive, intimidating figure who walked with a
surprising grace, he wore a battered felt hat pulled down over his
forehead and small round glasses with smoked lenses. He wore Irish
tweed jackets and yellow or white flannel trousers—always of the
finest quality—until they were ready to rot. Often he rolled his
trousers up to the ankles and looped a necktie around his waist

instead of a belt. His socks—when he wore socks—rarely matched. His white tennis shoes were almost black; no one could remember seeing them fresh and new.

Redolent of pipe tobacco, he was often covered in ash and broken bits of matches. Chewing his pipe, he frequently gnawed through the stem. At other times, he nervously cracked the stem in two with long, slender fingers.

He would chew to shreds the dozen or so handmade Irish linen handkerchiefs which his wife, Mary, a former army psychiatric nurse, stuffed in his hip pocket before he left for the studio every morning. Someone once said that when Ford was done with a handkerchief, it looked as though a flock of moths had destroyed it. The actors and actresses who formed a cult around Ford dared not interrupt when, lost in thought, he attacked a handkerchief with his teeth.

Ford had a mesmeric effect on actors; they loved to swap stories about the tricks he used to get them to do what he had in mind. He almost never gave specific direction. Sometimes he communicated wordlessly, as when he removed a bandana from his neck and gently tied it around an actress's waist before she played a scene. Often he proceeded indirectly, seeming to talk about everything but the material he wanted to shoot; yet actors swore that, instinctively, they understood what Ford was trying to tell them far better than if he had attempted to put his concept into words. It was as if they had experienced a kind of thought transference; they found themselves doing things on camera they had never really intended to do.

Among actors who worshipped Ford and longed to please him, by all accounts there was no greater thrill than to hear him respond to one's work in his low, melodious voice, "Jesus, that was nice."

Ford came to New York in search of an actor for *Up the River*, a prison picture then in preparation at Fox Films. The New York office provided theater tickets for the entire week. On the first night, he saw John Wexley's death row drama *The Last Mile*, starring Spencer Tracy as a condemned man named Killer Mears.

One look at Tracy's high-pressure performance and Ford had decided. In the role of the desperate convict who stages a bloody prison mutiny, Tracy's gestures were spare and understated, yet bulging eyes that darted right and left gave him the air of a man possessed. Ford discarded his tickets to all the other shows, returning to the Sam H. Harris Theater four nights in a row.

"I'm not handsome and I can prove it," Tracy joked when Ford visited him backstage. The actor's laugh had a wounded quality that Ford found very beautiful. Although "Spence" was only thirty, lines webbed his forehead and shot out from the edges of his restless blue eyes.

Tracy, an insomniac, liked to stay out all night, belting the brew and visiting brothels; among madams he had the reputation of a mean drunk, who had beat up a prostitute in a bordello called Lu's. His friends would often have to carry him home at dawn to the apartment he shared with his wife Louise and their deaf six-year-old son, Johnny, named after Tracy's father.

Offered $800 a week to appear in a single film, Tracy brooded about whether he deserved the big break Ford was giving him. His nature was deeply pessimistic; in any situation, he expected the worst. He had a very low tolerance for change and uncertainty. At a farewell party at the Lambs Club before he headed west, Tracy was in no mood to celebrate; he seemed terrified of disappointing Ford.

In Hollywood, Ford became Tracy's mentor and father figure. Ford, no stranger to self-doubt, knew how to handle Tracy's bouts of raging insecurity. When RKO nearly canceled *Up the River* on account of a rival prison picture, MGM's *The Big House*, Tracy went wild. Ford laughed and told him not to worry: "Since Metro made the picture we wanted to, we'll have to make a different one, but we can have some fun doing it." Ford, with his love of improvisation, deftly turned the story into a comedy, launching the apprehensive Tracy as a film comic. Spencer was a natural, Ford declared. He may not have been comfortable in his own skin, but he certainly appeared relaxed in front of a movie camera. Ford admired Tracy's technique precisely because it was barely perceptible; the actor hardly seemed to work to get his effects.

The successful completion of *Up the River* did little to assuage

Tracy's self-doubt. Before he started a second picture, Fox executives assigned him to learn something about film technique by observing Ford at work on his own next project, *Seas Beneath*. Tracy confessed to the actor George O'Brien, a leading member of Ford's informal "stock company," that he was "scared to death" of continuing in pictures.

Ford, for his part, did everything to put Tracy at ease. The director seemed eager to welcome Tracy into the small, loyal family of actors who regularly appeared in his films; some of them called Ford by the nickname "Pappy." His overtures to Tracy included frequent invitations to bring Mrs. Tracy and Johnny to the Santa Monica beach house Ford rented for Mary and their children, Patrick and Barbara; the two wives, married to similar men, saw much of each other in this period.

Tracy's initiation was to have taken place on the final day of filming *Seas Beneath*. After a day's shooting on board a U.S. Navy freighter, a small boat took Ford, Tracy, and George O'Brien to the Santa Monica pier.

Finishing a film was always a tense time for Ford, who seemed comfortable with life only when he was at work. Until a picture was in the can he steadfastly refused "the drink." Between projects, he liked to let off steam. Usually that meant locking himself in a room at home on Odin Street in North Hollywood for about three weeks. In search of oblivion, Ford stripped naked, wrapped himself in a sheet, and hit the bottle.

This time, however, he seemed to have devised another means of escape. As the three men walked along the pier, Ford, pointedly ignoring Tracy, invited O'Brien to leave with him at once for the Philippines. The freighter sailed that night. Insisting that there was no time to pack, Ford said they could buy fresh clothes in Manila in seven days. "The destroyers are there in the Philippines," Ford went on, seductively. "Dancing all the time, you know!"

When Ford produced a ticket from his coat pocket, O'Brien, in a frenzy of excitement, bought it on the spot; probably any actor in the stock company would have done the same.

All this time, it was as though Ford had forgotten Tracy. At the end of the pier, Tracy awkwardly wished them well on their trip.

"Spence!" said Ford, focusing on him suddenly with owlish intensity. "Don't you want to come?"

At that moment, it became evident that the performance on the pier had all been for Tracy's benefit. Ford clearly expected Tracy, like O'Brien, to drop everything in order to follow him to the Philippines. That was the degree of trust Ford demanded of the actors in his inner circle.

But however much Tracy admired Ford, something prevented him from saying yes. Attracted to the father figure as Tracy undeniably was, he remained ambivalent. As always, Tracy feared uncertainty. He resisted Ford's tricks. He was wary of being drawn into the director's orbit. Deeply suspicious, he questioned Ford's motives for seeking to draw him in. Very devious himself, Tracy questioned Ford's own deviousness. He did not want Ford somehow to get the better of him.

"What are you, a travel bureau?" Tracy laughed, implicitly refusing Ford's invitation.

With that, Ford and O'Brien were off to the ship *Tai Yang*. Tracy went home in a studio car. The encounter established the subtle but unmistakable tension that characterized relations between Ford and Tracy from then on.

Moments before the Norwegian tramp steamer left the dock that night, Mary Ford and the children screeched up in Ford's car. Mrs. Ford was a dark formidable figure with heavy eyebrows and a large aquiline nose. Her thick black hair, parted in the middle, was knotted in a huge bun at the nape of her neck. She wore a slash of crimson lipstick. On at least one occasion she had passed for a Navajo, dancing all night with cowboys who took her for a squaw.

"Don't cry, Mary, everything is going to be fine," O'Brien reassured her.

"You would cry too if you were me," said Mrs. Ford.

"Why?"

"You've got my ticket!"

To Ford's friends and associates, Mary was known as the lion tamer. The divorcee with the sandpaper voice had seemed a pretty tough character when Ford first introduced her to his film industry friends in 1920. Some of the wives, Victoria (Mrs. Tom) Mix and Ollie (Mrs. Harry) Carey, started a rumor that Jack's bride was a stunt rider from the east. Shrill and argumentative, she relished cutting this larger-than-life figure down to size.

Ford himself always seemed a little frightened of Mary. Rough-and-tumble fellows like John Wayne tiptoed around her. On visits to Odin Street, "Duke"—as Wayne was known—hid his cigarette ashes in his trouser cuffs.

In the beginning, Mary had filled the house with hard-drinking military personnel. During Prohibition, Mrs. Ford made bootleg gin in the bathtub: three drops of juniper juice to a pint of water. And on Sundays, her Navy pals brought quantities of the alcohol used to shoot torpedos; mixed with ginger ale, it made a concoction called torpedo gin.

As the years passed, however, Mary put on airs. She ceased to drink in public. She hit the bottle only when her husband was away or too drunk to notice. She spent so much time shopping and throwing around Jack's money that the care of their children was largely relegated to a governess. She wanted everything the other wives had. She seethed with jealousy that Victoria Mix used solid gold forks and knives instead of silver; and that Ollie Carey drove about Los Angeles in her own Lincoln Town car with a Navajo Indian in the back seat.

Although Mary had grown up a poor relation shuffled between family members in New Jersey, she made much ado of her aristocratic North Carolina background. She traced her lineage to Sir Thomas More and blamed her woes on General Sherman, who had torched the family plantation. When she berated Ford, sometimes she would affect a slight Southern accent and pepper her shouts with "you all." Mary believed that only if her husband remained convinced of her social superiority would she be able to keep him. The more successful he became in Hollywood, the more necessary it was to remind him of his inferiority. Fiercely protective of the money and power that came with being Mrs. John Ford, Mary never tired of denigrating the work that provided her privileges.

Abuse poured constantly from Mary's lips. She accused her husband of being weak and unmanly. She mocked his "shanty Irish" background. She bemoaned his failure to leave Hollywood and seek a proper job.

Ford, in turn, brooded about the fact that Mary, a Scotch-Irish Presbyterian, was a divorcee, whose first husband was still alive. That had made it impossible for them to marry in the Roman Catholic Church, which, to a devout Catholic like Ford, meant that they were not really married at all. At times, Ford regarded this as a shame and disgrace to them both; at other times, the lack of a Catholic ceremony offered a ray of hope that someday he might escape the unhappy marriage once and for all.

Meanwhile, Ford did everything to prolong the Philippine journey; he and George O'Brien pushed on to Hong Kong, Shanghai, Peking, and Japan. By the time they returned to San Francisco, four months had passed; Mary greeted her husband with a blistering tirade that Ford characterized to friends as her martyr act. To patch things up between them, he proposed to repeat the Philippine adventure with Mary as soon as he finished filming Sinclair Lewis's *Arrowsmith*.

They sailed in October 1931. The trip, marred by the usual bitter quarrels and heavy drinking, was a disaster. Ford was particularly irked by the many trunks of fancy clothing with which his wife insisted on traveling. He hated status symbols of any kind. At the Royal Hawaiian Hotel in Honolulu, Ford wrapped himself in a sheet and locked himself in a dark room with a stock of Irish whiskey; his binge lasted five days. Mary, breathing fire and fury, checked him into Queen's Hospital, where he was treated for alcoholic dehydration. The Fords' five months abroad had been intended to repair the marriage; but by the time they docked in San Francisco in March, it was evident to both partners that they would never really be happy together.

That spring of 1932, Ford met Kate Hepburn, then appearing in *The Warrior's Husband*, which Fox was interested in filming. Two years after he had discovered Spencer Tracy on Broadway, Ford was back in New York, shooting a screen test of Kate.

Eager to be thought of as a Philip Barry actress, Kate had selected a scene from *The Animal Kingdom*. She appeared with a touch of lipstick, her hair parted on the side and pulled straight back off her face.

When one considers all that would pass between Ford and Hepburn in years to come, her choice of material seems more than a little ironic. Kate played the scene in which Daisy Sage, a free spirit who would never have considered marriage before, proposes to her soul-mate Tom Collier. At the very moment Daisy has found it in herself to expose her feelings, Tom announces his decision to marry another—a woman who, at length, will do everything to extinguish the sensitivity and creativity Daisy has always cherished in Tom.

Staring at Kate through a haze of smoke, Ford marveled at her ability to seem sophisticated one moment, like a child of eight or ten the next. He described her as "a split personality, half pagan, half puritan."

For all of Ford's excitement, the test did not result in a movie offer for Kate; Fox did eventually film *The Warrior's Husband*, but neither Ford nor Hepburn were involved in the project. Years later, Ford and George Cukor would often joke about which director had really discovered her. Ford may have seen her first, but it had been Cukor who, on the basis of his screen test, persuaded David Selznick to bring Katharine Hepburn to Hollywood.

Kate called John Ford wayward and odd, and loved him for those very qualities. He was the sort of man—she said—who played a joke on someone but didn't wait for the outcome. Most people would stick around to watch the victim trip over the rope, but not Ford. Kate laughed that this characteristic, which seemed very Irish, had driven her absolutely mad.

In letters and private conversations when they knew no one was listening, she called him Sean, the Irish version of his name. Kate always knew that no matter what she did, she would remain close to Sean's heart. Yet she could never predict with certainty his reaction to anything.

She learned that their first day on the set of *Mary of Scotland*, February 25, 1936. Kate had a 9 a.m. call on Stage 9, but Ford had asked the company to assemble an hour before.

It was not Ford's way to appear on a set and tell actors exactly what he wanted. Instead, he would gather cast members for coffee and conversation. After looking over the set for a few minutes, he might ask one of the actors to read a few lines informally. At this point, Ford never asked the actor to move here or there—just to read and get a feel for the material. Then he might ask another player to chime in; and then, when there was (in the words of John Wayne) "a good feeling about the scene," Ford would summon the cameraman.

"What do you think about this?" Ford would say gently. "Run through it again, fellows."

With only a work light, the actors would read the lines again. After consultation with the cameraman, Ford might make a few suggestions. Asked whether he could do something, an actor's natural response was to say, "Sure."

Working in this manner, Ford—who tended to throw out lines from the screenplay and invent terse dialogue of his own—usually took about an hour to set up a scene.

Ford's acute sensitivity notwithstanding, actors were terrified of him, and with good reason. He had a stiletto tongue. He was known to single out an actor and pick on him throughout a production. He was famous for reducing tough guys like Victor McLaglen and John Wayne to tears. In a flat voice, he would attack, mock, and humiliate actors until they groveled: "D'ya know, McLaglen, that Fox are paying you $1200 a week to do things that I can get any child off the street to do better?" Or he would roar through a megaphone: "When does your contract come up for renewal?" This appeared to be malice, but close friends saw it as painful insecurity; Ford had a need to test people.

Ford's unwillingness to give specific instructions forced actors to hang on his every word and gesture. The dark glasses made him especially difficult to read. For all the camaraderie and good feeling, an undercurrent of fear permeated his sets. Actors waited for Ford to jump on them; not even a close personal friend was exempt from being designated his patsy. Actors who worshipped Ford—and most did—dreaded being "put on ice"; the slightest infraction on or off the set might cause him to ignore a man for years without explaining why.

Quite often, no one but Ford seemed to recognize the offense that caused a fellow to be banished. And no one could anticipate when Ford might acknowledge his presence again. Even a close friend like John Wayne once suffered that fate for reasons Wayne claimed not to comprehend. Ford, asked why he had put this or that man on ice, was likely to insist nothing of the sort had occurred. He enjoyed making people wonder.

With actresses he tended to be courtly and courteous; he affected a rare old-world formality. If a man used vulgar language in front of a woman, Ford, superstitious about such things, would instantly banish him from the set. Yet at times he could hardly conceal his own lack of pleasure in directing women. He was a man's director and proud of it. He always seemed more comfortable with the boys.

Paradoxically, while actresses raved about Ford's ability to practice a kind of thought transference, they found him hard to communicate with. His cutting, sarcastic manner frightened and intimidated even those against whom it was not overtly directed.

Kate Hepburn's brash behavior that first day was unprecedented on a Ford set. When the director arrived to prepare a scene in Mary of Scotland's chambers, Kate, in a white neck ruff, was sitting with her feet up on a table, smoking an Irish clay pipe. She seemed to imitate Ford's nervous manner of chewing on a pipe stem. All about her, the actresses who played the other Marys in the film—Mary Seton, Mary Livingston, Mary Beaton, and Mary Fleming—puffed on clay pipes of their own.

Ford appeared not to notice. To Kate's perplexity and fascination, he pointedly ignored the little tableau she had arranged. Pipe smoke wafted through the set, but he said not a word about it.

Yet it did throw him.

"Now, I tell you what I want you to do in this first scene," he began, most uncharacteristically. Anyone who had made a film with Ford before—and that excluded Kate—would have known he would never open a day's work like that. Somehow Kate's very presence had altered his work rhythm. Accustomed to inspiring fear and awe in his actors, he seemed grimly intent on showing no response to her playful insurrection.

Eventually the pungent smoke made one actress sick, and she dashed off the set. Even then, Ford refused to mention it. Determined to provoke some reaction, Kate blithely puffed on her clay pipe long after the others had stopped. But by 6:05 p.m., when the day's fifth scene was completed, not once had the director acknowledged the pipe-smoking Marys.

For all that, to those who had worked often with Ford and knew him best, he seemed a different man in Kate's presence. Ordinarily, at lunchtime, he would disappear to a portable dressing room, where he took off his shirt, undid his belt, and snoozed for about forty-five minutes. Then a prop man would bring him a large dish of ice cream. But on *Mary of Scotland*, Ford regularly presided over a big noisy table in the RKO commissary. Kate, in jodhpurs, sat at his side.

They joked, sang, told stories, baited, teased, and insulted each other mercilessly. Ford and his group employed ridicule to test a man's character. Cameraman Joe August, screenwriter Dudley Nichols, actor Harry Carey and other of Ford's cronies treated Kate like one of the boys; and she appeared to love it.

"You're a hell of a fine girl," Ford assured her. "If you'd just learn to shut up and knuckle under you'd probably make somebody a nice wife."

He watched her as though she were a little freckle-faced Irish girl. Kate's fearlessness, her relish for trading barbs, enchanted him. He marveled that she could take abuse as well as dish it out. He loved that she was irreverent and violently opinionated. He respected her intelligence and thirst for knowledge about every aspect of filmmaking.

His usual formality with women disappeared. He seemed less guarded. He egged her on. He could not get enough of her chatter. He lapped up her perpetual optimism and enthusiasm.

When a woman in a picture hat and white gloves approached the table to shake Kate's hand, Ford muttered, "So you won't shake hands with me, eh?"

"I had a clean glove on," said the visitor, a writer for one of the fan magazines.

Kate roared with delight: "I've been trying to think of a crack as mean as that for weeks!"

"Listen, Katharine," said Ford, who appeared to have slept in his clothes. "I'll play you a round of golf."

"For a hundred dollars a hole!" Kate shot back.

"All right, for a hundred dollars a hole. And if you lose, you'll agree to come to this studio at least one day dressed like a woman."

"And if I win," she countered, "will you agree to come to the studio at least one day dressed like a gentleman?"

Ford turned to the screenwriter. "Listen, Dudley, let's put that unhappy ending back on this picture. Let's behead the dame after all."

"Yes, sir," Nichols replied.

"And let's do it right now!" said Ford.

Director and actress discovered that they shared a passion for golf. They both played very quickly; and before long, after a day's filming they were regularly driving his dilapidated two-seater Ford roadster to the California Country Club. Ford detested the ostentation of a fancy car, and kept two sets of golf clubs in the rumble seat amid piles of script pages and eucalyptus leaves.

He adored Kate's competitiveness. They both made a great game of their fierce rivalry on the golf course. He loved pretending to be furious when she beat him.

One afternoon, Ford was on the green in two and had a three-foot putt.

"You concede this!" he barked.

"Putt it out," insisted Kate, never one to concede anything.

Ford glared at her—and missed. The ball rolled about a foot

and a half beyond the cup. He tried to tap it back and missed again. Instead of a par, he got a double bogey.

The director picked up his putter and hurled it fifty or sixty feet.

"If I were you," Kate crowed, "I'd use an overlapping grip to get those distances."

He had enormous faith in her abilities. There was astonishment at RKO when Ford—notorious for his insistence on making every last artistic decision himself—encouraged Kate to direct a scene in *Mary of Scotland*. If anyone had doubted her impact on the man, Ford's willingness to turn over the reins provided all the proof necessary.

It happened on Friday, April 10, 1936, when they were shooting the tower scene between Mary of Scotland and her lover, the Earl of Bothwell. Suddenly Ford cursed in exasperation: "This is a goddamn lousy scene!" He hated scenes with too much dialogue, and this had more than most. In such cases, his inclination was to rewrite—or rip out the pages and proceed as though they had never existed.

"Do you want to shoot it or just drop it out of the picture?" he asked Kate.

"It's the best scene in the picture!" she challenged him.

"You think so?"

"Yes, I do."

"Well, if you like it so much, why don't you shoot it?" he growled. Without another word, he retrieved his filthy old felt hat and marched off.

That had certainly never happened before; and at first, people had no idea how to react.

On the one hand, Kate figured Ford just wanted to call her bluff; on the other, she was very touched that he believed she could do it. In either case, it was vitally important that she direct the scene—and do it well. She turned to Joe August, who had worked with her on *Sylvia Scarlett*. An impish man who at times seemed almost totally inarticulate, his nickname was Quasimodo. In conversation, he tended to communicate with pantomime and sound effects rather than words. He had the reputation of being one of the best cameramen in the business.

"Joe, will you stay?" Kate implored.

He agreed, as did Fredric March; whereupon Kate directed for the first and last time in her career.

Two days later, Kate and George Cukor went sailing with Ford, George O'Brien, and others on the *Araner*, the double-masted 110-foot ketch named after the Aran Islands, birthplace of Ford's mother. The *Araner* was very special to Ford; he had grown up around ships in Maine and loved the feeling of freedom out at sea. For his wife, the yacht—purchased for $30,000 in 1934—was a treasured status symbol. Mary loaded the vessel with expensive silver, linen, and red carpets. But for Ford, the *Araner* was a place to relax, to feel "loose as a goose."

And it provided a means of escape. When a film was done, Ford sometimes stocked the *Araner* with cases of Irish whiskey and sailed to Mexico. He hired a mariachi band to follow as he made the rounds of whorehouses, where he drank and soaked in the atmosphere; sex itself was of considerably less interest. Eventually, when Ford was too drunk and sick to go ashore, he would order the band to play continuously on deck or in the mahogany-paneled main saloon. For days on end, he lay alone in a tiny, cramped cabin, preferring that to the master suite, whose ornate four-poster marriage bed he usually assigned to John Wayne or some other pal.

George Cukor was well aware of Kate's feelings for Ford and what that must mean for her present relationship. When Cukor signed the *Araner* guest-book on April 12, he wrote in the remarks column, "Poor Leland!"

That day, Kate wore a white mock-turtle T-shirt under a navy cardigan and brief navy shorts with a white stripe down each side. Except for a trace of crimson lipstick, she wore no makeup. Her chin-length hair blew back off her face as she sat cross-legged on the polished deck. Ford, in rumpled white trousers, perched in a chair as Kate vigorously massaged the soles of his feet.

Kate's background as a tomboy in a houseful of brothers made it easy for her to fit into Ford's masculine world. She could josh, spar, and compete with the toughest of his cronies. Life with Dr. Hepburn had taught a different lesson; watching her mother, Kate had learned to defer to the male, to do everything she could to comfort and protect him. At the dinner table, Mrs. Hepburn always made certain Dr. Hepburn was able to tell his best stories. With the right man—strong like Dr. Hepburn—that sort of behavior came naturally to Kate.

For all the banter, Kate was deeply respectful of Ford. This was a particularly exciting moment to work with him. Ford had long been held in high regard in Hollywood, but *The Informer*— made at RKO while Kate was shooting *Break of Hearts*—marked a watershed in his critical reputation. Based on a novel by Liam O'Flaherty, this highly stylized work was declared by critics of the day the finest sound film ever made.

Kate called Ford a big-time operator. It seemed to her that no one knew more about filmmaking than he did. He was never comfortable with the label "artist," but he took his craft very seriously indeed. She knew he had great ambitions about all he wanted to accomplish as a director. Ford was the sort of artist, Kate sensed, who cut his own path without regard to anyone's opinion. He had great nerve and was not afraid to fail. As a director, he was always quick and decisive.

Yet the absolute certainty he showed on a film set disappeared the moment he was not at work. Kate saw that filmmaking was far easier for him than day-to-day living. When Ford shot a picture, he always seemed to know exactly where the story was going; not so the story of his life.

Ford was a profoundly unhappy man—and stubbornly self-destructive. In 1934, Dr. Harley Gunderson had diagnosed an enlarged liver and other symptoms attributable to alcohol; Ford's drinking binges had become a kind of slow suicide. He drank in search of oblivion. He was a periodic alcoholic who exercised control over when he hit the bottle: never during a picture, always after. He sometimes signed pledges with his parish priest, promising never to touch the drink again; but he always reverted.

Ford religiously went on a binge when he finished a movie.

But *Mary of Scotland* would be different. By the time the day trip on the *Araner* ended, Kate and Ford had begun to plan a trip east together after the picture. They had discovered another shared passion, the sea; and Kate wanted Sean to experience the Fenwick waterfront where she had grown up. Vowing not to disappear to Mexico with the boys, he promised to accompany her.

John Ford was in love.

Every day on the set at 4 p.m., the entire company would break so that Kate could serve tea and biscuits to cast and crew while Ford looked on adoringly. There was always a torrent of words, yet discussion of work was strictly forbidden. Someone said it would be safer to face a lion than ask Ford a question about the picture during teatime.

Before he shot *Mary of Scotland*, in the course of nine consecutive evenings Ford had screened each of Hepburn's previous films to study, he said, "every angle of her strange, sharp face—the chiseled nose, the mouth, the long neck." And now, Ford and Joe August made her the focus of light in a world shrouded in shadow. Again and again, the figure of Mary Stuart, shimmering with light and life, pierces through the velvet blacks that surround her.

That was how Ford saw Kate. The vivid light–dark contrasts in *Mary of Scotland* suggest the chiaroscuro of the Hepburn–Ford relationship.

He almost lost her: In one scene, Kate was riding side-saddle at full gallop when Ford saw that her head was about to crash into a thick heavy tree branch.

"Kate, duck!" he cried. A second more and, by her own reckoning, she would have been decapitated.

Now it was Kate's turn to save him.

Ford completed work on *Mary of Scotland* on April 23. Ordinarily he would rush home, hand his wife $1000, and tell her to order a supply of liquor. A heavy drinker herself, Mrs. Ford did not mind her husband's binges; on the contrary, she seems to have viewed them as a way of keeping him in hand. As long as Jack was stinking drunk between pictures, nothing worse could happen to threaten Mary's position as Mrs. John Ford.

But this time, Ford and Kate headed to New York, where she met with the Theater Guild to discuss appearing in a stage version of *Jane Eyre* sometime in the 1936-7 season. When she signed a contract on May 19, she anticipated that after a Broadway run, Ford might do a film of the play with her in the starring role.

Ford met Kate's mother in Manhattan. Just then, Mrs. Hepburn was especially feeling the sting of Catholic charges that she was a member of the idle rich who only wanted to keep poor Irish and Italian immigrants from breeding. At a moment when she was being reviled as a "prophet of decadence" by prominent American Catholics like Patrick, Cardinal Hayes, Mrs. Hepburn seemed a bit wary of Ford.

"You are the youngest of thirteen?" Mrs. Hepburn confronted him. "Your people are Irish Catholics?"

"Yes," he replied.

"Thirteen!"

"You have plenty," he teased.

"Oh, yes," she said uneasily.

Usually Kate would have used a chauffeur to take them to Fenwick, but Ford hated that sort of thing; so Kate did the driving herself while Ford and her mother talked in the back seat.

Unlike Luddy and Leland, John Ford—then a self-described "socialistic democrat"—could hold his own in the kind of spirited political conversation Mrs. Hepburn favored. Despite the rough-and-tumble pose, Ford was a deeply learned man with a wide-ranging knowledge of history and politics. He had monitored the "Russian experiment," as he called it, with great interest, although he did not believe communism to be "the remedy this sick world is seeking." He feared communism would lead to another Bonaparte.

By the time they reached Fenwick, Ford and Mrs. Hepburn had disagreed often and become the best of friends.

"Look at that!" Kate cried. "Look at that! Look at that sunset!"

"Kate, why don't you just let us enjoy these things," Ford said softly, and her mother agreed. "We can see them just as well as you can."

The encounter set the tone for Ford's visit. He was there to have a quiet look about the place where Kate had grown up. They played golf, sailed on Long Island Sound, walked along the stony beach. John Wayne—who probably knew Ford better than most— once said that his genius was the ability to absorb: people, moods, places.

Kate soon learned that there was rarely any need to point things out; he saw and grasped things immediately, without discussion or explanation. He was always taking impressions of life. It seemed to her that Ford possessed antennae which very quickly received waves of thought from all around. Later she would tell him that he understood her as no one had before. At the heart of that understanding, no doubt, was Ford's trip to Fenwick. It was said in the family that to comprehend Kate, one had to know something of this place where she had sunk her emotional roots. One had to see the vast open horizon, and consider the sense of possibility and of openness to experience that it represented to her.

To Kate, the decrepit old cottage whose screens and porches rattled ominously in the north wind was more than just wood and nails. This house held memories of her brother Tommy and Aunt Edith; Kate had known paradise here.

At Fenwick, Ford loved the comfortable cottage where everybody could always hear everybody else. He loved the noisy dinnertable conversations, where each family member and guest was expected to do his or her little turn. He loved the egos and the characters and the comedy of it all.

Dick Hepburn was the focus of attention at that moment. After Dick graduated from Harvard in 1933, Dr. Hepburn had agreed to "let him alone" for two or three years while he tried to break into the theater. Kate persuaded George Cukor to give her brother a screen test; but when the role of Laurie in *Little Women* went to another actor, Dick returned to Connecticut to apply himself to playwriting.

At the family home in West Hartford, he turned out two dramas; the second, *Behold Your God*, had finally received a production at Jasper Deeter's Hedgerow Theater, a converted mill in Moylan, Pennsylvania. Unlike Mrs. Hepburn, who bristled every time newspapers linked her with a movie star daughter, Dick did not hesitate to use the connection to publicize his play. In anticipation of the opening on April 18, 1936, he suggested that Hedgerow might want to hint that Kate was flying east to see the play, although there was no chance of that happening. He discussed the possibility of exhibiting life masks of himself and Kate to emphasize the relationship.

Publicity linking Dick to his famous sister did nothing to help the production. *Behold Your God* received unfavorable reviews. "Even the name of Hepburn as author," wrote *Variety*, "is unlikely ever to persuade any ambitious producer to give it a Broadway presentation."

Kate, who had begun to pay Dick a $125 monthly allowance so he could rent an apartment of his own on East 19th Street in Manhattan, returned to find him undaunted. Doggedly he pressed on with his plans to become a successful playwright, putting in eight-hour days at the typewriter.

In New York, Ford visited Kate's East 49th Street townhouse. But he did not sleep with her. From the first, he made clear that he was not interested in an affair. He wanted marriage and a life together. To show Kate that he considered this relationship different, Ford talked about various women with whom he had had affairs in the past. Still, she sensed that he wasn't being entirely truthful. Kate could not believe he had ever really been unfaithful to Mary.

Unlike Leland Hayward, who always traveled with an extensive wardrobe, Ford brought only a single suit of clothes on the trip east. At a dinner party where Laura Harding and the other guests were dressed to the nines in anticipation of going on to a concert at Carnegie Hall, Ford arrived in a dirty old coat with patched elbows and rumpled gray flannel trousers with a shiny seat.

Kate called his manner of dress real style. She saw that the shabby clothes were his own form of snobbery. He dressed that way because he didn't need to dress like everyone else.

The hosts were *Fortune* editor Russell Davenport and his wife Marcia, the music critic for *Stage* magazine. Kate had come to know Davenport in the years since she had briefly shared his bachelor flat with Phelps Putnam. Now, she was eager to introduce Ford to her friends. When conversation lagged painfully at the dinner table, Ford and the guest-of-honor Henry Luce struggled to keep things going. Kate was very grateful; usually Ford tended to go stone silent in situations like that.

He did not accompany Kate and the others to their box at the concert, however. As a married man it would not do for him to be photographed with Kate in public before he had had a chance to talk to Mary.

For Ford, everything had happened quickly. He was not a man who had expected to find happiness outside work. Long ago he had accepted that marriage would always be a straitjacket. He had poured his energies into filmmaking. All he had ever looked forward to when he finished a picture was oblivion. But these few weeks suggested he was capable of something very different. He and Kate planned a trip to Ireland together; they would arrive at Galway, then sail about the Aran Islands. Kate was life-affirming; he had never experienced that in a woman.

Before he returned to California, Ford (who, in emulation of his older brother Francis, had dropped his family name of Feeney) wanted to stop in Portland, Maine, to see his ailing eighty-six-year-old father. John Feeney, a widower and retired saloonkeeper, had once hoped his son would be a priest. From Maine, Ford would go straight to Los Angeles to tell Mary everything. Although they had two pups, as he called them, the fact that they had never been properly married in the Roman Catholic Church made it seem easier to ask for a divorce.

Ford called Kate from Maine to say that his father appeared to be much better. Then he headed west.

Hardly had he reached home and had his talk with Mary when word came from Portland that old John Feeney had died. It was June 22. The news threw Ford into feverish uncertainty. Deeply superstitious, he seemed to take it as God's comment on the decision he had just made.

Distraught, he called Fenwick, but Kate wasn't there. Afterward, Peg and Mrs. Hepburn could not seem to agree on exactly what he had said. By the time Kate arrived, her mother and sister were uncertain whether Ford had already left for Maine or was still in California.

Kate, in anguish, realized she dared not contact him at home.

The Hepburns were a talkative family, yet they always left much unsaid. The children grew up with the tacit understanding that they must never ask about Fred and Carrie Houghton, whose framed photographs hung unexplained on the master bedroom wall. According to Bob Hepburn, if they did express curiosity about their grandparents, Mrs. Hepburn would merely turn her face away.

Friends like Jo Bennett perceived that Mrs. Hepburn's avoidance of any discussion of her past had created a physical "tension" in her. On political topics she was loquacious and argumentative; but there was much in her life she could not bear to give voice to. Her household rang with the din of incessant chatter, yet it was also a place of secrets and silences.

Even now, Mrs. Hepburn could not bring herself to talk of young Tom's death; and certainly no one spoke of the other suicides in the family. Dr. Hepburn eventually found some outlet in private conversations with Bob, whose attendance at Harvard Medical School made it possible to broach the unspeakable on what seemed like a professional basis. Yet after all these years, Dr. Hepburn—who never dared discuss Tom's death with Kate—continued to insist it had been an accident.

Kate, at whatever emotional cost, had made a tacit pact of silence with Dr. Hepburn in 1921. That so much remained pointedly off-limits gave her life a distinct tension of its own.

On June 22, 1936, the day Ford's father died, Kate wrote a letter of condolence on pale green tissue paper. She confessed she could hardly be philosophical about the death of a parent; she could not imagine how she would react if she lost Dr. or Mrs. Hepburn. She felt certain he would understand all she wanted to say. That was the way it was between them and always would be.

With him she did not have to give voice to her feelings; he

simply absorbed and comprehended. After years of silence, it must have come as a great relief to be able to communicate so easily.

Unable to mail the letter to Odin Street where Mary might intercept it, Kate sent it to Ford at his home studio, Twentieth Century–Fox. She marked the envelope "Personal." Ford did not receive it until after he returned from burying his father. By that time, he seems also to have buried any clear sense that he deserved a chance at life with Kate. His Catholic conscience—primitive and unshakable—took over.

Had Kate been at Fenwick to receive his call on the 22nd, perhaps she might have been able to work her magic on him. She had a way of piercing through his black moods. When he received word about his father, he had wasted no time in reaching out to Kate; hers was the voice he needed to hear. As it was, he had only Mary, who seized the opportunity to turn old John Feeney's death to her advantage.

Mary knew her husband. She knew the feelings of doubt and inadequacy that tormented him; and she knew his propensity for self-flagellation. Kate was not alone in sensing that Ford used a tough exterior to conceal that he was being torn up inside by a great many things; a number of the actresses who worked with him saw that. But only Mary seemed to grasp that he had always been attracted to her precisely because her negativity reflected his own; when Mary castigated Jack, she was only saying what he already thought of himself.

In his own strange way, he was fascinated by and drawn to Mary's darkness. It wasn't just her hair and thick eyebrows that were black; it was her cast of mind. When he photographed Mary not long after they were wed, he obscured her face and body with shadows; he envisaged his bride as a kind of silhouette.

"Jack is very religious, he'll never divorce me, he'll never have any grounds to divorce me on," Mary once vowed. "I'm going to be Mrs. John Ford until I die."

Mary called her husband Jack, Daddy, or Pa—but never Sean, the Irish name Kate called him in private. Kate valued everything Mary rejected: She adored the poetry and romanticism of Sean's

Irish roots; Mary was ashamed of Jack's "shanty Irish" family. Kate revered Sean as a filmmaker; Mary never gave up hope that Jack would find a manlier occupation. Kate saw Sean as sensitive; Mary thought Jack weak. Kate loved Sean precisely because he was the sort of man capable of being devastated by the world; Mary used Jack's burden of Catholic guilt against him.

By the time Kate Hepburn returned to Los Angeles to begin her next film, *A Woman Rebels*, on July 1, 1936, Mary Ford was geared up and ready for battle.

Mrs. Ford had often imagined herself in rivalry with the actresses who worked for her husband. Before they married, Ford had ordered her never to visit when he was shooting a picture; through the years, Mary always insisted she stayed away because she didn't want to give any leading lady the satisfaction of thinking she had outsmarted her.

Initially, Mary had been beside herself with delight at Jack's directing an actress of Hepburn's breeding and background. But now, those very credentials made Kate the most threatening sort of adversary, accustomed as Mrs. Ford was to claiming social superiority to most people in Hollywood. It did not help that studio publicity was just then touting Kate as a descendant of James Hepburn, Earl of Bothwell: a dubious claim.

Another thorn in Mary's side was the love of film Kate shared with Ford. He never so much as showed a script to his wife. By Mary's own account, Ford had badly hurt her feelings when he forbade her ever to visit a film set; since that time, she had affected disdain for his work. The actors and actresses who made up Ford's "stock company" regarded themselves as a family, and Mary felt excluded from all that. Besides, she lacked any sensitivity to her husband's accomplishments; she honestly failed to see why people called Jack a great artist.

Ford was almost another man from the one Kate had talked to the previous month when he called from Maine in anticipation of asking Mary for a divorce. It wasn't just the death of old John Feeney that had cast a gloom over his spirits; it was Mary's violent determination to hold on to her husband at any cost.

Of the two Ford children, fourteen-year-old Barbara (named for his mother) was the apple of Jack's eye. She bore a marked physical resemblance to Mary; but her intelligence, imagination, and hypersensitivity were her father's. Mrs. Ford responded to the threat of divorce with a threat of her own: Jack could take Patrick, fifteen, the sickly son for whom he showed little sympathy; but Barbara must remain with Mary.

To make matters worse, Ford had returned to Los Angeles to discover that in his absence, RKO had substantially recut *Mary of Scotland*; intolerant of anyone's being so bold as to comment on his work, let alone tamper with it, Ford did not take studio intervention lightly.

If Kate had expected Ford to have settled things with his wife by now, it was easy to understand why that had not happened—and continued not to happen all summer. They saw each other nearly every day at the studio, and he spent many happy evenings with her at Angelo Drive. Yet Ford, veering wildly between euphoria and despair, showed no sign of moving out of the house he shared with Mary and the children. Kate, for her part, appeared certain that the postponement was only temporary, and her optimism kept them both going through a very difficult period.

According to Ford's niece Cecile De Prita, at one point Kate offered Mary $150,000 to give Ford his freedom along with the daughter he cherished. Mary turned her down.

Ford had always seemed most at peace when he was working; but his next picture at RKO, *The Plough and the Stars*, based on the Sean O'Casey play, was a profoundly unhappy experience. The project had gotten off to a bad start when Spencer Tracy turned down the role of Jack Clitheroe. Ford believed that Tracy owed it to him to do the film whether or not he wanted to himself. Tracy, for his part, openly acknowledged his debt to Ford. But the same resistance to being drawn into the director's orbit that had prevented Tracy from going to the Philippines with Ford and George O'Brien after *Seas Beneath* led him to turn down *The Plough and the Stars*.

When shooting began on July 8, Ford lacked his usual intense focus; and it is not too much to suppose that the trouble stemmed from the conflicting demands of two women. Cliff Reid, the associate producer, viewed the rushes with grave concern. In the role of Fluther Good, Barry Fitzgerald, of Dublin's Abbey Theatre, was impossible to understand. Reid had worked with Ford on *The Lost Patrol* and *The Informer*; he knew well the director's fierce resentment of associate producers who gave advice based on the rushes. Once, when Reid had made the mistake of praising the rushes, Ford spitefully reshot an entire sequence. "Joe," he called to Joe August, "the front office likes the rushes, so there must be something wrong. We'll have to keep shooting until we find out what it is." Strictly to punish Reid, he worked for two days more, adding $25,000 to the budget.

Although Ford publicly insisted that he preferred never to look at rushes, he often ran them alone. At most the editor and assistant editor were permitted to attend. Others were strictly barred.

Cliff Reid thought that only one person on earth would be able to talk to Ford about the Fitzgerald problem without getting pitched out by the ear. "Come in and look at some of the rushes," he implored Kate, and discreetly arranged a time when Ford was unlikely to interrupt.

Kate, viewing the rushes, agreed that Fitzgerald was extremely difficult to understand. The screening room was dark, the projector running when the door suddenly flew open and Ford appeared in a stream of white light. Kate sensed that Reid and his associates were terrified of what Ford might do. But if they expected Ford to explode in rage, they were wrong. He said not a word, which Kate recognized as his most deadly means of attack. Finally she broke the awkward silence.

"They feel that Barry Fitzgerald can't be understood," she began, "and I don't think he can be understood."

"I'll tell you something," said Ford, giving them all a chilly look. "Anyone who is stupid enough not to understand him, I don't care whether they understand him or not."

Afterward, Ford never mentioned the incident. Kate was left to wonder how he had learned of the screening and whether he was furious at her for conniving with the associate producer.

She did know something Ford refused to disclose to anyone else: Part way through filming, he realized the picture was seriously flawed and that he had no idea how to fix it. Kate admired the coolness and objectivity with which he appraised his work. He was his own most severe critic. Ford held himself to a high standard; when he failed to meet that standard, disappointment tore him apart inside. His pain was all the worse for the struggle to conceal it with an attitude that struck some people as cavalier. Watching him like this pierced her through the heart.

In the end, RKO was unhappy with *The Plough and the Stars*. The studio demanded changes. But Ford believed the particular changes they wanted had nothing to do with the film's real defects.

"Why make a picture where a man and a woman are married?" production chief Sam Briskin asked Ford. "The main thing about pictures is love or sex. Here you've got a man and a woman married at the start—who's interested in that?" Ford, for his part, remained intent on filming O'Casey's play word for word.

Suddenly Ford did something that never happened while he was working: He went on a bender. Mary and the children were away—probably on the *Araner*—when Cliff Reid discovered Ford in a drunken stupor at home on Odin Street.

Famous for his ability to resist the bottle until a picture was done, Ford had cracked under all the pressure. Conflict with RKO was the least of it. Applying the same exacting standards to his personal relations that he did to his work, Ford seemed to believe he was letting everybody down: Kate, Barbara, Mary. Whatever he chose, someone would be hurt; and his indecision was hurting them all.

Reid needed Ford to put in an appearance at the studio; but the director refused to stop drinking. Again the associate producer appealed to Kate. There was no one else Ford would listen to.

Kate rushed to Odin Street. Usually the home behind the white picket fence would have been off-limits; but Mary was gone, so Kate let herself in. She found Ford in a dismal condition. With difficulty she got him up and out of the house.

Kate drove to RKO, where she spirited Ford into her dressing room. There, in a misguided attempt to help, she forced a potentially lethal mixture of whiskey and castor oil down his throat. He became very ill. He said he felt as though he were going to die. While he slept for some two hours, Kate agonized over what she had done to him. At times she was certain he was dead. When Ford's eyes opened, Kate rushed him to the Hollywood Athletic Club, where his cronies finally brought him round.

Kate's terror may have been a way of confronting the fact that her loving presence in Ford's life had thrown him into turmoil unlike any he had known. In the spring, saving him from the need to seek oblivion after a film had seemed a great accomplishment; but now, guilt, upset, and frustration about their relationship had caused Ford to do the unprecedented: drink during a picture. Had Kate, with the best will in the world, driven him to a new pitch of self-destructiveness? That was the very opposite of what she wanted. Kate's lifelong belief that she had nearly killed him seems to be a reflection of her own guilt at having failed to rescue him from his demons.

Ford was desperate to get away. More than ever, he felt the need to escape when he finished *The Plough and the Stars*. This time, there was no suggestion that Kate accompany him. Ostensibly the reason was that she owed RKO another film after *A Woman Rebels*; shooting was due to begin in September. For Ford, *The Plough and the Stars* was the last of a three-picture commitment.

When he sailed the *Araner* to Hawaii, no doubt he sincerely hoped to reach some decision on what to do about his marriage. Despite the black moods to which he was prone, Kate believed that hope was a defining characteristic of Ford's personality. And there is every evidence that he kept hoping to find a way for them to be together.

RKO voiced surprise and dismay that Ford would go off on his yacht when work remained to be done on *The Plough and the Stars*. In October, the studio assigned George Nicholls, Jr. to shoot the scenes Ford had declined to tack on. When Ford heard about it, he roared that he wanted his name removed as director, but the studio refused. He vowed never to work at RKO again.

Kate had serious problems of her own at the studio. Although RKO regarded her as one of its most valuable properties, her career had begun a distinct downward slide. Hepburn provoked powerful responses; filmgoers rarely reacted with indifference. In films like *A Bill of Divorcement, Morning Glory, Little Women*, and *Alice Adams*, she had strong appeal; but when audiences responded negatively, they did so with passion. The studio bosses pondered what to do about the "Hepburn Stigma." For a star of her magnitude, there had been too many box office debacles, not enough successes.

After duds like *Spitfire, The Little Minister*, and *Break of Hearts*, Hepburn had seemed to turn her fortunes around with *Alice Adams*. Yet no one appeared to learn its lesson; the studio failed to follow up with other modern comedies.

The damage *Sylvia Scarlett* did to her career was Hepburn's own fault—and Cukor's; that film, which lost more than $200,000, went down in history as RKO's "worst A-picture" ever. Next, Pandro Berman had poured every possible resource into *Mary of Scotland*; it was that year's second most costly RKO production. RKO hoped the John Ford–Dudley Nichols team, after a massive triumph with *The Informer*, could help Hepburn regain popularity; but *Mary of Scotland* also failed at the box office. Though the film was loaded with visual interest, there was no chemistry between Hepburn and Fredric March.

The lesson of *Alice Adams* continued to go unheeded. Thirties audiences showed scant enthusiasm for watching Hepburn in picturesque costume dramas; yet that was exactly the sort of film RKO gave her next. As eccentric Victorian firebrand Pamela Thistlewaite in *A Woman Rebels*, she succeeded only in further alienating the filmgoing public

Kate turned to George Stevens. Once before he had rescued her career; perhaps he could do it again. Stevens, for his part, expressed little sympathy for *Quality Street*, the Barrie play she wanted to do next. It would be another quaint costume film, precisely the sort of thing she should avoid. But Stevens was a man of fervent loyalties. Kate had given the director his first big opportunity; he did not question that he must return the favor.

Yet everything seemed different this time. Besides the wrong-headedness of the material, part of the problem may have been that Stevens, enjoying a love affair with Ginger Rogers, failed to focus on Kate with the intensity he had shown in *Alice Adams*. RKO executives who previewed *Quality Street* lamented what one wag called the "lace drawers atmosphere." To judge by studio records, there was growing concern that Kate was being very badly served by the costume pictures in which RKO repeatedly cast her. Such material, it was said, failed to suit "the temper" of the time.

But the problem wasn't costume pictures per se: Greta Garbo in *Camille*, Bette Davis in *Jezebel*, and Vivien Leigh in *Gone with the Wind* were wildly popular in the 1930s; and Kate had had a big hit with *Little Women*, in which she played Jo March as a hard-edged modern personality. The trouble with a vehicle like *Quality Street* was its cloying preciousness. It played to nearly empty houses and lost some $248,000.

Kate's career crisis had not been helped by her strained relations with Leland Hayward. After he learned of the romance with John Ford, "Uncle Leland," as Ford called him, had done nothing further to push her for the Edna Ferber play, *Stage Door*. Margaret Sullavan took the stage role Hayward had promised Kate. On the rebound, he began an affair with her. When Sullavan became pregnant, Hayward proposed marriage.

Kate, even at the height of their relationship, had shown no sustained inclination to marry Hayward. This contrasted markedly with her attitude to John Ford. Kate was still waiting for Ford to make up his mind to leave Mary when news of Hayward's wedding on November 15, 1936 plunged her into a fit of agitation.

"But you didn't want him, Kath," Mrs. Hepburn said on the telephone. "Maybe he just wanted to get married. Poor man. You can't blame him."

George Cukor agreed: "Kate, what's wrong with you? You could have married him if you wanted to. You didn't."

It was true. Still, Leland's marriage highlighted the uncertainty of her own situation. Since only a few close friends knew about Kate's love affair with John Ford, most people assumed Leland

Hayward had dumped her. Hayward himself would always eagerly encourage that version of events. Kate, for her part, was too protective of Ford to suggest otherwise.

Kate heeded her mother's advice and sent the bride a telegram: "Dear Maggie, You have just married the most wonderful man in the world. Blessings, Kate." Sullavan, in a jealous pout, set fire to the message.

Six months before, when Kate had agreed to appear in *Jane Eyre* for the Theater Guild, she had seemed about to begin a new life with John Ford. She had helped him break the pattern of seeking oblivion, and he had come east to explore Fenwick and meet the Hepburns. Everything had seemed so clear. Although much was left unsaid, Kate rejoiced that they were able to communicate without having always to put their feelings in words.

A great deal had changed since May. It was no longer certain that Ford would leave his wife. He returned from Hawaii still undecided. Always unwilling to show his pain, with Kate he constructed a defensive wall of jokes and banter. They talked and laughed, but the dream of going off together to the Aran Islands, with all that symbolized, became increasingly remote. He took up life again on Odin Street; and Mary resumed her practice of stuffing a dozen or so handmade Irish linen handkerchiefs into his back pocket every morning.

As Kate headed east for the first tryout of *Jane Eyre* in New Haven on December 26, the only thing she could still be certain of were her own feelings.

S E V E N T E E N

Many evenings, Kate spoke to Sean through the setting sun. On her dressing table at the theater, she kept his photograph propped against a toy elephant. As she studied the face in the picture, she imagined that Sean laughed at her. When she went on stage, in her mind's eye she saw him float in midair just beneath the balcony. She played every performance to him.

Although no one seemed to guess, she based her interpretation of *Jane Eyre* on their relationship. Instead of the mousy, quiet, modest Miss Eyre Helen Jerome had envisioned, Kate portrayed the governess as bold and provocative; Jane displayed the same fearlessness with gruff Mr. Rochester that Kate had always shown with Ford.

She dared not tell him any of this, at least not just now; the flurry of telegrams and letters between them were all jokes and raillery, as though to forestall the possibility of saying anything more serious.

Kate was anxious not to hurt Ford. She later admitted to one of Ford's friends that, putting aside what she wanted, she had refused to push him to act. For the moment, the only indication that something more than friendship was involved was that she always carefully wrote to him at the Hollywood Athletic Club or Fox Studios, never at home. A letter from Kate, however innocent, was likely to propel Mary into one of her shrieking fits.

In the weeks prior to the tour, Kate had scarcely concealed her own lack of enthusiasm for a commitment made under very different circumstances in May. Nothing about the production seemed to please her.

Kate had the right to approve the director and all cast members. Although initially there had been talk of Laurence Olivier as Mr. Rochester, that had come to nothing; and Cukor's suggestion of John Barrymore—reportedly on the wagon—was not well received at the Theater Guild. When the names of obscure actors were mentioned, Kate instructed Leland Hayward to tell the Guild that her co-star would have two weeks to prove himself. After that, Kate reserved the right to demand that the Guild replace him to her satisfaction or close the show altogether.

Before the Broadway opening, tryouts were scheduled for New Haven and Boston; but Kate's contract allowed her to demand further previews if she believed the production needed work. Jed Harris's decision to rush *The Lake* to New York when the show was still in a shambles was what led Kate to insist on this provision. The poor reviews she had received for *The Lake* made her exceedingly nervous about facing the *Times*'s Brooks Atkinson and other New York reviewers again.

Kate knew only too well that her career was on shakier ground than in 1933. In the interim, she had had one hit, *Alice Adams*, and several flops; the success of *Jane Eyre* was all the more essential.

By the final dress rehearsal, Kate doubted it would be successful. She bristled at the sight of a billboard where her name was printed in larger letters than those of Dennis Hoey, who played Mr. Rochester, and other company members. At once she complained to Lawrence Langner, who ran the Guild with Theresa Helburn.

"I want it understood," Kate barked, "that I object to having any more billing than the other actors."

"That's very generous of you," said Langner.

"Generous!" she said with disdain. "I just don't want to stick my neck out!"

Founded in 1919, the Theater Guild had enjoyed an immensely successful first decade with many famous productions. After that, its fortunes wavered. In March 1936, Langner, scouting for new plays in England, decided to buy the American rights to *Jane Eyre* if the Guild could get Ruth Gordon to play the governess. He wrote to Terry Helburn about the need to smash the star system in the American theater before it destroyed companies like the Guild. He insisted that everything expensive stars brought to the theater, they inevitably took out again. All the money lavished on big names, Langner declared, would be better spent on productions. Yet two months later, Langner and Helburn were thrilled to sign Kate Hepburn. For all their scorn of Hollywood, they counted on a movie star's name on the marquee to attract huge new audiences.

There was trouble from the start. Terry Helburn, small, slim, and dainty with lavender hair, recognized that part of the difficulty was the play itself. She was disturbed by Helen Jerome's decision to eliminate the childhood scenes Charlotte Brontë used to explain Jane's adult character. And she feared that somehow the third act didn't work. The Guild demanded substantial rewrites.

Kate posed another problem. Helburn insisted that despite the sparkle of her performances in New Haven, Kate lacked the technique to develop a character through three acts. Helburn blamed this shortcoming on Hollywood. Kate only knew how to create, in Helburn's words, "the little pieces of the mosaic by which a film is built up." With no theatrical training to speak of, she had little idea of how to modulate a performance.

But Kate proved a tireless worker and acutely intelligent. Undaunted, she was eager to get things right. She did not flinch at criticism; on the contrary, she enjoyed learning. She had an appetite for growth and experience. Indeed, by the end of the tour, Kate would confess to John Ford that she actually preferred the challenge of working in the theater.

From first to last Kate walked a tightrope with the Guild. She liked Langner and Helburn personally. She respected their experience and judgment and was eager to soak up what she could from them. At the same time, it was essential that she maintain a certain distance. For all her troubles in Hollywood, Kate remained a major star; everyone wanted a piece of her. There was nothing insidious about Terry Helburn and Lawrence Langner; but as producers, their inclination was to try to control Kate. It was in their interest to baby her and make her emotionally dependent. They did what they could to shift the relationship onto a personal basis.

Kate, for her part, struggled to keep things crisply professional without hurting anyone's feelings. This wasn't always easy. Helburn and Langner had known Kate when she was just starting out. Sometimes they talked to her as though she were still the understudy whom they had denied a five-dollar raise in 1930 when she took over for the actress playing the maid in *A Month in the Country*. At this point, it wasn't arrogance or willfulness that caused Kate to make sharp demands; it was the recognition that she needed to be businesslike and impersonal. She was a very valuable commodity. Helburn and Langner would swallow her up if she let them.

Although Leland Hayward continued as her agent, Kate had to defend herself on a day-to-day basis. To all intents and purposes, she did her own negotiating. Fortunately she had had years of experience watching Mrs. Hepburn—who had cut her teeth in conflict with Amory Houghton, Jr.—negotiate on behalf of women's suffrage and birth control. From her mother Kate learned that when associates like Margaret Sanger tried to get too close, it was often best to put up an icy front.

Loneliness was the price Kate paid for this self-imposed isolation.

For companionship she relied on her secretary Emily Perkins. The hearty Englishwoman, who spoke with a North Country brogue, called Kate "Baby." Em, as she was known, had worked as wardrobe mistress on *Mary of Scotland*, where she became one of John Ford's pets. Devoted to Ford and Hepburn, Em kept him apprised of how Baby was doing on the *Jane Eyre* tour.

In Boston, loneliness led Kate to accept a dinner invitation from Howard Hughes, thirty-one years old but already a millionaire film producer and daredevil aviator. She had known Hughes was after her since he landed his airplane on a field near the *Sylvia Scarlett* location. Cary Grant introduced his friend to Kate. But she encouraged the Casanova neither then nor when he landed on the golf course of the Bel Air Country Club, where she was playing with the club pro. Hughes emerged with his golf bag and insisted on finishing the nine with her.

His persistence paid off in Boston, where *Jane Eyre* played for two weeks at the Colonial Theater. Although business was excellent, Helen Jerome had yet to solve the play's structural problems, and Kate notified the Guild that she was going to insist on extending the tour. She dined with Hughes several nights in a row. His presence threw up a wall around Kate that helped distance her from Helburn and Langner.

Tall, stooped, and rawboned, Hughes had dark hair, pale skin, and gleaming white teeth. Kate, then twenty-nine, chuckled that he looked rather like John the Baptist.

He was as taciturn as Kate was talkative. She attributed his shyness to the fact that he was partially deaf. Avoiding eye contact, he tended to fold his hands between his legs and study the knuckles. He reminded people of a downcast, spoiled little boy. Only when Hughes talked of airplanes did his eyes burn and his language verge on the sensual. In Boston with Hepburn, Hughes was weeks away from an attempt to break his own transcontinental air record of nine hours, twenty-seven minutes, and ten seconds. He called his sleek silver and blue racer the *Winged Bullet*. A low-winged single-seater with an open cockpit, it was reputed to be the world's fastest plane.

In Hollywood, Ford was directing *Wee Willie Winkie* with Shirley Temple at Fox. At this point, Ford knew nothing about Kate's dinners with Hughes; nor could she have been certain how he would respond if he did. It was always difficult to know what Ford was thinking, especially as he still clung to a stiffly light-hearted manner. He set the tone and Kate followed.

Ford never missed a beat. After Kate complained of brutal cold in Buffalo—third stop of the abruptly extended tour—he sent a pair of white cotton longjohns to await her arrival in Chicago. On January 16, 1937, Kate sent an unsigned telegram thanking him for the longjohns and, tongue in cheek, asking for 100 percent wool next. He filled the request that afternoon.

Howard Hughes planned a considerably more dramatic approach. On January 19, he took off in the *Winged Bullet* from the

Hughes Aircraft hangar in Burbank. He bent forward over the instrument panel as a gale propelled the racer at enormous speed. Flying above the clouds at an altitude of 14,000 feet, he rarely saw the ground.

Over the Sierras, his oxygen mask gave out. Hughes tried to lift a hand to his face but lack of oxygen made that impossible. He felt drowsy. His arms and legs went numb. He was overwhelmed by a "helpless, hopeless feeling" that he was about to fall asleep— and die. Through an act of will, somehow he managed to lower the aircraft several thousand feet, where normal breathing could be restored.

When Hughes reached Newark Airport, he broke all speed distance records. Traveling an average of 332 miles an hour, he had crossed America in seven hours, twenty-eight minutes, and twenty-five seconds. Unfastening his oil-soaked flight jacket, Hughes flashed a boyish grin at reporters. The hero answered questions about the flight and his loss of oxygen. The New York papers reported that Hughes planned to remain in the city "for some time"; instead, he rushed to Kate in Chicago.

On the night of January 20, Hughes and Hepburn shared a suite at the Ambassador East Hotel. Luddy had once triumphed when Phelps Putnam failed to act; now, Hughes benefited from John Ford's vacillation.

The next day, word spread through Chicago that an attorney had notified County Clerk Michael Flynn that a "prominent couple" would appear at his office shortly after closing time to apply for a marriage license. The lovebirds were widely rumored to be Howard Hughes and Katharine Hepburn. Less than a month had passed since their first dinner in Boston. When newsmen turned up at the Ambassador East Hotel to question Kate, Em Perkins kept them at bay.

As it happened, Brooks Atkinson was also in town that day. The *Times* critic had learned of the Theater Guild's decision not to bring the play to New York that season while Helen Jerome continued to rewrite. Atkinson turned up, he said, with musket in hand to see what the problem was. This was no mission of mercy. The influential critic planned to defy tradition and review the play before Hepburn and the Guild were ready; everything Kate dreaded was about to happen. Terry Helburn and Helen Jerome were in the audience when Atkinson, notebook on lap, saw Kate enter in long, full skirts and skim across the stage.

Jerome watched in consternation as Kate suddenly changed line readings and stage business. Why would she do that tonight? The playwright complained that Hepburn seemed in a devilish mood. She was—although Terry Helburn and Helen Jerome can have had no idea why.

As Kate later admitted, she had played every performance of *Jane Eyre* to Ford. Everything about the show—the circumstances in which she had first agreed to do it, her conception of the character, her wistfulness at starting the tour—was saturated with thoughts of him. The added factor of Hughes threw everything off.

On January 22, the Los Angeles papers were full of stories about Hughes's plans to marry Hepburn. The air speed king and the movie star were reported together at the Ambassador East Hotel.

Raised to be matter-of-fact about sex, Kate seemed to find physical intimacy easy; it was emotional communication that was hard. For a very short time, she had established a powerful bond with John Ford. They did not sleep together, but they communicated in ways Kate had experienced with no one else. Yet at this point, she had cause to wonder whether she had presumed too much. Ford's exasperating refusal to do anything but joke would have left any woman to question whether he felt about her quite as she had believed.

Knowing how easily wounded Ford was, Kate would have realized that newspaper accounts of her romance with Hughes would provoke a powerful response. Whether Ford would show his feelings was another matter.

Ford was always quick to react to news of Kate. He would tell his intimates like Dudley Nichols, Cliff Reid, John Wayne, and assistant Meta Sterne that he had heard from her. He particularly enjoyed discussing "Miss Katharine" with her friend George Cukor.

Even in the midst of filming, he would fire off letters and telegrams to her at the slightest provocation.

This time, however, he waited three days to write.

Meanwhile, reporters chased Hughes and Hepburn all about Chicago. The press camped out at the Ambassador East. At one point, Em Perkins put on Kate's fur coat and trousers and drove off in the star's automobile, leading reporters on a wild goose chase while Kate left by a tenth-floor window, edged along the narrow parapet, turned a corner, and climbed down a rear fire escape. When she reached the bottom she was unable to get out and had to go all the way back up again. The newspaper stories dragged on for days and provided wonderful publicity for the show.

On January 25, Ford wrote a long comic letter in the voice of an American sailor who had expected to marry Em Perkins. The sailor has discovered that while he was at sea, a certain Mr. William Kilborne, English musician on the liner *Queen Mary*, has been secretly wooing Em. The letter, addressed to Kilborne, describes the sailor's upset that his fiancée has betrayed him at a moment when he was hoping to establish a home with her. Lamenting the money he has spent on gifts of expensive underwear, he demands to be reimbursed; otherwise, he threatens to punch Kilborne in the kisser or sue him for alienation of affection. Ford sent the letter to Kate at the Ambassador East without further comment.

He could not maintain this ironic pose for long, however. The Kilborne letter hardly did justice to his turbulent feelings. He needed to talk to Kate.

The day *Jane Eyre* moved on to St. Louis, Ford broke down. Repeatedly he called the Park Plaza Hotel but never reached her. On several occasions he talked to Em, who promised to tell Baby he had called.

When Em gave Kate the messages, she was thrilled. She had much to say to Sean and there was much she hoped to hear him say. But how could she reach him at night when he was still with Mary? Unable to call Odin Street, she would wait for him to contact her the next day.

That night, Kate had a serious problem with her voice. She

had spent the day testing the new theater. When the footlights went on, the heat caused fumes to rise from the stage surface, which had recently been treated with chemicals. Kate began to cough and choke. Afterward, she could barely speak. A physician ordered Kate to rest her vocal cords until the play opened the following night. She was to eat ice, spray her throat, and avoid cigarettes.

As if that were not enough, Kate faced an added pressure. The Guild board was due in St. Louis the following night to discuss the rewrites with her. Brooks Atkinson had published a devastating review that accused "La Hepburn" of playing Jane Eyre "with her fingertips." He wrote: "Miss Hepburn takes the whole play in one key, going through the love scenes very much as she tiptoes through the scenes of decorous parlor conversation. There seems to be no great fund of subdued emotion behind the unworldly mask of her personality." The play came in for worse criticism; Atkinson derided Helen Jerome for a "pedestrian adaptation" which failed to capture the novel's flavor.

Kate spent the day in bed. Em fed her ice and sprayed her throat. For hours she waited for Sean's call. Determined to spare her voice, she would speak to no one but him.

At one point the phone rang and the operator announced Cliff Reid. Em refused the call, saying that Miss Hepburn was ill. Soon afterward, the operator was back with a message from Ford. It had been he, not Cliff Reid, on the line; he would call again at 11:30 p.m.

But that was when Kate's meeting with the Guild was scheduled! Kate knew Ford would be hurt if she was not there to take his call. Always hypersensitive to a potential affront, he would think she was trying to avoid him. Hepburn sent word to the Guild that she must postpone the meeting until a quarter past midnight.

After the opening night performance, which was filled to capacity, Kate rushed back to the Park Plaza. She waited for forty-five minutes. At 12:15 she had no choice but to go off to meet the Guild; they could not be kept waiting any longer.

No sooner had Kate left than the phone rang. Afraid to talk to

Ford herself, Em asked the operator to explain that Kate had waited as long as she could. After that, Ford abandoned all attempts to reach her.

Em, sensitive to his insecurity and wounded pride, wasted no time in writing a long letter of explanation. She never mentioned the letter to Kate. Most of all, Em hoped to assure "Shoney" that Kate had wanted to talk to him very badly last night. Recognizing that Ford was probably much too cross to call, Em urged him at least to try writing again.

That was all he needed to hear. The flurry of letters and telegrams resumed; and by the end of February, Ford braced himself to drop the comedian's self-protective mask. He spoke seriously and directly about his feelings for Kate. She called it the best letter she had ever received. It was so perfect, Kate said, one despaired of finding words to reply.

In her suite at the Marott Apartment Hotel in Indianapolis, she wrote many drafts of a letter to him. Finally, on March 1 she found a way to say what was on her mind.

As she approached thirty, Kate was trying to make sense of what the next thirty years of her life would be like. She told Sean of her determination not to become a mess. She knew now that he really did understand her; and she prayed he always would. She confessed that she had often spoken to him through the setting sun. She longed to talk about herself, the future, and the two of them. She told him she would be back in Hollywood in May. Before that, however, they dreamed again of the Aran Islands. There was talk of a cruise on the *Araner*; a rendezvous in Honolulu; a visit from Ford to see *Jane Eyre* in Toledo, Columbus, Cleveland, Pittsburgh, Washington, or Baltimore.

Kate spent the rest of the tour in a state of euphoria. Any minute they were going to be together; they both seemed certain of that now. It was only a question of when. As the tour drew to a close, it seemed as though Kate had saved Sean from a lifetime of unhappiness. He was finally going to leave Mary. Although he had not shown up to see *Jane Eyre*, he promised to meet Kate in Honolulu.

At the last minute, he disappointed her with a letter full of the old vacillation.

When *Jane Eyre* closed in Baltimore, the company dispersed so that the rewrites might be completed before the production went on to Broadway. On April 10, Kate wrote to Ford from a bumpy southbound railroad train to say that she had had enough of his maybes and somedays. She needed clarity—either a yes or no—and hoped she could still get that from him when she returned to Los Angeles. For now, Kate was headed to Florida: Howard Hughes had invited her to sail to Nassau and Jamaica on his yacht, the *Southern Cross*.

When Kate sailed to Nassau with Howard Hughes, she wondered whether pride would prevent Sean from seeing her again. If that happened, she vowed to drive by his house in a Ford roadster and think about all that had passed between them.

It seemed to Kate that the man she called her dearest friend had given her the strength and courage to face the next thirty years. But when she returned to Los Angeles in May, Ford had decided nothing. Of course he wanted to see her; he used every opportunity to meet. Yet he could not bring himself to leave Mary and the children, however unsatisfactory he knew that would be to Kate.

She continued to demand clarity; maybe and someday, she told him, were nothing but feeble euphemisms for no.

Kate responded to Sean's paralysis by moving in with Howard Hughes, though she retained her rented hilltop house on Angelo Drive as a getaway. The Hughes house on Muirfield Road in Hancock Park was filled with torn red velvet couches and smoky-brown paintings in decrepit gilt frames. Hughes and Hepburn needed only to leap over a fence to play golf at the adjoining Wilshire Country Club.

Kate loved the theatricality of life with Hughes: the money, the power, the yachts, the airplanes, the crush of reporters and photographers wherever they went. In this, she was very much her father's daughter: Dr. Hepburn had always made a point of owning only two suits and two pairs of shoes, yet he thrived on the prestige of a grand house. He insisted on privacy, yet he constantly dramatized himself, whether in the operating room, at the dinner table or in the bath. There was a part of Kate that, like her father, adored being the center of attention even as she protested that she didn't want anyone to know a thing about her.

But Kate had another side, inherited from her mother. Mrs. Hepburn had craved emotional intimacy, communication, love: the very things Dr. Hepburn refused when, on their honeymoon, he warned his bride to keep her innermost thoughts to herself. This was the part of Kate that continued to be drawn to John Ford.

The relationship did not end when Kate moved in with Hughes; it entered a new, more tortured phase. Both Kate and Ford suffered for his failure to act. All he had to do was ask and almost certainly she would have left Hughes at once. But he could not bring himself to do that, much as it hurt him to think of her with another man. The instrument of Ford's torment was of his own making.

When Ford found a short story in *Collier*'s magazine called "Stage to Lordsburg," which he hoped to adapt as a film, it was Kate he longed to discuss the project with. And when she reported to RKO to discover that her stock at the studio had continued to fall, he was one of the few in the industry on whose loyalty and friendship she knew she could depend.

Kate's romance with Ford had caused her to lose *Stage Door* on Broadway when a jealous Leland Hayward decided not to push her for the role. Since then, however, RKO had purchased the screen rights for her. But it seemed a bad sign when RKO also put its other big female star, Ginger Rogers, in the picture. Ostensibly the studio just wanted to help Rogers get beyond her image as Fred Astaire's dancing partner; but the gesture could have been interpreted to mean that Hepburn wasn't popular enough anymore to carry the film herself.

As Kate would say, Rogers was on her way up at RKO at the very moment she herself was on her way down. Depression America experienced a backlash against the Twenties adulation of the rich and privileged. In many quarters, plebeian was in, patrician out.

Hepburn, who had started her career struggling to emulate Hope Williams, fell victim to growing public impatience with the American upper class. It was very much in Ginger Rogers's favor that no one was likely to mistake her for a finishing-school girl.

As far as much of America was concerned, the sort of superior person Hepburn typified needed to be cut down to size; and that is exactly what happens to the society-girl actress Kate portrays in *Stage Door*. By the end of the film, she's had a good deal of the smugness knocked out of her. She responds with genuine feeling to the suicide of a fellow actress. She ceases to hold herself above the other residents of the theatrical boarding house. She displays the kind of emotion people doubted she possessed. She finally allows herself to be just one of the girls.

Kate worked on *Stage Door* throughout June. That month, RKO purchased screen rights to a *Collier's* short story entitled "Bringing Up Baby" as her next comedy vehicle. The script was assigned to John Ford's friend and collaborator Dudley Nichols, who would work with the story's author, Hagar Wilde. Nichols had written the script for *Hurricane*, the film Ford was shooting that summer; and the two were in regular contact about that project, as well as the screenplay based on "Stage to Lordsburg" which they were planning to begin in August. Given Nichols's close working relationship with Ford, it would be hard to imagine that they failed to discuss the Hepburn project.

The original story "Bringing Up Baby" was a trifle about a couple who lose a tame panther in rural Connecticut. (In the film, the panther was changed to a leopard.) Told to tailor his script to Hepburn, Nichols drew on the bumptious, funny, touching girl he had observed at close range during the filming of *Mary of Scotland*. This was Kate Hepburn as he had seen her with Ford. Nichols captured the spirit of madcap teasing and banter that had characterized that brief, happy time in Ford's life.

Nichols endowed the screenplay's Susan Vance with Kate's optimism, enthusiasm, and irrepressible determination. She is the sort of woman who insists, "Everything's going to be all right." He made David Huxley a comic straight man, whose dignity Susan is forever puncturing, much as Kate had loved to do with Ford. And, as Nichols wrote the character, David loves to be tweaked although, like Ford, he prefers to conceal his feelings. David possesses Ford's exasperating ambivalence; he is the sort of man who says, "I love you, I think."

When shooting started on September 23, under the direction of Howard Hawks, Kate found herself surrounded again by members of the Ford group. Besides Dudley Nichols, there was Cliff Reid as associate producer, and Ford cronies Ward Bond, Barry Fitzgerald, and D'Arcy Corrigan in the cast. Ford himself visited the set on at least one occasion with Lord Killanin.

Howard Hawks, an admirer and close friend of Ford's, gave Cary Grant, who played David, the small round glasses that were Ford's trademark. Hawks saw Hepburn's as the dominant, more active part in the story. Susan chattered and David reacted, much as Ford had done with Kate.

"Cary, this is a good chance to do Number Seven," Hawks would often say, by which he meant the basic comic situation of trying to converse with a woman who was doing a great deal of talking.

At first, Kate had some difficulty with the comic aspects of the script, and Hawks realized that she was trying too hard to be funny. Afraid not to be seen to be superior to the material, she seemed to want to join her audience in laughing at Susan. Instead of playing her scenes deadpan, as Hawks urged, Kate preferred to signal that she knew it was all a lark.

Hawks approached Walter Catlett, a Ziegfeld Follies comic he had under contract.

"Walter, have you been watching Miss Hepburn?"

"Yeah."

"Do you know what she's doing?"

"Yeah."

"Will you tell her?"

"No."

"Supposing she asks you to tell her?"

"Then I'll have to tell her."

Hawks went to Kate. "We're not getting along too well on this thing," he explained. "I'm not getting through to you, but there's a man here who I think could. Do you want to talk to him?"

Catlett, a brilliant mimic, took the leading lady's place in one of her scenes with Cary Grant; using all the Hepburn mannerisms, he played the scene deadpan to show her how it ought to be done.

To Kate, watching Catlett was a revelation. Afterward, she ran straight to Hawks.

"Howard, hire that guy and keep him around here for several weeks because I need him." Hawks gave Catlett the role of Constable Slocum.

From then on, Kate changed her approach. She acted as though she had no idea there was anything funny about her behavior. She allowed the audience of *Bringing Up Baby* to laugh at her in a way that made her appear vulnerable. Her antics became charming rather than arrogant or off-putting.

As Kate worked on *Bringing Up Baby*, she engaged in intense negotiations with the Theater Guild. She minced no words about her unhappiness with Sidney Howard's rewrites for *Jane Eyre*. Increasingly, she resisted Terry Helburn and Lawrence Langner's efforts to get her to commit to bringing the show to Broadway. Kate had little idea of how desperate they were to cure the Guild's financial woes. By November, Langner pitched in to salvage the play to Kate's satisfaction.

There was resentment on both sides. Helburn and Langner were profoundly uncomfortable with the need to humor a leading lady whom they did not regard as a particularly important actress in the theater. Kate was a necessary evil, their need for her a symbol of the Guild's failing fortunes. At times, Helburn and Langner could not avoid a patronizing tone in their letters to the movie star. They set themselves up as the only competent judges of the sort of "import-ant" material to which Kate must limit herself. Yet they knew they must never go too far; the Guild could hardly afford to lose her. The financial success of the tour—Atkinson's pummeling notwith-standing—proved that.

Kate, for her part, often bristled at their condescension. She appeared to associate their attitude with Mrs. Hepburn's refusal to take her daughter's acting seriously. Her mother's opinion reinforced Kate's own insecurities about being less an actress than a personality. She longed to prove herself to her mother and the Guild.

Kate did not overestimate her abilities. Writing to Terry Helburn, she was honest about her limitations as an actress. When rights to *Jane Eyre* reverted to Helen Jerome, the playwright refused to renew the contract with the Guild unless they agreed to remove Kate Hepburn. She had never forgiven Kate for her performance on the night Brooks Atkinson saw the play. Eager for a scapegoat, Jerome blamed all of the play's problems on "the Hollywood Duse," as the playwright snidely called her. That finally ruled out *Jane Eyre* for Kate.

Terry Helburn urged her to consider opening on Broadway in a classic drama instead of the contemporary fare she seemed to prefer. With striking candor, Kate replied that she had not earned the right to assume that her performance in a classic would be worthy of the material. She confessed that it would be difficult enough to succeed in a new play when no actress had preceded her in the minds of the public. She was not ready to compete with the ghosts of all the great actresses who had appeared in the sort of play Helburn had in mind.

Kate was in a curious position with the Guild, whose producers seemed oddly oblivious to her problems in Hollywood. Even as Helburn and Langner were pressuring her to appear under their banner on Broadway, RKO was rapidly losing interest in her.

Initially, the critical success of *Stage Door* led the studio to urge that Kate steer clear of costume roles of any kind, *Jane Eyre* included. But *Stage Door* did not do as well as Pandro Berman had anticipated. For all the critical acclaim, it earned a meager $81,000 profit. A number of studio executives attributed the disappointing figures to the public's aversion to Katharine Hepburn. *Bringing Up Baby* further diminished her stock at RKO. The *Hollywood Reporter* hailed it as "unquestionably her best performance to date" and posterity would recognize it as a landmark in screen comedy. Yet contemporary audiences rejected the film, which lost $365,000.

When RKO agreed to loan Hepburn to Columbia Pictures to appear in *Holiday* for George Cukor, it was widely interpreted as a very bad sign. Evidently RKO had ceased to believe that Hepburn had a "unique value" to the studio which needed to be protected.

Kate was supposed to go off to Columbia in disgrace, but she certainly didn't act that way. Instead, she relished the opportunity to play the Hope Williams role she had understudied in New York. In 1928, the actress and the role had embodied everything to which Kate aspired.

A great deal had changed in ten years. Philip Barry had fallen off his throne. After *The Animal Kingdom*, the playwright had a string of flops; he was a has-been, a Twenties phenomenon who had failed to communicate with Thirties audiences. Donald Ogden Stewart, screenwriter of the film, had played Nick Potter, Johnny Case's best friend, in the original stage production. Very socially adept and very superior, he had gleefully conspired to prevent that irritating Hepburn girl from filling in for Hope Williams. In 1938, Stewart found himself in a different position; drunk, dissolute, and badly in need of money, he was required to dance attendance on Kate.

A decade before, Stewart had been "in Society," as he liked to say; the Depression made him a proponent of the Marxist gospel. He slipped some of his newfound political views into the screenplay, probably in hopes of giving Johnny Case's revolt a timely significance. Still, Philip Barry's message that we must take time off from work to experience life seemed naive and irrelevant in Depression America, when people were eager for any work at all. In 1938, not even adroit performances from Hepburn and Cary Grant could breathe life into this curio from a more innocent time.

At the wrap party, Cukor surprised Kate by showing the *Holiday* screen test she had made for him in 1932. Back then her film career had been about to soar; now it took a nosedive.

RKO's sole comment on Hepburn's plummeting prestige was to assign her to a picture called *Mother Carey's Chickens*. Kate interpreted the assignment as a signal that they wanted to get rid of her. She knew it was time to bail out.

Refusing the assignment, Kate offered to buy out the remainder of her studio contract. During the filming of *Holiday*, Cukor had been doing tests in anticipation of directing *Gone with the Wind* for David Selznick, who had formed his own production company. Kate had her eye on the part of Scarlett O'Hara. Although the public identified her with New England, the Hepburn family background in the South particularly attracted Kate to the part. Determined to have it, she enlisted Cukor's support; but Selznick, for his part, was not keen. Cukor vowed to keep pressing on her behalf.

On May 3, Hepburn and RKO jointly announced that they had agreed to part ways. She was free to go elsewhere. That same day, Harry Brandt of the Independent Theater Owners Association ran advertisements in the trade papers blasting Hepburn and a number of other stars as box-office poison. The exhibitors implored film studios to stop featuring stars who held little appeal for the American public.

Later that month, Kate gave up her rented house on Angelo Drive. Aware that she had come to the end of something and must decide what to do next, she headed east for an indefinite stay with her family. Hughes remained behind in Los Angeles. If Selznick agreed to cast her as Scarlett O'Hara, she would return immediately. Otherwise, she intended to take as long as she needed to figure out quite how to start anew.

E I G H T E E N

I n South Cove at Fenwick, strong breezes rocked Kate's sailing canoe from side to side. At least four times, the vessel almost capsized. Unable to attach her rudder, Kate screamed and cursed with frustration. When she glanced in the direction of the beach, she was taken aback to see Luddy filming her embarrassing outburst with a movie camera.

Kate wrote to John Ford that he would have died of laughter to see it all.

She sailed, swam, and played tennis and golf. She laughed that she spent days outdoors getting sunburned, then days indoors getting unsunburned. Her nose always seemed to be bright red, and she liked it that way.

She resumed fancy diving practice for the first time in a long while. When Kate attempted a one-and-a-half, she landed on her face with eyes wide open. Her eyelashes scratched the eyeballs. The next time, she landed on her chest. Kate wrote Sean that what little bosom she had had been lost in the plunge and might never emerge again.

Kate adopted a bufflehead duck whose wings someone had clipped so he could not fly, and christened him Donald. He appeared suddenly from up the river and spent several nights on the Hepburn beach. Whenever Kate approached, Donald would scurry off in fear. A storm caused him to retreat across the Hepburn lawn until he found refuge behind the cottage in the tranquil waters of the lagoon.

She often found herself thinking about Ford and how he would respond to the little things she saw and did. She knew he would love

Fenwick that season and told him so in charming letters that detailed daily life there. If she had come east hoping to forget him, it soon became evident that that was not about to happen. Kate seemed never completely to give up hope that they might be together yet. Now it was she who clung to maybes and somedays.

Meanwhile, she worried whether Ford received all her letters as she still could not write to him at home. When she went to stay at the Turtle Bay townhouse, she was sure to let him know at once. That way he could write her there directly and not a day would be lost.

Kate planned to remain in New York until Howard Hughes was ready to embark on his historic round-the-world flight in a Lockheed 14 twin-engine passenger plane. Just before takeoff she would rush back to Fenwick to monitor the spectacular adventure.

Privately Kate called Hughes "his nibs," a reference to his haughty, tyrannical character. As Em Perkins never tired of pointing out, Hughes was rude and boorish; his sole interest in Baby was to isolate and control her. Hughes insisted he wanted to marry Kate, yet he was often unfaithful. He had set her heart pounding when he rushed to her in a daring cross-country flight, yet he spent even more time running away from the woman he claimed to worship. She had endured days and weeks alone in the big, gloomy house on Muirfield Road while his nibs disappeared to hotels with a variety of women. At one point while Kate was in residence, he took off for a two-week cruise with Luise Rainer.

Much to Em's alarm, there were moments when Kate seemed to try very hard to convince herself that she was in love with Howard Hughes, as though that would put an end to things with John Ford. Someone once said that Howard Hughes employed his airplanes as a kind of "ultimate weapon" in pursuit of the women he desired. How could Kate, with her strong competitive streak and love of danger, resist a man who claimed to perform his record-breaking flights for her? He insisted that when he flew, Kate's face hovered in front of him the entire way. And he promised to dip his wings over the Hepburn cottage at Fenwick at the outset of his round-the-world flight.

As always, Kate thrilled to the game of cat and mouse she played with the reporters camped outside her house in the days before the flight. She and Hughes fooled them by moving to Laura Harding's apartment on East 52nd Street. His presence in New York was tinged with mystery. He had not yet been granted government permission to circle the globe. There was considerable danger involved: Others had lost their lives in similar attempts.

Back in Los Angeles, Hughes had told reporters that he intended solely to break the speed record from New York to Paris. But his real plans were no secret when he and a crew of four made a preliminary appearance at Floyd Bennett Field in Brooklyn, New York. It remained only for the authorities to give the go-ahead. The airstrip was mobbed with newsmen, who believed Hughes had taken up residence in one of the halls built to house the 1939 New York World's Fair. No one seemed to guess he spent his nights with Kate. Reporters and photographers outside her house saw no sign of him.

On July 10, Kate's chauffeur-driven Lincoln took the couple to Floyd Bennett Field. Hughes emerged, wearing a rumpled white shirt, gray trousers and brown snap-brim felt hat. In a paper bag, he carried the sandwiches Kate had prepared for the flight. With long strides and a pensive expression, he proceeded to Hangar 7.

The Lincoln sped Kate to Fenwick, where the Hepburns had placed a radio on the dining-room table. They put up a large map to follow the flight.

That evening radios throughout America announced that Hughes had dipped his wings over Fenwick before pointing the silver aircraft toward Paris. When word spread in the summer colony that Hughes promised to send word from various stopover points, neighbors who shared a party line with Dr. and Mrs. Hepburn picked up every time the Hepburn signal, one long ring and three short, sounded.

All the urgent news was not about the flight, however. It was a well-kept family secret that Edith Hooker was about to undergo major surgery on her right eye. Since March she had been suffering blurred vision, intense headaches, and an inability to work at her usual frantic pace. Full of life and passion, Edith had no intention of allowing infirmity to slow down her work for an Equal Rights Amendment to the United States Constitution. As might be expected, she did not want her enemies in the fight to know she was ailing, for the news might cause them to ease up on her; she swore everyone to secrecy about her surgery.

On July 14, the day Edith underwent her operation, Howard Hughes returned to America, setting a new round-the-world record of three days, nineteen hours, and seventeen minutes. The radio on the Hepburn dining table was blasting news of the aviator when word came from Baltimore that Edith had been wheeled out of the operating room.

Kate's Lincoln pulled up in front of her townhouse at 1:30 p.m. Dressed in polo shirt and shorts, with a bright red bandana wrapped around her head, she dashed past reporters into the house. She had left Fenwick as soon as she heard that Hughes was refueling in Minneapolis.

She threw open the large front windows. Out on the street the reporters could hear Kate's radio, turned up very loud, describing the scene at Floyd Bennett Field, where some 25,000 people had gathered. At 2:30 p.m. Kate, who had been joined by Laura Harding, called the airstrip. Told that Hughes had not yet touched down, Kate left a number for him to call.

Finally, Hughes landed, and after shyly greeting the crowd he was taken by limousine to the Greenwich Village mews house of New York World's Fair chief Grover Whalen. While Mayor La Guardia and other dignitaries waited in the living room, Hughes snuck out the back door. He took a cab to Turtle Bay, but when he saw the mob of newsmen outside Kate's house, he went on alone to the Drake Hotel on Park Avenue.

The next day, there was a ticker-tape parade in Hughes's honor attended by more than a million cheering spectators. At that moment, it seemed as though Hughes were the most celebrated man in America. His name appeared on the front page of every newspaper; his slight drawl blared from every radio. He delivered a speech at City Hall, then disappeared with Kate. Before they reached Fenwick, Hughes proposed marriage.

The visit with the Hepburns was a disaster.

From first to last Hughes declined to enter into the family spirit. He failed to grasp the magic of the place, where he was constantly complaining about the erratic plumbing and scarcity of hot water. On the occasions when he agreed to eat with everyone else, he sat glumly silent, refusing to do the little turn each family member and guest was expected to perform. Laughter and loud voices came from all sides of the table, making it especially difficult for Hughes to hear. He appeared at meals unshaven and unwashed. More often, Hughes demanded to be fed separately. Complaining of the large quantities of fish that Fanny Ciarrier tended to serve, his nibs would order Kate to prepare a lamb chop or some other meat dish; and even then, he groaned that it was undercooked.

Mrs. Hepburn disapproved of Kate's waiting hand and foot on this ungrateful fellow. She knew that Kate wanted children; she would be unlikely to have them with Hughes. According to Mrs. Hepburn, Kate, with her demanding career, would do better to marry a man willing to stay home with the youngsters.

Hughes was wildly jealous of Luddy, as always a frequent and often uninvited guest at Fenwick. He used every opportunity to kiss Kate and tell her he loved her. Hughes's presence did not seem to bother Luddy. Other men had come and gone; so would Hughes. Luddy was determined to outlast them all. Even if Kate did marry Hughes, Luddy was certain the marriage would not endure.

Hughes's demand that Kate banish Luddy won no friends among the Hepburns. The family had never stopped adoring the mad ex-husband, whom they accepted as one of their own. Luddy, for his part, insisted he was the sanest member of the household. When Hughes protested at Luddy's following him around the Fenwick golf course with a movie camera, Dr. Hepburn set the visitor straight: "Howard, Luddy has been taking pictures of all of us long before you joined us and he will be taking them long after you've left. He is part of this family. Go ahead. Drive. You need a seven iron."

Kate, for her part, alternated between glee at being fought over and embarrassment in front of the neighbors that Luddy was still on the scene. Defending Hughes to her family, Kate insisted he was shy. Yes, he was very strange, she admitted, but any man interested in marrying her would have to be strange!

Still, she could hardly overlook the fact that Hughes made no effort to fit in. Avoiding the Hepburns, he spent hours studying adventure magazines in the bathroom. He ignored Dick and was cruel to Aunty Towle. He seemed unappreciative of Mrs. Hepburn's efforts to make him feel at home. When Fanny took his clothes to be cleaned in Old Saybrook village, the millionaire refused to pay the bill. He offended everyone by declaring Long Island Sound a cesspool.

Before Kate decided whether to accept Hughes's marriage proposal, she had wanted him to see the waterfront where she grew up. She wanted him to know her in the setting she regarded as home. It was important that he love everyone and everything there as Ford had; instead, Hughes clearly could not wait to escape.

In the end, Hughes returned to the west coast without Kate. There was no formal break, but the subject of marriage did not come up again. Kate spent the rest of the summer at Fenwick.

She baked in the sun. She savored the summer waves and breezes. She imagined what it would be like if Sean were with her.

She read the endless scripts Terry Helburn sent, but none held the slightest appeal. She turned down various offers from Hollywood. She declared that she had no intention of performing any more roles in a "half-assed mood." She longed to be inspired. She would wait for a script that really thrilled her. Leland Hayward warned that her refusal to return to Los Angeles immediately could destroy her career. Kate wrote to Ford that she knew she might be doing damage to herself, but something kept her from leaving Fenwick just yet. She luxuriated in the cocoon her family provided.

Throughout the summer, Kate received mixed signals from the Selznick camp. Selznick feared she wasn't sexy enough to play Scarlett O'Hara, and all the "box-office poison" publicity certainly hadn't helped. At this point in her career, she did not wish to undergo the screen test Selznick demanded. She confided to Ford that although she didn't really believe she would get the role, *Gone with the Wind* remained the only project for which she would rush back to Hollywood.

Kate and Palache planned a three-week jaunt to Ireland. They would land in Galway as Kate and Sean had dreamed of doing. Kate called off the trip at the last minute; she sighed that she would probably attract too much attention in Europe on account of the Hughes flight. Besides, she wrote to Ford on August 15, she still hoped to see Ireland first with him.

That seemed unlikely to happen.

It had not been easy for Ford to live in the same town with Kate in the months after her return from Nassau with Howard Hughes. Ford cherished every opportunity to see her, yet the fact that she was living with another man remained a source of torment. While Kate shot *Bringing Up Baby*, Ford's heavy drinking necessitated a stay at a drying-out clinic in the east. Mary Ford had triumphed when Jack remained with wife and children; but Mary didn't let it go at that. Far from savoring the victory, she demanded an even greater capitulation. It was obvious that she had very nearly lost Jack to Kate; and the experience shook her to the core.

From the moment in 1920 when her husband first warned her never to visit him on a film set, Mary had felt deeply threatened by his career. A love of film was something Ford had permitted himself to share with Kate; Mary seemed determined to kill that in him forever. She wanted him to renounce his identity as an artist.

Ford was a Lieutenant Commander in the naval reserve; and the Navy was Mary's world. She constantly reminded Jack of her family's military ties. Several uncles and cousins were Annapolis and West Point graduates, and Mary herself had spent nine months as a nurse at the naval academy. Her uncle, Admiral Victor Blue, served as Chief of Naval Operations. Mary let it be known that only a military career would make Jack amount to something in her eyes.

At times, the wife could not resist bringing up his relationship with Kate, although she knew Jack would stuff his ears with cotton and ignore her. But he did react when Mary belittled his work as a director; he responded by doing everything in his power to prove her wrong. That had hardly been possible with Kate still in Los Angeles; her presence had made it hard for him to focus on his work. But her departure for the east in May 1938 changed things. The knowledge that she was gone seemed to trigger something in Ford.

Ending an interlude of uncertainty and poor concentration, he embarked on the richest and most productive period of his career. Over the course of the next three years, during which Kate was rarely in California, Ford would turn out his greatest films one after another in swift su_____ion. He would work in a fever. After *Stagecoach* (shot in the ____ and widely acknowledged to be Ford's masterpiece), h___ ___rect *Young Mr. Lincoln* (spring 1939), *Drums Along th___* summer 1939), and *The Grapes of Wrath* (fall 1939). The___ ___me *The Long Voyage Home* (spring 1940), *Tobacco Road*___ 1940–41), and *How Green Was My Valley* (summer 194___ ___eckoning, it was an amazing three years.

Ford seemed ___ ___ Kate's prolonged absence from California as a sign tha___ ___nally accept that he had lost his chance at happiness with ___ ___ow he poured heart and soul into his work. More than ___ ___ps, work offered a refuge from the pain of everyday exist___ ___med to Kate that storytelling provided the sense of reso___ ___ could not find in his own life.

At the end ___ ___mmer of 1938, Philip Barry appeared at Fenwick to pit___ ___dea. It was not the first time he wanted to write for Kate ___ ___ she was in a very different position from the fledgling ___ ___en fired from *The Animal Kingdom*.

As the *J___ ___ur had proved, Kate's name on the marquee guaranteed h___ ___t sales to a play. On top of that, the recent publicity sur___ ___her affair with Hughes had added immensely to the publi___ ___ion with her. A great many people wanted a peek at the ___ ___r whom Howard Hughes had dipped his wings over Fenw___

Phili___ ___had an idea for a play about a wealthy family whose pr___ ___violated when a magazine modeled on *Fortune* assigns a ___ ___ profile them; the writer's research threatens to unearth the family's well-kept secrets. Initially, Barry had planned to base his heroine on the dazzling Helen Hope Montgomery, who lived with her family on the Philadelphia Main Line. Barry now proposed to mix elements of Kate Hepburn and her family into the brew. At length, he would make his heroine a redhead who has been to Bryn Mawr and has a penchant for going naked. She is a fascinator, full of tricks. About to be married to a national hero, she cannot get rid of her comically devoted ex-husband, who insists on hanging about the property and making a nuisance of himself. Her brother is a writer, whose typing can be heard throughout the house. Her family despises publicity of any kind.

Kate was very excited. Her sole reservation was Barry's working title, "Gentle Reader"; but that seemed a small point. Kate joked that as far as she was concerned, the title ought to be "The Answer to This Maiden's Prayer." She sent him back to Dark Harbor, Maine, to start work immediately.

When Kate called Howard Hughes in California, he advised that if she did agree to do the comedy on Broadway, she must own the motion-picture rights from the outset. Film studios, scared off by the box-office poison label, might try to detach Hepburn from the project when it reached Hollywood; her only protection was to control the rights herself. If Kate liked the material Barry showed her, Hughes offered to purchase the rights for her for $30,000.

In September, Barry wrote to inform Kate that he had already finished the first act and would have all three acts to her by mid-October. But he declined to show her a word until the entire play was finished. He disclosed only that the heroine's name was Tracy. Kate wanted to keep the play secret until it was completed, believing they would benefit later from the element of surprise. She decided to remain at Fenwick until October 1 and begged him to get her the play as soon as possible.

Meanwhile, the tapping of Dick's typewriter keys was heard throughout the Hepburn cottage in September. In his room on the third floor, he was preparing a little surprise of his own.

Kate seemed not to notice that she was not the only family member to endure a career crisis that summer. Since *Behold Your*

God, Dick had been unable to get a play produced, although he appeared never to stop working. He wrote on New York City buses, in the waiting rooms of elevated trains, in Grand Central Station, and in an Italian restaurant. Dick believed writing in public would improve his plays by preventing him from over-analyzing his characters.

He was endlessly approaching producers, most of whom didn't even bother to answer his queries. He pestered them with letters that even he admitted were wild. On May 2—the day before the box-office poison advertisements in the Hollywood trade papers—Dick had approached Jasper Deeter of the Hedgerow Theater with his new drama *Cortez, Conqueror of Mexico*. Dick had dedicated the play to Deeter, whom he credited with saving his life by putting on his first production.

By this time, Dick had vacated his flat in New York and moved back in with Dr. and Mrs. Hepburn, though Kate continued to pay his monthly allowance of $125. On June 28, he was hard at work at Fenwick rewriting *Behold Your God* when Fanny brought in a postcard with Deeter's terse rejection. Dick was devastated.

While he admitted to heartbreak, Dick insisted he did not feel humiliated. Lawrence Langner, Guthrie McClintic, Arthur Hopkins, Orson Welles, and others may not have deigned to acknowledge receipt of *Cortez, Conqueror of Mexico*, let alone turn it down; but the Hepburns—principally Mrs. Hepburn—adored the play as much as Dick did and that made him feel triumphant, although he knew the outside world regarded him as a failure. Still, he worried that his family was suffering for him more than he should permit.

Aged twenty-six, Dick had no plans to give up. Kate had been supporting him for two and a half years, and it seemed to him that she could afford to be generous. He anticipated that she would keep paying his monthly allowance until her own money ran out. He sent a copy of *Cortez, Conqueror of Mexico* to John Ford, and finished the rewrite of *Behold Your God* (retitled *Prometheus*). He was also considering his options for what to do next.

On September 13, he informed Deeter that he was deciding

between a story about two piratesses and a Fenwick play. The latter, to focus on Howard Hughes's visit to Fenwick after the round-the-world flight, possessed distinct advantages to a playwright who liked to say: "My material is always first-hand. I never make up a line." In the past, Deeter had warned against historical subjects. A Fenwick play offered an opportunity to mine the rich material that was Dick's alone.

At least, Fenwick had been Dick's exclusive province until Philip Barry came there with an eye to incorporating details of the Hepburn family into his new play. Kate had welcomed the interloper into their nest and given him permission to write about the material Dick had been storing up for years. After Tom's death, Kate had usurped Dick's natural position in the family as the "oldest son"; now she was seizing his literary material as well. An explosion was inevitable.

On September 21, the Hepburn cottage shook. A massive wall of green and black sea water fell upon the old house built on a sandbar. Gale-force winds ripped into the windows. Glass shattered and rain tore through rooms. Two chimneys collapsed and a section of the house blew off.

Outside, cars, boats, and parts of neighboring cottages sailed through the air. The torrential rain seemed horizontal, not vertical. Tides rose to seventeen feet above normal. One witness recalled a persistent "whining shriek, demoniacal and dreadful." To some, the hurricane of 1938 felt like the end of the world. No one had been prepared for the disaster, which claimed 682 lives; the United States Weather Bureau then had no hurricane warning service in Connecticut.

Mrs. Hepburn, insisting that Dr. Hepburn had secured the cottage against disaster, demanded to remain. Dick dragged her out, along with Kate, Fanny, and a houseguest. Standing in a foot and a half of water, he caught his mother and the others as each climbed through the dining-room window. Then he slowly led them through pounding wind and spray to higher ground. By the time they found refuge at the Riversea Inn, about twenty minutes had passed. That was when the Hepburn cottage crumpled.

The third floor, where Dick's typewriter and files still sat, stayed above water as the remains of the house floated half a mile northeast. When Dick caught up with it the next day, he discovered that his notes for the new play were not even damp.

Connecticut lay in ruins. Power and telephone lines were down. Roads were impassable, cluttered with fallen trees and the twisted wreckage of cars sent hurtling through the air. Railroad tracks lay submerged beneath several feet of water. Fires blazed everywhere. Countless white houses had turned green, splattered with leaf pulp.

Much of the state was cut off from the outside world. Somehow, Luddy managed to reach Fenwick. He spent three days photographing Kate digging in the sand for the flat silver Amory Houghton, Jr. had given Dr. and Mrs. Hepburn as a wedding present in 1904. Howard Hughes sent a plane with food and water.

In the end, Kate and Dick retrieved eighty-five pieces of silver, which they placed on a tray amid the debris. They also unearthed their mother's tea service. Nothing else was left.

Later, Marion Hepburn would declare that the amazing thing was not that the rickety Fenwick-Gothic cottage had been washed away, but that it had managed to remain on the sandbar for forty years. It was said that George Roberts, Jr. had built the cottage so close to the sea precisely because of the danger; and now, Dr. Hepburn vowed to erect a grand new house on the same site, only three feet higher.

The new edifice would be his challenge to the wind and waves; let the forces of nature attempt to destroy Dr. Hepburn's sturdy brick house with steel supports! Kate gave her father the money to start building at once. Mrs. Hepburn was heartbroken to lose the old cottage where Tommy and Edith had lived, but Dr. Hepburn actually seemed happy for one more opportunity to erase the past.

After Hartford Hospital had failed to appoint him chief of surgery in 1927, Dr. Hepburn spent years fighting to stake out a turf; he did not win the battle until 1937, when colleagues ceded to him all operations on the urinary tract and Dr. Hepburn agreed to refer all other cases to fellow surgeons. The washing away of Fenwick provided a chance to build an enormous house befitting the chief of the new urological service. In size and grandeur the "new Fenwick" was designed to overwhelm the other cottages at the summer colony.

Dr. Hepburn, pointing out that with the exception of Peg the children were old enough to be planning homes of their own, encouraged them to design their rooms with wooden blocks. Yet from first to last, the father's psychological needs guided the project. Dick spoke for most when he called the new house stupendous. Of the children, only Bob seemed to think it extravagant; he recognized that Dr. Hepburn was building a "showpiece" rather than the sort of comfortable home they had known and loved.

Bob recognized another thing: There was something strange about the plans for the bedrooms. To enter her parents' room, Kate did not have to go out into the hall and knock on the door. A special passageway led from Kate's room to Dr. and Mrs. Hepburn's dressing room, whence she could walk directly into their sleeping area. It was as though her room had been "added on" to theirs. For all the changes since 1921, Kate and her parents continued to form a separate unit which excluded the other children. Kate's special, intense relationship with Dr. and Mrs. Hepburn, far from having evaporated through the years, was rendered concrete in the architecture of the new house.

Marion felt that sense of exclusion most deeply. She had grown up with the belief that Dr. Hepburn preferred Kate. Marion lacked her older sister's looks, brains, and talent. In a family that prized competitiveness, to be without some distinguishing achievement was a sorry fate. In her diary, Marion lamented her own absence of ability or ambition. She was not athletic like the other Hepburns. Whenever Dr. and Mrs. Hepburn tried to force Marion to play tennis, the child hid in the attic until her parents were gone; then she slipped downstairs to the kitchen, where kindly Fanny comforted her with food.

Marion was not old enough to remember much about Tommy, yet the mythical "best of the children" exerted a strong hold on her imagination. When she was in the seventh grade, she won a prize for a short story about a little boy—a baron's son—who mysteriously disappeared from the family castle many years ago. Marion imagines the child in the cold, lonely spot where he has slept all these years in a thin cotton tunic. Suddenly, the boy stirs uneasily; his eyes open as though by magic. It is time for the lost son to return to the castle.

Marion went to Bennington College, intent on becoming a writer. Her teachers subtly discouraged her; one remarked, "How much more of an achievement it really is to bake a good cake than to write a poor novel!" And Marion can hardly have failed to get the hint when Mrs. Hepburn quoted George Bernard Shaw at her: "To a woman without talent or money, a husband is more necessary than a master to a dog."

The Hepburns were delighted when Marion, as a senior at Bennington, received a marriage proposal from Ellsworth Grant, the son of a wealthy West Hartford family, whom she had known for five years. They planned to marry two days after she graduated in June 1939. Marion seemed to take comfort in the notion that marriage—the very thing Kate had failed at—would be her life's achievement. Yet there was always an air of sadness about her. Like her grandfather Fred, Marion suffered from paralyzing bouts of depression.

"Everyone thinks I'm insane," she would say. "They laugh at me behind my back. I'm never going to make any progress."

Bitter and unfulfilled, Marion would urge Dr. and Mrs. Hepburn to throw Dick out of the house; why should the family nurture Dick's dreams of literary success when Marion had agreed to abandon her own?

But it wasn't the family playwright Kate was worried about that fall of 1938—although perhaps she should have been. Philip Barry's promise to have the completed play in her hands by mid-October had been overly optimistic. The first act contained the material he had pitched to her at the end of the summer. As he started the second act, Barry lost track of the original story about a reporter who uses Tracy's brother to invade the Lord household so that he may describe the family circle from the inside. The tone shifted abruptly as the comedy Barry was supposed to be writing turned serious. As for the third act, Barry found himself hopelessly blocked.

Barry had little choice but to allow Kate to see the completed pages. The first act was much as she had hoped, but she saw the problems in the second act immediately. Kate flew to Dark Harbor in a seaplane to offer suggestions. Based on their conference, Barry revised the second act and Kate seemed pleased with the changes.

Still, there was no third act when Barry agreed to submit his work-in-progress to Terry Helburn. He did so reluctantly; he had been unhappy with the Guild's production of his *Hotel Universe*. But Kate felt honor-bound to do her next play for the Guild since Helburn and Lawrence Langner had not forced her to go to Broadway with *Jane Eyre* when she believed the play still needed work.

Langner greatly appreciated her sportsmanlike behavior. The Guild was then in desperate straits. In debt to the tune of $60,000, it verged on bankruptcy, and was rapidly losing its preeminent position in the New York theater world. Eager to do almost anything with Kate, Helburn and Langner closed their eyes to the fact that the play was unfinished. They wasted no time in signing the playwright, hiring Bob Sinclair to direct it, and starting to cast—although Sinclair urged them to defer decisions on important parts until they saw what happened to the characters in the last act.

In their glee at finding a vehicle that Kate was inclined to do, Helburn and Langner overlooked the fact that she was still seriously hoping to be cast in *Gone with the Wind*. As late as November 21, Hepburn was on Selznick's list of final candidates to play Scarlett. Had that role come through, there is no question she would have accepted, especially now that Philip Barry was having so much trouble. Still, Kate refused to take a screen test for Selznick; and by December 12, she was out of the running.

Only now was she prepared to sign a contract to do *The Philadelphia Story*, as the Barry play was being called. Hepburn signed with the Guild on December 29. Rehearsals were to begin no later than January 16.

Panic set in at the Guild when there was no word from Barry, who had been working with scant success in Hobe Sound, Florida.

On New Year's Eve, Terry Helburn sent him a frantic telegram, begging to know where the third act was.

Barry called Kate, who was careful not to agitate him. The playwright hadn't had a success in years. It certainly did not boost confidence that his latest play, *Here Come the Clowns*, had flopped when it opened on Broadway on December 7; even his admirers called the new work "mystifying." Now, Barry was terrified that the Guild would have *The Philadelphia Story* cast and ready to go before he had finished the third act.

"Oh, nothing much is going on up here," Kate lied. "We're seeing actors and we have a good director and we're trying to take real care." The conversation appeared to calm him. Four days later, the long-awaited third act arrived in New York.

Helburn and Langner thought the new material confused and disappointing, yet there was no time to waste. Rehearsals and tryouts proceeded as Barry, under immense pressure, revised day by day.

On the advice of Howard Hughes, Kate had waited to see all three acts before agreeing to pay $30,000 for the motion-picture rights. (Barry, in turn, used that money to invest in the Broadway show.) The contract, signed on January 16, 1939, gave Hepburn the title of film producer.

Kate's correspondence with Barry indicates that actress and playwright hoped to get more money from Hughes to do other film projects together; this was only the beginning. Hepburn joked about an office with their names on the door and their feet on the desk. But all that would have seemed a long way off as *The Philadelphia Story* had its first tryout at the Shubert Theater in New Haven, Connecticut, on February 16. Other previews were to follow in Philadelphia, Baltimore, Washington, and Boston.

The third act remained a shambles, and major problems vexed the script throughout. Langner groaned that Tracy's writer brother (played by Dan Tobin) seemed fuzzy; the ex-husband (Joseph Cotten) had little substantial action to perform and appeared to have sprung from nowhere. Langner urged Barry to consider allowing the more vital character of the reporter (Van Heflin), rather than the ex-husband, to marry Tracy at the end of the play.

By this time, Kate was understandably nervous about their chances for Broadway success. To John Ford and others, she confided a growing lack of faith in the material. She had little confidence that *The Philadelphia Story* would win praise from the New York critics. Barry had never quite written the wonderful play about the violation of a family's privacy that Kate had imagined when he first pitched the idea. Once again, Hepburn implored the Guild not to bring a show to Broadway. Pointing to the excellent box-office receipts, she recommended that they continue to tour; bad reviews in New York would almost certainly rule out a tour—and all that money!—afterward.

The debate came to a head in Washington when Barry turned in a third act that seemed to satisfy Langner. But Kate could hardly fail to notice that Langner was not exactly effusive in his praise. Terry Helburn, for her part, remained dissatisfied with the second act, although she kept that opinion to herself until after the play opened in New York.

Kate argued: "If I have a barrow and I'm selling my fruit very well on the side streets, why should I go to the marketplace where all the other barrows are, and where I may not do nearly as well?"

Barry and the Guild overruled her. The playwright and the producers were very eager to have their shot at success on Broadway, and this time Kate had little choice but to go along. They booked the Shubert Theater on West 44th Street for the New York premiere on March 16.

When the company arrived in Manhattan, Kate steered clear of her Turtle Bay townhouse. Pretending that they were still on the road and that this was an opening night like any other, she booked rooms at the River Club. She kept the curtains tightly shut to block out the view of New York.

In each city where they had played, prior to opening Kate had gathered the group of actors known as her four cavaliers—Van Heflin, Joseph Cotten, Dan Tobin, and Frank Fenton—to raise a champagne toast to their success. As they clinked glasses on March 15 in New York, Kate struggled unsuccessfully to hide her tension behind a masklike smile.

"We're simply in another tryout town!" said Kate.

"Like Akron," one of the cavaliers chimed in.

"That's right, like Akron," she agreed.

The next evening, Dr. and Mrs. Hepburn and Luddy were Dr. Florence Sabin's dinner guests at the Cosmopolitan Club before they all headed to the theater. Backstage, neither Cukor's bouquet nor Ford's telegram seemed able to soothe Kate's nerves. Frantically she paced back and forth, muttering "This is Indianapolis! This is Indianapolis!" Nothing kept Kate from remembering that Brooks Atkinson and the other critics were waiting with their muskets.

She was not the only one to suffer the jitters. Terry Helburn and Lawrence Langner knew that the survival of the Theater Guild was at stake that night. With a vehicle no one seemed to have much confidence in, everything rested on the leading lady.

The audience's reception of the first act seemed chilly, but by the third act the laughter and applause were warm and enthusiastic. Barry's last few plays had been serious and philosophical; in *The Philadelphia Story* he returned to the sharp, sophisticated, witty style of *Holiday* and *The Animal Kingdom*, but with a Thirties twist. Theatergoers relished the spectacle of his haughty heroine Tracy Lord losing her priggish, self-satisfied air as she admits her mistakes by the final curtain.

The notices in the morning papers were superb. Even Brooks Atkinson reckoned *The Philadelphia Story* to be Barry's finest play and Hepburn's best stage performance: "A strange, tense little lady with austere beauty and metallic voice, she has consistently found it difficult to project a part in the theater. But now she has surrendered to the central part in Mr. Barry's play and she acts it like a woman who has at last found the joy she has always been seeking in the theater."

Barry had put Kate back on top, and she was very grateful. He was no longer the godlike figure he had once seemed to Kate; and that endeared him to her all the more. Still, she privately confessed astonishment at the reception she and the play received. Kate seemed to have a clearer sense of the play's weaknesses than the audience did; but she was not about to point them out to anyone. As she told

John Ford, it was enough that she had triumphed; the success of *The Philadelphia Story* gave her the clout to do whatever she wanted.

After the show had been running for a while, Lawrence Langner visited Kate in her dressing room to discuss the future.

"Kate, what are you going to do next?"

"Good God, Lawrence, I'm doing this," she replied.

"Yes, but what sort of thing are you aiming at?"

He talked of Shakespeare, specifically *As You Like It*. "I think you should do Rosalind."

"Good God, Lawrence, I can't play Shakespeare!"

"How do you know? Try or learn."

On the morning of Monday, June 12, Kate put on a gown of dusty rose-colored linen trimmed with point lace. She adjusted a large white hat. She grabbed a bouquet of cornflowers and stood beside her sister Peg, who wore an identical costume and looked very like her. They were to serve as attendants at Marion's wedding. Dick and Bob were ushers.

Guests assembled in the garden might easily have imagined that they had stepped into the society wedding in *The Philadelphia Story*. Dr. Hepburn, peering out through the Boston ivy that clung to his dressing-room window, would have found that thought very pleasing. In a sense, this was his day every bit as much as it was Marion's.

But there existed another room in the house, where the view of what mattered in life was very different. Stacks of well-worn, carefully annotated books with markers jammed between pages crowded that room. The authors were Karl Marx, Friedrich Engels, Emma Goldman, V. I. Lenin, Leon Trotsky, Joseph Stalin, and various other radical economists, historians, theoreticians, and dreamers. There were numerous volumes on the history of Russia.

Mrs. Hepburn lived in her books as intensely as she did in the real world, perhaps more.

A long wooden desk overflowed with newspaper cuttings, correspondence, and drafts of speeches. File drawers held hundreds of index cards with the names and addresses of contacts in the suffrage and birth control movements. The signatures in the correspondence files read like a roll call of women's struggle in this century. The earliest documents related to the fight to abolish prostitution and the spread of venereal disease; the most recent, to the operation of illegal birth control clinics in Connecticut, where state law prohibited the use or dissemination of birth control.

When Clara McTernan interrupted Marion's wedding to report a police raid on her Waterbury birth control clinic that very morning, Mrs. Hepburn rushed inside to take the call. Far from being upset that a deputy sheriff and county detective had entered the clinic and "confiscated several bags and boxes of articles," Mrs. Hepburn exulted that this was precisely what she had been waiting for.

Most of her fellow activists seemed not quite to grasp Mrs. Hepburn's belief that at this point, the movement's only hope was to emulate the old NWP tactic of provoking violent confrontations with the authorities. Some who did understand called her mad. Mrs. Hepburn wanted police to invade the clinics. She wanted women to resist arrest, refuse to pay fines, and go to jail. She sought widespread publicity that would show the lengths to which men were willing to go to deny women basic rights.

She had all but given up hope of orderly change. As legislative chairman of Margaret Sanger's National Committee on Federal Legislation for Birth Control, Mrs. Hepburn had met with repeated frustration. A bill very nearly made it through the Senate in 1934, but was shot down at the last minute when one senator demanded a recall. The next year, both houses tabled the birth control bill without a hearing.

In 1935, when a backer offered to finance an illegal birth control clinic in Hartford, some activists expressed confidence that the state government would not enforce its unusually harsh 1879 anti-contraception law. Others believed that Connecticut would act; but they predicted a court case in which pro-birth control forces would emerge victorious. Neither view appealed to Mrs. Hepburn, who saw the clinic as a device like the Silent Sentinels, calculated to provoke repressive measures against women.

The Hartford clinic opened in July. It occupied the first floor of a brownstone on Retreat Avenue, opposite Hartford Hospital. When three months passed without a raid, Mrs. Hepburn decided that the time had come to provoke one.

It was no slip of the tongue when, speaking to a group at Connecticut State College in Storrs as acting head of the National Committee on Federal Legislation for Birth Control while Margaret Sanger was in Europe, she publicly referred to the clinic. Her remarks were reported in the press, and there was concern that the police would launch a raid. Mrs. Hepburn was quietly disappointed when they did not.

Police actions in Massachusetts captured her imagination. In 1937, an undercover policewoman gathered evidence at a clinic in Salem. A raid followed. Authorities seized the facility's records and charged employees with violating state law. Soon afterward, the vice squad raided a clinic in Brookline; another raid followed in Boston the next day. Mrs. Hepburn, exhilarated, rushed to Massachusetts to speak. This was the confrontation she had been hoping for. She urged women to refuse to pay fines and go to jail. She wanted women to resist!

Her battle cry fell on deaf ears. Hers was a voice from another generation of activists. She quivered with anger when a woman physician at the Brookline clinic announced that police had conducted the raid "in a very courteous manner." Mrs. Hepburn chastised Massachusetts women for closing the clinics and appealing their cases in court. The women responded by calling her ideas "insane" and "very harmful to the cause."

Mrs. Hepburn turned her attention back to Connecticut. Again her strategy was to pretend inadvertently to reveal the existence of an illegal clinic. Margaret Sanger, who had been arrested herself and understood the publicity value of confrontation, knew and approved.

On June 8, 1939, Mrs. Hepburn's ally and next-door neighbor Sallie Pease, president of the Connecticut Birth Control League, publicly disclosed that the new Waterbury clinic, located in a building owned by Waterbury Hospital, was the first in the state to occupy space in a public facility. Four days later—Marion's wedding day—police raided the clinic.

Mrs. Hepburn envisioned mass resistance, jail terms, sensational publicity, and an outpouring of public support for birth control activists. Nothing of the sort occurred. The matter was played out in court, not jail. Eventually, the clinics closed not with a bang but a whimper. Younger activists like Dr. Hilda Standish, the clinic's medical director, had a husband and children to consider; she could not see going to jail.

Mrs. Hepburn began to feel isolated in the movement. Years of struggle to subordinate herself to Dr. Hepburn at home had finally eroded her legendary patience and tact in public. Increasingly, she found herself losing her temper and having to apologize afterward. She had little choice but to allow the younger, more conservative women in the Connecticut birth control movement to fight the battle their own way: through the courts and in the legislature. She gave her full support and continued to hold meetings in her home and speak throughout the state. Her passion for the cause never diminished. But her days as a leader and master strategist ended.

More and more, Mrs. Hepburn found comfort in her volumes of radical political philosophy and a cup of tea.

Kate spent weeknights in the Turtle Bay townhouse, which she now owned but, according to Palache, never really considered home. After the Saturday night show, Kate religiously drove up to West Hartford to spend the weekend in "my father's house" on Bloomfield Avenue.

On the evening of Saturday, October 7, 1939, *The Philadelphia Story* had been running for seven lucrative months and Kate was in the middle of intense discussions with Howard Hughes and Philip Barry about the film sale, when Dick greeted her in West Hartford with a copy of his new play, *Sea-Air*. Kate believed that it was enough to destroy her.

She wept. She boiled with rage. She predicted a great scandal. She accused Dick of malice and of exploiting her private life. She shouted that he was either a fool or a fiend. She shrieked that although Dick had changed everyone's name, the characters were all clearly recognizable. Occasionally he forgot himself and used their real names by mistake. She called the play hateful—especially its unflattering portraits of Howard Hughes, Philip Barry, and Leland Hayward.

She demanded that he promise not to show the manuscript to Broadway producers. She warned that he was about to ruin her life. As Kate saw it, even as she had been appearing in a play about a reporter who uses false pretenses to observe a family from the inside, her own brother had been spying on her and writing up everything he saw and heard!

Dr. and Mrs. Hepburn and Marion all rushed in to take Kate's side. It seemed to Dick that the whole family was against him. When the shouting died down, Mrs. Hepburn—always the diplomat— professed to admire the play very much; but she too warned Dick against exploiting his sister.

Dr. Hepburn had the impression that Dick finally promised not to embarrass Kate with *Sea-Air*; but Dick later claimed to have done nothing of the kind, although he did consider using a *nom de plume* or excising a few of the more objectionable passages. Dick, for his part, seemed not to understand what all the fuss was about. He claimed to have had no desire to damage Kate. He could not agree with her that he was a traitor. He thought his sister tiresome to throw a fit over what he considered to be nothing.

He presented *Sea-Air* as a charming comedy, not the shameless exposé Kate accused him of having written. He portrayed himself as an artist untainted by crass commercial considerations. He defended himself by saying he would show the play only to reputable producers, not to anyone who would be interested in *Sea-Air* merely for its gossip value. He suggested that Kate show *Sea-Air* to Hughes and Barry and ask if they objected, or give it to a libel lawyer for his opinion. Dick freely admitted that he had modeled the heroine, famous actress Elizabeth Lascelles, on his sister; but he argued that the play would only enhance Kate, like a fine painted portrait.

Then there was the issue of Dick's freedom to write about whatever subject he chose; like any author who looks to what he know best for inspiration, Dick claimed Fenwick and the Hepburns—Kate included—as his material to use as he pleased. From this point of view, life at Fenwick was every bit as much Dick's possession as Kate's.

Eventually, Dick despaired of explaining himself. As far as he could tell, Kate's state of mind did not permit what he considered rational discussion of the subject. For the rest of the weekend, she became hysterical every time he so much as mentioned *Sea-Air*.

Aside from Dick's emotional investment in *Sea-Air*, there could be no denying that the play was his most technically accomplished to date. He wrote with a flair and assurance that had eluded him in previous efforts. He was certainly an expert on his subject. Anyone familiar with the old Fenwick would have instantly seen that he vividly captured the turbulent atmosphere of the place he knew so well. He included the whole cast of characters; Dr. and Mrs. Hepburn, Aunty, Luddy, Palache, Laura, Fanny, and Em. Even Dick's harshest critic would have had to admit that he had them all down to a tee.

In the old cottage where everyone could always hear everyone else, Dick had obviously been listening very carefully, especially that summer when Howard Hughes came to visit and Fenwick blew to bits in the hurricane. Dick put everybody's best lines and most embarrassing peccadilloes into *Sea-Air*. Although his main targets were Hughes and Barry, Dick spared no one—not even Kate's best friend Palache, who would have fainted if she found out that he had included details of her ongoing affair with a married man.

Dick claimed to have been inspired by Lillian Hellman's *The Little Foxes*, in which a power-hungry sister struggles to dominate her family. The main action of *Sea-Air* concerns Kate's attempt to decide whether to accept Howard Hughes's marriage proposal. In the meantime, Hughes, dirty and misanthropic, collides with everyone. He tries to eject Luddy from Fenwick. He tortures Aunty Towle by remaining in the bathroom for hours when the poor old woman desperately needs to get in. He is rude to Mrs. Hepburn. He spars unpleasantly with Leland Hayward, when the agent visits Fenwick to confer with Kate.

Finally, Kate blows up at Hughes. She accuses him of being selfish, neurotic, and superficial. She derides him for moping and grousing. She calls him greedy, conceited, and disgusting. She resists his attempts to fetter and control her. She compares him to an octopus who wants to wind his tentacles around her art and suck the creative urge away.

So much for the man who had given Kate $30,000 to buy the film rights to *The Philadelphia Story* and seemed likely to bankroll other Hepburn–Barry projects in the future! Dick's treatment of Kate's other principal business associates is little better. His Leland Hayward is a ridiculous popinjay, whom Kate mocks as "my old poodle"; his Philip Barry, an unctuous, shivering, drunken fraud eager to grind out any kind of pretentious trash so long as he and Kate can make a buck.

Part of the trouble was that Dick gave voice to an attitude which rarely traveled beyond the Hepburn family circle. Kate, for her part, had no illusions about Mrs. Hepburn's and Aunty Towle's low opinion of "la-di-da commercial" vehicles like *The Philadelphia Story* or the men associated with them. Mrs. Hepburn would rush into New York to see the latest O'Neill play; she worshiped Shakespeare and Shaw. But Barry's light comedies about the very rich struck her as worthless. Dick's brutal satire would have been particularly painful to Kate because it highlighted Mrs. Hepburn's quiet disappointment in her daughter's work and values.

After learning of *Sea-Air*'s existence, Kate went back to New York in a fury. Nothing had been settled, and there was no telling what sort of scene would occur when Kate returned the following Saturday night.

Dick was hurt, angry, and confused as Dr. Hepburn continued to badger him. Suddenly he was isolated in the family. Kate possessed a "terrific will" like their father's, as Bob said, and was unlikely to back down. On Friday, October 13, Dick made his move before Kate could say another word about the matter. Lying in bed in his room on Bloomfield Avenue, Dick scribbled a long, frantic letter to Jasper Deeter.

Dick described in detail the big blowup of the previous weekend. He reported all that Kate and his parents had said. He confessed that *Sea-Air* was indeed about his sister and the Hepburn circle. Assuring Deeter that he knew he was discreet and would not use the play to blackmail Kate, Dick asked him to study the manuscript. He needed an objective opinion on whether *Sea-Air* was any good and whether it would ruin Kate's life. Dick insisted he was prepared to admit to a terrible mistake, but not just because Kate and her allies said so.

Kate and the family were livid when they discovered that Dick had shown *Sea-Air* to an outsider. Had he given the play to Lawrence Langner, Arthur Hopkins, or one of the other New York producers Kate knew, she might have been able to get it back. They were unlikely to want to offend her now that she was back on top. But a little man like Jasper Deeter was a wild card. He and Kate moved in entirely different worlds. If Deeter decided to stage *Sea-Air* at the Hedgerow Theater, there was nothing Kate, or Philip Barry for that matter, could do to stop him.

To make matters worse, Deeter was engaged in a peculiar imaginary struggle with Kate. He enjoyed reminding Dick that he considered himself a far more important figure in the American theater than any movie star. *Sea-Air* provided an unexpected opportunity to vex the woman for whom he professed such contempt.

The angry scenes in the Hepburn household dragged on for weeks as Dick waited for Deeter's opinion. Kate had no clue that Dick was recounting her fits of rage in regular letters to the producer. On November 7, Dick could wait no longer. He sent word that he needed to see Deeter in person. Dick compared a trip to the Hedgerow Theater to visiting a shrine. He returned to Connecticut in a state of euphoria, declaring that his soul could go on now.

Deeter loved *Sea-Air*! The producer who had turned down Dick's last few efforts wanted to stage the play and promised to send the board's formal offer by November 25. Sensational material like this did not often find its way into Deeter's hands.

Kate cried and vomited. She said she couldn't bear the shame of Dick's having actually met with Deeter. She cursed the producer; she wailed that he was just like Jed Harris, happy to destroy her career. Screaming at the spy who had written down all her words, she lost her voice.

Mrs. Hepburn sat in silence as Dr. Hepburn roared at Dick. The father was not careful to spare his son's feelings. "Dad didn't mind hurting people," Bob would say years later. But Mrs. Hepburn did mind—very much. She was concerned about her son and daughter; both seemed to be at breaking point.

That night, the mother read *Sea-Air* for the sixth time. She waited until her husband went out in the morning before she had a long talk with Dick. She struggled to speak in the voice of reason, although at one point she too became hysterical. The conversation lasted all morning. Mrs. Hepburn assured Dick that she admired *Sea-Air* more than ever. Still, she was concerned that at the moment, it would hurt Kate with Hughes and Barry. Kate, she said, was already under enough strain; couldn't Dick put his play aside until it no longer posed a threat?

Mrs. Hepburn argued that if only Dick would be patient, Kate would want to appear in *Sea-Air* herself. She declared Elizabeth Lascelles a fine role for her daughter. She hinted that Kate no doubt secretly loved the play but could not show her admiration until after the business with Hughes was concluded. Mrs. Hepburn reminded Dick that he didn't need the money and that Kate had always done her best to assist him. She implored him to put off production for a year. Then the family could all have a wonderful time with *Sea-Air* instead of the heartache they were experiencing now. Wouldn't it be much better if Dick and Kate put on the play together as friends?

By the time Dick returned to his room, he was extremely depressed. The talk with his mother left him with little choice but to withdraw *Sea-Air*. Dick wrote to Deeter that although he didn't believe Kate would ever really like his play, he was willing to take the chance that she might agree to portray Elizabeth in the future. He asked permission to resubmit *Sea-Air* to Hedgerow as soon as Kate was done with Hughes and Barry.

Dick, suffering from sciatica, spent a few days in Boston for tests on his back. All seemed to have calmed down in the Hepburn household. Then on November 28, Dick sent *Sea-Air* to Arthur Hopkins; by now, he told Deeter, he was thinking of Greta Garbo or Helen Hayes for his leading lady.

This time, Kate put her foot down; in no uncertain terms, she forbade her brother to distribute *Sea-Air*. She was prepared to cut off Dick's allowance. Dr. Hepburn would not hesitate to throw him out of the house.

The threats seemed to work. *Sea-Air* was a dead issue in December and much of January, as Dick seemed to be preoccupied with his sciatica. He was planning to use his savings to finance a six-week South American cruise when he suddenly realized that only one thing would make him feel better. He needed to know what the New York theater world thought of his play.

Dick sent *Sea-Air* to fifteen Broadway producers including Lawrence Langner. Then he sent his sister a note, gleefully announcing what he had done. If Kate planned to sue or discontinue his allowance, Dick asked only that she do so before he had invested the last of his savings in the cruise.

Kate wrote back that she wished Dick would burn his play. When she arrived for the weekend, she took each family member aside to announce that Dick had put a knife in her back.

Already the rejections were starting to come in. Langner sent Dick a very nasty letter, declaring that the Theater Guild would never do anything to hurt "a decent, fine girl" like Kate. He predicted that no reputable producer would go near *Sea-Air* because of potential libel problems. He warned that if Dick did manage to get the comedy produced, it would ruin his reputation.

Despite the warnings and rejections, Dick felt much better for having distributed *Sea-Air*. A new man, he put in four hours a day on *Love Like Wild-fire*, his work-in-progress. The sciatica didn't seem to bother him so much anymore. He was still thinking of taking that South American cruise when Kate made serious noises about cutting off his income.

On February 21, Dick asked Deeter for a letter in praise of *Sea-*

Air to show Kate and the family that whatever they might think, his literary work deserved to be funded. Deeter responded with a testimonial beyond anything Dick might have hoped for. Pointing out that he had had similar correspondence with George Bernard Shaw and Eugene O'Neill at one time or another, Deeter hailed *Sea-Air* as a work of art. He insisted it was one of the few American plays to use the Shaw influence without merely imitating the master. He argued that Dick must be given the opportunity to go on writing without the need to support himself.

With that, the saga of *Sea-Air* drew to a close. Dick stopped trying to sell his play. He retrieved as many copies as he could.

Through the years, there were whispers about the existence of such a play, but few people could be found who had actually read it. Some who did claim familiarity with *Sea-Air* described it in ways that made clear they were merely repeating things they had heard, with subtle embellishments of their own. *Sea-Air* became a legend in the New York theater world.

And it became a legend in the Hepburn household. Jasper Deeter's letter made a lasting impression on Dr. and Mrs. Hepburn. They would always have reason to wonder whether all Deeter said had been true; perhaps they had forced Dick to give up his one chance at greatness. Kate too would wonder whether she had destroyed her brother. Had she allowed Dick to stage his play, he would have had his shot and that probably would have been that. As it was, she had denied him the opportunity to succeed—or fail.

Kate's suppression of *Sea-Air* guaranteed Dick's mythical position in the family. Untested, he became like his brother Tom; no one would ever know what either Hepburn boy might have been capable of in life.

N I N E T E E N

Many years later, when Kate visited John Ford on his deathbed, they talked about his troubled and ambiguous relationship with Spencer Tracy.

In the beginning the men had been the best of friends. It was well known in Hollywood that Tracy owed his film career to Ford. At a time when the studios declared Tracy "too ugly," Ford brought him west, along with Humphrey Bogart, to appear in *Up the River*. But then, suddenly, Ford put Spence "on ice."

Kate had devoted considerable thought to Ford's rift with Tracy. Ford tended to work repeatedly with actors he admired, so it was very strange that after *Up the River*, he did not use Tracy again until Kate intervened many years later.

As Sean lay dying, Kate told him the version of events Spence had once related to her. According to the actor, he and Ford had broken over his refusal to appear in *The Plough and the Stars*. In the end, Ford cast Preston Foster, and, said Tracy, held a grudge against him for years.

Sean pointedly said nothing when Kate told him Spence's account. As Kate knew, silence was often Ford's way of attacking most dangerously.

The conversation shifted to other matters as Ford presumably turned the subject over in his thoughts. Then, suddenly, he returned to it, protesting that Spence had it all wrong.

Kate seemed to have been waiting for him to say that.

According to Ford, there had been no disagreement. Yes, Ford had wanted Tracy for *The Plough and the Stars*; but when the director saw that the studio was going to interfere with the film he wanted to make, he advised his friend to turn down the part.

"This is going to be a lousy script," Ford claimed to have told Spence. "Duck out of it. Refuse to do it. I'm going to do this as quickly as possible and get it over with."

He insisted to Kate that he and Spence had never quarreled; they had simply drifted apart when Tracy left Fox for MGM.

Kate didn't believe it. She fondly accused Sean of being very devious. Although Ford, like Tracy, possessed that perfect memory which is characteristic of the old Irish, she suspected he could not be trusted to tell the real story. Spence was dead, she pointed out, so she couldn't very well ask him. And although she didn't mention it, she knew that Sean would soon be gone too. Then she would never find out what had passed between the two great loves of her life, once friends, to cause them to dance around each other so.

Once again, Kate found herself asking for the clarity Sean had always resisted.

In the spring of 1940 when Kate returned to Los Angeles after a two-year absence playing *The Philadelphia Story* in New York and on tour, her relationship with Sean was still somehow unresolved. Their correspondence shows that they had never stopped caring for each other. Gradually, the lovers became loving friends. Yet there was no demarcation, no definite, unambiguous yes or no. To read their letters from that time is to watch them struggle, sometimes uncomfortably, to forge a new kind of relationship.

Ford's friends continued to speak of Kate as the woman who had known him best; but there was a tacit acceptance that that must be over for him.

In September 1939, the news that Germany had invaded Poland had a profound effect on Ford. He told friends that time was running out; he needed to make as many more good films as fate would allow. He continued to work at the height of his powers; yet he seemed to accept, even embrace, the military destiny Mary had outlined for him. He recruited Hollywood professionals for a reserve unit known as the Naval Field Photographic.

Kate, for her part, would insist that Ford could have been very happy with her; yet she wondered whether that happiness might have destroyed him as an artist. She regarded Mary as crude and insensitive; yet she admitted to a grudging respect for her rival.

Sean had stopped saying maybe and someday. Still, never having married in the Roman Catholic Church meant that he and Mary, a divorcee, had never really been united in God's eyes. That meant a great deal to Ford. It provided at least a glimmer of possibility as he lived on unhappily with his wife, and Kate began to remind her worried friend George Cukor of a spinster.

Kate had spent a year on Broadway in *The Philadelphia Story*. She interrupted a national tour to make the film version at MGM. Her shrewd decision to tie up the motion-picture rights (actually Howard Hughes's idea) and her dealings with Louis B. Mayer were already legend. She insisted it wasn't money she wanted but the studio chief's promise of two major male stars; still smarting from the "box-office poison" label, Kate didn't want to take any chances the film would flop. She asked for Clark Gable and Spencer Tracy. Mayer gave her Cary Grant and James Stewart instead.

Mayer agreed to George Cukor as director but turned down Philip Barry, who demanded too much money to write the screenplay. MGM signed Donald Ogden Stewart in his place; but it was Joseph L. Mankiewicz, the producer, who solved some of the key adaptation problems.

As early as the play's previews, Lawrence Langner had complained that Tracy Lord's ex-husband C. K. Dexter Haven didn't have enough to do and that audiences didn't know enough about his background. For the film, Mankiewicz streamlined the narrative by combining the ex-husband's character with that of Tracy's brother Sandy; now Dexter, not Sandy, is responsible for bringing the reporter into the household. That made the part infinitely more appealing to a star like Cary Grant, who was given the opportunity to choose between playing Dexter or the reporter, Macaulay Connor.

To set up the story more fully than in the play, Mankiewicz devised a brief silent sequence that shows why Tracy and Dexter broke up two years before the film's action begins.

The Philadelphia Story was everything Kate might have hoped for in a comeback vehicle. It broke box-office records at the Music Hall in New York and earned a $1.3 million profit. It won six Oscar nominations, including that for Best Actress, although Kate lost out to Ginger Rogers for *Kitty Foyle*. Donald Ogden Stewart won for Best Screenplay Adaptation and James Stewart for Best Actor.

As Kate considered her next step, she resumed the national tour of the stage production. *The Philadelphia Story* had rescued the Theater Guild, allowing the organization to pay off its debts; still, Lawrence Langner would bitterly remark on all the money the film earned for MGM while the Guild made "peanuts."

"What shall I do next?" Kate asked Langner after the last performance.

He urged her to try something dangerous.

"What do you mean by dangerous?" said Kate.

"A play in which you'll aim high but risk falling flat on your face if you don't come through with a great performance. Shakespeare or Ibsen, for instance."

The Guild was terrified of losing Kate now that Hollywood wanted her again. Whenever Terry Helburn and Lawrence Langner could, they thrust contracts at her appointing them her theatrical managers. They sought to handle her future dealings with Philip Barry, who was then in the throes of writing a new Hepburn vehicle. They wanted to seek out other stage and film material on her behalf. They talked of asking Robert Sherwood to write a play for her.

Repeatedly, Kate refused to sign. She knew the Guild would go on looking for projects anyway. Besides, she was obviously more effective doing her own deals. Eager not to hurt anyone's feelings, Kate promised that if the Playwrights' Company or any other rival producing organization approached her, she would say she was under contract to the Guild.

Following the tour, she rented a house for a month in Hobe Sound, Florida, near Philip and Ellen Barry. Her sister Peg joined her there; they planned to drive north together afterward. With Barry's work-in-progress nowhere near completion, Kate spent the time reading plays, including Pat Coleman's *Oh Bury Me Not,* which

Terry Helburn had given to her. Whatever project Kate chose, she planned to do it on stage first, then on screen.

A few months earlier, George Bernard Shaw had rejected the Guild's request for permission to stage *Saint Joan* with Hepburn. Now they resumed negotiations when Kate asked the Guild to look into the possibility of hiring Orson Welles to direct. She had greatly admired Welles since seeing his *Julius Caesar* in 1937.

The Welles idea came to nothing. Kate and the Guild seemed to have settled on *Oh Bury Me Not* when suddenly she approached MGM with a proposal to skip the theatrical production and film the play immediately. After much frantic back and forth with Langner, Kate agreed to talk to MGM on the Guild's behalf. In exchange for abandoning plans to stage the play, Langner demanded $100,000, of which $40,000 would go the Guild, the rest to the author. Helburn and Langner also wanted Kate to negotiate their appointment as associate producers on the film.

On May 29, 1941, a confident Lawrence Langner wrote to tell Terry Helburn to put Kate to work on the deal immediately. Five days later, Kate surprised them both.

Helburn wired Langner the disappointing news that Kate had found a script on her own. The Guild had no claim to the new project, which Kate planned to shoot at MGM as soon as a screenplay could be completed. Helburn and Langner's sole consolation was that at this point, Kate planned to return to Broadway to do the new Philip Barry play under the Guild banner.

In Hollywood, there was a good deal of buzz about the vehicle which Kate had pitched to Louis B. Mayer without revealing the co-writers' names. If Mayer accepted her demands, he would pay the highest price ever for an original screenplay. She wanted $100,000 for the script, the same amount for herself, $10,000 for her agent, and another $1000 to pay her way between Connecticut and California.

Far from irritating the studio chief, Kate's air of secrecy seemed to pique his curiosity. When Mayer consulted Joe Mankiewicz, the producer speculated that Ben Hecht and Charles MacArthur had written the treatment about the unlikely romance between a Dorothy Thompson-like foreign affairs journalist and a gruff sportswriter. Mankiewicz guessed the "name" screenwriters had to sell it anonymously because they were under contract elsewhere.

Mayer agreed to Kate's tough terms and signed her to a multi-picture contract. The deal forever established Kate's credentials as a clever businesswoman, especially when it came out that the treatment had been written by the obscure Ring Lardner, Jr. and Michael Kanin, with uncredited assistance from Michael's brother Garson. Hepburn had calculated that Mayer would never meet her price if he knew their identities.

As she had done at the time of *The Philadelphia Story*, Hepburn requested Spencer Tracy. He made a perfect "counter," as Ford had taught her to call a strongly contrasting actor. Tracy's deadpan manner would play very nicely against hyperkinetic Kate.

Tracy, then forty-one, had come a long way since the early days with Ford. His many celebrated roles included Joe Wheeler, the man falsely accused of murder in Fritz Lang's classic *Fury*, and Academy Award-winning performances in *Captains Courageous* and *Boys Town*. He was widely revered as perhaps the greatest film actor of his generation.

For all that, insecurity continued to tear the man apart. He pawed old wounds. He endlessly rehashed insults real and imagined. He brooded over his father's look of astonishment when the squat plain boy with jug ears and cock eyes (as Tracy described himself) spoke of his plans to become an actor. Spencer's girlfriend had laughed when he told her his dream. He never forgot his hurt when he overheard her making cracks to one of her friends. And he frequently talked about it.

Even now that Tracy had proved them all wrong, he constantly doubted his own abilities. He believed he had put something over on the public. According to Louise Tracy, he lived in terror that "any minute now" people would "catch on to him" and he would suddenly lose everything he had. His wife told reporters how he lay awake at night "doing his figuring" about how much they needed to live on should his career collapse. He feared material that might expose his limitations as an actor.

When the Theater Guild invited Tracy to appear in a revival

of Shaw's *The Devil's Disciple*, he wrote to Terry Helburn on June 12, 1939 that the offer was way beyond anything he might have hoped for. Eager to flatter Tracy, Helburn had noted that *The Devil's Disciple* contained Shaw's most brilliant virtuoso part; Shaw, she pointed out, considered the play essentially a vehicle for a male star. The offer appeared to overwhelm him. What at first struck Helburn as humility quickly disclosed itself to be something quite different. Much as he seemed sincerely to want to do it, Tracy threw every obstacle in the path of actually appearing in the play. Negotiations dragged on for many months, frequently with the sensible, stolid Louise Tracy acting on her mercurial husband's behalf.

By spring 1941, Tracy was giving every indication of planning to do *The Devil's Disciple*, but nothing was definite yet. Lawrence Langner suggested to Mrs. Tracy that her husband might want to emulate Katharine Hepburn in buying the film rights before the play opened on Broadway.

Tracy was in the Everglades in south Florida filming *The Yearling* when Kate requested him for her new picture. At first it looked as though he would not be able to fit *Woman of the Year* into his schedule. But *The Yearling* was a troubled production. Location shooting in the hot, insect-infested swamps made Tracy miserable. He was unable to sleep or rest. He suffered anxiety attacks. He complained of difficulty breathing. His eyes burned. His flesh was swollen with insect bites. Swarms of mosquitoes clung to the camera lens, rendering the cameraman's job a nightmare. Shortly after Victor Fleming replaced King Vidor as director, the film was canceled.

Kate had moved in temporarily with George Cukor until she rented a house of her own in Beverly Hills. As her friend, Cukor expected Kate to offer him all her new projects, and he was badly wounded when she did not ask him to direct *Woman of the Year*. She believed him wrong for the material—and said so. Cukor—Hepburn observed—didn't know "a baseball game from a swimming match." Kate would insist that she wanted a more masculine director to handle the sports scenes, as well as to oversee Tracy, but her real reason for spurning Cukor probably would have been even more hurtful had he known it: As a director, Cukor was not strong on the visual gags and effects of comic timing Kate saw as the heart of the film.

"I want to see you about doing a picture," she told George Stevens on the telephone.

"I'm terribly busy," said the director, who had gone to work for Harry Cohn at Columbia.

"George, I have to see you."

"Okay, come over," said Stevens, who found it impossible to turn Kate down. He would always be very grateful to her for having given him the opportunity to direct *Alice Adams*.

She brought the screenplay, which was about two-thirds completed. Approximately forty pages remained unwritten. Kate had been working intensively with the writers, whom she referred to as "the boys."

"I want you to do this picture," Kate told Stevens. "I think it's just your dish."

"Well, tell me the goddamn story. Just tell it to me."

Kate told Stevens about the brilliant and beautiful Tess Harding's love affair with craggy Sam Craig. She was a superior woman, he a common man. She was talkative, he taciturn. She was devoted to world affairs, he to sports. She hobnobbed with intellectuals and world leaders, he with punch-drunk ex-fighters. She wanted marriage and career, he a traditional wife and plenty of children.

Stevens responded with his usual poker-face and forbidding silence.

"Read the script tonight," Kate implored.

"No, I haven't got time."

Kate looked heartbroken.

"You want me to do this picture with Spencer Tracy?" Stevens went on, hating to see her that way. "You want me to direct it? Okay, here I am. I'll do it."

There was one problem. Stevens insisted she bring the project to Columbia, where his arrangement with Harry Cohn prohibited the studio head from interfering with the way he shot a film. As Kate affectionately put it, Stevens liked to be "the boss of the whole shebang." He feared that wasn't about to happen at a "producer's studio," as he called MGM, where artistic decisions were made by committee. Kate kept pushing for MGM, because that was Spencer Tracy's studio, and Stevens finally agreed, despite the antagonism his decision would no doubt create with Cohn. She admired his insistence on doing what was right, whether or not it helped his career.

All that remained was for Hepburn to meet Tracy. There had been much talk about Tracy in the Ford circle at the time of *The Plough and the Stars*; but Kate had never actually encountered him. That happened now outside the Thalberg Building at MGM. The meeting was accidental. She was on her way in, Tracy and Mankiewicz on their way out to lunch.

To Hepburn, he was the brilliant actor Ford had nurtured, then broken with; to Tracy, she was the only woman Ford had ever really loved.

"Mr. Tracy, I think you're a little short for me," said Kate.

"Don't worry," laughed Mankiewicz. "He'll cut you down to size."

Tracy stared disapprovingly at the whipcord trouser suit Kate had ordered from the men's tailor Eddie Schmidt. That wasn't his idea of how a woman should dress.

"Not me, boy!" Tracy exclaimed to Mankiewicz once the actress was safely out of earshot. "I don't want to get mixed up in anything like this."

Tracy prided himself on his liaisons with co-stars including Loretta Young and Ingrid Bergman. On the one hand, the intensity of Ford's feelings for Kate would have made her seem all the more appealing to Tracy; on the other, her involvement with the father figure made her a kind of forbidden fruit. From the first, he was very edgy with her. In conversation with George Stevens, he pointedly refused to refer to Kate by name. Tracy spoke volumes when he called her only "the woman."

When Tracy appeared on the set on the first day of shooting, Friday, August 29, he affected a skeptical attitude, which consisted of a good deal of glowering, particularly at Kate. He sucked intently, almost defiantly, on a peppermint. For all his insecurity, Tracy expected to be kowtowed to. But that, apparently, was not about to happen on *Woman of the Year*. Kate, who had set up the deal and hired everyone, was clearly running the show.

"I sure as hell walked into a fine situation," Tracy groaned to Stevens. "Here I find myself doing a picture with a lady and her director. I ought to be old enough to know better than that."

George M. Cohan once said that his friend Tracy could "stare, glare, and finally scare the other actors, without batting an eyelash or making a peep." That, in essence, was Tracy's approach as Stevens shot a scene in the bar where Sam Craig takes Tess Harding after a baseball game.

Kate sensed Tracy staring at her dirty fingernails; she accidentally knocked over a glass, presumably ruining the shot. But Stevens kept the camera running. What followed set the tone of their onscreen relationship. Without a word, Tracy handed Kate his handkerchief, as Dr. Hepburn no doubt would have done with Mrs. Hepburn.

"Oh, you old so-and-so," Kate found herself thinking. "You're going to make me mop it up right in the middle of a scene."

When the water started to leak to the floor, Kate climbed under the table in an effort to jolt Tracy. But he just kept staring at her, and she saw the beginning of one of his tight-lipped grins.

Before long, the talk at MGM was that Tracy and Hepburn were having an affair; but as everyone knew, that was hardly unusual for Tracy. Catholic and guilt-ridden, he always crawled back to his wife after a fling. Louise Tracy was no Mary Ford, denigrating her husband's film career. Mrs. Tracy, a former actress, quietly played a surprisingly active role in Spencer's professional dealings.

If there was any reason to believe that Tracy's latest affair would last beyond *Woman of the Year*, it was that he and Hepburn both planned to be in New York in the spring. Kate was to appear in Barry's *Without Love on Broadway*, Spencer in *The Devil's Disciple*, Lawrence Langner having sent word to Tracy the day before shooting began that George Bernard Shaw had endorsed the Guild's plan to stage the play. As Kate told her family, she worshiped Tracy's talent. She emphasized that he had been trained in the theater and possessed an abundance of stage experience. The romantic prospect of going off together to New York greatly appealed to her.

Tracy, who had already angered Ford once before by refusing to appear in *The Plough and the Stars*, knew that Ford did not take betrayal lightly. Ford was rarely heard to comment on a friend who had committed an affront against him, but he always reacted, often in deliberately obscure ways; stock company members were forever trying to interpret some of his more oblique and enigmatic gestures. Ford would insist nothing was wrong, punishing a man by making him wonder whether he was only imagining that Ford was furious.

If Tracy wondered whether, or how, Ford would react to news of the affair with Kate, he did not have to wait long to find out. On September 3, five days after shooting on *Woman of the Year* began, Ford suddenly left town under mysterious circumstances. Telling Mary that he had to take a short business trip, he carried only a small briefcase. He traveled cross-country on the Union Pacific Streamliner. By the time he arrived in Washington, D.C., he had exchanged his decrepit Irish tweed coat and white flannel trousers for a military uniform.

With the exception of two brief visits, Ford would stay away from Hollywood for five years. The period of intense creative activity, from *Stagecoach* to *How Green Was My Valley*, that had begun after Kate's departure for the east in 1938 ended now that she was back for good.

Having proved for all time his worth as a director, now he would show Mary that he also could be the man she wanted him to be. Commander John Ford of the U.S. Naval Reserve swore off drinking. He took up residence in a fourteen-by-eight-foot room at the Carlton Hotel. He reported to Colonel William "Wild Bill" Donovan in anticipation of activating the Field Photographic Unit. With a symbolism that would have been lost on neither Mary Ford nor Kate Hepburn, he secured a desk in the former office of another of Mary's uncles, Rupert Blue.

Ostensibly, Ford's sudden, rather theatrical departure had nothing to do with Kate. Still, there can be no question that it shadowed her relationship with Tracy from the outset.

A man of Tracy's tormented and deeply suspicious nature could never accept that Ford's timing had been purely coincidental. As early as *Seas Beneath*, when Ford staged another abrupt and mysterious exit for his benefit, Tracy's fear of being controlled by Ford had led the actor to keep his distance. But now, whether Tracy liked it or not, he found himself drawn into one of Ford's famous mind games. It was as though Ford, in departing at that particular moment, had deliberately cleared the way for Tracy to proceed with Kate; but as so often with Ford, why he would want to do that, or whether he was doing it at all, remained an open question. The gnawing uncertainty was precisely the thing Tracy hated most.

At MGM, people were already thinking of Tracy and Hepburn as a team. From that first day when Kate knocked over a glass and Spencer willed her to mop up the water, George Stevens was reminded of Laurel and Hardy. As Sam Craig, Tracy played the Hardy role. Stocky and sour, he clings to his own rigid idea of propriety. He lives for the moment when he can glower at Hepburn for creating "another nice mess."

Stevens quickly took note of Tracy's "glacial" attitude to Hepburn's energy and enthusiasm, and put it into the picture. This made the dynamics of her comic pairing with Tracy very different from those of the relationship with Cary Grant in *Bringing Up Baby*, which was written to reflect Kate's romance with John Ford. *Bringing Up Baby* presents Susan Vance's antics as good for David Huxley. In the final scene, when Susan accidentally destroys the project David has been working on for ages, we know he's not completely unhappy about it. His day with her has subjected this stuffed-shirt to humiliations that include wearing women's clothes, but in the end he confesses it's been the best day of his life.

In *Woman of the Year*, Sam Craig would say no such thing of the grief Tess Harding has given him. *Bringing Up Baby* recognizes Susan as a life force; *Woman of the Year* sees Tess as a disruptive element that needs to be brought into line.

George Stevens, perceiving a certain narrative logic in Tracy's perpetual "putdown" of Kate, tacked on a final sequence that called into question everything the Hepburn image seemed to stand for. In this film, it is the woman who must be humiliated—and like it. While Tracy stares and glares, Hepburn makes a mess of the kitchen, struggling ineptly to prepare breakfast for him; it is the liberated woman's penance for having dared not to be a good, sweet, traditional little wife.

After Stevens finished filming on October 26, Kate headed east to see her family and confer with Lawrence Langner and Terry Helburn. Tracy plunged into preparations for his next picture, *Tortilla Flat*, which would begin shooting on November 23.

Mary Ford did not initially respond as one might have expected to her husband's military career. After years of begging Jack to abandon Hollywood, she had trouble adjusting to life on Odin Street with only Barbara for company; Patrick was at the University of Maine. Mary repeatedly telephoned the Carlton Hotel to complain of loneliness. Her first husband had died that year; and now, with war imminent, she feared for Jack. In frequent letters home, Ford warned Mary to prepare for the long haul. He asked Barbara to spend more time with her mother. Ward Bond and John Wayne frequently looked in.

Still, Mary insisted on traveling to Washington with Barbara to say a proper goodbye. On December 7, the Fords were dining at the home of Admiral and Mrs. William Pickens when a telephone call brought news of the Japanese attack on Pearl Harbor. The United States declared war the next day.

Ford seemed to take the conjunction of events—the death of Mary's first husband, her arrival in Washington, the bombing of Pearl Harbor, the declaration of war—as a sign of what he must do. Not wanting to face death before he had made peace with God, Ford married the widow Mary in a Roman Catholic ceremony at the National Cathedral in Washington.

By the time rehearsals of *Without Love* were due to begin in New York in February 1942, Tracy had decided not to do *The Devil's Disciple* that spring. Kate, committed to the Barry play, had to leave

Los Angeles knowing that she faced months away from Spencer. And she faced the possibility that he would settle back in with his wife as Ford had done when Kate went off on the *Jane Eyre* tour.

Ford's decision to marry in the Church redefined Kate's relationship with Tracy. It did not mean that Ford's feelings for Kate had changed; it meant only that he had abandoned hope of finding happiness with her. Ford had hovered in the background of the Hughes liaison, almost certainly making it impossible for Kate to consider his marriage proposal seriously. Now, however, she was free as she had not been in five years. News of the ceremony provided a definite end to her love affair with Sean.

As Kate's brother Bob perceived, she was drawn to Tracy precisely because he so desperately needed her. In the early days of their marriage, Louise had nursed him devotedly; but then her attention had been diverted by the demands of raising a deaf, sickly child. When Tracy met Kate, he seemed to sense her readiness to focus on him and his problems to the exclusion of all else. Her inclination to devote herself to him was potentially as extreme and excessive as his own desire for such an arrangement.

Tracy signaled his need for Kate loud and clear when he drank with particular ferocity during the filming of *Tortilla Flat*. As though courting his own destruction, he mixed alcohol with barbiturates and chloral hydrate. He was very manipulative. He did not want Kate to go off to the Barry play, but he would never say something like that directly. Instead, he made her fear what would happen if she left him.

Kate had failed to save Ford; that made it all the more vital that she rescue Tracy from his demons.

Yet there were also Langner, Helburn, and Barry to consider. Kate felt the tug of friendship very keenly. She owed them her comeback in *The Philadelphia Story* and knew they were all hungry for another success. She was particularly fond of Philip Barry and his wife, Ellen; he had started to write *Without Love* for Kate before she met Spencer Tracy. Conflicting loyalties tore her in opposite directions.

And Kate had much else on her mind. In December, Edith had

suffered a cerebral hemorrhage, her third attack since Christmas 1940. Florence Sabin, who had come to Baltimore to be with her, announced that Edith was unlikely to live. As far as Dr. Sabin could tell, from now on it was only a matter of time. Nonetheless, the life force continued to rage inside Edith. She was a fighter; she would not give up easily. Dr. Sabin, who called Edith's condition a kind of prolonged living death, sadly declared that it would be better for everyone when she died.

As it happened, the days would stretch into weeks and months, and Edith's condition would not change. For a time Don Hooker hoped that Edith might actually will herself to regain consciousness. Mostly she seemed peaceful and serene; but there were horrible moments, as when she suffered convulsions. Friends urged Dr. Hooker to take a rest, but he wouldn't hear of it. He said that although Edith seemed oblivious to his presence, he could not bear to leave her. On one occasion, she did seem to awaken; she smiled broadly at him with wide open eyes before slipping back into unconsciousness. Day after day, as though waiting for that to happen again, he would sit at her bedside as the months turned into years.

Deeply worried about both Spencer and Edith, Kate headed east for the first tryout of *Without Love* at the McCarter Theater in Princeton, New Jersey, on March 4; there followed Wilmington, Baltimore, Washington, Philadelphia, Boston, Hartford, Providence, Cleveland, and four other cities. But her heart wasn't in it.

In the role of Jamie Coe Rowan, Kate wore "hotdiggity" costumes designed by Valentina. She had crimson silk pajamas; a black silk day dress and black straw hat; a white silk day dress and large green straw hat; a pink and black striped evening dress; and an ivory and gray mousseline evening dress. She clutched a black silk bag; a blue silk bag; a white jersey bag; blue flowers; two bunches of violets; and five white orchids. She removed, put on, then removed a pair of white gloves. At moments, she seemed not to know what to do with her hands, although some reviewers wondered whether that might be a deliberate effect. She posed against furniture. She tilted her face. She threw in an impish double-take or two. When all else failed, she tried the old arm-swinging Hope Williams walk.

But every trick in Hepburn's book could hardly conceal the absence of a good play. As the Theater Guild company neared the end of its calamitous tryout tour, Philip Barry was still madly rewriting. He couldn't seem to straighten out the plot lines: one about a platonic marriage of convenience in which the partners finally fall in love; the other about the husband's efforts to reconcile England and Ireland.

The Guild's script doctors recognized the root of the problem in Barry's determination to reinvent himself as a serious dramatist with something important to say to wartime America. The role of political visionary did not suit him. The more Barry rewrote, the more *Without Love* turned into a propaganda play. Lawrence Langner chastised Barry for hurling his political message at theatergoers in a lump, and promised that *Without Love* could be Barry's greatest triumph if only he would emphasize the comedy.

Terry Helburn was less optimistic; on Broadway, she trusted Kate to carry the ramshackle vehicle through the power of her personality. Yet that seemed unlikely, if Kate persisted in her refusal to work with the leading man. By now, Helburn knew why Kate felt such obvious pain on stage with Elliott Nugent: She saw Spencer Tracy in the role of Patrick Jamieson and assumed the audience did too. Nothing Helburn said could convince her otherwise.

George Stevens once said that when things went worst on a production, Kate always knew how to pick up the entire company. According to Stevens, she was better at pep talk and psychology than any football coach. That was hardly the case on *Without Love*. Her distracted state of mind left little doubt that she would prefer to be with Tracy. She remained in the show solely out of loyalty to Barry and the Guild. Yet the prospect of an open-ended run in New York, should *Without Love* score a surprise hit as *The Philadelphia Story* had done, seemed almost too much for her to bear.

In April, Langner was dismayed by press reports that Kate planned to leave at the end of the tour to make another picture with Tracy at MGM. The rumors were accurate. On April 17, Kate told Langner of her decision.

After the critical and box-office success of *Woman of the Year,*

MGM was eager to get Tracy and Hepburn into another film as soon as possible. Also, the studio hoped that Kate's presence might deter the heavy drinking that had begun to interfere with Tracy's work. No matter what film Tracy was working on—good, bad, or indifferent—suddenly he would shoot out of bed one night, convinced it was "a stinker." No matter how enthusiastic he had been at the outset, his sense of doom would overcome him. Now he knew he had made a terrible mistake! This was the picture that was going to end his career! He often disappeared and could not be found for weeks.

Kate was due to begin *Keeper of the Flame* on June 1. Donald Ogden Stewart had written the maudlin melodrama, based on a novel by I. A. R. Wylie. Cukor was to direct. In MGM's view, Cukor's great success in "handling" the notoriously difficult John Barrymore on *A Bill of Divorcement* and other pictures suggested that he might work similar magic with Tracy.

Kate assured Langner that she would return to *Without Love* in September. Langner wasted no time in contacting Philip Barry in Hobe Sound, and urging him to call Kate at once. Mindful of Kate's sense of honor, Langner knew she was likely to keep any promises to this beloved old friend. So did Spencer Tracy.

On Monday, May 11, 1942, the house lights had begun to dim in Pittsburgh's Nixon Theater when Tracy slipped into the back row of the crowded auditorium. About 5 feet 10 inches tall, with massive shoulders, freckles, and a shock of unruly red hair streaked with gray, he seemed eager to escape notice. He wore a dark blue suit, a navy tie, and a crisp white shirt with a low collar for comfort. He slouched in his seat and stuck out a square jaw. As the curtain went up, he inserted a peppermint into his mouth like a coin into a slot machine. He sucked loudly and expressively through the first act of *Without Love*. During intermission, he hid in the box-office anteroom.

Tracy was intent on pressuring Kate to leave *Without Love* for good. He did not want her to return to the play in September. Aiming for a permanent arrangement with her, he planned for her to remain with him in Los Angeles after *Keeper of the Flame*. He saw Philip Barry, who desperately needed Kate in the show, as the enemy, who had to be obliterated at any cost.

When the house lights came on at the end of *Without Love*, Tracy tried to duck out without talking to the press. But when reporters asked how he liked the show, Tracy saw his opening. Throwing out one of his withering stares, he growled in reply, "How do you like Miss Hepburn?"

The stony face, the deeply furrowed brow, the refusal to answer directly said it all.

Before the week was up, the pressure began to show on Kate. She was on her way to her dressing room before the matinee when a photographer snapped her picture. She pounced, clawed his hands, and smashed the camera. A policeman heard the commotion and dashed in to pull the adversaries apart.

The sight of Tracy and Hepburn at close range made people uneasy. On the set of *Keeper of the Flame*, they appeared to exist in a world of their own. To watch them together was to wonder why this fierce, independent woman had so totally subordinated herself to Tracy's will.

She fussed over him incessantly, as if unable to keep still. She combed his hair. She arranged his collar. She wiped his face. She massaged his temples. She made certain he was comfortable and had everything he needed. No detail escaped Kate's attention so long as it concerned Spencer's well-being. There was seemingly no limit to her devotion.

She closely monitored every fluctuation of his chronic melancholy. She was producer, director, wardrobe mistress and makeup lady all rolled into one. She was warm, effusive, and loving. There could be no doubt that she worshiped the man.

When actors and crew gathered to hear Tracy tell stories, Kate sat at the foot of his chair. She pulled her knees up to her chest. She raised her heels and pressed down hard on her toes. She looked up at him with glittering eyes. She seemed to turn into a small child, innocent and vulnerable. She hung on Spencer's every word and laughed loudly in all the right places as though she had never heard anything so marvelous. She treated being near him as a very great privilege and expected everyone else to think the same.

Tracy, for his part, appeared to take Kate for granted. At times, he barely responded to her powerful presence. He showed no gratitude or affection. When he did take notice of her, he treated her as a sort of "backward little girl." She reacted to his abuse with a tight, tense smile that was enough to break one's heart.

John Ford, in love with Kate, wouldn't have changed a single thing about her; as far as Spencer Tracy was concerned, she could do nothing right. He was particularly critical of her speech. According to Tracy, she talked too loudly, too quickly, and too much.

Ford had loved her courage and spirit. He adored her when she was difficult and insisted on doing things her way. Theirs had been a battle of equals. With Tracy, Kate struggled to suppress herself and conform to his wishes—something she would have done for no other man but Dr. Hepburn.

Kate seemed to have found—in the words of her brother Bob— "a reasonable facsimile of Dad." Spencer Tracy shared Dr. Hepburn's bullish strength, but also his inability to praise and his willingness to hurt others. As with her father, Kate was sensitive to the pain beneath Tracy's bluster. Like Dr. Hepburn, Tracy would always have reason to wonder whether he bore responsibility for a son's fate. He believed in his Catholic conscience that Johnny's deafness was punishment for a father's sins. He blamed his own visits to brothels and the venereal infections he had contracted there. (The therapeutic potential of penicillin was not discovered until 1929.) According to Pat O'Brien, when Tracy learned that his ten-month-old son had been deaf since birth, he went on "the first big drunk of his life."

As he would many times through the years, Tracy disappeared to the Hotel St. George on Clark Street in Brooklyn. His only luggage was a case of Irish whiskey. He locked himself in a tiny room and lay in the bathtub for days, struggling to forget.

Yet there was a part of him that wanted to remember his own loathsomeness. Guilt did not cause Spencer to mend his ways. On the contrary, he carried on with greater abandon. Every woman with whom he betrayed his wife seemed to remind him of the one woman who must have caused Johnny's deafness. He put the good, gallant Louise on a pedestal; he never tired of pointing out her selfless devotion to Johnny; he treated her as a martyr doomed to unhappiness with the likes of him. Some said it was Catholicism that kept Tracy married to Louise; others thought guilt. The saintly, long-suffering wife played an important role in Tracy's scenario of self-flagellation. Betraying her, he proclaimed his own degradation.

When he returned to his wife after a very serious affair with Loretta Young, it must have been clear to nearly everyone in Holly-wood but Kate Hepburn that Tracy would never divorce.

From the moment Kate came into his life he cast her in the role of mistress. He lived at the Beverly Hills Hotel, she in John Gilbert's old house on Tower Drive. He visited in the evening and left when he was finished. The arrangement seemed to turn him on. In the mornings, she often drove down to the hotel to play tennis with the pro and have breakfast with Spencer.

He paid regular visits to his wife and children, Johnny and little Susie, at the family ranch in Encino. To all the world, Louise remained Mrs. Spencer Tracy. Publicity director Howard Strickling saw to it that Louise participated in the promotional push when MGM released *Tortilla Flat* in May; and in September, she was much in the press as founder and president of the newly opened John Tracy Clinic for deaf children. Spencer was the clinic's first financial backer.

In the beginning he had said something that always bothered Kate. She repeated it to George Cukor and other friends, as though wondering what it meant. According to Tracy, before he met Kate he had hoped to cast her in a dual role in *Dr. Jekyll and Mr. Hyde*. He wanted Kate to play Jekyll's virginal fiancée, but also the whore Hyde degrades and humiliates.

The idea incensed Cukor. Kate was so pure, innocent, and good, he argued; her standards of behavior were so very high. How could Spencer imagine casting her as a whore? Yet the fact remained that on some level Tracy did see her that way. Full of self-loathing as he was, he seemed to enjoy humiliating Kate by bringing her down to his level; turning a woman of that calibre into his mistress, Tracy reminded himself and others of the moral depths to which he had sunk.

As with her father in the aftermath of Tom's suicide, Kate may have seemed the weaker partner; yet her decision to care for Tracy attested to great inner strength. Once before at a pivotal moment, Kate had tacitly accepted that the man's need was greater. Spencer was weak, Kate was strong; she would try to protect him at whatever cost to herself. As Palache would say, once Kate had made that decision, everything seemed easy; Kate never had to question whose need to put first.

The Brooklyn hotel where Tracy disappeared on his worst binges was a short walk from Adams Street, where Kate's grand-father Fred Houghton used to "feel sick in the night." That proximity, however coincidental, highlights the psychological continuity between Fred Houghton and Spencer Tracy, with Charlie Hough-ton, Charlie Hepburn, Tommy Hepburn, and Sewell Hepburn in between. To outsiders, Kate's relationship with Tracy appeared so strange, intense, and mysterious because it was invested with the pent-up emotions of a larger family drama. That drama had begun with Carrie Houghton's failed attempt to prevent Fred from drifting too close to the edge.

T W E N T Y

Several times Kate changed the telephone number in her rented hilltop house on Tower Drive above the Beverly Hills Hotel. She remained incommunicado all through the summer of 1942.

Friends from New York who passed through Los Angeles were unable to contact her. At this point, they attributed her refusal to answer messages to script trouble on *Keeper of the Flame*. It was no secret that Kate had returned to Hollywood to discover Donald Ogden Stewart encountering the same problem Barry had on *Without Love*: Neither writer could seem to integrate the political and romantic elements of his story. Worse, Stewart appeared unwilling to accept the script's shortcomings; he went so far as to insist to his second wife, Ella Winter, that Kate was upset merely because he had written Tracy the stronger role.

With Kate scheduled to return east in September, the Theater Guild charged ahead with plans to bring *Without Love* to Broadway after two weeks in Detroit. Philip Barry spent the summer rewriting.

On August 12, Kate wired Terry Helburn to say that *Keeper of the Flame* was dragging on longer than anticipated. Cukor had brought in his friend Zoë Akins to see what she could do with the screenplay, and they had finally started shooting in July; even then, the material never seemed quite right to Kate. She urged the Guild to postpone *Without Love* until mid-October.

Helburn sniffed trouble when she discovered that she had no way of reaching Kate at home. "What are you up to that you keep changing your phone number?" she wired. "I will guard your secret if you will send it to me."

Kate never did. Instead, on September 2, she wrote a long, rambling, desperate letter to Langner, Helburn, and Barry. Dick Hepburn might have recognized the voice in that letter; but Langner and Helburn had never heard anything quite like it before, certainly not from Kate.

She begged them not to force her to leave Los Angeles. She insisted that for personal reasons, it would crucify her to be tied up in New York for four months. She threatened to walk out the minute her contract permitted. She warned that she would be frantic and miserable. She confessed she could not keep her mind on work. She implored them to remember that they were supposed to be her friends. She pleaded with them not to destroy her.

The letter left its recipients in shock. Philip Barry was devastated. Terry Helburn wrote many drafts of a reply expressing sympathy for the emotional disturbance Kate seemed to be in, yet reminding her of her duty. In the end, however, Helburn put aside the drafts in frustration.

Kate's refusal to provide a telephone number left one option. Helburn did not ask permission to come to Hollywood; on September 6, she wired Kate that she planned to arrive on Wednesday.

The meeting took place on the evening of September 9 at Helburn's hotel, the Château Elysée. Helburn steadied her nerves with a Scotch and soda. Only four months had passed since she had last met with Kate. Yet the actress seemed a changed person. Helburn found her cold, distant, unreachable. There were none of the usual kisses and hugs.

At first, Kate held herself very tightly in check. Then suddenly she burst out in anger, insisting that she could not honor her commitment to Barry and the Guild despite anything Helburn had come to say. As would happen again many times through the years, the need to suppress herself with Spencer caused her to lash out at others.

Helburn lost patience. Chain-smoking, she waved a cigarette in the air as she lectured Kate on responsibility. She announced that she and Lawrence Langner intended to hold Kate to her Guild contract. She reminded the actress that her MGM contract specified a release date: If the studio failed to honor that date, they would have to pay the Guild to hold the cast an additional two weeks; otherwise, Kate would have to pay.

Helburn pointed out that the Guild had invested a great deal of money in *Without Love*; indeed, the play had been written and produced expressly for Kate. They could not allow her to walk out at the last minute on a whim. She trusted that even Kate would see the logic of all this in a quieter state of mind.

Kate reacted with a screaming fit. She pleaded with Helburn to allow her to remain in Los Angeles. She accused the Guild of trying to ruin her. She threatened to retire from stage and screen if they forced her to come to New York. Then she stormed out.

Helburn had seen enough. She arranged to return to New York in the morning. On the train east, she scribbled a long, furious letter, informing Kate that they would expect her as soon as Cukor was finished. Insisting that she thought of herself as much as a mother as a manager to Kate, Helburn warned her to stop letting her emotions get in the way of business judgment.

Kate finally accepted that she had no choice. She would go east at the last possible moment and remain not a day beyond sixteen weeks.

On November 10, *Without Love* opened at the Saint James Theater on Broadway. Critics hated the show, but to Kate's astonishment audiences seemed to love it, and business was brisk. Yet she complained to Cukor that friends who came backstage rushed quickly to the subject of her Valentina clothes, instead of talking about her performance or the play. Kate took that as a dreadful sign and looked forward to the end of the run on February 13, 1943.

After Terry Helburn discovered that Kate was not leaving to fulfill a film commitment, she engineered a parade of petitioners to implore her to remain. While Kate had no contractual obligation to do so, perhaps Philip Barry and others could make her feel guilty about abandoning a show on which they had all worked so hard, and which meant so much to all of them. The show was making money and would have to close if she left.

It was not easy for Kate to turn down her old friend Philip Barry. But Tracy's looming presence at the River Club helped her to withstand the temptation to say yes. Barry would be the first casualty of Kate's single-minded devotion to Spencer.

"I go crazy," Kate told Cukor, before he too joined the chorus urging her to extend her engagement. Cukor dashed backstage and praised her performance to the skies.

At Helburn's behest, even Dr. Hepburn agreed to have a talk with his daughter—and failed. Kate remained firm in her plan to spend two weeks with the family in West Hartford, then return to the coast. On January 14, Terry Helburn, waxing ironic, wrote to Philip Barry that since Kate's father had been unable to influence her, perhaps the only person left for them to turn to for help was Spencer Tracy.

In those days, guests at the Beverly Hills Hotel were treated to a peculiar spectacle. Late at night, one might see Katharine Hepburn curled up asleep outside Spencer Tracy's door.

Hotel employees knew that meant the actor was on a bender. He locked himself in with a case of Irish whiskey, stripped naked, and drank himself blind. He would permit no one to enter, not even Kate. Still, she lay in the corridor all night in case he wanted her. She listened for the crash of furniture and glass. She did not budge for fear of what he might do to himself.

In 1921, she had failed to sense the danger when her brother, having complained of "the horrors," locked himself in a room at Aunty Towle's; Kate would never make that mistake again.

When it seemed almost too quiet in Tracy's suite, she sought a kindly member of staff who would agree to unlock the door. Often Spencer had barricaded himself in. She would have to dislodge chairs and tables to enter. Frantically she scanned the dark suite. There was no telling where she might find him. Sometimes he lay unconscious in his own filth. But at least he was alive.

She would clean his body and do what she could to soothe him. Then she would resume her post outside the door.

Kate maintained a watchful stance even when Spencer was not on a binge. In the best of circumstances, he almost always had "a buzz on," as he called it. She constructed her life around him. She arranged her work schedule to suit his needs. She drastically reduced her professional commitments in order to make herself available whenever he needed her. She would appear in as few films as possible, preferably with him. She would accept no assignment that interfered with her priority. When projects were offered that would take her away from Spencer, Kate, at thirty-six, insisted the part called for a younger woman.

It was especially difficult to curb Spencer's drinking in the war years. To Robert Sherwood, Tracy confessed great shame at having failed to join the military. At MGM, he was the biggest male star left; James Stewart, Robert Montgomery, Robert Taylor, and Clark Gable were all in uniform. Men much older than Tracy were rushing to sign up. Kate's brothers were both in the service. While his peers were at war, Tracy was much in demand to play soldiers in the movies.

Los Angeles teemed with military men waiting to be shipped out to combat in the Pacific. At the Hollywood Legion Stadium fights, sailors heckled Tracy; they mocked him as a shirker and a coward. The actor remained stone-faced while police removed the servicemen; then, humiliated, he slipped out of the stadium before the main event. His civilian status became a new source of guilt. Tracy, in constant, self-lacerating turmoil, appeared to welcome something new to brood about.

Meanwhile, John Ford performed feats of courage in the Navy. The Hollywood trade papers were full of his heroics. Meta Sterne kept Kate apprised of what he was up to.

In April 1942, Ford was on one of the sixteen North American B-25 medium bombers under the command of Lt. Col. James H. Doolittle, raiding Japanese military installations in retaliation for Pearl Harbor. As they flew over the military installations, Ford, filming the action with a movie camera, kept screaming at his pilot to fly lower.

In June, Ford would be wounded in the Battle of Midway.

Perched atop the wooden control tower of the U.S. Naval Air Station, he photographed the Japanese attack amid a storm of machine-gun fire. Shrapnel wounds in the elbow and shoulder knocked him unconscious, but he awakened after a few minutes and resumed filming. When he visited Mary on his way to Washington, his arm was swathed in bandages.

In Hollywood, Mary Ford became the scourge of all cowards and draft-dodgers. She castigated the miserable curs who remained behind, drinking and "chasing tail" while real men like Jack risked their lives in the war. Seven days a week, Mary's Rolls-Royce was parked outside the Hollywood Canteen, a former livery stable on Cahuenga Boulevard off Sunset. She ran the kitchen with Marlene Dietrich; they served dinner to the GIs in two shifts every night.

Ward Bond and John Wayne were not exempt from Mary's wrath. Citing the blind and lame twenty-year-old soldiers she saw every day at the Hollywood Canteen, Mary chastised Jack's old cronies for self-indulgence. She lambasted Bond for being drunk three-fourths of the time, and Duke for going berserk over Esperanza Bauer, a Mexican call-girl whom he insisted he wanted to marry as soon as he could divorce his wife.

Spencer Tracy came reluctantly when Mary Ford summoned him to the carnival setting of the Canteen. Cackling with malicious delight, she crowned Tracy and Cesar Romero "the handsomest men left in Hollywood" before packing them off to the kitchen to scrub dishes.

In the aftermath of Tommy Hepburn's suicide, Mrs. Hepburn had taught her children the usefulness of hard work and constant activity: "Don't forget your daily chores," Mrs. Hepburn would say. "They are what keep you from going insane." At first, this was the prescription Kate offered Spencer. She wanted him to have little free time to brood. With Kate's encouragement, between the summer of 1943 and the spring of 1944 Tracy made three films to her one. She theorized that like Sean, he was happiest on a film set; it was life that Spencer found difficult.

Kate read and discussed Tracy's scripts. She became a fixture in his dressing room. Yet her dedication seemed to have no impact.

His black moods and heavy drinking continued. There was no honeymoon.

Even at this early stage in their relationship, Spencer did not flinch from humiliating Kate in front of others. During the filming of Fred Zinnemann's *The Seventh Cross*, Tracy was having a drink in his dressing room with his co-star Hume Cronyn. Kate arrived after a day's work on *Dragon Seed*, based on a best-selling novel by Pearl S. Buck. She despised the kitschy superproduction which required her to be made up as a Chinese peasant. She told Lawrence Langner that the longer she remained at MGM, the more soggy-brained she seemed to become. To live at all now, she said, she just tried to survive from day to day; she shut out yesterday and tomorrow for fear of going mad.

Yet she scrupulously concealed her own problems in front of Spencer. When Kate appeared in his dressing room, as she did that day when Hume Cronyn was there, she was the soul of concern for all that ailed her lover.

Tracy, in foul humor, barely took note of her. Cronyn leapt to his feet and introduced himself.

"I hope I'm not interrupting anything—please sit down," said Kate.

As she shook hands with Cronyn, she seemed to study Tracy, gauging his mood. In any situation, that was her top priority.

"How are you doing, old man?" Kate said, full of sympathy and good cheer.

"On my ass."

"Problems?"

Tracy sipped his drink and declined to respond.

"I think I'll get myself a drink," said Kate, who prided herself on her ability to drink Spencer under the table.

"Can I get it for you?" asked Cronyn, rising again.

"She told you to sit down," Tracy barked.

By the time Kate joined them, Tracy appeared to have drifted off into his own thoughts. He pointedly did not participate as Hepburn and Cronyn chatted about *The Seventh Cross*, which Hepburn knew well. Cronyn found her look as firm as her handshake. Her charm and directness greatly impressed him.

Tracy sat in ominous silence until Kate took out a cigarette. Cronyn started to light it for her. That innocent, polite gesture threw Tracy into a fit of rage.

"Why don't you two find a bed somewhere and get it over with?" he exploded.

Cronyn, absolutely motionless, allowed the flame to singe his fingers.

"Sit down, for Christ's sake!" Tracy waved to Cronyn. "You keep bounding around like corn in a popper!"

Kate kept a smile plastered across her face. She took Spencer's abuse without a word of protest. She had become expert at pretending nothing was wrong.

But something was very wrong. Tracy's years of insomnia were beginning to take their toll. He slept at most two or three hours at a time. He spent so much time memorizing scripts that the lines seemed to "boil around" in his head all night. The minute he drifted off, he found himself dreaming lines that seemed "all wrong"; he shot awake, desperate to correct them. He kept a coffee-maker next to his bed and sipped cup after cup through the night. Exhausted by day, he drank more coffee and swallowed quantities of amphetamines. It was hardly surprising that he was constantly on edge, ready to snap.

John Ford returned to a hero's welcome in March 1944. During the fifteen days he was in Hollywood, MGM zealously courted him to make a picture there. Ford insisted that a man had better things to do in wartime; although he could not reveal his mission, he was headed to the south coast of England to oversee photography of the Allied invasion of Normandy.

And what was Tracy doing just then? He played Lt. Col. James H. Doolittle in Mervyn LeRoy's *Thirty Seconds Over Tokyo*, a movie about the daredevil bombing raid in which Ford had actually participated.

Eventually, Kate had to come to terms with the fact that a crowded work schedule had done nothing to improve Spencer's state of mind. He seemed more tormented than ever. In front of most people, Kate affected a cheerful air; but in private, she was frantic to solve the Tracy problem. She would not rest until he was safe.

In October, Tracy and Hepburn began their third project together, a film version of *Without Love*, directed by Howard S. Bucquet. There was considerable irony in Tracy's agreeing to the project after many months of denigrating Barry and his play. But as far as Spencer was concerned, he had forced Kate to choose; and he had won. He no longer saw Barry as the enemy.

Philip Barry, for his part, remained wary. Barry had been devastated, understandably so, when Kate withdrew from *Without Love*, forcing the successful Broadway show to close. And he hated Donald Ogden Stewart's screen adaptation for eliminating every trace of the play's political subject matter.

On the set, Kate used her copy of the script as a desk to write a long, confiding letter to Ellen Barry. She painted a picture of a man teetering perilously close to the edge. She described Tracy as a physical and mental wreck. She chronicled his inability to sleep. She reported his fear that he was about to go insane.

She was determined, she said, to beat the years of exhaustion and sleeplessness that were destroying Spencer, and had a plan to give the actor a year's rest away from MGM. She had been talking to him of Hobe Sound. Would the Barrys provide information about a hotel where Tracy might rent a secluded bungalow? Would it be too much trouble to take photographs? Could they jot down a few words in praise of Hobe Sound? And could they help with a question Kate herself had been unable to answer? Spencer wanted to know what month the insects came.

At one time, Kate would have been the first to see the awkwardness of asking the Barrys to help Spencer Tracy. Tracy, after all, had been responsible for her departure from *Without Love*; he had single-handedly closed down a show which meant a great deal to Philip Barry. By this point, however, Kate seemed oblivious to anyone or anything besides Spencer; her preoccupation with the man and his problems isolated her in ways that she appeared hardly to understand. She approached the Barrys without hesitation, as though it would be the most natural thing in the world for anyone, even them, to want to help rescue Spencer.

Kate had a theory that sooner or later, every artist must refill the reservoir. She believed that most artists have about fifteen years of creative capital. After that, they are likely to dry up unless they seek new ideas and stimulation.

When, as Tracy often did after making a decision, he suddenly changed his mind about taking the year off, Kate suggested that he return to the Broadway stage. Perhaps he had been in Hollywood too long. Perhaps the artistic challenge of an important new play would help him recapture his freshness.

Spencer always said that he wanted to keep life small. Kate encouraged him to open up and take a few risks. As far as she was concerned, that was the only way to live.

In March 1945, Tracy went to New York. Kate set up meetings with Lawrence Langner and Terry Helburn, as well as with the Pulitzer Prize-winning dramatist Robert Sherwood, the author of *Idiot's Delight* and *Abe Lincoln in Illinois*. The forty-eight-year-old Sherwood, a founding member of the Playwrights' Company, was regarded as one of America's finest playwrights. He served as a speechwriter to Franklin Delano Roosevelt and director of the Overseas Branch of the Office of War Information.

Over six and a half feet tall, with hollow cheeks and a delicate mustache, Sherwood cut a poignant and lugubrious figure; Noël Coward called him "a nine-foot tower of gloom." He spoke in a slow, soft, careful manner with many long, painful pauses. Acutely shy, he seemed to dredge up every word from the depths of his soul. He was earnest, intense, and highly principled. Many people found conversation with him excruciating.

When Sherwood spoke of "the ideals and aspirations for which so many men have fought and died," Spencer Tracy was very moved. Like a sinner in the confessional, Tracy poured out his guilt at not having served in the war.

With Kate's encouragement, Tracy had spent two weeks vis-

iting wounded soldiers at hospitals in Hawaii prior to filming
Without Love. He agonized that he should have done much more.
Yet something in his character almost always prevented him from
doing what he knew to be the right thing. He told Sherwood about
one mortifying incident when, scheduled to go abroad to entertain
the troops, he went on a bender instead; his next memory was
waking up in a padded cell in Chicago. Now he had a new anxiety
to churn him up at night: With the war coming to an end, how could
he possibly face the returning soldiers?

Sherwood offered a solution. He was planning a major new
political drama for the Playwrights' Company, entitled *The Rugged
Path*; if all went well, he wanted Tracy to play the role of a disillusioned newspaper editor who goes to war in search of what
America is all about. Perhaps Tracy could atone by using his great
talent to give voice to the dreams of the American fighting man.

Tracy, overwhelmed, declared that he would be highly
honored, but instantly the second thoughts rose up. He wondered
whether he was worthy of that honor. He was a drunk, a screw-up,
and a malefactor; as always, he took perverse pride in boasting of
his failings. In New York, the St. George Hotel beckoned at the
other end of the Brooklyn Bridge.

"You may be making a mistake with me," he warned Sherwood. "I could be good in this thing, all right. But then, who knows?
I could fall off and maybe not show up."

Sherwood, never one to respond quickly, stared long and hard.
Using prolonged silence to great effect, he gave Tracy a bit of his
own medicine.

"Spencer," he said thoughtfully, "all I want for myself is to see
this play played once by you." He counseled Tracy not to dwell on
the prospect of a long Broadway run; he urged him to take it one
day, one performance, at a time.

Tracy returned to Hollywood, convinced he had found sal-
vation at last. Sherwood, with his air of saintliness, was unlike
anyone he had ever met. Yet he continued to brood about his own
unworthiness.

When Lawrence Langner inquired whether Kate would be in

New York in the fall and available to appear in a Guild production, she replied that she might; for the moment, Spencer seemed very excited about *The Rugged Path*. But he dared not consider the part his until the Playwrights' Company officially offered it to him.

On April 12, 1945, Franklin Delano Roosevelt suffered a cerebral hemorrhage at the Little White House in Warm Springs, Georgia, and died two hours later. Tracy, holed up at the Beverly Hills Hotel, became emotional as he listened to Robert Sherwood on the radio, reading a tribute to his friend. He fired off a long telegram to Sherwood. He called the speech touching and beautiful. He declared that there was no writer who could have articulated the feelings of America at this moment better than Sherwood, and that it was now more important than ever that Sherwood complete *The Rugged Path*. Tracy reiterated that any actor chosen to speak Sherwood's words on stage or screen would be a lucky man indeed. Precisely who that actor might be did not matter, only that Sherwood have an opportunity to communicate with as large an audience as possible.

Sherwood did not receive the telegram until after he had returned from the president's funeral in Washington and burial at Hyde Park. In a letter written on April 16, Sherwood vowed to do everything in his power to impart Roosevelt's ideals in the new play, and he promised to keep Tracy informed of his progress.

Convinced that redemption was at hand, Tracy swore off the bottle. When Sherwood finished *The Rugged Path* in June, Tracy loved it. He agreed to start rehearsals in September.

As September approached, Victor Samrock, business manager of the Playwrights' Company, pointed out to Sherwood that Tracy had failed to sign the contract, which included a proviso Tracy demanded: he had the right to leave the production with only two weeks' notice. Sherwood insisted they had nothing to worry about.

The news that Kate planned to follow Spencer to New York led Lawrence Langner to step up his efforts to persuade her to do a play of her own. Elia Kazan was eager to direct her in S. N. Behrman's *Dunnigan's Daughter*. Kate, for her part, leaned more towards

As You Like It. Whichever Kate chose, Langner would be exceedingly enthusiastic.

Before long, however, it became clear to Kate that Spencer would need her full-time help to stay sober. *The Rugged Path* held great personal significance for him. He was eager not to disappoint Robert Sherwood. It was essential to Tracy's self-esteem that he get through the show without incident.

At this point, Spencer was much more important to Kate than her career. Ironically, now it was she who took the year off to play nursemaid. She moved into her house in Turtle Bay. Spencer and his brother Carroll took up residence in the Waldorf Towers on East 50th Street.

"Where's the contract?" Samrock asked Sherwood.

"We've got a deal with Tracy," the playwright replied. "I'm not concerned."

Two days before the first reading, Carroll Tracy called Samrock. "Spencer thinks the deal should be improved," he announced. He went on to explain that Tracy demanded a share of the profits.

"The deal has been agreed upon," Samrock insisted. "Spencer might get a share of the profits in some future deal, but it's not this one."

"In that case you have no contract," said Carroll, hanging up.

Sherwood decided to call Tracy's bluff. At the first rehearsal, which Tracy refused to attend, he explained the situation to the company. Tracy left him with no choice but to postpone the play until the following year when a new leading man could be found.

Word of Sherwood's speech soon got back to Spencer, and he called in a repentant mood. "I'm sorry," he told Sherwood. "I'm going to come to rehearsal."

It was a very bad start to what was to have been a noble project. Tracy's reason for doing *The Rugged Path* certainly had not been the money he could make from it. Yet by raising the issue of money now, he had quickly sabotaged any chance at personal redemption the play might have offered. Sensitive to charges that he had been earning top dollar in Hollywood while his peers were at war, he could not have chosen a better way of proving his detractors right about the sort of man he was. And he seemed oddly intent on punishing the one man who had reached out to help him. True to form, he did everything he could to proclaim his own unworthiness.

Tracy's tormenting fears became obvious at an early rehearsal when he asked Sherwood: "Suppose on opening night there's a polite round of applause as I make my entrance and I wait till it stops, and then I open my mouth to say something and I can't. What happens?"

His moods would change suddenly. One moment he seemed anxious, the next angry and sullen. Tracy was jelly inside, yet his mien was severe and strong. "He'd look at you and you felt as though all your clothes were coming off," recalled Victor Samrock. It was hardly the sort of situation Sherwood, sensitive and idealistic, had expected.

Rehearsals and out-of-town tryouts became an emotional roller-coaster, as Tracy criticized the material he had originally claimed to love. Again and again, the star threatened to walk out.

"We'll iron this out tomorrow, Spence, okay?" said the director Garson Kanin, after a routine quarrel.

"If I'm still here tomorrow," Tracy boomed for all to hear as he left the theater.

When he wasn't threatening to depart, Tracy tortured the management with the possibility that he would hit the bottle. "Vic, you know what will happen to me if I take one drink," he warned Samrock.

Kate went along on the tryout tour. In a characteristic tactic, she stuffed Spencer with chocolates to keep him from drinking.

After the company opened in Providence, Rhode Island, at the end of September, Tracy became violently ill with a high fever and chills. Declaring that his enemies wanted him to skip a performance so they could say he was drunk, Spencer insisted on going on in Washington, D.C. He vomited in the wings between acts. Kate wiped his face with a towel.

Louise Tracy arrived to see *The Rugged Path* in Boston, requiring Kate to keep a low profile. It was also in Boston that Spencer suddenly quit the play, then changed his mind hours later. Sherwood despaired when rumors of Tracy's departure damaged Broadway ticket sales. By the time they reached the Plymouth Theater in November, the playwright was no longer speaking to the actor. Sherwood wasn't angry so much as hurt and depressed.

Before the Broadway premiere on November 10, Kate cleaned Tracy's dressing room. She threw open windows. She dusted and scrubbed. She rearranged furniture. She changed curtains and floor coverings. If Kate hadn't been so easily recognizable, a casual visitor might have mistaken her for the maid.

Several times a week after the show, Tracy, dreading another sleepless night, invited Victor Samrock, along with actors from the play and various cronies and hangers-on, to the Waldorf Towers. There were always more people than chairs. Carroll served tea and sandwiches. Spencer, looking a bit like the Lincoln Memorial, held forth until 3 a.m. Kate sat at his feet. According to Samrock, Kate worked very hard at not being Tracy's equal in a group. Night after night, she declined to join the conversation. She resisted attempts to treat her as a person in her own right. She acted like one of those stagestruck young girls who attach themselves to an important old actor.

Tracy's favorite topics seemed to be the play's shortcomings and the stupidity of the people who came to see it. Concentrating his fire on poor Sherwood, he accused the playwright of "making cracks" about him. It did not improve Tracy's state of mind that the printed program contained a boxed announcement: "*The Rugged Path* employs fourteen World War II veterans."

By and large the critics disliked the play but praised Tracy for his "restrained" performance. *The Rugged Path* might have enjoyed a long run and gone on to a highly successful national tour strictly on the basis of star appeal. But the star had other ideas. Not wanting it to be said that *The Rugged Path* closed because he had walked out, Tracy pursued a devious course. He kept changing his mind about when and if he planned to quit. His leaks to the press created havoc at the box office.

On December 18, Robert Sherwood sent a telegram begging Tracy to remember the spirit in which they had begun. Sherwood declared that he had said not a word against him, praised his magnificent performance and expressed great sadness that their work should end in an atmosphere of recriminations and shabby gossip. Insisting that he understood the actor's problems and still had his best interests at heart, Sherwood implored Tracy to permit the Playwrights' Company to announce that he would remain for one hundred performances. Tracy refused; ticket sales plummeted; and *The Rugged Path* closed on January 19, 1946.

Kate returned to MGM to begin *Undercurrent* for Vincente Minnelli on February 5. Left behind in New York, Tracy went on one of the worst benders of his life. He woke up at Doctors Hospital. Attempts to dry him out were thwarted when a crony snuck in a bottle of booze. After guzzling the contents, Tracy suffered violent trembling and hallucinations.

Eager to hush up the incident, MGM dispatched Whitey Hendry, the studio security chief, who knew Tracy well. In 1937 Hendry had burst into a trashed sixth-floor room at the Beverly Wilshire Hotel, where Spencer, clutching Carroll's throat, was trying to throw his brother out the window. On numerous occasions, the MGM security staff, costumed as paramedics, had strapped Tracy to a stretcher and whisked him away in an ambulance.

At Doctors Hospital in 1946, Whitey Hendry's mission was to hide the MGM star from the public. He ordered Tracy, writhing in a straitjacket on a trolley, rushed to a room on the women's floor.

Kate, in Hollywood, found that John Ford's Navy life had allowed him to refill the reservoir. He returned from the war with a rich stock of images and impressions.

At war, as on a film set, Ford became another man, decisive and full of resolve. He assumed the role of Christian warrior fighting to protect wife, children, and all the other good things back home. To read Ford's wartime letters to Mary is to watch him play that role to the hilt. He dreamed of the war's end when he and "Ma" could live their lives with children and grandchildren gathered around. He praised Mary for showing plenty of guts. He exulted that he was proud as hell of her, and admitted to being tough to live with. Lamenting Hollywood's bad influence, he vowed that Mary was the only woman he had ever really loved; she would know what "Daddy" meant by that.

But he could not keep the mask in place for long after the war. It was one thing to play defender of the family far from home, another to find himself entrenched on Odin Street again. Ford lasted through the series of gala welcome-home parties Mary staged at Christmas 1945. Then, as he had so many times in the past, he sought oblivion. He secluded himself in an upstairs room with a large supply of liquor and a recording of Mexican revolutionary songs. He urinated out the window.

Barbara cared for her father by day. In the evening, John Wayne, in full makeup and costume, would arrive from the RKO studios. "I'll take my turn," Duke would tell Barbara, who was grateful for a few hours off. Upstairs, he found Ford wrapped in a sheet amid a display of empty whiskey bottles. The room was dark.

Ford and Wayne talked softly, the revolutionary songs blasting on the phonograph. Every time the record came to an end, Ford picked up the needle and started it again.

During the war, Mary had waged her own battle to prevent Josie Wayne from divorcing her husband on account of his relationship with a Mexican call-girl. By the time Ford returned from the war, Mary's efforts had failed. The Waynes were divorced. Duke would marry Esperanza Bauer on January 18, 1946. Ford disapproved and said so.

Sitting with him night after night in that dark room, Wayne began to understand the source of Ford's violent resentment of Esperanza. Ford hated the fact that Duke had left his wife when he himself had been unable to leave Mary for Kate Hepburn. Now that he had come home, he seemed to realize his own terrible mistake. But it was too late.

Or was it? That March, Ford reached out. He offered Kate the starring role in *The Ghost and Mrs. Muir*, which he planned to shoot as a last picture for Darryl Zanuck at Fox before starting his own independent production company.

Kate pondered the offer for weeks; but in the end, her commitment to Tracy made it impossible to accept.

That May, Laurence Olivier, Ralph Richardson, and John Burrell brought the Old Vic company to New York for a six-week engagement at the Century Theater, under the auspices of the American producing·organization Theater Incorporated. Night after night every seat and standing-room place was occupied. The repertory included both parts of Shakespeare's *Henry IV*, Chekhov's *Uncle Vanya*, the W. B. Yeats translation of *Oedipus Rex*, and Sheridan's *The Critic*. The last two appeared on a single bill. Olivier called the evening his "biggie". A twenty-minute intermission separated the actor's "titanic interpretation" of Oedipus and his farcical Mr. Puff. Lawrence Langner reported to Spencer Tracy in Hollywood that Olivier's *tour de force* caused theatergoers to go wild with enthusiasm, and offered Tracy a similar chance to demonstrate his versatility.

Intrigued, Tracy and Hepburn invited Langner to dine in Los Angeles. Langner and his wife, Armina Marshall, staying at the Beverly Hills Hotel, drove with Spencer up into the hills to Kate's rented house on Beverly Grove Drive. No alcohol was served. After the Doctors Hospital incident, Kate was frantic to keep Spencer on the wagon.

While Kate pacified Spencer with a double portion of chocolate layer cake and ice cream drenched with sauce, Langner made his pitch. He knew that Kate was restless. She had often complained of growing soggy-brained at MGM, where L. B. Mayer reacted with horror when she asked to do a film of Eugene O'Neill's *Mourning Becomes Electra*. The studio chief indignantly declared that no such picture would ever be made there while he still had "a breath to breathe." Although Kate found his response hilarious, it suggested the sort of attitude with which she had to contend. As she faced a new five-year MGM contract, she longed for fresh challenges and opportunities. If she wanted to make a change, now was the time.

Still, Tracy came first. As the debacle of *Without Love* had proved, a New York season was out of the question so long as he objected.

By this time, Langner understood that if he wanted Kate, Spencer must be part of the deal. He conveyed the Theater Guild's offer to back Tracy and Hepburn in a repertory company of their own, modeled on the Old Vic. He appealed to Tracy's vanity, imploring him to give Olivier some competition. And he played on the actor's nagging sense that he had not lived up to his potential. As Arthur Hopkins had once advised Tracy's idol John Barrymore, Langner urged him not to squander his gifts on mediocre material.

Tracy, able to speak volumes with a glance, was a great film actor; there was no question about that. On screen he was an artist of magnificent silences. But he would always wonder whether he should measure his abilities against another yardstick. He brooded about whether he must prove himself in roles that emphasized the text. The possibility that he had failed to use his gifts to the full became one more thing to chew over in the night.

Tracy wanted to try the great stage roles, yet he feared he would fail. Kate, brought up to be fearless, didn't mind taking risks. When Langner challenged Kate to test her talent, she responded as though Dick or Bob were daring her to do a fancy dive off the Fenwick pier.

Kate was forever pushing Spencer to take the plunge. She was forever conspiring with Langner to arrange a meeting between Tracy and Eugene O'Neill. Expecting, as always, everyone to share her feelings about Spencer, she was certain the playwright would find him fascinating.

Langner begged Kate not to sell herself into slavery for another five years when she could be performing *As You Like It* around the country. Tracy rubbed a heavy, hard-looking hand across the lower part of his ruddy face as Langner urged him not to renew his own studio contract.

Langner promised Tracy and Hepburn that they could "set the country on fire" by reviving "some of that real old-time theater." He proposed a repertory of four or five masterpieces, suggesting O'Neill's *Desire Under the Elms*, Ibsen's *The Master Builder*, and Shaw's *The Devil's Disciple*, among other possibilities. To sweeten the deal, the Guild offered to set up an independent production company, for which Tracy and Hepburn could make one film a year. That way, the couple would spend about twenty-five weeks a year in the theater and twelve on a movie set.

Kate was enthusiastic; but it was up to Spencer. The dynamics of her relationship with Tracy required Kate to insist that she was "quite dumb." Langner and others cringed to hear her say it.

Tracy, for his part, mulled over the Guild proposal for weeks. He assured Langner that he was seriously considering leaving MGM, but said he wanted to discuss it further in September after he and Kate had finished their next picture together, Elia Kazan's *Sea of Grass*.

Before Kazan started shooting, Pandro Berman warned the young director about Tracy: "You've heard the stories. Thank goodness Kate is with him now." But Tracy posed no threat on this picture. Kazan, disappointed by his leading man's lack of athleticism, watched Tracy "squeeze" out of the studio car the first day. Kate had fattened him up considerably. Kazan thought Tracy looked like one of the horses he was supposed to ride in *Sea of Grass,* the story of a cattle baron in the nineteenth-century New Mexico Territory.

Kate insulated Spencer from pressure that might drive him to drink. Concerned solely with keeping him sober, she encouraged him basically to walk through the film. Shrewdly, she made it impossible for Kazan to say a word about Tracy's listless performance. Hardly would he finish a take when Kate's voice resounded through the set: "Wasn't that wonderful? How does he do it? He's so true! He can't do anything false!" Kazan was defeated.

Kate's insistence on shielding Tracy suggested that he was hardly in any condition to face the demands of a repertory season. Nonetheless, she dutifully accompanied him east for a further round of inconclusive talks with Lawrence Langner and Terry Helburn.

But it was another encounter that seemed to shake Tracy to the core, despite Kate's best efforts to protect him. It was witnessed by Mrs. Hepburn's old friend Jo Bennett, who was visiting Fenwick when Kate brought Spencer Tracy to see the waterfront where she had grown up. Unlike Leland Hayward, John Ford, and Howard Hughes, Tracy did not see the old cottage, where Kate had known "paradise" with her aunt Edith and brother Tom; he saw the new Fenwick, the solid and proper vacation home Dr. Hepburn had built with his daughter's money.

Whenever Mrs. Hepburn and Mrs. Bennett got together, they reminisced about the many battles they had fought for women's rights. It was now thirty-five years since they had launched their campaign against prostitution and venereal disease in Hartford. As always, everyone in the family had something to say. The passions were operatic. No one seemed to keep still. Jo's daughter-in-law Thistle Bennett, also visiting at the time, thrilled to the complex choreography of Hepburns flitting in and out, each with his or her own important mission and point of view.

All of Kate's brothers and sisters had married. Dick's union with Elizabeth Ballard ended in divorce. Bob was very happily married to Susanna Floyd. Peg, married to Thomas Perry, and Marion, to Ellsworth Grant, had children of their own. Luddy was no longer on the scene, having finally divorced Kate in an American court and remarried.

Bob Hepburn watched Kate and Spencer. He sensed that Tracy could make neither head nor tail of the nonstop political conversation at Fenwick. Out of his element, he struck Bob as "a lost soul." Tracy, accustomed to have people sit at his feet, soon discovered that that was not going to be the case here.

Dr. and Mrs. Hepburn, Jo Bennett, and the others listened politely as Tracy told a few Hollywood and theatrical anecdotes. But his stories fell flat. No one but Kate seemed to get what he was talking about, or care. Hardly had he finished when Dr. and Mrs. Hepburn rushed back to their subjects. It was a terrible moment.

The Hepburns did not reject Tracy because he was a married man with two children. They did not find fault because he was an abusive alcoholic with a penchant for prostitutes and a history of venereal infection. They did not argue with his conservative views or ask whether he intended to marry their daughter.

Dr. and Mrs. Hepburn turned away because Spencer Tracy had failed to interest them; and in the Hepburn household, that was the greatest sin imaginable.

TWENTY-ONE

As Kate approached forty, she and Alice Palache began to re-evaluate their lives. Both women were involved in intimate relationships with married men who showed no sign of leaving their wives. Both women had begun to grow restless with circumstances they had once accepted unquestioningly.

Since meeting Russell Jones in 1932, Palache had accepted that he did not intend to do anything about an unhappy marriage until his son and daughter were grown up. At the outset, Jones stated his agenda. He made clear that his marriage to an Egyptologist, also named Alice, had been over before he met Palache. He complained that his wife, an invalid, could not participate in the sports and outdoor activities he loved.

Three or four nights a week, Jones visited Palache's Murray Hill apartment. He spent the evening with her, never the whole night. He cooked wonderful dinners in her closet of a kitchen. He advised Palache on her budding career as an investment banker at the Fiduciary Trust Company. They cultivated a small circle of friends who accepted their circumstances.

During World War II, Jones, who had served in the previous war, felt it was his duty to sign up. In the beginning he worked at the Pentagon; Palache traveled to Washington every weekend to see him. Later he was sent overseas.

The war created new opportunities for women on Wall Street. Financial institutions had little choice but to give women employees signing powers and official titles. Fiduciary Trust appointed Palache assistant vice-president, then vice-president.

She remained Rus Jones's mistress when he returned to his wife after the war. In the 1930s, Mrs. Jones had assumed that her husband was involved with several women in New York; by now, however, she was well aware of Palache's existence, and she began to drink heavily. Palache, for her part, started to feel the strain of a long-term relationship with another woman's husband. She wanted marriage, children, a family home.

When Rus suggested that they buy a piece of land together in the area of North Salem, New York, Palache had mixed feelings. She feared the community would not welcome an unmarried couple. Palache had been with Rus since she was twenty-six years old; she realized that had it been another man, she almost certainly would have had a baby. Finally, she confessed her upset. She told Rus that she no longer found their relationship "picturesque," as she put it. For the first time, she pushed him to get a divorce. But when, immediately, he tried to slide around the issue, she told herself that giving an ultimatum was not the best way to deal with the situation.

Palache knew that very early on Kate had decided motherhood would not mix with the demands of an acting career. But Kate did not lack the desire to be a mother; on the contrary, she wanted a child even more than Palache did. Palache knew Kate longed for a home and especially a garden of her own; but she was hardly about to have those things with Spencer. Instead, she lived in various rented houses in Los Angeles; and she treated the Turtle Bay house as though it were a hotel.

The best Kate could do was persuade Spencer finally to leave the Beverly Hills Hotel for his own small, dark, airless flat on South Beverly Drive in Beverly Hills. He also rented a small house on the ocean in Trancas, north of Zuma Canyon; allergic to strong sunlight, he would brood in the dark living room while Kate was on the beach.

Tracy and Hepburn did not go out together in public. Although Hollywood knew of the affair, the MGM publicity machine described them as "staunch friends." The press discreetly avoided the subject. To give their relationship a semblance of normality, Kate planned small Sunday dinners at her house high in the hills. Kate and Em Perkins would cook the meal. The regular guests were Donald Ogden Stewart and his wife, Ella Winter, and sometimes Kate's stand-in Eve March, known as "Murph." It was not unusual for Spencer to arrive direct from a Sunday visit with Mrs. Tracy at the ranch in Encino; his emphatic timing suggested a desire to make clear that Louise was still his wife, Kate his mistress.

Louise Tracy was a constant offstage presence in Kate's life. Louise was no invalid or alcoholic. She maintained a high public profile as founder, president, and director-in-charge of the John Tracy Clinic for deaf or hard-of-hearing children and their parents. She was a beloved figure in the film community. Her name and photograph appeared often in the press. She was a nationally recognized authority on the education of the deaf. She gave frequent newspaper and magazine interviews and lectured throughout the country. Articles inevitably identified her as the actor's wife, and Tracy often participated in publicity and fundraising for the clinic.

It had been easy for Kate to feel anger at Mary Ford. But what was there possibly to say against Louise Tracy? Spencer, indeed everyone, regarded her as a saint.

There can be no doubt that Louise knew about Kate. On at least one occasion, Terry Helburn mistakenly wrote to Tracy at the Encino address, openly alluding to the relationship. As Louise commonly did, she read the letter and passed it on to her husband. Unlike her old friend Mary Ford, however, Louise refused to fight. She took the high road. She appeared to sense that passivity was her strongest weapon.

Whatever Kate may have hoped in the beginning, by the time she approached forty it was evident that Spencer was never going to divorce. Kate wanted a child very badly. Finally she seemed to hit on a solution. She tried to persuade Palache to have Rus Jones's baby. According to Palache, Kate proposed to take the child and care for it as though it were her own. It seemed such a strange offer, yet Kate was obviously extremely serious. When Palache resisted, Kate became desperate, pleading with her friend, "You really ought to have one." She would not let up. Palache, however, refused even to consider a plan she called "reckless."

Kate's curious proposal to Palache expressed the discontent that had begun to gnaw at her. She had spent nearly six years with Spencer, but he had hardly changed at all. She had dedicated herself to diverting him and making him happy, yet he seemed as tormented now as he had been on the day they met. Fiercely protective, she continued to put his needs first at no matter what cost to herself. Yet to a close friend like Palache, there could be no question that Kate had become increasingly uneasy.

A week after Kate turned forty, she committed her first symbolic act of revolt. That May, J. Parnell Thomas, chairman of the House Un-American Activities Committee, took testimony in Hollywood to uncover communist infiltration of the film industry. Thomas announced that "hundreds of very prominent film capital people have been named as communists to us." Kate, enraged, wanted to speak out against censorship and the oppressive political atmosphere in Hollywood; Spencer, whose views were far to the right of hers, thought that show people ought to steer clear of politics.

In open defiance of Tracy, Kate spoke out anyway, ending six years of absolute deference. On May 19, 1947, she was the opening speaker at a mass rally for Progressive Party presidential candidate Henry Wallace, an advocate of social reform and friendship with the USSR, at the Gilmore Stadium in Los Angeles. Instead of wearing her usual costume of coat and trousers, Kate wore a bright red dress as a bold visual statement of where her political sympathies lay; immediately controversial, the costume was a flamboyant theatrical gesture worthy of her mother or Edith.

Kate, visibly excited by the stir her dress caused, used the occasion to attack the HUAC witch hunt. "Today J. Parnell Thomas is engaged in a personally conducted smear campaign of the motion picture industry," she told the crowd of 20,000. "He is aided and abetted in this effort by a group of super-patriots who call themselves the Motion Picture Alliance for the Preservation of American Ideals. For myself, I want no part of their ideals or those of Mr. Thomas. The artist, since the beginning of time, has always expressed the aspirations and dreams of his people. Silence the artist and you have silenced the most articulate voice the people have."

Kate was neither surprised nor repentant afterward when L. B. Mayer read her the riot act. Her speech, widely reported in the press, hurt her career when right-wing pickets warned theatergoers to boycott her new film, Clarence Brown's *Song of Love*. Kate's subsequent claims that she believed nothing would happen to her because, as she said, her family "came over on the *Mayflower*" were nonsense. She was well aware of the acute jeopardy in which her mother's open sympathy with Marxism and the Soviet Union put her. Like those suffragists of her mother's generation who were drawn to peril as an antidote to constraint and stultification at home, Kate thrilled to the danger of speaking out for her beliefs. The speech and its tumultuous aftermath offered a vivid reminder of all she had been missing for the past six years as she lived the "small life" with Spencer.

Tracy recoiled from risks as urgently as Kate longed to take them. When MGM wanted him to go to England to make *Edward, My Son* with George Cukor, he worried desperately about his ability to function in a foreign country. Kate, for her part, was eager for the new experiences that foreign travel would afford. She was like a bird who could not wait to be let out of her cage. At the moment her own film career was virtually at a standstill; there was no picture she particularly wanted to do. Excitedly proposing to accompany Spencer to London, Kate did everything in her power to persuade him to go.

Nervous and neurotic—as Cukor described him—in anticipation of going to England, Tracy suffered from the same fear of change that had afflicted him at the time John Ford brought him from New York to Hollywood. As it happened, once Tracy reached England he liked it so much that, according to Cukor, *Edward, My Son* was the first film in years on which he did not disappear for a drunken binge or some other self-destructive episode.

Kate, accompanied by Em Perkins, traveled to England separately. Planning to be with Spencer most of the time while he worked in London, Kate had also signed up to appear on stage in

The Philadelphia Story in Berlin. (At length the production would be canceled.) As Kate told Philip Barry, after years of being cooped up in Los Angeles it seemed strange to be starting off on an ocean journey.

While she and Em sat on the captain's deck, practicing her old lines in *The Philadelphia Story* made her feel as though she were in a time warp. She wrote to Armina Marshall and Terry Helburn that as she studied the role of Tracy Lord, sometimes she forgot what year it really was. Ten years before, *The Philadelphia Story* had represented a huge comeback for Kate, whose career had been at a nadir. With *Woman of the Year*, she had shrewdly consolidated her triumph. After that, as Lawrence Langner had recognized, she and Tracy should have been able to do almost anything together. But things had not worked out that way. Instead of reaching for new opportunities, she had willingly retreated into the kind of life Tracy demanded.

Reading aloud from *The Philadelphia Story* as she sailed to Europe reminded Kate of a time when everything had seemed possible. Her letters home suggested that she would like to start feeling that way again.

Mrs. Hepburn knew what it was to feel the need for escape. Every so often in her last years, she would suddenly announce plans to take off for a few days in her wood-paneled, pale yellow station wagon. Bob Hepburn and his wife, Sue, fondly called the vehicle the banana wagon. Always the adoring wife to a very demanding man, Mrs. Hepburn needed some time just to herself.

The nightmare of Edith's prolonged illness had been very hard on her sister. Dr. Hooker, under pressure from the hospital, which needed the bed space, consulted with Mrs. Hepburn before moving Edith to the Home for Incurables. Yet until his own death from cancer in 1946, Don never seemed to give up hope that Edith would awaken. As it happened, Edith outlived her husband by two years. She had been in a coma for almost seven years when she died on October 23, 1948.

Mrs. Hepburn still had the perfect posture she had possessed at fourteen. But in the banana wagon, she seemed to sink into the driver's seat. Watching her from a window on Bloomfield Avenue, Sue Hepburn could barely see her head over the top of the wheel as she drove off. "Do you think she's going to get there alive?" Sue would ask.

Mrs. Hepburn's destination was always the same. Forbidden to unburden herself to Dr. Hepburn, she visited Mary Towle in New York. Exactly what they talked about no one ever knew. But the visits always had a wonderful revivifying effect. Several days later, she would come home ready to resume her role as listener whenever a family member had a problem.

According to Bob, in these years Kate talked extensively to their mother about her relationship with Spencer Tracy.

Kate, too, had reached a point where she needed to discover a means of escape. The trip to Europe reminded her that there was a whole world out there even if Spencer, for his part, had no interest in exploring it. More than ever in the months following Edith's death, Kate showed signs of longing for a change. A lack of stimulation had affected her work. Kate hadn't been excited about a film since *Woman of the Year*; and it showed. Spencer preferred sameness; she found it suffocating. He avoided challenges; she thrived on adventure. She craved new ideas and information.

Although she had discussed various projects with the Theater Guild, most particularly a new play Philip Barry hoped to write, Langner had always sensed Kate's unwillingness to leave Tracy alone for extended periods. She feared he would drink; she feared he would destroy himself. Until now, nothing had been able to tear Kate from her post outside Spencer's door.

After Tracy and Hepburn finished filming Frank Capra's political drama *State of the Union*, Lawrence Langner called to say, "Kate, I want to talk to you. Now, where are you going? You are repeating yourself. You can't just travel one road. Take a chance. I want to see you play Rosalind."

In one form or another, Langner had been arguing that since *The Philadelphia Story*. On numerous occasions he had urged Kate to appear in *As You Like It* while she was still young and beautiful and had "the most attractive legs in the United States." He advised her to do it before she woke up one morning to discover that the opportunity had passed her by, and promised that the experience of appearing in Shakespeare would help her grow as an actress. Langner liked to say that he owed his success to persistence; he kept pushing when others would have stopped.

In New York on April 7, 1949, Kate finally agreed to portray Rosalind. Perched on the edge of a chair, she told Langner that she expected to be involved in every aspect of the production; for director she envisioned Tyrone Guthrie, for stage designer Oliver Messel. Now that she had decided, she could hardly wait to start. She hoped to go into rehearsal by mid-October, as soon as she and Tracy finished their next film.

When Langner left the townhouse, she cried out the window to him, "Don't be cheap! We only live once!"

Edith's death seemed to have jolted Kate back to life. She wanted to renew and reinvent herself. That meant sticking her neck out. It wasn't that she was any less dedicated to Tracy, only that the time had come when she needed to refill her reservoir.

She recognized that she was no better prepared to perform Shakespeare than she had been in 1938; back then, Kate had written to Terry Helburn that she had not earned the right to assume that her performance would be worthy of the material. Nor had she felt ready to compete with the ghosts of all the actresses who would have preceded her in a great role. And she did not feel ready yet.

"I wonder if Constance would work with me," Kate said to George Cukor. The flamboyant, sharp-tongued seventy-one-year-old Constance Collier, reputed to be the model for Max Beerbohm's Zuleika Dobson, was one of the *grandes dames* who frequented the Cukor table. She had appeared with Kate in *Stage Door*.

"I never allow myself to dwell on the past, and look very little into the future," Collier insisted in a husky contralto voice. "The world changes; points of view change; values change; and we must not go on clinging to the old and the past. We must go through the present to whatever the future brings us."

She cut a commanding figure. A mass of unruly curls cascaded over a dark Byronic brow. Her enormous black-brown eyes had overlong lashes. The nose was aquiline, the profile classic. A favorite dress was bright red clasped at the neck with a diamond pin. Full of life and ambition, Collier bravely refused to acknowledge the onset of physical decrepitude. There was little feeling in her fingers and she was losing her eyesight. Even so, she was deep in negotiations with the Theater Guild about staging a production of *The Mad-woman of Chaillot*.

Kate admired her nerve. And she recognized Collier as a fund of information. Coquelin had tutored her. Herbert Beerbohm Tree had hired her at His Majesty's Theater, London. She had played all of Shakespeare's great women. Kate treasured a photograph of Collier, strong and defiant with wild hair, as Nancy Sykes in *Oliver Twist*; the younger actress saw in that portrait an image to cultivate in her forties and fifties. She framed the picture and put it on her dressing table.

George Cukor approached Collier, who agreed to tutor Kate in Shakespeare three hours every evening for the next six months.

After Lawrence Langner revealed his personal dislike for Tyrone Guthrie, Terry Helburn brought the young director Michael Benthall, a Guthrie disciple, from London to meet Kate. Tall and powerfully built with a short thick neck, narrow eyes, and a matinée idol's chiseled features, Benthall, still only thirty, had the reputation of an "unrepentant showman." Terry Helburn much admired his *King John* and *The Merchant of Venice*; and Lawrence Langner and Armina Marshall had returned from England with nothing but praise for his staging of Webster's *The White Devil*. There were no promises on either side when Benthall agreed to visit America briefly before beginning rehearsals for *She Stoops to Conquer* at the Old Vic.

Kate strode into the meeting, wearing a white linen trouser suit. Benthall studied her undernourished face, her fine bones. He listened to her nasal voice and high-styled laugh. He was enchanted.

Benthall described his ideas for a production he insisted must be "lyrical" and "romantic." He used those words many times. He evoked the paintings of Watteau. He talked of trees and owl hoots and snowstorms. He wanted constant movement on stage, with every element calculated to set off Hepburn to the best advantage. For designer he proposed James Bailey, who had worked with him on a Victorian *Hamlet* the year before at the Stratford-on-Avon Memorial Theater. Knowing Kate's original preference, Benthall placed Bailey's talent somewhere between Oliver Messel and the late Rex Whistler.

Terry Helburn, now that she had brought Benthall to America, wondered whether she had made a mistake. She fretted that his concepts might be "a little too delicate and fancy" for the "direct and forthright" leading lady. Langner reminded Benthall that the Guild wanted to keep the production light for the tour. But it was too late. Kate championed Benthall in every dispute.

There was considerable awkwardness when George Cukor, knowing of Kate's plans, decided that he must direct *As You Like It*. In the past, he had told Constance Collier that Kate would make a splendid Rosalind because of that quality he called "garçonne." According to Cukor, too much femininity in the actress playing Rosalind makes it hard to understand why she should suddenly put on men's clothing. Kate, on the contrary, was precisely the sort of "high-spirited and quasi-arrogant girl" for whom the decision to dress as a boy would be but a "quarter-step." At a moment when Cukor was scheduled to direct the next Tracy–Hepburn vehicle, his offer to stage *As You Like It* posed a problem for Kate. She was immensely fond of Cukor; but the whole point of *As You Like It* was to escape Hollywood, not bring it with her!

Terry Helburn let Cukor down gently. She waited until June 2, during the first week of filming on *Adam's Rib*, to tell him of the Guild's decision.

Adam's Rib, the best Tracy and Hepburn film since *Woman of the Year*, was made in the afterglow of Kate's decision to seek new opportunities away from Spencer. Her mind made up, Kate was confident and eager; she felt good about herself. She could afford to relax in front of the camera. After hours, she explored Shakespeare with Constance Collier. The challenge seemed to renew her. She was no longer just going through the motions; people sensed she was "on" again.

Kate's excitement electrified her performance as Amanda Bonner, a lawyer who takes on the case of a downtrodden woman accused of shooting her unfaithful husband. Amanda's courtroom adversary is her own spouse, prosecutor Adam Bonner. Amanda turns the case into a referendum on equal rights by insisting that jurors would sympathize with the shooting were her client a man who found his wife in another man's arms.

Although *Adam's Rib* lacked the visual gags and beautiful, poignant, often sexy silent moments that had distinguished *Woman of the Year*, the Ruth Gordon–Garson Kanin screenplay used the same narrative formula: A superior, independent woman gets her comeuppance at the hands of a down-to-earth man.

Both films explicitly link the Hepburn character to the women's rights movement. *Woman of the Year* shows Tess Harding speaking on the legacy of the suffrage fight to an audience of activist women that might have included Mrs. Hepburn and Mrs. Hooker. And Amanda Bonner harps on the equal rights theme throughout *Adam's Rib*. In court, Amanda uses a tactic Mrs. Hepburn had employed in 1915 when she brought a contingent of working women to testify for women's rights at the state legislature. Implicit in the comic logic of both stories is the necessity of undermining the Hepburn character's principles; the solid, tradition-minded husband restores order by showing her the error of her ways. No wonder Mrs. Hepburn continued to look askance at her daughter's movie career; films like *Woman of the Year* and *Adam's Rib* called into question much of what she believed and had worked for.

After the film, Tracy spent a holiday with Kate in New York. He returned to Hollywood before Michael Benthall arrived to begin rehearsals on November 14.

The friendship between director and leading lady grew particularly intense. Even a strong personality like Benthall's companion, Robert Helpmann, felt painfully excluded. The ballet dancer and actor, one of the great protean talents of his generation, felt as though he were "on the outside, looking in." There was tension whenever the three were together. Helpmann, initially ill at ease with Kate, perceived she felt the same about him. To make matters worse, *As You Like It* was the first Michael Benthall production in which Helpmann, ten years his senior, had no involvement.

And there was tension between Kate and the Guild. Even before the show embarked on a brief tryout tour, Lawrence Langner and Terry Helburn struggled to suppress their own resentment over Benthall. He and James Bailey seemed to have cast a spell on Kate. Eager to absorb their sophisticated visual taste, she took their side on everything, down to the look of the deluxe souvenir program about which Benthall quarreled fiercely with the Guild. Langner ordered costs kept down; Benthall insisted on a production in which each element contributed to a single powerful visual impact, expense be damned. To pacify Langner, Kate volunteered to do the first twelve weeks on straight salary without her usual percentage of the gross weekly box office.

The show's ornateness proved its critical downfall when *As You Like It* opened at the Cort Theater in New York on January 26, 1950. It was compared to a brilliantly colored picture postcard, in which stylish scenery and costumes suffocated the play. Kate, in the words of Constance Collier, "charged onstage like a firehorse." Long and leggy in a pair of tights, she delighted fans and exasperated critics. "For much of the time she reads her lines with a strident insistency that becomes uncomfortable for the spectator," groaned Howard Barnes in the *New York Herald Tribune*.

"There is too much Yankee in Miss Hepburn for Shakespeare's glades and lyric fancies," sneered Brooks Atkinson in the *Times*. Returning in the Sunday edition to hurl a second inkpot, the critic discovered "more showmanship than acting" in Michael Benthall's "marshmallow contrivance."

Kate refused to read Atkinson; she asked Terry Helburn to send her mother Richard Watts, Jr.'s review in the *New York Post*: "As a long-time admirer of this frank and courageous young woman, I was proud of her last night."

Still, *As You Like It* was popular, and ran until June when Kate returned to Los Angeles to spend the summer with Spencer. She was due back in New York on September 5 to rehearse for the national tour. Dick Hepburn, who had served as assistant stage manager on Broadway, was hired to play Sir Oliver Martext on the road.

George Cukor was just then hatching a plan to build three income-producing cottages in the lower garden of his property, just above Sunset Boulevard. The heavily planted grounds, which included a grape arbor and a semi-circular rose garden arranged in pie-shaped wedges, hovered over the city. Situated downhill at the end of a wide walk with large orange trees on either side, the cottages would be secluded enough to preserve Cukor's privacy as well as that of his tenants. Kate seized the opportunity to propose that Spencer take up residence in one of the cottages on St. Ives Drive.

Kate's proposal had numerous advantages, not least of which was placing Spencer under Cukor's watchful eye. Despite studio-inspired stories that Tracy had stopped drinking entirely, Kate could harbor no such illusions. He often went off the wagon, and when he did Cukor would be nearby to look out for him in her absence.

That was asking a great deal of Cukor. But the director knew perfectly well what he was getting into. Cukor's willingness to babysit Tracy demonstrated his own intense loyalty to Kate. Only eight years older than Kate, Cukor acted the role of an indulgent uncle eager to do anything for the magical child who is his pride and joy. Even when she was well into middle age, Cukor reported her bright sayings and doings to their mutual friend Irene Selznick in a manner that made Kate sound like a precocious little girl.

Tracy was to occupy the cottage alone. Indeed, the plan seems to have been Kate's way of coping with Spencer's refusal to live with her. If they could not share the home and garden she dreamed of, perhaps they could be children together in Cukor's extended family. That was about as close as Tracy would allow her to get.

Spencer agreed to move to the cottage, which would be completed in the fall of 1951. He warned that Cukor must respect his privacy; no one was to enter without Tracy's permission, not even Kate. A wavy red brick wall at the rear would provide further seclusion.

That something had changed between Tracy and Hepburn

became clear as Kate lined up projects which would keep her away from Los Angeles much of the time. For now, devoted to Spencer as she remained, Kate made clear that she would not be drawn back into the claustrophobic "small life" he preferred. Kate began her national tour on September 22 in Hershey, Pennsylvania. Before the company arrived in Los Angeles for three weeks at the Biltmore Theater in December, she had agreed to go to Scotland and England the following summer to perform Shaw's *The Millionairess* under Michael Benthall's direction.

The *As You Like It* tour would end in March, giving Kate the possibility of several months with Spencer between assignments. As though she dreaded pausing even for that brief interlude, Kate signed a contract with independent producer Sam Spiegel to appear in John Huston's *The African Queen*. John Ford had had an option on the C.S. Forester novel in 1941, but had been unable to hold the rights until the end of the war, when he hoped to make the picture.

Tracy signaled that he and Kate were heading in opposite directions; shortly after she decided to go to Africa, he announced plans to extend his MGM contract for another three years.

Mrs. Hepburn, aged seventy-three, was in poor health when she traveled to Buffalo, New York, to see Kate in the final performances of *As You Like It*. Never one to groan, she hated any mention of her heart condition. Her childhood in the Buffalo area was another topic she preferred to avoid. Fifty-nine years before, her mother, Carrie Houghton, had proclaimed herself a survivor, refusing to allow Fred to drag her into darkness. Carrie set inflexibly high standards for her children; she encouraged the girls to grow and learn so that they might become strong and independent. She taught her daughters always to try, and to be willing to risk failure. That was what Mrs. Hepburn's own daughter seemed to be doing right now.

Appearing in Shakespeare, and having recently agreed to do Shaw, Kate seemed to justify Mrs. Hepburn's early support of her desire to become an actress. After years of tension over the direction Kate's career had taken when she went to Hollywood, Mrs. Hepburn's trip to Buffalo marked a time of healing and mutual acceptance. Kate, at forty-three, was finally realizing her mother's dreams for her.

After the play closed, mother and daughter returned to West Hartford, where the entire family gathered for dinner on Friday, March 17, 1951. On Saturday morning Dr. Hepburn went to work, leaving Kate alone with her mother.

In those years, Mrs. Hepburn liked to take her morning meal, usually a fried egg and a pot of tea, at a small three-legged table beside the fireplace in the dining room. It was one of many spaces in the household she had made distinctly her own. Seated bolt upright, she would study the *New York Times*, as she said, to start her mind going. Everyone else's breakfast was served at the large dining table. One approached "Mum" at one's peril.

At 8:30, Kate joined her mother near the crackling fire. Mrs. Hepburn always kept a collection of newspaper cuttings within reach. Her reading interrupted, she would use the cuttings to stimulate discussion of world events. This morning, however, she produced a scrapbook of a very different nature.

To Kate's astonishment and delight, Mrs. Hepburn had assembled a collection of *As You Like It* reviews. There were pans and raves and all possible shadings between; Mrs. Hepburn had kept everything. She certainly had never done anything like that before. For years, the mother had shown scant concern for her daughter's film career; it was tacitly accepted in the family that Kate's subjects were not Mrs. Hepburn's. But now, Kate and her mother sat for hours, reading the reviews aloud; they laughed at the opinions good and bad. When Dr. Hepburn arrived at 1 p.m., he was amazed to discover them still sitting there, reveling in each other's company.

Kate enjoyed a boisterous lunch with her parents. She and her mother took turns teasing Dr. Hepburn about his tendency to lay down the law. After lunch, father and daughter decided to drive to Fenwick while Mrs. Hepburn took her afternoon nap. They planned to return by teatime.

Anyone who entered the Hepburn house at 5 o'clock on a wintry afternoon would be likely to see Mrs. Hepburn reading a book and sipping tea beside the fire. That day, when Kate and Dr.

Hepburn returned from Fenwick at about 5:30, they found the tea set waiting where the maid had put it, but no sign of Mrs. Hepburn.

The doctor assumed she had overslept; or perhaps she had become engrossed in one of her Russian history books and forgotten the time. He called; she did not answer. According to Kate's letter to Margaret Sanger written ten days later, Dr. Hepburn went upstairs alone to find her.

"Oh no—no," he gasped when he opened the door.

Kate rushed up the curved staircase, then down the hall, to her parents' room. As she had done thirty years before, she acted instinctively to shield her father.

"Go down, Daddy. Go down—don't look—"

For the second time that day, Dr. Hepburn left Kate alone with her mother.

Lying in bed with her eyes closed, Mrs. Hepburn was not wearing the soft wooly robe she always wore for her nap. Her hair was partly done up. Her skin was still warm. Her fingers clutched the sheet with which she had been trying to cover herself when she suffered a cerebral hemorrhage and died.

Eager to spare Dr. Hepburn any inkling of his wife's pain, Kate unclasped the fingers and straightened the sheet. All sign of struggle vanished. Kate kissed her mother and went downstairs to fetch Dr. Hepburn.

Once again a pact of silence formed between father and daughter. Kate had erased details of the death scene to make it easier for Dr. Hepburn to cope with. Although he had glimpsed that hand struggling with the sheet, by the time Kate led him back in his wife appeared totally at peace.

He inspected the dressing room. He noted Mrs. Hepburn's robe in her closet next to the door. He found several hairpins on her dressing table. He could tell that the bathtub had been used. He declared that Mrs. Hepburn must have been fixing her hair before teatime when she suddenly felt dizzy and returned to bed.

Life with Dr. Hepburn had left her always to suffer alone; it would be no different in death. He pictured her smiling sweetly as she closed her eyes, and insisted that she looked too relaxed to have suffered. He assured Kate that her mother could not have known what was happening.

Three days later, Mrs. Hepburn was cremated in Springfield, Massachusetts, for burial beside her son.

Soon after his mother died, Bob Hepburn visited the family house to discover his father in the process of discarding Mrs. Hepburn's books, papers, and files.

"What are you doing?" Bob asked in dismay.

"I'm throwing away all of this socialist junk," Dr. Hepburn replied.

He methodically destroyed every trace he could find of Mrs. Hepburn's activity in the suffrage and birth control movements. He tossed out decades of women's history. Insisting that it was essential to be "objective about death," seventy-one-year-old Dr. Hepburn declared that the time had come to clean house and start afresh.

"What is past is past."

TWENTY-TWO

Kate's life with her family had always been a world apart from Spencer, and so it remained after her mother's death. He did not attend Mrs. Hepburn's funeral. About to begin *The People Against O'Hara*, the first picture under his new MGM contract, Spencer excused himself from coming east.

Kate permitted herself no time to mourn; as always, to avoid acknowledging her own pain, she plunged into any and all available activity.

Hardly had she buried her mother, and done her best to settle her father into a life alone, when she sailed to England in April. Pre-production work on *The African Queen* would occupy several weeks in London. There she would plunge into a world of strangers who knew little or nothing of her loss, and nothing of the state of mind she was in. Constance Collier, who accompanied Kate to London, did know the intensity of Kate's relationship with Mrs. Hepburn. Collier worried that Kate was taking things much too fast; sooner or later, the impact of Mrs. Hepburn's death was bound to catch up with her.

According to Collier, Kate always had a hard time admitting openly that anything was wrong; her instinct was to take care of other people, as she had just done with her father. On the boat to England with Collier, Kate assumed her usual pose of being perfectly all right. But it was evident that Kate was far from all right. As her letters to Terry Helburn attest, Collier recognized the degree of her friend's emotional turmoil long before Kate did herself. At this point, if Kate worried about anyone besides Dr. Hepburn, it was Spencer Tracy.

In London, Kate had her first sustained contact with John Huston and Humphrey Bogart. Neither man had any way of knowing that Hepburn was not behaving like herself. Neither had reason to suspect that it was out of character for Kate to spend a day in bed groaning about "the curse," as she did on arrival. Huston and Bogart assumed that she must always be like this: prickly, defensive, and irritable. She was critical of everything.

And everything seemed to upset her, not least John Huston's elusive, enigmatic character. His refusal to discuss the script or take a proper interest in her costumes exasperated her.

Much later, in a calmer state of mind, Kate would recognize that like John Ford, Huston was a director who preferred to take his time. He was not to be rushed. He could be maddeningly mysterious, but so could Ford. People who had worked with Ford often noted a similarity of manner in Huston. Huston's intuitive working method, his acute sensitivity to moods, people, and places, was precisely the sort of approach Kate would have instantly responded to under ordinary circumstances.

But these were no ordinary circumstances. Perhaps because Huston was very much Kate's type, she seemed to expect him to sense her pain, to connect with her immediately as Sean would have done. At the moment, however, Huston appeared to have no idea why Kate was reacting so strongly against him.

In Hartford she had received the director's message of condolence; yet in London he said not a word about her mother, leading Kate to believe that an assistant had sent the message. Perhaps Huston had already forgotten; perhaps he had never known.

It was typical of Kate's relationship with Tracy that she expressed no anger when he failed to fly east to comfort her after her mother died. That she held Huston to a very different standard, demanding the sympathy and comprehension she failed to get from Spencer, suggests that she had displaced a good deal of her suppressed anger onto the director. With Huston, Kate resented the very behavior she routinely tolerated in Spencer. She discussed her resentment with Constance Collier: It galled her that in Huston's presence, everyone was expected to focus attention on him as though on a small child. It galled her that everything always depended on his moods and whims.

"Would he come?" she complained. "Would he keep concentrating? Others were expected to be the solid rock on which he built." Had Kate set out to describe life with Tracy, she might have uttered those very words. Not surprisingly, Kate's dealings with Huston in London reminded her of "the last desperate moments of an extremely unsatisfactory love affair."

Huston went on ahead to Africa, leaving Hepburn, Bogart, and other company members to assemble in Rome for their own flight to Africa. That gave Kate an opportunity to spend a week or so with Spencer; he had promised to join her in Rome as soon as he finished his new film.

Tracy and Hepburn had been much apart recently, but this separation would be different. While Kate was in England, they remained connected by telephone, Spencer's favorite means of communication. On location in Africa, however, regular phone contact was ruled out. That was a big blow to Spencer, who had grown accustomed to his lifeline to Kate.

But it would be just as difficult for Kate. No matter where she might be, she liked to be able to check up on him. Kate may have temporarily abandoned her post in front of Tracy's door; but she was still there in spirit, acutely sensitive to all that might happen to him.

Tracy, who feared flying, was scheduled to arrive in Italy by ship. For ten years, Kate had showered him with tenderness and concern. She had put his problems first. Their week in Rome gave Spencer a chance to return the favor; it was his turn to comfort her for a change. As Constance Collier, who remained behind in London, saw all too clearly, for once it was Kate who desperately needed to be cared for.

Kate, excited at the prospect of seeing Spencer, arrived first. She stayed with the American sculptor Frances Rich, a friend of John Ford. Daughter of the film actress Irene Rich, Fran had studied with Malvina Hoffman, another of the intellectual women whose friendship Ford cultivated through the years. In Paris in the 1930s, Rich had carved in stone and studied fresco painting. When Kate visited Rome in 1951, she was working in bronze. Attracted to liturgical art, she characterized her own religious sense as "slightly pagan."

Two days with Fran seemed to work wonders on Kate. The women toured Rome by moonlight, went on picnics, talked, and saw the sights. Indeed, by the time they headed to the boat to collect Spencer, Kate's mood had started to lift.

The improvement did not last long. A forthright, rough-and-ready character in the Ford manner, Rich drove a nondescript Fiat station wagon. As Tracy stepped off the boat in Naples and glimpsed the little Fiat, his first words were a withering, "What's that?"

It was the first time he had seen Kate since her mother died. Part of the problem may have been that Fran Rich was Ford's friend; the Fiat was the sort of modest vehicle Ford preferred as a statement that he didn't need big flashy cars.

Spencer's comment, spoken with a dash of contempt, persuaded Kate instantly to change plans. That was how it always was between them; it would be no different this time. Tracy, Hepburn, and Rich piled into the limousine MGM had sent for its star. An arrangement was made to have someone drive the Fiat into Rome behind them.

In the days that followed, Kate stayed on in Rich's apartment; Tracy registered at the Grand Hotel, alone. If he recognized how emotionally fragile Kate was just then, he gave no sign, or perhaps he simply didn't care. She quickly fell into the habits of a decade. Her pleasure came from seeing him pleased. She catered to his every mood and whim. Once Spencer was firmly in charge, he did seem to enjoy himself in Rome—up to a point.

Though he was scheduled to remain until Kate flew to Africa, he suddenly announced plans to decamp for London a day early. Kate believed that he was having a wonderful time seeing Rome, yet before she knew what had hit her he was gone. He gave no reason for his abrupt departure.

"Did he leave because he was bored," Kate later asked, "or did he leave because he couldn't bear to say goodbye?" As always, it was being left with questions that seemed to disturb her most.

Her pent-up rage came to a boil when she got off the airplane in Stanleyville, the Belgian Congo, to learn that an hour before, Huston had left for the location in Biondo, in order to oversee the construction of bungalows out of bamboo and palm leaves from the surrounding bush. The native crew was to cut trenches around the compound which would be filled with kerosene; the trenches could be quickly ignited should deadly soldier ants attack.

If Hepburn's reaction seemed out of proportion to the news that triggered it, that was because her fury was probably a delayed reaction to Tracy. Unable to express resentment against Spencer for his abrupt departure, she transferred her turbulent feelings of hurt and perplexity to Huston for his. When she exploded angrily at the director on finally catching up with him in Biondo, he can have had no idea of what all the fuss was about.

The outburst appeared to relieve Kate. As the days passed, Huston emerged from under Tracy's shadow. Kate viewed her director in a new light; she liked what she saw. Interested in books, art, politics, and sport, Huston had an appetite for life to match her own. Kate belatedly recognized that Huston was precisely the man to help her refill the reservoir. She recognized that as a director, he had much to teach her.

They hunted together in the tall grass, and the experience permitted Huston to perceive Kate's essential fearlessness: a quality that director and actress would emphasize in their portrait of Rosie Sayer, sister of an English missionary in Africa.

When Kate became violently ill after drinking contaminated water, Huston took the role she usually played; he came to her cabin late at night to care for her. Powerful hands gently massaged her back, head, neck, hands, and feet.

"Just stay asleep, Katie dear," Huston murmured. "Stay asleep. Asleep—asleep."

Brought up never to moan, Kate luxuriated in this rare opportunity to have a strong man comfort her. With Dr. Hepburn and Tracy, it was always the other way around. No wonder Kate rhapsodized about the total separation from reality she felt in Africa.

The personal and spiritual bond Huston forged with Kate allowed her to give her richest and most multi-faceted performance. He saw her whole. He comprehended Kate's fierceness and indomitability, but also the childlike innocence at the heart of her appeal. Huston managed to capture that amazing combination on camera.

As always in her best performances, the beauty is in the details. It was Kate's oddity of gesture that first caught George Cukor's eye when she lowered a glass to the floor in her 1932 screen test. Nineteen years later, at the peak of her powers, she was still performing small, simple actions in unexpected ways that called attention to themselves. She moved with a dancer's intelligence.

In *The African Queen*, when Hepburn picks up a milk pitcher, instead of grasping the handle as most people would do, she gracefully cradles the jug with both hands. When she lifts a suitcase, she does not clutch the handle palm down; she inserts her hand palm up and pulls the suitcase toward her. When she reaches for a brown mug, she ignores the handle altogether, cupping long, slim fingers over the top.

Hepburn knows how to abort a gesture for effect, as when she reaches out to comfort her brother (played by Robert Morley), whom a German soldier has hit with a gun; she stops at the last moment, seeming to caress the air instead of his bloody face.

And she knows how to carry a long, virtually wordless scene, holding the eye as she communicates thought and emotion with the virtuosity of a silent film actress. In one impeccably choreographed long take, Rosie has just led her badly disoriented brother to his room, where he insists he wants to be alone. She pulls the door shut, looks toward the camera, then back at the door.

There follows an agonizing dance of uncertainty. Terrified of what is going on inside, she is drawn to re-enter. About to open the door, she cuts short the gesture, pauses, then moves away, hands tensely clasped in front of her. Again she looks at the door, then away. Her hands dart below frame, nervously fingering her belt. Her lower lip trembles. Her right hand starts to touch her face but abruptly pulls back.

Rosie senses that something is about to happen but has no idea what to do about it. Only when she hears her brother collapse does she throw open the door and gather him up in her arms. "Brother! Brother, dear!" she cries, but it is too late.

One can easily see why the character of Rosie Sayer so powerfully appealed to Kate. Rosie possesses many of the qualities she admired. Like Kate, Rosie reacts to tragedy by getting stronger; her response to a brother's death is to embrace life. Instead of allowing misfortune to crush her, she becomes more urgently alive.

And there is a good deal of Mrs. Hepburn in Kate's Rosie. Kate would always marvel at her mother's ability to keep her eye on the goal, whether in combat with Amory Houghton, Jr. or with opponents of women's suffrage and birth control. As Kate saw her, Mrs. Hepburn never took personally anything opponents said or did against her; she focused her energies squarely on the objective, whether getting the Houghton girls into Bryn Mawr or a bill through Congress.

In *The African Queen*, when a drunken Mr. Alnutt (Humphrey Bogart) hurts Rosie's feelings by calling her a psalm-singing skinny old maid, we see her pain but also her determination to resist being mired in that pain. Rosie's sole concern is to force Alnutt to go through with her plan of blowing up the German ship; she makes clear that nothing else matters.

Playing Rosie provided Kate with an opportunity to show a woman's excitement in the face of danger; that excitement is key to Hepburn's character, and to the character of suffragists like her mother and Mrs. Hooker, who shocked and bewildered men with their eagerness to plunge headlong into peril to get what they wanted.

Huston captures that excitement in the scene after Rosie and Alnutt have gone down the rapids together for the first time. Alnutt assumes that the terrifying experience will short-circuit Rosie's determination; and so perhaps do we as we watch Rosie, seemingly in a state of shock, pat the sweat off her face with the back of her hand. Like Alnutt, we may think the ordeal has been too much for her. But then the prim old maid is transformed before our eyes.

Kate's expressive blue eyes light up; she flashes enormous white teeth; her gaunt face literally glows. Rosie isn't sweating from fear or exhaustion, we learn, but from stimulation. The adventure thrilled her! Instead of discouraging Rosie, this first encounter with life-threatening danger hurls her relentlessly forward. She feels exhilarated. There will be no stopping her now!

The scene is quintessential Kate, as is a later scene where Huston highlights a very different side of Rosie's personality. Awed by her strength and determination, now we glimpse her girlishness. The moment comes soon after Alnutt kisses Rosie for the first time. As she adoringly brings his tea in the morning, Rosie realizes that she knows her beloved only as Mr. Alnutt.

"Dear, what is your first name?" Rosie hesitantly inquires.

Rosie, told that his name is Charlie, becomes a blushing, giggly girl. She repeats his name over and over with unabashed delight. Acted by another forty-four-year-old actress the moment might misfire, coming off as coy and ridiculous. With Kate it is irresistible. Watching Hepburn in this scene, one realizes that when John Ford and others spoke of her capacity in life suddenly to turn into a little girl, innocent and enchanting, this is what they meant.

A large part of Huston's achievement in *The African Queen* is to have caught Kate Hepburn in all of her magnificent complexity. The film, more than any other, is responsible for the enduring power of the Hepburn image. This is how we think of Kate: a strong, life-loving, indomitable woman, graced with vulnerability and a child's sense of wonder.

By the time Huston and company were ready to leave Africa on July 17 to finish filming in England, Kate, suffering from dysentery, had lost twenty pounds. She carried an ebony walking stick she had ordered carved as a gift for Dr. Hepburn. She arrived in London to learn of her father's marriage three days before.

Kate had been away for nearly five months when she returned to New York on September 22. As soon as she arrived she drove to West Hartford to see Dr. Hepburn. For years "my father's house" had provided a refuge, but that was hardly the case now. She entered Bloomfield Avenue to find her entire world turned upside down.

All traces of her mother's work and intellectual life had vanished. The books, the files, the correspondence, all had been tossed out as though to erase the contaminating presence of everything Mrs. Hepburn had worked for and believed in. An air of frenzy lingered in the house.

Dr. Hepburn had been in a great rush to tie the knot before Kate returned from Africa.

Madeline Santa Croce had been one of Dr. Hepburn's surgical nurses. He had met "Santa" years before when her father was a patient in his care. Watching her plump the old man's pillow, Dr. Hepburn had remarked that she would make a good nurse. When Santa, a worker in a rug factory in Thompsonville, explained that she had only an eighth-grade education, the handsome surgeon suddenly offered to pay her way through high school. From then on, Santa made no secret of her passionate devotion to Dr. Hepburn. "I look upon your father as a god," she once told Bob. "I worship him!"

Dr. Hepburn prized Santa's domestic abilities. She could cook. She could clean. She could take care of the garden. She could grow and can vegetables. She could darn socks and sew curtains. Marrying Santa allowed him to fire the maid and other household helpers.

Dr. Hepburn had spent a lifetime with a woman who had strong opinions of her own; the new Mrs. Hepburn agreed with everything he said. Although Santa was fifty years old, he regarded her as a *tabula rasa*. With immense relish, he began at once to fill her head with his own thoughts and views. She loved to parrot him. At the dinner table, Dr. Hepburn would produce a book after the meal. He read aloud while his bride listened adoringly. Later, he would encourage Santa to read to him. The scene suggested a travesty of countless evenings the children had spent listening to their parents read aloud from Shakespeare and Shaw.

According to Bob Hepburn, his sister Marion never forgave Dr. Hepburn for marrying beneath him and bringing Santa into their mother's house. Bob, for his part, wondered about the wisdom of the match. Kate, never one to question Dad, insisted that he must have married Santa to spare his children the chore of caring for him as he grew old.

The rear of the cottage that George Cukor built for Spencer Tracy gave out onto a small enclosed patio and manicured garden. Kate, appalled by the perpetual darkness of Spencer's tiny apartment on South Beverly Drive, asked Cukor to install floor-to-ceiling windows to permit sunlight to flood the living room and bedroom. Tracy's present accommodations allowed him to brood in darkness all day. Kate planned the cottage to ensure daily contact with light and life.

Not long after Tracy moved in in late fall, he subverted Kate's plan. He forbade the gardener to trim the trees and shrubs in his patio and behind the wavy red brick wall at the rear. Tracy preferred everything dense, tangled, and overgrown. He wanted an impenetrable jungle around him. As Tracy blocked the view and closed himself in, he transformed the cottage into an expression of his own dark state of mind.

He tended not to open the simple coarse curtains in the living room, whose walls were planks of wormy chestnut. He hardly touched the wooden shutters in the bedroom that Cukor compared to a monk's cell; the room, furnished with an oak chest, a chair, and a bed, had "the air of a place where a man might do penance."

The tiny house was designed for a single occupant; from the first, there had never been any question that Kate would live there with Spencer. Although a closet-sized maid's room adjoined the modest kitchen, he refused to have live-in help. A surprisingly spacious dressing room, out of proportion to the rest of the cottage, recalled Dr. Hepburn's dressing room in West Hartford.

Respectful of Tracy's privacy, Cukor might not see his tenant for days or weeks at a time. Yet they kept in frequent contact, often gossiping on the telephone for an hour or so during the day.

Kate installed telephones throughout the hilltop house on Beverly Grove Drive which Howard Hughes had arranged for her to rent during the four months she planned to stay in Los Angeles.

Spencer never had to wait more than one or two rings to reach her. Modeled on a château in the south of France, the cavernous house with a tennis court and a swimming pool came unfurnished. Kate raided the RKO and MGM warehouses for furniture to add to the pieces of her own she kept in Cukor's storeroom between rentals. Cukor, an inveterate collector, provided the odd bibelot.

Soon Kate was giving frequent dinner parties. She pressed a button and the roof of the large circular dining room slid open, so guests could eat under the stars. The dramatic gesture suited Kate perfectly. She was as eager to open things up as Spencer was to close himself in.

Now that she and Tracy were spending long periods apart, Kate worked hard to establish, if only to a small circle of married friends, that they were indeed a couple. The presence of Cary Grant and Betsy Drake, Humphrey Bogart and Lauren Bacall, and Ruth Gordon and Garson Kanin seemed to validate her own relationship.

Kate had returned to find Spencer in poor physical and mental condition. Following his abrupt departure from Rome, he had gone to England to see Laurence Olivier and Vivien Leigh. By this time Olivier had joined the chorus urging Tracy to test his abilities with more challenging material than MGM seemed inclined to provide. Olivier argued that Tracy had the equipment to be a great actor, if only he would try. Tracy basked in Olivier's praise, but refused to take his advice. In Los Angeles, he started to drink heavily again.

That October Kate began preliminary work on a new Cukor comedy with Tracy, based on a Gordon–Kanin screenplay; filming was scheduled to begin on December 1. All the while, however, Tracy was painfully aware that *Pat and Mike*, the story of a woman athlete and a shady sports promoter, was the last film under Kate's MGM contract; from then on, she would be free.

And she intended to use her freedom. Before leaving London, Kate had filled her work schedule for many months to come. After *Pat and Mike*, she planned to appear on stage in *The Millionairess* for the producer Hugh "Binkie" Beaumont in London; Michael Benthall would direct the production, which had been postponed on account of delays in filming *The African Queen*. Then she planned to do another film for John Huston, *Miss Hargreaves*; and after that, in all likelihood she would return to *The Millionairess*, which the Theater Guild hoped to mount on Broadway.

Cukor and Constance Collier worried that Kate was pushing herself much too hard. Africa had taken a terrible toll on her health. Sun-damaged skin draped the famous cheekbones. Kate confessed to Ella Winter that the dysentery had continued for six months. Yet she worked on several projects at once, juggling *Pat and Mike* script conferences with preparations for *The Millionairess*. She exuded a kind of manic vitality. Someone compared her to an alarm clock that couldn't be shut off.

She was constantly on the phone to Binkie Beaumont or Michael Benthall in London. On a free day with Irene Selznick, Hepburn talked from 7:30 a.m. to 5:30 p.m., detailing all that had happened in Africa and all she hoped to accomplish now.

When *The African Queen* opened that fall, it became clear that under Huston's impeccable direction Kate had given her most accomplished performance yet. Nominated for an Academy Award for Best Actress, Kate lost to Vivien Leigh in *A Streetcar Named Desire*. Still, there could be no denying that *The African Queen* marked a watershed in her career. She accepted that Lawrence Langner had been right; her efforts in Shakespeare had immeasurably broadened her range as an actress.

In *Pat and Mike*, the role of Pat Pemberton, gifted, versatile, and eager to try new things, would have seemed wonderfully appropriate at a moment when Kate was determined to do the same. Pat decides that she must quit her comfortable, unchallenging job as a physical education instructor at a small California college; with the film, Kate was wrapping up a longtime commitment to MGM. Pat realizes that she must break free from a boyfriend who is quite satisfied with things as they are; Kate faced the same problem.

Ironically, in the film it is sports promoter Mike Conovan (Spencer Tracy) who offers Pat the chance to seek fresh challenges. That was the very opposite of Tracy's role in Kate's life. It was no secret that Spencer was most unhappy about her decision to leave MGM.

While *The African Queen* suggested a brash new beginning, *Pat and Mike* feels like an end: The "battle of the sexes" theme, so vital in films like *Woman of the Year* and *Adam's Rib,* seems tired and routine. The script never transcends its formula. Tracy and Hepburn are called on to do nothing they haven't done before. Still, in the many shots of Hepburn on the golf course or tennis court with which Cukor has padded out a thin story, we glimpse the bold, competitive, irrepressible girl whom family and friends had often observed at Fenwick, showing the world, and herself, all she was capable of.

For four months, Kate reverted to the role she had often played with Spencer. Once again she sat at his feet; once again she hung on his every word and worked hard not to seem his equal in a group. Yet everyone knew she would be leaving as soon as she finished *Pat and Mike* on February 21, 1952. Tracy, complaining of his ulcer, treated Kate's impending departure as a public humiliation. But she had no intention of backing down.

Due in New York for intensive last-minute work on Shaw with Constance Collier, Kate was frantic that Tracy would go on a bender. She resolved that in the long run her own presence in Los Angeles would not stop Spencer from drinking; he was going to have to do that himself. By the time Kate headed east, a knot of overgrown trees and shrubs had begun to close off the rear of Tracy's cottage. But at least Cukor was nearby; the director would send Kate regular dispatches on the health and mood of "the old man who lives in the gully", as they called him, though he was only seven years older than Kate.

Cukor tried to keep the tone light and joky. Writing to Kate at the Connaught Hotel in London, he might report that Tracy had taken him to dinner at Romanoff's, where the actor often shared a booth with Pat O'Brien and other Irish cronies on Thursday nights. Cukor would be sure to mention that he had recently spoken to Spencer on the telephone. He would note if the old man had a cold or if his ulcer was acting up. He would comment fondly that Spencer was as verbally abusive as ever.

Cukor did not, however, mention that since beginning a new picture, *Plymouth Adventure*, on March 24, Tracy had begun an affair with his thirty-one-year-old co-star, Gene Tierney. Kate was going to have to find that out for herself.

On the morning of Tuesday, June 26, Kate, ensconced with Em Perkins at the Connaught Hotel in sweltering London, tore open a tiny package which John Huston had sent from Paris, where he was filming *Moulin Rouge*. She discovered a flat bronze miniature of an African wild boar with the message: "Portrait of your friend."

Hunting with Huston in Africa, Kate had been walking ahead on the trail when she sighted a wild boar. The 400-pound beast with immense tusks seemed to stare directly at her. Eager for a closeup, Kate aimed her 8-millimeter movie camera and approached; suddenly she heard Huston coax softly: "Kate . . . Kate. Come back, Kate." He did not want to provoke the animal.

Kate, annoyed that Huston was spoiling her shot, moved steadily toward the beast. Then she stopped to rewind her camera. Huston, certain the boar was about to attack, aimed his rifle but hesitated; he knew a bullet in the heart would not stop it from charging.

"Come back, Kate," he pleaded. Huston could feel his finger start to squeeze the trigger. "Slowly . . . "

Just then, the boar's family dashed across the path; he glanced at them, glanced at Kate, then followed the others into the jungle.

Hepburn found the episode exhilarating; Huston was nearly prostrate. And now again, on the morning of her London debut in the role of Epifania Ognisanti Di Parerga Fitzfassenden, Kate felt that she had been rushing headlong toward some terrible danger when Huston intervened.

On pale blue tissue paper, she asked what in the world he was doing in Paris, and she in London. Suddenly, Kate confessed, all she could think of was the tall grass and the early morning light and the slaughtered deer and that total separation from reality she had known only in Africa. Staring at the tiny bronze, Kate sensed that it was warning her not to return to the theater that night.

She did not heed the warning. That evening at the New Theater, Kate appeared on stage shouting at the top of her lungs; she hardly stopped screaming until the final curtain. Wearing a

Balmain gown as if it were a rag, she marched madly about; she bemoaned the mess of her life; she threatened suicide; she flounced on a fake Chippendale chair, broke its back with a loud crack, and leapt to her feet, insisting the violent experience had calmed and relieved her. She threw Cyril Ritchard to the ground as though he were a sack of potatoes; when the six-foot-two, 190-pound leading man painfully picked himself up, Hepburn cried "Vermin!" and knocked him down again. To another character's sneering charge that she was "off at the deep end again," Kate yelled on one note, in a single long breath: "The deep end! The deep end! Oh, what is life if not lived at the deep end?"

Kate hopped up and down; whooped with delight; descended a staircase three steps at a time; did a swan dive onto her face; wriggled about on the floor; pounded her fists; proclaimed men the inferior species; and generally abused her vocal cords with all manner of caterwauls.

Audiences loved it. The *Observer* crowned her Katharine the Great. Critics described Hepburn's performance as "dynamic," "electric," "blasting," "high-powered," "high-pressured," and "galvanic," leading one wit to protest that it was as though they were talking about a new jet project, not an actress. Binkie Beaumont exulted that *The Millionairess*, which had failed the last time he produced it, was playing to capacity audiences nightly. If now and then La Hepburn seemed a bit overwrought on stage and off, the management blamed it on the heat wave.

By contrast, Kate's friends had begun to worry. Her over-the-top performance greatly disturbed George Cukor, who saw *The Millionairess* in Liverpool at one of the provincial previews. He quietly urged Constance Collier to do what she could to help Kate calm down. Similarly, Lawrence Langner, who attended the opening night with Armina Marshall, expressed consternation that Kate was playing the role at much too high a pitch. For many months Hepburn had been driving herself at such a relentless pace that Cukor feared what might happen if she failed to relax.

But Kate could not relax. As he had done at the time of *Without Love*, Tracy turned up at the play and pressured her to come back to Los Angeles; he loomed over the production from first to last. This time, however, he had to counter Kate's strong determination to break away.

Spencer raised the stakes. Installed at Claridge's in London, he continued his affair with Gene Tierney, and flaunted the relationship under Kate's nose.

Tierney and her mother were renting an apartment in Grosvenor Square near the Connaught Hotel. Tierney noted that whenever she dined with Tracy, he would constantly look over at the restaurant door, as though Kate might arrive at any moment. It was as if he wanted her to find out. Tierney's mother declared Spencer "the most tormented man" she had ever met. Yet Tierney wanted to marry him. Spencer promised he would try to work things out so they could go off together. She told her friends that Tracy was in love with her.

"Gene, I don't believe it," said Kirk Douglas. "First, Spencer's married. He'll never get divorced. Second, he has a very intense relationship with Katharine Hepburn, and he'll never give it up."

Constance Collier told Cukor that by mid-August Kate was on the verge of a nervous breakdown. Desperately worried, she attributed Kate's upset to delayed shock; she pointed out that Kate had not stopped working since Mrs. Hepburn died. Kate had let things pile up for a long time; they all came crashing down on her in London.

Kate did not conceal her turmoil from Lawrence Langner; she wrote to tell him that she was convinced she was cracking up. Perhaps she should have listened when the bronze boar warned her to clear out. On August 14, she mysteriously developed a temperature of 103 degrees. She started to lose her voice. She complained that when she spoke it was as though she were being strangled.

Binkie Beaumont, summoned by Constance Collier to the Connaught, was greatly alarmed by the degree of agitation in which he found Kate. He wondered whether she would be able to complete the London run, let alone take the play to New York. Despite her fever, she demanded to go on that night, and again the night after that. At the insistence of a very worried Michael Benthall, Kate was not required to play matinées for the rest of the season.

On September 5, Tracy, still in London, called Ruth Gordon and Garson Kanin in New York, and gave them to believe that Hepburn was worn-out and exhausted. As the Kanins later told Cukor, Tracy gave every sign of being at loose ends himself. He announced that he would remain with Kate, then abruptly changed his mind and sailed home. At a meeting with the Kanins in New York, he seized on their proposal to write *It Takes a Thief*, a new Tracy and Hepburn vehicle about an international jewel thief and the woman who pursues him. Tracy, eager to lure Kate back to MGM, immediately pitched the idea to Cukor. As far as Spencer was concerned, that would fix everything.

After closing in *The Millionairess* on September 20, Kate, still in appalling condition, flew to New York the next day. Huston, for reasons of his own, had put off *Miss Hargreaves*, leaving her free to go directly to Broadway. But Benthall pressured Langner to postpone the opening so that she might have a long rest at Fenwick. Kate remained in Connecticut for three weeks, talking once a day on the telephone to Constance Collier, but to no one else associated with the production. Collier prayed that her Epifania would be as well received critically in New York as it had been in London.

It wasn't. At first, Kate appeared to have her voice back; but the problems with her throat quickly resumed. The dress rehearsals, on October 15 and 16, were a disaster. Langner offered to postpone the next night's premiere, but Kate wouldn't hear of it. "If you postpone it, I'll be worse," she insisted. "I'll be much more nervous waiting."

By and large, the New York critics dismissed her performance. "The tricks are fascinating, but they are all tricks," wrote Walter Kerr in the *Herald Tribune*. "Miss Hepburn's whole performance originates in the larynx; there is nothing deeper, more meaningful to tie the fireworks together and the razzle-dazzle becomes disconcertingly hollow before the evening is far advanced."

Running on empty, Kate propelled herself through ten weeks. When she became over-excited, she felt her neck and throat tighten. She had thoughts of suicide. She checked into Columbia-

Presbyterian Hospital and contemplated a leap from the window. Realizing that she had allowed herself to drift into perilous mental terrain, she decided that she must save herself by an act of will. Confronted with death, she embraced life.

Accompanied by Robert Helpmann, who played the eerie Egyptian doctor who falls in love with Epifania's throbbing pulse, Kate spent cold weekends at Fenwick. The two friends hardly talked for days at a time. Listening to the waves crash against the rocks, Kate slowly pulled herself out of her depression.

In the four years after Kate left Los Angeles upon completing *Pat and Mike*, she and Tracy spent a total of no more than six months together. Usually he saw her in New York, sometimes in London— an important retreat for her—or elsewhere in Europe.

On her rare visits to Los Angeles, Kate tended to stay in the main house at Cukor's. When she arrived, there was always a dish of fruit and a single orchid waiting in the guest room; a private entrance allowed her discreetly to slip out to see the old man in the gully whenever she liked. She ate most meals with Spencer, but was forbidden to spend the night. He could not bear to have anyone present when, in red flannel pajamas, he smoked in bed, sipped endless mugs of coffee, and read murder mysteries until dawn. She would climb a narrow flight of steps cut in the hillside; if she looked back, she could see Spencer's night lamp burning through the dense tangle of trees and shrubs.

As he did when Kate was away, Tracy kept in touch with the main house by telephone; no sooner would she return to the guest room than the phone might already be ringing.

The calls continued in New York or London, wherever Kate might be as she struggled to mount a film version of *The Millionairess* with José Ferrer playing the doctor. Her phone rang at all hours. No matter what Kate was doing, Spencer expected her to drop everything.

And she did. Kate might be in her light, airy sitting room overlooking Turtle Bay Gardens, but suddenly her mind was in the small, stuffy cottage where Tracy was calling from bed after another sleepless night. Kate might be at work on the screenplay of *The Millionairess* with Preston Sturges, but she would have to interrupt her concentration and listen to Spencer.

Friends knew that Tracy's daily consumption of coffee, dexedrine, and sleeping pills left him constantly frantic and on edge. One appeal of the telephone was the instant connection; he lacked the patience for letter-writing. When static interrupted, Spencer would scream and shout into the mouthpiece, frantic to be heard. He repeated his litany of complaints to Kate, Louise, and Cukor; at one point he even latched on to Robert Sherwood again. When other clients failed to reach the agent Bert Allenberg, they figured he must be on the line with Tracy.

Ruth Gordon sighed that she wished she thought Spencer was happy. He was constantly in crisis. He lamented that he was too old, fat, and ugly to be a leading man anymore. He protested that he had felt like a fool doing love scenes with Gene Tierney. He predicted that after the box-office failure of *Plymouth Adventure*, MGM would soon be looking for an excuse to kick him out.

Spencer interpreted everything as a portent of doom. He took nothing at face value. Every event seemed an oblique comment on him. When MGM production chief Dore Schary called off the upcoming Tracy vehicle, *Jefferson Selleck*, with the explanation that he didn't like Joseph Mankiewicz's screenplay, Spencer read that as a sign of his own failing fortunes. When the studio assigned him to shoot *Flight to the Islands* instead and Cukor promptly bowed out because of a prior commitment to Columbia, Spencer wondered whether his friend was reacting to the grosses on *Plymouth Adventure*.

Talking out his problems on the phone, Tracy would finally seem to settle on a course of action; he would hang up, then call back moments later, undecided again. His vacillation drove people crazy; Dore Schary dubbed it "the Tracy syndrome."

Now he was going to Paris to confer with Garson Kanin about the *Flight to the Islands* screenplay; now he wasn't. Ruth Gordon tried to entice him with the promise that she and Gar would serve as trained nurses. As always with Tracy, no one ever knew what he was going to do until he did it, and even then he was likely to change his mind many times en route.

Finally Tracy sailed from New York on the *Queen Mary* on February 25, 1953, only to be plunged into crisis soon after his arrival in Paris. As Kate was on vacation in Jamaica with Irene Selznick, Spencer, eager for a telephone fix, called Louise first.

Mrs. Tracy reported a message from Vivien Leigh, requesting the keys to Spencer's cottage! Vivien seemed to be under the impression that Spencer, whom she had run into in New York, had offered her the use of the cottage in his absence. The news drove Tracy wild. He was outraged that someone could be so insensitive as to mention the cottage's existence to Louise, although she certainly knew that he lived there.

As Cukor was soon explaining to his household manager, Elsa Schroeder, Spencer also loathed the thought that anyone would set foot in his quarters. Leigh had moved out before Cukor learned of the incident; still, he instructed Schroeder to get to the bottom of it, so he could give a full accounting to Tracy. Typically, Spencer was so restless in Europe that he cut the trip short.

For months Tracy would pour out his troubles to Kate several times a day. What did it mean that MGM had postponed *Flight to the Islands* until Cukor was free to direct? Should Spencer go back to France to see about a Benjamin Franklin script Garson Kanin had talked about writing in collaboration with Robert Sherwood; or the international jewel thief comedy that had yet to materialize? Then suddenly the frenzied calls would stop. Without warning Tracy disappeared. And Kate could only wonder what the silence meant.

When her phone stopped ringing, she would contact Cukor. Kate always appeared a bit embarrassed to show how worried she was. To all the world, she hardly seemed to spend any time with Spencer. Yet Cukor knew the extent to which the most trivial details of Tracy's daily life preoccupied her.

Kate may have distanced herself physically, but she had not pulled back emotionally. In fact, physical distance heightened the relationship, by making it even more a phenomenon of the mind. It had been one thing when Kate could let herself into Tracy's hotel suite to check that he was alive; it was quite another to have to rely on Cukor.

If Cukor had not actually seen or heard from Tracy, he would offer to walk down the hill, where he could see Spencer's lamp through the trees and shrubs. Or instead of continuing up Doheny to Cordell in his automobile, the director could make a right on St. Ives to check whether Tracy's black Thunderbird was in the carport.

It had been years since Kate had demanded clarity from a man. By this time, all she asked was to be reassured that at least Spencer was in his cottage. Cukor was not always able to tell her what she needed to hear. Sometimes he found it very difficult to disclose the truth. To spare her dignity, Cukor often pretended not to understand quite how serious all this was to her.

In February 1954, Kate was in London hoping to start filming *The Millionairess* as soon as the money was in place. Cukor nervously reported that Spencer seemed to be living elsewhere. He would arrive to pick up a few things, then slip off before Cukor had an opportunity to question him.

Was he having another fling? Had he moved to a hotel? Was he with Louise? Although in recent days Kate had heard from Tracy regularly on the telephone, it suddenly became clear that she never had any idea where he was calling from.

When the night lamp went on at the bottom of the hill, Cukor wasted no time inviting Tracy to dinner. Spencer certainly would never tell where he had been; but at least Cukor could give Kate a detailed account of his mood and appearance. She could only gauge his voice; Cukor could study Tracy's face and gestures. He milked every second of the two-hour visit for information to pass on to Kate; now that Spencer was back, she longed to know whether he seemed to have been eating properly.

And she worried how he would react to MGM's decision to loan him out to Twentieth Century–Fox for Edward Dmytryk's western, *Broken Lance*. Spencer was already interpreting the loan-out as a sign of his diminished status at the studio. He ruefully dubbed himself the St. Ives Roy Rogers. The perceived humiliation was precisely the sort of thing to cause him to hit the bottle. Cukor monitored Spencer until he left for Arizona; but when the Thunderbird roared out of the carport, there was no guarantee that he would actually reach the location in the Santa Cruz Valley. At first Spencer did not ring Kate, leaving her to wonder whether he was preoccupied with work or had disappeared on a bender.

Tracy had promised to come to London in May. Cukor knew how important that visit was to Kate; he contacted her the moment Spencer returned from Arizona. Production chief Darryl Zanuck had complimented Tracy on the rushes; and although Spencer remarked sarcastically that Zanuck always liked the rushes, the actor was obviously feeling very proud of himself. No one loved praise more than Spencer. He was in such a good mood that he had already booked a ticket to London; but Cukor reminded Kate that whether he would actually go was another matter.

By the time Tracy arrived in London, Kate's one and a half years of work on the film of *The Millionairess* seemed to have gone up in smoke. The English money was in place, but some of the American backing had failed to materialize. Writer-director Preston Sturges, declaring himself ready for the glue factory, decamped for Paris. Kate had to pay some of the bills herself; she would later call the entire experience the "greatest professional disappointment" of her life.

Kate was at the Connaught, Tracy at Claridge's. She visited him at least once a day, sometimes with a bag of scones and pies from Shepherd's Market.

One morning Claridge's assistant manager phoned, asking to see Tracy. Spencer, with typical paranoia, assumed the worst. Always sensitive about his extramarital relationship, he feared the hotel intended to protest at Kate's frequent visits. Unwilling to face the assistant manager on his own, Tracy summoned Garson Kanin, who happened to be staying in the hotel at the time. It was Kanin who let in a tall man in a cutaway coat and striped trousers.

The assistant manager began: "I've been asked by the management if it would be possible—you do understand, Mr. Tracy, this is not a personal matter, merely one of policy. The management has asked me . . . that is to say, Mr. Van Thuyne has suggested . . ."

"What matter?" Tracy interjected. "I still don't know what you're talking about."

"It's about Miss Hepburn, sir . . . It's a matter of dress, you see, sir. We do have certain regulations . . . Miss Hepburn wears trousers."

So it was hardly as Spencer had feared; Claridge's was upset that a woman in trousers was regularly crossing the lobby.

To avoid trouble, Tracy proposed to alter their routine; he would come to Kate's hotel. But she wouldn't hear of it. Nor would she agree to wear a dress. She continued to visit Claridge's; but from then on, instead of sailing through the lobby, Kate used the service entrance with the maids.

Spencer soon left for America, unusually enthusiastic about beginning his next film, John Sturges's *Bad Day at Black Rock*. Hardly was he back when he called Kate to report that he had changed his mind. He had decided not to do the picture after all. He dreaded the idea of location work in the Mojave Desert, where MGM had constructed an elaborate replica of a godforsaken little town in the middle of nowhere.

Dore Schary did not share Kate's willingness to coddle Spencer. When Tracy withdrew from the picture two days before shooting was due to begin, Schary, an old hand at dealing with the Tracy syndrome, threatened to sue him for the cost of the production. By the time Kate heard from him again, Spencer had reluctantly agreed to continue with the film.

Kate had once told John Ford that he understood her better than anyone. But now he miscalculated. He had watched Kate go into a cocoon with Spencer, then saw her re-emerge as she pursued a life apart. Ford misread Hepburn's long absences from Tracy; like many people, he guessed that the relationship had cooled. He thought he saw his chance and decided to seize it.

Since the war, Ford had kept track of Kate through mutual friends. He constantly sought information from Em Perkins, whose devotion to "Shoney" had not diminished. Meta Sterne, who always referred to Ford as "Himself," provided further details. Meta was notorious for her dislike of most women; Kate proved a rare exception. George Cukor, too, maintained a warm friendship with Ford, and never failed to report what Kate was up to.

Members of the Ford circle routinely recounted their own Hepburn sightings, no matter how fleeting; Ford was always eager for any scrap of conversation with her, especially when his name had been mentioned. The wisdom among Ford associates was that his and Kate's strong feelings for each other had made it impossible for them to work together again.

Since 1936, Ford had owned the rights to a Maurice Walsh short story entitled "The Quiet Man"; he had very much wanted to shoot in Ireland with Kate, but there was no backer. When Ford finally made the film for Republic Pictures in 1951, he changed the name of the fiery, freckle-faced, red-headed Irish girl Ellen to Mary Kate. In the screenplay, Shawn, the Irish-American who returns to his roots and falls in love, became Sean. Not surprisingly, at moments Maureen O'Hara, as Mary Kate, bears a distinct resemblance to Hepburn in *The Little Minister*, the picture she was filming when Ford first saw her around the RKO lot.

Ford filmed in Ireland while Kate was in Africa with John Huston. Unabashedly autobiographical, *The Quiet Man* is a rarity in the Ford oeuvre, a fully fledged love story. Less an account of anything that had actually happened, it was a fairy-tale projection of what might have been. John Wayne, in the role of Sean, sensed that Ford had him act out on camera what the director had failed to do in life: take the decisive action necessary to consummate his love. Sean's moment of decision comes when Mary Kate, weary of his refusal to act, boards the Dublin train to make her escape. He rushes to the station and drags her off, so that he may prove his love.

There had been no such happy ending in 1937 when Kate Hepburn made an escape of her own on a train to Florida—and Howard Hughes. The *Jane Eyre* tour had ended, and Kate's Sean had not kept his promise to take her to Ireland. It was on that bumpy train trip that she had written the devastating letter in which she announced that she had had enough of Ford's vacillation. Maybe and someday, Kate had insisted, were just feeble ways of saying no.

Filming in Ireland was an emotional experience for Ford. After years of thinking of himself in Mary's terms as "Admiral Ford," he was eager to rediscover "Sean," the romantic Irishman Kate Hepburn had once loved.

To the horror of Mary who continued to scorn her husband's "shanty Irish" background, Ford became a director of Four Provinces, Lord Killanin's new Irish film production company; worse, he seemed ready to give up lucrative Hollywood assignments so that he might work in the native Irish film industry. He agreed to work for free, and slowly evolved plans for an anthology film based on three Irish tales. Ford told Lord Killanin that Orson Welles's film of *Othello* had sparked the idea for an Irish ghost story with an Ascendancy background. Ford wanted to shoot at Powerscourt or Lisemore Castle. And he wanted Kate Hepburn for his leading lady.

Before he could approach her, illness intervened. Ford began to lose his eyesight, and feared he was going blind. Confined to a dark room, he was forbidden to read or work. The croaker, as Ford called his physician, diagnosed conical myopia and external cataracts; he predicted that in surgery he might be able to save one eye.

Ford emerged from the operating room temporarily blind; the slightest exposure to light caused him excruciating pain. Dictating to Meta Sterne, Ford told Lord Killanin of his immense frustration at not being able to proceed with his plans. At length, however, his sight was partially restored, and he went back to work. Wearing a black patch to protect his left eye from the light, Ford dictated a letter to Kate.

It was August 1954. Ford had heard that Kate was in Venice at the Palazzo Papadopoli, playing the role of an American spinster secretary who falls in love with Rossano Brazzi in David Lean's *Summertime*. When Binkie Beaumont corresponded with Kate, it seemed to him that she was terribly lonely in Venice. According to Constance Collier, who was with her, Kate often worked in the punishing heat from 8:30 a.m. to almost 9 p.m. What with the lights and the blazing sun, Kate thought Venice hotter than Africa.

Ford, in his letter, announced that since he and Kate were both abrupt New Englanders, he would get right to the point. He sounded tense, nervous, poised for rejection. He was not above a little emotional blackmail. He told Kate that as his days were drawing to a close he would love to direct her again. He uttered the words she had been waiting to hear in 1937; he asked her to come to Ireland with him.

He was seventeen years too late.

Kate promptly signed up for a six-month Old Vic tour of Australia with Robert Helpmann. Rehearsals of *Measure for Measure, The Taming of the Shrew,* and *The Merchant of Venice* began on March 1, making it impossible for her to consider Ford's offer.

No one but Meta Sterne seemed to understand Ford's prickly mood as he began shooting *Mister Roberts* for Warner Bros. on location at Midway Island that September. He sipped beer every afternoon, something he never did on a picture. A great wounded bull of a man, he sought a target, any target, for his rage.

Henry Fonda, who had starred in the long-running Broadway play, could not comprehend why Ford seemed to botch the job so badly. Fonda loved and worshipped Ford; yet there could be no denying that the director's rhythms and story sense were drastically off. Ford had secretly fought to keep his old friend in the picture when Jack Warner wanted to replace Fonda with Marlon Brando. Yet when Fonda respectfully differed on a matter of direction, Ford went wild. He rose from his chair and punched the actor in the jaw. Fonda's chair flew back, knocking over a pitcher of water.

The drinking escalated. In Honolulu, Ford secluded himself on the *Araner,* causing the production to grind to a halt. Locked in a dark cabin, he went on a binge that lasted five days. According to Fonda, Ford finally had to enter a hospital to dry out.

Ford was not alone in reacting strongly to Kate's Old Vic tour. Tracy too took the six-month commitment very hard.

Spencer had quietly signed a new contract that required him to make one MGM picture a year; the non-exclusive deal permitted him to shoot as many outside films as he liked. The terms were extremely favorable to Tracy, who had scored a critical and commercial triumph in *Bad Day at Black Rock;* studio executives were very excited about his next picture, *Tribute to a Bad Man*. Unfortunately, filming in the Rocky Mountains coincided with Kate's trip to Australia. Spencer turned up at the location five days late, then disappeared the next afternoon; he went on a bender and was absent for another eight days.

Slurring his words, Tracy called a friend, Peter Viertel, in Los Angeles. He sounded upset, and Viertel asked where he was.

"Colorado," Tracy replied. "But I'm not going to be here much longer. See you later. At eight o'clock. Chasen's."

"Have you finished the movie?" asked Viertel.

"No, but I'm coming back anyway," Tracy declared and hung up.

Instead, he phoned the film set from Grand Junction, Colorado, about sixty miles from the location. Announcing that he had just landed at the airport, he demanded a studio car to pick him up.

Things got worse from there. Tracy lasted a mere three days on location. Insisting that he could not work at an 8000-foot altitude, he wanted the set moved about 2000 feet lower. Transporting the nine ranch buildings could take as long as three months. Tracy's disappearing act had already cost MGM about $200,000. When the exasperated director protested, the studio was only too willing to remove Tracy from the picture.

But it was the decision to terminate his MGM contract that apparently reduced the actor to tears. Schary had had his fill of the Tracy syndrome. Distraught, Spencer wept in his motel room: "It's the end of my career, I'm finished, it's never happened to me before."

Tracy might have been finished at MGM, but other studios seemed eager to take him on. He signed with Paramount to shoot Edward Dmytryk's *The Mountain* on location in the French Alps at Chamonix. After a pie-eyed Tracy hurled an empty liquor glass at a French waiter's face, Kate dispatched a secretary to look out for him. The arrangement worked well enough until the last day on location, when someone offered Tracy a beer. That was all it took.

By the time the studio car headed to Geneva, Spencer was

drunkenly flinging empty beer bottles out the window. At the airport, he graduated to wine; in Paris, he shifted to hard liquor. On the flight home, stewardesses couldn't bring enough alcohol to keep him happy. The pilot radioed Los Angeles. When Spencer staggered off the plane, Louise was there to collect him.

Tracy was like a child who misbehaves to get attention. Whether consciously or not, he had done everything to persuade Kate to give up the independence she had demanded since *As You Like It*. His message was clear: If you continue to stay away, I will destroy my career, and drink myself to death.

As it happened, the effect of John Ford's letter in August 1954 had been the opposite of anything he intended. Kate had reacted to that letter by fleeing to Australia. In turn, her six-month commitment to the Old Vic tour had driven Tracy to the self-destructive episodes which finally broke her resolve to lead an independent life. Greatly alarmed by his behavior, Kate decided that she must remain at his side until he was out of danger. After she fulfilled a commitment to appear with Robert Helpmann in *The Iron Petticoat*, filmed at Pinewood Studios in England, she would dedicate herself to caring for Spencer.

Ford had to confront the fact that, far from having lured Kate away, almost certainly he had propelled her into a much closer bond with Tracy.

TWENTY-THREE

I n March 1956, Tracy and Hepburn were in New York, preparing to fly to Cuba. Director Fred Zinnemann and agent-turned-producer Leland Hayward waited with Ernest Hemingway in Havana, where Spencer was to appear in *The Old Man and the Sea* for Warner Bros.

The usual anxieties plagued Tracy, but this time he seemed particularly concerned about Hemingway. Actor and novelist had gotten along perfectly well when they met to discuss the film three years before. But Tracy had been on the wagon at the time; he certainly wasn't now. When he sent word to Havana that he was detained with a cold, everyone knew what that meant.

As always, he was having second thoughts. He wondered whether the script was right for him. He brooded over his exclusion from the final story conferences. And he worried about Hemingway's reputation as a bully. Tracy predicted that Hemingway would drag him over the coals when he saw the shape Spencer was in.

Arriving in Cuba drunk, Tracy guaranteed the rough treatment he dreaded. By the time Hemingway saw him, Spencer was sober, but that didn't stop Hemingway. He seemed to smell Tracy's fear. When Hemingway attacked, Kate intervened. Unable to deny that Spencer had been drinking on the turbulent flight from New York, she insisted that was the first time he had had a drop in more than a decade. Hemingway countered that he knew Tracy had been drunk on *Tribute to a Bad Man*, the picture that cost him his MGM contract.

471

It was all downhill after that. Hemingway would snidely refer to Tracy as "the artist"; he made endless remarks about Spencer's girth.

"Have a drink," Hemingway taunted.

"No, thanks," the artist replied.

"Go on, have a drink."

"I'd just as soon not."

"What are you? A rummy? Can't you just have a drink or two? Do you have to go till you're insensible? Is that your problem?"

Tracy threatened to quit; Warner Bros. threatened to replace him. John Sturges took over when Zinnemann walked out. Eventually, Jack Warner shut down the troubled production and ordered everyone home. *The Old Man and the Sea* would be completed at a later date in a tank on the Warner lot.

Tracy returned from Cuba in perilously low spirits. According to Cukor, when Spencer seemed about to take a drink, Kate would tie him to his bed until the impulse passed. She had always said that at least Spencer was able to find peace in his work; but now, he had lost even that. After the battering he had received from Hemingway, Kate was determined to shore up Tracy's self-esteem.

It was no longer a matter of finding the sort of challenging role Kate, Langner, Olivier, and others had long urged Spencer to try; he needed something much more basic. He had been stripped of the security of his MGM contract; three films in a row had ended in debacle. Spencer needed reassurance that his career was not over. He needed to work with an important director who could convince him that his talent was intact.

John Ford called Kate after he returned from Ireland. While she was in Cuba, Ford had shot his long-delayed *Rising of the Moon*, the anthology of Irish stories in which he had asked Kate to appear in 1954. Now, in 1956, Ford's life was still apparently drawing to a close as he asked Kate again to accompany him to Ireland—this time for another role. His latest "last" picture was to be *Drama at Inish*, a farce about a touring theatrical company's visit to a small seaside resort. The starring roles called for actors "of mature years." Ford and Lord Killanin had Hepburn and John Gielgud in mind.

Kate did not say yes; she did not say no. She left it at maybe.

Just now, she was appearing in *The Rainmaker* at Paramount; after that she planned to team up with Spencer in *Desk Set* at Twentieth Century–Fox. She offered Ford hope that she might consider his offer. They agreed that Lord Killanin would send her a copy of the Lennox Robinson play. Meanwhile, Kate had another matter she wanted to discuss with Sean. It was no secret that he had signed with Columbia's Harry Cohn to direct *The Last Hurrah*, based on the Edwin O'Connor novel. Kate asked Ford to cast Spencer as Frank Skeffington, the crusty Irish-American mayor of Boston.

This was no small request. Although Ford would certainly never admit it, he and Tracy had been at odds for years. No one but Kate would have dared intervene for a man whom Ford had put on ice.

At a moment when the director was trying to lure Kate away, she asked him to rescue his rival in love. She asked Ford to assist the one man he was most eager to defeat. And she asked him to postpone filming *The Last Hurrah*, scheduled for April 1957, until Tracy finished *The Old Man and the Sea*. She wanted Ford to indicate that he needed Tracy, although he and Kate both knew it was very much the other way around.

Kate's request shows how much she trusted Sean. He would never direct his biting sarcasm at Tracy if Kate asked him not to. Though he was notorious for his ability to reduce tough guys like John Wayne and Victor McLaglen to tears, Ford would be the soul of kindness if that was what Kate wanted. Whatever Ford's true feelings about Tracy, she knew she could safely put Spencer in his hands.

Ford did not say yes; he did not say no. Both Kate and Sean were capable of much deviousness; no doubt she had picked up a good deal of that from him. By the end of the conversation, the only certainty was that Lord Killanin would soon be in touch with her.

Ford agonized for months. He confided to John Wayne that his mind was going round and round. Now he planned to use Tracy; now he didn't. Swearing Duke to secrecy, he disclosed that he was about to settle on Ward Bond. A month later Ford turned up on the set of *Touch of Evil* to offer the role to Orson Welles. And a month after that, he wrote to Lord Killanin that his first and only choice was Spencer Tracy.

Even then, the need to postpone the production provided an excuse to keep changing his mind. Ford wondered aloud how he could play such a scurvy trick on the Irish players who had already made plans to come to Hollywood in April. The idea of deferring to Tracy stuck in the director's craw. Spencer had once pointedly refused to join the Ford stock company; letting him think he was more important than any other member of that select circle was almost too much for Ford to bear.

Kate kept lobbying; as always, she was full of tricks. She talked to Lord Killanin on the telephone about *Drama at Inish*; she made a show of offering dates when she might be available.

Ford gave in first. After months of hesitation, he made his final decision in April 1957. He postponed *The Last Hurrah* to allow Tracy to complete *The Old Man and the Sea*. Before Spencer reported to Ford, Kate hoped to take him to Harbour Island near Nassau for at least a month to get him in shape. As for *Drama at Inish*, she agreed to discuss it on the set of *The Last Hurrah*.

Now that Spencer's immediate future was settled, Kate headed east at Lawrence Langner's invitation to appear in *The Merchant of Venice* and *Much Ado About Nothing* at the Stratford Memorial Theater in Stratford, Connecticut. While Spencer fulfilled his commitment to Warner Bros. that summer, Kate, who had just turned fifty, lived in a red fisherman's shack on piles at the edge of the Housatonic River. Living nearby was her secretary Phyllis Wilbourn, inherited from Constance Collier who died in 1955; Em Perkins had left to open a restaurant.

Spencer had assured Kate that he would join her as soon as he finished *The Old Man and the Sea*, but his repeated failures to show up were humiliating. For all of her efforts on his behalf, he showed little sensitivity to her feelings. According to John Houseman, artistic director of the American Shakespeare Theater, Hepburn would happily declare that Tracy was on his way, only to announce soon afterward that he had been detained. Time and again he broke his promises to come to Connecticut.

On one occasion in August, Kate seemed certain that Spencer was to arrive that evening. Excitedly she told the company that she was driving to the airport to pick him up. When she got there, however, Spencer was not on the flight. In Los Angeles, he had stopped for a few drinks on the way to the airport and was not heard from for days. Kate returned to Stratford alone.

On February 24, 1958, Spencer Tracy, fifty-seven, and John Ford, sixty-three, prepared to work together for the first time in more than a quarter of a century.

Tracy, his eyes darting right and left, lumbered onto Stage 8 at Columbia Studios at about 8:30 a.m. As always, he bit his lower lip or poked his tongue in his right cheek. Someone said his weather-beaten face resembled a map of Ireland. His hair was a silver thatch. His great ham hands were swollen with edema. His breathing was heavy and laborious. Now and then he seemed to panic, gasping for air.

Ford appeared unsteady on his feet, although it was impossible to tell whether that was merely part of his act. He wore a cap of Donegal tweed; the black patch over his left eye made Duke Wayne's young daughter think Ford looked like Death. He was said to have split vision in his right, "good" eye. Lifting his smoked glasses off his nose, he would hold Frank Nugent's screenplay very close, as though trying to read the year on a tarnished penny.

Spencer had anticipated the reunion with Ford with great trepidation. The fear of being dominated and manipulated by Ford that had led Tracy to turn down his invitation to go to the Philippines, and later his offer to appear in *The Plough and the Stars*, had not diminished. His anxiety about the meaning of Ford's dramatic gesture of suddenly leaving town at the very moment Tracy and Hepburn began their affair in 1941 was as strong as ever. If Ford had felt betrayed by Tracy's refusal to act in a film, what must he feel toward him for having taken up with Kate? And what punishment would he devise for Tracy on the set of *The Last Hurrah?*

Spencer, who dreaded a repeat of Hemingway's needling, knew that Ford had every reason to make him his patsy on this film. Some victims loved Ford so much that they let his barbs roll right off their back; but Spencer couldn't do that. He could not bear to be made a fool of by Ford. As Kate understood, like Ford himself, Tracy was hypersensitive and easily broken. At the same time, Tracy wanted no favors or special treatment. Always alert to potential insult, he expected Ford to be as demanding of him as he was of everybody else.

George Cukor prided himself on never offering Tracy even the most minimal direction. According to Harry Carey, Jr., a Ford stock company member, many Hollywood directors quaked at the prospect of telling Tracy to cross the room. When a director did offer strong ideas of his own, the "actor's actor" might smother his forehead with his palm as though absorbing all he had been told; then do whatever he felt like doing.

In contrast, with Ford he expected to be corrected and criticized. He did not want Ford to ride him; yet he did not want to be coddled either. He feared the director's abuse; but more than that, he dreaded his pity.

Spencer would have been furious if he knew the extent to which Kate had engineered things behind his back. She explained to Ford that Tracy had no trouble starting first thing in the morning; but he required a nap at lunchtime, and even then he had a tendency to wilt early. That first day on the set, Ford completed his first shot by 10:15. Explaining that he wouldn't need Tracy in the afternoon, the director sent him home before lunch.

According to Barbara Ford, whenever her father sensed that Spencer was petering out, he pretended to be tired himself.

"God, I'm exhausted," Ford would moan. "You know, I think we've done a full day's work and I don't know why the hell you don't go home."

Ford was such a good actor that Tracy never understood this was all for his benefit; he just thought poor Ford was getting old.

In an effort to make Spencer feel secure in the midst of the stock company, Ford had cast several of Tracy's "playmates"—as he called Pat O'Brien, Jimmy Gleason, Wally Ford, and Frank McHugh. Even so, when all the actors marched off to lunch, it was tacitly understood that Tracy would not join them. Nor was he expected when Barbara Ford cooked for the boys at her house near the Columbia ranch, where some sequences were shot. Instead, he took a nap in his dressing room.

Only once were Tracy's problems obliquely referred to, and that was when Carleton Young offered to bring a case of Irish whiskey to the set for St. Patrick's Day.

Ford blew his top: "On this set?! Are you kidding?! What do you want to do, Carleton, shut down the set for a month? We've got a bunch of drunks on the set!" Barbara Ford counted eight periodic alcoholics, including Spencer and her father.

Kate was not present for the first week of filming. Since December, she had been touring with *Much Ado About Nothing*; the tour ended on March 1. Her absence allowed the men to work things out themselves. When she finally appeared on Stage 8 at Columbia Studios on Monday, March 3, it seemed to her that Tracy and Ford were stalking around each other like prize bulls in a ring. She imagined that each had a deep understanding of the other's cunning.

She threw back her head and laughed out loud at the sight of them together again. Obviously the pairing had worked. Ford pointedly treated Tracy like a member of the football team and Spencer exuded confidence, knowing he was doing some of his best acting in years.

Kate joined the company for 4 o'clock tea. At a moment when Sean dreamed of having her back in his life, it cannot have been easy for him to sit there with Kate and Spencer; but for love of her, he did. Meta Sterne, in picture hat and pearls, remembered that the ritual of tea and biscuits on every Ford set had begun with Kate during *Mary of Scotland*. That afternoon, besides the usual jokes and songs at the table, there were emotions that Spencer could scarcely understand.

Or maybe he did. The next morning he called in sick. If Ford worried that Spencer had taken one of his notorious two-week lunch breaks, he did not show it. Yet he must have breathed a sigh of relief when Tracy, making no excuses, turned up at 8:45 on Wednesday morning. That day, Ford sent him home twenty minutes before teatime.

By the time *The Last Hurrah* wrapped on April 24, an air of normality seemed to have settled over Ford's dealings with Tracy and Hepburn. Ostensibly the old tensions dissolved as Ford appeared to accept Kate's relationship with Spencer; but in reality, things became more complicated than ever. Kate's visits to the set had churned up a great many feelings, and not just on Ford's side.

As always, his oddness fascinated her. And she loved being admired unreservedly; there could be no question that he adored everything she did. That was so unlike Tracy. Ford was forever encouraging Kate to perform her little tricks. Yet no sooner would she drift into the old intimacy, laughing and telling stories, than she would pull back suddenly lest she go too far. Kate seemed frightened of his feelings, and of her own.

He loved that in private she still addressed him as Sean. He cherished her visits to his office. He devoured every letter. He leapt on every reference to their shared past. He was very moved when Kate alluded to his visit to Fenwick in 1936 as though to signal that, yes, she remembered all that had passed between them.

Sometimes he pressed too hard and she became skittish. She turned down repeated pleas to make a movie in Ireland. She declined his invitation to use the *Araner*, moored in Honolulu, as a refuge for herself and Phyllis while Spencer worked on a film in Hawaii.

Each time, Ford withdrew without protest, returning with another offer soon afterward. He had no intention of giving up. He kept looking for his opening. He even offered Tracy another project, if that was what it took to allow him to steal more time with Kate.

For a long time, Kate at least had the comfort that her best friend was also involved in a relationship with a married man. With Palache she could talk about her difficult personal situation as perhaps with no one else. But the dynamics of the friendship changed when Rus Jones finally reached an understanding with his wife.

In 1954, the Cosmopolitan Club blackballed Palache's membership application out of respect for Mrs. Jones. The outcome of this action was unexpected: Mrs. Jones seemed mortified that a public issue had been made of her wrecked marriage, and after years of denial she suddenly agreed to divorce. Rus married Palache in a small ceremony in Lakeville, Connecticut, soon afterward.

Finally Palache could have a real home of her own with the man she loved. She abandoned her Manhattan apartment for a spacious house high on a windy hill in North Salem, New York. She supervised the construction of terraces and stone walls; she created a garden and drove her own tractor over the steep meadows of their property. She and Rus raised Norfolk terriers.

She was hurt by Kate's response to her good fortune. Instead of being happy for her, Kate appeared to envy Palache's marriage and home, clearly pained by the contrast to her own life with Tracy.

The friendship was strong enough to withstand the tension. Kate and Palache had always been fiercely competitive; in the beginning, Palache had prided herself on being the better tennis player and the better student. In later years, she earned Kate's respect as a prominent investment banker and Bryn Mawr board member. Palache's own large ego allowed her to maintain equal footing with her famous friend. But of the two, homely Alice was certainly not supposed to be the one who finally got her man to marry her.

Sometimes it was as though Kate were still waiting for her life with Tracy to begin. Renting a series of houses in Los Angeles, she seemed poised for the moment when the old man would finally settle matters with Louise. There was always something determinedly transient about Kate's living arrangements; were she to buy a property, that might seem like an admission that her situation with Tracy was permanent.

It was. Mrs. Tracy had moved to a house in Benedict Canyon. She sent Christmas cards from Spencer and Louise. She kept up pretenses. She ignored press reports that described the Tracys as estranged. Spencer fulfilled a psychological need of his own by keeping Mrs. Tracy on a pedestal; he visited "the Hill"—as he called the new place—and talked to Louise on the phone regularly.

Cukor was Tracy's witness when he wrote a will, leaving everything to Louise. Plagued with respiratory problems, he feared each breath might be his last. His liver, bladder, and kidneys no longer functioned properly. He had an enlarged prostate. He suffered from high blood pressure. He was terrified that years of drink were destroying his memory. His rapidly deteriorating physical condition offered Mrs. Tracy hope that he might soon come home for good.

Anyone who saw Tracy on a film set in those days needed only to look around to find Kate, his nurse. After eighteen years with Spencer, her devotion to him had not diminished. She usually chose a spot behind a tangle of equipment, so that her presence would not "throw" the old man while he worked. The knitting needles in her freckled hands moved swiftly, methodically. Her emaciated face reminded Tennessee Williams of the image of a medieval saint in a Gothic cathedral.

Off camera, Spencer slouched in a canvas chair beside her. She gave him his pills. She plied him with milk for his ulcer, water for his "plumbing problems." Again and again, she rushed over to the director to coo, "Boy, he's really something, isn't he?"

Much as Kate had hoped, *The Last Hurrah* enabled Spencer to function on a film set again. Working with Ford had calmed him considerably. Once more, work provided the escape he so desperately needed. Although the new Ford project, *The Judge and his Hangman*, never came to fruition, Tracy soon found a champion in Stanley Kramer. Kramer planned shooting schedules around Tracy's inability to work long hours. But the situation remained tenuous. Kate lived with the threat that at any moment Spencer could be plunged into a new bout of self-destructive behavior.

There was no longer any question of her accepting an open-ended commitment, such as a play in New York or London. Determined to keep a watchful eye on Tracy, Kate limited her own assignments to the gaps in his schedule. On this principle, she slipped off to make two pictures of her own, in addition to a second summer season at Stratford performing *Twelfth Night* and *Antony and Cleopatra*.

While Tracy waited to report to Stanley Kramer for *Inherit the Wind*, she played Violet Venable in a film version of Tennessee Williams's *Suddenly Last Summer* at Shepperton Studios near London. Kate thought Williams America's finest living playwright; she was eager to tackle one of his great women's roles. From the first, however, *Suddenly Last Summer* proved an unhappy experience; the material seemed to trouble Kate, although no one could quite understand why.

Kate grew increasingly agitated in the role of a doting mother whose only son, Sebastian, has died under mysterious circumstances. Mrs. Venable has fabricated an elaborate story to explain what happened to Sebastian. Her niece Catherine (played by Elizabeth Taylor), who witnessed the young man's horrific death, poses the sole threat to Mrs. Venable's sanitized account. Mrs. Venable seeks to have Catherine lobotomized at a state mental hospital so that the truth will never come out.

In the story of the traumatized young witness and the parent eager to prevent her from remembering, the parallels to Kate's own past were inescapable.

"If you only knew what it means to me when I have to say those things!" she shouted at Joseph Mankiewicz, who was directing the film.

Mankiewicz and the producer Sam Spiegel presumed Hepburn was merely being prudish about Williams's treatment of homosexuality and other sexual themes. "That's the play, and that's what we have to do," the director replied.

Hepburn decided that she must distance herself from the material by making Mrs. Venable seem mad. Mankiewicz, mistaking her agitation for a desire to take over the picture, fought her every step of the way. The result was unbearable tension on the set. On the last day of filming, Hepburn spat in Mankiewicz's face as a parting gesture.

She strode into Spiegel's office. "You're just a pig in a silk suit who sends flowers!" Kate informed him. Then she spat on the floor and marched out.

After Tracy completed *Judgment at Nuremberg*, his second picture for Stanley Kramer, Kate seized the opportunity to do a screen adaptation of Eugene O'Neill's *Long Day's Journey into Night*. When producer Ely Landau and director Sidney Lumet offered Hepburn the role of Mary Tyrone, they asked whether Tracy might be interested in playing her husband, James.

For a long time, Spencer had been making noises about wanting to do an O'Neill play; for a long time, Kate and others had been urging him to try. Landau's offer appeared virtually risk-free. The film would be shot quickly, and Kate would be there to cushion Spencer at every step. When Kate inquired whether Landau intended to tamper with the text, the producer told her he intended to shoot the play in its entirety. The project seemed like an actor's dream.

Yet Tracy turned Landau down. Ostensibly the reason was money; Tracy made a big point of refusing to work for the $25,000 Kate happily accepted. Complaining about the fee, however, was probably just a reversion to Spencer's tactic, noted by Terry Helburn, of throwing every obstacle in the path of actually appearing in an O'Neill play. Even at this late stage, Spencer was plagued with insecurity which prevented him from accepting a last chance to prove, to himself as much as to others, all he was capable of as an actor. Landau and Lumet cast Ralph Richardson in his place.

Kate gave one of her strongest performances. As in *The African Queen*, she drew on her mother for inspiration. Rosie Sayer embodied Mrs. Hepburn's air of fearlessness; Mary Tyrone hinted at her fears.

Kate created enormous psychological tension by emulating the physical evidence of Mrs. Hepburn's lifelong struggle to conceal turbulent emotions. She clutched herself defensively. She played with her arms. She touched her breasts. She tightened her jaw. She covered her lower face with her hand, curling her fingers inward and poking the index finger between her lips. One moment her voice was taut and constrained; the next, she allowed all the pent-up rage to spew out. Now she turned down the sides of her mouth; now she flashed a broad, tense, heart-piercing smile. In another role, such gestures might come across as mannerisms, but here they powerfully communicate Mary Tyrone's inner turmoil.

Long Day's Journey into Night was filmed in thirty-seven days in September and October 1961, in Manhattan and on City Island in the Bronx. Only the dubbing remained to be done when Kate sailed with Spencer on the *Queen Mary*; he was due in Berlin for the world premiere of *Judgment at Nuremberg*.

Kate later told Cukor that the trip nearly finished Spencer off. He fell ill at the screening on December 14 and had to be rushed back to his hotel. They went on to London as scheduled but left before the English premiere on account of Spencer's kidney disorder.

Tracy felt certain he was dying. As soon as Kate finished dubbing in New York, she took the old man to Palm Springs for a rest. Hardly had they settled in, when Kate was called to her ailing father's bedside.

Thus began a frantic year of rushing between Tracy and Dr. Hepburn. After a week in California, Kate would find herself abruptly summoned to Connecticut. She put her career on hold; whatever time she could snatch from Spencer must now be devoted to Dad.

Until the age of eighty, Dr. Hepburn had remained remarkably vigorous. It was no secret in the family that he had quickly grown bored with Santa; his efforts to educate her were soon abandoned. Yet "poor old Sant"—as Kate called her stepmother with a dash of condescension—continued to worship Dr. Hepburn "as a god"; when his health began to fail in 1960, she dutifully attended to his every need. He suffered from arteriosclerosis and a burst gall bladder. Bob performed prostate surgery; he told Kate that their father must be in great pain. But unlike Spencer, who constantly whined about ailments real and imagined, Dr. Hepburn refused to complain.

A new era began when Kate asked Palache, senior vice president at the Fiduciary Trust Company, to take over from Dr. Hepburn as her financial manager.

In May 1962, Fran Rich reported to John Ford that she had just spent a good deal of time with Kate in Hartford. Dr. Hepburn appeared to be failing rapidly. Too weary to speak, he withdrew into himself. Yet there could be no doubt that his mind was intact. He was clearly aware of everything that went on in the room. And he remained as stubborn as ever. His balance became so poor that he required two people to help him walk. Nonetheless, Dr. Hepburn insisted on getting out of bed himself. On one occasion he fell, smashing his forehead against a desk.

"Damn fool!" he growled when his children rushed in to pick him up.

He grew unresponsive. Often he did not speak or communicate for days. Yet when Bob rolled him onto his left side, so that Dr. Chester Fairlie could listen to his lungs, Dr. Hepburn gave a long, slow wink, which the son interpreted to mean, "These darned medical men; just what do they think they can do!"

Dr. Hepburn contracted pneumonia. On the night of November 19, Kate, now fifty-five, joined her brothers and sisters at the bedside.

"Is that oxygen mask comfortable, Dad?" Bob asked.

Dr. Hepburn replied with a firm squeeze of the hand.

He slipped into a coma at about 11 p.m. and died at 8 the following morning. He was eighty-two.

It was forty-one years since Kate, as a thirteen-year-old child, had tacitly accepted the pact of silence that condemned her to a lifetime of unanswered questions. Now her father was dead, his needs no longer a concern. Yet the repercussions of their pact continued to play out in Kate's struggle to protect Tracy from himself. With Tracy, she asked the questions she had been forbidden to ask about Tom. In trying to salvage him, she devoted years to trying to salvage the past.

Kate spent Thanksgiving with her brothers and sisters at Peg's farm in Canton, Connecticut. When she returned to California, she committed herself totally to the task of keeping Spencer alive—as she had failed to do with Tom. From then on, as Palache said: "There was nothing that could happen that could interfere with anything that had to do with that relationship or with him: nothing, nothing, nothing."

To reach the famous Hollywood house called the Aviary, you drove up a long, steep, winding road to the former John Barrymore estate. Also known as the Birdcage, the whimsical, airy, high-ceilinged Mediterranean-style house on Tower Grove Drive was once a menagerie of rare tropical birds. There were French windows, skylights, and a leaded stained-glass window depicting Barrymore and his wife, Dolores Costello. When the marriage ended, Barrymore was said to have slaughtered the birds and used them as tiebacks for curtains in the main house.

Kate had rented one of Hollywood's most fabled hilltop properties with panoramic views across the city and the ocean, but she spent most nights in the tiny maid's room off the kitchen at Spencer's cottage. Tracy wanted her nearby in case he could not breathe. He was terrified of death. He could not bear to have anyone in his room, so she lay in the maid's room, listening for a cry in the dark.

Kate was careful always to refer to the cottage as his. Spencer had not invited her to share his home; he had allowed Kate in strictly "in a nursing capacity," as Palache explained the arrangement.

There was plenty of work available in Hollywood if Kate wanted it. In recent years she had earned Academy Award nominations for *Summertime, The Rainmaker, Suddenly Last Summer,* and *Long Day's Journey into Night.* The O'Neill film, in particular, had marked a turning point as the critics hailed, in Dwight MacDonald's words, the emergence of "a superb tragedienne." The praise thrilled her; but, as Irene Selznick explained to Binkie Beaumont, at this point Kate would be interested in a role only if Tracy could co-star. Spencer, ill and depressed, desperately needed the refuge of work; but there were no offers. The studios knew that he could no longer work a full day.

Kate played tennis at the Beverly Hills Hotel most mornings; afterward, she often stopped at John Ford's office on Palm Avenue in West Hollywood, about five minutes from the Tracy cottage. The walls were cluttered with photographs of the cowboys and other actors he had worked with: Harry Carey, Tom Mix, Duke Wayne, George O'Brien, Hank Fonda, Ward Bond, John Carradine, Victor McLaglen, Andy Devine and many others. The air was thick with cigar smoke. Ford would strike a match on the sole of his shoe, then toss it on the floor. Two dachshunds chased each other on the filthy rugs.

Sean's face was very pale, his hair white and wispy. Meta Sterne would rush in with a tray of tea and biscuits. In the nearly three decades she had worked for Ford, most stock company members had assumed she was a spinster; now it came out that she had been married from the start. Some said Meta's husband was a gangster, some said an invalid paralyzed from the waist down.

About this time, George O'Brien began to worry about Ford. More and more he spent his days reading and chainsmoking cigars in bed.

"Winston, do you want me to get General Eisenhower up here?" O'Brien joked.

"Jesus, I'm tired, George," Ford replied.

He and Mary were constantly at each other's throats. The Ford home in Bel Air, a white Colonial house purchased when Odin Street was torn down, rang with shrieks and shouts. Aside from the passions involved, Jack was now hard of hearing. He accused Mary of spending more than his annual income; he confronted her with having squandered $7000 on a wardrobe for Barbara; he waved receipts for $760 spent between 10:30 a.m. and noon; he described her spendthrift ways as a mania.

"It's a conspiracy!" Mary would yell. She laced her tirades with phrases like "separate maintenance" and "community property rights." She accused him of concealing enormous holdings in A.T. & T.

He insisted he had turned the stock over to the bank for loans to pay taxes. He said he was going broke. He talked of donating the *Araner* to the Navy. He threatened to give Mary the house and all he owned, then run off to Europe on a tax dodge. But she would probably "piss everything away" in a year, he predicted, forcing him to return.

"Where is the money going?" Mary lamented. "I'm not spending it! You must be keeping another woman!"

Ford did not escape to Europe, but he did often travel up the steeply winding road to the Aviary. His driver, Bill, took him through a tall, spiked iron gate and up to the front door past Italian cypresses and pine trees. Tubs overflowed with Kate's roses and sweet peas.

Fresh air swept through open windows. She and Ford would sit in the sunny upstairs studio, where she kept her easel, paints, and brushes beneath a row of skylights. He examined her canvases. Kate read and gave detailed opinions on his new scripts. She listened to his problems as he faced the fact that the studios were no longer eager to back him.

His powers were failing; he could hardly deny it. His eyesight and hearing were terrible. As he worked, he could no longer see a completed film in his mind. He abused prescription drugs. He was afraid to go to the croaker for a complete checkup.

In April 1963, Warner Bros. threatened to cancel *Cheyenne Autumn* unless he added a few stars to the cast. In the new Hollywood, his name was no longer enough. Kate wasted no time in engineering a cameo for Spencer. Ford gave him a small role he could easily handle when shooting began in Monument Valley in September; another cameo went to Jimmy Stewart.

In mid-June, Kate moved Spencer to a rented house on Trancas Beach for the summer. She gave their address to Ella Winter and a few other close friends.

If you passed the simple wooden house at 30842 Broad Beach Road, you were likely to see Spencer's black Thunderbird in the carport. When the couple went out, Tracy waited, head lowered, in the passenger seat while Kate loaded the car with his oxygen tank and anything else they might need. If she didn't move quickly enough, he pressed the horn impatiently.

That was the scene on July 21 as Tracy and Hepburn prepared to go off on a Sunday picnic. It was a few minutes past noon. Kate wore a white sunsuit, Spencer an open-necked gray shirt and gray trousers. She had just put the picnic basket and oxygen tank in the back seat when suddenly Tracy went ashen and flailed for breath.

Kate ran inside to summon the Zuma Beach fire department; she reported a man with a heart attack. While she waited for them, she tried to administer oxygen. She held Tracy's hand and whispered to him. He refused to lie down.

The rescue unit arrived at 12:31. Fire Captain Robert M. Robb found Tracy breathing laboriously.

"Be calm and just relax," Kate told Spencer. "Everything is going to be all right." She herself seemed very calm and in control.

A physician from a nearby house gave Tracy an injection, which appeared to soothe him. The fire department administered oxygen for about forty-five minutes. Kate brought a glass of milk with ice cubes for his ulcer. Finally, a private ambulance, siren blaring, took Tracy to St. Vincent's Hospital in Los Angeles. As attendants wheeled the stretcher to the emergency entrance, Tracy pulled a sheet over his face to hide from the flashing cameras and reporters' questions.

The doctors told Kate that he had not had a heart attack after all. Pulmonary edema, or fluid on the lungs, had hindered his breathing. That night, Kate slipped out a side entrance at the hospital.

Shortly before midnight, reporters were still outside the hospital when Louise Tracy emerged. In appearance and manner, the actor's wife was said to resemble Eleanor Roosevelt. Louise had rushed to St. Vincent's the moment she heard what happened, nursing the hope that illness would finally cause Spencer to come back to her.

Louise paused to tell reporters: "He is doing as well as can be expected. He seems to be coming along very nicely. We hope he will be able to come home in two or three days."

Once Tracy was home—though in his cottage, not in Benedict Canyon with Louise—Kate began to leave the light on in the kitchen. She would close the maid's room door, get into bed, and turn out the lamp. Many nights she could not fall asleep until she heard Spencer in the hallway. Sometimes she waited for hours.

She knew the rhythms of his walk. If Spencer moved too slowly, Kate wondered why. If she heard the creaking of the table that faced the hall door, she knew he had paused to lean against it.

Kate listened as Spencer padded into the kitchen, where she kept the water kettle on a very low boil. She always left a cup and saucer nearby. She might put on slippers and join him. Other times she lay in the dark, waiting for Spencer to prepare his nightly cup of tea and return to his room.

She slept lightly. A long portable cord connected the buzzer beside his bed with the maid's room. Even during the day, if Tracy was feeling sick Kate would take the cord with her whenever she stepped outside. He must not be left alone, struggling for breath. She kept an oxygen tank in the hallway.

Tracy's hospitalization had given them both quite a scare. Spencer remained at St. Vincent's for twelve days. After several weeks back with Kate, he had to check into the hospital again on August 30 for further tests. Carroll Tracy and his wife, Dorothy, no supporters of Spencer's relationship with Kate, handled the press.

Spencer was too weak to go to Monument Valley for *Cheyenne Autumn*, so Ford agreed to shoot his material in the studio afterward. In December, Tracy, still ailing, had to back out altogether; Edward G. Robinson replaced him.

Spencer's health improved a bit in the early months of 1964. Kate moved a stationary bicycle into his room. She bought a police dog named Lobo to encourage Spencer to take long walks at the reservoir. She played Brahms recordings and brought him books on Catholicism. She spoiled him with rich soups and hot fudge sundaes. According to their friend Jean Negulesco, when Kate invited Tracy's cronies in for lunch, she always served Spencer first.

He had a hair-trigger temper. When she expressed an opinion he would suddenly cut her off: "For Christ's sake, come on!"

"Well, I think that—"

"That's what you think!"

Soon Tracy seemed well enough for Kate to resume her morning tennis game with the pro at the Beverly Hills Hotel. She would drive up to the Aviary and spend hours happily painting in her light-filled upstairs studio. She described herself as an insane spirit who danced around the trees when she was alone.

In February, when Stanley Kramer offered Kate the role of the middle-aged Southern belle in *Ship of Fools*, she assumed he was about to ask Spencer to play the doctor. When the director awkwardly announced that he had decided to cast a younger actor, Kate grew indignant. She turned down the role, refusing to appear without Tracy. The following month, MGM announced that in May Tracy would play a veteran poker player in *The Cincinnati Kid*, co-starring Steve McQueen; but once again, he withdrew at the last minute.

Now that Tracy had pulled out of two pictures, film offers were very unlikely to continue. That summer, he visited the *Ship of Fools* set at Columbia two or three days a week. Ostensibly he was there to learn to direct by watching Kramer. He gave press interviews and was much photographed in a canvas director's chair with his name on the back. He hoped to send out the message that he was in good health and ready to return to film acting.

Meanwhile, Kate agreed that George Cukor should approach Walter F. Wanger with a proposal to direct a new Tracy and Hepburn vehicle at MGM. Kate and Spencer met with Wanger, who appeared most enthusiastic. Cukor assumed they had a firm commitment; but in September, he sadly reported to Kate that the producer seemed to be politely backing off. MGM would have been happy to sign Hepburn, but at this point Tracy was another matter. The news left Spencer's ego in tatters.

John Ford, in a black mood of his own, picked a terrible moment to call Kate from Honolulu, inviting her to make a picture at MGM. The previous July, Ford had gone to Ireland to shoot *Young Cassidy*, based on Sean O'Casey's autobiography. Ford had wanted to turn the project down; but when he showed the script to Kate she urged him to do it. Two weeks into shooting, he felt too sick and weak to continue and flew home in despair that his career was over; another director finished *Young Cassidy* in his place. But Ford wanted one last chance to work with Kate. In late September, he did everything in his power to persuade her to accept the role of Miss Andrews in *7 Women*. She knew how much it meant to him. But the situation with Tracy forced her to turn him down.

Tracy's health deteriorated. A prostatectomy at Good Samaritan Hospital in Los Angeles left him near death. At first he seemed to get through surgery nicely, and the tumor was non-malignant. Three days later, his condition took a drastic turn for the worse. Irene Selznick talked to Kate in the midst of the ordeal; she found her more upbeat and composed than she would have believed possible.

The doctors soon announced that Tracy was out of danger. But he faced another lengthy recuperation; worse, this time he and Kate could hardly deceive themselves that he would be offered new film roles when he was better.

Stanley Kramer surprised them. Kramer worried that Tracy was spending too much time feeling sorry for himself. "He was sitting at home doing nothing," the director recalls. "He wasn't amused. He wasn't interested. He wasn't driving to go on." Kramer offered Tracy and Hepburn the lead roles in *Guess Who's Coming to Dinner*; they would play a couple whose daughter announces plans to marry a black man.

Kate loved the idea; Spencer was resistant. "But I get tired," he groaned.

"You won't get tired," Kramer promised. "I'll send you home every day at one."

Tracy hesitated.

"Spence, are you going to sit there in your rocker and wait for oblivion?" Kramer challenged.

Tracy agreed to take the part; Hepburn, standing behind him, silently applauded Kramer's victory.

The film provided an opportunity to engineer the screen debut of Kate's niece Katharine Grant, an aspiring actress. Marion's daughter, using the stage name Katharine Houghton, was cast as Kate and Spencer's daughter.

One problem remained: Tracy was uninsurable. To get the picture made, both Kramer and Hepburn agreed to put their salaries in escrow. Should Spencer drop out, the money would be used to reshoot with another actor.

Less than a month before rehearsals were set to begin, Spencer, fighting for breath, collapsed at home. The fire department rescue squad administered oxygen. He did not require hospitalization; but press reports made the executives at Columbia nervous.

"Spence, nobody wants you to do it if you're not up to it," Kramer told him. "There are no obligations. It isn't too late to call the whole thing off, and I will, if you can't make it. But I'm not going to make the picture without you, and that's final."

Tracy, thinking it over, stared at him for a moment.

"Okay," he decided. "Let's go."

When Tracy and Hepburn appeared for the first day of rehearsals on Monday, March 13, 1967, Kramer had no way of knowing whether Spencer would make it through the picture. There was a good chance he wouldn't. He had always been the sort of actor who prefers to play a full scene on camera; he believed the long take allowed him more perfectly to capture the arc of a character's emotions. Emphysema kept him from doing that any more; he had to keep stopping to catch his breath. One long, complex speech posed special difficulties. In his prime, Spencer would have insisted on shooting it in a day, possibly in one take. On *Guess Who's Coming to Dinner*, the speech took six days.

There were other problems. Much as Tracy had long dreaded, he now had great difficulty remembering lines; he persistently forgot cues in dialogue. As usual, his fear and frustration erupted in displays of anger at Kate.

"What the hell are you doing, kneeling?" he shouted during rehearsal.

"Spencer, I just thought it would be appropriate," Kate replied.

"Spencuh!" he imitated her accent and brittle voice. "Christ, you talk like you've got a feather up your ass all the time! Will you go out and come in like a human being?"

To the end, Kate permitted Spencer to talk to her in a way that she would accept from no one else. On their last picture together, everything had changed, and nothing.

"All right," Kate said softly, and did as commanded.

"She was vulnerable," says Stanley Kramer. "Now that's a great, great virtue to be vulnerable. Many people spend their lives trying not to be vulnerable. She was vulnerable and she could handle it."

In May, there was an uncomfortable sense on the set that Tracy had entered the last days of his life. On Monday, May 22, as the production began its final week, Tracy took Kramer aside: "You know, I read the script again last night, and if I die on the way home tonight, you can still release the picture with what you've got."

On Wednesday morning he completed his last shot, the scene in the drive-in after Tracy bumps another car. Back at the cottage, he called everyone he could think of with the news. "I made it! I made it!" he crowed repeatedly on the phone.

After that, the nights were particularly bad. Tracy swallowed sleeping pills and turned out the light, but still he could not rest. In those last three weeks, Kate would slip into his room in the night. She would put her quilt and pillow on the floor beside his bed. Sometimes she brought the sofa cushions from the living room.

She said: "I'll just talk and talk and you'll be so bored you're bound to drift off."

She kept her distance. She remained on the floor. She did not climb into bed with him. As she talked the old man to sleep, she caressed Lobo. Watching Spencer toss and turn and sigh, Kate tried to understand the sources of his torment, something which she had been forbidden to do with Tom.

Eventually Spencer lay still. She would take the long portable cord attached to his buzzer and return to the maid's room. She closed her door, climbed into bed, and turned off the lamp.

At about 3 a.m. on Saturday, June 10, Kate was awakened by Spencer's footsteps in the hallway. She heard the creaking of the table opposite the hall door as he paused to lean against it. By the time he entered the kitchen, Kate had put on her slippers. She was about to leave her room when she heard the crash of his cup, followed by a loud thud as he hit the floor.

She threw open the door, kneeled, and held him in her arms.

His eyes were closed; the red flannel pajamas were splattered with tea. Spencer Tracy had died of a heart attack at the age of sixty-seven.

Kate summoned Phyllis Wilbourn from the Aviary. She summoned Willie and Ida Gheczy, the couple who worked on the Cukor property. They carried Spencer to his bed. Kate covered him up and lit candles.

Phyllis helped move her clothes and other personal possessions to the car, so there would be no sign of her when Mrs. Tracy arrived. Then, on second thought, Kate decided to stand her ground. Now that Spencer was dead, she need have no compunction about claiming the cottage as her home. She and Phyllis moved everything back inside.

Soon the tiny cottage swarmed with people. George Cukor rushed down the narrow flight of steps cut in the hillside. Howard Strickling, retired from his post as MGM publicity director, came to control the inevitable press onslaught. Spencer's family appeared: Carroll and Dorothy, Johnny and Susie, and of course Louise.

She, too, would lay claim to a status Spencer had denied her; now that he was dead she need not hesitate to insist on all the rights and privileges due to Mrs. Spencer Tracy.

When Kate told the undertaker—hired by the family—which suit she wanted Spencer buried in, Louise spoke up.

"But he's my husband. I should pick out the—"

"Oh, Louise, what difference does it make?" Kate cut her off.

The battle lines were drawn. As the family left, Dorothy Tracy demanded the keys to the cottage.

"What did you say, Dorothy?" Phyllis shot back. "The keys to this house—our house?"

The Monday morning funeral was a family affair; Kate did not attend. But at the last minute, she decided to see the old man off at the undertaker's. She and Phyllis slipped into the rear of Cunningham and Walsh, where the driver allowed them to help lift the coffin into the hearse. The women discreetly followed the cortège until Immaculate Heart of Mary Church on Santa Monica Boulevard came into view. Kate was gone by the time the hearse arrived at the church; someone waited there to take over for her.

The lead pallbearer, with wispy white hair, smoked glasses, and a black patch over his left eye, stepped up to the wagon's back door. John Ford gripped Spencer Tracy's coffin and helped guide it into the service.

TWENTY-FOUR

Spencer's death left Kate in an awkward position. Whatever she told herself, friends and colleagues knew that the cottage had never really been her home; now, some wondered where to reach her to express condolences. And they wondered whether she would want to hear from them. Gladys Cooper felt uneasy writing directly; she asked Cukor to speak to Kate on her behalf. Cathleen Nesbitt feared that somehow it would be presumptuous to reach out, yet thought she must; she, too, wrote to Cukor.

A good many people experienced similar qualms. Kate wasn't the widow; she and Tracy had always kept their relationship so private. Would she be offended if one spoke openly now? Did she want others to acknowledge her role in Spencer's life?

Laurence Olivier and Irene Selznick worried about where Kate would live, now that she was alone. Selznick, about to leave for London on a business trip, canceled her hotel and took a large apartment instead. Whether Kate actually came to London didn't matter; Selznick wanted her to know that she had a roof for her.

A few days after the funeral, Kate called Louise Tracy. Like Alice Palache, who eventually became friends with Rus Jones's ex-wife, Kate reached out to her longtime adversary.

Kate had stepped back and allowed Mrs. Tracy to run the show at the funeral. Newspaper photographs showed Louise on Howard Strickling's arm, as though clinging to the studio-manufactured version of the marriage which Strickling had spent many years publicizing. On the day of Tracy's death, Strickling had put out one last story to conceal the truth: Press reports fixed the heart attack at approximately 6 a.m. and portrayed Louise and other family members arriving at the cottage before Spencer's friends George Cukor and Kate Hepburn appeared.

In the aftermath of all that, Kate seemed to want Louise to acknowledge her, if only just between the two of them.

"You know, Louise, you and I can be friends. You knew him at the beginning, I at the end—or we can just pretend that—I might be a help with the kids."

"Well, yes," said Louise. "But you see, I thought you were only a rumor."

No doubt the remark stung because the word "rumor" so perfectly suggested the strangeness of Kate's twenty-six-year relationship.

Because Tracy and Hepburn took unusual pains to keep that relationship private, people sometimes wondered whether perhaps, as the studio insisted, they were no more than "staunch friends." Through the years, it was obvious that they often spent months apart. Word got around among Cukor's friends that Kate stayed in George's guest room; or, in later years, that she slept in the maid's room at the cottage. Based on these arrangements, their affair was sometimes mistakenly described as platonic; Kate and—occasionally—Spencer were rumored to be homosexual.

At first, after Spencer died, Kate wanted everything exactly as he had left it. She clung to the physical remains of their intimacy. She kept his books on the oak table, his medicine on the shelf. She moved into his room. She sat in his chair and wore his old shirts. She complained to Irene Selznick when this person or that failed to contact her, either directly or through Cukor; yes, Kate wanted friends to recognize her life with Spencer and was hurt when they did not.

Overgrown trees and shrubs had long ago crowded out the light in Spencer's cottage; all remained dark, shadowy, ambiguous. Kate realized she could not recall whether he had ever told her he loved her. She admitted that she really did not know how he had felt about her.

For years, Kate had wondered whether Tom had really said "You're my girl, aren't you? You're my favorite girl in the whole world" before he went upstairs to die. To protect her father, she had told so many versions of her brother's death that she could no longer remember the truth. Something like that happened now with Spencer. She had spent twenty-six years pretending there was nothing between them. How could she expect people to acknowledge what she had had with him when she was no longer certain herself?

Kate had just turned sixty. Exactly three decades had passed since Ford finally wrote to tell her how he felt about her; and Kate wrote back, speaking of her thirtieth birthday and the struggle to make sense of what the next thirty years would be like. In 1937, she had every expectation of spending the rest of her life with him. Sean was her dearest friend; he provided a strength and understanding she could expect from no one else. Now those thirty years were over. Their lives had not worked out as either had anticipated, yet Sean was still there for Kate.

What did he want or expect following Tracy's death? For all the fantasies of leaving his wife now that they were both old and sick, surely Ford did not really intend to walk out. In his own peculiar way, he was devoted to Mary, or "Nana" as he called her. Still, he remained hopeful; Kate saw hope as one of Sean's defining characteristics. He pressed ahead determinedly; he worked at breaking down Kate's emotional resistance, although it would be some time before he let her know quite what he wanted. For now, he appeared content to resume the role of dearest friend, the one who understood Kate best. They agreed it was time for her to refill the reservoir.

Kate lined up an ambitious series of projects. By July 18, she had agreed to appear in *The Madwoman of Chaillot* for Ely Landau, the producer of *Long Day's Journey into Night*. The Giraudoux play, which had been a pet project of Constance Collier's, possessed the added attraction of reuniting Kate with John Huston; he had wanted to film it since 1952, when he had hoped to cast Greta Garbo.

Before Kate left for a week on Martha's Vineyard with Ruth

Gordon and Garson Kanin, she received a call from Abe Lastvogel. The agent asked her to read *The Lion in Winter*, a script about Eleanor of Aquitaine. Martin Poll, who often played tennis after Kate with the Beverly Hills Hotel pro, was producing the film. Kate and the Kanins checked into the Harbor View Hotel on Martha's Vineyard on July 27. She spent her days at Palache's beach house, where she read *The Lion in Winter*.

The script enthralled her. The story of Henry II's attachment to two women, his wife Eleanor and his young mistress Princess Alais, held a strong attraction for Kate, who had known first-hand what it is to be caught in a triangle with a married man.

With Ford and Tracy, however, Kate had been the mistress, the younger woman. *The Lion in Winter* called on her to inhabit the withered skin of the older rival, the wife who struggles to retain the power and status of her position. It called on her to imagine what it must be like to be Mary Ford or Louise Tracy. It called on her to explore why such a woman keeps fighting despite all humiliation, and to what degree love may remain a factor for both the husband and the betrayed wife. It called on her to make audiences understand and sympathize with the female figure who, in life, had been Kate's rival and enemy. She leapt at the challenge.

The Lion in Winter, to be directed by Anthony Harvey, had the added advantage of offering Kate an opportunity to co-star with Peter O'Toole, whose acting she much admired. It had been Kate who urged Sam Spiegel to cast O'Toole as Lawrence of Arabia when the producer wanted Albert Finney. Now, she welcomed her pairing with O'Toole as a chance to play all out in a battle of equals, much as she had done with Bogart in *The African Queen*.

"When do we start the picture?" Kate excitedly asked Poll when he called for her reaction. Her instinct was correct, of course; she would win an Academy Award for the role.

Poll explained that he was in the middle of preparations for a film based on Romain Gary's *The Ski Bum* and hoped to get to *The Lion in Winter* sometime after that.

"I must play this right away!" Kate insisted. "Suppose I get hit by a truck and don't play this role?"

Soon afterward, script problems forced Poll to withdraw from *The Ski Bum.* "When are we going to make this picture?" Kate demanded when he called with the news.

Hepburn's only stipulation was that she finish *The Lion in Winter* in time to start work with Huston on *The Madwoman of Chaillot* on February 12. That gave Poll six weeks to cast and prepare the entire production.

Back in Los Angeles that August, when she learned that Irene Selznick was planning her film-producing debut with *Martha*, based on two novels by Margery Sharp, Kate astonished her friend by offering to direct. Sean had been urging her to try since she directed the tower scene in *Mary of Scotland* in 1936. Kate dazzled Selznick with her ideas for the picture, which included hiring Jean Renoir as a technical adviser. She also considered Alan Jay Lerner's offer of the lead role in a Broadway musical based on the life of Coco Chanel. To avoid thinking about her troubles, she wanted to be certain that her schedule was filled for many months to come.

Yet her trip to Ireland to shoot the first part of *The Lion in Winter* unavoidably stirred up thoughts of Spencer and Sean. In December, swimming in the Irish Sea off Bray every morning at five, she meditated on the national character.

"You're known to be late!" Kate lectured Peter O'Toole on the first day of shooting. "I intend for you to be on time. I hear you stay out at night. You'd better be rested in the morning if you're going to work with me!"

That was her public persona. Letters home testify to a more wistful mood. The Irish landscape, which she had so often dreamed of with Sean, affected her powerfully now that she was seeing it at last—alone.

Once before, John Huston had offered comfort and caring at a time when she most needed it. Once before, in the aftermath of the death of someone close to her, Kate had depended on Huston to provide her with what she later described as that total escape from reality they had experienced in Africa together. In *The African Queen*, Huston had captured her as no other director had managed to do. He resembled Spencer and Sean in so many ways, yet he lacked their streak of self-destructiveness; it is no wonder, perhaps, that she instinctively turned to him now.

At Christmas Kate went to Galway. She spent four days at St. Cleran's, the Georgian manor house she dubbed Castle Huston. She slept in the Gray Room, in which a huge old crucifix hung over the bed, where she was served breakfast. Out the window she saw cows and horses, endless gray stone walls, and windswept beech and ash trees. Overflowing with art and artifacts, the house seemed like an image of John Huston's mind.

Childlike she explored the room full of African objects in the basement. She wandered among large Mexican figures and Japanese screens. She admired Italian bronzes and Etruscan vases. She marveled at the huge Monet painting of water-lilies in the drawing room. She peeked in at Huston's Venetian bed; eight or ten Japanese robes were draped over a screen.

She loved the sight of her host bowing and grinning in his too-perfect Irish casuals. They sat down to lunch, Huston at the head of the table, Kate and Phyllis, and Huston's assistants Betty O'Kelly and Gladys Hill. To Kate's exasperation, he talked of everything except *The Madwoman of Chaillot*; but by now she had accepted that Huston was not to be pushed.

One day they drove out to a stone cottage in Connemara, where she swam in the icy Atlantic. The barren, rocky coast fascinated her. Cromwell had pushed Sean's ancestors out of Galway and into the wilds of Connemara. Kate declared that one would have to be very tough to survive there.

She thought it typically perverse of Huston to allow her to leave after Christmas never having discussed the Giraudoux play. When she returned to St. Cleran's for New Year's, however, they had a very satisfying talk about the project.

Ely Landau did not share her enthusiasm for Huston's ideas. While Kate was in Arles, finishing *The Lion in Winter*, Landau and Huston quarreled at a script conference. On January 25, 1968, Huston called Kate to say he was off the picture. Landau checked in an hour later.

"If John's off, I'm off," Kate announced. But Landau soon

persuaded her to change her mind; he replaced Huston with Bryan Forbes.

George Cukor saw this as a period of healing for Kate, a time to make up for the years of immobility with Spencer. In her absence, Cukor cared for Lobo; every day his assistant drove the dog to the reservoir in Tracy's Thunderbird.

Kate rented a villa in St. Jean–Cap Ferrat, a bicycle ride from Victorine Studios in Nice, where *Madwoman* was filmed. Paul Henreid, also in the picture, thought Kate had changed markedly since Spencer's death: "He had constantly put her down, telling her what to do, and as he put it, he had 'kept her in her place.' Without him she seemed much freer, much more her own person."

In April, Kate was having breakfast on her large terrace high above the Mediterranean when Irene Selznick called with news of an Academy Award for her performance in *Guess Who's Coming to Dinner*. Kate released a statement declaring that she considered the Oscar to be for Tracy and Hepburn as a team. Privately, however, she wrote to Ella Winter that she was disgusted by the Academy's failure to name Spencer Best Actor.

Kate returned to Los Angeles to work on *Martha* with Irene. There were problems with the script. After Selznick completed a financing and distribution deal, they traveled to Jersey in the Channel Islands, to see what William Rose, the Academy Award-winning author of *Guess Who's Coming to Dinner*, could do with the material. Script conferences with Rose, a raconteur and heavy drinker, were great fun; but a suitable screenplay never materialized.

Meanwhile, Alan Jay Lerner pressed Kate to do *Coco*. She protested that she couldn't sing a note. She expressed reservations about the script. She insisted that she was too much the "country bumpkin" to play a *grande dame* like Coco Chanel. She predicted that audiences would stone her. Even as she said all that, however, the sheer risk of doing a musical obviously intrigued and excited her. Eager to try everything life had to offer her, Kate confessed to Ella Winter that she was sorely tempted to go ahead and make an ass of herself on Broadway.

Much remained unresolved between Kate and Sean. She would never know why he had failed to come to see her in *Jane Eyre*; he would never understand how he could have let her go. A sense of something unfinished permeated their encounters.

In June 1970, Kate grew very emotional when Ford, frail and in ill health, appeared at the Mark Hellinger Theater as *Coco* neared the end of its successful Broadway run. From the start, theatergoers had flocked to see Kate; one critic called the show "a form of endearment, a gesture of assent, an open palm of respect." For the first time in her life, Kate felt that audiences were rooting for her.

7 Women had indeed been Ford's last film. These days, unable to attract backing for a new picture, he often remained in bed, surrounded by stacks of books and crumpled candy wrappers, for days at a time. Determined to blast Jack out of bed, Mary would turn up the volume on her record player; but he had little reason to come downstairs anymore.

Kate knew what this trip cost him. For her, he pretended to be light on his feet. She loved that the entire company seemed to peek when Sean visited her dressing room after the performance. His desire to show that he remained passionately interested in everything Kate did moved her deeply.

Kate told everyone that Ford had come all the way east just to see her. But somehow, she didn't believe it herself. She was certain his main purpose was to visit Wild Bill Donovan in Washington, D.C. When she hinted that to Sean after he returned to California, he wrote back immediately, emphasizing that she was his sole reason for traveling cross-country. At seventy-six, he wanted Kate to know exactly how he felt. There was no time for anything else.

Two days after Ford wrote that letter, he and Mary celebrated their fiftieth anniversary; they repeated their marriage vows before a crowd of old friends ranging from John Wayne to George Cukor. Kate's role in Ford's emotional life was no secret to either man; and there had been other, less significant affairs through the years. Still, Mary had what she always wanted: She remained Mrs. John Ford to the end. Asked the secret of her long marriage, Mary said dryly: "Believe nothing you hear and only half of what you see."

Sean's visit seemed to free something in Kate, then sixty-three. After years of resisting his approaches, she was eager to entertain and flirt with him again. To read Kate's letters from this period is to be reminded of the songs she used to improvise for Phelps Putnam.

In bed in his dark room on Copa de Oro Road in Bel Air, Ford would have to hold Kate's letters almost to his nose to make out her tiny pen-and-ink drawings of Atienza, Spain, the walled city where she was filming Euripides's *The Trojan Women*, in which Michael Cacoyannis had cast her as Queen Hecuba. Kate described herself sipping coffee in bed at dawn; she evoked the blue light on the horizon, and the sounds of sheepbells, roosters, and crows; she told how the heat and dust felt on her skin and eyes.

She knew the kinds of images that would stir Sean. She marked on the drawings where the sun rose and set. She pictured the view from her adobe peasant house some 4000 feet above a vast brown valley. She spoke of the howling winds and the changing clouds and light. The stark, rocky landscape, which resembled Monument Valley, made Kate think of him. She sent her telephone number, and he called her often. From time to time, he would seek out Cukor just to talk about Kate.

Hepburn was in London filming Edward Albee's *A Delicate Balance*, under the direction of Tony Richardson, when Cukor wrote that Ford was dying. Cukor, who had recently hosted a Hollywood directors' luncheon in honor of Luis Buñuel, reported that Ford had been very brave to attend; but he was too ill to remain for the entire event. Afterward, Cukor learned that he had terminal cancer.

Kate became more open and direct. Each time Sean called, she let him know how much it meant to her to hear his voice. On an occasion when Kate could not talk freely because she was entertaining friends, she hurriedly wrote to explain why she had had to hang up so quickly. Easily wounded, Sean was likely to detect the slightest reserve in her voice; he had never stopped testing her. Kate wanted there to be no ambiguity about her feelings for him.

"Come for the death watch, Duke?" Ford asked when John Wayne visited the ranch house on dusty Old Prospector Trail in

Palm Desert, about 140 miles from Los Angeles, where the Fords moved in December 1972.

"Hell, no, Jack," Duke answered. "You're the anchor. You'll bury us all."

"Oh, well," said Ford, propped up on pillows in a small, shuttered, candelit room. "I think I'll stick around a while longer then."

A black, silver-mounted saddle loomed at the foot of his hospital bed. To his side were a portable television, a night table with a bottle of Guinness stout, and a statue of the Virgin Mary. A plastic bucket held an assortment of the old cigar butts he liked to chew.

"Like a cigar?" he would ask, offering the bucket to a guest. Most refused.

Barbara Ford or a nurse informed visitors that they could have five minutes with the old man.

Mary Ford, crippled with Parkinson's disease, usually received guests in her bedroom in a separate wing off the living room. Next to her bed stood the metal walker she used to move about the house. She could no longer belt the brew on account of an ulcer; age and illness had knocked much of the fight out of her.

But Mary waited intently in the living room the day in March 1973 when Kate Hepburn came to say goodbye. She posed, gripping her walker, among Jack's trophies: the six Academy Awards, the Legion of Merit and other military medals, the framed citations, the admiral's sword on the wall.

Ostensibly, Mary and Kate were on decent enough terms; in truth, they despised each other. To Mrs. Ford, Hepburn would always be the woman who had offered her $150,000 to give up Jack and allow him to take Barbara. While Kate remained closeted with her husband, Mrs. Ford talked loudly to Barbara, as though intent on reminding Kate just whose home this was.

Kate did not stay long that first day; she planned to spend a full week in Palm Desert. She fussed over Sean and chattered nervously. But the sight of him, thin and fragile in a nightshirt, was obviously very painful. His freckled hands with their delicate, long, slender fingers were still beautiful.

At first he pretended to feel better than he did. Always proud, he insisted that he had just gotten into bed, having spent the morning up and about. He watched intently as Kate talked; sometimes it was as though he had stopped listening, preferring to concentrate on every angle of the "strange, sharp face—the chiseled nose, the mouth, the long neck" that had fascinated him when he screened her films over and over in anticipation of shooting *Mary of Scotland.*

Kate struggled to seem calm, but now and then a high-pitched voice betrayed her.

Ominously silent, Sean would suddenly burst out with a comment on how beautiful she was. His timing was perfect; his words, so abrupt and emotional, completely destroyed her composure. She reacted with a blush in her voice as though no one had ever complimented her before. He enjoyed throwing her off like that.

As Kate leaned over him and smiled, she appeared to suppress a surge of feeling; suddenly she was reprimanding him for dropping cigar ash all over the bed. It was one thing to write letters and talk on the phone, another to be this close and not know what to do or say.

Insisting that she needed to rest, Kate promised to return in the morning. When she kissed him, Ford put his arm around her and asked if she knew he loved her. He had been waiting to do that for a very long time.

She indicated that she did.

Then he looked down at his wasted body and said that it was all over for him.

Kate said she knew and left.

She drove on a winding highway up into the mountains above Coachella Valley. She passed the 3000-foot altitude sign, then a marker announcing Pinyon Crest. The road turned to dirt. She kept climbing.

Lately, Kate had been taking stock. In recent days she had been about to launch a major lawsuit against MGM. After many months of work on a script based on Graham Greene's *Travels with My Aunt*, which she hoped to film with George Cukor, Kate found herself abruptly dismissed without compensation when MGM turned over the material to another writer. Cukor, indignant on Kate's behalf, urged her to go to court. Confident she would win, Kate sat with lawyers shortly before leaving Los Angeles. As they pored over documents showing how much work she had done, Hepburn suddenly declared to Phyllis, "This is the biggest bore!" Then she told her lawyer, "I think I might die of boredom suing Metro."

And that was that. The suit was off. At sixty-five, Kate had better things to do.

For one, she planned to return to Bryn Mawr for the first time since 1928. Although Kate refused to give that year's commencement address, she did finally allow Palache to convince her to meet the senior class on March 20 after her week in Palm Desert. The prospect terrified her.

She climbed the rugged dirt road past a sign announcing Shumway Ranch. After two miles, she reached the gate to what Fran Rich liked to call "the top of the world." At cliff's edge, a seven-foot bronze St. Francis, arms outstretched, loomed over the valley.

The artist's modern house and studios were hidden just over a hill. Massive sculptures erupted among the rocks as though from nature. One bronze portrait bust depicted Kate Hepburn as Cleopatra in an ornate headdress; Kate had asked Fran to capture that moment in *Antony and Cleopatra* when the queen reacts scornfully to Antony's decision to abandon his troops and follow her to Alexandria.

Not for Kate men like sweet, dear, devoted Luddy, prepared to give up everything for her. She was drawn to enigmatic, elusive figures "born to dark hysteria"; Phelps Putnam's self-characterization applied equally to John Ford and Spencer Tracy.

As Kate confessed to Sean in the days that followed, she had devoted years to trying to figure out both men.

"Takes a lot of time," Ford laughed ruefully.

Neither sat easily in this world, she pointed out. They came by rest and peace of mind with great difficulty. At times, they seemed to work very hard against themselves. One needed only to listen to Mary banging about in the living room among trophies and awards that, Kate believed, meant little to Sean. Mrs. Ford had spent decades making her husband feel inadequate. Yet when Kate offered light and life, he chose darkness.

He did not know why. As he told Kate now, he knew only that he had never meant to hurt her.

"I took life as it came along," Ford insisted.

"Yes," she said softly.

"You're an amazing woman, Kate," he said in a strong, resonant voice.

He would die in that room five months later. For now, they talked and talked. When Kate said it was time for his nap, he insisted he wasn't tired.

He asked about her brother—was he still writing?

Dick never changed, Kate replied. He wrote, he enjoyed life, he remained at Fenwick.

Mention of the place seemed to tear Sean apart inside; the old cottage had long since washed away, but that was the Fenwick he remembered.

"Look at that! Look at that sunset!" Kate had shouted as they first crossed South Cove together in 1936.

"Kate, why don't you let us enjoy these things," said Sean from the back seat with Mrs. Hepburn. "We can see them just as well as you can."

Kate had visited Fenwick the other day, she told him now. At high tide, the family house was nearly under water. As the north wind blew the waves off Long Island Sound, she thought she might never get out alive.

After Tracy and Ford, the emotional center of Kate's life shifted back to Connecticut and the world of her brothers and sisters.

When Dr. Hepburn died, Kate had devoted herself to caring for Spencer; there had been little time for family. Nor had she been a presence in Connecticut as she rushed from one project to another in the aftermath of Tracy's death.

Although Kate would rent Spencer's cottage until 1978, she

really had no reason to remain on the west coast. When she wasn't working, more and more she tended to spend the week in New York, weekends at Fenwick. Santa had lived on alone in the stately "new Llangollen" on Bloomfield Avenue in West Hartford; but now, Kate gave the property to the University of Hartford. "Poor old Sant" moved in with her sister, and Bob Hepburn cared for her until she died in 1990.

In the parents' absence, the family dynamics changed drastically. The major drama had always been between mother and father; Kate and the others were the audience. Now and then, Mrs. Hepburn would encourage the children to have their say; but there was never any doubt that the parents were the stars of the show. Kate's celebrity did nothing to change her subordinate role. In "my father's house," she immersed herself in her parents' concerns as all the children were expected to do.

No matter how large the egos of the Hepburn children, they were as nothing compared to those of the parents. When someone once asked Dr. Hepburn, "Aren't you Katharine Hepburn's father?", he indignantly replied, "Katharine Hepburn is my daughter!" In other words, however famous Kate may have become, in his eyes she took her identity from him, not the other way around.

As Kate returned to the family fold, the brothers and sisters assumed center-stage for the first time. Very quickly, Kate, Dick, and Bob formed a triumvirate; they had known Tom, the babies Marion and Peg had not. But there was also a sense in which Kate moved to set herself apart as the one who, after all, had been closest to Tom and knew him best.

Outsiders might have guessed that Kate dominated the family because of her wealth and fame; but it wasn't that at all. She risked her brothers' and sisters' irritation by claiming that the mother and father she remembered were different from the parents they had known. Kate's superior knowledge of the Eden before Tom's suicide gave her immense power over the others.

As Palache said, Kate became quite "imperious" in old age. Kate, for her part, exulted that people were afraid of her now, as once they had been afraid of John Ford and Spencer Tracy! Palache finally despaired of trying to convince her old friend to do anything; it was easier to go along with Kate than to fight her.

On occasion, Kate's brothers did fight her. According to Bob, although Kate did not defer to her brothers as she used to defer to Spencer or Dr. Hepburn, she would give in now and then if he pressed hard enough. But it had to be an issue he believed in passionately; Kate remained a "tremendous force," not easily swayed.

And she remained fiercely loyal. Palache called Kate "one of the most loyal people in all creation." Close friends and family knew that when she loved you, it was forever. She was capable of enormous warmth and emotional generosity.

Bob smiled to himself when, late in life, Kate suddenly accepted Luddy back into the fold. Now a widower in his seventies, Luddy began to visit her at Fenwick; after many years of fighting him off, Kate was clearly delighted to see him again. She would rush into the kitchen to cook for the long-suffering ex-husband; and Luddy would try to make himself useful around the house. He fixed leaky faucets and completed other repairs that the Hepburns prided themselves on not being able to do. When Luddy became ill with prostate cancer, Kate would bring meals to him in New Canaan, Connecticut. He died in 1979 at the age of eighty.

According to Bob, as they all grew old Kate had great difficulty accepting the approach of death—her own and those of her brothers and sisters. Kate was too much of a life force to confront death easily. Besides, she always insisted on doing everything her way; for once, that would be impossible. "See, Kate has always controlled her life," her brother explains. "Now death controls you."

Her later years were filled with achievement. Kate did about one project a year. She worked in film, television, and theater. Her lifelong determination to refill the reservoir had paid off; she had her choice of vehicles.

She won a record-breaking fourth Academy Award as Best Actress for Mark Rydell's *On Golden Pond*. She returned to Broadway in plays by Enid Bagnold and Ernest Thompson. She published two best-selling volumes of memoirs.

At the Turtle Bay townhouse which she had first rented in 1933 as a temporary measure until she had her life in order, Kate groused about the way the light was altered when new office buildings shot up all around. In contrast, at Fenwick the view of wide open horizon, of sea and sky and billowy clouds, had not changed since the Hepburns and the Hookers moved to the spot in 1912. When the brothers and sisters glanced out the window, they might have thought themselves in another time.

Dick, divorced from his second wife, lived at Fenwick full-time. Kate came on weekends. Peg might visit from her farm, about an hour away, as did Bob and Sue from West Hartford. Until she died in 1986, Marion and her husband occupied a nearby cottage of their own. Kate often spoke of the "magic" of remaining at Fenwick, where she could still feel the presence of those she had known and loved there.

Through an open window drifted cries of delight as boys and girls leapt off the Fenwick pier. Children roughhoused on the lawns of the same old brown shingled cottages where the Hepburns had once played capture the flag, prisoners base, and kick the can. In South Cove, a small, shirtless boy racing past in his sailboat might have been Tommy.

The sights and sounds of the past kept a great many questions alive with unusual intensity. Much remained painfully unresolved. In the absence of Dr. and Mrs. Hepburn, the children might have talked openly about all that had long remained unspoken; but they did not. Certain topics had been forbidden for too many years. Kate insisted she could no longer be sure what was true and what wasn't in her memories of that terrible April morning in 1921. Yet Bob would always wonder whether his sister knew something she refused to tell.

There were other questions. As though sensing some connection with what had happened to Tommy, the brothers and sisters pursued the larger family past, which Mrs. Hepburn had kept off-limits. Each Hepburn went off in his or her own direction, independently of the others; by now, secrecy came naturally to them.

Marion became obsessed with genealogical research, but her findings were seriously flawed. Kate quietly visited her mother's half-sister Mary Houghton, who spent her last years in East Aurora, New York, living with three Chestnutwood cousins; she talked with her there on several occasions. Bob conferred with his cousin, Arthur Houghton, Jr., Amory's grandson, who indicated that the family had long been deeply ashamed of Fred. Arthur, beset by questions of his own, repeated Amory's claim that the strain of madness must have come from his mother's family, the Oakeses. Bob, for his part, savored the irony that Fred's daughter and granddaughter, the two Kates, had become the family's great achievers. Amory, contemptuous of all women, would have hated that!

At Fenwick, the light in Kate's second-floor room goes out very early most nights. Dick still sleeps on the third, "children's" floor, as he did when he was a boy. The timeless sound of waves crashing on the rocks pours in through open windows.

Downstairs, the blazing fire Kate insists on in all weather has been extinguished. Before the fireplace is the portable table where the brothers and sisters, now in their seventies and eighties, still play noisy, fiercely competitive games of parcheesi, always with an open box of candy nearby.

Among a group of old photographs hanging on one wall is a picture of a mother and her young son. It is the strange, sad, awkward little boy of about eight whom one notices immediately. His stiff, high-collared black cloak trimmed with grosgrain ribbon completely obscures his arms and body; the pale child appears trapped. In this early portrait, little Fred Houghton peers out at the world with the unutterable sadness that would one day consume him.

Although the Hepburns rarely talk about Fred, there is a sense among them that their tumultuous family saga began with his decision to kill himself in 1892. At Fenwick, in a house dominated by light and life, Fred's dark photograph, prominently displayed, is a reminder of the power of the past, and of the agonizing questions that have shaped and driven Katharine Hepburn.

ACKNOWLEDGMENTS

I would like to thank Katharine Hepburn for agreeing to talk with me for this book. I cannot imagine having written her biography without having had the opportunity to meet her, ask her questions, listen to her talk, and see for myself the enormous complexity of this astonishing woman. She has given us all a triumphant sense of what it is to embrace life, to dare, and above all to strive to be everything that one can possibly be. Her life has been a tribute to the struggles, both public and private, fought by her grandmother, Carrie Houghton, her mother, Katharine Houghton Hepburn, and her aunt, Edith Houghton Hooker.

I owe an immeasurable debt of gratitude to Dr. Robert Hepburn, Katharine Hepburn's brother. It was Bob who convinced his sister to allow me to interview her for this biography. Bob also talked with me himself at great length, in the course of repeated meetings, about everything and anything I wanted to ask. Highly educated, deeply devoted to history and the search for truth, gifted with the frankness and objectivity of a great doctor, and above all a fine and decent man, Bob Hepburn was the one person without whom I could not have written the book I hoped to do.

I would also like to thank Sue Hepburn for her constant kindness, her astute perceptions, and her help with many aspects of this project.

Allegra Huston, my editor at Weidenfeld and Nicolson in London, has worked with me on three books and has shaped me as a writer. From first to last, we have worked very closely on this project, and her contribution has been immense. There is no way adequately to acknowledge all she has done to make this biography what it is. To have had the benefit of her dazzling intelligence for the past seven years has been a great gift. My life is the richer for the honor of her friendship.

Betty Prashker, my editor at Crown in New York, has done everything imaginable to make this book possible. At our first meeting, she fired off a series of questions she wanted a book about Katharine Hepburn to answer; these questions became the focus of my research. Betty read the manuscript with great intelligence, sensitivity, and care, and I have benefited enormously from her many insights and suggestions. I am in awe of her talents as an editor.

Lois Wallace, my long-time agent, has made it possible for me to have a life that I love. From the moment I decided to do this book, she was, as always, involved at every turn, offering her wisdom, affection, and patience. I cannot imagine how to thank her. Also at the Wallace Literary Agency, I would like to thank Tom Wallace for much excellent advice.

At Crown, a great many talented people worked very hard on behalf of this project; my thanks to all, especially Laurie Stark, for dragging me into the computer age.

At Weidenfeld and Nicolson, I have been very fortunate to have the support of Ion Trewin. I hope he knows how grateful I am for all he has done on my behalf. And of course, I would like to thank all of the other wonderful people at Weidenfeld who did so much for this book.

Among archivists who have assisted my research, I would particularly like to thank Dr. Howard B. Gotlieb and Karen Mix of the Department of Special Collections, Mugar Memorial Library at Boston University; Saundra Taylor, Rebecca Campbell Cape, and Heather Monroe of the Lilly Library at Indiana University; Sam Gill of Special Collections at the Academy of Motion Picture Arts and Sciences; and Arian D. Ravanbakhsh of the Alan Mason Chesney Medical Archives at Johns Hopkins University. Without the dedication of such brilliant archivists, our history would be lost to us.

At Bryn Mawr College, which plays such an important role in

this story, I want to thank President Mary Patterson McPherson for her decision to unseal Alice Palache's oral history so that I might use it for this biography. I am deeply indebted to Caroline Rittenhouse, the college archivist, who contributed much to my understanding of what Bryn Mawr meant to Carrie Houghton and her girls in the "golden age" of M. Carey Thomas. I must also acknowledge the great kindness of Leo Dolenski, the manuscripts librarian, who assisted me in countless ways.

A great many people provided the information I needed to tell Katharine Hepburn's story. They include: Lew Ayres, Eleanor Beatty, Dr. Debra E. Bernhardt, Theodore Bikel, Alice Birney, Jon Bloom, Joan Boer, Robin Brown, Arthur M. Burr, Jim Campbell, Rebecca Campbell Cape, Kenneth R. Cobb, Michelle Cotton, Mrs. Marvin B. Day, John Dooley, Elizabeth Dribben, Peter Engelman, Rick Ewig, Candace Falk, Jane Fredrikson, Mrs. Frederick S. Fried, Judy Gomez, Ray Gosnell, Dr. Howard B. Gotlieb, Idilio Gracia-Pena, Julia Grimsman, Bert Hartry, Elizabeth Hodges, Carol Hodson, Sue Hodson, Ross Hunter, Suzanne Jacquin, Joe Keller, Chuck Kelly, Mike Klein, Jane Knowles, Brigitte Kueppers, Stanley Kramer, Barbara Kravitz, Barbara Krieger, Francis L. Lamb, Richard Lamparski, the late Ely Landau, Mary S. Leahy, Carmel Lofredo, Bernard McAneney, Robin McIlhenney, Linda McIlveen, Dr. Thistle M. McKee, President Mary Patterson McPherson, Jacque Mapes, Catherine L. Mason, Lisette Matano, Robert Merritt, Barbara Minsker, Karen Mix, Warren Moffett, Heather Monroe, Nancy Nunn, Robert Oakes, Sharyn M. Oakes, Cassie Pabst, Edward Papenfuse, Ruth Penkala, Martin Poll, Charles Pollock, Arian D. Ravanbakhsh, Richard Richardson, Victor Samrock, Jenifer Sigafoes, Marjorie Sly, Mrs. Lester Smith, Joseph G. Streamer, Ron Sutz, Frederick R. Swan, Inez Swimelor, Marta Sykes, Kathy Tallalay, Saundra Taylor, Wendy Thomas, Mrs. Norman A. Walker, Virginia Wright, Suzanne Zack.

And I want to thank the staffs of the archives, libraries, historical societies, and other institutions, who contributed material to this biography: The Alan Mason Chesney Medical Archives, The Johns Hopkins Medical Institutions; New York State Library,

Albany; Ontario Historical Society, Canandaigua, New York; Buffalo & Erie County Historical Society, Buffalo, New York; Hamburg Historical Society, Hamburg, New York; Town of Hornellsville, Registrar of Vital Statistics; City of Hornell, Registrar of Vital Statistics; New York State Archives and Records Administration; New York City Municipal Archives; Rare Book and Manuscript Library, Columbia University; Academy of Motion Picture Arts and Sciences, Center for Motion Picture Study; Bryn Mawr College Archives; Special Collections Department, University of California, Los Angeles; Schlesinger Library, Radcliffe College; The Houghton Library, Harvard University; Sophia Smith Collection, Smith College; Special Collections, Vassar College; Vassar College Library; The Library of Congress, Special Collections; Lincoln Center Library of the Performing Arts, Special Collections; Kent County, Maryland Historical Society; Department of Special Collections, Mugar Memorial Library, Boston University; The Beinecke Rare Book and Manuscript Library, Yale University; The Lilly Library, Indiana University; Georgetown University Library, Special Collections; The Huntington Library, Pasadena; University Research Library, University of California, Los Angeles; Special Collections, Arts Library, University of California, Los Angeles; Film Archives, University of California, Los Angeles; University of Wyoming, American Heritage Center; The Bancroft Library, University of California, Berkeley; Stowe-Day Foundation, Hartford; The Maryland State Archives; Vital Records, City of New York; Hartford Probate Court; Yale University Alumni Records Office; Radcliffe College Alumnae Association; Registrar, City of Albany, Albany, New York; Vital Records, Buffalo, New York; Free Library of Philadelphia; Hartford Library; Connecticut State Library, Hartford; The New York Public Library, Main Branch, New York City; New York City Medical Examiners Office; Court of Appeals, Albany, New York; Hamburg Town Historian; The Baldwin School, Alumnae Office; Tamiment Institute Library, New York University; Corning Corporate Archives; Corning Glass Museum; Corning Public Library; Manuscripts Department, Dartmouth College Library; East Aurora, Town Historian; Emma

Goldman Papers, University of California, Berkeley; Hornell Town Historian; New Haven Historical Society; Prospect Lawn Cemetery.

Finally, special thanks to my husband, David, whose love, constant encouragement, and willingness to share in the intensity of the search made this book possible.

N O T E   O N
S O U R C E S

PART ONE

The reconstruction of events in Part I is based almost entirely on letters and documents written at the time by the principal players in this family drama, as well as by their friends and associates. The enormous volume of primary source material permitted me to rely on contemporary accounts of events, rather than on family legend.

CHAPTERS 1–2

No source was more vital than the hundreds of papers collected by Amory Houghton, Jr. while he supervised the lives of Katharine Hepburn's mother and her two sisters. Had Amory not so relentlessly, indeed compulsively, documented the years between 1892, when Fred Houghton committed suicide, and 1904, when Kate Houghton married Tom Hepburn, it probably would have been impossible to recover the full story at this late date. Amory hoarded the family's minutiae with the dedication of an animal preparing for a long winter.

Fred's widow, Carrie, and later her daughters, Kathy, Edith, and Marion, were required to document virtually their every move and motive in order to justify their actions and expenses to an uncle who was intent on controlling them. No detail was too private for Amory's scrutiny. He monitored the hot water the girls used for their baths; reprimanded them for changing their lace nightgowns too frequently; and charged to the penny for the telephone calls made to notify them of their mother's imminent death.

The paper trail that remains, in the form of letters, notes, memos, bills, receipts, and inventories, is astonishing. These voluminous records, which apparently had lain untouched for more than eight decades since Amory put them away, allowed me to glimpse the day-to-day life of Carrie and her daughters. Seeing the shaky hand in which Carrie attempted to write her final instructions to the girls as she lay on her deathbed, or the angry scrawl in which a fifteen-year-old wrote a note asking Amory's permission to purchase her first corset stays, gave these people an immediacy they could not otherwise have had for me.

In addition to Amory's records, I was able to locate hundreds of letters written by key participants in the story. There was a good deal of correspondence among the Houghtons, and those related to them by marriage, who resided in Corning, Buffalo, and Brooklyn, New York. These letters, intended by and large for no eyes but those of the close relatives to whom they were addressed, provided exceptionally revealing glimpses of my cast of characters.

For instance, I derived a particularly strong sense of Fred Houghton from the letters of his young first wife, Ollie Chestnutwood, to Fred's sister Nellie, to her own sister, Frankie Linen, and mother, Mrs. Levi Chestnutwood, as well as to Fred himself. These letters, written by a guileless, loving, often frightened girl, who had not yet developed the defenses of maturity, brought her tormented husband vividly to life for me.

Another important source was the correspondence of Nellie Abbott, the last family member to see Fred alive. Since, by all accounts, it was Aunt Nell who became the emotional center of Kathy Houghton's life after Carrie's death, it is not surprising that in these letters I discovered a depth of feeling and a sensitivity to tragedy totally lacking in the letters of her brother Amory.

The letters of Fred's second wife, Carrie, while less revealing about her husband than those of Ollie, permitted me to know first-hand the source of the strength and courage her daughters and granddaughter inherited. I was able to observe a master tactician as she fought the battle for her daughters' future in the face of her own knowledge that she was soon going to die.

In addition to letters, I made use of the considerable legal documentation of the lives of the Houghton sisters. From the moment Fred Houghton committed suicide, the courts became involved in the affairs of Carrie and her daughters. Because minors were involved—and because Fred had children by two wives— the court records are exceptionally complex and detailed. When Carrie died two years later, the court's involvement became even more intense.

One other piece of written testimony was critical throughout Part One. After I had completed several years of research, Dr. Robert Hepburn gave me his mother's unfinished autobiography, a project which she undertook sometime in the early 1940s. Bob had asked his mother to write down her story because she had always been extremely reticent about her early life. Mrs. Hepburn believed that her very sanity and survival depended on suppressing her memories of certain tragic events. The last thing one would expect to find is a frank autobiography; indeed, I suspect that her memoir remained unfinished because of the intense psychological pressure she must have felt in writing it. Mrs. Hepburn had so little experience with introspection—by her own account, she avoided it all her life as a survival tactic—that she often commits to paper stories to whose meaning she

seems oddly blind; some of these stories seem almost to erupt from her unconscious. Reading this remarkable document enabled me to know her as I might
not otherwise have done.

Vital information in Chapters 1 and 2 came from the following sources:
Amory Houghton, Jr.'s letters and memos to Mack Smith, Frederick Gar-
linghouse, Katharine Houghton, Edith Houghton, and Marion Houghton; Fre-
derick Garlinghouse's letters to Amory Houghton, Jr.; Katharine Houghton's
letters to Amory Houghton, Jr. and Mack Smith; Ollie Houghton's letters to Fred
Houghton, Frankie Linen, Mrs. Levi Chestnutwood, and Nellie Abbott; Fred
Houghton's letters to Ollie Houghton; Katherine (sic) Houghton's letters to
Frankie Linen; Nellie Abbott's letters to Ollie Houghton and Frankie Linen;
Carrie Houghton's letters to Amory Houghton, Jr., Mack Smith, Frederick Gar-
linghouse, and Sarah Deane; Sarah Deane's letters to Carrie Houghton; Marion
Houghton's letters to Amory Houghton, Jr. and Mack Smith; John Linen's letters
to Frankie Linen; Frankie Linen's letters to Ollie Houghton and John Linen; Levi
Chestnutwood's letters to John Linen and Frankie Linen; Sara Chestnutwood's
letters to Frankie Linen; Mrs. Levi Chestnutwood's letters to Frankie Linen; Ellen
M. Chandler's letters to Amory Houghton Jr.; George W. Wheeler's letters to
Henry Lyon and Amory Houghton, Jr.; Henry Lyon's letters to Amory Houghton,
Jr.; Victor Bentley's letters to Edith Houghton; Mrs. C. Hirsch's letters to Kathy,
Edith, and Marion Houghton; Mack Smith's letters to Kathy, Edith, and Marion
Houghton; W. G. Rappleye's letters to Carrie Houghton and Amory Houghton,
Jr.; Martha Washburn's letters to Amory Houghton, Jr.; Last Will and Testament
of Alfred Augustus Houghton, July 11, 1885; Last Will and Testament of Carrie
Houghton, August 15, 1894; Carrie Houghton's death certificate, #105, September
2, 1894; Affidavits of George Linen, William A. Tuttle, and Carrie Houghton,
November 29, 1892; Affidavit of Roland Crangle, November 5, 1892; Order
Appointing Special Guardian for interests of Catherine (sic) Martha Houghton,
Edith Houghton, and Marion Houghton, November 29, 1892; Willis Jacus's
Inventory of Alfred A. Houghton Estate, January 16, 1895; Estate of Caroline G.
Houghton, Schedule "A".

Information on Fred's attendance at Harvard came from the Harvard University archives; information on his legal training, from the Court of Appeals in
Albany. The Baldwin School furnished data on Edith and Marion.

Additional background on the Houghtons came from a privately printed
family study, which Bob Hepburn received as a gift from his cousin, the late
Arthur Houghton. John Westley Houghton's study, published in 1912, supplied
further details.

CHAPTERS 3-5

Kathy's struggle to enter Bryn Mawr is documented in the letters and records Amory assembled. He has inadvertently made it possible to trace the furious battle, which started within days of her mother's funeral, between a grief-stricken sixteen-year-old and a "savage" captain of industry. At times, Amory appears to view himself as the representative of an entire class of men who saw all too clearly the threat a Bryn Mawr education posed to their way of life. As Katharine Hepburn would say to me of all such men as Amory: "I think they were furious at the women. Disgusted! The women upset the whole fucking situation!"

Amory's letters of these months reveal that no tactic to thwart and defeat his niece was beneath him. He would use any weapon at his disposal, consciously trying to trick and defeat her by any means possible. Equally clear in her own letters and records is Kathy's determination to be true to her promise to her mother. To measure the level of her desperation, one has only to see the dates of that first trip to Bryn Mawr for entrance exams she knew she must fail. In the months that follow, Amory's files document Kathy's single-mindedness; there are records of endless hours of tutoring, and of purchases of books to stuff her head with knowledge that a normal student would take years to acquire. The correspondence between Florence Baldwin and Amory Houghton, Jr. discussing the arrangements to be made for Edith and Marion are among the most poignant documents of this period, for it is in reading them that one is struck by just how young and alone these children were—and by how thoroughly the real responsibility for her sisters now lay with Kathy herself.

To understand what Kathy was up against, I examined copies of the Bryn Mawr entrance exams from this period and consulted college records to determine the timing and nature of Kathy's own exams. That she was able to pass a sufficient number to be admitted, in her state of emotional turmoil, with worries about her sisters complicating her every decision, and with her uncle working against her at every step, was nothing short of a miracle.

In this period, the detail available to the biographer is almost overwhelming. The records maintained by Mack Smith made it possible for me to know precisely how much horsehair Kate purchased to line the clothes she ordered for Bryn Mawr, as well as why she felt it necessary to make a special trip to Buffalo to rescue her mother's cut-glass scent bottles.

Besides Amory and Mack, there is another vast source of primary material: the papers of M. Carey Thomas. The Thomas papers, originals of which are held at the Bryn Mawr archives, contain thousands of letters, diaries, minutes, reports, and other documents, recording not just the life of Bryn Mawr's second president—who was herself a major player in this story—but what I have come to think of as perhaps the greatest experiment in women's education: the first forty years of Bryn Mawr College. The papers, which occupy some 163 reels of microfilm, made it possible for me to inhabit the world of that now largely vanished experiment.

For several months, I put in eight-hour days at Vassar College, where a microfilm copy of the papers is held; it was one of the most rewarding periods of my research. Carey Thomas—for all of her limitations, which I believe to have been largely those of her day and class, however serious—is one of the most astonishing and powerful figures I have ever encountered. One cannot understand the profound effect that Bryn Mawr had on Kate and Edith, and later on the young Katharine Hepburn, without coming face to face with the spirit of Carey Thomas—extreme, violent, excited, outrageous, full of limitless possibilities and expectations.

It was also in the Thomas papers that I discovered the details of many of Kate and Edith's activities in that period, in particular the two great crises of their Bryn Mawr careers: Edith's expulsion for hazing in the fall of 1898, and Kate's mysterious fall and subsequent strange behavior in the early months of 1899 and later that spring. Had I decided to limit my reading simply to indexed citations for Kate and Edith, however, I might never have discovered that these critical events took place. For example, fragments of the hazing story may be found in the minutes of the Student Self-Government Association; other pieces turn up in the files for the Low Buildings; others, in Carey Thomas's letters to Mary Garrett, Mary Stevens, and various college trustees; and finally, the letters of a graduate student named Mary Helen Ritchie complete the picture.

The Thomas papers contain key insights into the personalities of Kate and Edith; there are important assessments of them in Thomas's own letters, as well as in the letters of Gonzalez Lodge and Mary Stevens. Amory Houghton, Jr.'s letters to Carey Thomas are extraordinary for what they reveal of this man, so utterly sure of himself that he seems unashamed and even rather proud of his own worst qualities.

To get the texture of college life, I made extensive use of student scrapbooks held in the Bryn Mawr archives. I studied the scrapbooks of Mary Grace Kilpatrick, Sylvia Scudder, Marion Parris, Margaret Hilles, Elizabeth Congdon, and Edith Dabney, all of whom (with the exception of Hilles) were at Bryn Mawr with the Houghton girls. As aesthetic objects, some of these books are astonishingly beautiful, and each possesses its own unique voice. Kilpatrick was particularly important for her diary-like account of Edith's Lantern Night. Without Kilpatrick's descriptions of girls breaking windows and attempting to fling themselves through the jagged glass, I would not have completely grasped the impulses driving Edith during the later hazing incident.

Charles Houghton's suicide was reconstructed from numerous sources, perhaps the most surprising of which was a diary kept by Mary Higgins, Margaret Sanger's older sister. Higgins was Nellie Abbott's maid, and the diary provides a vivid sense of the impact of Charles's death on the family, especially on Nellie.

In some genealogies, the name of Amory's mother, Sophronia Oakes, is spelled Oaks. I have chosen to rely on the earliest mentions of her name in documents which use the "Oakes" spelling.

Among the most important documents on the hazing incident were the following letters: Howard Comfort to Carey Thomas, November 5, 1898; Mary Stevens to Carey Thomas, November 10, 1898; Evelyn Walker to Carey Thomas, December 6, 1898; Carey Thomas to Edith Houghton, November 4, 1898; Evelyn Walker to Carey Thomas, November 2, 1898; Carey Thomas to Edith Houghton, November 8, 1898; Carey Thomas to Mary Stevens, November 7, 1898; Carey Thomas to Amory Houghton, Jr., November 4, 1898; Carey Thomas to Edith Houghton, November 7, 1898; Carey Thomas to Evelyn Walker, November 8, 1898; Evelyn Walker to Carey Thomas, December 10, 1898; Edward Bettle, Jr. to Carey Thomas, December 1, 1898; Edward Bettle, Jr. to Carey Thomas, November 29, 1898; Amory Houghton, Jr. to Carey Thomas, November 6, 1898; Carey Thomas to Mary Garrett, November 8, 1898; Carey Thomas to Mary Garrett, November 9, 1898; Carey Thomas to Mary Garrett, November 29, 1898; Carey Thomas to Mary Garrett, December 14, 1898; Mary Garrett to Carey Thomas, November 7, 1898; Carey Thomas to Gonzalez Lodge, December 15, 1898. On May 26, 1899, Thomas wrote to Amory Houghton, Jr. about Edith's wish to graduate in three years. Thomas's continued interest in Edith is evident in many letters between them in the years to come.

On Kate's fall and its aftermath there is testimony from Walter Christie, M.D.; Gonzalez Lodge; Helen Thomas; and Carey Thomas. Of particular importance was Gonzalez Lodge's long letter to Carey Thomas on May 19, 1899.

I checked the records of the now defunct Granger Place School for details of Edith and Marion, and verified Kate's attendance at Radcliffe in the college archives.

The Alan Mason Chesney Medical Archives at Johns Hopkins University provided a wealth of information on the Hopkins Medical School—particularly the situation of women there. The letters of Mary Garrett and Florence Sabin supplied much invaluable material.

Edith wrote at length about her experiences at Hopkins. In June 1904 she published an essay, "Medicine as a Profession for Women," in *The Triennial Magazine*. In 1916 she published a series of articles in *The Survey* under the collective title "Life's Clinic" (later published in book form), detailing her work in the dispensary clinic. There is also much relevant material in her book *The Laws of Sex*, published in 1921, a rare copy of which I located in Margaret Sanger's papers in the Sophia Smith Collection at Smith College. Other information about Hopkins came from Eleanor Bluemel, *Florence Sabin: Colorado Woman of the Century;* and from memoirs of Bertram Bernheim, Dorothy Reed, and Lillian

Welsh. An unpublished essay by Edith's friend Elizabeth Daly shed light on her departure from Hopkins. Don Hooker wrote about their trip to Germany together in the October 1919 issue of *Social Hygiene.*

Mack Smith's records enabled me to track Kate's travels in Europe, and later as a "visiting girl." She also discusses this period in her memoir, in addition to describing her early encounters with Tom Hepburn at Hopkins. Bob Hepburn filled in additional details, both from his father's and his mother's points of view.

Amory's letter of February 4, 1904 is reproduced in Katharine Hepburn, *Me: Stories of My Life.*

Amory Houghton, Jr., Frederick Garlinghouse, and Mack Smith wound up the affairs of the estate in a document entitled "Estate of Caroline G. Houghton, Schedule 'F'."

CHAPTERS 6–10

For this section, which covers the first thirteen years of Katharine Hepburn's life, I made extensive use of the documents of the women's suffrage movement, collected in various archives throughout the country. Hundreds of letters written by Mrs. Hepburn allowed me to follow her as she developed into the woman her mother had hoped she might become: a strong, gifted leader.

I devoted months to reading widely in the history of the women's movement in an effort to understand the atmosphere of violence and upheaval in which Kathy Hepburn spent her girlhood. Kathy grew up in what was, I learned, the equivalent of a military command post, where her mother functioned as a power-ful officer, planning strategy and issuing orders to her troops on a daily basis. To read the letters of the suffragists is to understand that their struggle was nothing like the sentimental picture many of us have of a few women in white gowns floating down the avenue with their banners. It was a revolution: a violent seizure of power.

When I asked Katharine Hepburn about the violence, she recalled that as she listened to her mother's friends tell of having tubes shoved down their throats and nostrils, causing them to spit up blood, she was excited by their accounts. I knew then that to understand the woman little Kathy became, I would have to listen intently to the voices she had heard as a child.

I found a great many relevant letters in Washington, Boston, Hartford, Baltimore, and New York. I examined the massive suffrage collections on micro-film at Vassar College and in the Sophia Smith Collection at Smith College. I worked through the papers of the National American Woman Suffrage Associ-ation and the National Woman's Party, as well as the files of the Connecticut and Maryland branches of those organizations.

I studied the correspondence of Mrs. Hepburn's circle of intimates: Jo

Bennett, Toscan Bennett, Katharine Beach Day, Valeria Parker, Emily Pierson, Annie Porritt, Florence Sabin, Grace Seton, Mary Towle—and of course of her sister and brother-in-law, Edith and Don Hooker.

And I read the letters of her other associates: Lillian Ascough, Alva Belmont, Lucy Burns, Carrie Chapman Catt, Rosamond Danielson, Catherine Flanagan, Mrs. Gilson Gardner, Elsie Hill, Maud Hincks, Hazel Hunckins, Florence Kelley, Dora Lewis, Katharine Mullen, Alice Paul, Anita Pollitzer, Daphne Selden, Anna Howard Shaw, Doris Stevens, Mrs. Carlos Stoddard, Mabel Vernon, Mabel Washburn, Helena Hill Weed, and Maud Younger.

Because the activities of the suffragists often placed them in great peril, they had to learn to trust and depend on each other. As a result, their letters are filled with news of everyday life; they provided me with a wealth of information about the daily lives of the Hepburns, details which otherwise would have vanished from memory. I could not have told this story without them.

In the papers of Florence Ledyard Cross Kitchelt in the Schlesinger Library at Radcliffe College, I came upon a memoir Mrs. Hepburn had written describing her entry into the suffrage movement. In the scrapbooks of Mary Bartlett Cullen at Smith College, I found extensive documentation of Mrs. Hepburn's and Mrs. Hooker's activities. And in Alice Paul's immense oral history at the University of California at Berkeley, I was pleased to discover important insights into the personalities of both sisters.

On Tom Hepburn's background, two family histories by Frank Snowden Hopkins, *The Hepburn Family of Kent County, Maryland* and *The Powell and the Lloyd Family*, provided much important material. I was also able to draw on a collection of Hepburn family letters, which was provided to me by Francis Lamb, who is distantly related to the Hepburns. The essays by various family members in *Marion Hepburn Grant: A Biography* furnished additional detail.

In her autobiography, Mrs. Hepburn talks at length about her early relationship with and marriage to Dr. Hepburn. On the dynamics of that marriage, I had the benefit of conversations with Bob Hepburn and Katharine Hepburn. Bob was particularly illuminating on his father. My portrait of Dr. Hepburn owes much to Bob's willingness to spend day after day, hour after hour with me patiently discussing his father's character, speculating on his motives and drives, and explaining in detail his work as a doctor. Tom Hepburn was a man who provoked strong reactions; some of Mrs. Hepburn's women friends expressed considerable distaste for him in their letters. There can be no question that Bob loved and respected his father, but he was also able to see his faults; and he understood as clearly as anyone, I believe, the forces that drove his father to act as he did.

On Katharine Hepburn's youth, I learned much from the testimony of her childhood friends and neighbors and their spouses: Arthur M. Burr, Mrs. Marvin Day, Mrs. Frederick Fried, Mrs. J. Edward Lumbard, Robert Merritt, Nuala Smith, Frederick Swann, and Mrs. Deborah Walker.

The manuscript of James Thrall Soby's unpublished autobiography provided a vivid picture of the boyhood world he shared with his best friend Tom Hepburn.

Charles Hepburn's Certificate of Death is #12208. Thomas Houghton Hepburn's Certificate of Death is #9018. Dr. Sewell S. Hepburn's Certificate of Death is #5594.

Bob Hepburn recalled the scene in the dining room when Mrs. Hepburn received the news about Tom, and the trip home from the crematorium with his brother's ashes in a candy box.

Jo Bennett's daughter-in-law, Dr. Thistle McKee, discussed Jo's sense of the impact Tom's suicide had on Kathy and Mrs. Hepburn.

PART TWO

Katharine Hepburn was a prolific letter-writer. She always seemed to be dashing off a letter in her racing script, which grew bolder as she became more famous and powerful. Countless pre-dawn hours, especially after she went to California to begin her film career, were spent sitting in bed with a pad of paper, writing to a friend or family member in the east. On a movie set, she might use her copy of the screenplay as a desk to write more letters; others were penned on bumpy railroad journeys or in hotel rooms as she toured the country in one play or another. The result is an enormous body of correspondence, which permitted me to follow Katharine Hepburn's actions, thoughts, and motives up close throughout much of her adult life.

Notoriously evasive in interviews with journalists, as well as in her autobiography, *Me: Stories of My Life*, Hepburn was often astonishingly frank and confiding in letters to intimates—although she rarely told the whole story to any one person. Her own letters, which I tracked down in many odd corners, were invaluable to me in writing Part Two of this book, as were hundreds of letters written by her friends, lovers, family members, and business associates.

CHAPTERS 11–15

For the aftermath of Tom Hepburn's suicide, my most important source was the testimony of Bob Hepburn, who described his sister's "sea change," as he called the sudden alteration in her behavior. Other vital material for this period came from the correspondence of Jo Bennett, Toscan Bennett, Katharine Beach Day, Donald Hooker, Edith Hooker, Alice Paul, Annie Porritt, Florence Sabin, Margaret Sanger, and Mary Towle.

I discovered perhaps the most vivid picture of the young Katharine Hepburn in an oral history deposited by her lifelong friend Alice Palache in the Bryn Mawr archive. Although the oral history had been sealed since the time of Palache's death, I was able to gain access to it through the kindness of President Mary Patterson McPherson, who allowed me to use it for this book. Brilliant, loving, perceptive, and witty, Palache has a great deal to report about life among the Hepburns in those years. With an eye for detail, she describes everything from her encounters with a naked Dr. Hepburn to her adventures with Kate as they toured Europe together. One of the very few outsiders to become a permanent part of the Hepburn family circle—Aunty Towle and Luddy were others—Palache saw a Kate Hepburn unknown to many of her closest friends in Hollywood.

Transcripts of Katharine Hepburn's own speeches to Bryn Mawr students, delivered at Palache's behest, supplied much additional detail about their experiences at school. I also consulted Kate's archival files, and those of her friends Alice Barbour, Elizabeth Rhett, Alice Palache, and Alita Davis. Further material came from the letters and papers of Helen Taft Manning, Alice Palache, Marion Edwards Park, and M. Carey Thomas. Kate's exploits were widely reported in issues of the *College News* (1924–28), where I also found relevant information about college life in the period.

In her autobiography, Mrs. Hepburn recounted the tempest in the household when Kate announced her plans to become an actress. Further details were provided in the transcript of a talk Marion Hepburn Grant gave at the Stowe–Day Foundation in Hartford. Robin Brown (Marie Simpson) described Kate as she prepared to make her theatrical debut in the stock company of which Robin was also a member.

My account of Kate's experiences in New York, and of the story of the poet H. Phelps Putnam, is based on letters written by Ellen Barry, Philip Barry, Stephen Vincent Benet, Malcolm Cowley, Katharine Hepburn, Mrs. Thomas N. Hepburn, Edith Hooker, Arthur Hopkins, John Houseman, Lawrence Langner, Archibald MacLeish, F. O. Matthiessen, George Middleton, Alice Palache, H. Phelps Putnam, Florence Sabin, Donald Ogden Stewart, Allen Tate, and Edmund Wilson. I also drew on memoirs by Malcolm Cowley, Cheryl Crawford, Ruth Gordon, Katharine Hepburn, Lawrence Langner, George Middleton, Donald Ogden Stewart, and Edmund Wilson. Other material came from the Philip Barry papers in the Beinecke Library at Yale University, as well as from the small but significant Barry collection at Georgetown University.

I found a most unusual perspective on Phelps Putnam, as well as on Leland Hayward and Jed Harris, in the transcript of story conferences with the director Mark Rydell and the screenwriter Ernest Thompson for the film *On Golden Pond*. A tape recorder was running during the long sessions of intensive work on the screenplay, and Kate, in an oddly reflective mood, frequently interjected remarks about her own life. References to long-forgotten figures like Phelps Putnam seemed to make no sense to her young listeners at the time, but they were of course immensely useful to me throughout the writing of Part Two of this biography. Reading the transcript again and again, I was reminded of Bob Hepburn's perception that while his sister was by nature "not introspective," she did often use her own experiences to understand the characters she was playing on screen.

Kate and Luddy's marriage license was issued in West Hartford on December 6, 1928. Bob Hepburn discussed Luddy at length with me.

The file on *A Bill of Divorcement* in the George Cukor papers at the Academy of Motion Picture Arts and Sciences provided documentation on Kate's Hollywood debut, including a May 26, 1932 interoffice memo from Katherine Brown to Cukor about testing her in New York. John Ford's screen test, showing Kate in a scene from Philip Barry's *The Animal Kingdom,* has been preserved at the UCLA Film Archives.

The Cukor papers were invaluable for the vivid picture they offer of the man and of his complex friendship with Katharine Hepburn. Cukor's extensive correspondence with a wide circle of friends and professional associates provides many revealing glimpses of the milieu in which Kate lived during most of her years in Hollywood. Although Cukor appears to have regarded Kate as a kind of prize possession, the letters make clear that he felt a deep, if nervous, affection for her. His letters to—and about—her are often written in the tones of a proud parent or uncle; and to judge by her own letters, there would always be something of the child in her behavior with him. Their relationship mingled extremes of intimacy and reserve. Kate might swim in the nude in front of him; she might live in his house for weeks at a stretch; yet each maintained a distinct zone of psychological privacy which appears to have made their friendship possible.

In addition to examining Cukor's correspondence with Kate, I had the opportunity to read letters to Cukor from other players in the Hepburn story including Zoë Akins, Tallulah Bankhead, Merian C. Cooper, Laura Harding, Natalie Paley, and Irene Mayer Selznick. I also consulted transcripts of taped conversations between Cukor and Hepburn, which took place in conjunction with Cukor's attempts to gather material for a projected autobiography.

Outside the Cukor papers, I tracked down other pertinent letters by Zoë Akins, Dorothy Arzner, Pandro Berman, Alan Campbell, Merian C. Cooper, Jed Harris, Leland Hayward, Katharine Hepburn, Kenneth MacGowan, David Selznick, Irene Selznick, Myron Selznick, Ned Sheldon, and George Stevens.

On Leland Hayward, I found further information in Brooke Hayward, *Haywire*; Slim Keith, *Slim*; and in the Leland Hayward Collection at Lincoln Center Library.

Additional material for this period came from Pandro Berman's oral history; from George Stevens's papers at the Academy of Motion Picture Arts and Sciences; from the Zoë Akins collection at the Huntington Library; and from the Jed Harris collection at the Library of Congress.

CHAPTERS 16–18

To say that the John Ford papers at the Lilly Library in Bloomington, Indiana, were an important source for my portrait of Katharine Hepburn would be the most absurd form of understatement. Like the family history of suicide, the letters revealing Kate's relationship with John Ford are a piece of the puzzle that suddenly makes everything look and feel dramatically different. Once we know about the major role Ford played in Kate's emotional life, a great many elements of the story take on a new and altered meaning.

I have come to believe that only when placed in the context of Kate's love for Ford can some of the deepest enigmas of her relationship with Spencer Tracy be understood. As we view the two men side by side, the underlying psychological pattern of her motivation emerges in sharp relief. It is precisely that potential revelation which, I suspect, has led Kate herself to play down in public Ford's significance in her life. As her biographer, however, I realized early on that if I was to understand the forces that drove her, I needed to know more about that untold story.

The John Ford papers document the life of a great American artist, one of the most fascinating and complex men I have ever tried to comprehend. The archive exists due to the historical foresight of Ford's grandson Dan, who collected some of the most important material and preserved the rest at a moment when it might have been lost forever. Dan Ford wrote a wonderful memoir, *Pappy: The Life of John Ford*, published after his grandfather's death, and he has deposited at Lilly much of the material he assembled for that book. I am forever in his debt, both for the wisdom and sensitivity of his memoir and for his generosity in preserving these materials for history.

It was during the several weeks I spent in Bloomington studying the Ford papers that Katharine Hepburn first came alive for me in a way that made this book possible to write. Day after day, I would arrive at the library as the doors opened and begin to read Kate's letters to Ford—letters unlike any others of hers I was ever to see. Kate told him in one of her letters that no one else had ever understood her as he did; but then, she probably never showed herself to anyone as fully as she did to Ford.

I must admit that at first I felt uncomfortable reading these intensely private letters of a vulnerable, open young woman, deeply in love. But it proved impossible to resist their spell—and somehow, in that thickly carpeted, high-ceilinged room at the Lilly Library, I began to lose all sense of time or place as I became completely absorbed in the details of their love affair, and in the strange and colorful world of John Ford.

I read at breakneck speed, all the while marking pages to be photocopied, pages I was later to read countless times until the words and phrases were carved in my memory. When I finished reading Kate's letters to Ford, and copies of his letters to her, I turned to his correspondence with his wife Mary. Ford was a prolific letter-writer. During the war, for instance, he wrote to Mary nearly every day, and as I read those letters, the other part of John Ford, the part that would forever keep him from seizing his happiness by starting a new life with Kate, began to emerge for me.

I will never forget my sense of disorientation as I shifted from being immersed in the voice of the man who loved Kate Hepburn, to the very different voice of Mary Ford's husband. It was hard to believe that one man could contain within him two such distinct selves. Even more perplexing was the contrast between Mary's voice in her letters and Kate's voice in hers. Kate addressed a brilliant romantic Irish rebel named Sean who seemed to have nothing to do with Jack, the "man" Mary kept urging him to be.

And there were other letters, boxes and boxes of them; no matter how many I read each day, there were always more, containing new clues to the mystery of Ford's personality, a mystery which Kate once said she had spent much of her adult life struggling to comprehend.

In addition to preserving these letters, Dan Ford made tape recordings of his grandfather telling the stories of his life, as well as recordings of Mary Ford, Barbara Ford, John Wayne, Henry Fonda, Jimmy Stewart, Olive Carey, Harry Carey Jr., and others. At first I read transcripts; the reminiscences were extraordinary, providing a powerful portrait of the man who had held them all in thrall for nearly all their lives. But it was only when I listened to the tape recordings themselves that the full impact of this material became clear to me.

Orson Welles once told me that every great director must first be a great seducer. To listen to John Ford's strong, sweet, melodious voice, bottled at the Lilly Library, is to begin to comprehend why so many actors and actresses, the members of his informal "stock company," were prepared to devote their lives to him. I cannot imagine how I possibly could have written about Ford without having heard him speak like this.

No less vivid was the sound of the fascinating, monstrous Mary: talking on and on, uncensored, in that harsh roughneck's voice. Mary was so fully present on these tapes that suddenly I could believe in her power; for the first time, I could understand how it had been possible for her to have fought Kate—and emerged the victor.

And there were tapes of Ford and his beloved daughter, Barbara, which allowed me to see why Ford had been unable to bring himself to go off with Kate, Mary having vowed to keep his daughter from him if he did. Listening to father and daughter talk, I sensed the exceptionally strong bond between them and knew, as I had not known before, that Ford could never have left Barbara—or perhaps that he could never have survived that leaving.

But of all the tapes I listened to, none were more important than those of

Kate and Ford together during her last visits with him shortly before he died in 1972. If reading their love letters had at first made me uncomfortable, that was nothing compared to what I experienced as I played these tapes. Indeed, in the beginning, I felt so uneasy that I mentally turned off their voices and had to go back and forth numerous times before I could allow myself to register how intimate—and final—were the conversations I was hearing. But in the end I did listen, memorizing their voices so that I can hear them now. I will never forget the sound of John Ford, straining to express his love before it was too late. I have tried to capture something of that passion in the chapters I have written about Kate and her Sean.

In addition to Dan Ford's memoir, a number of books provided important information and insights into Ford's character: Lindsay Anderson, *John Ford*; Peter Bogdanovich, *John Ford;* Tag Gallagher, *John Ford*; Robert Parrish, *Growing Up in Hollywood*; Andrew Sinclair, *John Ford*; and Pilar Wayne, *John Wayne*.

It is in this section of the book that another massive source of letters and documentation first comes into play: the Theater Guild papers in the Beinecke Library at Yale University. With her appearance on stage in *Jane Eyre* in 1937, Kate entered a long and close professional association with the Theater Guild. For years to come, Kate's involvement with the Guild's directors, Lawrence Langner and Theresa Helburn, would be central to both their lives and hers.

There is a reason why there is such an abundance of material on Kate's personal life in the Guild papers; her ability to sell tickets to shows at a time when the Guild's finances were faltering made it essential for Langner, Helburn, and Langner's wife, Armina Marshall, to chart the slightest fluctuations of Hepburn's moods. Turmoil in her relationships with John Ford and later with Spencer Tracy could have a disastrous impact on Kate's ability to bring in the money the Guild desperately needed to survive.

Although it would be wrong to say that Kate's relationship with Langner, Helburn, and Marshall was one of close friendship, they were in intimate personal contact until the late 1950s. There was a pretext of friendship—but the core of their dealings was always business. Not only does the Guild archive—as yet only partially catalogued—contain many confiding letters from Hepburn herself, but there are also endless communications back and forth between Lawrence Langner and Terry Helburn, monitoring every aspect of the actress's emotional life. Very often throughout the writing of the latter part of this book, I knew exactly what Kate was feeling at a particular time because Langner and Helburn had made it their business to find out.

My discussion of the tours of *Jane Eyre* and *The Philadelphia Story* is based on letters by Zoë Akins, Vera Allen, Philip Barry, Joseph Cotten, Frank Fenton, John Ford, Laura Harding, Leland Hayward, Katharine Hepburn, Van Heflin, Theresa Helburn, Helen Jerome, Lawrence Langner, Armina Marshall, Warren

Munsell, Emily Perkins, and Robert Sinclair. I consulted the Guild production files for both plays, as well as Barry's extensive script notes for *The Philadelphia Story*. Other information came from the Barry collections at Yale and at Georgetown.

In a book project full of twists and turns, none was more surprising to me than the discovery of a selection of the extraordinary letters of Richard Hepburn, Kate's brother, in the Hedgerow Theater Collection at Boston University. Written during the 1930s and 1940s, these letters afford a unique window into Kate's behavior in the Hepburn household; not only was Dick able to see a private Kate Hepburn off limits to most people, but as a writer he was capable of making wonderfully vivid all he saw and heard. These letters—written mainly, but not entirely, during the crisis over *Sea-Air*—are full of fire and high drama. In addition to Dick's letters to Jasper Deeter, I read other letters of his to Theresa Helburn and Lawrence Langner, as well as Mrs. Hepburn's letters to them on the subject of Dick's career. And, by a stroke of luck, I was able to secure one of the few existing copies of *Sea-Air,* Dick's legendary play about Kate and the Hepburns.

Mrs. Hepburn's activity in the birth control movement is extensively documented in the Margaret Sanger papers at the Library of Congress and at Smith College. I read widely in both the state and national papers.

CHAPTERS 19–24

I discussed Katharine Hepburn's relationship with Spencer Tracy with her brother Bob, who vividly described Tracy's calamitous trip to Fenwick to meet the Hepburns. Dr. Thistle McKee, Jo Bennett's daughter-in-law, offered her own recollections of the visit.

Katharine Hepburn herself documented the relationship in a great many letters, often surprisingly candid, to friends and associates including Ellen Barry, Philip Barry, George Cukor, Theresa Helburn, Lawrence Langner, and Ella Winter. Cukor's own letters on the subject were invaluable, allowing me to pinpoint many dramatic changes in the Tracy–Hepburn relationship.

Further information on their life together came from letters by Philip Barry, Hugh Beaumont, Constance Collier, Ruth Gordon, Theresa Helburn, Garson Kanin, Lawrence Langner, Vivien Leigh, Armina Marshall, Laurence Olivier, Irene Selznick, Robert Sherwood, Donald Ogden Stewart, and Ella Winter. My portrait of Tracy also drew on his own letters and a good many telegrams (his preferred method of communication) to George Cukor, Lawrence Langner, and Robert Sherwood.

A number of memoirs and biographies provided revealing glimpses of Tracy: Lauren Bacall, *By Myself*; Hume Cronyn, *A Terrible Liar*; Bill Davidson, *Spencer Tracy: Tragic Idol*; Kirk Douglas, *The Ragman's Son;* Paul Henreid, *Paul Henreid:*

An Autobiography; Katharine Hepburn, *The Making of The African Queen*; Katharine Hepburn, *Me: Stories of My Life*; Garson Kanin, *Tracy and Hepburn*; Elia Kazan, *A Life*; Vincente Minnelli, *I Remember It Well*; Jean Negulesco, *Things I Did and Things I Think I Did*; Dore Schary, *Heyday*; Larry Swindell, *Spencer Tracy: A Biography*; Peter Viertel, *Dangerous Friends*; and Ella Winter, *And Not To Yield: An Autobiography*.

The story of the *Without Love* debacle is documented in a large selection of letters by Philip Barry, Theresa Helburn, Katharine Hepburn, Lawrence Langner, Elliott Nugent, and Robert Sinclair; and in the Theater Guild production files. Helburn's angry meeting with Kate is detailed in undated notes which Helburn wrote immediately afterward; in wires dated September 6 and September 10, 1942; and in a long letter to Kate on September 12, 1942. In a letter deposited in the Houghton Library at Harvard University, Kate wrote about her troubles to the poet Witter Bynner.

On *The Rugged Path*, I drew on letters by Robert Sherwood, Garson Kanin, and Spencer Tracy; and on an interview with Victor Samrock.

Kate's withdrawal from Tracy and return to the theater in *As You Like It* is documented in the Guild's production files, and in letters by James Bailey, Michael Benthall, George Cukor, Theresa Helburn, Katharine Hepburn, Lawrence Langner, Armina Marshall, and Spencer Tracy.

Edith Hooker's long illness and death are detailed in many letters by Donald Hooker and Florence Sabin.

On the subject of Mrs. Hepburn's death, in March 1951 Katharine Hepburn wrote a long letter to Margaret Sanger, describing her last morning with her mother and the discovery of her body early that evening. In a series of letters to Terry Helburn during the filming of *The African Queen*, Constance Collier reported in detail her fears for Kate, based on recent observation and on Kate's own letters to her from Africa. Kate's nervous breakdown during *The Millionairess* is documented in letters by Hugh Beaumont, Michael Benthall, Constance Collier, George Cukor, Theresa Helburn, Katharine Hepburn and Lawrence Langner.

Letters in the Cukor papers supplied details of the Tracy cottage; but I could never have grasped its psychological significance without the help of Charles Pollock, who arranged for me to visit the strange little place where Tracy spent his final years. I needed to walk the property and gauge the cottage's relation to the main house; I needed to look out Tracy's bedroom window; and I needed to see the layout and the size of the rooms, especially that of the maid's room where Kate finally slept when Spencer was too sick and afraid to remain in the cottage alone, as he had long preferred to do.

For these last years of the Tracy–Hepburn relationship, I drew on letters of James Bailey, George Cukor, John Ford, Ruth Gordon, Robert Helpmann, Katharine Hepburn, John Houseman, Lord Killanin, Frances Rich, Irene Selznick, John Wayne, and Ella Winter. I talked to the late Ely Landau about Tracy's refusal to appear in *Long Day's Journey into Night*, and about Kate's state of mind during filming. On the subject of *Guess Who's Coming to Dinner*, I consulted the Stanley Kramer collection at UCLA, and interviewed Stanley Kramer and Ray Gosnell. Information on the years after Tracy came from letters by Hugh Beaumont, Gladys Cooper, George Cukor, John Ford, Ruth Gordon, Katharine Hepburn, John Huston, Cathleen Nesbitt, Laurence Olivier, Irene Selznick, Donald Ogden Stewart, and Ella Winter; from Alice Palache's oral history; and of course from conversations with Bob and Sue Hepburn.

I N D E X

KH   = Katharine Hepburn
KHH = Katharine Houghton Hepburn (KH's mother)
EHH = Edith Houghton Hooker
ST   = Spencer Tracy

Relationships shown are to Katharine Hepburn. Films planned or made by Katharine Hepburn or Spencer Tracy are listed under those names; others are listed under the name of the director. Books and plays are listed under the name of the author.